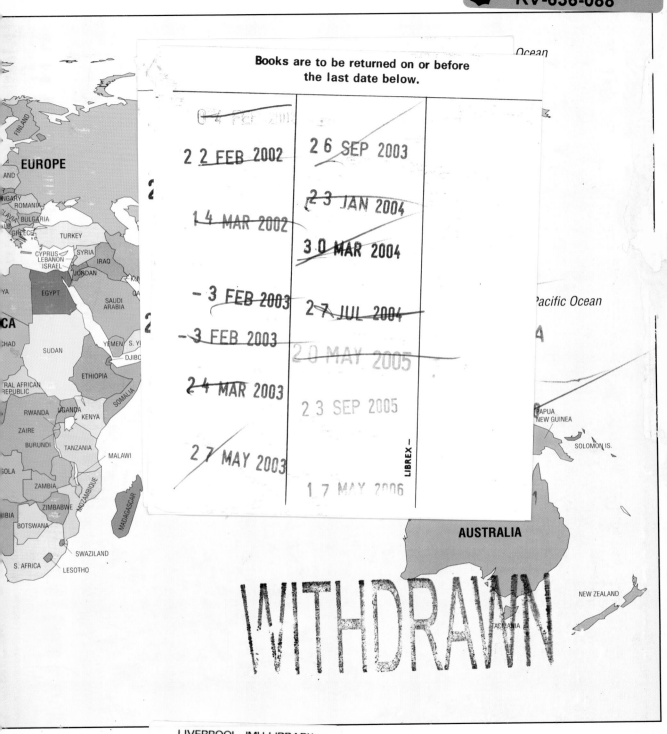

**Books are to be returned on or before
the last date below.**

0 4 FEB 2002

2 2 FEB 2002   2 6 SEP 2003

                    2 3 JAN 2004

1 4 MAR 2002

                    3 0 MAR 2004

- 3 FEB 2003   2 7 JUL 2004

- 3 FEB 2003   2 0 MAY 2005

2 4 MAR 2003   2 3 SEP 2005

2 7 MAY 2003

LIBREX —

1 7 MAY 2006

WITHDRAWN

INTERNATIONAL MARKETING
A GLOBAL PERSPECTIVE

Lee D. Dahringer
Emory University

Hans Mühlbacher
University of Innsbruck

ADDISON-WESLEY PUBLISHING COMPANY
Reading, Massachusetts   Menlo Park, California   New York
Don Mills, Ontario   Wokingham, England   Amsterdam   Bonn
Sydney   Singapore   Tokyo   Madrid   San Juan   Milan   Paris

To MD, HD, RAM, and ESM.

To Helga and Heike.

Library of Congress Cataloging-in-Publication Data

Dahringer, Lee.
  International marketing: a global perspective/ by Lee D. Dahringer and
Hans Mühlbacher.
      p.   cm.
  Includes bibliographical references and index.
  ISBN   0-201-50354-9
  1. Export marketing--Management.   I. Mühlbacher, Hans, 1949-
II. Title.
HF1416.D34   1991
658.8′ 48--dc20
                                                                    90-36665
                                                                          CIP

CREDITS

p. 7: Photo reprinted with permission from Wide World Photos, Inc.

pp. 8–9 (Map 1.1): Adapted with permission from *The Economist World Atlas and Almanac*, The Economist Books/ Prentice-Hall Press.

p. 11 (Exhibit 1.2): Reprinted with permission of Industrieverlag Peter Linde, Gesellschaft m.b.H.

p. 14 (Exhibit 1.5): Reprinted from May 1, 1989 issue of *Business Week* by special permission, copyright © 1989 by McGraw-Hill, Inc.

pp. 16–17 (Exhibit 1.6): Reprinted from July 17, 1989 issue of *Business Week* by Special Permission, copyright © 1989 by McGraw-Hill, Inc.

p. 18 (Exhibit 1.7): Data adapted from *Business America*, September 11, 1989, p. 7.

p. 19: Photo reprinted with permission from Wide World Photos, Inc.

p. 19: Cartoon courtesy of THE FAR SIDE COPYRIGHT 1985 (pg. 55) UNIVERSAL PRESS SYNDICATE. Reprinted with permission. All rights reserved.

p. 35: Photo reprinted courtesy of Longines Watch Co. Francillon Ltd.

p. 36 (Map 2.1): Adapted with permission from Honda Motor Co., Ltd.

p. 39 (Exhibit 2.4): Reprinted with permission from *The Columbia Journal of World Business*.

Credits continue on p. 663, which constitutes a continuation of the copyright page.

4 5 6 7 8 9 10-HA-95949392

PREFACE

Each student who embarks on a course in international marketing brings with him or her a rich view of the world and marketing that was acquired within that student's particular domestic culture. Nevertheless, to be successful as an international marketing practitioner, the student must open his or her "world view" to permit a thorough and objective analysis of opportunities in other cultures. The primary goal of this book is to broaden the way business students view international markets and marketing in order to encourage such an expanded view.

Most marketing managers view world markets internationally, or multinationally, as a series of discrete markets that do not share many characteristics. Yet international markets are currently changing. Worldwide opportunities and challenges presented by recent events—the sweeping changes in Eastern Europe, the economic integration of the European Community, the political and economic turmoil in the Middle East, the growth of markets in the Asian Pacific area, and the changing economic strength of the North American market— require new marketing management approaches to deal successfully with global competitors, suppliers, and markets. Most important, international marketers require a **global** perspective to compete successfully.

This text discusses the experiences of marketing authorities from around the world, then examines how successful companies decide which products to market, how best to market them, and how to find and take advantage of similarities across national markets. Benetton clothing, for example, appeals to young consumers in almost every economically developed nation. BankAmerica services corporate customers interested in low-interest loans and investment advice around the world. In addition, Sony sells consumer goods globally.

The text does not argue that a marketer should sell the same thing, the same way, everywhere. But a company that believes it *must* overhaul its marketing mix for each separate national market errs as much as one that applies only domestic marketing solutions to international marketing problems.

International Marketing: A Global Perspective is written for the student who is interested in international business and who has completed a principles of marketing course. Thus, some knowledge is assumed on the part of the student, as basic concepts are applied internationally. Terms and principles, however, may be reviewed briefly before a discussion that examines how moving across national borders affects those concepts.

Philosophy

The underlying assertion of this book is that *any firm—regardless of size—can compete globally.* Success is a function of opportunity, perspective, motivation, and knowledge. International opportunities are plentiful. The challenge for today's marketing manager is to identify those opportunities appropriate for the firm.

Approach and Organization

The book's five sections, as illustrated in the Exhibit, make the global approach to international marketing accessible to the student.

*   Part One deals with the factors **motivating** a marketing manager to enter international markets.

*   Part Two looks at the process of **assessing** a potential market, then matching market potential with a company's ability to market effectively.

*   From that assessment, Part Three takes the student through the process of **building** a marketing strategy. Managers must make basic strategic decisions, choose market positions and market entry methods, and develop marketing plans.

*   Part Four then discusses the process of **implementing** this strategy and addresses distribution, promotion, pricing plans, and implementation.

*   Part Five addresses the process of **managing,** by examining marketing management, business systems, marketing finance, and the future of global marketing including careers in the field.

To develop and implement successfully a global marketing perspective, an international marketer must be systematic in dealing with opportunities and problems. This book presents a systematic approach to these concepts. Part Two, for example, which deals with assessing potential markets, addresses the important issues in the same logical order used by a global marketer. While the marketer first examines the potential of markets, classification and assessment procedures are used. Then the marketer assesses the economic, political and legal, and cultural and social environments. The firm's potential itself is then evaluated and compared to the market opportunities identified. Subsequent sections of this book approach the information to be gathered, analyzed, and used from an international marketing manager's perspective.

This process may be applied to any size firm. In fact, many small firms worldwide, such as HIRSCH, a smaller manufacturer of high-quality watchbands based in Austria, competed successfully in global markets because of high motivation to be successful, and because the company approached international problems in the structured manner described in this book.

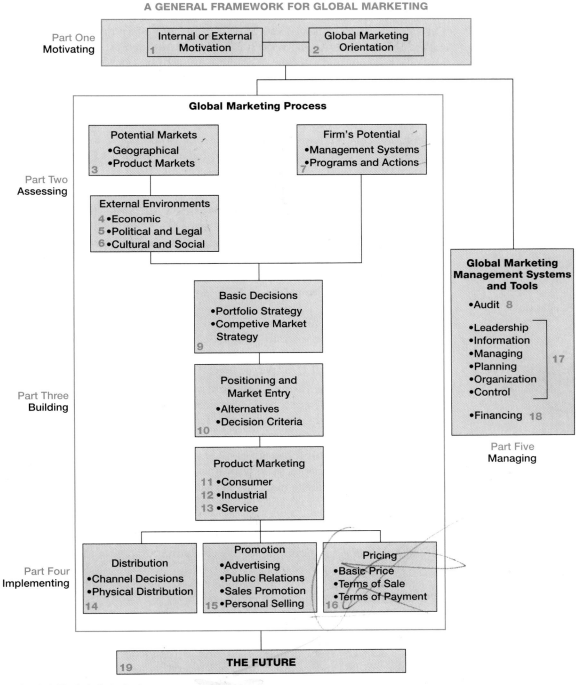

A GENERAL FRAMEWORK FOR GLOBAL MARKETING

Part One
Motivating

| Internal or External Motivation 1 | Global Marketing Orientation 2 |

Global Marketing Process

Part Two
Assessing

Potential Markets
•Geographical
•Product Markets
3

Firm's Potential
•Management Systems
•Programs and Actions
7

External Environments
4 •Economic
5 •Political and Legal
6 •Cultural and Social

Part Three
Building

Basic Decisions
•Portfolio Strategy
•Competive Market Strategy
9

Positioning and Market Entry
•Alternatives
•Decision Criteria
10

Product Marketing
11 •Consumer
12 •Industrial
13 •Service

Global Marketing Management Systems and Tools
•Audit 8

•Leadership
•Information
•Managing
•Planning
•Organization
•Control
17

•Financing 18

Part Five
Managing

Part Four
Implementing

Distribution
•Channel Decisions
•Physical Distribution
14

Promotion
•Advertising
•Public Relations
•Sales Promotion
•Personal Selling
15

Pricing
•Basic Price
•Terms of Sale
•Terms of Payment
16

19   **THE FUTURE**

Numbers in bold color indicate chapter

Why You Should Use This Text

The 1990s promise to be economically, socially, and politically turbulent. Radical changes in Eastern and Western Europe, the Middle East, Asia, and North America will continue to occur. Although any textbook can become somewhat outdated, this book will remain useful because it provides a structured approach for *analyzing* dynamic changes. The student is responsible for remaining current with world affairs. Both the analytical framework, which addresses such issues, and the global marketing perspective in this book will be valid in rapidly changing environments. Perhaps the global approach is necessary, not only to help a firm be aware of changes and their impact, but also to help it adjust successfully to such changes, which is the key to long-term survival.

To support this approach, this text offers several unique features.

- **Global perspective.** The horizontal search for strategically equivalent segments, across national markets, is a predominant theme.
- **Management orientation.** The organization of this book introduces students to international marketing through the decisions that international marketing managers must make.
- **Authors from two cultures.** Both authors of the text (one is American; the other is Austrian) have extensive experience in international-marketing teaching, researching, and consulting in North America, Eastern and Western Europe, Australia, India, and Lesotho, Africa. This experience resulted in a truly international outlook on marketing issues, versus the more conventional U.S. perspective.
- **Eastern Europe.** Because one author is from Austria, a nation that has traditionally served as a bridge between Eastern Europe and much of the rest of the world, the coverage of Eastern Europe in this text is more extensive than in other texts.
- **Services marketing.** Instead of a cursory discussion, this book has dedicated an entire chapter to services marketing because of the current high level of international trade in services and their unique dimensions as products.
- **Current.** Every effort has been made to ensure that the material in the text is as current as possible in discussions of global trends, environments, and relations. For example, we have included coverage of the radical political and economic changes in Eastern Europe as well as a look at the marketing implications of the debate over whether or not the European Community is a single unified market.

Teaching and Learning

The text has several features designed to motivate students' interest in the material, help them learn more efficiently, and make this text an effective teaching tool. Throughout, we have tried to present complex material in a straightforward manner, without oversimplifying the concepts. Various teaching and learning aids include the following:

- **International Incident.** Every chapter begins with an International Incident, a factual illustration of the chapter's international marketing concepts with a global perspective.

- **Glossary.** A glossary with key terms and definitions appears at the end of the text.

- **Key Terms and Margin Notes.** Key terms and their definitions are identified by boldface in the text. Key concepts are also summarized for learning reinforcement in the margin of the text.

- **Global Dimensions.** Discussions in boxed material highlight global approaches to social, cultural, political, and environmental issues that affect marketing.

- **End-of-Chapter Discussion Questions.** These questions provide a way for students to check their comprehension of the key issues discussed in the chapter. Some questions are appropriate for mini-projects, while others will stimulate class discussion. These questions also serve as an excellent vehicle for review of the chapter material.

- **Cases.** Each chapter concludes with a short case that allows for application of chapter material.

- **Art, Photos, and Maps.** Each chapter contains artwork, tables, photos, and maps that supplement and illustrate the chapter discussion. Four full-color maps, which serve as a general reference for students, also illustrate both the diversity and similarities among global markets.

- **Impact on the Marketing Mix.** Several chapters contain this section, which encourages the student to be sensitive to how each element in the international mix affects the others, and to recognize the highly dynamic nature of marketing management.

Instructor's Manual

An Instructor's Manual is also available to adopters of this text. This manual is designed to provide assistance to the professor in several ways.

- **Sample syllabi**—both semester and quarter system sample syllabi options are described.

- **Format options**—teaching format options include projects, cases, and lectures, with a brief explanation of the best use of the material, including advantages and disadvantages.

- **Student projects**—an author-provided, cross-culturally tested outline describes a student project option that guides the student through the development of an international marketing mix; shorter class projects that can be assigned throughout the semester are also provided.

- **Teaching aid resources**—a section that describes the film, video, and secondary data sources that are readily available for use by the professor either in the class, or for supporting materials for class projects.

- **Chapter overviews**—each chapter is summarized and outlined, topics are highlighted and prioritized, and timing issues are discussed.

- **Teaching suggestions**—hints for presenting key points and concepts for each section and chapter are provided.

- **Answers for End-of-Chapter Discussion Questions** are proposed.

- **Case teaching notes**—for each case, the instructor is provided with a synopsis, objectives, teaching notes, socioeconomic data, responses to case issues, and a case summary.

- **Additional cases**—additional cases and teaching notes not in the text are provided in the Instructor's Manual.

- **Transparency masters**—these are provided for the most important key figures and tables in the text, as well as for additional figures, tables, and illustrations to further highlight international marketing issues.

ACKNOWLEDGMENTS

All textbooks are the result of a team effort. In this case, with parts written on three different continents, it is especially true. We appreciate those educational institutions that provided support and encouragement during the writing and revision of the text: Emory Business School, Atlanta, Georgia, USA; University of Innsbruck, Innsbruck, Austria; Nijenrode—The Netherlands School of Business, The Netherlands; and The Graduate Business School, University of Queensland, St. Lucia, Australia.

Even more important than institutional support is the professional support, encouragement, and input provided by colleagues throughout the world. A partial list of those to whom we owe a special thanks include as follows: Dean No Knubben and Maria Meyer of Nijenrode; Dr. Oliver Yau and Dr. Ken Tucker of the Graduate Business School, University of Queensland; the late Dr. George M. Parks of Pace University; Roger Heisler of Emory Business School; Mary Ellen Templeton and David Vidor of the Emory University Libraries; Dr. Wilfried Vyslozel, University of Innsbruck; Magistrate Joachim Schwabe of Schwabe and Ley, Gesmbh., Vienna, Austria; and William E. Reinka, vice-president of Ocean Export, Expeditors International, Los Angeles, California.

Several reviewers in the United States and Europe also provided extremely valuable input, which helped the authors to polish drafts of the textbook and to communicate their ideas more clearly. These reviewers, who often worked under tight guidelines with rough manuscripts, include the following:

Gerald Albaum	University of Oregon
Erin Anderson	The Wharton School
Jessica Bailey	The American University
Phillip D. Grub	George Washington University
Sudhir H. Kale	Arizona State University
Algin B. King	Towson State University
Saul Klein	Northeastern University
Bertil Liander	University of Massachusetts—Amherst
James E. Littlefield	Virginia Polytechnic Institute & State University
Stan Paliwoda	University of Calgary
Judith D. Powell	University of Richmond
Manuel Rodriguez	California State University—Fullerton
Ron Savitt	University of Vermont
Jesper Strandskov	Copenhagen Business School
James K. Weekly	University of North Carolina—Charlotte

The Addison-Wesley team who worked on turning this manuscript into a text, across continents and time zones, deserves a special note of thanks. We are especially grateful to Christine O'Brien and Peggy J. Flanagan. Others who provided valuable assistance include Chip Price, Beth Toland, Mary Clare McEwing, Dick Morton, Mary Dyer, Maribeth Jones, and Mary Fisher. I would also like to thank Ann T. Kilbride, an independent packager, who supervised the production coordination of the text.

The strong Instructor's Manual, which adds significantly to the educational value of this text, was completed under tight guidelines at a remarkably high professional level thanks to Dr. Algin King, Towson State University, and Dr. Manny Rodriguez, California State University at Fullerton.

Finally, a special thanks must be given to the hundreds of students and practitioners, in many nations, who enthusiastically participated in classes, discussions, and consulting projects, helping us develop and test the material presented in this book. Any errors, of course, remain our responsibility. To the students and professors who use this book, any ideas, suggestions, comments, or recommendations would be most appreciated and considered in preparing future editions.

L. D. D.
H. M.

CONTENTS

LIST OF MAPS

MOTIVATING

PERHAPS THE MOST IMPORTANT CONTRIBUTING factor to the success of an international marketer in the world market is attitude. Today's marketplace is global, yet many firms continue to act as if they were involved only in domestic markets. Competitors, suppliers, and customers can come from around the world—these are some of the external factors discussed in Chapter 1, The Challenge of Global Business.

Success in any international business is built on the proper application of sound marketing principles. Then, a firm may analyze a foreign market to determine whether a marketing program should be modified, by how much, and what the expected profit from such modification might be.

A firm may also be motivated into international activity by internal motives, perhaps taking advantage of their distinct product, for example, or top management's vision. Internal motives and external motives stimulate the firm to be more active internationally and to address basic international business realities such as economic integration, the growing importance of the Triad (Western Europe, the United States/Canada, and Japan), and global competition.

Such realities and challenges require a carefully planned response if they are to be managed successfully. For today's firm challenged by global business, that response is the adoption of a global marketing perspective. This view of international markets and marketing gives the firm the advantages of economies of scale and experience curves to allow a more competitive edge through lower costs and increased effectiveness. Chapter 2 discusses the why of global marketing, as well as how to know when to use similar marketing campaigns across nations, when to use individual campaigns, and how to manage that process.

THE CHALLENGE OF GLOBAL BUSINESS

INTERNATIONAL INCIDENT

Procter & Gamble: Global Marketing in the 1990s?

In January 1990, Edwin Artzt took over as Chairman and CEO of Procter & Gamble, the company that helps Americans and the world wash their clothes (Tide and Ariel), brush their teeth (Crest and Blend-a-med), and diaper babies (Pampers).

Artzt was selected for many reasons, but chief among them was his extensive international experience, helping P&G's products become more competitive against strong competitors overseas such as Unilever (in Europe) and Kao (in Japan). The choice of an internationally experienced manager was a reflection of P&G's global activities and its view of the importance of international marketing in the future.

By the year 2000, estimates are that 60 percent of P&G's total sales will be from outside the United States, up from 27.4 percent in 1978. Much of this growth in P&G's international presence is a result of a more customer-focused decision-making process. For example, Japanese women who buy diapers prefer to change diapers more frequently than Americans do. After P&G changed its products to respond to national differences, sales increased dramatically. But at the same time, good ideas are shared across national markets. With diapers, for example, P&G popularized the concept of differently colored diapers for boys and girls in the United States. After careful testing, however, it discovered the same concept was well received in Japan, increasing sales even more.

As for P&G's future managers, Mr. Artzt says, "I'm not going to suggest everyone needs experience in three or four countries, but, increasingly, managers of multinational companies will have multinational experience."

Sources: Adapted from "P&G's New Boss Wants a More World Company," *Business Week*, October 30, 1989, pp. 40–43; "Artzt Puts Global Stamp on P&G," *Advertising Age*, October 16, 1989, pp. 1, 79, 82; and "P&G Rewrites the Marketing Rules," *Fortune*, November 6, 1989, pp. 43–48.

The history of world trade is one of exotic products coming from faraway lands to customers eager to buy something new. The southern islands of the Philippines, for example, were the center of a trading hub throughout Southeast Asia in the fourth century. Camphor from Borneo, cloves from the Moluccas, and parrots from New Guinea were all traded in the area. Today's "typical American consumer" may wake up to an alarm clock from Korea, drink coffee imported from Latin America, drive a Volvo from Sweden, and let the kids watch the "Smurfs" (originally from Germany) on a TV from Japan, while keeping track of the time with a Swiss watch. From the early days of direct trade or barter between neighboring communities to today's large-scale international trade, the result has been the same: more and different goods at lower prices than would have been possible if international trade had not occurred.

International trade increases consumer choice and lowers product prices.

When there are barriers to trade, whether natural or artificial, customers' choices are limited and they must pay higher prices. For example, when India limited imports of automobiles to that country, the cars that were available there were much more expensive than comparable models in Europe. Moreover, because domestically produced cars did not have to compete with imports, Indian manufacturers did not use the latest technology, in either styling or engineering.

In the twentieth century the importance of international trade has increased greatly. In fact, international trade has been growing faster than domestic economic activity. In the late 1980s, for example, world exports grew to a record total of $2,450 billion.[1] This remarkable level of trade has led to an economic environment in which no country is economically self-sufficient. To give just one example, the United States imports almost all of its VCRs, bananas, and coffee, while Japan depends on imports for 90 percent of its energy needs.

Increasingly open national markets make today's business environment a global one.

Where once many national markets were difficult to enter because of natural or artificial barriers, the growth of world trade is opening up new markets everywhere. As a result, buyers around the world—especially in the Triad markets (the Western European countries known as the European Community, the United States and Canada combined, and Japan)—have become accustomed to being able to obtain goods that have been produced in many other nations. Customers want to obtain the best products at the best possible prices. Hence, to be successful today most businesses must be able to satisfy customers in a global marketplace.

MARKETING—THE KEY TO BUSINESS SUCCESS

Marketing to global customers is the key to business success.

Before we explore the nature of **global marketing**, which is a business view of selling products to customers around the world, it is necessary to devote some attention to the importance of marketing in general. Although there is much discussion of the need for rapid technological development and high manufacturing productivity, as well as the problems of financing large-scale corporate operations, in the customer-dominated markets of economically developed nations marketing must be the focus of management's efforts if the firm is to remain competitive and profitable. (The role of marketing in less economically developed and centrally controlled economies is more controversial;[2] this is reviewed later in the book.)

On the one hand, marketing may be described as a bundle of management techniques (often referred to as **marketing technology**). These techniques guide a company in searching for appropriate markets and in gaining and maintaining a competitive position in those markets. On the other hand, marketing can be viewed as a basic approach to doing business; this is the so-called **marketing philosophy.** An organization that takes this approach focuses in a planned and systematic way on its exchange (including buying and selling) relationships with market partners.

EXHIBIT 1.1
THE MARKETING
PHILOSOPHY

The three core marketing
orientations must be
viewed from *both* the
long-term and global per-
spectives in order to ap-
ply the marketing philos-
ophy, the key to business
success.

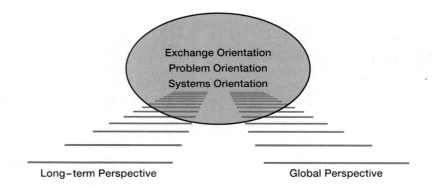

Exchange Orientation
Problem Orientation
Systems Orientation

Long–term Perspective   Global Perspective

Marketing is a philoso-
phy—an approach to
business—as well as a
set of techniques.

The marketing philosophy may be characterized by a number of basic orientations, as illustrated in Exhibit 1.1. An **exchange orientation** is the belief that a lasting business relationship can be established and maintained only if all the exchange partners are willing and able to contribute to the relationship so that each benefits. An Infiniti automobile, for example, is exchanged between the customers and the Nissan dealer. The exchange takes place only as long as the customer gains (reliable transport, status, attractive styling, and so on) as much as he or she gives up (money). The dealer gains the money; uses some for salary, profits, and office expenses; and exchanges the rest with Nissan for another car for a future sale.

Balanced exchange relationships cannot be built and maintained unless the partners adhere to the second basic orientation of the marketing philosophy: the **problem orientation**. Each exchange partner (especially a potential seller) needs to be aware of the actual or potential problems of the other partners and must help solve them. Thus, the first question to ask when analyzing a potential business relationship is not what the organization can gain from the deal but whether it can make a substantial contribution toward solving the problems faced by its exchange partner. If so, then sales and profits result.

A business firm should not overlook the fact that it has other exchange partners besides its customers and that its long-term success depends on satisfactory relationships with all of those exchange partners. The marketing philosophy should therefore include a **systems orientation**—an awareness that the organization's well-being depends on a continuous flow of resources from raw materials through distributors. This resource flow can be maintained only if decisions concerning one exchange relationship do not interfere with other relationships. If, for example, the solution to a customer problem (such as a new fertilizer that increases farm production) creates unacceptable living conditions near the company's production facilities (air pollution, for example) or violates government regulations (perhaps by exposing workers to dangerous fumes), the organization may not be able to offer that particular solution.

The marketing philosophy requires that the organization undertake the three orientations from a **long-term perspective**. One of the manager's most important duties is keeping track of current trends, anticipating future trends,

In 1989, Nissan Motor Corporation launched the Infiniti, their new entry into the luxury automobile market. This car was designed to compete with other world class luxury cars like Mercedes, Volvos, Peugeots, and Audis.

and assessing their implications for the organization. Managers must understand that while present success is a result of past efforts, it is no guarantee of success in the future. Future success can be achieved only by preparing for likely changes in the organization's exchange partnerships and in the nature of the problems it will be called upon to solve.

The information required for marketing decisions, and the resources to carry out those decisions, can come from locations throughout the world. So can potential competitors. Nissan, for example, competes against Mercedes-Benz, Volvo, Peugeot, and Audi. An organization's potential markets may also be located in many different geographic areas. The marketing philosophy in most businesses, therefore, should have a **global perspective**, that is, a strong orientation toward nondomestic markets. Amway, the U.S.-based home care products company, for example, found its marketing campaign in Japan to be so successful that sales were over $524 million in 1988.[3] Indeed, in view of the increasing internationalization of markets, competition, and resources, a global orientation is practically a prerequisite for successful business activities today.

WHY GO GLOBAL?

Often, a firm is at first reluctant to become involved in international marketing. But experience and a product-market orientation lead to many new opportunities.

A firm's initial reasons for entering foreign markets often are not clearly defined. Sometimes international sales are achieved at a low marketing cost as a result of unsolicited orders from nondomestic customers. The firm's reactions to such opportunities are not governed by traditional business strategies, profit-and-loss evaluations, or capital budgeting schemes.[4] Usually they are based on *psychic distance*, that is, the perception of large differences between foreign and domestic markets. "Going global" exposes managers to unknown environments, such as different buyer behavior, which increases perceived risk. For example, white is

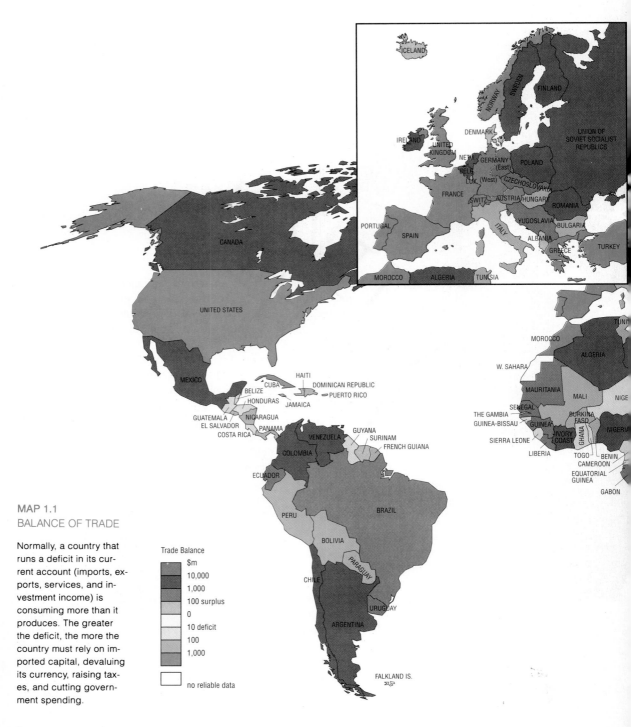

MAP 1.1
BALANCE OF TRADE

Normally, a country that runs a deficit in its current account (imports, exports, services, and investment income) is consuming more than it produces. The greater the deficit, the more the country must rely on imported capital, devaluing its currency, raising taxes, and cutting government spending.

Trade Balance
$m

	10,000
	1,000
	100 surplus
	0
	10 deficit
	100
	1,000

☐ no reliable data

8

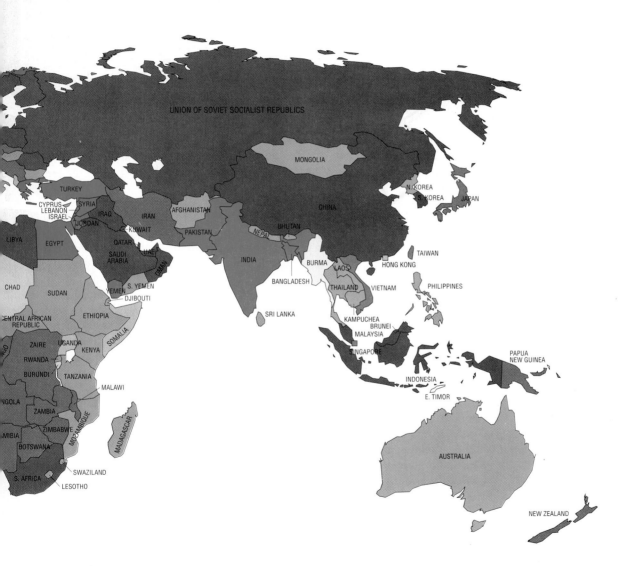

UNION OF SOVIET SOCIALIST REPUBLICS

MONGOLIA

TURKEY

CYPRUS
LEBANON
ISRAEL
JORDAN

SYRIA
IRAQ

IRAN

AFGHANISTAN

CHINA

N.KOREA
S.KOREA

JAPAN

KUWAIT

PAKISTAN

NEPAL

BHUTAN

LIBYA

EGYPT

QATAR
UAE
OMAN

SAUDI
ARABIA

INDIA

BURMA

LAOS

TAIWAN

HONG KONG

CHAD

SUDAN

YEMEN
DJIBOUTI

S. YEMEN

BANGLADESH

THAILAND

VIETNAM

PHILIPPINES

CENTRAL AFRICAN
REPUBLIC

ETHIOPIA

SRI LANKA

KAMPUCHEA

ZAIRE

UGANDA

SOMALIA

KENYA

RWANDA

BRUNEI
MALAYSIA

SINGAPORE

BURUNDI

TANZANIA

MALAWI

PAPUA
NEW GUINEA

NGOLA

ZAMBIA

MOZAMBIQUE

MADAGASCAR

INDONESIA

E. TIMOR

MIBIA

ZIMBABWE

BOTSWANA

SWAZILAND

AUSTRALIA

S. AFRICA

LESOTHO

NEW ZEALAND

a symbol of death in Japan, so international managers need to know that products packaged in white boxes do not sell as well there as they do in the United States, where white symbolizes purity. The desire to maintain a rational management approach in the face of such uncertainty often prompts managers to limit expansion to geographic markets that are perceived to be similar to the firm's domestic market—in other words, to minimize psychic distance by expanding, for example, from U.S. to British markets.

To take just one example, a U.S. company may respond immediately to an order from a Canadian firm because it feels comfortable selling to a "well-known" trading partner. Yet a potentially more profitable order from a German firm may receive no response because the U.S. firm's managers feel uneasy about the large number of unfamiliar tasks and unknown risks involved.[5]

A better approach to global marketing is to define *product markets* based on fulfilling the needs of specific groups of customers through the application of specific company capabilities. When defined in this manner, foreign market behavior may be very familiar to the decision maker even if the environments are new. Customers in many nations may seek the same benefits; they may be satisfied by the same product or service.

When a firm has gained some international experience, it may begin to recognize the long-term growth potential that results from a global perspective. When the resulting opportunities to develop new capabilities (technologies, expertise, experience) and new products become evident, the firm will routinely consider nondomestic business opportunities as part of its strategic decision making.[6]

Stimuli, motives, and objectives all influence the firm's globalization process.

There are three basic factors, each with two different elements, that govern a firm's globalization process: stimuli, motives, and objectives. Two general sources of stimuli may cause a firm to begin the process of expansion into nondomestic markets. **Internal stimuli** may include strong marketing skills, unique products (such as Apple computers), or excess capacity in the areas of management, marketing, production, or finance. A firm may be able, for example, to produce 100 units a day, but the domestic demand may be only 65 units; this might encourage the firm to find a nondomestic market that will buy the remaining 35 units. **External stimuli** may include unsolicited orders from foreign customers, perceived market opportunities, competitive pressures in the home market, or government programs to encourage exports.[7] Honda, for example, found competition so strong in the Japanese market that it entered foreign markets in order to grow.

A company's top managers become aware of these stimuli as a group. But each manager is likely to have a different set of motives.[8] Their motives may be classified as either defensive or offensive. When **defensive motives** dominate, management is reluctant to become involved in international business. **Offensive motives** lead to aggressive and systematic efforts to locate or respond to global opportunities. Austrians, for example, tend to be aggressive in response to external stimuli. (See Exhibit 1.2.) Their motives are very similar to those reported by Italian[9] and British[10] managers.

EXHIBIT 1.2
MOTIVES OF
AUSTRIAN TOP
MANAGERS WHO
DECIDE TO "GO
INTERNATIONAL"

	Companies with up to 499 people		Companies with 500 people or more	
	Rank	Frequency	Rank	Frequency
Our company exports because the production capacities can be better used or extended in the long run.	1	93.0	1	100
The home market does not grow fast enough.	2	78.7	2	92.9
Exports provide us with the necessary cash flow to modernize production.	3	71.3	4	70.1
Through exports the firm's image can be improved in the home market.	4	69.7	5	56.7
The Austrian market is saturated.	5	57.0	3	73.2
We want to neutralize our competitors in the home market (or get an advantage).	6	55.3	7	37.8
We want foreign currency.	7	46.3	7	37.8
Profit margins are higher in foreign markets.	8	37.1	11	26.0
Prices for our products are better in foreign markets.	9	36.5	9	32.3
We want to fight foreign competitors in their own markets.	10	36.1	6	43.3
Our products are difficult to sell in the home market.	11	35.3	10	28.9
We have foreign know-how.	12	29.2	12	18.9
Competition is weaker in foreign markets.	13	26.1	13	10.2

Source: H. Mühlbacher and G. Mitterhuber, "Die Internationali sierung der Geschafstatig-keit osterreichischer Unternehmungen, Motive und Tendenzen," *Journal fur Betriebswirtschaft* 2(1983): 103–116.

Together with the strategic objectives and operational objectives, or goals, set for the firm (discussed in Chapter 2), and the stimuli that induced the company to start a globalization process, top management's motives will lead to a predominantly defensive or offensive posture. Whether the motives are defensive or offensive largely determines the firm's commitment to global expansion, the resources allocated to such expansion, and the ways in which new markets are entered. In the first case, low-risk alternatives with a minimum of resources required, like indirect exporting, will be favored. An offensive posture will lead the company to take bolder steps, such as direct investment in new markets.

THEORIES OF WORLD TRADE

Many theories help explain why international trade occurs, but the end result is why it continues—better products at better prices.

A variety of theories attempt to explain why goods and services are sold internationally. Among these are the concept of an international product life-cycle, the theory of comparative advantage, direct investment theories, historical models, the technological forces, and others.

Although all of these explanations have merit, it should be remembered that nations don't trade, companies do. And companies can become much more efficient and effective through specializing in business areas such as improved technology, production, or marketing.[11] Through corporate specialization, just as for labor specialization, a greater output results from a given level of input. As output increases for the given input, total costs per unit fall, permitting lower prices. But a larger market is needed for the larger output. Thus firms can become more powerful competitors, producing more and better products at lower prices, if they pursue larger markets.

At some point, even the largest domestic markets, such as the United States, become mature and firms must turn to international markets to extend (find additional) sales and profits. This process is described by the international product life-cycle (Exhibit 1.3). For example, UPS (the parcel-delivery company), faced with a maturing U.S. market, expanded into 175 countries during the late 1980s in order to maintain sales.

The theory of **comparative advantage** underlies most other theories of world trade. It argues that trade occurs because a nation has a relative or comparative advantage in the production of a product compared to another nation. If two nations specialize in production of different products, a larger total output at lower costs results than if both nations tried to produce both goods. For purposes of discussion, comparative advantage theory frequently assumes there are only two nations, producing two products, and there is only one factor of production, labor. Obviously world trade is more complicated. But the model still holds if expanded to include more nations and products.

To illustrate, assume two nations, Korea and Denmark, are capable of producing wheat and steel. (See Exhibit 1.4.) Korea can produce in one labor day either 120 bushels of wheat or 20 tons of steel. In one labor day Denmark

EXHIBIT 1.3
INTERNATIONAL
PRODUCT LIFE CYCLE

As a product matures in a domestic market, its sales and profit curve begins to "flatten" and decline. In order to continue sales and profit growth, companies may seek out (extend to) new markets. Increasingly, those markets are international ones.

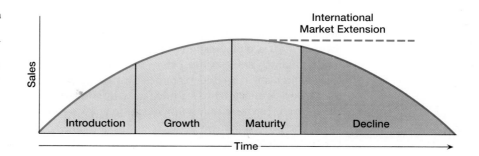

EXHIBIT 1.4
COMPARATIVE
ADVANTAGE

Korea		
Exports	=	100 bushels wheat
Imports	=	20.0 tons steel
Self-production of steel	=	<u>16.7</u> tons (100 ÷ 6)/6:1 = opportunity cost
Net gain	=	3.3 tons steel

Denmark		
Exports	=	20 tons steel
Imports	=	100 bushels wheat
Self-production of wheat	=	<u>80</u> bushels (20 × 4)/4:1 = opportunity cost
Net gain	=	20 bushels wheat

(Terms of trade = 5:1)

can produce either 40 bushels of wheat or 10 tons of steel. That is, Korea has an absolute advantage in the production of both goods. But Korea has a *comparative* advantage in the production of steel. (120:40 bushels of wheat = a 3:1 absolute advantage. 20:10 tons of steel = a 2:1 absolute advantage, comparatively less than the 3:1 wheat advantage.) If it were to focus on the production of wheat, Korea might produce and export 100 bushels. If the terms of free trade in our example are 5:1 (5 bushels of wheat for 1 ton of steel), Korea would receive 20 tons of steel. But if Korea were to produce its own steel with the labor it takes to produce 100 bushels of wheat, it would have only 16.7 tons (100 ÷ 6). Thus it gains 3.3 tons from international trade. Denmark exports 20 tons of steel for 100 bushels of wheat. But if it were to grow its own wheat instead of producing steel, it would produce only 80 bushels (20 × 4); thus it gains 20 bushels through international trade. As this example illustrates, nations engaged in international trade, even if one enjoys an absolute advantage in the production of all goods, can both enjoy greater total output, and lower costs, than if trade did not occur.

Direct investment theories examine world trade from the perspective of the corporate need to access business resources (markets, labor, raw materials, and so on). As Western Europe becomes increasingly economically integrated, now a market of 320 million consumers, for example, U.S. firms are increasing their investment in order to be close to this larger market and because they fear Western Europe might increase its protection of its home markets from imports. Worldwide, nearly 17 percent of total U.S. corporate assets are held outside the United States, more than for any other industrial nation. Investment into the United States is dramatic also. (See Exhibit 1.5 for recent trends.) In fact, since 1979 direct foreign investment in the United States has been greater than U.S. direct foreign investment abroad.

Traditional trade and investment patterns, or **historical models**, contribute to today's international business activities. Kenya, for example, was once a

EXHIBIT 1.5
JAPAN: NOW THE TOP
FOREIGN INVESTOR
IN THE UNITED
STATES

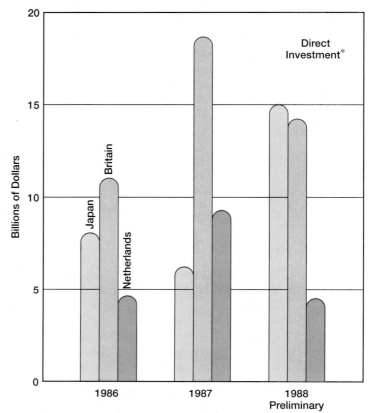

*Includes only investment where foreign company has control of U.S. operations. All portfolio investment is excluded.

Source: Business Week, May 1, 1989, p. 20.

colony of Great Britain. Today its major trading partner continues to be Great Britain. Another example is the United States, in which political stability, a relatively accessible market, and a relatively large and affluent market have made it an attractive international market for some time. Governments may establish policies, however, that try to alter historical patterns. The USSR, for example, in recent attempts to attract much needed foreign investment, passed laws that establish preferential tax treatment for foreign firms.

Perhaps the most current theory of why international trade is expanding so rapidly is that of *technological forces*. (For a business leader's opinion on the need for sharing technology internationally, see Global Dimensions 1.1.) Selling computer parts overseas, developing engineering skills through education, sharing production skills with business partners in other countries, and broadcasting TV programs across national borders all indicate how easily technology can be transferred. Borrowing technology, then creating new and better products based

GLOBAL   DIMENSIONS   1.1

The Need for Technological Innovation

"We live in a world of exploding scientific and engineering change. In such a world, no single country can hope to produce within itself all the breakthroughs it needs to remain competitive. It has only two choices: to become a technological backwater, or to let those innovations flow in from countries around the world while sending its own innovations to consumers far from its own shores."
John Akers, IBM chairman

on that technology, is Japan's strongest competitive advantage, according to Akio Morita, co-founder of Sony.[12]

Consumers are increasingly exposed to higher-quality products made by foreign companies. They are traveling more than ever before. And technology and communication increase the transfer of information around the world. (Cable News Network, for example, broadcasts in the United States and Western Europe.) Consumers are becoming more concerned about product quality and price than where the product was produced.

Domestic firms must recognize and adapt to customers' rapidly changing preferences or risk losing their business. A classic example is the U.S. automobile industry, which lost touch with American consumers during the 1970s. Japanese automakers filled the void, and the U.S. automobile industry has been struggling to regain lost sales ever since. By 1990 only Ford and General Motors were still among the ten largest automotive firms in the world. In fact, the largest companies in a given industry have changed from being almost all U.S.-based, to being headquartered around the world, as illustrated in Exhibit 1.6.

In sum, world trade increases in response to customers' desires for better products at better prices. And firms that discover their *competitive advantage* (what they do better than other firms in their industry) are in a better position to do business in any market, domestic or global. The difference today is that the markets and competitors are spread around the world.

WORLD ECONOMIC INTEGRATION

International trade has also resulted in economically interdependent nations.

Today no nation is economically independent. For example, the financial ministers of the six leading industrial nations meet regularly to "cooperate closely to foster stability of currency exchange rates."[13] Economic integration, of course, also has political and social dimensions. Thus, the European Community (EC)—composed of the United Kingdom, France, Germany, Spain, Greece, The Netherlands, Italy, Portugal, Belgium, Denmark, Ireland, and Luxembourg—is committed not only to economic integration by 1992 but also to greater political integration in the long run.

EXHIBIT 1.6   THE WORLD'S LARGEST 100 COMPANIES

Rank 1989	1988			Market Value Billions of U.S. Dollars	Rank 1989	1988			Market Value Billions of U.S. Dollars
1	1	Nippon Telegraph & Telephone	Japan	163.86	31	24	British Telecommunications	Britain	24.29
2	9	Industrial Bank of Japan	Japan	71.59	32	39	Bellsouth	U.S.	24.17
3	2	Sumitomo Bank	Japan	69.59	33	20	British Petroleum	Britain	24.15
4	5	Fuji Bank	Japan	67.08	34	25	Ford Motor	U.S.	23.93
5	4	Dai-Ichi Kangyo Bank	Japan	66.09	35	43	Amoco	U.S.	22.93
6	3	IBM	U.S.	64.65	36	34	Bank of Tokyo	Japan	22.46
7	10	Mitsubishi Bank	Japan	59.27	37	55	Chubu Electric Power	Japan	21.97
8	6	Exxon	U.S.	54.92	38	23	Sumitomo Trust & Banking	Japan	21.86
9	7	Tokyo Electric Power	Japan	54.46	39	66	Coca-Cola	U.S.	21.50
10	12	Royal Dutch/Shell Group	Neth./Britain	54.36	40	60	Wal-Mart Stores	U.S.	21.49
11	13	Toyota Motor	Japan	54.17	41	26	Mitsubishi Estate	Japan	21.45
12	14	General Electric	U.S.	49.39	42	116	Kawasaki Steel	Japan	21.30
13	11	Sanwa Bank	Japan	49.29	43	46	Mobil	U.S.	21.15
14	8	Nomura Securities	Japan	44.44	44	29	Tokyo Gas	Japan	21.13
15	27	Nippon Steel	Japan	41.48	45	32	Tokio Marine & Fire	Japan	20.91
16	21	A T & T	U.S.	38.12	46	108	NKK	Japan	20.15
17	17	Hitachi Ltd.	Japan	35.82	47	63	Atlantic Richfield	U.S.	19.63
18	15	Matsushita Electric Industrial	Japan	35.70	48	28	NEC	Japan	19.61
19	41	Philip Morris	U.S.	32.14	49	30	Daiwa Securities	Japan	19.11
20	38	Toshiba	Japan	30.91	50	50	Asahi Glass	Japan	19.05
21	33	Kansai Electric Power	Japan	30.89	51	37	Fujitsu	Japan	19.05
22	16	Long-Term Credit Bank	Japan	30.85	52	52	Chevron	U.S.	18.90
23	18	Tokai Bank	Japan	30.54	53	36	Nikko Securities	Japan	18.84
24	19	Mitsui Bank	Japan	29.69	54	54	Japan Air Lines	Japan	18.03
25	35	Merck	U.S.	27.52	55	98	Mitsubishi Electric	Japan	17.94
26	53	Nissan Motor	Japan	26.98	56	131	Sumitomo Metal Industries	Japan	17.86
27	48	Mitsubishi Heavy Industries	Japan	26.65	57	59	Nippon Credit Bank	Japan	17.71
28	40	Du Pont	U.S.	26.08	58	42	All Nippon Airways	Japan	17.65
29	31	General Motors	U.S.	25.25	59	79	Sears, Roebuck	U.S.	17.50
30	22	Mitsubishi Trust & Banking	Japan	24.67	60	84	Procter & Gamble	U.S.	17.40

EXHIBIT 1.6   *(continued)*

Rank 1989	1988			Market Value Billions of U.S. Dollars	Rank 1989	1988			Market Value Billions of U.S. Dollars
61	94	GTE	U.S.	17.33	81	49	Yamaichi Securities	Japan	14.96
62	68	Bell Atlantic	U.S.	17.12	82	75	Assicurazioni Generali	Italy	14.79
63	62	Dow Chemical	U.S.	17.00	83	44	Takeda Chemical Industries	Japan	14.75
64	83	Pacific Telesis	U.S.	16.86	84	73	Eastman Kodak	U.S.	14.52
65	45	Taiyo Kobe Bank	Japan	16.63	85	91	Bristol-Myers	U.S.	14.39
66	64	Unilever	Neth./Britain	16.60	86	65	Daimler-Benz	West Germany	14.36
67	61	Mitsubishi Corp.	Japan	16.50	87	122	Pepsico	U.S.	14.22
68	74	Johnson & Johnson	U.S.	16.45	88	77	Kinki Nippon Railway	Japan	14.14
69	56	Daiwa Bank	Japan	16.25	89	111	American Home Products	U.S.	13.58
70	70	Minnesota Mining & Mfg.	U.S.	16.09	90	114	Kajima	Japan	13.53
71	47	Mitsui Trust & Banking	Japan	16.09	91	101	American Express	U.S.	13.49
72	76	Nynex	U.S.	16.05	92	102	B.A.T. Industries	Britain	13.46
73	86	Ameritech	U.S.	16.02	93	69	Yasuda Trust & Banking	Japan	13.46
74	88	Glaxo Holdings	Britain	15.92	94	96	Imperial Chemical Industries	Britain	13.43
75	171	Kobe Steel	Japan	15.79	95	115	Siemens	West Germany	13.39
76	51	Seibu Railway	Japan	15.67	96	78	Nestlé	Switzerland	13.39
77	100	Southwestern Bell	U.S.	15.51	97	124	American International Group	U.S.	13.38
78	120	Sony	Japan	15.19	98	112	Abbott Laboratories	U.S.	13.35
79	104	Eli Lilly	U.S.	15.19	99	80	Fiat Group	Italy	13.32
80	109	Osaka Gas	Japan	15.05	100	85	Honda Motor	Japan	13.30

Source: *Business Week*, July 17, 1989, p. 140.

Not only Europe, but the entire world, is increasingly economically integrated. As of 1987, for example, the United States was the world's leading debtor nation, owing over $400 billion to foreign investors. The payments on that debt would be equivalent to some $2,600 per year for an average family of four. As a result, other nations have an unprecedented degree of influence on the U.S. economy. More U.S. farmland than Japanese farmland, for example, is used to feed the Japanese.[14] (For illustrations of the composition of U.S. trade see Exhibit 1.7.)

EXHIBIT 1.7   COMPOSITION OF U.S. MERCHANDISE TRADE

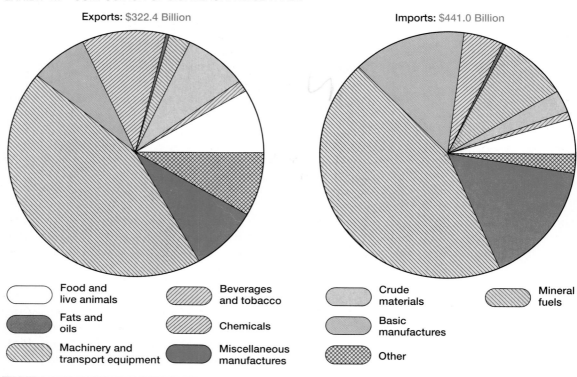

Exports: $322.4 Billion   Imports: $441.0 Billion

Food and live animals | Beverages and tobacco | Crude materials | Mineral fuels
Fats and oils | Chemicals | Basic manufactures
Machinery and transport equipment | Miscellaneous manufactures | Other

Source: *Business America*, September 11, 1989, p. 7.

World economic integration carries with it both social costs and social benefits. For example, steel can be manufactured in Pjonjang, South Korea, and sold in Pittsburgh at a lower price than steel manufactured in Pittsburgh—a fact that affects employment rates in both Pittsburgh and Pjonjang. In 1987, for the first time, more Japanese cars than cars made by Swedish manufacturers were sold in Sweden, a change that became a subject of political controversy. Movies and TV programs produced in various nations are exported throughout the world. (Sales of U.S. TV programs to Europe alone are expected to be more than $2 billion by 1992.[15]) Critics charge that the global spread of fast-food restaurants, together with large-scale agricultural production and foreign investment in wine facilities, is undermining the gastronomic traditions of France.[16] And foreign investment that tends to be controversial, such as the purchase of CBS Records by Sony, is increasing in almost every nation.[17]

The Triad

Much of the increasing integration of the world economy is occurring in the Triad—some 880 million consumers in all. Consumers in these markets are

The "I Love Lucy" show exemplifies the global popularity of U.S. TV programs. Currently the show is on the air 24 hours a day, since it is broadcast somewhere in the world at all times.

argued to be increasingly similar.[18] According to the chief executive officer of the Olivetti Company, in order to be globally competitive "a business must increasingly feel comfortable in Europe, Japan, and the United States, all at once."[19]

The Triad—880 million relatively affluent consumers—forms the basis of international trade.

In essence, the **"Triad view"** of marketing requires that the firm assess opportunities to standardize its marketing mix for the Triad markets or determine the degree of modification required for particular national markets within the Triad. A firm does not have to be a global giant like Toyota or Ford to take the Triad view. Smaller firms like Waterford Wedgwood, a manufacturer of fine china based in the United Kingdom, compete successfully in Japan, the United States, and Europe. Medium-sized U.S. firms like Scientific Atlanta, a global marketer of telecommunications systems, compete successfully throughout the world against much larger corporations such as Alcatel (Belgium) and NEC (Japan). The critical element is not size but an approach or philosophy that views the world as consisting of many potential markets; it is, in short, a global perspective.

The greatest international business opportunities for a firm may result from being aware of external opportunities—sometimes such opportunities may even happen by chance.

"*Now* that desk looks better. Everything's squared away, yessir, squaaaaaared away."

· ·
GLOBAL COMPETITION

Today's marketers face global competition in all industries.

For most firms, the primary stimulus to enter global markets is **competition**. Business today is increasingly characterized by competitors operating on a worldwide level. In addition, foreign competitors are claiming an increasing share of domestic markets. Many companies based outside the United States are heavily supported by their governments in the companies' quest for international sales. Airbus Industrie, for example, which competes against Boeing and McDonnell Douglas, has been supported by several Western European nations for twenty years, but has yet to make a profit. One frustrated U.S. executive even claims, "American companies are not competing with other companies but with the treasuries of other governments, and that's the problem." Others, however, argue that U.S. firms' poor global competitive position is due more to U.S. management paying too little attention to global business.[20]

Also becoming more frequent is **cross-subsidization** of markets, in which a corporation uses cash generated in one market to subsidize marketing programs in another. Thus, the Michelin tire company uses revenues from its domestic market in France to support its marketing campaigns in the United States.

In recent years entire industries have become global in their competitive scope. They range from multidomestic industries, in which competition in each country (or small groups of countries) is relatively independent of competition in other countries, to truly global industries, in which a firm's competitive position in one country is significantly influenced by its position in other countries.[21] In a multidomestic industry, which was common two decades ago and still exists today, the firm can choose to remain domestic or become multinational, applying different strategies depending on local market conditions. In a global industry, on the other hand, the firm that wants to survive must be active on a global scale and must develop an integrated worldwide strategy for all of its operations.[22] Examples of global industries include commercial aircraft, automobiles, and watches. But extreme caution must be used in developing and executing an integrated worldwide strategy, as the risks and potential for mistakes are greater than for a multinational approach.

Most industries are somewhere between these two extremes. However, there is a clear trend toward increasingly global industries. The importance of purely national competition is decreasing in computers, pharmaceutical products, consumer electronics, chemicals, machinery, and industrial control systems. Similar developments are being seen in consumer and service industries such as soft drinks, clothing, tourism, insurance, shipping, and banking. (See Global Dimensions 1.2.)

In an industry that is becoming global, it is no longer effective to use national boundaries as a basis for market segmentation. This means that large national companies (which may be small in global terms) must change their strategies. As is illustrated by companies like U.S. Steel and British Leyland Motor Corporation, strong national firms that may even have been leaders in

GLOBAL DIMENSIONS 1.2

Banking and Global Business

"Unfortunately, many U.S. exporters face foreign competition with a serious handicap: they cannot rely on their hometown banker to provide a full range of international financial services." This complaint signals the lack of a national policy in the United States to support exports through an array of integrated banking services and the inability of small banks to deliver the full range of banking services that companies need to compete in international markets. Since foreign competitors can count on national banking networks that do provide those services, this situation places U.S. firms at a disadvantage.

Only about 60 of the more than 14,000 banks in the United States offer international banking services. And only a handful have a complete global network of foreign subsidiaries and branches. In contrast, European, Canadian, and Japanese banks commonly offer a wide range of services both domestically and globally. Even in the small Dutch town of Breukelen, businesses have access to a banking network that spans the globe. In a typical American bank, in contrast, it can take six weeks to cash a foreign check.

Source: H. R. Heller, "U.S. Exporters Need First-Rate Global Banking Networks," *Business Week*, June 8, 1987, p. 20.

their industry at one time may find their positions eroded as the industry becomes global in scope.[23]

Companies that operate globally treat the world as a source of supply as well as demand. They obtain the resources they need wherever they can buy them at the best price. Manufacturing spare parts or even entire products in low-wage countries allows global firms to engage in intensive price competition against domestic firms in many markets. (Wage rates do change, however. Tandy recently closed a computer-component plant in Korea, due in part to Korea's industrial wage increasing 110 percent since 1984.[24]) Technological know-how gained in different parts of the world is quickly applied to new products. Cooperation with firms in other nations can reduce costs and increase management knowledge, further enhancing the competitiveness of global firms relative to domestic firms. (See Global Dimensions 1.3.)

Small companies may still be competitive in a global environment.

Smaller companies are not necessarily forced out of the market as their industry becomes global. Instead, they may perceive opportunities in special market segments. These may be defined either by specific customer needs or by characteristics such as license requirements, contract-negotiation procedures, governmental control, or payment in products instead of money. The Australian Pie Company, for example, sells high-quality meat pies to customers with similar tastes in both Australia and Japan.

GLOBAL DIMENSIONS 1.3

Global Insurance Partners

Japan-based Nippon Life Insurance Company has bought part of a U.S. firm, Shearson Lehman Brothers, in order to gain training and exposure to more sophisticated financial operations. Shearson Lehman will train Nippon Life employees in corporate finance, stock and bond trading, and asset management. Shearson Lehman's primary owner, American Express, is offering its credit cards through Nippon Life's sales force, which consists of some 80,000 salespeople. In the long run, Nippon Life intends to enter the U.S. insurance market. But the company's managers realize that they must first study the market carefully, because it differs significantly from the Japanese market in marketing methods, products (such as insurance policies), and actuarial assumptions.

Source: J. Heins, "No Place Like Home," *Forbes*, November 16, 1987, p. 104.

In sum, no member of a global industry, whatever its size, can continue to focus solely on domestic business. Even small firms have to reach out and serve special markets on a global level in order to survive.

Even if firms do not expand their business across national borders, their competitors are increasingly likely to be based in other countries. Both local and national firms are confronted with foreign competitors in their home markets. Since the mid-1980s, more than 70 percent of all goods produced in the United States have faced competition from nondomestic sources.[25] For example, in addition to purchasing business software from U.S. vendors, American Express obtains high-quality software at a lower cost from a firm based in India.[26] Similarly, consumer electronics firms in Taiwan and South Korea sell their products in the U.S. market.[27]

Instead of competing with local firms, new entrants to the market may simply buy them. In 1987 British Petroleum, Unilever, and Hoechst, all European corporations, took three of the seven highest positions on *Fortune*'s list of "U.S. Deals of the Year" when they bought U.S. companies.[28] As long as the value of the U.S. dollar is low compared to that of other currencies, foreign companies will find such deals attractive. (See Exhibit 1.6.)

Foreign ownership does not seem to have adverse effects on the sovereignty of governments or the welfare of citizens in the host country. On the contrary, the intensification of competition in domestic markets, or international market potential, should encourage entrepreneurs and managers of smaller companies to enter nondomestic markets themselves. For firms with high-quality products that have gained customer acceptance, it may actually be easier to expand into other markets than to increase their share of the domestic market. If a firm has recognized expertise in a specific area, it may be able to "export" its know-how, thereby obtaining a considerable amount of global business.

Resources

Resources and supplies have become global as well.

In many industries the rate of innovation is less than dramatic. As a consequence, domestic as well as global competition for market share often boils down to a race to lower prices. Hence, opportunities to reduce costs and/or increase efficiency are welcome. Again, the firm with nondomestic business has an advantage. It has access to cheaper sources of raw material, capital, and labor. Research and development can be conducted wherever the necessary resources in terms of brain power, technological know-how, and capital are located.

Firms of any size can engage in this type of competition. For example, a family-owned maker of industrial uniforms in Georgia recently installed a computer system that will make its entire production and marketing process more efficient, thereby helping the company compete more effectively against imported products. In the opinion of its managers, "The competition is so global today that a small company in little-town Georgia has to be as concerned with competition in Italy and Taiwan as General Motors is."[29]

New developments in process technology (such as improvements in manufacturing equipment) can be recognized and applied on short notice in many foreign countries. The report of the President's Commission on Industrial Competitiveness states that one of the biggest mistakes of U.S. industrial policy has been to overlook the importance of production-process technologies. A company cannot maintain a competitive advantage in industries with rapid new product development based on the latest technology when foreign competitors can quickly produce the same products far more cheaply.[30] U.S. companies were slow to grasp the importance of robots, automation, and statistical quality control—all of which were commercially developed in the United States but were applied with much more rigor and success in other countries, including Japan, Germany, Sweden, and France.

Markets

To attain and maintain global competitiveness, however, it is not enough simply to keep abreast of technological developments. The firm must have a "portfolio" of markets that allows it to balance lower cash flows in some markets against higher cash flows in others. Moreover, when a competitor attacks it in its home market, the firm should be able to mount a counterattack in the competitor's own domain. This ability made it possible for Goodyear to slow the pace of Michelin's attack on the American tire market.[31] And, increasingly, small U.S. companies are beginning to establish their own sales forces, or to invest in factories overseas.

In order to remain healthy, most companies must grow. However, many home markets in the industrialized nations are saturated. For many small to medium-sized firms, growth through additions to the existing product line is also difficult. These firms may have limited financial resources, production capacities, or technological know-how, or they may encounter competitors offering the same products. Diversification into new areas of business is always risky. The most viable alternative may be to enter less saturated foreign markets.

Many foreign markets offer more opportunity for business expansion than the home market does. Among the high growth members of the American Business Conference, whose annual revenues average $360 million, foreign sales grew at a 20 percent annual rate from 1981 to 1986, five times faster than the average U.S. domestic growth rate.[32] The United States regained its role as the world's largest exporter in 1989, beating out West Germany, and it continues to be the world's largest importer too. Overall, Canada is the largest U.S. trading partner, followed by Japan.

Increasingly, global marketing is not only a route to growth but also a necessary means of survival. In Europe, stagnant growth, competitive pressure, and the need to reduce costs have made nondomestic business a must for many firms. European firms have reacted positively to this challenge. For example, 54 percent of the gross national product (GNP) of The Netherlands, 22 percent of Britain's GNP, and 26 percent of Canada's come from exports. In the mid-1980s Germany's machinery industry had an export rate of 62 percent.[33]

In the United States, in contrast, only 250 companies accounted for 80 percent of exports in 1987.[34] In 1988 only 39,000 U.S. manufacturers, or about one in ten, were engaged in exporting.[35] There were at least 30,000 small U.S. companies that had export potential but were not conducting business in foreign markets.[36] Although U.S. exports totaled over $217 billion in 1986, only 5.1 percent of the nation's GNP was derived from export transactions. Much smaller West Germany, with exports of over $230 billion (29 percent of its GNP), was the world's leading exporter.[37]

Some small, locally operating businesses do not perceive the threat embodied in these statistics. They feel certain that their markets are too small and too specialized to be entered by global competitors. Or they put their faith in economic, political, and legal barriers to entry by foreign firms. But is any business's current success and future profit potential really independent from developments in other parts of the world? Even the owner of a drugstore in Winslow, Arizona, needs to take a more global view. From the prices of the products sold in the store to the rate of interest on the mortgage, many elements of day-to-day business reflect the impact of decisions made in London, Tokyo, or Frankfurt. In the following chapter we will take a closer look at the challenges and opportunities that await a firm that broadens its horizons and assumes a global marketing perspective.

Market growth and opportunity is usually greater in foreign markets than in domestic ones.

Global marketing is increasingly necessary for the survival of the firm, but U.S. firms have been slow to adapt to the global marketplace.

SUMMARY

In the consumer-dominated markets of developed nations, marketing must be the focus of management's efforts if the firm is to remain competitive and profitable. A marketing philosophy is characterized by a number of basic orientations. One of these is the exchange orientation, the conviction that a lasting business relationship can be established and maintained only if all the exchange partners are willing and able to contribute to the relationship in such a way that each will benefit. However, balanced exchange relationships cannot be maintained unless the partners adhere to a problem orientation, in which each partner is aware of the actual or potential problems of the other partners and contributes to efforts to solve them. The marketing philosophy also includes a systems orientation: managers are conscious of the fact that the organization's well-being depends on a continuous flow of resources.

The marketing philosophy requires that the organization maintain a long-term perspective. The marketing philosophy should also be combined with a global perspective, a distinctive orientation toward nondomestic markets.

Marketers have traditionally defined foreign markets on the basis of geographic boundaries. A more realistic approach to global marketing is to define product markets based on the benefits provided to specific groups of customers through the application of specific technologies. There are two general sources of stimuli that may cause a firm to begin the process of expansion into nondomestic markets: internal stimuli, such as a unique corporate competence, and external stimuli, such as unsolicited orders from foreign customers.

In responding to these stimuli, the company's managers may be dominated by different sets of motives. When defensive motives dominate, management is reluctant to solve a problem or respond to a stimulus by becoming involved in international business. Offensive motives lead to more aggressive and systematic efforts to locate global opportunities.

Organizations operating at a global level are continually searching for areas of specialization that will give them a competitive edge. Underlying this process is the buyer's desire to purchase the best product at the best price. World trade increases in response to that desire.

One effect of the increase in world trade is that today no nation is economically independent. Much of the increasing integration of the world economy originates in the Triad—the United States/Canada, Japan, and the European Community. Customers in these markets are increasingly similar, a fact that encourages firms to standardize their marketing mixes for the Triad markets. This approach can be extended to potential markets throughout the world, thereby becoming a global perspective.

For most firms, the primary stimulus to enter global markets is competition. In recent years entire industries have become global in their competitive scope. In such industries it is no longer effective to use national boundaries as a basis for market segmentation. Companies that operate globally view the entire world as a source of both customers and resources.

Even if firms do not expand their business across national borders, their competitors are increasingly likely to be based in other countries. Both local and national firms are confronted with foreign competitors in their home markets. Firms of all sizes also compete for resources, such as cheaper raw material, capital, and labor.

Another stimulus to "go global" is the search for new markets. To remain healthy, most companies must grow—but many home markets in the industrialized nations are saturated. Many foreign markets offer more opportunity for business expansion than the home market does. Indeed, for many firms global marketing is a route not merely to growth but to survival.

Today no business's current success and future profit potential are independent from developments in other parts of the world. Almost any firm may benefit from broadening its horizons and assuming a global marketing perspective.

DISCUSSION QUESTIONS

1. What are the three basic orientations underlying a marketing philosophy? What are their roles in international marketing?

2. What is psychic distance? How does it influence a firm's motives for engaging in global business?

3. Suppose your company is based in Minneapolis and manufactures fish-smoking equipment for the home market. A Brazilian firm inquires about your company's products. Illustrate how the company would react to this external stimulus if its managers' motives were defensive, compared to how it would react if the managers' motives were offensive.

4. Why has world trade developed to such an extent if a country like the United States can produce just about everything it needs?

5. Why is world economic integration increasing?

6. Why is the Triad so important to marketers today?

7. "The importance of international or global business to large firms is real. But small firms that sell only in the domestic market do not need to be concerned." Do you agree with this statement? Why or why not?

8. What major trends are making it more important than ever for firms to pay attention to opportunities for international trade?

9. In your opinion, why aren't more U.S. companies involved in international trade?

NORRELL TEMPORARY SERVICES

Doug Miller, president of Norrell Franchise Division, was concerned about the future of Norrell Temporary Services, a leader in the U.S. temporary services industry. While domestic growth and profits had been heartening, he believed the future held competition from overseas, as well as potential opportunities in other national markets. Initial exploration of the market in the United Kingdom had been undertaken, with potential opportunities identified. Mr. Miller thought now was the time to act.

Norrell Temporary Services provides temporary personnel to corporations in almost every business. The temporary services industry had seen rapid growth in the United States, and signals from international markets indicated strong potential there, too. Additionally, competition was becoming more global. For example, although experiencing considerable internal reorganization problems, Blue Arrow, a British company, had recently bought Manpower, one of Norrell's biggest U.S. competitors. A Swiss temporary services company had established a significant U.S. subsidiary, and a Canada-based company had entered Australia, possibly as a "bridge market" into Asia.

Although firm data on the international temporary services market were difficult to find, changing European Community laws concerning permanent employment and increasing economic activity in Asia both pointed to possible growth markets for companies providing temporary personnel services. France, for example, traditionally barred temporary personnel hiring for all jobs classified as permanent. But Mr. Miller knew that the coordination of EC member nations' laws expected in 1992 might well significantly alter such a restriction.

Norrell wanted to move quickly; it believed the future of the temporary services industry had to take into account international competitors and markets. The question was how best to proceed. Should the European Community be of primary interest? Certainly, temporary services companies existed in the United Kingdom, with strong national and international competitors. Large regional competitors were to be found in West Germany. And Kelly Services, a major U.S.-based competitor, had already begun to move into Europe. But Norrell was aware of the other third of the Triad. Japan, with its tremendous economic growth and shifting labor demands, might be worth considering. Norrell was also interested in the rest of Asia, in particular the Newly Industrialized Countries (NICs). A member of Norrell's board of directors suggested that nations such as Hong Kong, Taiwan, Singapore, Malaysia, Korea, and Indonesia would become particularly important. Many of these nations were experiencing rapid economic growth, outpacing the growth in the labor supply. Australia and New Zealand were of interest, too, because of similarities in the marketplace and operations observed by Norrell's CEO during a trip there.

Norrell, of course, had a wealth of experience in franchising operations in the United States. In fact, much of its success was based on its strong franchise system of offices throughout the nation. Extending such experience might be the best way to enter other markets. But Mr. Miller was well aware that Norrell needed to consider the problem more fully before developing an international marketing plan.

Case Issues

1. What factors contribute to Norrell's desire to further explore the international market? Be sure to look for internal stimuli, external stimuli, a defensive versus offensive approach, and strategic versus operational issues.

2. The book discusses basic stimulations for an increased interest in international marketing activities. Which of these are in force in the Norrell case?

3. What recommendations would you make to Mr. Miller?

N O T E S

1. "The Changing World Trade Structure," *Focus Japan*, November 1988, p. 1.

2. See I. P. Akaah and E. W. Riordan, "Applicability of Marketing Know-how in the Third World," *International Marketing Review*, Spring 1988, pp. 41–55; N. Dholakia and R. R. Dholakia, "Marketing in the Emerging World Order," *Journal of Macromarketing*, Spring 1982, pp. 47–56; and J. Naor, "Toward a Socialist Marketing Concept—The Case of Romania," *Journal of Marketing*, January 1986, pp. 28–39.

3. "Amway's Big, Happy Family Is All Smiles—In Japan," *Business Week*, September 4, 1989, pp. 47, 50.

4. N. J. Barrett and I. F. Wilkinson, "Internationalization Behavior, Management Characteristics of Australian Manufacturing Firms by Level of International Development," in P. W. Turnbull and S. J. Paliwoda, eds., *Research in International Marketing* (London: Croom Helm, 1986), pp. 213–233.

5. A. Yaprak, "An Empirical Study of the Differences Between Small Exporting and Non-Exporting U.S. Firms," *International Marketing Review*, Summer 1985, pp. 72–83.

6. Barrett and Wilkinson, op. cit.

7. F. Wiedersheim-Paul, H. C. Olson, and L. S. Welch, "Pre-export Activity: The First Step in Internationalization," *Journal of International Business Studies*, Spring/Summer 1987, pp. 47–58.

8. E. Dichtl, M. Leibold, H. G. Koglmayr, and S. Muller, "The Foreign Orientation of Management as a Central Construct in Export-centered Decision-making Processes," *Research for Marketing* 10, no. 1 (1983):7–14; and S. Reid, "Firm and Managerial Determinants of Export Market Expansion Strategies, An Empirical Investigation," in S. Barone and V. M. R. Tummala, eds., *Proceedings, Midwest AIDS Annual Meeting*, Academy of Decision Sciences, pp. 96–99.

9. S. Reid, "An Anatomy of the Export Expansion Process," paper presented at the Third International IMP Research Seminar on International Marketing, Lyon, 1986.

10. J. C. Leontiades, *Multinational Corporate Strategy* (Lexington, Mass.: Lexington Books, 1985), pp. 66–67.

11. See R. D. Robinson, "Some New Competitive Factors in International Marketing," in *Advances in International Marketing*, vol. 1 (Greenwich, Conn.: JAI Press, 1986), pp. 1–20.

12. "A Japanese View: Why America Has Fallen Behind," *Fortune*, September 25, 1989, p. 52.

13. T. May, Jr., "Fortune Forecast: Equilibrium Ahead for Interest Rates," *Fortune*, March 30, 1987, p. 63.

14. "Tailored Trade: Dealing with the World as It Is," *Harvard Business Review*, January–February 1988, pp. 88–89.

15. "Why U.S. Flicks Are Foreigners' Faves," *Fortune*, August 29, 1988, p. 82.

16. S. Sachs, "France Draws the Line at Wine, Won't Let Japanese Butt Into Firm," *Atlanta Journal and Constitution*, September 11, 1988, p. 18-A; and P. Wells, "A Taste for France," *Wisconsin Alumni*, July–August 1988, pp. 28–29.

17. See "Foreign Investors Are Keeping the Pot Boiling," *Business Week*, November 24, 1986, p. 84.

18. K. Ohmaie, "Becoming a Triad Power: The Global Corporation," *International Marketing Review*, Autumn 1986, pp. 7–20; R. Abravanel, "Shaping Effective Responses to the Globalization Challenge," in R. Varaldo, ed., *International Marketing Cooperation: Conference Proceedings* (New York: Praeger, 1986); and S. Jameson, "Japan Industry Hears a Faint, Growing Call: The Yanks Are Coming," *Los Angeles Times*, December 26, 1988, pp. I, 16–19.

19. *Wall Street Journal*, April 7, 1987, p. 1.

20. George Rubstejnek, "Let's Get Back to the Basics of Global Strategy," *Journal of Business Strategy*, September–October 1989, pp. 32–35; and "The Captains See a Tilted Field," *Fortune*, November 6, 1989, p. 93.

21. M. E. Porter, "Changing Patterns of International Competition," *California Management Review*, Winter 1986, pp. 9–40.

22. G. Hazel and C. K. Prahalad, "Haben Sie wirklich eine globale Strategie," *Harvard-Manager* 1 (1986):90–97.

23. J. Leontiades, "Market Share and Corporate Strategy in International Industries," *Journal of Business Strategy*, Summer 1984, pp. 30–37.

24. "Is the Era of Cheap Asian Labor Over?," *Business Week*, May 15, 1985, pp. 45–46.

25. President's Commission on Industrial Competitiveness, *Global Competition—The New Reality*, vol. 1, January 1985, p. 9.

26. R. I. Kirkland, "Entering a New Age of Boundless Competition," *Fortune*, March 14, 1988, p. 40.

27. V. Sharan, "Internationalism of Third World Firms: An Indian Case Study," *International Marketing Review*, Summer 1985, pp. 63–71.

28. Kirkland, op. cit.

29. C. Burritt, "Computers Are Called Crucial to Competitiveness," *Atlanta Constitution*, October 31, 1986, p. 1-D.

30. President's Commission on Industrial Competitiveness, op. cit.

31. G. Hazel and C. K. Prahalad, "Do You Really Have a Global Strategy?," *Harvard Business Review*, July–August 1985, pp. 138–148.

32. Kirkland, op. cit.

33. H. Siebert, "Perspektiven der internationalen Arbeitsteilung—Thesen zum deutschen Aussenhandel," *Marketing ZPF*, 7 June 1985, pp. 109–118.

34. J. B. Treece, "Most U.S. Companies Are Innocents Abroad," *Business Week*, November 16, 1987, p. 168.

35. "The Long Arm of Small Business," *Business Week*, February 29, 1988, p. 32.

36. J. A. Tannenbaum, "Weaker Dollar Enriches Some Exporters," *Wall Street Journal*, October 5, 1988, p. B-2.

37. J. Schafer, "Foreign Trade Shows Are a Timely Way to Cut Trade Deficit," *Marketing News*, November 20, 1987, p. 12.

RESPONSE TO THE GLOBAL CHALLENGE

GLOBAL MARKETING

Companies Without Borders

Exxon and General Motors may be large companies, with sales around the world, but are they *global*? Not necessarily. They do business around the world, but they traditionally have been oriented toward one market (the United States), although this is changing. A global corporation looks at the whole world as one potential market—manufacturing, buying, researching, raising capital, and selling wherever the job can be done best.

National markets are really too small to support a company if that company wishes to remain competitive in a global industry. Imperial Chemical Industries (ICI), a Britain-based company with a pharmaceuticals division, competes in an industry where developing a drug takes twelve years and $250 million. David Friend, who directs the pharmaceuticals division, says, "No major pharmaceuticals company is in the game for anything other than global products."

While niche players such as Mercedes-Benz continue to survive globally through superior products exported from one country, at least one expert believes that 136 different industries are moving globally, and companies must be able to produce, distribute, and market products in North America, Europe, and the Pacific Rim to be competitive. Companies that are leading this global trend include General Electric, whose diagnostic-scanning systems division is run by a Moroccan who attended school in France, but got a Ph.D. at UCLA; Ford Motor Company, which is dedicated to creating global products, such as the Tempo; and American Express, Citicorp, and Texas Instruments. Other companies with increasingly global views include Sony, Toyota, Procter & Gamble (see Chapter 1), Rolex, BSN, and Samsung.

Going global has high risks, particularly if there is insufficient research and poor follow-up. Many national differences still exist and will not disappear simply because corporations might wish them to. Even in the laundry detergent industry, where P&G enjoys success with its pan-European brands, Henckels, its German–based competitor, still has strong national brands that are quite successful.

But, increasingly, companies are following a global marketing approach, looking for similar markets to serve across national boundaries, instead of the traditional approach, which views each nation as a separate and distinct market requiring an individualized marketing mix. The global business race of today means companies must change the way they think, are organized, and conduct business daily if they wish to maintain their business leadership throughout the 1990s.

Sources: Adapted from Jeremy Main, "How to Go Global—and Why," *Fortune*, August 28, 1989, pp. 70–76; Marina Specht, "Henckel Thinks Pan-Europe," *Advertising Age*, January 30, 1989, p. 44; "The Race to Stock Europe's Common Supermarket," *Business Week*, June 26, 1989, p. 80; and Kamran Kashani, "Beware the Pitfalls of Global Marketing," *Harvard Business Review*, September–October, 1989, pp. 91–98.

As the experience of a
corporation increases (it
sells more units of its
product), its costs per
unit decrease. This expe-
rience curve effect is a
basic foundation of glob-
al marketing. For exam-
ple, Company A sells 100
units at a cost of $1.00
per unit. Company B sells
50 units at a cost of $3.00
per unit. Company A in
this case enjoys greater
price flexibility or a higher
profit than Company B.

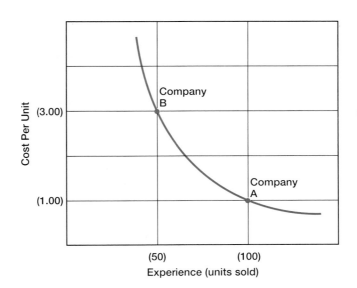

Experience (units sold)

. . . .

WHAT IS GLOBAL MARKETING?

The traditional international or multinational approach to marketing concentrates largely on geographic markets, developing a distinct marketing mix for
each market. Traditional approaches sacrifice the *experience curve effects* (defined
below) that can be gained by using the same marketing mix in more than one

Global marketers look
for product markets
that are as similar as
possible, instead of
national markets that
are dissimilar.

market. **Global marketing**, in contrast, concentrates on **product markets** (groups
of customers with shared needs), emphasizing their similarities regardless of the
geographic areas in which they are located. However, it does not ignore differences among markets. These differences are taken into account when implementing the marketing program. For example, advertising is translated into
different languages for different national markets. "Coke is it," for example, is
translated into *Echt is echt* in Dutch (literally "the real thing is the real thing").
And different distribution strategies are developed for areas with different distribution structures. Most Indian grocery stores, for example, are quite small,
requiring more frequent delivery of smaller quantities than in U.S. supermarkets.

Experience Curve Effects

Capturing experience
curve effects is the un-
derlying argument for
adopting a global mar-
keting orientation.

The most powerful argument in favor of a global marketing orientation is the
opportunity to benefit from **experience curve effects**. (See Exhibit 2.1.) This
concept has two dimensions: increased efficiency due to economies of scale and
increased effectiveness due to accumulated know-how. The principle of economies of scale states that whenever the production or sales volume of a product
increases, total costs per unit (including production, marketing, and administrative costs) fall. Economies of scale accrue in large businesses because they are
able to operate at a lower cost per unit than their smaller competitors.

For a global marketer, an important source of economies of scale (in addition to purchasing and production) is the marketing mix. When a company can use the same marketing mix in several different countries, with only a few adjustments such as translation of advertising copy, the average cost of marketing per unit declines. An example is the advertisement for Longines watches in the European edition of *Cosmopolitan* magazine, which uses the same model and slogan (in English) for several national markets (see Exhibit 2.2). The company gains experience curve effects by appealing to highly educated, wealthy consumers everywhere.

Experience curve effects also occur when a company "learns by doing." The second time a worker or manager does a job, he or she usually does it better than the first time, thereby becoming more effective. Similarly, when a company enters its second foreign market using what it learned when it entered its first such market, it should be more effective.

Corporations that sell more of a product in markets that combine several nations (resulting in a larger overall market) benefit from both dimensions of the experience curve. Companies like Philips (in The Netherlands), which produces consumer electronic products such as VCRs, have used this approach to lower their prices, because experience curve effects have reduced their costs and increased their effectiveness. Global marketing is sometimes referred to as the *new competition*. Although the new competition has many elements, experience curve effects are central. Thus, a key to the success of Japanese companies such as Sony in the U.S. and European markets is their use of sophisticated business and marketing strategies that are developed on the basis of experience.[1]

Global Market Analysis

If markets throughout the world become more similar, a global marketing orientation is more likely to be successful.

A controversy exists as to whether markets around the world are becoming increasingly similar. Evidence that suggests they are leads some experts to argue that the effect of this trend is to "homogenize world tastes, wants, and possibilities into global market proportions, which allows for world-standardized products."[2] If markets are indeed becoming more similar, such as markets for sports equipment, firms would be wise to develop standardized marketing mixes, thereby realizing the maximum possible experience curve effects. This point of view is challenged by other experts, however. They argue that nations—hence, markets—are becoming increasingly *dissimilar*. In their view, distinct rather than standardized marketing mixes are necessary. For example, some national markets are heavily influenced by religious fundamentalism. When those religions (for example, Judaism and Islam) disagree, distinct marketing mixes are required.

For organizations that adopt a global perspective, the critical point is not whether buyers are the same everywhere, but to what extent shared customer needs exist in different nations. If they do, the company can develop a relatively standardized marketing program to appeal to those needs.

Exhibit 2.3 illustrates a marketing approach based on the analysis of product markets. A marketer of a line of cosmetics, such as Revlon, might identify a target market consisting of high-income, fashion-conscious women in several

The celebrated Longines Hour Angle navigational watch, made by Longines to a design by Charles A. Lindbergh, who completed the first solitary non-stop transatlantic flight in May, 1927.

Today, people going places, as well as those who have already arrived, still rely on Longines for the elegant approach to their timekeeping needs.

countries (France, Brazil, and the United States, for example). This product market is larger than a single domestic market. Thus, it offers a greater opportunity to take advantage of experience curve effects in purchasing, production, and marketing. In this case, a standardized global marketing mix could appeal to the target market.

MAP 2.1   GLOBAL PRODUCT FLOWS—HONDA

Another example of a globally oriented firm is Honda. Map 2.1 illustrates the flow of Honda's motorcycles, automobiles, and power products. For example, its French built lawnmowers and tillers are exported throughout the European Community. It also imports motorcycles from Taiwan to China and Central America, and cars from the U.S.

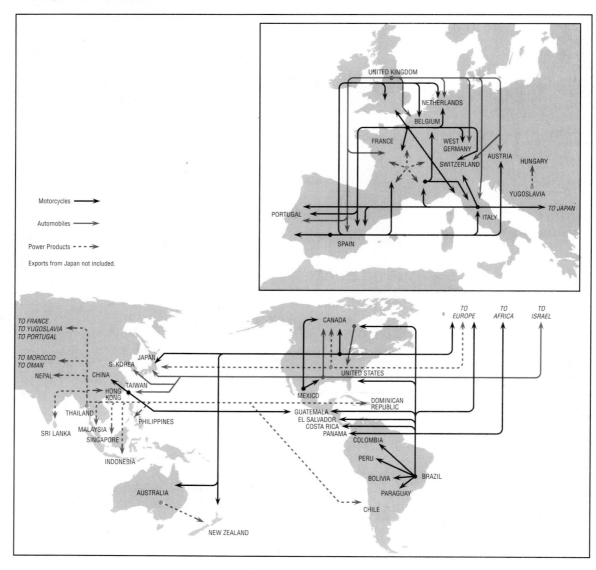

When market needs are different, a global company can develop individualized strategies for consumers in different parts of the world and still benefit from experience curve effects. Nestlé, for example, sells different blends of

EXHIBIT 2.3
A GLOBAL
MARKETING
SEGMENTATION
APPROACH

A global cosmetics mar-
keter may find that high-
income, highly fashion-
conscious women in dif-
ferent nations all share a
similar desire for aesthetic beauty. This product
market could be ap-
pealed to through a rea-
sonably standardized
marketing mix.

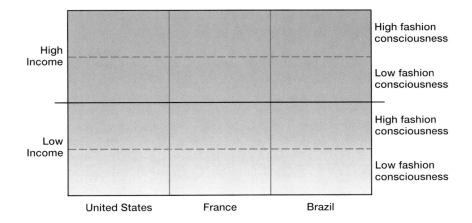

Product: Cosmetics
Target Market: High-income, highly fashion-conscious women
Price: High, for enhanced status
Distribution: Selective, through high-fashion outlets
Promotion: High fashion, status, exclusivity

coffee in different national markets. But it coordinates the marketing planning process for all of those markets, sometimes even using the same brand name, thereby benefiting from the sharing of ideas and more effective allocation of corporate resources.

Concentration and Coordination of Activities

Experience curve ef-
fects may be gained
from two sources, con-
centration and
coordination.

A global marketing orientation allows a company to achieve experience curve effects in two basic ways: concentration and coordination of activities.[3] **Concentration** means centralized decision making, which is normally combined with a high degree of standardization of marketing activities. Because cultures differ greatly and buyer behavior reflects those differences, concentration with respect to all elements of the marketing mix is rare. But concentration is not necessary for a firm to have a global marketing orientation. Experience curve effects may also be gained through the **coordination** of marketing activities—for example, by sharing information about customer preferences.

Richardson-Vicks, a manufacturer of health care products, coordinates its product-line planning for numerous markets. When evaluating a product line in one country, marketing managers also evaluate its potential in other countries. In a similar vein, Caterpillar sets the same standards of service for customers in all of its national markets. This policy serves to reinforce the brand's image as well as the company's image. Coordination of activities might also mean that product designers design products that will be accepted in many national markets.

Most important, coordination allows a company to put the lessons gained in one market to work in another market, thereby moving down the experience curve more quickly. Thus Nutrasweet, for example, learned valuable lessons regarding competitive markets in Europe, which should prove useful when its patent expires in the United States.

. . . .
STANDARDIZING THE MARKETING MIX

To exploit the experience curve, global marketers attempt to standardize the marketing mix as much as possible.

As discussed, the degree of similarity among a company's markets largely determines the extent to which its marketing programs and processes are **standardized**. A company's marketing mix can be totally standardized, totally individualized, or, more frequently, somewhere between these two extremes.[4]

The Coca-Cola Company has almost totally standardized the marketing program for its flagship brand, Coke. Travelers to all parts of the world readily recognize the product's red-and-white logo, whatever language is used to identify it. The company's goal is to achieve "one sight, one sound" brand recognition throughout the world.[5]

Either standardization or individualization of the marketing mix may be successful; the key to success is evaluating national markets as to their standardization potential and then developing the appropriate marketing mix.

Corporations like McDonald's, Benetton, and British Petroleum have also followed a standardized marketing strategy with considerable success. Other companies, such as Nestlé, have taken a more individualized approach with their marketing programs, yet have realized experience curve gains by sharing marketing ideas among their various national markets. Still other companies (often smaller ones, such as the Lindeman Vineyards in Australia), while exporting only, consistently take foreign markets into account in their marketing planning. All are examples of global marketers.

Forms of Standardization: Programs and Processes

Standardization may occur either in marketing programs or in marketing processes. The greatest experience curve effects occur when both programs and processes are standardized.

Programs. The degree of standardization that exists in Coke's global marketing program is rare due to legal, cultural, and other differences. Most standardized marketing programs can be placed in one of the four stages illustrated in Exhibit 2.4.[6] Stage I represents a product that is essentially the same in all markets but is marketed through varying promotion, price, and distribution strategies for each market. An example is Canon's 35 mm camera. It was conceived and designed as a global product. But in the United States it is promoted as a "mistake-proof" camera, whereas in Japan it is presented as the leader in state-of-the-art photographic equipment. In other markets different price, promotion, and distribution strategies are followed.

At the other extreme, a company in Stage IV offers the same product, promotion, price, and distribution mix to all of its markets. This level of standardization is not found often, partly because pricing and distribution are very difficult to standardize. A company can adopt a standardized pricing strategy— for example, being the low-price provider in all markets—but the actual price

EXHIBIT 2.4
STAGES OF
MARKETING MIX
STANDARDIZATION

A fully standardized mar-
keting mix is not often
found. More frequently
the mix will progress to-
ward complete standard-
ization, starting with
product (Stage I), then
adding promotion (Stage
II), price (Stage III), and
finally distribution (Stage
IV). A firm may, of course,
stop at any stage, de-
pending on the markets
which it is serving.

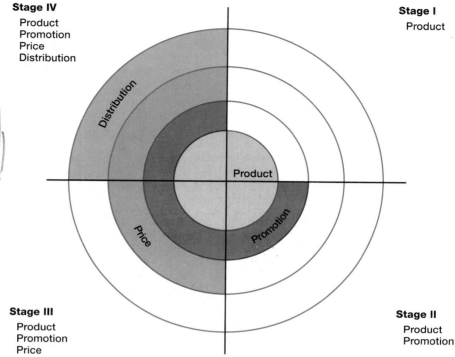

Stage IV
Product
Promotion
Price
Distribution

Stage I
Product

Distribution

Product

Price

Promotion

Stage III
Product
Promotion
Price

Stage II
Product
Promotion

Source: Adapted from S. M. Huszagh, R. J. Fox, and E. Day, "Global Marketing: An Empirical
Investigation," *Columbia Journal of World Business*, Winter, 1985, Twentieth Anniversary Issue, pp.
31–43.

charged will almost always vary in response to demand, competition, and regulation. Distribution, by its nature, is a marketing activity that is performed
close to the market. It frequently varies according to national differences in
transportation systems, regulations, geography, and tradition.

The gains that are achieved through concentration increase as a company
moves from Stage I to Stage IV. Techniques like **pattern advertising** can ease
this process. In pattern advertising, the theme and components of the advertising
campaign are designed for use in several national markets. This "pattern" gives
the campaign a uniform direction and appearance. An example is the advertising
of Benetton clothes, in which the themes of modernity and fun are used in all
markets, regardless of location.

Processes.   The procedures followed by a firm in making marketing decisions
are known as **marketing processes**. These, too, may be either standardized or
individualized. Henckels, the Germany–based manufacturer of industrial and
consumer products, for example, spent five years orienting its local managers
to the company's new global approach. It used standardized processes—sharing
personnel, training, and a common corporate culture—so that its managers

would work and think in the same ways. In a similar manner, the manager of the Finnish market for *Reader's Digest* was sent to a management development seminar at an American business school, so that he could learn American management techniques and coordinate his planning processes more closely with those at corporate headquarters. Companies are often able to standardize their marketing processes more easily than their marketing programs, because they have more control over their own procedures than over their markets.

Deciding Whether to Standardize

When evaluating foreign markets and deciding whether to standardize the marketing mix for those markets, several factors must be taken into consideration.[7] These factors are shown in Exhibit 2.5. They are (a) the market, (b) external environments, (c) the product, (d) financial factors, and (e) the corporate environment. Since many of these factors are difficult to measure precisely, they are best described in terms of a continuum extending from factors favoring individualization to factors favoring standardization.

The Market.   If a standardized strategy is to succeed, the markets of interest must have certain characteristics in common, at least to some degree, and be of sufficient size, with low barriers to entry. (Barriers to entry are often the result of government policies such as an import tax, which make it artificially difficult to enter a market.)

The degree of perceived *similarity* among markets affects a firm's perception of the degree of risk associated with strategic decisions. For example, if a firm that is currently operating in Sweden, France, and Norway evaluates expansion opportunities in Switzerland and Mexico, it is likely to perceive expansion into Mexico as riskier (higher psychic distance) than expansion into Switzerland. Markets that are similar are more likely to be entered successfully using a standardized campaign, although they may or may not be perceived as less risky. Basically, the firm must decide what level of risk actually exists, and is acceptable, when entering a particular market. As information and experience increase, perceived risk decreases and companies generally enter more dissimilar ("riskier") markets. In fact, a study that examined the marketing of 954 different products found that as the experience of a firm in foreign markets increases, reliance on similarity among markets decreases.[8]

The degree to which a market is *urbanized* is an important factor in deciding whether to standardize a marketing program. A marketing strategy that was developed for a highly urbanized market like The Netherlands might not be able to reach enough potential customers in places like Ireland, where more than half the population lives in rural areas or very small towns. In another country with a high level of urbanization, such as Australia, such a strategy would be more likely to succeed.

External Environments.   A number of environmental forces affect a firm's ability to market successfully with a standardized strategy. The most important of these forces are economic, political, legal, cultural, and geographic.

EXHIBIT 2.5
INDIVIDUALIZED
VERSUS
STANDARDIZED
MARKETING MIXES

The decision to standard-
ize or individualize is influenced by many factors
that are actually the op-
posite ends of a continu-
um. If the analysis indi-
cates that more factors
are on the standardiza-
tion end, that becomes
the correct decision. On
the other hand, if all or
most factors support an
individualized marketing
mix, the firm should then
market on a nation-by-na-
tion basis.

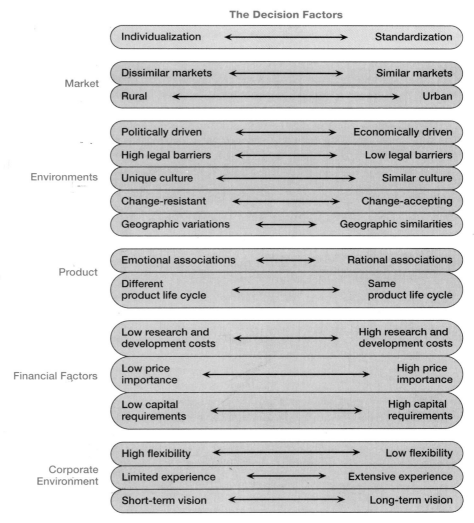

Source: Based on L. D. Dahringer and E. Cundiff, "To Globalize or Not—A Managerial Decision Framework," *Journal of Marketing Management*, Winter 1986, pp. 171–180.

Numerous economic and political-legal forces combine to influence all
aspects of a global organization's activities. (See Chapters 4 and 5.) Economic
and political-legal forces continually interact, both within and between nations.
For example, the difficult political relationship between the United States and
Iraq directly affects their economic relationship.

When a product is politically sensitive in a particular national market, an
individualized marketing campaign is called for. For example, Hollandsche Beton
Maatschappij B.V. is a construction company in The Netherlands with projects
throughout the world. It must meet the unique requirements of each host-

country government regarding plant construction, the number of host-country contractors that must be hired, and the amount of training of local personnel that must accompany the project. Thus it prepares a campaign specifically for each market.

At the other extreme, many products that are less politically sensitive—often, items that are purchased largely on the basis of price—can be marketed through relatively standardized campaigns. For such products, global marketers are able to take advantage of large markets and pass the resulting economies along to buyers in the form of lower prices. Thus, an inexpensive washing machine developed in Italy was marketed successfully throughout most of Western Europe because of its low price.

The *legal* environment (see Chapter 5) includes such factors as tariffs (taxes) and other barriers to trade. The higher those barriers are, the more difficult it is to launch identical marketing strategies in new markets. In such instances an individualized strategy may be mandatory. Another key aspect of the legal environment is patent and trademark protection. In countries that do not offer mutual registration of trademarks, a company may be unable to operate under its standard brand or trade name.

Cultural-social factors (see Chapter 6) involve a wide variety of patterns of living, including behavior norms like those regarding diet or styles of dress. They play a major role in determining what can and cannot be done in a given market. For example, the prohibition against the consumption of alcoholic beverages in Moslem countries affects the design of hotels, as well as the services hotels offer. In markets with unique cultural characteristics, a standardized strategy from another nation is likely to be unsuccessful. Where cultural factors are fairly similar, as is true of Germany, part of Switzerland, and Austria, a standardized campaign for hotels might be viable.

A society's attitudes toward change or the rate of change also affect the degree of standardization that may be used in particular markets. Consumers in a highly traditional market may not accept a marketing strategy that originates in a more dynamic society. Resistance to change can be especially difficult to deal with when the product itself represents a marked change in the way people do things. This can be seen in the case of telephone communication. The telephone has changed the way people live, work, and play in virtually every corner of the world. Today it is so much a part of the way most of us live that it is difficult to imagine the resistance it faced when it was introduced in the late nineteenth century. To give just one example, Emperor Franz Josef of Austria refused for many years to allow telephones to be installed in his palace.

Variations in *geography*, such as climate, may make it necessary to adapt either a product or its promotion for different markets. For example, a computer that operates satisfactorily in an ordinary office in a temperate climate may require design adaptations or special handling if it is to be used in a tropical climate. Where technologies, such as heating and air conditioning systems, exist to control environmental conditions, like temperature and humidity, a more standardized approach is possible.

The Product.   The nature of the product—whether it is a consumer good, a service, or an industrial good—also affects global marketing strategies. Holiday Inn, for example, uses similar design and marketing strategies around the world. Many industrial goods, such as computer chips, are well suited to a standardized approach. But many food products, especially those that have been popular for years, thus having highly emotional associations, must be sold through individualized campaigns in different nations. Corn flakes, for instance, are sold as a breakfast food in the United Kingdom but as a snack in Japan.

It is often argued that economically rational industrial products and consumer goods are most easily standardized. There is evidence, however, that marketing mixes for such products often are not standardized, due to substantial differences in market and buyer behavior.[9] (Issues related to marketing mix composition for consumer and industrial goods and services are discussed in Chapters 11–13.)

Another important factor in global marketing strategies is the **product life-cycle**. Although there are numerous life-cycle models,[10] most experts argue that as a market matures, the organization may successfully enter a similar market elsewhere (as illustrated in Chapter 1). For example, IBM might be able to take its older computer models, which are in the maturity stage of the product life-cycle in the United States, into another market where they would be in the introductory or growth stage. But for a standardized campaign to be successful, the product should be in the same stage of the life-cycle in all of the markets involved. Otherwise, differences between stages in such factors as degree and type of competition, rate of growth in sales, the most effective form of promotion, the most desirable distribution strategy, pricing, and the nature of the product itself will prevent a standardized approach from being successful.

When the stages of the life-cycle are different in different markets, as illustrated in Exhibit 2.6, individualized strategies are required. If, for example, personal computers are in different stages of the product life-cycle in Egypt and Sweden, companies that wish to compete in both of these markets would have to adjust their marketing mixes to take this difference into account. Although their physical products might be similar, the rest of the marketing mix would have to be individualized for each country.

Whether a product life-cycle is driven by technological or cultural factors is another important consideration. A firm that is faced with two markets in which its product is in the maturity stage of the life-cycle might assume that a standardized marketing program could be used in both markets. But if one market is driven by technology and the other by cultural factors, a standardized campaign is unlikely to be successful.[11] For example, computers might be in the growth stage of the product life-cycle in two markets, but in one of those markets sales may grow slowly due to the expectation that new technology will soon be available (a technological factor), while in the other market sales may grow slowly as a result of customers' fear of automation (a cultural factor). A standardized campaign would not have the same results in both markets, because

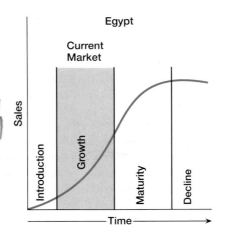

Egypt

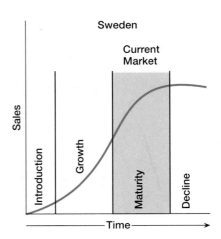

Sweden

it would be unable to overcome the differing sources of sales resistance in the two markets.

Cost and Other Financial Factors. If research and development costs for a product are low, an individualized strategy may be appropriate. But if research and development costs are high, such as for pharmaceutical products, it is more difficult for small-scale competitors to enter foreign markets. Small producers are not able to justify the expenditures required to be competitive, nor are they able to spread those costs over larger global markets. This means that smaller competitors are less able to offer competitive products at competitive prices. Hence, for such products global strategies are essential. As one writer on the subject has stated, "Businesses today have to solve an impossible economic equation: how to amortize the higher development costs of new products over their increasingly shorter lives. Globalization is the only answer."[12]

Price also plays a role in the development of a global strategy. When potential buyers are willing to give up individualized products in exchange for a standardized product with a lower price, as is true in the case of automobiles and major appliances, a standardized strategy is more likely to succeed. This is particularly true if increases in sales volume result in sizable savings in per unit production or marketing costs. In the case of products for which price plays a less important role, individualization is more likely to succeed; luxury yachts, which are custom-built at great expense to suit specific customer tastes, and nuclear power plants are examples of this.

A standardized strategy normally requires a larger capital investment for large-scale production facilities and for marketing, because the marketing system used in the home market may need to be duplicated in each new market. But the cost per unit of the product will be lower, enhancing price competitiveness. At the other extreme, an individualized strategy allows the firm to enter smaller markets by using existing, often less expensive, facilities and procedures for both production and marketing. The usual trade-off is, of course, higher per unit costs.

The Corporate Environment.   The attitude of corporate management has a strong influence on the success of a global strategy. A high degree of flexibility and acceptance of change may result in individualization of marketing strategies. Lack of flexibility, in contrast, tends to result in standardization. However, a low tolerance for differences does not necessarily mean that a standardized strategy will be successful. The organization may be unable to accept the amount of change required. Marketing managers, for example, tend to think in terms of their own national markets; it is difficult for them to think in cross-national terms, that is, in ways that cross other national markets. In such cases top management must help them develop a global orientation—as we saw in the example of Henckels earlier in the chapter.

Corporate experience also influences the firm's ability and willingness to develop a global orientation, as does the corporation's short- or long-term vision. As mentioned in Chapter 1, a long-term perspective is necessary to be successful in international marketing.

Evaluation Techniques

The potential for a standardized marketing program can be evaluated through a benefit-cost approach or a use-need model.

There are several techniques that can be used to evaluate the potential for standardization of a marketing program. One is the **benefit-cost approach**, which analyzes the balance between the customer's perceived benefits and the costs of the product in different markets. Another is the **use-need model**, which examines the way a product is used in comparison with the need it fulfills.

The Benefit-Cost Approach.   This technique evaluates the potential for standardization by looking at customers' perceptions of benefits and costs.[13] Customers buy when the "bundle" of perceived benefits is greater than the bundle of perceived costs. Exhibit 2.7 illustrates these benefits and costs.

A benefit associated with place, such as convenience, may lower the related place costs, thereby encouraging a purchase. (For example, Convenient Food Mart offers a quick way to purchase groceries on the way home.) In societies that value convenience highly, such as the United States, consumers will pay a higher price to gain convenience; in other societies, such as Pakistan, convenience may be perceived as irrelevant or of low value.

Different perceptions of the value of convenience, or any other benefit offered by the marketing mix, suggest that the company needs to individualize the marketing mix for different consumer groups. On the other hand, if perceived benefits are similar—for example, the sensory benefits of color and style—the company may offer a more standardized marketing mix. Benetton provides an example of the successful application of this approach in the fashion world.

EXHIBIT 2.7
ILLUSTRATIONS OF
PERCEIVED BENEFITS
AND COSTS

Type	Customers' Benefits	Customers' Costs
Sensory	Appealing appearance, feel, sound, smell, or taste	Unpleasant appearance, feel, sound, smell, or taste
Psychological	Positive state of mind (feeling good, generous, satisfied)	Negative state of mind (feeling bad, guilty)
Place	Attractive, convenient, or comfortable	Unattractive, inconvenient, or uncomfortable
Time	When desired	Time spent in obtaining information, purchasing, or using product
Economic	Potential for resale, enhanced earning power, lower relative financial costs	Higher relative financial costs, high total costs

Source: Adapted from C. Lovelock and C. Weinberg, *Marketing for Nonprofit Organizations* (New York: Wiley, 1984), p. 48.

One reason for using an individualized strategy may be that technical specifications are different in the target markets. For example, U.S. producers of manufacturing equipment are at a disadvantage against local competitors in Europe because they have to adapt every machine and tool for those markets—a costly process. Similarly, cars may have to be adapted for different markets, depending on the pollution-control standards of the country in which they are sold.

The Use-Need Model.   A popular framework for making strategic marketing decisions is the **use-need model,** which evaluates the market need that is met by a given product as well as how the product is used. Exhibit 2.8 illustrates this model.[14] Five combinations of use and need determine the degree of product and promotional standardization that is desirable and their related costs. For example, if a product is to be used differently in different markets but it meets the same basic need, individualizing the product while standardizing its promotion would be an appropriate strategy. Thus, TVs need to be reengineered for different markets to allow for differences in broadcast standards, electrical service, and quality of transmission, but the promotional theme of "best picture" could be standardized.

Only when use and need conditions are the same is a fully standardized program appropriate. On the other hand, when differences between markets in both use and need are great, a totally individualized program is needed. The long-term perspective taken by Japanese automobile manufacturers, and their willingness to develop products and promotional campaigns specifically for the U.S. market, illustrate the latter strategy.

EXHIBIT 2.8
THE USE–NEED
MODEL

Analyzing the conditions
under which the product
is used, along with the
buyer's need to be satis-
fied, gives the global
marketer insight into
whether the product and
promotion can be the
same or whether adapta-
tion is necessary.

Use Condition

	Same	Different
Same	Same product Same promotion Cost = 1	Adapt product Same promotion Cost = 3
Different	Same product Adapt promotion Cost = 2	Adapt product Adapt promotion Cost = 4

Buyer Need

Cost 1 = lowest
Cost 2 = highest

Unique promotion
Cost =

Source: Based on W. J. Keegan, "Multinational Product Planning: Strategic Alternatives," *Journal of Marketing*, January 1969, pp. 58–62.

MANAGING THE PROCESS OF GLOBAL MARKETING

A global marketing ori-
entation is more of a
business perspective
or philosophy than a
form of organization.

Responding to the global marketing challenge requires a global perspective, but it does not entail a specific form of organization. In fact, at any one time several alternative forms of organization might be appropriate. The firm must examine all available options and decide on the most appropriate.

Traditionally, firms have been classified according to the political boundaries they cross in conducting business and the importance of those boundaries to the organization. Exhibit 2.9 illustrates this approach. **National** firms focus on domestic markets; an **international** firm also has a domestic market focus, but it serves other national markets in addition; **multinational** firms view some

EXHIBIT 2.9
CLASSIFICATION OF
FIRMS IN THE
GLOBAL
MARKETPLACE

Firms that operate in the global marketplace may be classified depending on their view of the relationship between domestic and international markets. *National* firms see the domestic market as being most important and world markets as being of secondary importance. *International* firms are more interested in global markets, but as secondary to the domestic one, with decisions still driven by domestic market issues. *Multinational* firms see their competitive world as consisting of a series of separate domestic markets, each of potentially equal value. *Transnational* firms strive for product market linkages that cross national boundaries.

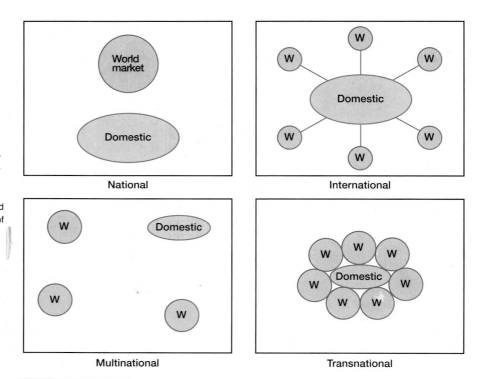

Source: Adapted from S. M. Huszagh, R. J. Fox, and E. Day, "Global Marketing: An Empirical Investigation," *Columbia Journal of World Business*, Winter, 1985, Twentieth Anniversary Issue, pp. 31–43.

foreign markets as at least as important as the domestic market; and **transnational** firms have a worldwide market focus.*

Considerably more important than the form of organization is a firm's *view* of its markets. One classification of the firm's view is **EPRG** (ethnocentric, polycentric, regional, geocentric).[15] An **ethnocentric** firm views its domestic market as most important, perhaps reacting defensively to international markets, if at all. A **polycentric** firm sees international markets as a series of domestic (or national) markets, similar to the multinational organizational form. A firm with a **regional** orientation seeks opportunities for coordinated and possibly concentrated marketing programs, but usually within a geographic or perhaps culturally homogeneous region. For example, a firm that focuses its marketing on the high-growth Asian nations of Taiwan, Hong Kong, Singapore, and Malaysia has a regional view.

International usually refers to any business activity across national boundaries; *multinational* normally means multiple national markets, each treated as a separate national market; *transnational* refers to linking international markets together.

A **geocentric** firm is most committed to a global orientation, continually seeking out worldwide opportunities for coordination and concentration. Diet Coke, for example, is marketed in such a manner. The product formula, positioning, and advertising are uniform across nations. But the brand name varies slightly due to various legal regulations. In some Western European countries the word *diet* has medical implications. So *Coke Light* or another name is used instead of *Diet Coke*. The artificial sweetener and package also differ in some countries, and promotional programs are localized.[16] Despite the variations, Coca-Cola clearly has a geocentric view.

A Global Marketing Framework

A decision framework is necessary to ensure all elements of the global marketing process are included in management's decisions.

The exhibit in the preface to the student illustrates the specific decisions an international marketing manager must make. But these decisions must be made in a manner that is consistent with overall corporate policy (see Global Dimensions 2.1).

After a global corporate policy has been developed, the product markets in which the firm will compete are chosen and resource-allocation decisions are made, based on the firm's competitive strengths and an environmental analysis. IBM, for example, is very active in the Japanese market, not only to increase sales and profits but also to maintain a strong global competitive position vis-à-vis NEC, a global information management corporation based in Japan. One of IBM's strengths is excellent service. As part of its competitive strategy, it can use this strength to support global marketing programs in the mainframe computer market.

After competitive market strategy is formulated, specific forms of market entry are selected. IBM often prefers to directly invest abroad, for example, to maximize control. Then specific decisions are made about the marketing mix: product, distribution, promotion, and pricing. At this level, a company also establishes objectives, such as market share and sales level.

Advantages of Global Marketing

Compared with domestically operating companies, globally operating companies have a much greater range of potential customers, needs, and technologies to choose among. Potential customers may not only be citizens of different nations who share needs, but they may differ in terms of social class, income, and education. A manufacturer of video cameras, for example, may offer its products to middle-income customers in North America and Europe and upper-income consumers in developing countries, like the Philippines.

Similarities among customers are most evident to marketers of industrial products. A European manufacturer of heavy gas engines, for example, may define its market as all potential customers, anywhere in the world, that need

Global Policy

Corporate Mission. Any firm's statement of corporate policy should contain information about the organization's mission and objectives. A company's **mission** is a statement of what it seeks to do in the long term, the rationale for its existence, and the major objectives it hopes to achieve. It is the vision that guides the decisions and actions of all the members of the organization. A global firm should state its mission in a way that will provide guidance to managers in the formulation of strategies without unduly limiting their ability to react appropriately to changes in the global environment.

The mission statement begins by defining the general purpose of the company. For example, Liechtenstein-based Hilti, one of the world's biggest suppliers of hand-powered fastening devices, defines its purpose as follows: "We satisfy market needs in the field of fastening technology for customers involved in small and industrial construction and for all other industrial purposes by offering tools, equipment, and elements in combination with pre- and after-sales services from the detection of the customer's needs to their satisfaction."

Objectives in the corporate policy statement may include growth versus stability, return on investment, market share, acceptable level of risk, approach to technology and innovation, image and goodwill, establishment of a specific working climate within the organization, and independence versus cooperation as a business strategy.

Business Definition. Another part of the firm's corporate policy statement is the business definition—which customer needs the company will satisfy and which technologies it will use. Theoretically, the company can choose among alternatives ranging from focusing on one specific need of one customer segment, applying a single technology, to trying to serve all needs of all potential customers, applying all available technologies. In practice, the decision depends on the company's resources and skills, as well as on market opportunities.

Business Philosophy. Every company should have a unique identity, which may be more or less formal or consciously managed. A firm's culture depends mainly on the basic values shared by its members and on the norms of behavior derived from those values. It is the driving force behind the firm's policies and activities. It is represented in statements regarding appropriate internal and external behaviors. Whereas the corporate mission basically determines the *why*, *what for*, and *where* of a company, its business philosophy states *how* relationships with different exchange partners should be managed. Such statements express top management's basic orientations and hence affect decisions regarding resource allocation and competitive strategies.

Although bus and train transportation are popular, the streets of Beijing are also filled with people using bicycles as a form of basic transportation.

both energy production and air-conditioning capabilities. In this case customers in many different nations have needs that are very much alike.

There are also situations in which a single product may satisfy a variety of needs. Bicycles produced in France may satisfy the social needs of groups that spend their leisure time together in Italy and France. They may also satisfy the individualistic needs of fitness-oriented consumers in the United States. In China, they may meet the basic need for transportation, combined with the need for prestige (in this case, the prestige that comes from being able to afford a foreign-made product). In such cases, product markets are defined by cultural, economic, geographic, and other boundaries, and they can be analyzed by the use-need model.

The company must also decide which technologies it will use to meet customer needs. The choice of specific technologies may result in the exclusion of certain markets, but it may also generate useful competitive strategies. In the case of French bicycles, the manufacturer will not need to change its technologies to satisfy the social or fitness needs of customers, but it might develop a strategy focused on premium pricing for specific customer segments. However, to satisfy the need for cheap transportation, the manufacturer will need to modify the product somewhat, simplifying the design so that the product will be easier to make and thus can be sold at a lower price. Depending on how the manufacturer has defined the technological dimensions of its business, one or more of the product's potential markets may not be appropriate and may therefore be excluded from consideration.

Finally, to insure the global marketing process is properly managed, a **global marketing management system** must be put into place. Such systems enable the organization to plan, implement, and evaluate marketing decisions. Without a management system in place, objectives, strategic decisions, and resource allocations may be incompatible, or even contradictory. For example, a firm may wish to be the technological leader in its industry, but it may be managed as if a maximum return on investment were more important. A marketing management system makes sure that trade-offs are identified and resolved, and that all members of the organization work toward a common goal.

SUMMARY

Global marketing is a corporate philosophical orientation in which strategic decisions are oriented toward product markets rather than national markets. The most powerful argument in favor of a global marketing orientation is experience curve effects, which occur when a company becomes more efficient as a result of economies of scale or more effective due to accumulated know-how. Corporations that sell more of a product in larger markets benefit from both dimensions of the experience curve.

Experience curve effects may be gained through concentration (centralization of decision making and standardization of marketing activities) and coordination of marketing activities in different markets. Standardization may occur either in marketing programs or in marketing processes. If marketing programs are standardized, the experience curve effects of concentration are realized. If marketing processes are standardized, the experience curve effects of coordination are realized. The greatest experience curve effect occurs when both programs and processes are standardized.

For a standardized strategy to succeed, the markets of interest must have certain characteristics in common. Markets that are similar are more likely to be entered successfully using a standardized campaign, and they are usually viewed as less risky. Another characteristic that must be taken into consideration in developing a global strategy is degree of urbanization.

A number of environmental forces also affect a firm's ability to market products successfully using a standardized strategy. The most important of these forces are economic, political, legal, cultural, and geographic. The nature of the product—whether it is a consumer good, a service, or an industrial good—and its stage in the product life-cycle also affect global marketing, as do costs and other financial factors. In addition, the attitude of corporate management has a strong influence on the success of a global strategy.

Two frameworks are often used to evaluate market and product characteristics in determining the potential for standardization. In the benefit-cost approach, the marketer attempts to determine how customers perceive the benefits of a purchase relative to its costs. In the use-need model, the market need that is met by a given product or service is compared with the way it is actually used.

Responding to the global marketing challenge does not entail a specific form of organization; the firm should examine all available options and decide on the most appropriate one. Traditionally, firms have been classified according to the political boundaries they cross in conducting business and the relative importance of those boundaries to the organization. National firms focus on domestic markets. International firms serve other national markets in addition to the domestic market. Multinational firms view foreign markets as at least as important as the domestic market. Transnational firms have a worldwide market focus. Another classification scheme, known as the EPRG, is based on the scope of the firm's orientation—ethnocentric, polycentric, regional, or geocentric.

In developing its global strategy, a firm must make a series of basic decisions, starting with the development of a corporate policy statement. A globally oriented firm's statement of corporate policy should contain information about the organization's mission and objectives. A company's mission is a statement of what it aims to do in the long term, the rationale for its existence, and the major objectives it hopes to achieve. Objectives are often used as performance measures that permit evaluation of results, to determine whether the company has accomplished its mission. Another part of the firm's corporate policy statement is business definition, in which the organization identifies the customer needs it will satisfy and the technologies it will use. Compared with domestically operating companies, globally operating companies have a much greater range of potential customers, needs, and appropriate technologies among which to choose. Further, every company has a unique identity, which depends mainly on the basic values shared by its members. Identity is the driving force behind a firm's policies and activities. Careful management of the firm's identity is crucial to success in the global marketplace.

Next, the markets in which the firm will operate are chosen and resources are allocated to those markets. The firm's competitive strengths and resource-allocation decisions help determine the opportunities open to it and hence affect the selection of a competitive market strategy.

Finally, the global marketing process must be planned, implemented, and evaluated through a global marketing management system. This system insures that the firm's objectives, strategies, and resource-allocation decisions support each other.

DISCUSSION QUESTIONS

1. What is the basic distinction between global marketing and the more traditional approach, international marketing?

2. How does a corporation that adopts a global marketing orientation benefit from experience curve effects?

3. What are the two main sources of experience curve effects?

4. Which of the EPRG categories is correlated with the least global marketing orientation? Which is associated with the most global orientation?

5. What basic decisions must a company make in developing a global corporate policy?

6. Domestic and global organizations have different perspectives on potential customers. Which has the broader view? Why?

7. Refer to Exhibit 2.5. Discuss three of the factors listed in the exhibit in terms of how they influence decisions regarding standardization or individualization of the marketing mix.

8. Using the benefit-cost approach, evaluate the potential for standardization for a toy that is designed to be played with by children between the ages of 18 and 36 months. Assume that the potential markets are the United States and the People's Republic of China.

9. How can the use-need model be helpful in evaluating the appropriateness of standardization versus individualization?

CASE

THE GLOBAL KANGAROO?

SmartAlex is a small public relations company based in Queensland, in northeastern Australia. Two entrepreneurs, Jan Power and Chris Dobinson, founded the company with the idea of having fun while making money. They had initial success with public relations and promotional programs, freelance writing and journalism, and high-quality promotional food photography. They then began to explore new products to tap into the Japanese market.

Early in 1987, the tourist market in Queensland was undergoing rapid expansion, particularly from Japanese visitors. Australian products were also gaining popularity in Japan. SmartAlex wanted to promote its novel Australian food photography in the Japanese tourist market or in Japan itself. It approached the Queensland Tourist and Travel Corporation (QTTC) for assistance. The QTTC was not able to help SmartAlex, but it was sufficiently impressed to suggest that SmartAlex talk with the Australian Trade Commission (Austrade) about international market opportunities. (Austrade is similar to the U.S. Department of Commerce in its support programs for companies interested in developing overseas markets.)

After some discussion, Austrade recommended that SmartAlex use its photographs to develop a calendar for the Japanese market. SmartAlex developed twelve photographs for the calendar. The calendar was to be produced and distributed by a Japanese partner, leaving SmartAlex free to focus on the creative elements of the product.

Late in 1987, Austrade took SmartAlex's samples to Japan to test response to the photographs. The result indicated a clear difference between the Australian and Japanese senses of humor. The potential Japanese buyers liked the four photographs that depicted kangaroos in human form, but they were not enthusiastic about the humorous settings in which the animals were placed. Additionally, they showed no interest in the other photographs, which featured Australian wildlife in more conventional settings.

Austrade suggested that koalas might have more appeal to Japanese buyers, but Jan and Chris did not like the suggestion. They preferred to use kangaroos as a focus and did not find much entertainment in producing photographs that excluded SmartAlex's characteristic humor. Jan, for example, thought that if they did use koalas, they should "have them sitting in rows under old hair dryers and things," an approach that probably would not be acceptable in Japan.

Despite this setback, Jan and Chris did not want to give up the idea of developing international markets. Recognizing the growing market for Australian products in the United States, they turned their attention to the U.S. greeting card market, where appreciation of SmartAlex's humor did not seem likely to be a problem. At considerable expense, they created a series of greeting cards that combined humorous photographs and messages. There were no greeting cards on the market at the time that treated kangaroos in a humorous manner. A colleague took samples to the United States on a business trip, but the U.S. buyers thought the humanized kangaroos looked like rats! Jan summarized the American response as:

> They think [the kangaroos] are very large majestic things that sail over wheat fields but don't ride racing bicycles. So he and most of his friends thought that they looked more like stuffed rats, for which there is not a huge market. . . ."

As with the photographs proposed for the Japanese calendar, it was suggested that SmartAlex might consider adapting its products to fit U.S. tastes. One specific suggestion was to follow the "Garfield model," using kangaroos as the basis for a range of items such as notepaper and memo pads, in addition to the greeting cards. However, this would require SmartAlex to use a "cutesy" kind of kangaroo rather than its current model. Once again there was little in this idea that was immediately attractive to Jan and Chris, because it ran counter to their particular style of creative humor.

This case is an abridged version of "SmartAlex—Double or Nothing?" by Jacqueline A. Flint. Reprinted by permission of the publishers from J. R. McColl-Kennedy, O. H. M. Yau and R. Hardman (eds), *Australian Marketing: A Casebook*, © by Harper and Row.

NOTES

1.   P. Kotler, L. Fahey, and S. Jatusripitak, *The New Competition* (Englewood Cliffs, N.J.: Prentice Hall, 1985), p. xi.

2.   T. Levitt, "The Globalization of Markets," *Harvard Business Review*, May–June 1983, pp. 92–102.

3. M. E. Porter, "The Strategic Role of International Marketing," *Journal of Consumer Marketing*, Spring 1986, pp. 17–21.

4. This section is based in part on P. G. P. Walters, "International Marketing Policy—A Discussion of the Standardization Concept and Its Relevance for Corporate Policy," *Journal of Business Study*, Summer 1986, pp. 55–69.

5. A. B. Fisher, "The Ad Biz Gloms onto Global," *Fortune*, November 12, 1984, p. 78.

6. The discussion of standardization is based in part on S. M. Huszagh, R. J. Fox, and E. Day, "Global Marketing: An Empirical Investigation," *Columbia Journal of World Business, Twentieth Anniversary Issue*, pp. 31–43; and John Thackery, "Much Ado About Global Marketing," *Across the Board*, April 1985, pp. 38–46.

7. This section is based in part on L. D. Dahringer and E. Cundiff, "To Globalize or Not—A Managerial Decision Framework," *Journal of Marketing Management*, Winter 1986, pp. 171–180.

8. W. H. Davidson, "Market Similarity and Market Selection: Implications for International Marketing Strategy," *Journal of Business Research*, vol. 11, December 1983, pp. 439–456.

9. P. D. White and E. W. Cundiff, "Assessing the Quality of Industrial Products," *Journal of Marketing*, January 1978, pp. 80–86.

10. G. Day, "The Product Life Cycle: Analysis and Applications Issues," *Journal of Marketing*, Fall 1981, pp. 60–67.

11. J. C. Camillus, "Technology-Driven and Market-Driven Life Cycles: Implications for Multinational Corporate Strategy," *Columbia Journal of World Business*, Summer 1984, pp. 56–60.

12. "Global Salesman," *Wall Street Journal*, April 7, 1987, p. 1.

13. C. Lovelock and C. Weinberg, *Marketing for Nonprofit Organizations* (New York: Wiley, 1984), pp. 47–51.

14. W. J. Keegan, "Multinational Product Planning: Strategic Alternatives," *Journal of Marketing*, January 1969, pp. 58–62.

15. Y. Wind, S. P. Douglas, and H. Z. Pearlmutter, "Guidelines for Developing International Marketing Strategy," *Journal of Marketing*, April 1973, pp. 14–23.

16. J. A. Quelch and E. J. Hoff, "Customizing Global Marketing," *Harvard Business Review*, May–June 1986, pp. 59–68.

ASSESSING

AFTER UNDERSTANDING THE CHALLENGE OF global business and establishing a global marketing orientation (Part 1), firms need to go through a process of global market opportunity assessment. In brief, not all market opportunities translate into corporate opportunities. Firms need to determine which represent real opportunities for them. This process entails three major steps: preliminary assessment, screening, and matching market opportunities to the firms' potential, thus determining competitive advantages.

The market-selection process starts with a preselection of potential markets based on the strategies of the company as expressed in its statement of corporate policy. Markets that seem promising are identified. Then market environments—economic, political and legal, cultural and social—are to be examined closely in order to assess the opportunities and risks involved in serving them. The screening procedure applies a variety of criteria to evaluate the similarity and attractiveness of the markets under consideration.

Knowing there is an opportunity, however, is not the same as being able to take advantage of that opportunity. Heading into global marketing can be disastrous without examining the company closely. Any assessment of opportunities in a global marketplace must include an in-depth analysis of the company's potential. Only those geographic and product markets where the company has a sustainable competitive advantage, or at least significant and communicable differences compared to competitive offerings, should be included in final market choice.

After a market is selected, data on what the firm should do and the firm's potential are evaluated in a global marketing audit. Then a marketing strategy designed for that market and consistent with overall corporate strategy is planned and implemented, as discussed in Part 3.

POTENTIAL
MARKETS

INTERNATIONAL INCIDENT

Hirschmann GmbH

Hirschmann GmbH is a German producer of special electrical plugs for industrial customers. It has developed its own technology, called *Anspritztechnik*, which is superior to the technology of competitors from East Asia, but more expensive to produce. The company is active in Germany, The Netherlands, France, Italy, Switzerland, Austria, Belgium, Spain, Canada, and the United States.

Looking for attractive new markets, Hirschmann GmbH first applied criteria specific to the firm's success in its product markets: the existence of a modern electrical infrastructure; a sufficient number of large, potential industrial customers; and a price level in the industry compatible with successful competition. These criteria led to a significant reduction in the number of potential markets. The company screened out all less-developed countries in Africa, Asia, and South America with an insufficient infrastructure, leaving South Africa in the pool of potential markets. The developing countries in the Far East and their highly industrialized neighbor, Japan, had to be ruled out as well, due to low price levels in their product markets.

The potential markets left after the first screening were reanalyzed for political and legal restrictions. Because Hirschmann GmbH offers customer-specific solutions to electric-contact problems, it must be able to directly reach its customers. So all centrally controlled economies had to be screened out, even if they had a large number of potential industrial customers. South Africa was ruled out, too, because its political system was not consistent with the moral standards of the firm as stated in its corporate policy. Legal dimensions that were considered included quality norms, which would increase the already relatively high cost of production (the U.S. market was ruled out); prohibitions on importing finished goods; the respect given to patent rights; and whether funds could be freely transferred.

The application of these criteria to the screening process resulted in the following group of markets left for in-depth analysis: the Scandinavian countries (Sweden, Norway, and Finland), Australia, and Brazil. Because economic indicators—such as per capita income, level of industrialization, and number of large potential customers—as well as market openness, political stability, and physical distance pointed in the direction of Sweden, Hirschmann GmbH chose this country as the most attractive market.

When a company applies a global approach to marketing, it views the entire world as made up of a variety of potential markets. Limited resources as well as the size and diversity of markets throughout the world, however, mean that the most appropriate markets for the company must be selected. To insure an efficient and effective selection process, marketers generally follow a progressive screening process (as illustrated in the International Incident).

Global marketers clus-
ter markets according
to their attractiveness
to the firm before ana-
lyzing them in detail.

They group potential markets into clusters on the basis of their attractiveness to the firm before they analyze the most attractive markets in detail.[1] The
criteria used for the clustering process and the assessment of a market's attractiveness will vary from one company to another, depending on general objectives
and priorities as well as on the product market served.

This chapter provides an overview of the criteria most often used in the
analysis of potential markets. It also discusses the criteria in terms of helpfulness
for global marketing. Finally, it outlines a procedure for assessing the attractiveness of potential markets and selecting a market to serve.

MARKET CLASSIFICATION CRITERIA

The first source of criteria to be used in screening potential markets is the
corporate policy statement. As we have seen in Chapter 2, it clarifies the
mission and philosophy of the business. Both affect market choice. In addition,
three general external environments are often used to describe market clusters.
These environments are economic, political-legal, and cultural-social. Together
they form a more complex criterion: **level of economic development**. Other
criteria sometimes used for the clustering of potential markets are inclusion in
a cooperative agreement between nations—for example, the European Free Trade
Association (EFTA)—or a sphere of common political interest—such as the
Council of Mutual Economic Assistance (CMEA)—that shares approaches to
international trade. In the following section we will see the application of these
criteria in the market-selection process.

General Objectives and Priorities

Clustering objectives
are derived from cor-
porate policy
objectives.

Corporate objectives and priorities can be used to cluster potential markets
according to their attractiveness to the firm. Growth goals influence market
choice, for example. A company that wishes to grow fast will choose a geographic and/or product market that is large enough and has sufficient purchasing
power. A company that is determined to be stable or to grow slowly may look
for markets that are in the later stages of development.

If a company seeks a high return on investment, it must select markets in
which it can achieve a leadership position, in which demand is high in relation
to supply, and in which customers have sufficient purchasing power. Small
geographic markets and markets in which competition is already strong would
be avoided.

Top management's orientation toward risk influences the company's allocation of resources and its competitive strategies. Risk-averse managers will
avoid certain markets for many reasons. Small European producers, for example, may avoid direct investment in some Latin American markets because of
the risks posed by political instability.

Companies that give a high priority to technological innovation tend to do business primarily in markets characterized by high levels of technological sophistication, as in Japan, where customers seek technical solutions that require significant research and development. Other companies select markets in which their level of applied technology fits the needs of the targeted customers. Thus, a Portuguese producer of hand scythes may not consider exporting its product to Denmark but may be very interested in potential markets in sub-Saharan Africa.

Companies that rely on their global identity and the goodwill of intermediaries, customers, and suppliers will look for markets in areas where their home country or company name has already earned a positive reputation. A German marketer of heavy machinery, for example, will focus on markets where Germany is known as a country that manufactures high-quality machinery. It will not consider markets in which German products are avoided for ideological reasons.

Finally, the organization's priorities regarding independence or strategic cooperation affect the choice of markets and competitive strategies. If a company has special technical or management know-how and does not wish to give away its secrets, it will not consider markets in which wholly foreign-owned subsidiaries are prohibited and joint ventures required, as is the case in some developing nations. On the other hand, a small company with limited financial resources may gain access to markets throughout the world by cooperating with regional or local business partners.

External Environments

External economic, political-legal, and cultural-social environments are common market-screening criteria.

The primary **external environments** are economic (including technical), political and legal, and cultural and social. In the next three chapters these environments will be discussed in terms of their effects on customer behavior in national markets and their impact on marketing decisions. Here we will briefly consider the factors that are commonly used in the preliminary screening of potential markets, including fairly simple economic characteristics such as geographic location and climatic conditions, political and legal systems, and cultural and social characteristics such as language and religion.

Economic Factors.   The location of national markets is often used as a basis for classification. As discussed in Chapter 1, minimal psychological distance (or even physical distance) results in a perception of lower market-entry risk. Thus, a U.S. firm may perceive the Mexican market as being less risky than the New Zealand market, even if this is not the case.

Classifying countries along geographic lines sometimes makes sense. For example, if the costs of transporting a product are high relative to production costs, the company may decide to export only to neighboring countries; this helps to explain the high level of U.S.-Canadian trade. However, a different market-entry technique, such as direct investment, may be appropriate for a more distant market and yield considerably higher long-term profits.

It is tempting to argue that markets located in the same geographic area are likely to share cultural traits and geographic conditions, and that they should therefore be grouped together as a potential target market. Certainly, a geographic grouping makes it easier for the company to organize its structure and activities. Multinational companies like Nestlé, Mobil, and Hilti structure their divisions according to geographic market clusters.

But geographic proximity does not guarantee that two target markets will be similar. To cite just one example, Austria, Czechoslovakia, and Hungary have a long history of similar cultural development. A closer examination of these countries, however, reveals that Hungary's and Czechoslovakia's political systems differ from Austria's. Moreover, these nations differ considerably in social structure, economic conditions, language, infrastructure, and natural resources. Therefore, grouping them together in a single target market would not result in a reliable evaluation of their potential or lead to the best marketing decisions.

Grouping countries according to their natural environments—that is, climate, mineral resources, water supply, or other resources—may help identify clusters with high or low potential. In some cases, such as the tourism industry, climate plays a major role in marketing decisions. In tropical areas, like Papua New Guinea, climatic conditions necessitate special packaging and storage techniques. Mountainous areas, like the Andes, may lack adequate transportation infrastructures. And countries that are rich in natural resources like oil (Nigeria), productive farmland (Colombia), or coal (Australia) have a better chance of increasing the purchasing power of their citizens than do countries that lack such resources. Even so, using these measures alone is not much more effective than using geographic location alone; the resulting clusters overlook the complexities of customer needs and behavior that largely determine market potential.

Political and Legal Systems.   Political and legal systems strongly affect whether a company can enter a national market, the risks associated with entering a market, and the conduct of business in a market. Therefore, a preliminary grouping of countries according to their political and legal systems is a useful way to classify markets.

However, this approach presents several problems. The first is defining appropriate groups; forms of government vary considerably, ranging from democracies to autocratic systems. Such differences are important because democracies are generally more politically stable than autocratic systems, or if change does occur in democracies it is usually less radical. (Compare Britain's elections, for example, with the overthrow of the Shah of Iran.) Political stability promotes business stability and market predictability.

The second problem is that similar political systems may generate quite different public policies. Even in countries with relatively similar political systems and ideologies, economic conditions may differ significantly. For example, Cuba, North Korea, and China have some political similarities, but their economic situations and the resulting business opportunities are quite different.

A country's legal system determines the rules that govern the conduct of business in that country. Because there is no international commercial legal system, global marketers must analyze the opportunities and threats associated with the different "rules of the game" in various potential markets. They may group companies according to whether their legal systems are based on common or code law (discussed further in Chapter 5). For example, most countries that have been under British influence at some time in their history have common law systems. Even so, they may have very different regulations governing business activities. New Zealand, for instance, regulates advertising much more strictly than the United States does. Thus, clustering markets according to their legal systems will result in broad categories that do not provide the precise information necessary for a full assessment of opportunities in those markets.

Cultural and Social Influences.   The cultural and social environment of any country strongly influences the needs, tastes, and wants of customers, as Chapter 6 will discuss in detail. The social organization of a society influences disposable income and purchasing processes. For example, who makes the decisions in the purchase of a family car? Do the children influence the choice of model, do Mom and Dad play an equal role, or does one family member dominate product choice? Education and living conditions influence product choices as well as the communication methods available to marketers. While other cultural and social characteristics play a role, here we will focus on those that are most often used in the preliminary classification of markets: language and religion.

A nation's language (or languages) affects the way marketers communicate with customers, suppliers, and intermediaries. The use of brochures, advertising, or packaging, for example, is greatly simplified when the same language can be used in different geographic markets. There are some drawbacks to grouping markets into language clusters, however. Grouping together countries in which the dominant language is derived from Latin, for example, would result in a heterogeneous set of markets including Argentina, France, Italy, Peru, and Romania. Even sorting out the Spanish-speaking group, including countries like Mexico, Spain, Honduras, and Venezuela, would result in a cluster of very dissimilar markets. Thus, although language should be considered in selecting markets and developing a marketing mix, it cannot be used by itself as a basis for classification.

Religion is an important cultural element in most societies. Many kinds of behavior, including buying behavior, are based on religious beliefs. Therefore, religion represents an interesting criterion for grouping countries into clusters. One might think that markets in which Christianity is the dominant religion differ significantly from markets in which Hinduism, Buddhism, Islam, or Animism is dominant. Yet a closer examination of each of these groups reveals enormous differences between markets. In Bangladesh and India, Pakistan and

Saudi Arabia, El Salvador and Italy, high percentages of the population belong to the same religion. But each market must be treated very differently, due to other distinctions. Thus, like language, religion is an element that needs to be considered in developing a marketing mix, but it is not by itself a viable criterion for evaluating and selecting markets, except in the case of religious products.

In sum, each of the external environments that are commonly used to group markets may be useful for preliminary screening. But for most products other factors must be considered as well. For example, Sweden has one of the highest rates of ice cream consumption per capita in Europe, a characteristic that would not be revealed by a classification of countries according to climate. It is necessary to examine other variables that more fully describe the market and its potential. One such variable is the level of economic development.

Level of Economic Development

Nations can be clustered by their level of economic development, which may include social and environmental variables in addition to economic ones.

There are more than 150 nations in the world, and their levels of economic development range from very low to very high. Grouping them on this basis results in clusters of markets with comparable purchasing power, demand for industrial products, and development of infrastructure. Several approaches can be used in classifying markets according to economic development.

The simplest approach is to use gross national product (GNP) or gross domestic product (GDP) per capita as a basis for classification.[2] This results in a cluster of countries that can be considered affluent, with per capita GNP over $4,500. These countries account for over two-thirds of the world's total GNP, but they contain less than one-third of the world's population. At the other extreme are countries that belong to the lowest-income category, with per capita GDP below $410; they contain 55 percent of the world's population. (See Exhibit 3.1.)

This classification not only lists high- and low-income countries, it also illustrates one of the problems of classification of data—inconsistent data. Although these listings are based on the same source, high-income (or "industrial") countries are classified by GNP, while low-income countries are classified by GDP. GNP and GDP are not the same, of course. GNP includes export and import data; GDP does not. Data available to the international marketing manager is frequently inconsistent, but the alternative would be to make no classification at all. Inconsistent data make it even more important to use classifications that use multiple criteria to assess markets.

Classifying markets on the basis of GNP or GDP alone, however, can be misleading. For example, some oil- and gas-producing countries, such as Saudi Arabia, Kuwait, and Libya, have very high national incomes and small populations. This results in a high per capita GNP figure, so these nations are in the same income group as Switzerland, Norway, the United States, and Canada. However, their level of economic development is not directly comparable.

To overcome this problem, more complex economic approaches can be used. Simple income measures can be combined with other characteristics of

EXHIBIT 3.1
HIGH-INCOME AND
LOW-INCOME
COUNTRIES

High-Income Countries

Australia	France	Kuwait	Saudi Arabia
Austria	West Germany	Libya	Spain
Belgium	Iceland	Luxembourg	Sweden
Canada	Ireland	Netherlands	Switzerland
Denmark	Italy	New Zealand	United Kingdom
Finland	Japan	Norway	United States

Low-Income Countries

Afghanistan	Comores	Laos	São Tomé
Bangladesh	Equatorial Guinea	Madagascar	and Principe
Benin	Ethiopia	Malawi	Sierra Leone
Bhutan	Gambia	Maldives	Somalia
Burkina Faso	Ghana	Mali	Sri Lanka
Burma	Guinea	Mauritania	Sudan
Burundi	Guinea-Bissau	Mozambique	Tanzania
Cape Verde	Haiti	Nepal	Togo
Central African	India	Niger	Uganda
Republic	Democratic	Pakistan	Vietnam
Chad	Kampuchea	Rwanda	Zaire
China	Kenya		

Source: Adapted from *International Monetary Fund, Annual Report, 1987* (Washington, D.C., 1988) pp. 171, 174.

national markets—such as social-class structure,[3] national resources, environmental conditions, level of technological sophistication, existing infrastructures, and cultural and behavioral variables—to create a more realistic picture of the markets in question.[4] This approach results in five or six clusters ranging from highly developed to very undeveloped. These categories are sometimes referred to as First, Second, Third, Fourth, and Fifth World.[5] (See Exhibit 3.2.)

At first, such classifications seem to result in useful groupings for purposes of global marketing. It might be assumed that the members of the First World, for example, are a homogeneous target market for prestigious consumer durables, high-tech industrial products, and expensive services. A closer look, however, reveals that such a classification is still oriented too much toward national averages and does not result in groups of markets with the same needs. There may be some homogeneous product markets, such as for designer boots or vinyl extruders, but what does such a grouping of countries do for a marketer of ravioli or security services?

Other attempts to use clusters of nation markets based on stages of economic development lead to similar results. The Third World, for example, includes countries such as Oman, Brazil, South Korea, Morocco, and Taiwan. They are similar in that they do not need massive foreign aid to develop their economies. But the goods desired by consumers in Oman are so different from those desired by consumers in Brazil or Taiwan that this grouping is of limited value to

EXHIBIT 3.2
THE "FIVE WORLDS"

The "Five Worlds" classi-
fication helps illustrate
how *level of economic
development* provides
added insight to the
global marketing manag-
er. Not only is the nation's
level and type of eco-
nomic activity analyzed,
but also its technological
know-how and role in the
global economy.

First World	Advanced industrial nations of the Triad, with a more-or-less capitalistic, market-oriented economy. Includes the high-income countries listed in Exhibit 3.1.
Second World	Eastern European members of COMECON, except Yugoslavia.
Third World	Nations that need time and technology, rather than massive foreign aid, to build their economies. Includes oil-exporting nations as well as others rich in natural resources.
Fourth World	Unlike Third World countries, these economies need significant financial help and special treatment from industrialized nations to export their goods, acquire technology, and develop natural resources.
Fifth World	Over 200 million inhabitants live in poverty in these nations, which have few known natural resources. Usually the population is engaged in subsistence farming or nomadic herding, often isolated from the outside world.

Source: Based on R. D. Staede, "Multinational Corporations and the Changing World Economic Order," *California Management Review*, Winter 1978, p. 7.

marketers of consumer goods. On the other hand, the industrial products needed in Morocco may not be very different from those needed in Poland, which is classified as Second World. High-income nations also differ in a variety of ways. Sweden's social-class structure is very different from that of the United States (see Exhibit 3.3), while Japan is characterized by a system of economic coop-eration that is unparalleled in either Sweden or the United States.[6] Even a single nation like the United States may be far from homogeneous.[7]

In sum, although grouping nations according to economic variables can be useful in the early stages of market selection, the marketer must be aware of specific differences between markets that may be obscured by aggregate eco-nomic data. (Some of these differences are discussed in Global Dimensions 3.1.)

EXHIBIT 3.3
SOCIAL STRATA—
UNITED STATES AND
SWEDEN

Sweden and the United
States traditionally have
had a similar social class
distribution (although the
United States has a lower
class that is larger than
its upper class). Due
mainly to dual career
households, the U.S. dis-
tribution seems to be
changing: Upper and
lower classes are in-
creasing, while the mid-
dle class is shrinking.

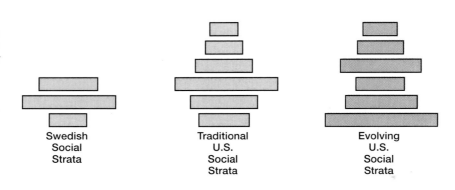

Swedish Social Strata   Traditional U.S. Social Strata   Evolving U.S. Social Strata

GLOBAL   DIMENSIONS   3.1

Developing Countries

A firm that assesses developing countries as potential markets should keep in mind that there is a big difference between the well-educated and affluent members of a society and its workers, unemployed, and rural poor. Even if many urban dwellers in developing countries have the same low income as the rural population, there are significant differences between the consumption patterns of the two groups. Thus, differences in income, age, and educational level within a population together with the environment they live in give rise to different life-styles that must be taken into account in marketing consumer products or services to developing countries.

Another factor that has to be considered is the dynamics of economic development. By the end of the 1980s countries like Thailand, Malaysia, and Indonesia had not yet achieved high per capita income. Yet their populations are not only numerous but also skilled and industrious. Low wage levels, political stability, and targeted industrialization programs in these countries have recently produced more rapid economic growth rates. Economic development similar to that in their very successful neighbor countries, Singapore and South Korea, can be expected. As a result, these countries represent markets that should not be overlooked.

Sources: L. A. Amine and S. T. Cavusgil, "Marketing Environment in the Middle East and North Africa: The Forces Behind Market Homogenization," in S. T. Cavusgil (ed.), *Advances in International Marketing*, vol. 1 (Greenwich, Ct.: JAI Press, 1986), p. 128; G. Rice and E. Mahmoud, "The Prospects for Export Marketing to Egypt," in E. Kaynak (ed.), *International Business in the Middle East* (New York: Walter de Gruyter, 1986), p. 219; and T. Straka, "In Asien wachst der fünfte Tiger heran," *Standard*, January 25, 1990, p. 12.

Less-developed countries contain a great percentage of the world's population, but a small percentage of the world's wealth.

Less-Developed Countries.   Most of the world's poorest countries are located in sub-Saharan Africa. Countries like Benin, Burkina Faso, the Central African Republic, Ethiopia, Mauritania, Somalia, and Sudan repeatedly experience devastating droughts, as well as civil strife and enormous refugee and health problems. Today they are the largest recipients of foreign assistance.[8] Their stagnant economies lack almost all the resources necessary for development: capital, infrastructure, trained industrial and agricultural workers, and political stability. To do business in such nations, the marketer must identify the nation's most urgent needs, develop specific solutions, assist in financing, train personnel, and maintain products. For example, companies that have sold baby formula in these countries found it necessary not only to create distribution channels and promotional campaigns, but also to hire women to visit villages to teach mothers how to use the product properly.

Asia contains another group of very poor countries, including Afghanistan, Bangladesh, Burma, Democratic Kampuchea, and Vietnam. All have recently suffered from war, floods, overpopulation, and political instability. Burma, for example, was one of the world's primary exporters of rice until 1962, when an autocratic government took power. It is now one of the poorest countries in the world and continues to be plagued by political turmoil. In Afghanistan, differences between rival groups of Mujahadhin (freedom fighters) will almost certainly lead to civil strife for several more years.

The potential for conducting profitable business in these countries is very low. It is difficult to classify and analyze **less-developed countries (LDCs)** in ways that are meaningful from the standpoint of global marketing strategy. Low income, restrictive legislation, and poor infrastructures present major obstacles to marketing in these countries. Why, then, should global marketers be interested in these markets at all?

The answer lies in both current and future opportunities. Many markets in industrial nations are almost, if not entirely, saturated. Markets in LDCs are therefore becoming increasingly important. Indeed, LDCs already provide better returns on investment than industrial countries.[9] For example, in 1984 LDCs accounted for less than 23 percent of U.S. direct investments but about 30 percent of income from those investments. Developing economies with the natural and human resources to overcome periodic financial and political crises are becoming prime target markets. To be successful in these markets, companies will have to take a long-term view. They must be willing to train local residents and facilitate the transfer of technology, and they must be adept at cultivating relationships with local firms and influential individuals.[10]

Sometimes governments attempt to attract the participation of nondomestic firms by providing financing for projects with potentially high sales volume.[11] Often these opportunities focus on a product that is deemed necessary or socially useful, such as fertilizer. The host country might provide credit assurances or low-cost capital to the foreign firm to lower its risk of doing business in that country, as an incentive for the foreign firm to sell its product there. Opportunities may also arise because many LDC governments want technology from more advanced economies. But technology transfers do not occur in a single step. Rather, there is a multistage flow of technology and managerial expertise between countries at different levels of economic development. Korea, India, Brazil, and the Eastern European countries import significant amounts of advanced technology. At the same time, they are playing a growing role in the transfer of technology to developing countries. For example, Eastern German and Czechoslovakian firms have cooperated with Western German engineering firms in industrial projects throughout the developing world.

Newly Industrialized Countries. The **newly industrialized countries**, or **NICs**, include Hong Kong, Singapore, South Korea, and Taiwan, all located in Southeast Asia. They are highly competitive, export-oriented manufacturing countries characterized by high rates of economic growth and low rates of inflation and unemployment. Low wages, long working hours, and strong management are the basic ingredients of their success. Political stability and market-oriented public policies have been top priorities in these countries in recent years. All of them import technology and consumer products. South Korea, for example, is the fourth-largest importer of U.S. farm products.[12]

Upon closer examination, the so-called "four tigers" just mentioned turn out to be quite different in basic economic structure. South Korea has become the twelfth largest industrial nation in the world. The country's economy is characterized by a few very large industrial conglomerates, called **chaebols**, that are efficient, high-volume producers. Samsung's sales, for example, reached more than $200 billion in 1988. Chaebols specialize in low-cost mass production, and they cooperate closely with their governments.[13] By gradually opening up its own markets, South Korea tries to avoid major trade imbalances with the industrialized nations. A marketer interested in doing business in South Korea must be aware that there are three different import categories. For luxury goods and products that compete directly with local production, the exporter needs a special import license, which should be confirmed in the sales contract. For another group of products, import quotas exist. All other products can be brought into the country without restrictions.

Taiwan's economy is characterized by a host of small and medium-sized privately owned companies with highly skilled workers and a high level of technical expertise. The companies are extremely flexible in their response to changes in customers' needs, but vulnerable to low-price competition from neighboring developing countries. During the mid 1980s Taiwan's economy grew at a yearly rate of 7 percent. Because companies had profited for decades from low wages, production technology was rather low. In the years between 1980 and 1985, however, wages went up 60 percent, resulting in pressures to increase productivity. In spite of the high barriers against imports erected by its government to protect the domestic economy, Taiwan has become a viable market for high technology. Recently, the high surpluses in its trade balances, in particular with the United States, forced the Taiwanese government to open up its markets.

Hong Kong is a densely populated British colony without its own constitution. It is self-administered, with a British governor. In 1898 the "New Territories," most of today's Hong Kong, were leased from China for 99 years. Hong Kong will be handed over to China in 1997, but it is supposed to stay a special region, keeping its current economic, social, and legal system as well as its autonomy for another 50 years. The insecurity of this agreement has resulted in an ongoing process of emigration and departure of capital. Nevertheless, at present Hong Kong has the second-largest per capita income in East Asia, after Japan. With approximately 150 banks, it is the world's third-largest center of financial transactions, behind New York and London; banking represents more than one-fifth of Hong Kong's GDP.

Singapore, meanwhile, is one of the busiest ports in the world and has a strong shipbuilding industry. It possesses the second-largest concentration of banking and financial institutions outside of the industrialized nations, after Hong Kong. These institutions actively attract foreign investment.

The high economic growth in Southeast Asia has spread considerably further than Japan into the NICs.

The NICs are obviously not a homogeneous group. But their economies are growing, their markets are increasingly viable, and their standard of living is improving.

Highly Industrialized Countries. The seven nations with the highest GNP, collectively referred to as the **highly industrial countries**, are Canada, France, Germany, Italy, Japan, the United Kingdom, and the United States. They form the core of the Triad market. Several other countries can be classified as highly developed even though they are not part of the Triad, including Australia and New Zealand. Large numbers of consumers with sufficient economic resources make these strong potential markets. However, economic potential is not the sole determinant of the attractiveness of a specific market.

Cooperative Agreements

Economic cooperative agreements between (or among) nations result in improved market opportunities.

As the volume of international trade has increased, various forms of economic cooperation among nations have emerged. These take the form of *bilateral* or *multilateral* arrangements, ranging from simple agreements on tariff reduction to full-scale political integration.

Economic cooperation can be expected to have the following effects on global marketing:

1. Larger markets, accompanied by opportunities for mass production, mass marketing, and more efficient use of resources.

2. Higher income in those markets, which in turn stimulates internal trade and creates opportunities for external suppliers of industrial goods, consumer goods, and services.

3. The possibility of direct investment, to avoid tariff and nontariff barriers and to profit from the increase in internal trade. Extended tariff barriers may result if the members of a cooperative agreement abolish all tariffs among themselves, but keep tariffs for nonmembers. Such a decision would automatically give a cost advantage to companies located inside the "tariff wall." Nontariff barriers include quota regulations and administrative hurdles. Italy and France, for example, have established fixed percentages of total car sales in their countries that Japanese car exporters are not allowed to exceed. Meanwhile the members of the European Community (EC) are involved in a heated discussion about whether to transfer these barriers to the entire community. Some Japanese companies have overcome the quotas by investing directly in car production in Great Britain.

4. An increase in the number of mergers and acquisitions initiated by firms outside cooperative agreements. This helps foreign firms insure that they will have a local subsidiary that will allow their business to avoid the negative effects of cooperative legislation that might confront a "pure" foreign firm. AMAG, an Austrian manufacturer of aluminum products, for example, has acquired or become a partner in a whole series of companies in different EC countries, to be prepared for such an event. The

GLOBAL   DIMENSIONS   3.2

Barter Clearing Ageements

Bilateral Barter Clearing Agreements between governments have been reached mainly between less-developed countries and members of COMECON, but they are becoming increasingly common between less-developed countries themselves, as well. Under such an agreement a clearing account is established by the participating countries. A clearing account works in a similar manner to a checking account. Traded goods are valued in clearing-account units. A balance sheet showing the number of clearing-account units exchanged is maintained by the central banks of the countries involved. Participating companies are paid in their domestic currencies; there is no direct barter relationship between firms in the two countries.

India maintains barter clearing agreements aimed at balancing its trade with a number of trading partners. Recently, the British firm Rank Xerox established a joint venture to assemble copying machines in India. Unable to export its products directly to the Soviet Union, because the latter makes little hard currency available for copiers, Rank can take advantage of India's need to export goods to the Soviet Union to pay for oil and steel plants under a barter clearing agreement between these two nations. Rank sells European-made components to the assembly plant in India, taking payment in Dutch guilders.

Source: "New Restrictions on World Trade: Governments Link Imports to Exports—Bartering Goods and Protecting Jobs," *Business Week*, July 19, 1982, pp. 118–122.

partnerships would also be able to take advantage of subsidized research programs within the cooperative agreement, which would not be available to the foreign firm on its own.

Each type of economic cooperation has different effects on the conduct of business and the nature of competition. Therefore, it is important to devote some attention to economic agreements in evaluating a potential market.

Bilateral Agreements.   The simplest cooperative international agreement is the **bilateral agreement**, a pact between two countries concerning trade in one or a few product groups. The purpose of the agreement is to reduce or even abolish barriers to trade. Bilateral agreements often serve as the basis for trade between industrialized countries and countries with restrictive conditions, such as nonconvertible currencies or centrally controlled economies. For example, Austria has signed separate bilateral agreements with all of its Eastern European neighbors. Each agreement regulates the amount and timing of trade between Austria and its trading partner, as well as the categories of products that may be traded. (For an example of a bilateral barter-clearing agreement, see Global Dimensions 3.2.)

There is a growing tendency for industrialized nations to sign bilateral agreements among themselves. One such agreement is the Free Trade Area Treaty between the United States and Israel, which was signed in April 1985. It provides for the eventual elimination of virtually all barriers to trade between the two countries. It is also the first trade agreement ever to cover explicitly a full range of services, including transportation, travel, tourism, communications, banking, insurance, construction, accounting, education, law, management consulting, computer services, and advertising.[14]

Another major U.S. bilateral agreement is the free trade pact between the United States and Canada. This agreement eliminated all tariffs on bilateral trade within ten years of 1988, reduced nontariff barriers, and established rules for the conduct of bilateral investment and resolution of trade disputes. In effect, it lowers the remaining barriers to trade of some $150 billion in goods and services annually between these two major trading partners.[15]

A variety of multilateral agreements exist, which add additional levels of economic integration as nations move from one level to a higher level.

Multilateral Agreements.   **Multilateral agreements** regulate trade among more than two countries. Their basic purpose is to facilitate trade by reducing tariffs and other barriers to trade. (See Exhibit 3.4.) For the global marketing manager, the most important multilateral trade agreement is the General Agreement on Tariffs and Trade (GATT). The most important feature of GATT is its *most favored nation* clause. As long as this clause is respected by a host country, marketers can count on fair treatment in relation to domestic competitors in that country. (GATT is discussed in more detail in Chapter 11.)

When a multilateral agreement removes all formal impediments to trade for a specified group of products, a **free trade area** is established. For example, the European Free Trade Association (EFTA)—which includes Austria, Finland, Iceland, Norway, Sweden, and Switzerland—removed all tariffs on manufactured goods traded by these nations. However, these nations maintain independent policies with regard to nonmembers; a company based in a nonmember country faces different barriers to entry with each EFTA member.

A less successful attempt to establish a free trade area is the Latin American Integration Association (LAIA), which includes Mexico and the countries in South America (except the Guianas). LAIA's progress toward free trade has been slowed by uneven economic development in the region.

EXHIBIT 3.4
A CONTINUUM OF
DIFFERENT FORMS
OF ECONOMIC
COOPERATION

As economic cooperative agreements move from the most basic (reduction of tariffs) toward the most complex (economic or political unions), the greater the degree of economic integration. This continuum is progressive; a common market, for example, has reduced tariffs plus movement toward removal of internal tariffs, plus harmonization of external tariffs, plus the free movement of factors of production.

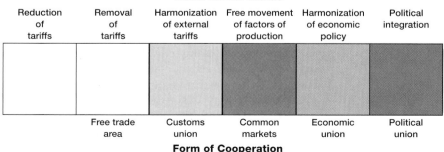

The European Community

Members of the **European Community** as of 1990 are Belgium, Denmark, France, Germany, Greece, Ireland, Italy, Luxembourg, The Netherlands, Portugal, Spain, and the United Kingdom. These nations have agreed to attempt to achieve a fully integrated market by 1992. Once this goal has been reached, the EC will be the most populous market in the industrialized West, with a total population of over 320 million, and it will represent the second-largest concentration of purchasing power in the world ($2,840 billion, compared to the United States' $3,140 billion as of 1988).

As a result of economic integration, it is anticipated that consumer prices in the EC will decrease by 2–4 percent; the number of jobs will increase by 2–3 million, and the GNP will grow by 1.5–3 percent. One effect will be an increase in the economic power of the Triad. Other nations, as well as companies within them, are devising strategies for responding to the EC's new role. For example, EFTA members are trying to establish a common strategy for joining or at least participating in the EC. Austria and Turkey have applied for membership, and Morocco has officially expressed a desire to become part of the EC.

Sources: M. Barrett and P. King, eds., "Towards a Single Market in 1992", *Euromoney*, September 1988; and J. A. Quelch, R. D. Buzzell, and E. R. Salama, *The Marketing Challenge of 1992*, (Reading, Mass.: Addison-Wesley, 1990).

The next level of economic cooperation is the **customs union**. This type of agreement has the characteristics of a free trade area, but in addition the members establish consistent tariff policies vis-à-vis nonmembers. An example of such an agreement is the Southern African Customs Union, which includes the Republic of South Africa (the dominant member), Botswana, Lesotho, and Swaziland. An exporter to any of these countries will receive the same tariff treatment. This has the effect of creating a larger market with a shared "tariff wall."

A **common market** is formed when member countries, in addition to removing tariffs between them and harmonizing their tariff policies vis-à-vis nonmembers, remove all barriers to the free movement of production factors among them. For example, capital can be transferred without any restrictions, workers have the freedom to look for jobs throughout the common market, there is free trade in services, and manufacturing plants can be built in the member countries that seem best to the companies. The European Community is the most familiar example of a multilateral agreement resulting in a common market (see Global Dimensions 3.3).

GLOBAL   DIMENSIONS   3.4

The European Monetary System

The **European Monetary System (EMS)**, created in 1979 to guarantee the internal and external stability of currencies of member countries and to coordinate their economic policies, has been a success so far. The most important part of the system is the fixed parities (rates) between the currencies of the participating nations. They are determined by their value against the **European Currency Unit (ECU)**, an artificial currency created to facilitate transactions. The currency exchange rates are allowed to fluctuate around the fixed levels in a predetermined percentage. If two currencies arrive at the upper and the lower end of their allowed zone of fluctuation, the national banks involved must buy and sell the respective currencies to stabilize their exchange rates.

If the European Community is to become an economic union, the EMS has to be replaced by a more restrictive one, such as absolutely fixed exchange rates. As of 1990, however, such a development seems rather unlikely, because of the dispute between member governments over the necessity of a common central bank.

Source: U. Ramm, "The Next Step on the Road to a United Europe," in M. Barrett and P. King, eds., "Towards a Single Market in 1992," Euromoney, September 1988, pp. 23–24.

The EC member nations have also agreed to harmonize their tax and subsidy policies as a precondition for the unification of their fiscal and monetary policies. The result should be an **economic union**, in which member nations will be fully integrated economically and will eventually adopt a common currency. (Such a process is subject to major political difficulties, however. See Global Dimensions 3.4.)

The most advanced form of economic cooperation is the **political union**, in which the agreement among the signing parties results in a new nation. To a certain extent, Australia and the United States are successful historical examples of this type of agreement. Two African nations, Senegal and Zambia, may be coming close to a political union; another recent example may be the reunification of Germany. Today, however, most governments believe that they would have to give up too much political sovereignty if they were to enter into such an agreement; political unions, therefore, are unlikely to be formed frequently.

The various forms of economic cooperation among nations influence the environment in which global marketing takes place. Whatever the specific arrangement, these agreements broaden the market and often unify conditions of market entry for companies based in nonmember nations.

It is important to note that none of the existing arrangements fall neatly into any of the above categories. The European Community, for example, is a

The most visible sym-
bol of decades of cold
war, the Berlin Wall,
came down in 1989,
signalling a new era of
political cooperation
between East Europe
and the rest of the
world.

full customs union, a well-developed common market, a partially developed economic union, and a weak political union. Moreover, there is no automatic progression from agreements on tariff reductions to full-scale political union.[16]

Depending on the objectives of the partners in a multilateral agreement, different patterns of regional market development may occur. Economic cooperation among LDCs, for instance, is aimed largely at the creation of a larger, protected market to stimulate the production and exchange of goods among the member nations. It should also create opportunities for profitable investment, especially for firms already conducting business in these markets. The Central American Common Market—consisting of Costa Rica, El Salvador, Guatemala, Honduras, and Nicaragua—has reached the first objective; it has established a free trade area for a wide range of products. But the unequal participation of the member nations and political disputes among the governments of some of these nations have made it impossible to establish a customs union. Failure to achieve faster economic development has resulted in frustration and a decrease in efforts to create a common market. It may even lead to disintegration of the agreement, as in the case of the East African Community, which broke up in 1978.[17]

Economic cooperation among communist countries was intended to maximize gains from economies of scale, specialization, and using natural resources in one nation for the benefit of all. In practice, however, the Council for Mutual Economic Assistance (CMEA, also called COMECON) developed primarily into a political group under the control of the Soviet Union. By early 1989 the CMEA consisted of Bulgaria, Cuba, Czechoslovakia, East Germany, Hungary, Mongolia, Poland, Romania, the USSR, and Vietnam. The absence of market forces, coupled with nonconvertible currencies (calculation was done in "transfer rubles") and distrust of the Soviet Union by most other CMEA members, resulted in a situation in which success was limited to bilateral agreements for specific projects. In 1989, the further existence of the agreement was challenged by Czechoslovakia, in connection with the political changes in all the East European member countries. Hungary and Poland demanded a change to free market exchanges based on convertible currencies. The situation became further complicated by the plans of the German Federal Republic and the German Democratic Republic to join forces in a currency union in 1990, leading to a political union shortly thereafter. The results of such radical political and economic changes are uncertain. But if economic progress is achieved, it opens up new market opportunities for firms worldwide.

Special Geographic Zones

For U.S.-based marketers, several geographic zones have special significance for reasons of proximity, raw materials, or politics.

Grouping countries into geographic market clusters is rarely enough for strategic purposes, but it has some value. In this section we discuss such groupings from the standpoint of their importance to U.S.-based marketers and the U.S. economy. From this perspective, there are four groupings or zones that are of interest because of their proximity to the United States, their supplies of critical raw materials, and their changing political environments.

Latin America

Due to its proximity to the United States, Latin America is of particular interest to U.S. marketers. But they have lost many markets in this zone to global competitors who seemed more willing to take a long-term view as to profitability. Many Latin American countries have vast supplies of natural resources, but a constraint on the viability of most of their markets is that to date more than half of their exports have consisted of simple commodities. They have little value-added manufacturing, which keeps incomes low. In addition, the Latin American countries are in very different stages of economic development, resulting in distinctive market characteristics.

Brazil is the most economically developed Latin American country, with an improving infrastructure and a high rate of economic growth. It has an export-oriented automotive industry, and it exports many consumer goods; for example, it is the largest exporter of shoes to the United States. In 1988 Brazil's trade balance surplus was $13 billion, third in the world behind Germany and Japan. Mexico possesses many valuable natural resources, especially oil and gas. It also has a strong industrial base and a large, skilled work force with work values similar to those of U.S. workers. Argentina, with its large agricultural sector, is among the world's most competitive suppliers of grain and beef. Venezuela, a member of OPEC, has used its oil income to underwrite industrial development. Chile and Peru have significant mineral resources.

Together, these countries account for more than 90 percent of Latin American exports of manufactured goods. But their growth in basic industries like steel, machinery, pulp and paper, gas, hydroelectric power, and home appliances is based on imports of capital, machinery, materials, and intermediate goods, resulting in huge deficits in the national balance of payments. These deficits, combined with high inflation, low productivity, and political instability, have driven several countries to the edge of bankruptcy. In response, they have instituted import surcharges, quotas, and tariffs; restrictions on currencies that may be used to pay for imports; and other measures aimed at limiting imports. These protectionist policies have had negative side effects, such as reducing the competitiveness of domestic industries.[18] In the long run, a protected industry loses its capacity to compete internationally, because it no longer has to offer the highest quality products, produced with the latest technology. When protectionist policies are repealed, as they almost always are, the companies not only find themselves at an international disadvantage, they even lose in their domestic market as superior foreign products become available. In sum, even though Latin American markets offer great opportunities, they also present many problems for global marketers.

The Middle East

The rich, oil-producing countries of the Middle East include Kuwait, Saudi Arabia, and the United Arab Emirates. In spite of their capital resources, these countries are still developing economically. Their normally stable governments are encouraging industrialization by importing high-tech industrial goods, turnkey plants, maintenance contracts, and industrial services. In order to obtain new technologies, they often require involvement by local firms when awarding major contracts. Saudi Arabia, for example, requires that at least 30 percent of the total value of a contract be provided by local firms. A foreign firm that enters into such a contract must be certain that the local companies can fulfill their part of the agreement.

The Middle Eastern countries constitute a generally promising market for industrial goods. There are also markets for many consumer goods, provided that they are not prohibited by Islamic religious principles. However, because of small populations these markets are limited.

Two other oil-producing countries, Iraq and Iran, would be included in this category if the long war between them had not seriously interfered with their economic development. Both countries have been important markets for weapons and other military equipment and for pharmaceutical products. Iran has also bartered its oil for such products as feta cheese and lawnmowers. If these countries can recover from the effects of war and political instability, they will be very promising markets in the 1990s.

Still another group of Middle Eastern countries is made up of those that are directly involved in the Arab-Israeli conflict: Lebanon, Syria, Jordan, Egypt, and Israel. In addition to their large military expenditures, these nations have been investing heavily in economic and human development. Egypt, for example, has developed a large cadre of trained administrators. However, it suffers from a population explosion and the declining importance of the Suez Canal, long a source of a significant portion of its foreign-currency income. Lebanon (especially its capital, Beirut), once the center of commerce and banking in the Middle East, has been devastated by war, political instability, and civil strife. Most of its commercial business has been lost to its oil-producing neighbors.

Israel is by far the most economically developed country in this group. It has strong agricultural and tourism sectors and many high-tech companies, especially in defense-related industries. The imbalance in Israel's international trade accounts, caused by its need to import many consumer goods, and its high spending on national defense are offset by large inflows of capital from the western industrial nations. Nevertheless, a high inflation rate and problems with its Palestinian population have created serious political and economic difficulties for Israel.

Finally, Turkey offers a market that is growing in importance. Turkey has achieved political stability after years of turmoil and military rule, and its liberal economic policies have encouraged foreign investment. Moreover, Turkey's location between Europe and Asia enables it to easily engage in trade with countries on both continents.

Eastern Europe

Until 1989 all Eastern European countries were centrally controlled economies (CCEs). Their foreign trade was a state monopoly. Traditionally, only official foreign trade organizations (FTOs) were authorized to make international purchases and sales for these nations. FTOs had to conform to annual and five-year plans that were developed, supervised, and administered by the nation's ministry of foreign trade. FTOs received information about product requirements and specifications, even the number of items to be produced, from an office of central planning. These products were manufactured internally whenever possible. Orders were placed with outside firms only when product requirements could not be met by domestic sources. Priority in permitting imports was generally given to sophisticated machinery and equipment for the chemical, energy, and automotive sectors, as well as agriculture, food processing, and packaging. By and large, consumer goods were given much lower priority. Because of such centralization of planning, it was usually difficult for a company accustomed to conducting business in market economies to enter Eastern European markets. Lack of direct information about customers created a barrier, as did the FTOs' inability to react quickly to changes. On the other hand, once a company had established a foothold in a centrally controlled economy it was likely to encounter less competition than is typically found in market economies.

An important factor for business success in a centrally controlled economy has always been participation in exhibits and trade fairs. (See Exhibit 3.5.) At these fairs, a wide variety of products and services are displayed by firms inter-

EXHIBIT 3.5
IMPORTANT TRADE
SHOWS IN EASTERN
EUROPE IN 1990

Trade shows are of great-
er importance for con-
ducting business in East-
ern Europe than in most
other parts of the world.
As this exhibit illustrates,
the shows vary by nation
as well as by their prod-
uct emphasis.

- **Bulgaria**
  International Consumer Goods Fair, May 7–13, Plovdiv.
  International Technical and Industrial Goods Fair, Sept. 24–30, Plovdiv.
- **Czechoslovakia**
  BW International Consumer Goods Fair, April 7–12, Brno.
- **East Germany**
  Leipzig Trade Fair, March 11–17 and Sept. 2–8.
- **Hungary**
  International Exhibition and Fair of Tourism, March 16–23, Budapest.
  Budapest International Fair (of consumer goods), May 23–31.
  Omek Exhibition of Agriculture and Food Industry, August, Budapest.
  International Fair (of consumer goods), Sept. 21–30, Budapest.
  International Exhibition of Packaging and Materials Handling, October, Budapest.
- **Poland**
  Agpol International Exhibition of Consumer Goods, Feb. 27–March 2, Warsaw.
  Poznan International Fair, June 10–17.
- **Romania**
  Bucharest International Fair, Oct. 14–22.
- **Soviet Union**
  TV, Cinema & Radio Engineering, April 10–18, Moscow.
  Public Health Show '90, May 22–31, Moscow.
- **Yugoslavia**
  International Automobile & Motorcycle Show, March, Beograd.
  International Tourism and Sports Fair, March, Sarajevo.

Source: "Eastern Europe," *Advertising Age*, February 19, 1990, p. 45.

ested in doing business with the country. Such participation may not result in immediate sales, but contact with end users, technical experts, and administrators may be established, enabling the marketer to learn the needs of potential customers and influence the technical specifications of future purchases. Another way to at least partly overcome the problem of limited marketing information has been to hold seminars in conjunction with state committees for science and technology, FTOs, or foreign companies that have already gained entry to the market of interest. Such events help familiarize end users with potential solutions to their problems and influence decision makers at the relevant FTO or ministry.[19]

Some of the similarities among the Eastern European economies just mentioned have gradually disappeared since 1989. Economic and political reforms made possible through the *glasnost* and *perestroika* policies of the Soviet Union have developed in the direction of market economies (see Global Dimensions 3.5). But because actual change is much slower than political declarations and legislative changes,[20] it is important to know how business was done under the old centrally controlled system in order to understand the existing peculiarities of business with Eastern European countries.

GLOBAL DIMENSIONS 3.5

Dynamic Developments in Eastern Europe

Decentralization of International Business. One of the most important changes in the markets of Eastern Europe, from a marketer's point of view, is the authorization of a growing number of ministries, foreign trade organizations, and individual companies to do international business on their own. Bulgaria canceled the state monopoly on international trade in 1989. In Poland each company is allowed to establish trade relationships with international partners. By 1990, 900 Polish companies already had their own foreign currency accounts. Hungary has followed a similar path. By 1990, Hungarian companies could import more than 260 goods without licenses, including metal-carving machines, paper, and fish.

Individual companies in Eastern Europe have become more and more independent. In the Soviet Union, for example, 20,000 of the existing 46,000 companies have become self-directed since January 1988. They are financially responsible for their own performance; the government is no longer liable for their debts. Companies that are not able to eliminate their deficits will be closed. But decentralization still has to go a long way before the economic system is comparable to Western industrialized nations. For example, some Soviet ministries had to order the companies in their field of responsibility to introduce marketing by January 1, 1990.

Private Enterprise. Bulgaria introduced shareholder companies, which can be completely private or even foreign-owned, in 1989. In Poland the "Act on Business Activities" legalized private enterprise (in most cases without limitations concerning public permission or size) in January 1989. Poles have begun to buy formerly public companies. A major barrier to faster development of private initiatives, however, is the lack of management know-how, capital, and a sufficient supply of products. In Hungary, there is a strong tendency to privatize industrial companies, commerce, and restaurants. In August 1989, Getz, a U.S. trading company, was the first Western company to own 100 percent of a formerly public Hungarian company, Intercooperation. IKEA, the Swedish furniture retailer, opened up its first outlet in Budapest in the spring of 1990.

Joint Ventures. In Poland and Hungary the legislation regarding joint ventures is the most advanced of all Eastern European countries. Since January 1, 1990, joint ventures between Polish and foreign companies can be established without any restriction as to ownership. The minimal capital share is $50,000, which can be in cash, equity, or technology. Management positions can be filled with non-Polish citizens. Joint ventures are exempt from sales taxes for their first three years. Taxes on profits are 40 percent. Profits from exports can be transferred to other countries. Most of these regulations were in place by 1989 and led to a joint venture boom that year, with 120 new joint ventures, 60 of them with German companies. This trend should continue in 1990.

Hungary has formed "Investcenter," which facilitates contracts between potential Hungarian and foreign joint venture partners. Nearly 400 joint ventures had been formed by early 1990, many of them in services or the construction business, and some of them in manufacturing. Suzuki, for example, will produce 50,000 of its Swift models in Hungary, while General Motors will produce car engines and Philips has entered the light bulb business.

Joint venture regulations were liberalized in all the other Eastern European nations, too. The changes in the Soviet Union, for example, led to fast growth in the number of joint ventures (more than 1,200 by early 1990). Roche, a Swiss chemical company, for example, founded Diaplus with the Soviet NPO Biotechnologia to produce and market products for medical diagnosis. Five U.S. companies, one of them Eastman Kodak, signed 25 contracts for joint ventures with Soviet partners worth $10 billion.

Banking Systems. The banking systems in Eastern European countries are also developing. In the Soviet Union, for example, new banks such as Promstroj-Bank (Bank for Industry and Construction) and Schilsoz-Bank (Bank for Housing, Communities, and Social Infrastructure) have been founded. They give potential foreign investors and business partners information about the solvency of Soviet companies. Five big Western European banks, together with three Soviet banks, founded the first real commercial bank in the Soviet Union. This bank will lend money to industrial joint ventures and train the other Soviet banks in Western bank-management methods.

In Poland, new legislation permits the foundation of independant commercial banks, which can finance themselves under free-market conditions. In Hungary, private banks were created in 1988. The Creditanstalt, an Austrian bank, founded the first broker house in Eastern Europe with a bank located in Budapest. The London Stock Exchange and New York–based Bear, Stearn & Co. joined forces to help set up a Hungarian stock exchange.

Sources: "Der steinige Weg zur Marktwirtschaft; Polnische Wirtschaftsreform mit Luecken," *Neue Zuercher Zeitung*, March 1989; "Les Investisseurs Américains Participent à Deux Privatisations en Hongrie," *Le Monde*, August 19, 1989; Arthur Anderson & Co., "Gesetz der Wirtschaftsgesellschaften und deren Rechtsnormen in Ungarn," August 1989; "Polen liberalisiert nun seinen Aussenhandel," *tw*, February 9, 1990, p. 5; "Ober 1200 joint ventures in der USSR," *Der Standard*, February 15, 1990, p. 17.

The People's Republic of China

China represents a special case. In 1988 it was by far the most populated country in the world (1,095 million), and it had a GNP of $378 billion.[21] In 1987 the GNP grew at a rate of 9.4 percent, and the industrial growth rate was 6.5 percent. China's exports expanded by 28 percent, whereas its imports stagnated. Such economic success mainly resulted from two factors: political liberalization, which allowed small private enterprise, and the setup of so-called special industrial zones along the coastline, which were opened for foreign investors. Guandong may be taken as an example; in 1987 this province was China's leading export area, with $5.5 billion worth of exported goods and $5.4 billion worth of foreign investments.[22]

Encouraged by such successes, for a while the government leaders seemed to be ready to open up the entire coastline for private industries, from the Gulf of Tonkin to the North Korean border. Their goal was to integrate China with the world trade system. They believed that China would compete well against Taiwan, South Korea, Hong Kong, and Singapore in labor-intensive industries such as shoes, toys, and textiles. Their biggest problems seemed to be to find enough foreign investors, to train a sufficient number of qualified managers, and to market products globally. The events of 1989, however, showed the underlying instability of such developments in authoritative political systems. Economic liberalization had led many Chinese citizens to greater awareness of social inequalities. Their calls for democratization in the country's capital, Beijing, resulted in the contrary—an overthrow of liberal officials, who were replaced by "hardliners." Concerned about the risk of investing under such conditions, many global marketers withdrew. The further economic development of the biggest nation in the world had become very uncertain.

A MARKET ASSESSMENT PROCEDURE

Market clustering may be done through either a statistical or a strategic approach.

The basic procedure used in assessing potential markets is market clustering. This consists of the following steps:

1. Splitting the global market into groups of submarkets so that the resulting clusters are more homogeneous than the global market as a whole.

2. Describing the "typical" member in each cluster.

3. Choosing a cluster or clusters for further analysis.

To be effective and efficient, the market clustering process must be carried out systematically (see Exhibit 3.6). The company may use either a statistical or a strategic approach.[23]

Statistical Clustering

This clustering system uses statistical procedures to examine variables such as demographics, stage of economic development, or population density to establish clusters of similar geographic markets. For example, on the basis of per capita GNP, countries can be divided into groups according to their level of economic development. An initial analysis using such a statistical process might indicate that Norway holds greater potential for selling VCRs than Burma.

The results of this approach depend heavily on the availability and quality of data about geographic markets. **Statistical clustering** can generate useful general information about market characteristics, but specific information about

EXHIBIT 3.6
THE PROCESS OF
POTENTIAL MARKET
ASSESSMENT

As the potential market
assessment process pro-
gresses, markets are
classified by certain criteria to narrow their se-
lection to the geographic
markets of greatest interest. At the end of the
process, product markets
are identified, then individually analyzed for their
potential. As the process
moves forward, the em-
phasis on research shifts
from secondary to prima-
ry, as the marketing man-
ager moves closer to the
establishment of specific
marketing mixes.

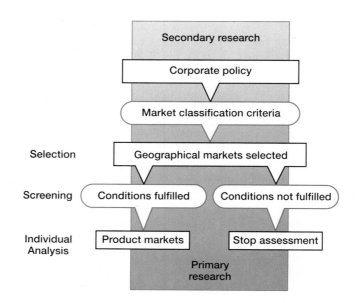

product markets may be overlooked. India, for example, is usually classified as
a developing nation, with per capita income of about $250 per year. A marketer
of color TVs might, therefore, be tempted to eliminate it from its list of potential
target markets. But India has a population of some 800 million. The vast majority
of Indians are very poor, but 10 percent of the population—about 80 million
people—have sizeable incomes; 1 percent, or 8 million, can be described as
affluent. Thus, opportunities to market color TVs in India are more attractive
than the per capita income figure suggests. Market clustering on per capita
income alone, therefore, would be misleading for a range of consumer products.

A similar statement holds true for industrial goods. In India, to continue
the same example, the manufacturing sector is developing rapidly. In recent
years Indian firms have become increasingly competitive in such markets as
machinery, computer software, and railroad construction. Consequently, there
is a growing market for industrial goods. Problems still arise, however, from the
complicated administrative process that must be followed to obtain an import
license. In effect, an exporter to India must prove that there is no local supplier
that is able to manufacture the same product. In addition, India does not respect
international conventions on the protection of patents. All this specific information, which strongly influences the attractiveness of the country's markets,
could be lost with a statistical clustering approach.

Strategic Clustering

In evaluating global markets, a strategic approach is more appropriate. Using
strategic clustering, the company groups the potential markets according to
strategic criteria. It chooses criteria that are important for the specific product

market to be served and that will help the firm achieve its goals. A marketer of video products for training nurses, for example, should consider the number of hospitals and nurses, the certification requirements, and the amount of public and private money available to sponsor training programs in various geographic areas.

Geographic markets will be most effectively clustered with criteria that consider not only the product market, but also the company's ability to successfully serve the product market. Characteristics often used include number, sizes, and purchasing power of potential customers; availability of technologically skilled personnel; product market growth rate; transferability of funds; number and size of competitors; availabilty of intermediaries; and specific market knowledge and local subsidies readily available to the company. For example, Japanese companies often enter the markets of the European Community via Spain. They do so because wages are relatively low in Spain and the Spanish government offers high subsidies for new industrial plants. Assessment and market selection in such a case depend on strategic considerations, not just easily accessible, general data about potential markets.

In each case the global marketer will have to evaluate the advantages and disadvantages of the clustering approaches available. The use of criteria that directly influence the attractiveness of a product market, in most cases, is appropriate. Sometimes a combination of statistical and strategic procedures may be chosen, depending on the time available.

Analysis of Product Markets

After analysis indicates that a specific geographic market contains potential, it may be subjected to specific examination to see if it is really viable.

The geographic market analysis may identify high-potential market clusters. The firm should then analyze specific product markets in detail. But if important criteria are not met, the assessment process is halted. A U.S.-based firm, for example, may have a policy of entering only markets characterized by low political risk. It would consider Canada or the United Kingdom for further market assessment, but it would screen out Libya.

Whether a company's product market is located in particular countries, extends over one or more geographic regions, or is global, it should be evaluated according to the criteria of substance, accessibility, and responsiveness. In addition, the marketer should examine the industry as a whole, major competitors, existing intermediaries, suppliers, and the available labor force.

Substance.   The **substance** of a product market is determined mainly by its size, that is, the number of customers, their expenditures, and the rate of growth. A market's size may be expressed in terms of sales, measured by some standard unit such as tons, or in terms of value (dollar volume); the latter is referred to as **market volume**.

There are different ways to estimate the volume of a geographically defined product market.[24] If neither the number of customers nor their purchasing power can be determined from available statistics, total exports of similar products from the most important industrialized countries may provide a simple

EXHIBIT 3.7
MARKET POTENTIAL,
MARKET VOLUME,
AND MARKET SHARE

Market share, or sales volume, is a function of what volume can be taken away from competitors, what new customers can be attracted, and what share of the current (growing) market can be obtained.

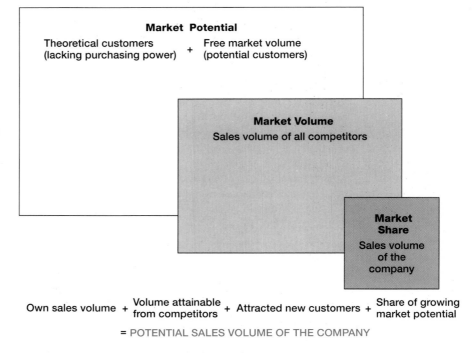

Market Potential

Theoretical customers   Free market volume
(lacking purchasing power) + (potential customers)

Market Volume
Sales volume of all competitors

Market Share
Sales volume of the company

Own sales volume + Volume attainable from competitors + Attracted new customers + Share of growing market potential

= POTENTIAL SALES VOLUME OF THE COMPANY

estimate of market volume. However, such an estimate does not account for exports from the country in question or for the activity of domestic competitors.

If more market data are available, more complex indicators can be used to estimate market volume. The volume of the market for disposable diapers, for example, can be estimated from the number of babies born per year, minus deaths, weighted by average household income. Although such a simple indicator does not take into consideration consumption behavior or the activities of competitors, it will give the marketer a good estimate of the approximate size of the market.

It may still be rather difficult, however, to assess the company's ability to achieve a substantial market share. For that reason the marketer should consider not only market volume, but also market potential, that is, existing volume plus potential additional sales. Exhibit 3.7 illustrates the relationship among market volume, market potential, and market share. To assess the substance of a potential market, the marketer should determine its rate of growth. This rate can be viewed as an indicator of the product's life-cycle stage. Early stages are associated with greater potential, growing market volume, and an improving return on investment. Later stages are characterized by stagnant or declining sales accompanied by low potential return on investment for new entrants to the market. For example, compact disk sales are growing rapidly in the United States. Many marketers are entering the market, their sales are rising rapidly, and their profits are increasing. But when market growth slows, marketers will be faced with lower profits as they increase promotion but lower prices in an attempt to keep sales active.

Besides the market's existing growth rate, the company should consider potential additional sales that may be generated through its specific marketing mix. Even such a rather complex approach to the estimation of market substance, however, will not reveal regional concentrations of potential customers, local customs regarding product use, and other special market characteristics, which will be discussed further in Chapters 4–6.

Accessibility. **Accessibility** refers to the marketer's ability to reach a market effectively. Global marketers may have to invest considerably to build an infrastructure (for example, a system of warehouses); to obtain a high degree of product differentiation, if there is no market niche left; or to adapt their production technology. Accessibility is enhanced by adequate distribution channels, promotion, and local government subsidies (but not if the subsidies go to competitors). On the other hand, legal measures that restrict import licenses can be effective barriers to entry in a market that otherwise would seem attractive to the company. Chapters 4–6 discuss various barriers to access faced by global marketers. Chapters 11–19 show how proper management can help overcome those barriers.

Responsiveness. **Responsiveness** refers to whether potential intermediaries and customers will react favorably to the company's offer. First estimates may be wrong in this respect. Shredded wheat has never become well accepted in the French market, for example, because it is too "British," yet the very "American" McDonald's has become a big success in France. To overcome the risk of guessing, the most important factors that influence responsiveness have to be determined and measured by thorough marketing research. (See Chapter 8.)

Analysis of the Industry

The final analysis of a market's potential should consider whether there is a profitable position for the firm within the industry that competes in that market.

The assessment of a potential market's attractiveness is incomplete without an analysis of the industry in question, including competing firms, intermediaries, suppliers, and the labor force. The form of the **industry analysis** varies depending on whether the product market is defined globally, regionally, or locally. The marketer should keep in mind that other companies in the same industry may define their markets differently. For example, a Norwegian marketer of cross-country skis may consider its business to be restricted to the Scandinavian countries, while a global competitor like Fischer Ski defines its market much more broadly. In that case, the Norwegian marketer should change its industry definition in order to analyze the situation more competitively.

Competitors. The **competitive structure** of an industry may be defined in terms of the number, size, relative market share, rate of growth, and technical sophistication of firms in that industry. To determine the number of competitors in an industry and the threat they represent, the marketer should decide on its definition of a relevant competitor. Relevant competitors may include not only domestic or international suppliers of similar products, but also marketers of substitute products, that is, any organization supplying products that satisfy the same customer need. From this broader perspective, for example, Coca-Cola competes against Grolsch beer.

The size of competing firms can be estimated from such data as number of employees or annual sales volume. These numbers should be evaluated carefully, because they are influenced by the nature of the product and the production technology used. The number of people working for a shoe manufacturer in Brazil, for example, may be similar to the number working for a competitor in Italy. But this doesn't mean the companies are the same size, because different production technologies may be employed by the two firms. In many cases, therefore, it will be necessary to estimate competitors' production capacities.

The market shares of competing firms are a measure of their competitive strength. They indicate what portion of total sales volume in the product market has been captured by each competitor. They may also be viewed as indicators of competitors' strategies. A large market share points toward cost leadership, whereas smaller shares may be a result of niche strategies. Such conclusions can be misleading, however, without knowledge of how stable the competitive situation is. Growth or decline in competitors' market shares must therefore be monitored.

Barriers to leaving a market can be economic, technical, social, or emotional. They may result in an intensification of competitive action, because they prevent competitors from going out of business. If a government is interested in a firm, for example, it may try to ensure its survival. Barriers such as this result in biased competition. In the evaluation of potential markets, therefore, a global marketer must include such barriers.

The attractiveness of a product market is influenced not only by the intensity of existing competition, but also by the expected reactions of major competitors to the market entry of a new contender. A competitor's reactions will depend on the new firm's strengths, weaknesses, and strategy, as well as the competitor's view of the threat posed by the new firm. The impact of competitive reactions on the company's success will depend on their intensity and speed. The global marketer, therefore, should analyze both the predictable reactions of competitors and the company's own strengths and weaknesses, to find out if entry to a potential market is attractive or not.

Intermediaries.   The existence, availability, and negotiating power of intermediaries influence the attractiveness of any market. A marketer needs to obtain information about available intermediaries, their organization, the portion of the market they serve, their approach to doing business, their level of information, the product range they cover, their capital equipment, and so forth. The special conditions faced by marketers in centrally controlled economies and less-developed countries have already been described. But even in an industrialized country there may be special problems to overcome. For example, in Japan it is highly unusual to transfer business from one intermediary to another. There, close inspection of potential intermediaries is more important than in other countries, such as Germany, where such changes can be made without a serious loss of goodwill and thus customers.[25]

The experiences of Western companies in Japan suggest that in most markets the marketer should pay attention to existing networks among producers and intermediaries.[26] It may be very difficult to enter the market, even with a superior product, if the intermediaries necessary to reach the ultimate customer are linked to domestic firms or other international suppliers.[27] (This is discussed further in Chapter 14.)

Suppliers. When evaluating potential suppliers of services, parts, or raw materials, the global marketer should consider the size and number of such firms, the potentially available substitutions, the marketer's importance as a customer, the importance of the supplied service or good to the marketer's product, and the threat of potential forward integration (when the supplier gains control of the next level of distribution, toward the customer) by the supplier. Like intermediaries, suppliers may be linked to certain competitors. Companies such as Ford, Honda, and Volkswagen commonly sign long-range contracts with (or even hold equity shares in) small or medium-sized suppliers. The suppliers conform strictly to the larger company's product specifications and profit from its technical and financial assistance.

Even in such cases, however, supply risks should be evaluated. If a manufacturer relies on just-in-time delivery of parts, disruptions of supply can be very expensive. Quality is also critical. Suppliers in China or Indonesia, for example, may seem attractive because of the low wage rates in these countries. But they do not yet have the skilled labor force necessary to deliver consistently high-quality parts for many sophisticated products.[28]

Labor Force. The number of potential employees seeking a job and, more important, their level of education and skill have a direct impact on a company's success in the market. So does the existence of strong labor unions. Many joint ventures in Eastern Europe, for example, have experienced serious trouble because of the lack of personnel with the management training expected in their western counterparts. Cultural factors also must be considered. Western companies that have founded sales offices or subsidiaries in Japan, for example, have found out to their great dismay that few Japanese like to work for foreign companies. And if they are ready to do so, they expect very high increases in salary.

Data Requirements

Data needed during the market assessment process can come from either secondary or primary research. **Secondary** or **desk research** is the gathering and analysis of data that have already been published by or are available from an existing source. Its major use is in the evaluation of each market's general potential and fit with corporate policy, for the purpose of identifying markets that are worthy of further analysis. Chapter 8 discusses the sources and the reliability of secondary data.

Primary or **field research** is the collection and analysis of new or as yet unpublished information. Such information may come from customers, intermediaries, competitors, suppliers, or experts in a particular field. It is most useful during an in-depth analysis of product markets, because it helps to identify the behavior, needs, and benefits sought by customers in those markets. The feasibility and cost of obtaining primary data vary considerably with the product category and the geographic area. Chapter 8 also addresses how to gather primary data.

When both secondary and primary data have been analyzed and combined with an assessment of the firm's special abilities, market opportunities can be matched with organizational strengths to determine which potential markets are most viable for the firm.

SUMMARY

For a company that regards the entire world as a marketplace, there are many potential markets. In order to restrict the number of options to groups worth further investigation, the global marketer should go through a process of increasingly precise data collection and analysis. The process starts with a definition of the product market in the company's corporate policy statement. From this definition, criteria for selection can be developed for grouping and selecting geographic markets, focusing on economic, political and legal, and cultural and social characteristics. Most of the necessary data for this purpose is available from secondary sources.

Cooperative agreements, which take several forms, affect the viability of the market and the ability of the marketer to conduct business in the expanded market. Several zones of interest exist, which deserve special attention due to their physical proximity, resource base, or political importance.

Before any target market is finally selected, the firm must analyze its viability on the basis of substance, accessibility, and responsiveness. The industry the marketer belongs to must be investigated as well. This step is crucial for the determination of the company's competitive advantages and its market-entry strategy. In most cases it necessitates some primary research and results in a clearer definition of potential markets.

DISCUSSION QUESTIONS

1.   What is market segmentation, and how should a global marketer go about "segmenting the world"?

2.   What are the basic arguments in favor of and against the use of geographic segmentation to form market clusters?

3. Would you choose a market clustering approach based on stages of economic development measured by GNP or GDP, or one that combines income measures with other characteristics of national markets? Explain why.

4. "Less-developed countries do not represent a real potential market for global marketers." Do you agree or disagree with this statement? Why?

5. What are the major issues you would identify in evaluating a less-developed country's attractiveness as a market for personal computers?

6. What value is there in the creation of an economic cooperative agreement for a marketer based in a nonmember nation?

7. Refer to Exhibit 3.4. Describe the basic differences among the various forms of multinational agreements.

8. How does trade with centrally controlled economies differ from trade with market-oriented nations?

9. Market segmentation on the basis of language and religion does not seem to result in homogeneous market clusters. Why?

10. Describe the product market criteria of substance, accessibility, and responsiveness, and illustrate how these criteria must be met for a product market to be considered viable.

C A S E

SCHMIDT WEAVING CORPORATION

Schmidt Weaving is a Western German producer of high-technology machines for the industrial weaving market. Its total sales in 1988 were over 300 million marks. Schmidt focuses on a product market that needs a high-quality, high-technology weaving machine. The Schmidt machine employs a flexible rod to weave material from yarn, instead of the classic shuttle used by the competition. The Schmidt technology provides more flexibility in using different yarns in weaving cloth or garments.

Demand worldwide for textile fibers is growing at an average rate of 2.6 percent per year. Historically, there has been a high positive correlation between purchasing power and the use of textile fibers. Saturation of the market is estimated to be at 40 pounds per person, some three times today's usage rates.

Although the textile industry uses some very sophisticated production processes and equipment, it is still relatively labor-intensive. As labor costs went up in Europe and the United States, many companies moved their production facilities to less-developed countries in Latin America or Asia. However, these companies usually kept their research and development and design facilities in the home country.

Europe and Asia are predicted to be the most important markets during the 1990s. Although Asia will surpass Europe in sales volume, in terms of profit Europe will continue to be the most important market due to less-intense price competition. Schmidt is currently doing business in all of the Triad, and quite successfully.

Schmidt has begun to evaluate Latin American markets, due to increased competition and management's desire to explore all market opportunities. The most important markets are Brazil, Argentina, Colombia, Mexico, Ecuador, Chile, and Venezuela. Schmidt's management has performed an initial analysis of the total Latin American market and discovered the following issues of importance.

Economic. The textile industry needs an industrialized environment in order to obtain supplies and production facilities, so the technical systems of different national markets must be considered. Although most of the countries in Latin America have the relevant industry, consumer income in these countries varies considerably. For example, the yearly average income in Mexico is about $2,000, but in Peru it is only about $800.

Political and Legal. In most Latin American countries, there are no political barriers to establishing a subsidiary (Schmidt's previous approach to entering an international market). There are some trade barriers, however, that make it more difficult to transfer money and financial investments to some Latin American countries and transfer profits back to Germany. In some countries, like Brazil and Argentina, Schmidt would have to prove that domestic machines could not produce the same quality cloth before Schmidt would be allowed to export their machines to those countries.

Culture. In Latin America, managerial decision making is more paternalistic and centralized than in Germany. In order to establish an ongoing exchange relationship in Latin American nations, a close personal contact between seller and buyer must be established.

Competition. Major Japanese and European companies are the chief competitors in Latin America. These companies—from Japan, Belgium, Italy, Switzerland, and France—have combined sales of 138.6 million marks. They sell not only weaving machines, but also control systems and other technical equipment, to the same customers as those that are attractive to Schmidt. A distribution system for such equipment is already established; Schmidt could enter the system and use it very efficiently.

Market research indicates that the total potential market in Latin America for industrial weaving machines is 500–600 units a year, at an average price of 80,000 marks. Schmidt's corporate objective is to achieve a market share of 25–30 percent. It thus expects to reach sales of 12–15 million marks a year.

Case Issues

1. Would you recommend Schmidt proceed further, and why?
2. Schmidt is considering using its current U.S. operation as a base for entering the Latin American market or choosing a country in Latin America and establishing a subsidiary. What elements should be taken into consideration in making this decision?

NOTES

1. A. Rizkallah, "Multiple Product–Multiple Market Allocations—A Portfolio Approach," paper presented at the Annual Meeting of the Academy of International Business, New Orleans, 1980, pp. 8–9.

2. W. W. Rostow, *The Stages of Economic Growth* (New York: Cambridge University Press, 1960).

3. E. Dichter, "The World Customer," *Harvard Business Review*, July–August 1962, pp. 119–121.

4. B. Liander, V. Terpstra, M. Y. Yoshino, and A. A. Sherbini, *Comparative Analysis for International Marketing* (Boston: Allyn and Bacon, 1967), pp. 63–90.

5. R. D. Staede, "Multinational Corporations and the Changing World Economic Order," *California Management Review*, Winter 1978, p. 7.

6. P. Choate and J. Linger, "Tailored Trade: Dealing with the World as It Is," *Harvard Business Review*, January–February 1988, p. 89.

7. J. Garreau, *The Nine Nations of North America* (New York: Avon, 1981).

8. "Most Developing Economies Are Growing, Although Slowly, Says DAC Chairman," *IMF Survey*, February 22, 1988, p. 61.

9. U.S. Department of Commerce, *Statistical Abstract of the United States, 1986* (Washington, D.C.: GPO, 1986), p. 804.

10. M. Lugmani, G. M. Habib, and S. Kassem, "Marketing to LDC Governments," *International Marketing Review*, Spring 1988, p. 65.

11. Ibid., pp. 56–67.

12. "Korea: A Nation That Works," *Newsweek*, June 23, 1986, special advertising section.

13. A. Kupfer, "How to Be a Global Manager," *Fortune*, March 14, 1988, p. 58.

14. A. A. Hanafy, "Free Trade Agreement May Mean Quadruple U.S.-Israeli Trade in Decade," *Marketing News*, June 19, 1987, p. 11.

15. I. A. Litvak, "Free-Trade Strategies with Canada," *Journal of Business Strategy*, November–December 1988, p. 34–39.

16. "Single European Market," in *Survey of Current Affairs* (London: Central Office of Information, January 1988).

17. P. W. Wood and R. F. Elliott, "Trading Blocs and Common Markets," in I. Walter and T. Murray, eds., *Handbook of International Business* (New York: Wiley, 1982), pp. 4.8–4.10.

18. Ibid., pp. 4.32–4.35.

19. D. Ford et al., "Managing Export Development Between Industrialized and Developing Countries," in P. J. Rosson and S. D. Reid, eds., *Managing Export Entry and Expansion, Concepts and Practice* (New York: Praeger, 1987), p. 72.

20. A. Zwass, "Zwischen Markt und Plan gibt es keinen Weg," *Der Standard*, February 1990, p. 19.

21. E. C. Baig, "Where Global Growth Is Going," *Fortune*, July 31, 1989, p. 76.

22. D. J. Yang and M. Shao, "The Reformers Say: Let a Thousand Businesses Bloom— Zhao Aims to Turn China's 'Gold Coast' into an Export Powerhouse," *Business Week*, April 11, 1988, pp. 36–37; and D. K. W. Chu and G. W. K. Wong, "Foreign Direct Investment in China's Shenzhen Special Economic Zone: The Strategies of Firms from Hong Kong, Singapore, U.S.A. and Japan," pp. 35–42.

23. P. E. Green, "A New Approach to Market Segmentation," *Business Horizons*, February 1977, pp. 61–73.

24. B. Katz, *Managing Export Marketing* (Hants, England: Gower, 1987), pp. 178ff.

25. See, for example, "Indicators of Market Size for 131 Countries," *Business International*.

26. W. Laxer, "Different Perceptions of Japanese Marketing," *International Marketing Review*, Autumn 1985, pp. 31–38.

27. H. Simon, "Eintrittsbarrieren und Eintrittsstrategien im Japanischen Markt," in H. Simon, ed., *Marketfolg in Japan* (Wiesbaden: Gabler, 1986), pp. 53–73.

28. N. Campbell, "Japanese Marketing as an Interaction System," paper presented at the Third International IMP Research Seminar on International Marketing, Lyon, 1986; and M. T. Cunningham, "Interaction, Networks and Competitiveness in Industrial Markets: A European Perspective on Business Marketing," paper presented at the European-American Symposium on the Worldwide Marketplace for Technology-Based Products, Enschede, 1987.

EXTERNAL CONSIDERATIONS

THE ECONOMIC ENVIRONMENT

INTERNATIONAL INCIDENTS

Global Stock Markets

Investing in stocks and bonds is no longer a domestic issue. The linkages among major markets in New York, Tokyo, London, Frankfurt, and elsewhere mean not only are corporations able to raise funds globally, but individual investors are influenced in one stock market by what is occurring in another.

In January 1990, for example, the 1,300-point drop in the Nikkei Stock Average (about a 5.5 percent decline) helped kick off a 71-point drop in the Dow Jones average. In fact, the two averages used as measures of Japanese and U.S. stock market strength move closely together (see Exhibit 4.1). So when a New York trader gets to work and sees that the Tokyo stock market has closed down, there is usually a negative reaction. Usually, a 10 percent change in the Nikkei Stock Average brings a 5 percent change in the Dow.

The United States, of course, for many years was the major supplier of investment funds for the world. But the positive balance of trade (exports more than imports) enjoyed by Japan and Western Germany means that a considerable amount of U.S. money has been transferred to their companies and stock markets.

Some of that has been "recycled" to the United States in the form of investment in U.S. companies, real estate, and purchases of U.S. government securities. But if the Tokyo stock market sinks, and Japanese investors' assets at home go down, they are more likely to invest less, or even sell off, overseas investments. That means less money in the United States at higher interest rates.

Another indication of the global linkages of stock markets is the effect that German reunification and the opening of Eastern Europe has had. Optimism over Germany's growth potential, as it takes advantage of the new markets in Eastern Europe, has led to a sharp increase in foreign investment in Germany, much of it through the Frankfurt stock market. At the same time, the surge in economic growth has led to higher interest rates in Germany. Those higher interest rates have begun to push up interest rates in the United States and Japan, as well. Higher interest rates attract investors, which in turn leads to lower stock prices. Even political changes in a non–stock market economy, such as Yugoslavia, can have a powerful impact on stock markets throughout the world.

Sources: "When Japan Gets the Jitters, the World Trembles," *Business Week*, February 12, 1990, pp. 83–84; "The Tokyo Stock Market and How Its Swings Affect You," *Business Week*, February 12, 1990, pp. 74–82; and "The Vertigo Felt 'Round the World," *Business Week*, January 29, 1990, pp. 80–81.

A firm that plans to move into a new market must first make a careful assessment of that market. Does it contain enough customers, with enough purchasing power, to be economically viable? What other factors in the economic environ-

EXHIBIT 4.1 THE NIKKEI AND THE DOW

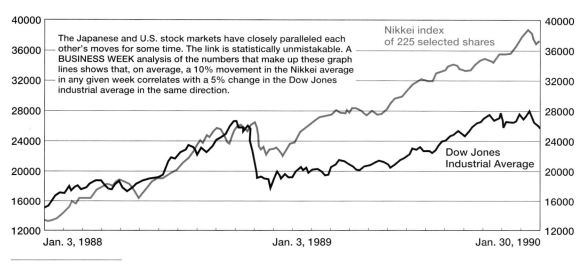

The Japanese and U.S. stock markets have closely paralleled each other's moves for some time. The link is statistically unmistakable. A BUSINESS WEEK analysis of the numbers that make up these graph lines shows that, on average, a 10% movement in the Nikkei average in any given week correlates with a 5% change in the Dow Jones industrial average in the same direction.

Nikkei index of 225 selected shares

Dow Jones Industrial Average

Jan. 3, 1988   Jan. 3, 1989   Jan. 30, 1990

Source: "The Tokyo Stock Market and How Its Swings Affect You," *Business Week*, February 12, 1990, p. 83.

The first international marketing evaluation is whether the market is economically viable.

ment affect the marketer's ability to reach a new market and the methods for doing so? These and similar questions are of prime importance to global marketers.

This chapter examines factors external to the firm that affect both the economic viability of particular markets and the ability of the firm to operate effectively in those markets. These factors may act as constraints or provide opportunities, depending both on the firm's situation and on shifts in the world economic system.

THE WORLD ECONOMIC SYSTEM

The most salient characteristic of the world economic system today is its increasing integration. There is no lack of evidence for this. By late 1988, for example, Japan had invested over $54 billion in the United States, while the United Kingdom had invested close to $102 billion.[1] In Czechoslovakia alone, Japan proposed a $5 billion investment just in 1990. (See Exhibit 4.2.) An additional sign of economic integration is the fact that financial institutions are becoming more closely linked, in order to better manage the international flow of funds. The London financial community has attempted to position itself as a leader in the world financial market, partly due to the time differences that allow a London-based financial trader to make deals on the New York and Tokyo stock exchanges on the same day.

The trend toward worldwide economic integration can be seen in the effects of the crash of the U.S. stock market on October 19, 1987. The impact of the crash reverberated around the world. The London and Tokyo stock mar-

EXHIBIT 4.2
FOREIGN DIRECT
INVESTMENT
POSITION IN THE
UNITED STATES

Foreign direct investment in the United States comes from a wide range of sources. This table illustrates some of the major sources of that investment, as well as how the historical patterns of investment are changing.

	Direct investment position			Change			
	Millions of dollars			Millions of Dollars		Percent	
	1986	1987	1988	1987	1988	1987	1988
All areas	**220,414**	**271,788**	**328,850**	**51,374**	**57,062**	**23.3**	**21.0**
Petroleum	29,094	35,598	34,704	6,504	− 894	22.4	− 2.5
Manufacturing	71,963	94,745	121,434	22,782	26,690	31.7	28.2
Wholesale trade	33,997	39,754	50,160	5,757	10,406	16.9	26.2
Other	85,360	101,691	122,552	16,331	20,861	19.1	20.5
Canada	**20,318**	**24,013**	**27,361**	**3,695**	**3,348**	**18.2**	**13.9**
Petroleum	1,432	1,426	1,614	− 7	188	− .5	13.2
Manufacturing	6,108	7,636	9,391	1,528	1,755	25.0	23.0
Wholesale trade	1,496	2,264	2,548	768	284	51.4	12.5
Other	11,282	12,688	13,808	1,406	1,121	12.5	8.8
Europe	**144,181**	**186,076**	**216,418**	**41,895**	**30,341**	**29.1**	**16.3**
Petroleum	26,139	32,957	31,536	6,817	− 1,421	26.1	− 4.3
Manufacturing	56,016	73,981	91,932	17,965	17,952	32.1	24.3
Wholesale trade	16,430	20,202	24,825	3,771	4,624	23.0	22.9
Other	45,596	58,938	68,124	13,342	9,187	29.3	15.6
Of which:							
Netherlands	40,717	49,115	48,991	8,398	− 124	20.6	− .3
Petroleum	(D)	(D)	(D)	(D)	(D)	(D)	(D)
Manufacturing	13,293	16,137	17,153	2,843	1,016	21.4	6.3
Wholesale trade	2,621	2,250	3,270	− 371	1,020	− 14.1	45.3
Other	(D)	(D)	(D)	(D)	(D)	(D)	(D)
United Kingdom	55,935	79,669	101,909	23,733	22,241	42.4	27.9
Petroleum	11,758	(D)	18,779	(D)	(D)	(D)	(D)
Manufacturing	16,500	27,061	37,021	10,561	9,960	64.0	36.8
Wholesale trade	5,676	8,200	10,049	2,523	1,849	44.5	22.6
Other	22,001	(D)	36,060	(D)	(D)	(D)	(D)
Japan	**26,824**	**35,151**	**53,354**	**8,327**	**18,202**	**31.0**	**51.8**
Petroleum	− 34	− 2	− 79	32	− 77	(1)	(1)
Manufacturing	3,578	5,345	12,222	1,767	6,877	49.4	128.7
Wholesale trade	13,687	15,352	18,390	1,665	3,038	12.2	19.8
Other	9,593	14,456	22,820	4,863	8,364	50.7	57.9
Other	**29,091**	**26,547**	**31,718**	**−2,544**	**5,171**	**−8.7**	**19.5**
Petroleum	1,556	1,218	1,633	− 339	416	− 21.8	34.1
Manufacturing	6,261	7,783	7,890	1,522	107	24.3	1.4
Wholesale trade	2,384	1,936	4,396	− 448	2,460	− 18.8	127.1
Other	18,890	15,610	17,799	− 3,280	2,188	− 17.4	14.0

D Suppressed to avoid disclosure of data of individual companies.
1. Percent change is not defined because the position is negative in 1 of the 2 years.
Source: *Survey of Current Business*, August 1989, p. 55.

kets closed much lower on the following trading day. While the New York market plunged 23 percent, the London market dropped 30 percent and the Tokyo market 15 percent.[2] The more recent January 1990 crash was led by the Tokyo market, as reported in the International Incident.

The Balance of Trade

A nation's trading accounts are recorded in the merchandise, or balance of trade, account.

Financial markets throughout the world are affected by a variety of economic factors, of which one of the most important is the balance of trade. Nations, like firms and individuals, need to keep track of their financial transactions. The account that records all the economic transactions that take place between a nation and other nations is the **balance of payments**. This account is divided into several categories, including military and foreign aid, capital invested abroad, return on investment, tourism, and the **merchandise account**. The merchandise account keeps track of the nation's exports and imports; it is commonly known as the **balance of trade** (see Exhibit 4.3).

By definition, the balance of payments must balance—it cannot be either a credit or a debit. But within the balance of payments account any given category, such as the balance of trade, can be either positive or negative. In 1989 the United States imported about $110 billion more than it exported (down from $120 billion in 1988); hence, it had a negative balance of trade. In contrast, in 1988 Japan exported an estimated $95 billion more than it imported. This resulted in a positive balance of trade and allowed Japan to maintain its position as one of the world's leading trading nations.[3]

In the short run a nation may be able to offset a negative balance of trade by borrowing, using savings, selling off assets, and the like (as the United States, for example, is doing). But most economists agree that in the long run it is not healthy, or even possible, for a nation to sustain a negative balance of trade. Thus, the enormous negative U.S. trade balance of recent years has caused concern among economists around the world.

One reason for this concern is the fact that the United States is the world's largest national market. American spending on imports is responsible for much of the spectacular economic growth enjoyed by such nations as Korea in recent years. Korea's 8 percent annual rate of growth in gross national product can be traced to its success in selling manufactured goods in American markets.[4]

The negative balance of trade in the United States has several deeply rooted causes.

The negative U.S. trade balance has several causes. Chief among them is the fact that fewer than 10 percent of American firms engage in exporting. In addition, labor costs have traditionally been higher in the United States than in other nations. Also, the relatively high value of the U.S. dollar compared to other currencies in the mid-1980s meant that American exports were expensive for consumers in other nations, while imported goods were relatively cheap for American consumers. Finally, American consumers have expressed a preference for high-quality imported products.

The U.S. government's high budget deficit has also been a factor in the negative balance of trade. The United States supported its budget deficit by borrowing from people in other nations. This borrowing made it possible to

EXHIBIT 4.3   U.S. BALANCE OF TRADE

The balance of trade is basically an accounting of the relationship between imports into, and exports from, a nation. This exhibit shows the latest balance of trade figures for the United States.

	1980	1981	1982	1983	1984	1985	1986	1987	1988
EXPORTS									
Merchandise exports, Census basis, including reexports and including military grant shipments	220,626	233,677	212,193	201,656	218,722	212,606	226,471	253,934	322,471
Adjustments:									
Private gift parcel remittances	156	178	163	166	169	194	175	243	245
Gold exports, nonmonetary	317	1,285	883	350	330	406	457	718	592
Inland U.S. freight to Canada	1,043	1,151	967	1,164	1,373	1,345	1,298	1,609	1,845
U.S. Canadian reconciliation adjustments, n.e.c., net	5,103	5,108	4,485	5,014	5,164	6,771			
Merchandise exports transferred under U.S. military agency sales contracts identified in Census documents	−3,317	−4,921	−7,369	−6,546	−5,719	−5,461	−4,550	−5,686	−5,221
Other adjustments, net	341	607	−124	16	−139	74	−484	−552	−681
***Equals:* Merchandise exports, adjusted to balance of payments basis excluding "military"**	224,269	237,085	211,198	201,820	219,900	215,935	223,367	250,266	319,251

IMPORTS

Merchandise imports, Census basis (general imports)	**244,871**	**261,305**	**243,941**	**261,724**	**330,514**	**336,228**	**365,672**	**406,283**	**441,351**
Adjustments:									
Electric energy	664	940	910	999	1,067	1,022	872	986	844
Gold imports, nonmonetary	2,772	1,816	1,462	290	474	559	2,163	2,133	3,576
Inland freight in Canada			1,118	1,325	1,504	1,376	1,643	1,830	2,254
U.S.-Canadian reconciliation adjustment, n.e.c., net	419	623	115	1,292	−841	−708	−645		
Merchandise imports of U.S. military agencies identified in Census documents	−394	−307	−427	−446	−774	−1,005	−1,199	−1,330	−1,686
Other adjustments, net	1,418	686	523	3,716	478	611	−81	−136	127
***Equals:* Merchandise imports, adjusted to balance of payments basis, excluding "military"**	**249,750**	**265,063**	**247,642**	**268,900**	**332,422**	**338,083**	**368,425**	**409,766**	**446,466**

Source: *Survey of Current Business,* June 1989, p. 68.

EXHIBIT 4.4	Controlled		Mixed		Open Market

DEGREE OF MARKET
ORIENTATION

Romania	USSR	India	U.K	U.S.	Hong Kong

Nations vary consider-
ably in their degree of
market orientation. This
exhibit illustrates the
range that an international marketer might
encounter.

maintain consumption at high levels. U.S. foreign debt has climbed to over $300 million, more than three times the amount owed by Brazil, the nation with the second-largest national debt. Yet in 1984, the United States was the world's leading creditor nation! This dramatic shift has economists speculating about whether the United States can sustain its present consumption levels or whether the drop in the value of the dollar that occurred in 1985 will result in increased exports and a lower trade deficit. Throughout the 1990s, the United States will most likely run a negative balance of trade and increase its level of foreign debt.[5] (See Global Dimensions 4.1.)

Market Orientation

Nations vary in their degree of free-market orientation, although several are evolving rapidly toward greater market orientation.

Economic systems vary considerably in their approaches to economic decision making. The economic systems associated with socialist or communist political systems traditionally rely on central decision making to allocate scarce resources, to meet industrial as well as consumer demand. In other systems market forces guide these decisions. Most economies lie somewhere between these two extremes (see Exhibit 4.4). They are considered "mixed" economies, because they are guided partly by market forces and partly by centralized decision making.

The degree of market orientation exhibited by a particular economic system can change over time. The French economy, for example, has traditionally been characterized by centralized planning, but in recent years it has moved toward greater market orientation.[6] A more radical change is China's establishment of "special industrial zones" to spur production and trade. Although the results of this policy have been mixed, in 1985 such zones accounted for about $550 million worth of products.[7] Perhaps most radical of all are the changes initiated in the USSR under Gorbachev. The Soviet economy went from a highly centralized to a mixed market in just a few years' time, even granting the right to hold private property, with as yet unclear results.

The United States is generally considered to have a highly free market, yet its economic policies in effect establish production quotas for some agricultural products, limit automobile imports, and protect domestic manufacturing in such areas as textiles and shoes.

A **centrally planned economy** offers the global marketer fewer opportunities than an economy that is more market-oriented. In the former, decisions regarding what goods will be offered to consumers, and their prices, are made by a government agency as part of an overall economic plan. Thus, degree of market orientation serves a "gatekeeper" function. It affects a firm's ability to reach target markets in other countries.

GLOBAL DIMENSIONS 4.1

A Persistent Negative Balance of Trade

Since the decline in the U.S. dollar beginning in the mid-1980s, the prices of U.S. exports have decreased while prices of products imported into the United States have increased. This should result in an increase in exports and a decrease in imports, thus eliminating the negative balance of trade. But in the late 1980s the U.S. balance of trade remained negative. Why?

The answer goes beyond the prices of exports and imports. Higher prices are acting to reduce the level of imports, but such products have proven to be fairly price-inelastic. That is, volume has not decreased as much as prices have increased, so that the effect on the balance of trade is negative. For example, importing 1,000 units of a product at $5.00 apiece results in an outflow of $5,000; importing 900 units at $6.00 apiece (a 20 percent increase in price) results in an outflow of $5,400.

Moreover, it takes more to increase exports than simply lowering their price. Business relationships, level of service before and after the sale, product quality, continuity of supply, and many other factors influence the attractiveness of goods on the world market.

Another factor contributing to the continuing negative balance of trade is the fact that firms exporting to the United States may accept a lower profit margin in order to remain price-competitive. They take a long-range view of profits, choosing to maintain market share until profit margins can be increased.

Ultimately, consumers and industrial buyers like imported goods. The price inelasticity mentioned earlier is a result of buyers willingly paying more for imported products than for domestic ones, because they associate higher quality or greater value with those products. As long as buyers see imports as a better value, the balance of trade is likely to remain negative.

Source: Adapted from W. Carl Kester and Timothy A. Leuhrman, "Why Dollar Bashing Doesn't Work," *Fortune*, October 27, 1986, p. 137.

Foreign Investment

The globalization of financial markets has been accompanied by an increase in foreign investment. In 1987, for example, foreign investment in Australia increased by 100 percent as a result of relaxed legal controls.[8] In effect, foreign investment is simply capital flowing from one nation to another according to the theory of relative advantage presented in Chapter 1. That is, in the absence of artificial barriers such as tariffs, investment funds can be expected to seek the highest real rate of return. This explains why the United States was popular with foreign investors in the mid-1980s, even though the dollar was highly valued relative to other currencies. The rate of return (adjusted for inflation) was among the highest in the world. With the devaluation of the dollar in the late 1980s, U.S. real estate and other investments became even more attractive. For Japanese investors, the devaluation of the dollar meant that a Manhattan office building that cost $100 million, the equivalent of 26 billion yen, in 1985 cost the equivalent of about 15 billion yen in mid-1987.[9]

At present a popular corporate strategy is to buy market share instead of developing it. (This occurs when a firm purchases or otherwise links up with a firm that is already operating in a specific market. The entering firm is quickly established as a competitor, instead of having to slowly develop a position in the market.) This trend, coupled with the increased tendency of investors to look abroad for opportunities, has led to stronger and more complex linkages among national economic systems. Even in the United States, the world's largest economy, "prosperity . . . increasingly will rely on economic viability—and politics— in other countries."[10]

In view of these trends, business as well as government must become more sensitive to political and social issues in other nations. This explains the interest shown in the foreign policy statements of the candidates in the 1988 U.S. presidential election. Newspapers in other nations reported on the candidates' views regarding foreign trade. Of particular interest were statements about tariff and nontariff barriers; many commentators speculated about the possibility of a shift away from the relatively free trade policies of the Reagan administration.[11]

Currency Systems

The interlinking of national economies has even led to multi-national efforts to influence floating exchange rates, to increase currency stability.

One effort to improve multinational economic coordination is a move by the so-called Group of Five (the United States, Japan, West Germany, France, and England) to realign the value of the U.S. dollar with that of other major currencies. In 1984 these nations took steps to coordinate their monetary policies in a way that would decrease the value of the U.S. dollar relative to other currencies. Prior to this agreement the exchange rate for French francs hit a high point of $1.00 = 10 francs. After the agreement it fell to $1.00 < 6 francs. The objective was to make U.S. goods more competitive in world markets (decrease the prices of U.S. exports) and to increase the prices of goods imported into the United States.

The reason the Group of Five needed to coordinate their monetary policies is that most national currencies are subject to a **floating exchange rate**. Floating currencies can be bought, held, and sold like any other commodity. This helps ensure the availability of foreign currencies for conducting international transactions, but it can also result in an "overvalued" or "undervalued" currency. In 1984, while American tourists in Paris enjoyed the high number of francs their dollars would buy, American products were 30 to 40 percent more expensive than competing French products. And French products were relatively cheaper in the United States.

Currencies that do not float are subject to a **fixed exchange rate**. The Mexican peso, the Indian rupee, and the Russian ruble are examples of such currencies. Fixed-rate currencies can be bought or sold at specific rates that do not vary. Governments can change those rates, but compared to the minute-by-minute fluctuations of floating exchange rates, fixed exchange rates offer the advantage of predictability to organizations that need to exchange currencies. (Rupees and rubles are also controlled currencies; they can be bought and sold only in specific cases.)

Fixed exchange rates can sometimes create shortages of particular currencies. For example, if the U.S. dollar is set at $1.00 = 8.25 Indian rupees, an Indian company that wants to buy dollars to pay for imports may not be able to find anyone who is willing to sell dollars at that rate. People with dollars may want, say, 12 rupees for $1.00. They won't sell at the lower rate, but the fixed rate prevents the buyer from buying at the higher rate. The impact on trade can be quite negative; in fact, a fixed exchange rate may actually act as a barrier to trade. At the other extreme, if a country's floating currency moves out of its "normal" range (that is, if it is "undervalued" or "overvalued"), products from that country will be underpriced or overpriced in the world market, as in the example of American products marketed in France in 1984.

When currencies fluctuate greatly, they may have a dramatic or even destabilizing effect on world trade. Thus, after the Group of Five coordinated their monetary policies, the value of the U.S. dollar dropped about 50 percent against that of the Japanese yen, but only 10 percent against that of the Korean won. This reduced Japanese exports by some 30 percent but caused a dramatic 46 percent increase in Korean exports.[12] (Exhibit 4.5 shows that the value of some currencies actually rose against that of the dollar.) In sum, global marketers must take into account the exchange rates of various national currencies, whether fixed or floating, in setting prices.

International trade has even generated international currencies.

For the past thirty years international trade has increasingly been financed through **international currencies**, money deposited in banks that are not located in the home country. The most familiar example of an international currency is **Eurodollars**, U.S. dollars that are held by other nations, or by companies based in other nations, and are not deposited in U.S. banks. This "currency" was created by the Soviet Union in the 1950s as a means of preventing its dollar deposits from being frozen in the United States in the event that political relations between the two nations worsened. Eurodollars (which actually include German marks, French francs, Japanese yen, and other currencies deposited outside their home countries) today amount to some $1,000 billion.[13]

International currencies may play a significant role in a nation's monetary policies, because they represent deposits of home-country currencies that are outside the control of those countries. For example, in trying to control the money supply in the United States, the Federal Reserve System must deal with the fact that large amounts of "American" money lie beyond its control. The banks that hold this currency may do anything they wish with it, including

EXHIBIT 4.5
THE CHANGING U.S.
DOLLAR AND TRADE
DEFICITS

As the dollar went down against most currencies, such as the yen, mark, or franc, imports from those countries went up in price. But the trade gap did not narrow. Consumers of imports such as automobiles, proved to be less concerned about the dollar price than the price–value relationship. Thus they continued to buy the same quantity of imports, but at higher prices; this resulted in more money flowing out of the United States. A further problem is that the dollar actually went up against other currencies (or went down very little). In those cases, imports became relatively cheaper, increasing demand and increasing the amount of the trade gap.

| Country | Deficit | | U.S. Dollar vs. Foreign Currency 9/85-12/86 | Products Exported to U.S. |
	a-1986 9 Mos	a-1985 9 Mos		
Japan	$43,871	$34,659	− 34.0%	automobiles and parts, steel, electronics
Canada	18,803	16,474	+ 0.3	automobiles and parts, lumber, machinery
West Germany	11,415	8,367	− 32.0	automobiles and parts, chemicals, machinery
Taiwan	10,716	9,085	− 12.0	apparel, electronics, telecommunications gear
South Korea	4,788	2,926	− 3.0	textiles, electronics, automobiles, steel
Italy	4,549	3,711	− 29.0	apparel, footwear, machinery
Hong Kong	4,303	4,150	− 0.2	apparel, electronics, telecommunications gear
Mexico	4,013	4,326	+ 135.0	automobiles and parts, oil, machinery
Britain	3,534	2,540	− 7.0	oil, vehicles, chemicals, machinery
Brazil	2,516	3,622	− 109.0	iron, steel, coffee, oil
Switzerland	2,485	1,026	− 31.0	chemicals, machinery, pharmaceuticals
France	2,455	2,656	− 25.0	automobiles and parts, steel, machinery, wine
Indonesia	1,981	2,898	+ 47.0	oil, rubber, coffee
Sweden	1,886	1,751	− 19.0	automobiles, steel, machinery
Venezuela	1,659	2,025	0.0	oil, metals
Nigeria	1,591	1,568	x	oil
Algeria	1,042	1,473	x	oil
Singapore	1,017	635	− 0.9	apparel, electronics, telecommunications gear
South Africa	891	631	− 17.0	metals, chemicals
Denmark	712	671	− 28.0	furniture, meat
Ecuador	639	886	+ 34.0	wood, oil, textiles
India	633	602	+ 8.0	fibers, apparel, oil, misc. manufactured items
Malaysia	512	513	+ 4.0	rubber, apparel, electrical machinery
Philippines	493	590	+ 11.0	apparel, electrical products, wood
Angola	438	629	x	oil

a-In millions.   x-No quotes available—insufficiently traded.
Source: "The Other Deficit: Dollar's Decline Fails to Have Intended Effect of Narrowing the Trade Gap," *Wall Street Journal*, January 7, 1987, p. 8.

MAP 4.1
SOUTH AMERICA,
GDP AND DEBT

Most of the nations in
South America have the
twin problems of low
growth in their economies
(as measured by GDP)
and high growth in their
debt. Thus they not only
owe more money, they
have relatively less re-
sources with which to pay
their debt.

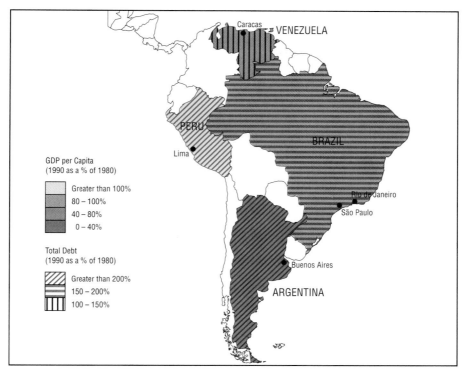

financing international transactions. An Ecuadorean bank, for example, may
have U.S. dollars as a result of its customers' trading with U.S. companies. If
an Ecuadorean company borrowed the dollars from the bank to finance an export
shipment from the United States, those dollars would end up being deposited
in a U.S. bank. In effect, the U.S. money supply would be expanded independently of any action by the Federal Reserve.

THE DISTRIBUTION OF INCOME AND WEALTH

Although there are some 150 national markets in the world, 24 of them account
for 66 percent of the world's gross national product. These countries belong to
the Organization for Economic Cooperation and Development (OECD), a multinational forum based in Paris that allows the major industrialized nations to
confer with one another about economic policies and events. The fact that the
OECD countries together represent less than 20 percent of the world's population illustrates the impact that the distribution of wealth can have on global
marketing.

In less economically de-
veloped countries, pover-
ty and affluence can exist
side by side. In New Delhi,
the plush Ashoka Hotel
sits next to a colony of
one-room, four-foot-high
mud huts.

A global marketer must
be concerned about
the level of wealth and
its distribution in
national markets.

In general, the higher the level of economic development in a national market (as measured by per capita GNP), the more economically viable it is likely to be. By this standard Singapore, with a per capita GNP of $7,420, would be more attractive than India, with a per capita GNP of $250.[14] Still, even within the poorest country there may be a certain number of affluent customers. By looking at both the size of the population and the distribution of income, the global marketer can see that the affluent market in India might be very attractive. The higher per capita GNP in Singapore must be viewed in the context of a much smaller total population—only 2.6 million.

Level of Economic Development

The distribution of income and wealth is affected by many factors. One of these is the nation's overall level of economic development. A low level of economic development means quite simply that there are not enough people with enough money to buy certain products. Thus, after the value of the dollar dropped some 40 percent between 1985 and 1987, U.S. exporters were still constrained by the fact that foreign customers had to be wealthy enough to buy their products, even at relatively lower prices.[15]

An extreme example of national poverty is Mozambique, which currently is suffering from the combined impact of war, drought, and economic decay. Living conditions there are considered to be the worst in the world. The economy has declined so far that one shopkeeper keeps ten-year-old shirt boxes on the shelves just to have something to display.[16] Such a low level of overall economic development contrasts sharply with the level of development found

GLOBAL DIMENSIONS 4.2

Income and Expenditures in a Less-Developed Country

Marketing in a less-developed country requires a careful analysis of income levels and distribution to determine whether a viable market exists there or not. In developing economies 80 percent of the population must share just 33 percent of the wealth; often as little as 10 percent of the population controls 90 percent of the wealth and income. This pattern is referred to as **dual income distribution**.

In most less-developed countries the majority of the people exist on a few hundred dollars of cash income per year, most of which is spent on food. What most Americans would consider a low price for a product, therefore, is usually a high percentage of total income. For example, in China an average meal at a Kentucky Fried Chicken store in Beijing costs $1.89. This may sound inexpensive, but it is equivalent to two days' wages for the average Chinese worker.

Source: Adapted from "The Great Mall of China," *Australian Business*, February 24, 1988, p. 36.

in the Triad markets. In the United States, for example, the number one nutritional problem is obesity. In most of the rest of the world it is starvation.

Income Distribution and Ability to Buy

The contrast between Mozambique and the United States illustrates the enormous differences a marketer may encounter when examining potential markets. Although such differences do not mean that all nations with low levels of economic development lack appeal for global marketers, they do require that the marketer address the issue of distribution of income and wealth. This is true even in the United States, where analysts have pointed out that the middle class is shrinking while the richest and poorest economic groups are growing. If this is true, marketers like Sears Roebuck, which have traditionally catered to the middle class, may lose market share while marketers of such products as "yuppie" baby clothes can expect higher sales volume.[17] By comparison, the middle class in China (people with an average income of $300 per year) is growing rapidly. With rent pegged at $2–5 per month, the Chinese middle class is gaining purchasing power; in other words, it is becoming an economically viable market for certain goods. (See Global Dimensions 4.2.)

Inflation

Inflation is an increase in prices in an economy that results in a decline in purchasing power for consumers in that economy. Global marketers must watch trends in inflation for two reasons. First, inflation increases the prices of factors

Inflation affects a market's ability to buy goods and services, as well as its economic and political stability.

of production, including raw materials, capital, and labor. Increased costs are reflected in higher prices. Second, inflation can affect the economic viability of a market.

In some countries the rate of inflation is so high that it has a dramatic effect on prices; for example, in 1983 and 1984 Israel's inflation rate was 370 percent, making goods and services nearly four times more expensive in 1984 than they were a year earlier.[18] Even more drastic was Brazil's 5000 percent inflation rate in 1989. While the adverse effects of high inflation rates on consumers are obvious, the effects on marketers are equally serious. Coca-Cola once had to decide in the space of 4 hours whether to purchase a fleet of trucks to distribute its products in one of its Latin American markets. The rate of inflation was so high that the price quoted was good only for that length of time. (The relationship between inflation and pricing is discussed further in Chapter 17.)

Governments often try to avoid the political and social unrest generated by inflation by freezing retail prices. When this happens, businesses are unable to pass along higher costs to customers. McDonald's, for example, was barred by the Brazilian government from passing along cost increases ranging from 70 percent for hamburger buns to 1,000 percent for milk and meat. Faced with the prospect of selling its products at a loss of $500,000 per month, McDonald's raised its prices and was immediately fined. It then shut its doors in protest, whereupon the government abandoned retail price controls out of fear that other businesses would follow McDonald's lead. McDonald's was able to raise its prices and resume profitable operations. However, this meant sacrificing some customers; lower-income families could no longer afford to eat at McDonald's.[19]

POPULATION, NATURAL RESOURCES, AND ECONOMICS

A large number of factors affect a nation's ability to provide the resources required for production or to offer a viable market for finished goods and services. These factors include the composition and distribution of the population, degree of urbanization, the presence or absence of natural resources, and geographic features such as topography and climate. Because this chapter focuses on the economic environment, the relevance of these factors to economic development is emphasized here. Other chapters deal with the effect of geography and natural resources on the design of the marketing mix.

Population and Market Viability

The population and its purchasing power are prime economic indicators of a market's attractiveness to global marketers.

The total population of a nation, its growth rate, and the distribution of age groups within it are of interest to global marketers. After all, the size of a potential market is a key element in its viability. As pointed out earlier, however, size without purchasing power is not meaningful. Sometimes population growth outpaces economic growth. This is a particular problem in developing countries, notably those in Africa. Even when these countries experience positive economic growth, their per capita economic growth is negative due to the rapid rate of population growth.

Brazil, considered by many observers to be the greatest economic success story in Latin America, must balance the need to create more than 1 million new jobs a year (to absorb the increase in its population) against the need to spend more than 4 percent of its GNP to pay the interest on its foreign debt.[20] Many other nations with high population growth rates, including India and Mexico, face similar economic dilemmas. At the other extreme, political leaders in West Germany traditionally had been concerned about that nation's negative population growth rate. They feared that there would be too few workers to maintain the economy and support the retired population. Indeed, the shortage of trained workers contributed to West Germany's willingness to accept East German refugees after the opening of the East German borders.

Clearly, the rate of population growth and the size of the population affect a society's ability to progress economically and provide for the future. They also affect the distribution of current and future wealth. Within a nation, it is often the poorest economic classes that exhibit the highest population growth rates. From the standpoint of the individual, there may be strong economic reasons for having a larger family. In Tunisia, for example, there is no social security system to help support elderly people who can no longer support themselves. Therefore, the more children one has, the greater one's chances of living comfortably in old age.

Religious beliefs can also contribute to higher birthrates. For example, according to Hindu doctrine funeral rites must be performed by the eldest son if a dead parent is to progress to the next life. Families thus are encouraged to have several sons, to ensure that the rites will be carried out properly. Regardless of the motivation, however, the results are similar: larger families reduce per capita income. Ironically for the global marketer, the markets that are growing fastest in terms of number of consumers are usually those that are increasingly unable to afford the marketer's products.

Age Distribution

Many marketers are interested in developing markets in China and India, which together represent some 70 percent of Asia's population (close to 2 billion consumers) and about 40 percent of the population of the world. The attractiveness of large markets also helps explain why multinational cooperative agreements like the European Community have such immense appeal.

The proportion of the population in particular age groups also affects the market's economic viability.

But the age composition of a population is also of interest to global marketers. Increases and decreases in the proportion of the population in specific age groups are closely related to the demand for particular products and services. As fertility increases, new markets emerge for products and services for young families and children. As death rates decrease, the same phenomenon occurs

MAP 4.2 POPULATION DENSITY AND GROWTH

Population density is measured by dividing population by land area, as illustrated in this map. But, like all national statistics, care must be taken in interpretation. For example, excluding the uninhabitable areas of Japan changes its population density from 324 to 1,500 people per square kilometer.

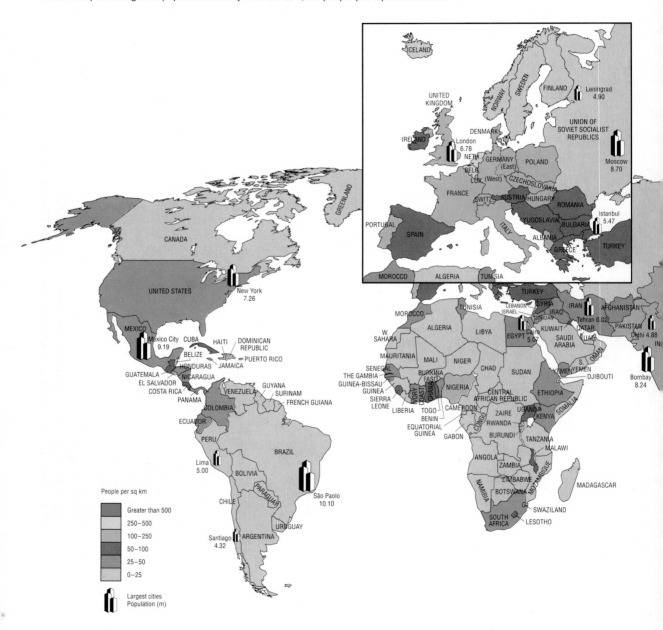

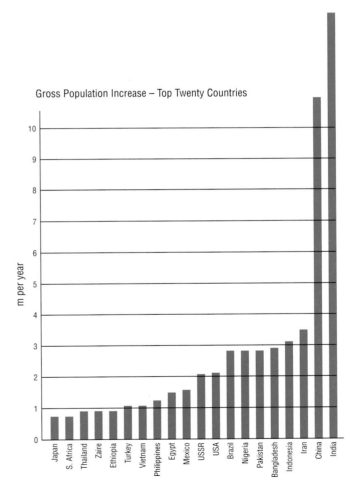

Gross Population Increase – Top Twenty Countries

113

EXHIBIT 4.6
PROJECTED
POPULATION AGED
65 AND OVER IN THE
OECD NATIONS

The "aging of America,"
which has received much
attention in the press, is
really part of a worldwide
demographic change.
This table projects in-
creases in the over-65
age group in highly de-
veloped nations.

Population as % of total population[a]

	1990	2000	2010	2020	2030	2040	2050
Australia	11.1	11.7	12.6	15.4	18.2	19.7	19.4
Austria	14.6	14.9	17.5	19.4	22.8	23.9	21.7
Belgium	14.2	14.7	15.9	17.7	20.8	21.9	20.8
Canada	11.4	12.8	14.6	18.6	22.4	22.5	21.3
Denmark	15.3	14.9	16.7	20.1	22.6	24.7	23.2
Finland	13.1	14.4	16.8	21.7	23.8	23.1	22.7
France	13.8	15.3	16.3	19.5	21.8	22.7	22.3
Germany	15.5	17.1	20.4	21.7	25.8	27.6	24.5
Greece	12.3	15.0	16.8	17.8	19.5	21.0	21.1
Iceland	10.3	10.8	11.1	14.3	18.1	20.1	21.1
Ireland	11.3	11.1	11.1	12.6	14.7	16.9	18.9
Italy	13.8	15.3	17.3	19.4	21.9	24.2	22.6
Japan	11.4	15.2	18.6	20.9	20.0	22.7	22.3
Luxembourg	14.6	16.7	18.1	20.2	22.4	22.0	20.3
Netherlands	12.7	13.5	15.1	18.9	23.0	24.8	22.6
New Zealand	10.8	11.1	12.0	15.3	19.4	21.9	21.3
Norway	16.2	15.2	15.1	18.2	20.7	22.8	21.9
Portugal	11.8	13.5	14.1	15.6	18.2	20.4	20.6
Spain	12.7	14.4	15.5	17.0	19.6	22.7	22.9
Sweden	17.7	16.6	17.5	20.8	21.7	22.5	21.4
Switzerland	14.8	16.7	20.5	24.4	27.3	28.3	26.3
Turkey	4.0	5.0	5.5	7.0	8.9	10.2	11.5
United Kingdom	15.1	14.5	14.6	16.3	19.2	20.4	18.7
United States	12.2	12.2	12.8	16.2	19.5	19.8	19.3
OECD average[b]	**13.0**	**13.9**	**15.3**	**17.9**	**20.5**	**21.9**	**21.2**

[a] 1980 actual; 1990 to 2050 projections.
[b] Unweighted.
Source: OECD, *OECD Observer*, Paris, October-November 1987, p. 5.

among older age groups. Developing countries, with close to half their population under the age of 15, have major drains on their economic resources (children are not as economically productive as adults).

In the Triad Markets, such changes have resulted in a variety of new
market opportunities. For example, retirement villages are becoming popular in
the United States, Australia, and much of Western Europe, and the smaller
number of children in those markets, combined with the increased resources of
dual-career households, mean that parents have more money to spend on their
children. (Exhibit 4.6 shows population trends in OECD countries.)

Urbanization

The degree of urbanization in a society is of interest to global marketers because it represents concentrations of potential customers. The term **urbanization** refers to the proportion of a population that lives in cities. It may come as a surprise to discover that Australia is the world's most urbanized nation, with 86 percent of its 15 million people living in urban areas.

Too rapid urbanization can lead to high unemployment, harsh living conditions, and frequent episodes of political and social unrest. An example is Mexico City, the most urbanized area of Mexico, which has such a high population growth rate that its population could double every twenty years. Much of this growth results from rural-urban migration—people moving away from poor rural areas in search of better opportunities. Jobs cannot be created at a fast enough pace to absorb this rapid increase in the urban work force. In contrast, the United States and Japan have long histories of slow but steady urbanization. Their active and growing economies, coupled with a lower rate of urbanization, have allowed them to absorb new urban dwellers and workers without a dramatic increase in unemployment.[21]

Urban and rural dwellers often have very different consumption patterns. In the United States, for example, Sears Roebuck built a tremendous business by catering to the rural population through catalog sales. But, as an increasing proportion of the population moved to the cities, Sears found it necessary to follow its customers; it changed its product offerings and placed more emphasis on stores in suburban shopping centers.

More than twenty years ago it was noted that urban dwellers in different nations are more likely to have similar consumption patterns than urban and rural consumers within the same country.[22] For example, urban women in Argentina, Brazil, and Peru have more similar consumption patterns with regard to cosmetics than do urban and rural women within any one of those nations. In developing countries, global marketers are often unable to reach consumers outside the relatively affluent cities. In China this represents only 20 percent of the population. Yet that market contains 200 million potential customers![23]

> Urban areas are important not only because they represent a concentration of customers, but also because urban and nonurban areas have different consumption patterns.

Natural Resources

Natural resources are actual and potential forms of wealth that are provided by nature. They include minerals, water and water power, land, geography and climate, and energy sources (such as oil, coal, and gas). A nation's natural resources are a major determinant of the type of economic system that can develop there. The Netherlands, for example, is rich in natural gas but has limited mineral resources. Therefore, it has had to depend on international trade to sustain its economy—exports and imports account for over 50 percent of The Netherlands' GNP. The United States, on the other hand, is blessed with an abundance of minerals, water, and energy sources. These resources, in addition to a sizable labor force, have led to the development of a relatively self-sufficient economy.

> Natural resources form the economic backbone of a nation.

Some nations are overly dependent on a single natural resource. Lesotho (a politically independent nation surrounded by the Republic of South Africa), for instance, has traditionally supported itself by supplying labor to mines in South Africa. As a result of the unstable political situation in South Africa in recent years, many of the men who worked in those mines have been sent home. To broaden its economic base, Lesotho has developed plans to export another abundant resource, water, to farms and industry in South Africa. In addition, many labor-intensive construction projects have been initiated in Lesotho with funds provided by the United Nations Development Program and the World Bank. These not only offer employment but also provide improved roads, air-fields in remote areas, and increased soil conservation.[24]

Geography

Geography also affects global marketing in fundamental and enduring ways. It is, after all, geographic factors that result in the presence or absence of natural resources. Geographic factors also affect the decisions of marketers; they may act as resources, as constraints, or as influences on market viability.

Geography is a resource, constraint, and major influence on market viability.

Geography as a Resource.   The Netherlands is one of the leading trading nations of Western Europe. Rotterdam is the busiest port in the world, and the country is crisscrossed with canals and rivers bustling with commercial traffic. Part of the reason for this is historical—The Netherlands has a strong tradition of trade and exploration. Another part is geographic. The Netherlands is located at the mouth of the Rhine River. Half of the exports and imports that move through The Netherlands are on their way to and from Germany, France, and Switzerland. Goods can be shipped to The Netherlands for distribution throughout Europe, or for export to the rest of the world via Rotterdam.

Geographic features like rivers, waterfalls, and beaches not only constitute resources, such as natural trade routes, but also can be viewed as products. The beautiful Maldive Islands off the southwestern coast of India attract $30 million worth of tourist income annually.[25] Niagara Falls, located on the border between the United States and Canada, is a source of electric power for both nations as well as a tourist destination. The oil wells of the Middle East and the North Sea are a major source of export income for Saudi Arabia and England. And mineral exports—copper from Chile, coal from Poland, lead from the United States—add to the economic well-being of the nations in which they are found.

Climate is a dimension of geography that is closely linked to a nation's economic development and functioning. The importance of climate as a resource is illustrated by the ability of Central American nations to produce tropical fruits for export to nations where they cannot be grown, because of different climatic conditions.

Geography as a Constraint.   If you want to go from the coast of Brazil west-ward to Peru, or to transport products between those two points, the only

Rotterdam Harbor, located at the mouth of the Rhine river in The Netherlands, is the world's busiest port.

efficient way to do so is by air. The surface route up the Amazon River and across the Andes Mountains would take many weeks and expose both travelers and products to considerable risk. The Andes thus act as a geographic constraint on both domestic and international travel and commerce.

Many other examples of geographic or climatic constraints can be given. The lack of rivers, or the presence of rivers that flood regularly, influences the location of agricultural processing plants. In nations with rainy seasons, trade is often hampered by mudslides or washed-out roads. Nations with no coastline, such as Zimbabwe and Switzerland, must rely on the ports of neighboring nations to export goods by sea. And in places like Siberia, where natural resources are plentiful, the extremely cold climate makes it difficult to exploit available resources.

Geography and Market Viability.   Clearly, geography has a major impact on market viability through the presence or absence of natural resources, which go a long way toward determining how far the economy can develop. Another area in which geography has a major impact is the cost and ease of distributing products. The inventory-carrying costs associated with transportation time are so high that Volkswagen flies spare parts from its German factories to the United States rather than send them by cheaper sea routes. In addition, the elevation of a market may affect product choices—consumers who live at sea level have different consumption patterns than those who live in mountainous areas.

Climate has a great deal to do with market viability. Consumers living near the equator prefer different food products than those living in milder climates. Heat and humidity result in lower levels of production, particularly in countries with limited energy for climate control, and poorly developed infrastructure systems (such as roads and bridges).

Patterns of consumption and production are, of course, influenced by many other factors besides geography. For example, ownership of in-home air conditioners in Brisbane, Australia, is estimated at 8 percent. In New Delhi, where the heat and humidity are so oppressive that they severely limit economic activity, the proportion of homes with air conditioners is even lower. Yet in Atlanta, Georgia, where the climate is far milder than that of either Brisbane or New Delhi, 80 percent of the homes are air-conditioned. Obviously, cultural norms, economic resources, and many other variables affect the purchase of goods such as air conditioners. Nevertheless, it remains true that geography is an important element in market viability.

OTHER DIMENSIONS

Any economic system has numerous additional dimensions, each of which is important in determining market viability. They include technology, infrastructure, industrial development, financial institutions, and the administrative function of government. These dimensions not only affect the global marketer's ability to reach target markets, but they also help marketers assess in some detail the relative viability of different markets. However, it is not always easy to obtain information about these dimensions, especially in developing nations. Even specialists have to rely on a variety of sources, piecing together their final impression in much the same way that one puts together a jigsaw puzzle.[26]

Technology

Both the level and the concept of technology within the potential nation market must be considered.

Global marketers must consider not only the *level* of technological development in a society (such as use of robots in computer-aided manufacturing systems) but also the *concept* of technology that is characteristic of that society. Concepts of technology can vary considerably from one society to another. The significance of such differences can be seen in the following example. Several years ago small tractors were supplied to Latin American farmers who had traditionally used oxen to plow their fields. Some time later the suppliers of the tractors returned to find them unused. The farmers, unfamiliar with the concept of preventive maintenance, had failed to change the oil or otherwise maintain the tractors. When the tractors broke down, they returned to plowing with oxen, a technology that they understood and knew how to maintain.

Marketers need to be attuned to differences between the technological environment of the home country and that of the target market. For example, U.S. computer manufacturers, eager to close a sale in China, did not learn that air conditioning is not readily available there. As a result, their computers, which require a temperate environment, did not perform as expected.[27]

Differences in technological development offer opportunities to market new production technologies. Thus, Austria's Voest Alpine Industrial Services has been successful in marketing advanced steel-production methods to less-developed countries. In much the same way, the technology gap has created opportunities to market services such as training and maintenance.

Even if the general level of technology in different nations is similar, as is the case, for example, in the United States and France, there will be differences in the specific technologies employed. A U.S. marketer who wants to show a videotaped product demonstration at a Paris trade show must realize that not only do the French machines use a different electrical current, they also use a totally different recording technology. The tape has to be "technologically translated" before it can be used as a sales aid.

Industries within the same nation can also differ in degree of technological development. In the United States, for example, electronic banking techniques such as electronic funds transfer and automatic teller machines are quite sophisticated. On the other hand, the United States is considerably less advanced than other nations, such as Germany, in the use of robotics in manufacturing.

Infrastructure

A nation must have sufficient communication, transportation, and energy systems to take advantage of its economic potential.

Lesotho's efforts to export water to South Africa illustrate the importance of a nation's **infrastructure**—its communication, transportation, and energy systems. Lesotho had the resource (water), but it did not have the infrastructure (dams and pipelines) to allow it to export this resource; these infrastructure elements had to be built before exporting could begin.

The level of development of a nation's infrastructure affects the extent to which its natural resources can be used. Alaska's vast oil reserves could not be used until the Alaskan pipeline was built. The water that powers turbines to generate electricity in northern Canada would be useless if there were no electrical system to transport power to industrial sites in the south. Infrastructure also determines whether global marketers can reach viable markets. A large target market with substantial buying power is of little value if goods and services cannot be sold to consumers because of faulty communications or poor roads.

Transportation infrastructure is especially important to global marketers. Triad marketers often take for granted the availability of distribution systems made up of good roads, railways, waterways, and air cargo systems. But India and Australia both have railroads with different gauges (track widths). To get products from one place to another via these rail systems, it is necessary to unload freight cars at various points and reload the contents onto cars that fit the second gauge. Similarly, roads and dependable trucking lines are not equally available throughout the world. The freeways of the United States may have their counterparts in the autobahns of Germany, but in Chad dirt roads connect one market to another, and these may be almost impassable in the rainy season, when the roads turn into mud.

Communication systems also pose challenges to global marketers, not only from the standpoint of availability (see Chapter 15) but also from that of quality. Global networks using satellite transmissions, telephones, FAX systems, computers, and telexes permit daily communication among far-flung business units. However, communication systems can sometimes cause problems. In some African countries telephone connections with other nations are easier, faster, and clearer than connections within the same country. The home office may be able to communicate with the local representative, but that representative may not be able to communicate easily with local customers. Clearly, the ability to reach an economically viable market is heavily influenced by the availability and quality of the communication infrastructure.

Industrial Sectors

An economy is composed of numerous industrial sectors, and the balance of those sectors is important to the economy's health.

Industrial sectors are categories of economic activity, such as mining, manufacturing, agriculture, wholesale and retail trade, construction, transportation, and business and personal services. In identifying and evaluating potential markets, the global marketer must determine which industrial sectors are of greatest importance in any given nation. A nation in which a single industrial sector dominates the economy is referred to as a **monoculture**. Chile, for example, has frequently suffered economically because much of its GNP is derived from the mining of copper. When the world price of copper fluctuates, so does Chile's GNP. Moreover, when good substitutes for copper were developed (such as high-quality plastics for pipes used in construction), Chile's economy suffered. Recently Chile has diversified its economy by increasing its exports of grapes, timber, fish, and wine. This policy resulted in a $1 billion surplus in its balance of trade in 1987.[27] (Exhibit 4.7 presents a measure of instability in export earnings among countries that export a single commodity.)

Many less-developed economies are monocultures, often relying on the agricultural sector, and frequently on just one or two crops, to generate a high proportion of their GNP. In such countries opportunities for growth are limited by dependence on prices in world markets, which the country cannot directly affect.

Global marketers must examine the balance among the industrial sectors of the nations they wish to serve, and they must be familiar with the growth pattern of each sector. Considerable insight regarding the economic viability and stability of a potential market can be derived from information about the level of activity in various industrial sectors. Exhibit 4.8 lists the industrial sectors found in a typical economy and indicates their relative importance in the U.S. economy.

Financial Institutions

International Institutions.   A nation may belong to one or more of several international financial institutions and agreements. (See Exhibit 4.9.) The function of these institutions is to contribute to the stability of the world economy and assist in the economic growth of member nations. The International Monetary Fund (IMF), for instance, acts as a lender of last resort. If a nation is

EXHIBIT 4.7
COMMODITY
DEPENDENCY AND
INSTABILITY

Historically, a monocul-
ture economy is more un-
stable than one that is
more balanced. In partic-
ular, a monoculture econ-
omy that is based on an
agricultural product, over
which the country has little price influence and for
which there are many al-
ternative suppliers, experiences greater instability.

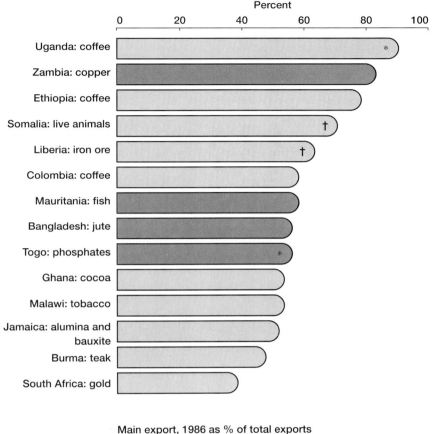

Main export, 1986 as % of total exports
*1984 †1985

Source: *The Economist*, December 19, 1987, p. 65.

Domestic and interna-
tional financial institu-
tions lend stability to
an economy and facili-
tate trade.

experiencing economic problems, such as high rates of inflation and unemployment combined with mounting external debt, and is unable to pay the interest
on that debt, it usually cannot borrow additional funds from private sources.
In such a situation the IMF may assist it through a "soft loan" (one with a low
interest rate and a long payback period). In exchange, the borrower nation must
adopt economic reforms suggested by the IMF, such as eliminating currency-
exchange controls, attempting to control inflation, and lowering restrictions on
international trade.

Other international institutions that affect global marketers include stock
markets and similar trading centers. As noted earlier in the chapter, financial
markets around the world are linked together by communication systems that
allow investors to be active in several financial markets at once. The existence
of closely linked financial markets on a global scale enables corporations and

EXHIBIT 4.8 GROSS NATIONAL PRODUCT (billions of dollars)

Most economies are made up of several industrial sectors, each of which contributes to the economic
health of the nation. This exhibit shows the economic diversity and health of the U.S. economy.

	1988	1989	Seasonally adjusted at annual rates					
			1988		1989			
			III	IV	I	II	III	IV
Gross national product	**4,880.6**	**5,234.0**	**4,926.9**	**5,017.3**	**5,113.1**	**5,201.7**	**5,281.0**	**5,3402.0**
Personal consumption expenditures	**3,235.1**	**3,471.1**	**3,263.4**	**3,324.0**	**3,381.4**	**3,444.1**	**3,508.1**	**3,5506.0**
Durable goods	455.2	473.2	452.5	467.4	466.4	471.0	486.1	469.5
Nondurable goods	1,052.3	1,123.4	1,066.2	1,078.4	1,098.3	1,121.5	1,131.4	1,142.4
Services	1,727.6	1,874.4	1,744.7	1,778.2	1,816.7	1,851.7	1,890.6	1,938.7
Gross private domestic investment	**750.3**	**773.4**	**771.1**	**752.8**	**769.6**	**775.0**	**779.1**	**770.1**
Fixed investment	719.6	746.3	726.5	734.1	742.0	747.6	751.7	744.0
Nonresidential	487.2	511.7	493.2	495.8	503.1	512.5	519.6	511.4
Structures	140.3	144.9	142.0	142.5	144.7	142.4	146.2	146.4
Producers' durable equipment	346.8	366.7	351.3	353.3	358.5	370.1	373.4	365.0
Residential	232.4	234.6	233.2	238.4	238.8	235.1	232.1	232.6
Change in business inventories	30.6	27.1	44.6	18.7	27.7	27.4	27.4	26.1
Nonfarm	34.2	22.2	41.5	40.8	19.1	23.6	19.8	26.4
Farm	−3.6	4.9	3.1	−22.2	8.6	3.8	7.5	−.3
Net exports of goods and services	**−73.7**	**−47.1**	**−66.2**	**−70.8**	**−54.0**	**−50.6**	**−45.1**	**−38.8**
Exports	547.7	625.9	556.8	579.7	605.6	626.1	628.5	643.5
Imports	621.3	673.0	623.0	650.5	659.6	676.6	673.6	682.3
Government purchases of goods and services	**968.9**	**1,036.6**	**958.6**	**1,011.4**	**1,016.0**	**1,033.2**	**1,038.9**	**1,058.3**
Federal	381.3	403.2	367.5	406.4	399.0	406.0	402.7	405.1
National defense	298.0	302.2	296.1	300.5	298.7	301.3	307.8	300.9
Nondefense	83.3	101.1	71.4	105.9	100.4	104.7	94.9	104.2
State and local	587.6	633.4	591.0	604.9	617.0	627.2	636.2	653.2

Source: *Survey of Current Business*, March 1990, p. 4.

government entities to raise capital at the lowest cost. Thus, to raise capital to
improve its electrical infrastructure, the government of Queensland, Australia,
sold over $100 million worth of bonds in the United States.[28]

National Institutions. Of course, stock and bond markets function at the national
level also. Indeed, most securities trading is done by home-country corporations
and other investors. National and local banks also operate to stabilize the econ-

EXHIBIT 4.9
SELECTED
INTERNATIONAL
FINANCIAL
INSTITUTIONS

Development Banks and Funds	
The World Bank	Makes loans to economically developing countries throughout the world. Provides financial and technical assistance to aid in development across a variety of projects, including water supply, tourism, infrastructure development, population planning, and industrial development. Loans exceed $8 billion per year. Funds are generated through member nations and borrowing in capital markets from private investors.
Asian Development Bank and Fund	Focuses on similar development needs in the greater Asian community.
Inter-American Development Bank	Established by 19 Latin American countries and the United States in 1959. It is the executing agency of the United Nations Development Bank. IDB funds are currently used to improve social services in member nations.
African Development Bank and Fund	Established in 1964, it is also an executing agency for the United Nations Development Bank. The ADBF is particularly involved in providing funding to sub-Saharan Africa.
International Monetary Fund	Established in 1944 at the Bretton Woods Conference, along with the World Bank. Promotes international monetary cooperation, expansion of trade (along with the General Agreement on Tariffs and Trade), and provides funding to improve economic conditions in the 140 member nations. Provides loans, along with economic guidelines and structures, to nations that are in economic difficulty (that, for example, cannot pay the interest on their external debt).

Source: OECD *Development Co-Operation Report, 1986*, Paris, 1986.

omy. National banking systems, like the Federal Reserve System in the United States, contribute to economic stability by regulating the money supply and banking operations. If the money supply grows too quickly, the result may be inflation; if it grows too slowly, the economy may stagnate. The national banking system influences the growth of the money supply through policies that govern interest rates, the amount of money in circulation, and the lending practices of banks, savings and loan associations, and other financial institutions.

Some countries do not have a national banking system. In those countries the money supply is potentially unstable, a situation that can result in high inflation rates. Thus, the existence of a national banking system may be a sign of a relatively stable economy, but it is by no means a guarantee—too many other variables determine the extent to which an economy is stable over time.

National and international financial institutions are of interest to global marketers because they affect customers' purchasing power and the availability of capital. A customer in a particular market may be interested in a product but unable to buy it. Prices and credit terms may have to be adjusted, depending on the monetary policies of the national banking system or other financial institutions. If the government of the host country has local participation laws that require businesses to raise capital locally, management needs to examine the policies of the institutions that influence the supply of capital in that country. Also of interest is the national saving rate, which is translated into funds for investment. Higher saving rates create a larger supply of money at lower interest rates to invest in the corporation.[29] For example, the saving rate in Japan is approximately three times higher than in the United States. This enables Japanese firms to take a longer-term perspective on marketing activities than is typical of U.S. firms. (Exhibit 4.10 compares saving rates in various industrialized countries.)

Governmental Policy and Administration

Ultimately, the economic attractiveness of a market is dependent upon government policy and stability.

The policies of a government are reflected in its official proclamations and laws, which regulate the society and allocate its resources. Political influences and legal issues derived from governmental policies are discussed in Chapter 6. But governments also influence the economic process through their administrative practices, that is, the way the bureaucracy or executive branch operates.

In many countries the political and administrative functions of government are distinct and separate. For example, in most European countries governments change but administrators stay. On a daily basis, companies do business with "the administration," not with "the government." Personal contacts, long-standing relationships, and an understanding of how the administration functions may make it possible to do business even if official policies are unfavorable. In addition, the continuity of employment that is characteristic of administrative workers lends stability to the bureaucracy. Because of these factors, global marketers must look beyond the official policies of a government and evaluate the stability of the administration as well.

The global marketer may need to consider regional, state, or local administrations as well as the national or federal governments. Strong local administrators, such as mayors and council members, make or at least influence decisions that affect plant location, land allocation, taxes, utilities, and other matters. National TV advertising in France, for example, has traditionally been limited because of pressure by the mayors of small towns. The mayors need the support of the local newspapers to be reelected. In return for that support, they put pressure on regional and national administrators to limit TV advertising, so that advertising in newspapers will be higher than it otherwise would be. As a result, it is difficult for global marketers to obtain as much national TV advertising

EXHIBIT 4.10
COMPARATIVE
SAVINGS RATES

Nations save at different
rates. This influences the
availability of funds for
companies to borrow and
the interest rate they must
pay, which in turn affects
their competitive position
internationally.

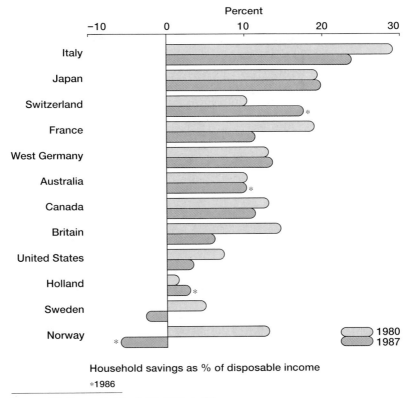

Household savings as % of disposable income
*1986

Source: *The Economist*, March 19, 1988, p. 76.

time as they would like, and regional or local TV advertising is often not available at all.

The economic environment is the first set of factors to be studied in assessing the potential of any national market. If the market does not contain enough customers with the purchasing power to buy the product, it is not economically viable. When the economic analysis yields positive results, global marketers should continue the evaluation process by examining the political, legal, and cultural and social environments.

S U M M A R Y

The most salient characteristic of the world economic system is its increasing integration. This is especially evident in financial markets, but those markets are affected by a variety of other factors, of which one of the most important is the balance of trade (merchandise account). The balance of trade is an account that keeps track of a nation's exports and imports. When imports exceed exports, the balance of trade is said to be negative; when a nation exports more than it imports, it has a positive balance of trade.

Economic systems vary considerably in their approach to economic decision making. The economic systems associated with socialist or communist political systems rely on central decision making; in other systems market forces guide economic decisions. Most economies lie somewhere between these two extremes. An economy's degree of market orientation affects a firm's ability to reach target markets there.

The globalization of financial markets has been accompanied by an increase in foreign investment, which is, in effect, simply capital flowing from one nation to another according to the theory of relative advantage. This means that business as well as government must become more sensitive to political and social issues in other nations.

An important aspect of international economic coordination is currency exchange rates. Under a floating exchange rate, a currency may be bought and sold for differing amounts of another currency. Currencies that are subject to a fixed exchange rate, on the other hand, may be bought or sold only at specific rates that do not vary. For the past thirty years international trade has increasingly been financed through international currencies such as Eurodollars.

The distribution of income and wealth in a nation is of vital interest to global marketers. In general, the higher the level of economic development in a national market, the more economically viable it is likely to be. The distribution of income and wealth is affected by the nation's overall level of economic development, by the purchasing power of particular markets, and by the rate of inflation.

Also of interest to global marketers are the total population of a nation, its growth rate, and the distribution of age groups within it. The rate of population growth and the size of the population affect a society's ability to progress economically and to provide for the future, as well as the distribution of current and future wealth. Large population centers are of great interest to marketers because they contain concentrations of potential buyers. Increases and decreases in the proportion of the population in specific age groups are closely related to the demand for particular products and services.

Other significant aspects of the economic environment include urbanization, natural resources, and geography. Rapid urbanization can lead to high unemployment, harsh living conditions, and frequent episodes of political and social unrest. A nation's natural resources are a major determinant of the type of economic system that can develop there, and geographic factors can also act either as resources or as constraints on marketing activities.

Global marketers must consider the level of technological development in a society. Differences in technological development limit the potential of some markets, but they also offer opportunities to market new technologies. Also important is the nation's infrastructure—its communication, transportation, and energy systems. The level of infrastructure development affects the extent to which a nation's natural resources can be used.

Other economic factors of interest to global marketers are industrial sectors, or categories of economic activity; financial institutions, both international and national; and governmental policy and administration. In the latter case, personal contacts, long-standing relationships, and an understanding of how the administration functions may make it possible to do business in a nation even if official policies are unfavorable.

DISCUSSION QUESTIONS

1. What are the chief characteristics of the world economic system, and how do they affect global marketing?

2. What is meant by the balance of trade? What determines whether it is positive or negative?

3. What are the different types of exchange rates, and how do they affect global marketing decisions?

4. "The only economic system in which a marketing organization can make money is a free-market economy like that of the United States." Do you agree or disagree with this statement? Why?

5. List the three major elements in the distribution of income and wealth, and discuss how each affects marketing.

6. Why are the size and growth of a population of importance to global marketers?

7. What impact does a nation's geography have on the potential for marketing in that nation?

8. Discuss and illustrate the impact of technology on a particular national market.

9. Discuss and illustrate the role of financial institutions in maintaining the economic viability of a national market.

10. What effect does the governmental bureaucracy have on a nation's economic health?

CASE

STROTHER'S SHOES

Strother's Shoes, based in Rocky Mount, North Carolina, was interested in entering the international shoe market. In 1989 the depreciation of the U.S. dollar against other major currencies presented Strother's Shoes with an improved opportunity, it believed, to export some of its low-priced shoes to developing countries. Strother's Shoes knew it might have problems in countries where income-distribution patterns meant that most people have very little discretionary income. But competitive pressures in the United States and Europe, where Strother's Shoes already enjoyed strong sales and profits, were increasing. When Erin Strother, founder and president of Strother's Shoes, looked at economic and population growth patterns in the world, she became increasingly convinced that a less-developed nation might present an opportunity for at least the low-priced product line.

Strother's Shoes, founded in 1971, specializes in making moderate- and low-priced shoes for the mass market. Thanks to modern equipment and a work force that participated in a profit-sharing plan, and thus was willing to work for a relatively low hourly wage, Strother's Shoes were competitively priced. With the appreciation of the U.S. dollar in the late 1980s, Erin Strother believed her products could be sold at competitive prices in developing countries as well. Although the profit would not be great, spreading production costs across more units would result in a large economies-of-scale effect, lowering costs for the company.

As a child, Erin had lived in India, and she had since kept informed about the political and economic trends in that country. She believed India was in the early phase of what would be a long, positive economic-growth cycle. India had improved its economic performance and increased the general standard of living for its citizens. Tariff and nontariff barriers to entry had been lowered. Re-export opportunities to neighboring countries and even the USSR existed. Combined with its large population, almost 800 million, India at first glance presented a very interesting market.

However, Erin Strother knew a more thorough investigation into the economic viability of that market should be conducted before making a decision. Her vice president of marketing, Joe May, had gathered the information shown in Exhibit A. While developing his economic profile, Mr. May had learned of several political, legal, and cultural factors that he thought should also be considered in the market assessment. For example, the Sikh religious group based in Punjab, one of India's most prosperous states, had been increasingly violent in its calls for political freedom. Another concern was the stories Joe had heard

---

EXHIBIT A
A PROFILE OF INDIA

Population: 789,120,000 Urban = 26%   Growth rate is about 2%

Capital: New Delhi

Ethnic Groups: Indo-Aryan 72%, Dravidian 25%, Other 3%

Languages: English, Hindi, Hindustani, others

Religions: Hindu 84%, Muslim 11%, Christian 3%, Sikh 2%

Life Expectancy: 55 years female, 56 years male

Literacy: 36%

Economy: GDP $193,820,000,000   Per capita $272   Real Growth rate averaged in the high 3% range.

Trading Partners: Exports: USSR 18%, U.S. 11%, U.K. 6%, Japan 9%
                    Imports: Iran 11%, U.S. 12%, USSR 8%, West Germany 6%

Exports: Clothing and other manufactured products, food, crude materials, machinery, chemicals

Imports: Petroleum, iron, steel, manufactured products, machinery, chemicals

---

Sources: *World Facts & Maps* (Chicago: Rand McNally, 1989), p. 131; and World Resources Institute, *World Resources, 1986* (New York: Basic Books, 1986), pp. 235–246.

about the necessity to offer "additional payments" to Indian government officials to receive permission to import products. Additionally, Joe had heard that the Hindu religion might influence the sale or repair of shoes.

Much of India has a warm climate, so shoes are not necessary for much of the year. The rainy summer months make the ground so muddy some people actually go barefoot, in order to keep their shoes from getting ruined. But Western styles of clothing and footwear were increasing in popularity in India.

A preliminary market investigation, based on some magazine articles Joe had found, indicated that the channel of distribution for clothing, although slower in India than in the United States, would not present a problem to Strother's Shoes. Joe was unable to find much information on advertising and promotion. Erin Strother called a meeting for Wednesday morning to focus on the question of whether Strother's Shoes should proceed with a market analysis of India.

Case Issue

1. Would you recommend that Erin Strother tell Joe May to go ahead with the market analysis? Explain why.

NOTES

1. U.S. Department of Commerce, *Survey of Current Business*, vol. 67, no. 8 (Washington, D.C., August 1987); and "The Japanese Want to Be Your Bankers," *Fortune*, October 27, 1986, p. 96; A. Clark, "Japan Goes to Europe," *World Monitor*, April 1990, pp. 36–40.

2. "International Stock Markets," *Bulletin: Swiss Banking Magazine*, January 1988, pp. 16–17.

3. "Made in the U.S.A.," *Business Week*, February 29, 1988, pp. 28–30; "The World Economy After the Crash," *Bulletin: Swiss Banking Magazine*, January 1988, p. 18; and C. H. Farnsworth, "Down to the Wire on Trade," *New York Times*, March 20, 1988, p. 3-1.

4. "The Pacific Century," *Newsweek* (Australian ed.), February 23, 1988. pp. 3–5.

5. "Looking Beyond America's Means," *The Economist*, September 19, 1987, p. 72; and "New World—New Markets," *Business Review Weekly*, February 12, 1988, pp. 38–41.

6. L. Rukeyser, "Latest French Moves Could Be Revolutionary," *Atlanta Journal*, July 26, 1986, p. C-1.

7. "China Throws Open Its Seaboard," *The Economist*, March 12–18, 1988, p. 65; and "Foreigners Crucial to Success of Reform Drive," *Financial Review*, October 10, 1986, pp. 16–17.

8. "Foreign Funds Flood into Australia," *Financial Review*, February 19, 1988, p. 3.

9. "I'll Take Manhattan—and Waikiki," *Time*, March 9, 1987, p. 62.

10. "Engine That Could Is All out of Steam," *Los Angeles Times*, February 7, 1988, p. IV-1.

11. "Making Sense of the Presidential Race—An Australian's Guide," *The Bulletin*, March 8, 1988, pp. 48–49; and "White House '89," *Asia Week*, February 19, 1988, p. 45.

12. "Dubious Honor," *Time*, February 8, 1988, p. 16; "Fear and Trembling in the Colossus," *Fortune*, March 30, 1987, p. 32; and "The Other Deficit," *Wall Street Journal*, January 7, 1987, p. 18.

13. Tan Chwee Huat, "The Asian Dollar Market," in P. D. Grub et al., eds., *East Asia Dimensions of International Business* (Englewood Cliffs, N.J.: Prentice-Hall, 1982), pp. 1–13; and P. Drucker, *Managing in Turbulent Times* (London: Pan Books, 1981), p. 154.

14. "Economic Data of DMCs," *Asian Development Bank Annual Report*, vol. 86 (Manila, 1986), p. 120.

15. "U.S. Industry Closing Trade Gap," *Atlanta Journal*, December 6, 1987, p. M-1; and "Made in the U.S.A.," *Business Week*, February 29, 1988, pp. 28–30.

16. "African Tragedy," *Wall Street Journal*, April 17, 1987, p. 1.

17. "Growing Gap," *Wall Street Journal*, September 22, 1986, p. 1.

18. International Monetary Fund, *International Statistics* (Washington, D.C., 1985), p. 71.

19. "São Paulo McDonald's in a Pickle," *Atlanta Journal and Constitution*, March 29, 1987, p. E-2.

20. "Dissimilar Debtors," *Wall Street Journal*, March 24, 1987, p. 1.

21. For a more complete discussion of the "sea change" caused by shifts in population structure, see P. Drucker, *Managing in Turbulent Times* (London: Pan Books, 1981).

22. E. Dichter, "The World Customer," *Harvard Business Review*, July–August 1986, pp. 113–123.

23. "The Great Mall of China," *Australian Business*, February 24, 1988, p. 36.

24. "Lesotho Deals Itself 'Ace in the Hole' Against Labor Woes," *Report: News and Views from the World Bank*, July–August 1979, p. 1.

25. "A Separate Paradise," *Asia Week*, March 25, 1988, pp. 42–49.

26. "Quixotic Quest," *Wall Street Journal*, January 9, 1986, p. 1.

27. "Why Chile's Economy Works," *Business Review Weekly*, February 12, 1988, pp. 20–23. (Reprinted from *Forbes*.)

28. "QLD to Use US Money for Development Works," *Financial Review*, February 18, 1988, p. 61.

29. "The Pacific Century," *Newsweek* (Australian ed.), February 23, 1988, p. 92.

EXTERNAL CONSIDERATIONS
THE POLITICAL AND LEGAL ENVIRONMENTS

INTERNATIONAL INCIDENT

Beeg Mek and Ketoflio Fry

On January 31, 1990, McDonald's opened the first of twenty restaurants planned for Moscow. Over 20,000 Muscovites stood in line that first day. But behind the highly successful opening were over 14 years of political negotiations.

George Cohon, president of McDonald's Canada, initiated discussions in Montreal, at the 1976 Olympics, aimed at opening a McDonald's restaurant at the 1980 Olympic games in Moscow. Discussions proceeded after that, but the Western nations' boycott of the 1980 Olympics resulted in a decision by Soviet officials to call off the talks. Cohon was advised by Alexander Yakoulev, Soviet ambassador to Canada at that time, "At the moment this is ideologically impossible. One day you will be able to do it." After Mikhail Gorbachev came to power in the USSR in 1984, political relations between the USSR and Canada, as well as many other nations, changed dramatically. Yakoulev became a close advisor to Gorbachev. Discussions regarding a joint venture between the city of Moscow and McDonald's became serious in 1987, after passage of a new joint venture law.

After devoting about half of his time during 1988 and 1989 to the joint venture, Cohon opened the world's largest McDonald's—with 27 serving lines and seating for over 700 people—on Pushkin Square. The British Broadcasting Corporation's report called the restaurant's signs "garish." But Soviet response was overwhelmingly positive, despite the 5-kopeck price of a "beeg mek and ketoflio fry" (high by Soviet standards—roughly half the daily salary of the average Soviet worker).

The world's largest McDonald's opened in Moscow in January 1990, 14 years after negotiations began.

McDonald's showed considerable political savvy by charging rubles. Although rubles couldn't be exchanged for other currencies, McDonald's could use them to finance the extensive vertical marketing system it established in the USSR to support its restaurants. Cucumber and potato seeds from The Netherlands were imported for use by Soviet farmers, who were taught how to grow produce to meet McDonald's exacting standards. McDonald's also helped to establish a bakery and meat processing plants, improving cattle production standards—in total a $50 million investment.

Although the changed political climate allowed McDonald's to enter the USSR, the political (and economic) system is still a source of potential problems. To the extent that production decisions are made by a central government body in the USSR, new businesses like McDonald's find it difficult to obtain supplies. Their needs simply don't "fit in the 5-year plan."

McDonald's second Moscow restaurant will appeal primarily to international tourists. By selling meals at foreign currency prices, McDonald's can obtain unblocked currencies, which it can transfer back to Canada. The royalties it can transfer back will be based on revenues from all of its Moscow restaurants.

Sources: Based on "McDonald's in Moscow—Slow Food," *The Economist*, February 3, 1990, pp. 74, 79; and B. Keller, "Of Famous Arches, Beeg Meks and Rubles," *New York Times*, January 31, 1990, pp. 1, 7.

The political and legal environments determine whether a business has the right to do business in a particular country.

The right to do business in any country is controlled by its government and is granted through the political process, that is, through the formulation of administrative rulings and laws. The role of governmental administration was discussed in the preceding chapter. This chapter focuses on governmental policies and the laws that result from them, which provide the guidelines for conducting business in a particular nation. The examples are not complete, of course, because national political and legal environments are quite different. But this chapter helps illustrate the differences, as well as the need for a global marketer to evaluate the political and legal environments carefully.

THE POLITICAL ENVIRONMENT

The current trend toward economic integration of nations has significant political implications.

Nation-states are formed in order to manage and control a political territory and its economy.[1] Ironically, as their economic interdependence increases, nations tend to move apart politically. An important exception to this general trend is the European Community, where economic, military, legal, political, and foreign policies are becoming increasingly similar. Even the socialist governments of Greece and Spain review their policies to make them at least somewhat compatible with those of other EC nations.

Several recent trends have decreased the ability of a nation to control its own economy. Global corporations, currencies, and banks have become increasingly numerous and powerful; as a result, assets and factors of production are continually transferred across national boundaries. Efforts to increase international economic integration, such as the European Community and the cooperative trade agreement between the United States and Canada, require that member nations give up some of their political sovereignty. France, for example, no longer benefits as much from protective farm tariffs, because the United Kingdom argued successfully for lower tariffs as a means of reducing food prices in the Common Market.

As a result of these and other trends, governments are faced with a dilemma: they need to promote economic cooperation and integration, but they do not wish to give up their political sovereignty. This dilemma results in a constantly changing political environment. In the following section we will examine several dimensions that illustrate the political environment and its impact on global marketing.

Political Stability and the Structure of Government

Political stability is the most important aspect of the political environment for a global marketer.

For the global marketer, the most important dimension of the political environment is the stability of the nation's political system. Events like the military coup in Burkina Faso or the continuing civil war in Sri Lanka produce changes in the "rules of the business game."[2] Political instability makes the business environment far less predictable—and predictability is a key to long-term business success.[3]

In Chapter 4 we pointed out that the administration continues for a time as a nation's political leadership changes. But in the face of radical political changes like those that occurred in Iran in the late 1970s, even the governmental bureaucracy may be unable to continue to operate. Sometimes when radical changes take place, opportunities to conduct business increase, as they did when Mikhail Gorbachev came to power in the Soviet Union. In some cases, however, they decrease, as occurred in China as a result of a shift toward a more conservative political climate after the Tiananmen Square incident in 1989.[4]

Of course, the bureaucracy may sometimes provide "too much" stability. For example, the government of Argentina attempted to privatize state-owned businesses and reduce governmental intervention in the private sector. But many members of the bureaucracy, apparently feeling threatened by these changes, joined forces with trade unions to block the reforms.[5]

Form of Government.   The form of government in a nation is of particular significance to global marketers. Form of government should be distinguished from degree of market orientation. Capitalism, communism, and socialism are sociopolitical philosophies that lead to economic systems characterized by varying degrees of market orientation. Democracy, monarchy, and dictatorship are forms of government.*

The degree of political participation by the citizens of the country defines the form of government.

Various forms of government differ in the extent to which they permit political participation by the general population. **Democracies** provide opportunities for the population to take an active role in the formulation of governmental policies. Although they vary greatly, the United States, Mexico, France, United Kingdom, and Japan are all democracies. Japan and the United Kingdom are **constitutional monarchies.** Each has a royal head of government with limited and specified roles. For example, in addition to performing important ceremonial roles, the Queen of England can convene Parliament and take an active role in shaping policy. But she does not rule by holding centralized power, in contrast to the royal heads of **absolute monarchies,** like the King of Saudi Arabia.

Dictators may be either monarchs or civilian or military rulers with centrally controlled power. Chad and Hungary were ruled by dictators. Hungary, however, has had some success in combining its form of government with "free-enterprise socialism" (that is, a relatively high degree of market orientation). Initially Hungary "legalized" its underground economy; as a result, about half of the country's workers took second or third jobs in order to raise their standard of living.[6] Now that Hungary is moving toward a more democratic state, due to recent political changes, the economy should become even more of a free enterprise orientation.

The philosophies of the political parties help determine what role a foreign business is allowed to play in the domestic economy.

Political Parties and Interest Groups. Political parties are important to global marketers because they channel public opinion into the formulation of governmental policies and laws.† Thus, the role that foreign businesses are allowed to play in a given nation are influenced by the philosophies of the political parties and other interest groups in that nation, as the opening incident illustrated.[7]

Political systems can be classified according to the number of parties they contain and their relative importance. The United States and the United Kingdom are essentially **two-party systems,** although both have minority parties as well; in fact, in the United Kingdom the minority parties often play a significant role in the political process. Mexico and Japan, in contrast, are basically **one-party systems**: Candidates who gain the nomination of the dominant party are virtually assured of election. Single-party democracies exist either when the dominant party is the only one that is officially allowed to exist (as was the case

---

*There is often some overlap between form of government and degree of market orientation. However, France, which is certainly a democracy, has traditionally had a high level of central planning. And socialist and communist nations are currently moving away from state control of the economy, toward increased reliance on market forces.

†Even communist regimes, which traditionally install a dominant political party and severely limit opposition to that party, may use political polls to obtain information about the attitudes and concerns of members of the society. Before opening its system, Hungary conducted forty public opinion polls each year.

in the USSR) or when the dominant party relies on political power or coercion to limit opposition (as was the case under the Marcos regime in the Philippines). **Coalitions** are formed when there are several parties, none of which receives a majority vote. Under such conditions parties must cooperate and form a power bloc that, if successful, will become the government. This enables a party to govern without obtaining a majority of the vote. For many years Italy has been ruled by a series of coalitions. Every time a coalition breaks up, a new government must be formed.

One difference between the United States and most other democracies is that in other countries a party representative almost always conforms to the party's official policy. But in the United States a Republican may vote with the Republican administration on one issue and against it on another. In a sense, then, the U.S. two-party system is a series of coalitions that are formed as various combinations of party members come together to support particular positions on specific issues.

Special-interest groups also play an important political role and may affect the attractiveness of particular markets. For example, the Greens, a small but vocal political party in West Germany, have taken a strong stand on environmental issues. They work very hard to defeat any business activity (such as nuclear power) that they believe will contribute to environmental pollution.[8]

> Special-interest groups, lobbyists, organizations, and even individuals can influence the political environment.

Lobbyists also influence international trade. Representatives of the U.S. automobile industry have called for higher tariffs or quotas on imports of foreign cars; they are countered by Japanese lobbyists working to keep trade barriers low. In fact, Japanese businesses employ over 100 registered lobbyists in Washington, D.C.[9] And Motorola's success in selling computer chips to Japan is due in part to lobbying on the part of the U.S. government to the government of Japan.

Powerful organizations and individuals can also influence the global marketing environment. Japanese rice farmers, for example, dominate Japan's ruling Liberal Democratic Party. Thanks largely to their efforts, the rice industry in Japan is highly subsidized; rice imports are banned, and Japanese consumers pay 500 percent more for rice than American consumers do.[10] As for powerful individuals, an example is Mahatma Gandhi, who strongly influenced Indian policies, including some that discouraged activity by foreign businesses, without ever holding formal office.

International interest groups also exist. In the mid-1980s a combination of interest groups became concerned about Nestlé's marketing of powdered baby formula in developing countries. Nestlé's marketing programs had to be altered as a result of a boycott organized by those groups.[11]

Intergovernmental Relations.   **Intergovernmental relations** (relations between home- and host-country governments) are a key determinant of the political environment. The degree of friendliness or hostility between governments influences the ease with which business can be conducted between citizens of those nations. The flow of trade between two nations reflects the extent to which

> Political relations between home and host countries influence the type and amount of trade that occurs between nations.

relations between those nations are positive (the United States and Japan, for example) or negative (the United States and Iraq). Indeed, the level and type of trade that occurs between nations may tell us more about intergovernmental relations than official governmental statements. For example, statistics on trade between the United States and the Soviet Union suggest that the two countries were on friendlier terms during the last years of the Carter administration than they were during most of the Reagan administration. In 1979, U.S. exports to the USSR totaled $3,967 million, with imports totaling $823 million. Nine years later, U.S. exports totaled $1,373 million and imports $550 million.[12] Under Gorbachev, trade increased once again.

Intergovernmental relations can also have the effect of isolating one nation from others in world political opinion. This occurs when a government pursues policies that most other governments consider inappropriate. Thus, the Republic of South Africa became increasingly isolated both politically and economically as a result of its policy of apartheid (racial segregation).[13] The release of Nelson Mandela, jailed for 27 years due to his leadership in the antiapartheid movement, was due in part to international political and economic pressure.

At worst, highly negative intergovernmental relations can result in a **boycott,** or refusal to permit trade with a particular nation. Companies that trade with Israel, for instance, are subject to boycotts by Arab nations. The U.S. government has responded to Arab boycotts by passing laws that deny foreign income tax benefits and export privileges to firms that comply with the boycott, as well as imposing heavy fines on those firms.

Current Government. The policies and practices of the government that is currently in power must be considered in assessing the political environment of

Widespread international opposition to South Africa's apartheid policy was one of the factors that led to the release in 1989 of Nelson Mandela, who spent 27 years in prison for anti-apartheid activities.

a foreign market. We noted in Chapter 4 that the 1988 U.S. presidential election campaign was followed throughout the world. Of particular interest was the potential for changes in U.S. international trade policy in the next administration.[14]

The government formulates policies and guides a nation's businesses in their interactions with foreign companies. Therefore, its beliefs about the appropriate role of foreign business have a significant effect on market opportunities. For example, the reunification of West and East Germany was in part motivated by the migration of East German workers to West Germany. But a united Germany also increased East Germany's attractiveness to foreign investors and its openness to foreign investment. This attitude has opened up new opportunities for foreign firms.[15]

Government and the Economy

Governments play multiple roles in their economies, all of which affect the global marketer.

In addition to the structural and administrative dimensions of government, there are economic dimensions that must be assessed by global marketers. Governments not only set policies that affect investment and international trade but also play a variety of economic roles, including those of regulator, buyer, supplier, competitor, and partner.

In all societies the government plays a regulatory role. In centrally planned economies, the government regulates almost all economic activities—allocation of raw materials, number and type of goods produced and shipped, time and place of sale of those goods, ways in which goods may be promoted, and prices charged. In market-oriented economies, the government also acts as a regulator, but it is less involved in day-to-day business decisions. Instead, it regulates by defining the rules of competition, often with the objective of maintaining a "level playing field." Thus, the antitrust legislation enacted in the United States early in this century was intended to give competitors a roughly equal chance of success.

Governments are also buyers of goods and services. Military procurement, for example, may constitute a large market. In the United States, military expenditures account for 6 percent of the gross national product. In Algeria, 40 percent of the national budget goes toward providing education.[16] Normally governments buy from domestic producers, but when only a limited number of companies produce certain products, governments may become major global customers. In the mid-1980s, for example, Jordan purchased twenty fighter planes worth about $23 million each from France.[17]

As suppliers of goods and services, all governments offer the members of their society such services as health care, social security, national defense, public safety, and education. These services vary widely in number and quality. In countries where the government provides many services, citizens often pay for those services indirectly through high taxes (as in Sweden) or low wages (as in the USSR).

Some governments are fierce competitors. They may even provide goods or services that directly compete with those offered by foreign marketers. In Japan, the Ministry of International Trade and Industry (MITI) provides consulting services to Japanese firms that want to enter foreign markets. Thus, the market for similar consulting services is smaller in Japan than in the United States, where fewer such services are provided by the government.

Finally, the government may play the role of partner, setting policies that benefit business and achieve social goals at the same time. The term **social partnership** is used to describe the alliance among government, labor, and management in Austria. This alliance has resulted in a very low strike rate and a high degree of industrial stability. In an average year there are 4 work disputes in Austria, compared to over 1,300 in the United Kingdom, where government, labor, and management act more as adversaries than as partners.[18]

A government's trade policy influences whether a firm can take advantage of the opportunity which a particular national market provides.

International Trade Policy. As mentioned earlier, a number of economic dimensions of government affect global marketing. Foremost of these is **international trade policy,** a set of laws and rules that regulate the flow of goods and services across a nation's boundaries. The trade policy provides a framework for policies regarding exports, imports, and foreign investment.

When nations run large trade deficits or believe they are being exploited by foreign investors or traders, there may be an increase in **nationalism,** the belief that a nation should have complete control over its own affairs. A frequent outcome of nationalism is **protectionism,** the use of legal controls to protect specific domestic industries or businesses against foreign competition. Often the emotional appeal of nationalism is used by businesses to gain public support for such controls. The impact of such policies, of course, is to raise the prices of imported goods; in effect, they are indirect subsidies. Thus, while some 200,000 American auto workers were laid off in the early 1980s, protectionist measures saved between 20,000 and 35,000 jobs in the auto industry, at a cost of between $93,000 and $250,000 per job.[19]

The same kinds of policies do not always have the same effects on the economies that employ them. Japan's policy of restricting imports, encouraging exports, and supporting overseas investment has produced remarkable economic growth over the past 20 years. In contrast, India's attempts to protect its markets have led to higher prices, limited product choice, and continued use of outdated technology. India is now in the process of removing such controls as part of a program to restore vigor to its economy. Exhibit 5.1 illustrates some of the historical effects of trade policies in the United States, Japan, and Europe.

Exports and imports are restricted or supported by all governments to some degree.

Export/Import Policy. All nations control exports and imports to some degree, providing both barriers to trade and supports for certain domestically produced goods and services. Barriers to trade include tariffs, nontariff barriers, quotas, and trade embargoes. Often specific products or technologies are controlled. Of special concern are products that might affect national security or are in limited supply. For example, exports of products and technologies related to nuclear power are restricted because of concern about the proliferation of nuclear weapons.* The United States also did not permit the export of supercomputers to nations that are viewed as security risks, such as India.[20] The United States, Japan, Australia, and members of the European Community control such trade through a multilateral agreement known as the Coordinating Committee on Multilateral Export Controls (COCOM). This group is currently reducing the time it takes to review applications for export licenses for sensitive products and reacting to political changes in Eastern Europe and the Soviet Union—easing curbs on the sale of computers and telecommunications equipment to these countries, for example.[21] Despite such controls, legal exports of sensitive products to friendly countries are sometimes reshipped to a third, higher-risk nation.[22] Moreover, such policies allow suppliers from other countries to gain a competitive edge.

Other export policies assist corporations that wish to export their products. The Japanese approach of identifying key industries and then developing an export policy for those industries has proven especially effective.[23] The Japanese External Trade Organization (JETRO), the counterpart of the U.S. Department of Commerce, has been so successful in implementing an aggressive export promotion policy that the Japanese government has asked it to help marketers in other countries increase their exports to Japan.

Another way of encouraging exports is to provide financial assistance. The United States has granted its Export-Import Bank (Eximbank), for instance, a $300 million "war chest" to provide financial support to U.S. exporters.[24] When such programs and policies are lacking, exports can be severely limited by noncompetitive prices.[25]

There are also policies that either limit or encourage imports. For example, a restriction in India on imports of weaving machines required foreign companies to prove that no producer in India could make the same kind of machine. To circumvent the restriction, one company entered into a joint venture with an Indian producer. Indeed, import quotas and nontariff barriers have an even greater constraining effect on trade than tariffs do.[26]

Sometimes governments support imports of particular products, services, or technologies. One of the reasons that China established special industrial zones was to encourage imports of technology from Western nations. The United States has an import-support program that offers tariff preferences for selected products from developing countries, in order to stimulate their economies. When these products are viewed as fully competitive, they no longer qualify for import support and the tariff structure is changed.[27]

---

*In the United States, most exports require only a general, unwritten export license. But for sensitive goods, or goods exported to politically sensitive countries, a validated, written export license must be obtained after appropriate governmental agencies (such as the Departments of Commerce and Defense) have been consulted.

EXHIBIT 5.1
RESULTS OF DIFFERENT TRADE POLICIES: THE UNITED STATES, JAPAN, AND EUROPE

Many factors contribute to a nation's balance of trade. Chief among these is the nation's trade policy. This exhibit illustrates some of the differences among U.S., Japanese, and West European nations' trade policies and the impact those differences have had.

		United States	**Japan**	**Europe**
After WW II until 1970	Policy	Market domination, exports > imports	Rebuild industry, spend less on R&D	Rebuild industry, spend less on R&D
	Results	Wages soar, collective bargaining	Depend on copying, new management style, lifetime employment	Improve techiques, new management style of codetermination
1970–1980	Policy	Cut taxes, boost spending, tight monetary policy, open market/free trade	Economy slows down, reduced production, closed market	Slow economy down, reduce production, spend less on R&D, nationalize important industry, closed market
	Results	High interest rates, other countries dump products into market, domestic demand increases by 15%	Domestic demand increases by 6%	Domestic demand increases by 3%
1980	Results	$32.2 billion trade deficit	$414.4 million trade deficit	*France:* $83.8 million trade deficit *Britain:* $1.3 billion trade surplus *Italy:* $6.9 million trade deficit
1986	Results	$169.8 billion trade deficit	$51.5 billion trade surplus	*France:* $5.0 billion trade surplus *Britain:* $4.2 billion trade surplus *Italy:* $3.8 billion trade deficit

Source: A. F. Alkhafaji and E. R. Hill, "A Comparison of Trade Policies: U.S., Japan, and Europe," *Proceedings, Academy of International Business*, 1988, p. 109.

Buying assets in another nation is often politically controversial in that country and is controlled by the government of that country.

Investment Policy. A nation's **investment policy** consists of all the laws and regulations that govern private participation (domestic as well as foreign) in the equity or ownership of businesses and other organizations in that nation. These laws can act as either aids or deterrents to foreign investment. Services, in particular, are constrained more by investment policies than they are by international trade policies.[28] (Many services are directly related to the flow of funds—banking and insurance, for example. It has traditionally been very difficult for foreign companies to invest in these areas.)

Governments may change their policies to encourage foreign investment in an attempt to spur domestic economic growth or underwrite a high trade deficit, in effect substituting investment funds for the outflow of money resulting from a negative balance of trade. Thus, Malaysia attempted to increase production by changing its rules governing how much of a company may be foreign-owned. Companies that export 50 percent or more of their production may now be up to 100 percent foreign-owned.[29]

Market orientation is reflected in governmental policy toward investment, which can be viewed as a continuum between two extremes: *no* private investment (either domestic or foreign) and *only* private investment. As a nation's degree of market orientation changes, the rules of investment also change. When they change dramatically, the government may have to undertake a campaign to change the investment habits of potential investors. For example, when France began to privatize publicly held corporations, ranging from glassmakers to insurance companies, the government undertook a massive advertising campaign to persuade French citizens to invest in these industries.[30]

Foreign direct investment occurs when a company invests in a subsidiary or partnership in a foreign market. An example is Nissan's $660 million investment in an automobile assembly plant in Smyrna, Tennessee. In contrast to investments in stocks, bonds, or funds deposited in a bank, which are generally left alone by the investor, foreign direct investment entails some degree of control by the investor.

The potential for control of the economy by foreign investors makes many governments nervous. This can lead to more restrictions on marketing activity. In the United States, there is growing concern about the economic impact of foreign multinational corporations. In the case of Nissan's assembly plant in Tennessee, if the company's traditional supplier relationships are maintained there will be a dual impact. First, new jobs will be created as Nissan's Japanese suppliers develop production facilities near the new plant to meet Nissan's "just-in-time" delivery requirements. Second, U.S. parts suppliers will be excluded from these special arrangements, and a larger portion of automobile industry profits will go to foreign investors. Some experts claim that this pattern represents "creeping colonization";[31] others maintain that the jobs created by foreign investment are important to the economy. In any case, foreign investments are controversial, and investment policies are therefore subject to considerable political pressure.

EXHIBIT 5.2
TEN LOW-RISK AND
TEN EXCESSIVE-RISK
COUNTRIES

Political risk assessment, even if it proceeds systematically and follows a list of indicators, is still somewhat subjective. This exhibit lists what two respected risk-assessment sources believe to be the ten best and worst nations in the world in terms of political risk. Note that the lists vary somewhat.

The 10 Best		The 10 Worst	
WPRF	*BI*	*WPRF*	*BI*
United States	Singapore	El Salvador	Iran
Denmark	Netherlands	Iran	Yugoslavia
Singapore	Norway	Nicaragua	South Korea
Finland	Kuwait	Zaire	Algeria
West Germany	Saudi Arabia	Zambia	Brazil
Austria	Switzerland	Libya	Nicaragua
Canada	West Germany	Bolivia	India
Japan	Britain	Turkey	China
Malaysia	Malaysia	Pakistan	Thailand
Netherlands	Japan	Philippines	Philippines

Identified by Frost and Sullivan's World Political Risk Forecast Services (WPRF) and Business International (BI).

Source: A. Desta, "Assessing Political Risk in Less Developed Countries," *The Journal of Business Strategy,* Spring 1985, p. 47.

Assessing Political Risk

Nations are not perfectly politically stable, so some degree of political risk always exists. A global marketer needs to assess that risk in order to evaluate the market opportunity.

A company that is interested in a foreign market naturally would prefer a stable, friendly, and known political environment. But this ideal is rarely found, so global marketers must be able to evaluate the degree of political risk in a potential market. Exhibit 5.2 shows two different assessments of which countries are the riskiest and the most risk-free.

High levels of political instability normally mean high risk. A country with a history of military or popular revolts (such as Peru) usually is less stable than either a balanced democracy (Canada) or a powerful dictatorship (Paraguay). Political instability is a problem for businesses because governmental policies and administrators may change radically—often with results that are unfavorable to business activity. For example, the changes in Cuba that occurred when Fidel Castro came to power resulted in the **expropriation** of American business interests—private property was seized by the government "in the public interest."

Less radical than expropriation is **domestication,** in which domestic control over foreign investments is increased gradually. The effect may be a partial loss of foreign control, or the loss may be total, similar to expropriation. Expropriation and domestication affect a firm very differently. With expropriation, the company suddenly loses all control over its assets and investments. With domestication, the firm usually has enough time to manage the transfer of ownership (and potential profit) in a systematic way.

Assessing political risk is a real challenge for global marketers. There are many approaches to the measurement of risk. Some assessment techniques include

I. Developmental aspirations of host countries
   A. Investment benefits to host countries
   B. Investment benefits to MNCs

II. Operational factors of the enterprise
   A. Product (nature, relevance, etc.)
   B. Structure (organizational setup, infrastructure, etc.)
   C. Policies (employment, ownership, labor relations)
   D. Company-community/government relations

III. National and environmental factors
   A. Economic factors
     1. Internal
       a. Real GNP and real GNP growth
       b. Growth rate in population and GNP (annual growth in GNP per capita)
       c. Sectoral and employment trends
       d. Inflation rate
       e. Investment/GNP
       f. Net government budget/GNP
     2. External
       a. Foreign public debt/GNP
       b. Debt-service ratio
       c. IMF holdings of domestic currency as a percentage of growth
       d. Current account/GNP
       e. Average external debt
       f. Leading export/total export
       g. Balance of payments outlook
       h. Stability of currency convertibility
       i. Remittance and repatriation regulations
   B. Sociopolitical factors
     1. Integration
     2. Capacity
     3. Social welfare system

IV. External influences
   A. Those that affect the national environment
     1. Border conflicts
     2. Alliance commitments or alliance shifts
     3. Embargoes/international boycotts
     4. International economic instability
     5. Position of the host country vis-à-vis the investor's government.
   B. Those that affect the foreign enterprise
     1. Selective international terrorism
     2. International boycott of selected firms

V. Political risk
   A. Microrisk
     1. Breaches of or unilateral revision of contract

(Continued)

EXHIBIT 5.3 *(Continued)*

    2. Change in the composition of ownership

    3. Selected operating restrictions

    4. Selected boycott

    5. Imposition of special operating taxes, fees, and other charges not levied on domestic operating firms

    6. Blanket regulation on certain exports/imports

B. Macrorisk

    1. Expropriation with or without compensation

    2. Nationalization or indigenization of all foreign assets

    3. Default or government repudiation of external debt

    4. Restriction on profit remittance

Source: A. Desta, "Assessing Political Risk in Less Developed Countries," *The Journal of Business Strategy,* Spring 1985, p. 53.

cultural and economic factors in their models; others consider risk on investment separately from risk on cash flow.[32]

Exhibit 5.3 illustrates the indicators that need to be considered when assessing political risk. Although Exhibit 5.3 focuses on less-developed countries, similar indicators exist for developed countries. Exhibit 5.4 illustrates what one consulting organization presents to a company when it prepares a political-risk analysis.

No matter what approach is used, the marketer needs to assess the exposure of a proposed venture to political risk and the possible outcome of encountering that risk, weighted according to probability. For example, the probability and likely outcome of expropriation for a U.S.-based company in Ethiopia are quite different from those faced by a Switzerland-based company doing business in the United States. Loss of control and return on investment are almost certain in the former case, but are highly unlikely in the latter case.

Multiple political environments exist, at the national, state, and local levels.

Just as government administration at different levels affects companies in various ways (see Chapter 4), so too the political environment may have varying impacts at the national, state, and local levels. Different sets of laws and regulations, usually not standardized, regulate the marketing of goods and services within as well as between nations. A U.S. importer of French wines, for instance, must deal with different state regulations on matters such as whether or not prices may be advertised. In Georgia, advertising of alcoholic beverage prices is prohibited; in California it is permitted.

Foreign investment is also influenced by variations in the amount and degree of support provided by state and local governments. Such support may take many forms, including tax breaks, such as accelerated depreciation or lower income taxes, and provision of electric power or water at a subsidized rate. State and local governments may even establish their own "foreign policies"—for example, by taking formal positions on investment in South Africa.[33]

 *POLITICAL RISK SERVICES*

Country Reports
85 authoritative, independent analyses

More than 1,000 businesses and government agencies depend on one or more of these 50-page reports. Through a worldwide network of 250 proven analysts, the reports cover the 85 countries most important to international business

- Valuable in planning for changes in government and policies
- Up-to-date references for preparing reports and in-house briefings
- Reliable resources to help executives brief themselves for country visits
- Essential in making decisions about new and ongoing projects, developing markets, currency values, political risk insurance, foreign credit risks, capital investments, and corporate security.

Each report follows a standard format:

EXECUTIVE SUMMARY
A succinct presentation of political and economic conditions with 18-month and five-year forecasts.

Fact Sheets — Up-to-date political, economic, demographic, and social data, with rankings of five-year averages relative to all 85 countries covered by the Country Reports, plus a chronological listing of key events pertinent to business over the past 12 months.

BACKGROUND
General Briefing — Pertinent geographic and historical details, territorial and maritime disputes, social and economic conditions, the power structure, and the present business climate.

Political Actors — Profiles of individuals and institutions affecting the business climate, in the context of the current regime, political turmoil, investment and trade restrictions, and economic policies.

18-MONTH FORECASTS OF CONDITIONS FOR INTERNATIONAL BUSINESS
Regime Stability — Probability of regime change, descriptions of likely alternative governments, and a chart of political support and opposition.

Turmoil — Sources of unrest and violence, risks for disruption in the international business climate, and tables recording terrorist incidents, where applicable.

International Investment Restrictions — Current levels of restriction on foreign equity, local participation, taxation, repatriation, and exchange controls, as well as political support, and forecasts for business conditions under the three most likely regimes.

Trade Restrictions — Analysis of support and opposition, current restriction levels, and risk forecasts of payment delays, tariffs, and other trade barriers.

Economic Policies — Current economic data and forecasts of risk in three policy areas: fiscal and monetary expansion, labor costs, and foreign debt.

FIVE-YEAR POLITICAL AND ECONOMIC FORECAST
Five-year projections for GDP growth, inflation, and current account under each of the three most likely regime scenarios. Also, levels of political risk and policies toward international business for each regime scenario.

Note: For clients with extensive multinational concerns, we offer substantial savings with Regional packages and our World Country Report Service. On the reverse side, indicate the countries you need to know about.

*   *   *

Our Country Reports are also available electronically on Data-Star, other online services, and diskette! For more information, call us.

Directors: William D. Coplin
          Michael K. O'Leary

407 University Ave.
Syracuse, NY 13210, USA
Tel: (315) 472-1224
Fax: (315) 472-1235

Political Risk Services
a division of IBC USA (Publications) Inc.

Source: Political Risk Services, a division of IBC USA (Publications) Inc., 407 University Ave., Syracuse, NY 13210.

Managing the Political Environment

Global marketers have a range of options to choose among in order to manage the political environment.

In attempting to manage the political environment, global marketers can choose among a variety of options. These options are not mutually exclusive; one or more of them may prove useful in a given situation. They include strategic alliances, the good-citizen approach, insurance, predetermined domestication, and portfolio management.

The word foreign often has a negative political connotation, especially in high-risk countries. Even in Triad markets like Japan, it is politically more acceptable to enter into a **strategic alliance,** that is, to join forces with a local partner (often referred to as a **joint venture**) to enter a particular market. Another approach is to play the **good-citizen role.** A company that plays a supportive role in a host country and hires that country's citizens to conduct its operations there may eventually be thought of as a domestic company; this has the effect of reducing political risk.

Insurance against political risk is available from some governments as part of their international trade policy. Thus, Eximbank offers U.S. exporters and investors opportunities to insure themselves against political as well as commercial risks. Austrade, an Australian government agency, provides a similar service in its efforts to encourage exports.[34]

Predetermined domestication can be an effective strategy for dealing with political risk. In this approach, which is common in developing countries, a company agrees to turn over its operations in a country to the host-country government according to a specified timetable. This technique often takes the form of a **turnkey operation,** which features training of future managers and workers. The host country gains an ongoing operation with current technology that can be operated efficiently by host-country personnel; the investing company receives a business opportunity with a known time horizon, which enables it to calculate profit flows. Often the company also receives a training and consulting contract that extends beyond the turnover date.

Additionally, **portfolio management**—spreading production, distribution, transportation, research and development, financial activities, and facilities across nations—may be used. This approach, discussed in more detail in Chapter 9, provides a "portfolio" of politically risky nations (ranging from high to low). This approach to political-risk management is similar to an individual investing in more than one stock in order to spread investment risk.

THE LEGAL ENVIRONMENT

Political policies that are formalized become laws, the guidelines for conducting business in a nation.

Government policies are established within the nation's political environment. When those policies are turned into formal rules and regulations, they are known as laws. The legal environment is the set of laws established by a society to govern its members' behavior. When global marketers are assessing the political and legal viability of a potential market, it is important that they consider certain aspects of the legal environment. In this section we discuss each of those aspects, how it affects the marketer, and what the marketer can do to manage it effectively.

International Business Law

No single international business law exists, so a global marketer must be aware of individual agreements among nations.

There is no international business law in a formal sense. Courts, laws, and regulatory agencies are national, not international, in scope. No agreed-upon regulations exist that can be applied to transactions across national boundaries. There are some treaties and agreements among nations that provide frameworks and guidelines for such transactions, but by and large the global marketer must work with different legal systems in different nations. Thus, when a company does business in over 120 countries, as Coca-Cola does, it must contend with over 120 different legal systems. (See Global Dimensions 5.1.)

It would be much easier, of course, if there were a standard legal system that applied to all nations. Current laws vary considerably, sometimes in what seem to be quite silly ways. For example, it is illegal to send soap through the U.S. mail to Paraguay. To establish a standard system nations would have to give up too much political sovereignty. Nevertheless, faced with the reality of economic interdependence, many nations have signed multinational agreements and conventions to give some degree of consistency to the international legal environment. These agreements may be *bilateral*, such as the agreement between the United States and The Netherlands that helps prevent double taxation of firms and personnel doing business in both countries. Or they may be part of a *multilateral* understanding like the Paris Convention, which established a patent-filing process that covers patent applications in eighty nations. If an application is filed in one member nation, that company has priority over companies filing similar applications in all member nations for up to 12 months. (Other multilateral conventions and agreements are illustrated in Exhibit 5.5.)

The laws of the home country usually follow the corporation as it does business in another country.

Another aspect of the international legal environment that can give rise to problems is the **extraterritoriality** of national law: the laws of the home country govern the operations of a corporation, including its subsidiaries or branches located in another country. For example, the U.S. government prevented Caterpillar's French subsidiary from participating in the building of a natural-gas pipeline from the Soviet Union to Western Europe. Although French law permitted the subsidiary to participate in the project, Caterpillar would have violated the U.S. Trading with the Enemy Act.[35]

In addition to preventing companies from engaging in some international transactions, extraterritoriality creates a double legal standard. A practice that is legal in a host country may be illegal in the home country. To take just one example, in Hong Kong it is legal to discuss prices with a competitor; in the United States it is not. Thus, global marketers must be concerned not only about having to operate under more than one legal system but also with the fit between different systems.

Legal Systems.   A major reason for the differences among national legal systems is their legal heritage. Canada, the United Kingdom, the United States,

GLOBAL DIMENSIONS 5.1

The Changing Face of Europe

Perhaps more dramatic than any other political revolution in the history of the world was the rapid political change experienced recently in Eastern Europe. After four decades of communist rule, seven nations in Eastern Europe (often referred to as the Warsaw Pact countries—see Map 5.1 on p. 153) underwent a largely nonviolent political revolution. Even in the USSR, the communist party voted to give up its monopoly on power.

What the outcome of this unprecedented change will be is uncertain. Hardly anyone predicted the changes that have already occurred. Few would dare to predict whether the political changes underway will continue, and if so if they will continue peacefully.

Even more complicated is predicting what the economic results of the political changes will be. Some of the Eastern European countries, such as Hungary and Czechoslovakia, had experimented for some time with mixed economies, permitting some independent economic activity outside the planned economic system. Even the Soviet Union had a flourishing black market for many years, a silent admission that the central planning system was not successful.

But the transition from a basically centrally planned economy with assured employment to one that closely follows free-market principles of supply and demand has been painful. Some early East German emigres to West Germany, for example, returned to East Germany because they decided they did not want to compete in the West German system. Even calls for a strong, Stalin-like leader in the USSR have been heard.

The difficulty seems largely to be that economic change has been painful, with economic progress slow to follow. China, on the other hand, had experienced significant economic change and progress under Deng Li, but it ignored its citizens' needs for an improved standard of living (which is in part delivered through the political process). In 1989, calls for political change were met with strong force against the student-led uprising.

Each of these crises provide evidence of the close interconnection between politics and economics. Instability is inevitable if a nation does not manage to keep both in balance with one another.

Sources: Nesha Starcevic, "Hardships Lie Ahead in Europe," *St. Louis Post-Dispatch*, February 11, 1990, pp. D1–D2; and "Communism in Crisis," *The Economist*, July 1, 1989, p. 11.

and some other nations have legal systems based on **common law,** which is an outgrowth of English law. **Code law,** which is found in many non-English-speaking nations, is based on Roman law. Islamic law is based on a different set of codes entirely. To further complicate matters, many countries have more than one set of laws. In the United States, for example, laws may be commercial,

Berne Convention

The Berne Convention created a union of nations in 1886 to protect literary and artistic works. Seventy-four nations are members of the union, including most European countries and some Asian, African, and Latin American nations. The principal nonmembers are the United States, USSR, and China.

The convention stipulates:

1. A work whose country of origin is in the union receives the same protection by other union members as is conferred on works of that country's nationals.

2. The enjoyment of protection in countries other than the country of origin is automatic and subject to no registration formalities.

3. The protection of an author's work does not rest upon whether it is protected in his home country.

The Berne Convention is administered by the World Intellectual Property Organization (WIPO) in Geneva, a specialized agency of the union.

Universal Copyright Convention (UCC)

The United Nations Education and Social Counsel (UNESCO) administers this major copyright convention, established in 1952. The purpose of the convention is to link countries with high levels of copyright protection, from the Berne Convention, with those of limited protection, as well as to secure the membership of the United States in an international copyright system. The UCC seeks to protect the rights of authors of literary, scientific, and artistic works. UCC member nations are required to accord the same protection to foreign works as to their own.

International Convention for the Protection of Performers, Producers of Phonograms, and Broadcasting Organizations (Rome Convention)

This convention originated in 1964 and is jointly administered by the International Labour Organization (ILO), UNESCO, and WIPO. Only 23 nations have joined; Germany and the United Kingdom are its leading members. This convention, like the Berne and UCC conventions, requires the same protection for foreign as for national works. The convention seeks to protect performances, sound recordings, and broadcasts, but not films, which are protected by the Berne and UCC conventions.

Convention for the Protection of Producers of Phonograms against Unauthorized Duplication of their Phonograms (Geneva Convention)

Adopted by an international meeting in 1974 in Geneva, there are 36 member nations. Three important nations who signed this convention, but not the Rome Convention, are France, Japan, and the United States. This convention seeks to limit record piracy, that is, duplicating records without permission. The convention requires that member nations protect sound-recording producers from other member nations against duplication and importation for distribution to the public. As with the Rome Convention, if the nation's domestic law prescribes formalities prior to protection, these are fulfilled if all authorized duplicates issued to the public bear the "P" notice.

(Continued)

EXHIBIT 5.5 *(Continued)*

Convention Relating to the Distribution of Program-carrying Signals Transmitted by Satellite (Satellite Convention)

This convention was established at Brussels in 1974 and is administrated jointly by UNESCO and WIPO. Seven nations are members. The convention seeks to prevent satellite piracy or the transmission and distribution of "poached signals" to unlicensed audiences. Member states are to prevent unauthorized distribution of a signal in their territory.

Multilateral Convention for Avoidance of Double Taxation of Copyright Royalties (Madrid Convention)

Established in 1979, only 4 states have signed this convention. It does not require compliance with certain minimum standards of protection; rather, it prescribes a model bilateral agreement for member nations to prevent double taxation.

Hague Agreement Concerning International Deposit of Industrial Rights

This convention enables an international application for design protection to be regarded as the equivalent of a national application. Membership is restricted to Paris Convention members. The agreement is effected by deposit of a sample registered at WIPO by a national of a member state. That deposit is then regarded by all member nations as if the formalities of the domestic laws of those nations had been met.

Paris Convention for Protection of Industrial Property

The basic principle is national treatment for patents and trademarks for all member nations. The principal advantage of the convention is that it allows persons who have sought protection (registration) in one member nation priority in another member nation for six months for trademarks and one year for patents.

Nice Agreement Concerning the International Classification of Goods and Services for the Registration of Marks

This provides a system of common classification of goods and services to use in the registration of trademarks. It does not bind member nations who may use it, or not, as they wish.

Trademark Registration Treaty

With only five members, this treaty provides for the international registration of trademarks.

Patent Co-operation Treaty (PCT)

This treaty is an agreement to provide for international cooperation in patent law and, especially, procedures to obtain patent protection. It was established in Washington, D.C., in 1970 and has 32 members, including the United States, USSR, United Kingdom, and France. It is administered by the WIPO.

Principal features include:

(Continued)

EXHIBIT 5.5 *(Continued)*

1.   An application filed in one's national patent office will extend to as many PCT countries as the applicant may designate.

2.   The application is researched and findings are sent to each designated national patent office.

The PCT thus facilitates examination of a patent in a national office, although it does not prescribe what each nation's substantive patent law should be.

International Patent Classification (Strasbourg Agreement)

This agreement was established in 1971 and has 27 member nations. It seeks to have a universal system of patent classifications and certificates. This is aimed not at the patent law of a nation, but to facilitate its administration.

Sources: S. Ricketson, *The Law of Intellectual Property*, Law Book Company, 1984; and J. Lahore, *Intellectual Property Law in Australia* (Sydney: Butterworths, 1977).

civil, or criminal. In most other common-law countries such distinctions are not made.

Under common law, precedent is critical in resolving any given issue. In reaching a decision, the court will examine existing laws and regulations, customary procedures, and previous cases dealing with similar issues. Under code law, in contrast, formal laws spell out precisely what constitutes proper behavior, although sometimes some interpretation is required.

Different legal systems are based on different principles, which leads to a large variety of laws and interpretations.

An example of the potential impact of these differences can be seen in the case of rights to brand names. Under common law, prior use is the most significant determinant in deciding who has the right to use a specific brand name. But under code law whoever registers a brand name first controls the rights to it. Thus, in a code-law country a company that uses a brand name first does not necessarily have the legal right to continue doing so. Anyone could register the same name. A company that wants to enter a market in a code-law country might have to purchase the rights to its "own" brand name or even operate under a different brand name.

Even the terms under which parties to a contract can be released through an "act of God" differ considerably in different legal systems.[36] This distinction is important, because an "act of God" normally releases a party from having to fulfill the terms of a contract. Thus, a labor strike might be viewed as an act of God in some countries but not in others, where strikes are considerably more predictable and manageable. In view of such differences, it is increasingly important to employ international legal counsel in making global marketing decisions.

Deregulation is growing throughout the world, but governments still oversee competition to varying degrees.

Regulation of Competition.   Just as governments differ in degree of market orientation, so too do they differ in the extent to which they regulate competition. The Reagan administration, acting through the U.S. Department of Justice and the Federal Trade Commission, relaxed antitrust rules and thereby made possible a series of mergers and acquisitions that was unparalleled in U.S. eco-

MAP 5.1
CENTRAL AMERICA

The five nations of Central America throughout the 1980s have been politically unstable to some degree. Guatemala, El Salvador, Honduras, Nicaragua, and Panama (militarily important because of the Panama Canal) have experienced low economic growth, warfare, and political unrest that could continue throughout the 1990s.

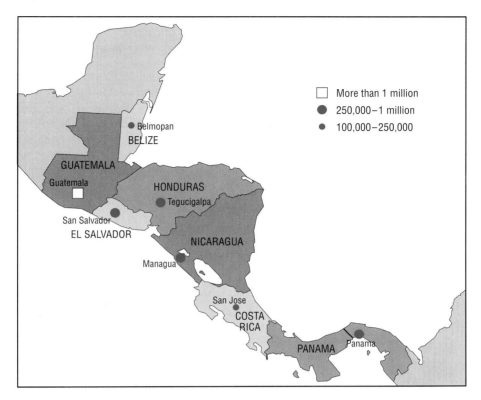

nomic history. At least some of this change was intended to permit U.S.-based companies to enter strategic alliances with overseas companies that would help them become more competitive in the world marketplace.*

This shift in the legal environment, part of the trend toward **deregulation,** has occurred in most of the Triad markets. It is reflected in Spain's and England's privatization programs, as well as in China's special industrial zones.[37] Deregulation results in increased market opportunities, but also in increased competition. Large corporations are often better equipped to move quickly into recently deregulated markets. Such opportunities, for example, are behind the increase in mergers, acquisitions, and joint ventures in the European airline industry. Executives there, anticipating deregulation, became very active attempting to make their airlines bigger in order to be more competitive as markets begin to open. Small and medium-sized companies may find niche opportunities, and often they can successfully form a joint venture or strategic alliance. Domestic companies within the deregulated market find that competition becomes very

---

*A strict antitrust policy would mean that U.S. firms were not given the same freedom as their foreign-based competitors to make international acquisitions and strategic alliances.

aggressive very quickly. They must adjust, possibly through joint ventures with foreign companies, in order to survive.

Dumping products in another country has significant political impact, because it affects competition.

Dumping, or selling products in foreign markets below cost or below domestic prices, is another economic activity that can give rise to international legal problems. Dumping is similar to **predatory pricing,** which has long been outlawed by U.S. antitrust legislation. Both practices are aimed at capturing market share, injuring competitors, and in the long run giving the company a high degree of market control. Companies ranging from Japanese computer-chip manufacturers to U.S. agricultural concerns have been charged with dumping products into foreign markets.[38] Eastern European shipping lines, for example, charge very low prices in order to bring foreign currencies into Eastern Europe. Western competitors have lost sales, and they could bring a charge of dumping in order to gain protection against underpricing. Charging competitors with dumping can also serve as a means of gaining information about them. The foreign competitor has to provide data on costs and pricing in order to prove that dumping did not occur.

It is not difficult to bring charges before a commission that hears dumping cases, such as the U.S. Treasury Department, but it is often difficult to prove such charges. The definition of cost (such as marginal versus average cost) may be central to the case.[39] Thus, accusations often focus on the difference between the price on the imported good and its price in the home market.

A piece of legislation that deserves special attention because of its potential impact on the competitiveness of U.S. firms in world markets is the Foreign Corrupt Practices Act (FCPA). This act, passed in 1977, forbids bribery of foreign public officials, allows payments for services (known as "grease," because it lubricates the business transaction), and stipulates criminal penalties for violators. Critics of the act charge that it is unclear and ambiguous. They also claim that the act places restrictions on U.S. corporations that are not faced by their foreign competitors. The act's supporters point out that international bribery is not only immoral but a bad business practice in the long run. At this writing, the FCPA has received so much criticism that several proposals for revision are before Congress.[40]

More recently, the U.S. has turned again to increased regulation of foreign trade. The "Super 301" law was passed to provide the threat of retaliatory import taxes of 100 percent. The intent was to try to force foreign nations to drop their "unfair trade barriers" against U.S. firms, aiding exports.

Protecting industrial property rights is a major concern for today's global marketers. They are the ultimate asset of most organizations.

Protection of Property.   Still another concern of global marketers is the protection of **industrial property rights,** or corporate assets that have the potential to generate funds, such as brand names, patents, trademarks, and technology. The loss of the trademark *Coca-Cola*, for example, would be devastating to the Coca-Cola Company's sales and profits, because then any soft-drink maker could bottle a sweet, brown carbonated beverage under the Coca-Cola name. No uniform international legal code addresses this issue, although there are several multinational agreements in this area.

Differences between common-law and code-law approaches to such rights also present problems for prospective marketers. For example, U.S. law protects patent holders against violation of process patents. But it does not apply to foreign companies that pirate those processes, even when the product ends up in the U.S. market.[41]

A major problem related to the protection of industrial property rights is **counterfeiting,** the intentional production or sale of a product under a brand name or trademark without the authorization of the holder of that name or trademark. It is difficult to estimate total corporate losses due to counterfeiting, but one source has calculated such losses at over $60 billion per year.[42] Counterfeiting causes not only the direct loss of sales but also longer-term losses that may be even more serious. For example, counterfeit products usually are of inferior quality, and some such products may even be harmful to their users; examples include fake birth-control pills and dangerous toys.[43] When these items cease to function properly or cause injury or other problems for their users, the negative image is transferred to the corporation whose product, technology, or brand name was used in an unauthorized manner. In such situations the manufacturer may have to change details of product design or construction. In other instances a more tightly controlled distribution system must be employed.

Even when conventions and agreements exist, protection of industrial property rights is difficult and expensive. In addition to legal action, an option available to large companies is retaliation. This may take the form of saturating the market with authentic goods at low prices or opening up outlets near the offender. Cartier Jewelers of Paris was able to retaliate against a Mexico City retailer that was selling other manufacturers' products under the Cartier name.[44]

Regulation of the Marketing Mix

The laws of a nation affect each element of the marketing mix: product; place, or distribution; promotion; and price.

Each element of the marketing mix is subject to legal regulation; detailed discussions of specific forms of regulation can be found in Chapters 12–16. Here we present an overview of the impact of the legal environment on each of those elements. We also discuss the combination of the various elements into an optimal mix in order to further illustrate the challenges facing global marketers.

Product. Legal systems vary considerably in their treatment of product issues. One of the most important areas in which such variations occur is product liability. The strict product-liability laws found in the United States are often a source of surprise and alarm to global marketers.[45] For example, regulations established by the Consumer Product Safety Commission set limits on the portrayal of all-terrain vehicles in use and prohibit advertising directed toward young children. When put in place, these regulations had a direct and negative impact on sales. Even similar product-use situations may be subject to different product-liability interpretations. Thus, theme-park rides that are considered safe in Queensland, Australia, are not subject to the same level of crowd control as similar rides in theme parks in Texas. By U.S. standards, such rides may be dangerous. Eliminating the product-liability hazard in this case would require more equipment and personnel, which would increase costs and affect profits.

Product-safety laws also vary from one nation to another. When sales of the pesticide DDT were banned in the United States for safety reasons, such sales continued to be legal in most other parts of the world. U.S. manufacturers of DDT found themselves unable to sell the product in their own country, but they were able to exploit a ready export market. Ironically, as U.S. food imports increase, more contaminated produce is purchased in stores in the United States because of the relatively relaxed controls on pesticide use in exporting countries.[46]

Different legal systems also regulate products differently from the standpoint of the product's impact upon the environment. Acceptable levels of air pollution, for instance, are defined differently in India, Germany, and the United States. India has decided to accept higher levels of pollution in order to facilitate production and economic development. The high levels of air pollution in Germany can be traced both to polluted air drifting across the border from France and to the European Community's inability to agree on pollution-control standards for automobiles.

Packaging and labeling are also subject to different rules and regulations. The packaging unit (such as quarts versus liters), requirements for listing ingredients, and the manner in which the package must be labeled are among the factors that must be considered in this regard. To give just one example, an Italian court ruled that a soft-drink manufacturer could not list ingredients on the bottle cap. The manufacturer had to modify its bottling procedures in order to print the ingredients on the bottle itself.[47] Complying with different packaging and labeling standards caused the company to lose the advantages gained from economies of scale.

Place. Distribution channels and the legality of agreements between manufacturers and distributors can differ considerably under different legal systems. For example, **tying contracts** specify that a retailer must buy all of a manufacturer's products in order to buy one particular product line (thereby "tying" the distributor to the manufacturer). Although they are illegal in the United States, in other countries tying contracts not only are legal but may signify the existence of a long-term relationship. Similarly, the establishment of exclusive territories for intermediaries is prohibited by antitrust laws in the United States. In contrast, it is an accepted practice in Europe and Latin America.

The legal environment also affects the distribution channels available to global marketers. Door-to-door selling, for example, is prohibited in France. In Australia, a customer can send liquor anywhere in the nation via a system similar to that used by florists in the United States, but in the United States most states do not allow the sale of liquor in that manner. In Saudi Arabia, global marketers must cope with the fact that official religious holidays close most wholesalers and retailers for about ten weeks each year!

Promotion. Promotion is a heavily regulated element of the marketing mix in many nations. Most societies attempt to protect their members against deceptive, misleading, or fraudulent marketing practices. In addition, every society attempts to regulate advertising from the standpoint of propriety and taste. Of course, all of these issues are defined quite differently in different societies. For example, in highly traditional religious societies, such as Saudi Arabia and India, nudity in advertising would be illegal, whereas in Holland it is commonplace. In Scandinavia, advertising directed toward children is prohibited; such advertising is permitted in the United States. Since promotion is the most visible element of the marketing mix, global marketers who are planning promotional campaigns must be particularly sensitive to these and other differences in the legal environment with respect to promotion.

Price. The pricing of products, especially "essential" products such as basic foods, is tightly controlled in many countries. In nations with highly inflationary economies, such as Brazil and Argentina, it is common to find price controls on food and beverage products. American antitrust laws limit marketers' discretion in setting prices for intermediaries. Some countries, such as Ghana, control the manufacturer's profit margin, which has the effect of controlling the price paid by the consumer. Value-added, import, and excise taxes have an even greater influence on retail prices. So do exchange controls, which selectively alter the rate at which currencies are exchanged, in order to encourage or discourage trade in particular products.

Profit Regulation

Companies are subject to regulation as to the amount of profit they can make.

At one time or another almost every nation has engaged in some form of profit control. In the United States, during the energy crisis of the late 1970s, oil companies were investigated and fined for making profits that were "too high." Other nations control profit levels through administered prices or by setting maximum profit margins.

Of equal concern to global marketers is the amount of profit that can be transferred from a subsidiary to the parent company. Companies frequently are interested in remitting as high a level of profit as possible, to be reinvested or issued to stockholders as dividends. On the other hand, national governments are interested in keeping profits in the country, in order to increase their tax revenues. Moreover, when profits are reinvested in the host country they help create more jobs.

To deal with this dilemma, many corporations employ **transfer pricing**— they set internal prices for the transfer of products, technologies, or services to their subsidiaries. If transfer prices are set artificially high, the effect is to transfer extra profits to the parent company. For example, a company based in Switzerland could charge its Brazilian subsidiary $2,000 for a part for which it charges other subsidiaries $1,500. In effect, an extra $500 of what would otherwise have been recorded as profit in Brazil has been transferred to the Swiss parent company.

Taxes

Both corporate and individual tax laws affect global marketing. Adjusting executive salaries to allow for higher taxes in host countries or to compensate for double taxation increases the costs of employing home-country personnel in foreign countries up to 300 percent.

Corporate tax rates influence not only personnel and pricing decisions but even location and investment decisions. For example, the Bahamas and the Channel Islands are often used as "tax havens" because they have low corporate tax rates. Companies establish subsidiaries in such countries and use transfer pricing to remit as much profit as they can to the low-tax-rate subsidiary. In this way they maximize their overall profits. Of course, governments attempt to tax these funds.

The interconnectedness of tax systems is illustrated by the impact of the recent tax reforms in the United States. The new, lower tax rates were expected to result in an increase in foreign investment in the United States, as well as an increase in the number of foreign managers and professionals working there.[48] This policy sparked debates in many nations about whether they should change their own tax structures in order to halt the outflow of capital and talent from those nations to the United States.

Governments may use tax laws to either encourage or discourage domestic companies from engaging in foreign trade. The U.S. government in effect applies lower tax rates to profits generated through exports by permitting the creation of **foreign sales companies (FSCs)**. These are corporations that are not located in a U.S. Customs Zone. An FSC is allowed to export products and pay little or no income on those sales, thereby increasing its profits considerably. This sounds like a strong export-support program; however, interested firms must meet so many qualifications that export levels are not as high as might be expected under such a program.[49]

Tariffs are an example of taxation used to discourage trade, because they either compensate for subsidies by foreign governments or protect domestic industries by raising import prices to noncompetitive levels.[50] Another form of tax disincentive is taxing foreign-earned income or profits at a higher rate than domestically earned income, on the premise that foreign companies should contribute something extra to the host country's economy. The impact of such policies is to discourage foreign investment as well as to raise prices for consumers.

The Court System

Just as there is no international business law, there is no international court system. However, the World Court, located in The Hague in The Netherlands, provides a forum in which nations can air their political grievances. And a

No international court system deals with business disputes, but the European Community court is increasingly serving that role across the EC.

European Community court in Luxembourg tries to apply uniform standards to all members of the European Community. Member nations now follow the European Community court's interpretations in applying national law. This court thus is beginning to function as a supreme court for the European Community. In addition, the European Community continues to work on directives that will standardize laws across the member nations.

Such situations are unusual, however. More commonly, the problems caused by the lack of an international legal system are confounded by the lack of courts to hear international cases. Companies facing international legal action encounter difficulties similar to those faced by Union Carbide after the tragic chemical leak at its plant in Bhopal, India. The company must defend itself against lawsuits related to the loss of over 2,000 lives as a result of the accident. The plaintiffs prefer to bring these suits in U.S. courts, where penalties and fines are much stiffer than in India.

Host-country courts often exhibit bias against foreign companies, particularly in countries where nationalism is running high or there is a history of exploitation by multinational corporations. A company that loses a case in a host-country court has little recourse. About all it can do is attempt to influence intergovernmental relations in the hope of getting the ruling overturned. Only large corporations with ample resources are in a position to exercise such influence.

Managing the Legal Environment

Personal relationships as well as contractual ones are important to the proper management of the legal environment.

Like other environments that affect global marketers, the legal environment is best managed by understanding the total environment in which the company will operate and choosing a business partner that can help minimize the risks of operating in that environment. However, the ways in which companies formalize their partnerships vary greatly and require sensitivity to cultural as well as legal differences. Japanese firms, in particular, place a great deal of emphasis on personal trust between partners. Americans, on the other hand, tend to rely on formal contracts.[51] The use of formal contracts means that business can be conducted much more quickly, but it also leads to more disputes and lawsuits.

When contracts are used, global marketers must make sure a **jurisdictional clause**—a formal statement of which nation's laws will apply—is included. If no jurisdiction is specified, each party to a suit will insist that it be heard in its home-country court system, where it can expect more favorable treatment. When clear jurisdictional clauses are lacking, courts usually decide jurisdictional disputes on the basis of where the contract was entered into or where the activity in question occurred.

When disputes arise, a lawsuit should be the last option considered. Businesspeople in many nations believe that going to court is a bad business practice. A company should undertake good-faith negotiations before resorting to legal action. Not infrequently, contractual disagreements can be resolved by improving communication between the parties or increasing mutual understanding of the legal and cultural environments. Some problems are caused by differences

EXHIBIT 5.6
INTERNATIONAL
ARBITRATION
RESOURCES

For the global company
following the preferred
dispute-resolution
process of negotiate-ar-
bitrate-litigate, several international arbitration resources exist.

International Chamber of Commerce (ICC)

The International Chamber of Commerce counsels and arbitrates in Paris. It is controlled by an Administrative Commission constituted by one member of each country whose business organizations are affiliated with the ICC. The commission attempts to counsel a resolution to disputes after a hearing. If that fails, the matter is referred for arbitration to the Court of Arbitration, chosen by the parties and the ICC.

American Arbitration Association (AAA)

The American Arbitration Association enables foreign businesses to use arbitration in the United States and avoid the complex and costly U.S. legal system. An arbitrator may make an award that seems just and equitable under the AAA rules. The association appoints the arbitrator, giving consideration to the parties' preferences and objections.

Geneva Conventions on Arbitration

The Geneva Protocol (1923) provides that member nations recognize the validity of arbitration agreements made between parties who are under the jurisdiction of the member nations, irrespective of where the agreement was executed.

The Geneva Convention (1927) provides that member nations recognize as binding and enforce under the rules an arbitration award made under an agreement covered by the Geneva Protocol.

New York Convention

The New York Convention, created in 1958 by the United Nations Conference on International Arbitration, has no requirement of reciprocity. This means a member nation may apply the convention to awards made in the territory of another member nation, and not its own. However, each member nation must refer parties to a written arbitration agreement. Important member nations include the United States, Germany, France, Japan, United Kingdom, and USSR.

UNCITRAL Arbitration Rules

These rules were published by the United Nations Committee on International Trade Law in 1976. They are a model for international arbitration, but are not embodied in a convention.

Convention on Settlement of Investment Disputes

This convention provides for the formation of a Center for Settlement of Investment Disputes at the principal office of the Bank of Washington, to settle investment disputes between member nations.

Sources: A. Walton and M. Vitoria, *Russell on Arbitration*, 20th ed. (London: Stevens E. Sons, 1982); and E. A. Marshall, *The Law of Arbitration*, 3rd. ed. (London: Sweet and Maxwell, 1983).

as simple as the way a date is written—for example, 3/5/88 is March 5, 1988, in the United States but May 3, 1988, in France.

If improved communication and negotiations fail, the next step in managing international legal disputes should be arbitration. Exhibit 5.6 lists some of the forms of international arbitration that can be pursued. Whether it is voluntary or binding, arbitration involves bringing the dispute before an informed, neutral party to help resolve differences of opinion. Today international contracts frequently include an arbitration clause as well as a jurisdictional clause.

If all attempts to resolve a dispute fail, litigation may be necessary. The negative social implications of court action, the possibly unfavorable view of foreign companies by home-country courts, and the problem of jurisdiction all mean that international court action is expensive, time-consuming, and even less predictable than domestic litigation. These difficulties, combined with the possibility of generating a negative public image, mean that international disputes should be settled out of court if at all possible.

SUMMARY

As their economic interdependence increases, nations tend to move apart politically. Governments need to promote economic cooperation and integration, but they do not wish to give up their political sovereignty. This dilemma results in a constantly changing political environment.

For the global marketer, the most important dimension of the political environment is the stability of a nation's political system. Also significant is its form of government, since various forms of government differ in the extent to which they permit political participation by the general population. In addition, political parties are important, because they channel public opinion into the formulation of governmental policies and laws.

Special-interest groups, such as environmentalists, may affect the attractiveness of particular markets. Lobbyists also affect international trade, for example, by demanding higher tariffs on imported goods. Powerful organizations and individuals can also influence the global marketing environment.

Intergovernmental relations influence the ease with which business can be conducted between citizens of different nations. The policies and practices of the government that is currently in power must also be considered in assessing the political environment of a foreign market. The government's beliefs about the appropriate role of foreign business have a significant effect on market opportunities.

Governments play a variety of economic roles. In all societies the government plays a regulatory role. In centrally planned economies, the government regulates almost all economic activities; in market-oriented economies, it regulates by defining the rules of competition. Governments are also buyers and suppliers of goods and services, and in some societies the government may enter into partnership with business and industry.

A nation's international trade policy is the set of laws and rules that regulate the flow of goods and services across its boundaries. Nationalism, or the belief that a nation should have complete control over its own affairs, often leads to protectionist trade policies, whose effect is to raise the prices of imported goods. However, all nations control exports and imports to some degree. Often specific products and technologies are controlled, particularly products that might affect national security.

A nation's investment policy consists of all the laws and regulations that govern private participation in the ownership of businesses and other organizations in that nation. Governments may encourage foreign investment in an attempt to spur domestic economic growth, or discourage such investment out of fear of control of the economy by foreign investors.

In attempting to manage the political environment, global marketers can choose among several approaches. These include forming a strategic alliance (joining forces with a local partner); the good-citizen approach (playing a supportive role in the host country); insurance; predetermined domestication, in which the company agrees to turn over its operations to the host-country government according to a specified timetable; and portfolio management.

The legal environment is the set of laws established by a society to govern its members' behavior. There is no international business law, and the laws of the home country govern the operations of a corporation in other countries. At the same time, a corporation's foreign subsidiaries and branches must conform to the laws of the host country, which may differ considerably from those of the home country.

Governments differ in the extent to which they regulate competition. In the Triad markets there has been a trend toward deregulation in recent years. Issues related to the regulation of competition include dumping, or selling products in foreign markets below cost or below domestic prices, and violations of industrial property rights. A major problem with respect to property protection is counterfeiting, or the intentional production or sale of a product under a brand name or trademark without the authorization of the owner of that name or trademark.

The legal environment also affects the marketing mix. For example, legal systems vary considerably in their treatment of product issues, notably product liability. The legality of agreements between manufacturers can also differ under different legal systems. In many nations promotion is heavily regulated, and the same is true of pricing, especially for "essential" products.

Governments sometimes control the level of profit that can be earned or the amount of profit that can be transferred from a subsidiary to the parent company. In addition, governments may use tax laws to either encourage or discourage domestic companies from engaging in foreign trade.

The legal environment is best managed by understanding the total environment in which the company will operate and choosing a business partner that can help minimize the risks of operating in that environment. When contracts are used, the global marketer must make sure that a jurisdictional clause is included. If a dispute does arise, a lawsuit should be the last option considered.

DISCUSSION QUESTIONS

1. Describe a current trend in global trade that affects a nation's ability to control its own economy.

2. What basic elements influence the political stability and structure of a government? How do they affect marketers?

3. What roles does a government play in an economy? Give two examples of such roles.

4. Should a federal government have an international trade, export-import, or investment policy, or should these issues be left to market forces? Why?

5. Why is it important for a company to assess the degree of political stability in a potential market?

6. What options does a firm have in trying to manage the political environment?

7. Briefly describe the impact on global marketers of the absence of a body of international law.

8. What are the basic differences between common and code law? What impact do these differences have on global marketing?

9. What is dumping, and why is it controversial?

10. Which is subject to more regulation, domestic or global marketing? Why?

CASE

EASTERN EUROPE: A REAL OPPORTUNITY?

Hellen Beatty knew that Eastern Europe was in political turmoil. More specifically, she was concerned about the possibility of political instability in Hungary, where her firm was interested in doing business. Hellen was vice-president of strategic planning for a medium-sized firm based in Baton Rouge, Louisiana. Her company sold computer control software to the chemical processing industry, including pharmaceutical companies. She knew that the chemical and pharmaceutical industries were among the healthiest in Hungary and among those that showed the greatest long-run potential. The products she could offer to Hungarians would permit stronger quality control, and help minimize waste in the production process.

The political and economic changes that had happened throughout Eastern Europe since late 1989 had caught her company by surprise. The company's usual international program would include a slow, careful analysis of the market, and if potential were indicated, the company would usually enter the market through exporting. They would sell the products to a reseller in that nation after having customized them to be technically appropriate for the market. Rarely did the company become more directly involved or assume greater risk.

But the political, economic, and cultural changes she observed, and the speed with which they occurred—not to mention the speed with which competitors were entering the Hungarian market (several had formed joint ventures in the past year)—led Hellen to believe it might be time to consider a new strategy for her company. Basically, her concern was that their traditional approach to international marketing might be too little, too late.

She was concerned, however, about how stable the political situation was in Hungary. If the changes that had occurred were to be rolled back, the market opportunity might disappear and a company rushing into the market would be at tremendous risk of losing everything. On the other hand, to be early into a fast-changing, and potentially profitable market would be desirable. And she hoped that as tensions between Western and Eastern European countries decreased, money that was once spent on defense would be spent on production of industrial and consumer products—which would benefit the industries she sold to. Further, as COMECON became less important, Hungary would be able to import more U.S.-based products, which had once been prohibited.

Hellen shared her thoughts with the company president, and was asked to prepare an analysis that would help the company determine whether to pursue the Hungarian market in a more aggressive manner than usual.

Case Issues

1. What are the major variables that should be included in such an analysis?

2. What is the current state of the political environment in Hungary, and what would your recommendation be as to pursuing that market?

NOTES

1. For further discussion of this point see Peter Drucker, *Managing in Turbulent Times* (London: Pan Books, 1981), pp. 159–165.

2. "Coup Reported in African Nation of Burkina Faso," *Atlanta Journal and Constitution*, October 16, 1987, p. 17; and S. R. Weisman, "Sri Lanka—A Nation Disintegrates," *New York Times Magazine*, December 13, 1987, pp. 34–93.

3. R. Cohen, "Struggling Back," *Wall Street Journal*, September 12, 1986, pp. 1–26.

4. F. Kempe, "Li, Conservative Chinese Official, to Meet Schultz," *Wall Street Journal*, March 2, 1987, p. 1.

5. E. Helguera, "A Prisoner of the Past," *Forbes*, November 3, 1986, pp. 132–136.

6. For a complete discussion of the difficulties of managing a partial free-enterprise system under a socialist form of government, see "The Soviets Are Now in a Very Romantic Period," *Forbes*, December 14, 1987, pp. 62–73.

7. For a more complete discussion of how parties and interest groups combine to influence political and economic policy in Japan, see S. Chira, "The Fragmented Factions That Make Policy in Japan," *New York Times*, April 26, 1987, p. F6, and R. Matthews, "Japanese Happy to Have Leaders Picked for Them," *Atlanta Journal and Constitution*, November 1, 1987, p. A19.

8. "Suddenly, a Deathwatch on the Rhine," *Business Week*, November 14, 1986, p. 52.

9. "Out of Touch," *Wall Street Journal*, April 1, 1986, p. 1; and "U.S. Business Needs More Muscle in Japan," *Business Week*, November 13, 1989, p. 186.

10. "Powerful Bloc," *Wall Street Journal*, December 4, 1986, p. 1; and "Rebel with a Cause," *Forbes*, March 23, 1987, p. 23.

11. R. D. Pagan, Jr., "The Nestlé Boycott: Implications for Strategic Business Planning," *Journal of Business Strategy*, Spring 1986, pp. 12–23.

12. IMF, *Direction of Trade Statistics* (Washington, D.C., 1987), pp. 88–90, 130.

13. For more information about this political and economic battle, see P. Norman, "EC Ministers Fail to Reach Sanctions Pact," *Wall Street Journal*, September 16, 1986, pp. 1–33; "How Not to Fight Sanctions," *Fortune*, October 27, 1986, pp. 9–10; R. Thurow, "Sanctions Force South Africa to Rely on Itself to Achieve Economic Growth," *Wall Street Journal*, September 18, 1986, p. 36; and P. Brimelow, "Why South Africa Shrugs at Sanctions," *Forbes*, March 9, 1987, pp. 101–104.

14. "Policies—White House '89," *Asiaweek*, February 19, 1988, p. 45.

15. "Up Against the Wall in East Berlin," *Business Week*, November 20, 1989, pp. 48–49; and "Reunification? East German Industry Says 'Not so Fast,'" *Business Week*, December 29, 1989, pp. 66–67.

16. E. Thomas, "Is America in Decline?," *Newsweek* (International ed.), February 23, 1988, p. 103; and "Different Drummers," *Newsweek* (International ed.), February 23, 1988, p. 106.

17. "Jordan Signs Deal to Buy Mirage 2000s, Update F-1s," *Jane's Defense Weekly*, February 13, 1988, p. 239.

18. International Labor Office, *Yearbook of Labour Statistics, 1984* (Geneva, 1985), pp. 828–830.

19. OECD, *OECD Observer*, February–March 1988, p. 6.

20. "Bureaucratic Battle," *Wall Street Journal*, February 24, 1987, pp. 1, 24.

21. J. W. Kennedy, "Risk Assessment for U.S. Affiliates Based in Less Developed Countries," *Columbia Journal of World Business*, Summer 1984, pp. 76–79; and P. Baker, "You're the Best Judge of Foreign Risks," *Harvard Business Review*, March–April, 1983, pp. 157–165.

22. "The Computers That Got Away," *Fortune*, November 10, 1986, p. 14.

23. P. D. Grub, "Outlook for International Business in Asia: Economic Conditions and Prospects," in P. D. Grub et al., eds., *East Asia: Dimensions of International Business* (Englewood Cliffs, N.J.: Prentice Hall International, 1982), pp. 248–251.

24. J. E. Yang, "House Approves Bill to Aid Ex-Im Bank in Boosting Sales of U.S. Goods Abroad," *Wall Street Journal*, September 23, 1986, p. 64.

25. R. J. McLean, *Exploiting Opportunities in the Pacific Basin: Survey Results*, Monograph no. M82 (Committee for Economic Development of Australia—Strategic Issues Forum, June 1986).

26. "A Yardstick for Protection," *Economist*, March 5, 1988, p. 77.

27. "U.S. Will Curtail Some Trade Benefits to Taiwan, South Korea, Brazil, Mexico," *Atlanta Journal*, January 3, 1987, p. D6.

28. "Services Also Feel Sting of Global Barriers," *Marketing News*, February 13, 1987, p. 13.

29. "Malaysia Revises Rules on Foreign Investment," *Wall Street Journal*, October 1, 1986, p. 37.

30. "Selling Capitalization," *Wall Street Journal*, November 5, 1986, p. 1.

31. C. L. Suzman, "What Are the Trends for Foreign Direct Investment in the Southeast?," *Economic Review* (Federal Reserve Bank of Atlanta), January 1986, pp. 42–47.

32. For a more complete discussion of alternative techniques and models, see D. Lamont, "Risk in World Markets: The Use of International Business Decision Rule #1 to Assess Country Risk," *Proceedings*, *Academy of International Business*, Fall 1982, pp. 8–15; A. Desta, "Assessing Political Risk in Less Developed Countries," *Journal of Business Strategy*, Spring

1985, pp. 40–53; and C. W. Hofer and T. P. Haller, "Globescan: A Way to Better International Risk Assessment," *Journal of Business Strategy*, Fall 1980, pp. 41–45.

33.   P. Spiro, "Get State and Cities off Foreign-Policy Stage," *Wall Street Journal*, September 24, 1986, p. 32.

34.   "EFIC Gives Support in Four Ways," *Overseas Trading*, April 1986, p. 15.

35.   "When Political Masters Fall Out, Whom Does Business Obey?," *The Economist*, July 10, 1982, pp. 63–64.

36.   W. Chan Kim and R. A. Mauborgne, "Cross-Cultural Strategies," *Journal of Business Strategy*, Spring 1987, pp. 33–35.

37.   L. Wentz, "Big Bang Set to Explode," *Advertising Age*, October 13, 1986, p. 62; and Shawn Tully, "Europe Goes Wild Over Privatization," *Fortune*, March 2, 1987, pp. 68–70.

38.   D. Bunnell, "Fighting PC Protectionism," *PC World*, December 1986, pp. 17–26; and Geraldine Brooks, "Australia Seethes at U.S. Farm Subsidies," *Wall Street Journal*, August 14, 1986, p. 20.

39.   B. Uttal, "How Chipmakers Can Survive," *Fortune*, April 13, 1987, p. 92.

40.   See L. Seagull, "Ethical Codes in Industry: Dealing with the FCPA and with Ambiguity," paper presented at the Winter American Marketing Association Conference, 1988; D. Fanning, "Am I My Brother's Keeper?," *Forbes*, May 4, 1987, p. 66; T. Goldwasser, "Don't Make Foreign Bribery by U.S. Firms Easier," *Wall Street Journal*, October 1, 1986, p. 32; and J. G. Kaikati and W. Label, "American Bribery Legislation: An Obstacle to International Marketing," *Journal of Marketing*, Fall 1980, pp. 38–43.

41.   "Patent Pirates May Soon Be Walking the Plank," *Business Week*, June 15, 1987, pp. 62–63.

42.   J. R. Chiles, "Anything Can Be Counterfeited—and These Days Almost Everything Is," *Smithsonian*, July 1986, pp. 35–43.

43.   "The Counterfeit Trade," *Business Week*, December 16, 1985. p. 64.

44.   Ibid.

45.   For a more complete discussion of the degree of product liability faced in U.S. markets, see M. Manlye, "Product Liability: You're More Exposed Than You Think," *Harvard Business Review*, September–October 1987, pp. 28–40.

46.   B. Meier, "Poison Produce," *Wall Street Journal*, March 26, 1987, pp. 1, 26.

47.   D. A. Ricks, *Big Business Blunders: Mistakes in Multinational Marketing* (Homewood, Ill.: Dow Jones-Irwin, 1983), p. 34.

48.   B. Bartlett, "How Many Border Crossings?," *Wall Street Journal*, September 10, 1986, p. 17; "Europe and Japan Are Catching Tax-Reform Fever," *Business Week*, September 1, 1986, p. 65; and R. I. Kirkland, Jr., "U.S. Tax Cuts Now Go Global," *Fortune*, November 24, 1986, pp. 131–132.

49.   For a more complete discussion of such support programs, see D. C. Bello and N. C. Williamson, "The American Export Trading Company: Designing a New International Marketing Institution," *Journal of Marketing*, Fall 1985, pp. 60–69.

50.   J. Urquhart, "Canada Sets Duty on U.S. Corn Imports After Ruling Growers Are Subsidized," *Wall Street Journal*, November 10, 1986, p. 5.

51.   "The 'Eastern Capital' of Asia," *Newsweek* (International ed.), February 23, 1988, p. 100.

EXTERNAL CONSIDERATIONS
THE CULTURAL AND SOCIAL ENVIRONMENTS

INTERNATIONAL INCIDENT

Those Rude Foreigners

"Rude" is a negative judgment for one business person to make about another. But what is rude behavior in one country is completely acceptable, even proper, in another. By American standards, some Germans and Indians are "pushy." By their standards, Americans too often are insufficiently motivated, also "rude." Americans are considered rude by some Italians, too, because Americans want to get to business "too quickly" and don't combine "the heart with the head." Iranians think the Japanese stand too far away, at a "rude" distance. And Chinese business leaders don't understand why the French open gifts when received, in front of the giver—that's "rude."

What determines what is rude? Our culture—our system of living, learned at an early age in our homes and schools. In the same way, we learn how to negotiate, how to dress, what to buy, when and where to buy it, and even how to dispose of products once they are used.

So business behavior, even to the level of detail on how to present a business card, is shaped for us, in subtle and deeply imbedded ways we often don't even recognize. Americans, for example, most often present a business card informally, between two fingers, and even immediately turn the card over and take notes on the back. In Japan, a business card is an extension of the person—to be handled with both hands, carefully and with respect. It is laid on the table and only put in one's pocket or written on after the meeting is over and the guest is gone.

Culture also shapes what we buy as consumers. Dutch children often eat chocolate shavings on buttered bread for breakfast. American children frequently have fried eggs. Indian children may have a spicy hot *sambal*, and Malays have rice. All are culturally acceptable and appropriate within their culture, but seemingly strange, even humorous, in others.

There lies the problem for international marketers. Most people, no matter where they are from, are culturally trained in consumption and business behavior. But once national or cultural borders are crossed, the rules change, to a set of unknown ones, which are often difficult to understand. Confronted with other cultures, our secure knowledge of how to behave, how others behave, and how to market to them disappears.

The final environmental analysis a company performs is cultural—what impact does the culture of the target market have upon its viability?

Culture (learned patterns of behavior) is the last critical factor that determines market viability. If the economic, political, and legal analyses prove positive, then a global marketer should proceed with a cultural analysis. Cultural factors play a "make or break" role in global marketing. Even within a nation there may be a variety of subcultures that complicate the task of the global marketer. In the United States, often referred to as a "melting pot" and sometimes as a "salad

Cultural sensitivity is just as essential for global marketers as for international marketers. Not knowing the cultural "rules of the game" has been the downfall of many international marketing campaigns.

"Well, I guess I'll have the ham and eggs."

bowl," there are numerous subcultures. These include ethnic groups (such as Spanish and Irish), religious denominations (Jewish and Catholic), and regional subcultures (the midwestern "breadbasket" and California's "utopia").[1] Each in its own way influences the conduct of business as well as buyer behavior.

In fact, all market behavior is culture-bound. Both consumer behavior and business practices are determined to a large extent by the culture within which they take place.[2] Thus, in order to match the marketing mix with consumer preferences, purchasing behavior, and product-use patterns in a potential market, global marketers must have a thorough understanding of the cultural environment of that market.

Global marketing seeks out cultural similarities while paying attention to important distinctions.

Until recently, most international marketing focused on cultural differences, adjusting marketing programs to make them acceptable to consumers in foreign markets. In contrast, successful global marketers seek out cultural similarities, in order to identify opportunities to implement a standardized marketing mix, as described in Chapter 2. Both the international and the global marketing approaches require that the marketer determine the cultural viability of markets.

This chapter discusses the relationship between culture and marketing and illustrates the elements of both the consumer culture and the business culture that must be considered in assessing a market's cultural viability. In addition, it provides guidelines for analyzing the cultural environment.

CULTURE AND MARKETING

Just what is **culture?** One definition that is useful to global marketers is the following: "Culture gives people a sense of who they are, of belonging, of how they should behave, and of what they should be doing."[3] A nation's culture provides a learned, shared, and interrelated set of symbols, codes, and values that direct and justify human behavior. Some of the many different elements of culture are:

*   Social organization, roles, and institutions

*   Norms and values

*   Religion

*   Language

*   Education

*   Art and aesthetics

*   Material culture and living conditions

Purchasing and business behavior are both learned behaviors, part of the overall culture.

All human behavior, including market behavior, takes place within a cultural context. Individual tastes and preferences are shaped by what society accepts and values. As Global Dimensions 6.1 shows, even the "meaning" of color is defined by culture. By influencing the set of rules governing how a firm competes, culture also has a major impact on business strategy.[4]

Not only does culture influence marketing; marketing also influences culture. Marketers act as agents of change within a culture. The two-way relationship between marketing and culture can be examined from three perspectives: (a) culture's influence on patterns of behavior, (b) culture's influence on the marketing mix, and (c) the influence of marketing on culture. In the rest of this section we will explore each of these perspectives in some detail.

Culture's Influence on Patterns of Behavior

Culture establishes acceptable purchasing and product-use behavior for both consumers and businesses. For example, Chinese culture places great emphasis on gift-giving to build relationships between friends. The gift should be "expensive enough to match the income of the givers, so that they are giving face (moral character) to those who receive their gifts, and that they gain face at the same time because they are thought of as being sincere."[5]

Applying one's own culture and rules for behavior to another culture almost always leads to marketing failure.

In the United States, test markets are often used to project the reaction of consumers to a new product. But when entering foreign markets, marketers frequently fall into the trap of the **self-reference criterion,** the unconscious application of one's own cultural experience and values to a market in another culture.[6] Consider the following example: In Egypt, giving one's word commits

GLOBAL DIMENSIONS 6.1

Fiasco in Hong Kong

John Player, the English cigarette maker, wanted to introduce its brand in Hong Kong. Marlboro was the leading brand there at the time, and Player wanted to compete directly against it. The John Player brand comes in a distinctive black box with gold trim. At the time, black dresses were the leading fashion item in many markets, including Hong Kong. Player's Hong Kong marketing agency decided that the best time for the product launch would be the Chinese New Year. An extensive introductory campaign was designed and executed. Samples were distributed, coupons were provided, and an expensive advertising campaign was undertaken.

The results were disastrous. Not only did the product not sell well, but people took the free sample packages to stores and traded them in for their usual brand. John Player had inadvertently violated an enduring cultural value, the association of the color black with bad luck and bad fortune. The timing of the launch made matters worse. At a time when people were in a happy, festive mood, they were especially sensitive to the negative connotations of the color black. The fact that black was popular among fashion-conscious consumers did not help John Player in its appeal to the mass market. Fashions are temporary and change rapidly. Underlying cultural values are enduring and change very slowly. John Player mistook one for the other and paid the price—market failure.

one to an agreement. This behavior stems from the religious values of Islam, in which God holds people responsible for keeping their word. An Egyptian would be shocked by an American marketer's request for a written contract. Such a request would be an insult to a Moslem's honor—a serious error caused by application of the self-reference criterion.[7]

Even more dangerous than the self-reference criterion is **ethnocentrism,** the belief that one's own culture is superior to any other. During the 1960s and 1970s American executives were noted for their ethnocentrism. Because U.S. companies led the world in product quality and technology, they felt that the "American way" was better than any other. Such extreme pride places serious limits on a marketer's ability to conduct business successfully in another culture, especially on a long-term basis. For example, the culturally based belief in being direct, even critical, in business negotiations often leads to failure when American businesspeople negotiate with Asians. In Asian culture, "face" must be preserved and criticism is an insult. To avoid the pitfalls of ethnocentrism and the self-reference criterion, global marketers must develop sensitivity to their own culture, how it differs from other cultures, and most important, the reasons for those differences.

Even consumption versus savings rates are influenced by culture. The U.S. culture largely supports consumption, with its short-term orientation and "live for today" attitude. The longer-term orientation that is part of Japanese society, where savings rates are three times greater than in the United States, supports saving and self-sacrifice for the long-term good.

Distribution systems and even stores vary by culture, too. Nations where women's major role is defined as homemaking, for example, are more often served by distribution systems that include bargaining. Arguing about the prices on products requires that considerable time be spent in shopping. Where women are more likely to have a career outside the household, time becomes more precious—a constraint on bargaining. In those cultures, fixed prices are more common.

Culture's Impact on the Marketing Mix

The key to global marketing is to develop marketing mixes that appeal across cultures.

Each element of culture influences each component of the marketing mix. An optimal marketing mix therefore can be developed only after examining each culture element to be sure that none presents an obstacle to successful implementation of the proposed plan. Such an analysis will also help the global marketer determine to what extent (if any) a standardized marketing mix would be acceptable in its target markets, or whether individualized market-by-market campaigns would have the best results. Following are examples showing how each element of the marketing mix is influenced by an element of culture.

1. *Promotion* is strongly influenced by language. Advertising copy may need to be changed because a campaign or slogan used in one culture has a negative meaning in another. Parker, the well-known maker of ballpoint pens, had to change its advertising in Latin American markets after learning that *bola* means "ball" in some countries but "revolution" or "lie" in others.[8]

2. *Product* acceptance is affected by norms, attitudes, and values.[9] For example, West Germany banned sales of three computer games to children because it was felt that they glorified war.[10] Similarly, a pervasive perception among Hong Kong residents that chicken fried in deep fat is tasteless was responsible for Kentucky Fried Chicken's inability to successfully enter that market in the 1970s.

3. *Pricing* is often affected by culturally based attitudes toward change. In the United States, where change is viewed relatively positively, new fashion items are given high prices partly because they symbolize change. But in countries where change is viewed negatively, a premium price for a new product would simply make the product too expensive for the average consumer.

4. *Distribution* is influenced by social institutions. In Asian and Arabic countries, for instance, ties to suppliers and buyers are often based on kinship, no matter how distant. Nonfamily members may be excluded from business transactions within a specific channel of distribution.

The Colonel's first location in Beijing overlooks the Ming dynasty front gate. The combination of food, service, and colors (red is a lucky color in Asia) has led to Kentucky Fried Chicken franchises' success throughout Asia after failure to enter that market some years earlier.

Marketing's Influence on Culture

Cultures change in part because they are exposed to new marketing mixes from other cultures.

Because culture is passed from generation to generation, it lends continuity to human behavior. It can also be a source of resistance to change. In fact, the more deeply held a cultural value, the greater the resistance to change in that value. Religious values, for example, change more slowly than less strongly held values.

But change does take place, partly because cultures borrow from each other. Buyers in less-developed countries improve their living conditions by purchasing more modern products from other nations.[11] The popularity of ethnic foods in any culture is a result of borrowing from other cultures. Goods and services of all types are increasingly popular in nations other than those in which they originate, a result of the globalization of markets.

Marketers and corporations conducting business across national boundaries also affect the cultures in which they operate. U.S.-based multinational corporations (MNCs) like McDonald's are often accused of "cultural imperialism," that is, exporting American values and life-styles.[12] At the other extreme, MNCs have also been accused of removing raw materials from less-developed nations without transferring needed production technologies into those nations.[13] Either way, corporations and marketers are involved in a two-way process of implementing and reacting to cultural change.

In the long run, as more markets become global and standardization of marketing mixes increases, the rate of cultural change will also increase. Indeed, the processes of cultural change and standardization reinforce each other. The more standardization occurs, the more cultural change can be expected. And the greater the change, the greater the opportunity for standardization. Thus, companies that use standardized marketing mixes have a cultural as well as a market impact. They are contributing to the sharing of ideas, attitudes, and images among cultures.

Many examples of the interaction of marketing and cultural change can be given. Australia became more popular among American tourists after the great success of the movie *Crocodile Dundee*. The increased interest in Australia provided new opportunities for marketers of Australian wines. Similarly, in opening its economic doors the People's Republic of China has set in motion an inevitable process of cultural change, as the Chinese people become accustomed to ideas and consumption patterns from other nations.[14]

Despite the efforts of marketers, cultures may change slowly, and specific products may meet with protracted resistance. Fundamentalist Protestant subcultures, for example, refuse to buy products that are not mentioned in the Bible. Later in the chapter we will discuss some of the means by which marketers can overcome such resistance. Before we do, however, the various elements of culture and the way they affect buyer needs and wants, and hence demand, must be understood.

. . . .

ELEMENTS OF CULTURE

The elements of culture and their influence on each other must be understood by the global marketer.

As noted earlier, a culture is a set of symbols, codes, and values. Each element of a culture reinforces all the others, and in addition has a direct influence on market viability. The global marketer must understand the elements themselves as well as how they are interrelated. Only on the basis of such an understanding can the marketer identify the elements of the buyer's culture that are critical to the success of a particular product or marketing mix.

Social Organization, Roles, and Institutions

The framework of a society shapes the behavior of its members, and, if understood, makes it easier to predict their behavior.

Social organization provides the framework of a culture. It includes virtually every aspect of how people live from day to day, the assignment of social tasks, and how and why people join together to meet their shared needs.

Information on social organization is extremely important to marketers of a wide variety of consumer and industrial products. An example of this can be seen in the definition of what constitutes a household and how many households there are in a potential market. In the United States, for example, a "typical" household is a nuclear family—one or two parents and their children. In Kenya, a typical household is an extended family—a nuclear family plus grandparents, aunts, uncles, and cousins.

Another aspect of social organization that is important to marketers is the roles people play within a household: who influences, makes, and carries out purchasing decisions, as well as who actually uses products. People's **social roles**

As societies change, women can assume non-traditional work roles to gain higher income and greater career opportunities. The rate of such change varies from country to country.

include their privileges and their responsibilities toward other people. We all play many roles in society—child, parent, sibling, student, boss, worker—and in each of these roles we have needs and wants that are important to marketers. For example, a mother buys consumer products for her children, but as a boss she may also buy industrial products.

The complexity of social organization and the stability of social roles and relationships are related to technological and economic development. In more advanced countries, social relationships tend to be more ambiguous and dynamic. In the United States, for example, gender roles are rapidly evolving toward more individualized and less predictable forms. The changing roles of women, in turn, are generating other types of change throughout the society. For example, 70 percent of American women of working age are employed outside the home and need services such as child care and household products that save time. The fact that roles are undergoing change makes it more difficult to predict behavior. Global Dimensions 6.2 illustrates how social roles are related both to one another and to other elements of culture.

In contrast, in less-developed nations, where many roles are strictly defined on the basis of gender and changes in social roles are taking place slowly, if at all, the task of predicting buyer behavior is primarily a matter of understanding existing social roles. In Saudi Arabian households, for example, food products are purchased almost exclusively by women in their role as head of the household. There, it would be inappropriate to advertise food products to men. But

GLOBAL   DIMENSIONS   6.2

Primary Education in Japan

Primary education in Japan embodies a much higher level of pressure than primary education in the United States. Young children spend several years preparing for the examination to enter prestigious private schools. Juku, or "cram" schools, typically offer fourth- through sixth-graders review programs that last three hours a day, three times a week. Summer jukus may last eight hours a day.

Not all the pressure is on the child. In Japan, mothers are traditionally responsible for assuring that their children do well in school. This means that mothers also attend juku—to learn how to help their children with their extra work and to provide them with a socially acceptable lunch. When students do well, their success reflects not only on them but also on their mothers.

One benefit of Japan's educational system is that 90 percent of Japanese students graduate from high school, compared with 76 percent of American students, and after high school the Japanese are better prepared to be productive participants in the work force. But the pressure has high social costs. Suicides among students who fail to do well on entrance exams are not uncommon. The Japanese system is also accused of producing students who memorize well but are not strong in original thought. When the students become adults they continue to suffer from high levels of stress. And Japanese mothers must cope with the fact that they are judged largely by how well their children perform in school.

Sources: Based on C. Simons, "They Get By with a Lot of Help from Their Kyoiku Mamas," *Smithsonian*, March 1987, pp. 44–52; "Memorizing vs. Thinking," *Newsweek*, January 12, 1987, pp. 60–61; and "The High Price Japanese Pay for Success," *Business Week*, April 7, 1986, pp. 52–54.

even in societies where men and women tend to be limited to traditional roles, the marketing manager must be aware of how those roles influence product acceptance in the context of that culture.

When people join together formally and informally to meet shared needs, they create **social institutions,** including the family, reference groups, and social classes.* The *family,* however it is defined by a given culture, is the most powerful institution in any society. Within the family children learn what is important, what to believe, and how to behave, including how to satisfy their needs and wants in the marketplace. Variations in this process from one culture to another can have significance for the global marketer. In Sweden, for example,

*Religious organizations, while they are part of the larger network of social institutions, also are another major element of culture and are discussed separately in a later section.

children are not encouraged to be the center of attention, as they often are in the United States. Thus, children's products must be marketed differently in the two countries.

Everyone belongs to a variety of reference groups, which help define how we should behave.

Reference groups are groups to which a person looks for guidance regarding behavioral norms. There are three types of reference groups: **membership groups** (groups we belong to), including the family, peer or friendship groups, **anticipatory groups** (groups we would like to belong to), and **dissociative groups** (groups we would *not* like to belong to).[15] Reference groups are particularly important for global marketers, especially in the case of products that are socially visible, unfamiliar to the buyer, or expensive. The same product may be classified differently by similar reference groups in different cultures. For example, an item that is a "must" for Norwegian teenagers might be rejected or ignored by teenagers in Taiwan.

In all societies people are divided into social categories or status rankings known as **social classes.** The distribution of people among classes and their ability to move from one class to another (that is, social mobility) vary from one society to another. In the United States, social class is defined in part by occupation (and, hence, income) and education, and it is evidenced by where and how well a person lives and with whom he or she associates. The key components of social class in the United States—occupation and education—can be changed; therefore, they create opportunities for upward mobility. In fact, such mobility is widely viewed as a legitimate personal goal. In Hindu India, in contrast, social class is defined by birth. A Hindu achieves upward mobility in the next life as a reward for accepting his or her current station in this life. Thus, while positioning a product as a sign of upward mobility may work well in the United States, such positioning would be entirely irrelevant in a Hindu market.

Norms and Values

Norms, values, and the social contract underlie the cultural rules that govern appropriate behavior.

Social norms are accepted rules, standards, and models of behavior; **values** are the deeply held ideas that underlie norms and guide social life. Greeting gestures, such as shaking hands (U.S.) or bowing (Korea), reflect social norms. Beliefs about what constitutes ethical business behavior are often based on religious beliefs and morals, that is, values.

The **social contract**—the generally accepted relationship between society and the individual—is the foundation of a culture's norms and values. It encompasses not only what the individual owes to society, but also what he or she can expect from society. The social contract for any given society can be placed somewhere on a continuum extending from highly individualistic to highly collective. In individualistic societies (such as North America), the social contract assigns most of the responsibility for effort and support to the individual. Members of such societies are also permitted to reap the rewards of their efforts. In collective societies (such as many Asian nations), more responsibilities are assigned to the society and more collective effort is required. In turn, individuals in these societies accept more support from others, and they provide such support. Tax rates tend to be higher in collective societies than in individualistic ones, and social services and other types of public support are usually more comprehensive.

A society's position along this continuum may affect the marketing of many products and services, particularly from the standpoint of promotion. For example, in a society with a collective social contract, energy-efficient devices are likely to be promoted successfully on the basis of their social benefits; in an individualistic culture, it would be more appropriate to promote them as money-saving devices.

Certain other cultural norms also have special significance for global marketers. The extent to which change is accepted in a culture, for example, affects the speed of product acceptance. More economically advanced nations usually are characterized by greater acceptance of change than less-developed nations. For them, the financial risk of poor product performance is relatively lower than is true for a low-income country. Norms related to acceptance of change are often rooted in religious traditions, but they are influenced by the living conditions and material culture of a society.

Another norm that can have a major impact on global marketing is the view of foreigners that is characteristic of a given culture. This norm influences not only product acceptance but also whether international trade can occur at all. A variant of this norm is the **country-of-origin effect,** the transfer of a particular country's image to products made there. Both industrial and consumer buyers rate products as more or less acceptable depending on where they are made. For example, industrial tooling machines made in West Germany are rated higher than machines with the same technical specifications made in Brazil.[16] Honda automobiles sold in Korea are imported from Honda's manufacturing plants in the United States, because Koreans don't like Japanese products. Attitudes toward foreigners are part of a larger set of cultural attitudes toward differences in general. Some cultures are notably more tolerant of differences of all kinds than others. The Netherlands is well known for tolerating wide differences in behavior and beliefs among people who live or visit there. In other countries, differences—whether religious, racial, ethnic, or political—are viewed with skepticism at best and bigotry at worst. In more tolerant environments marketers naturally find it easier to introduce products that set a person apart. In less tolerant societies it is necessary to play down or avoid any association of "difference" with a product.

Religion

The dominant religion of a culture is the basis of much behavior.

The dominant religious values in a society determine many other cultural norms and values.[17] Morality, etiquette, gender roles, and attitudes toward individual achievement and social change are all derived from religious values. Thus, Confucianism in China, Shintoism in Japan, Islam in Saudi Arabia, and Judeo-Christianity in Western Europe and North America have a strong influence on norms and values in those societies.[18]

Some religious subcultures resist change. The Amish do not use electricity or motor vehicles in their everyday life, which is dominated by agriculture. Moslems and Jews shun pork; Hindus refuse to eat beef. Religions also differ in the extent to which they value individual economic achievement. Exhibit 6.1 illustrates the relationship between religious beliefs and economic performance. Religion may also affect political stability and intergovernmental relations. The Sikh separatist movement has created instability in India; the conflicts in the Middle East and between Great Britain and Northern Ireland are also related to religion.

Even in societies where active participation in organized religion is declining, the influence of religious values should not be underestimated in assessing cultural viability. Although changes in some norms may create new market opportunities, emerging trends must be balanced against long-standing religious traditions in designing an effective marketing mix.

Language

Language not only permits communication, but it is also part of the culture itself.

Language is much more than a formal written and oral structure that permits communication. It is an essential element of culture. Understanding another language not only allows one to conduct business in that language but, perhaps more important, it also provides insight into the social organization and values of those who speak it. In addition, because of its obvious connection to advertising and other forms of promotion, language is a central consideration in the execution of a marketing plan.

EXHIBIT 6.1 DOMINANT RELIGIONS AND ECONOMIC PERFORMANCE

Religion, as a core belief system in a culture, has a strong impact on the economic achievement of that culture.

	Per Capita GNP in 1978 U.S. $
Protestant polities—North Atlantic	5,030–12,100
Catholic polities—Europe	1,990–9,090
Islamic polities—OPEC	1,260–7,690
Eastern Asian eclectic polities	1,160–7,280
Jewish polities—Israel	4,120
Protestant polities—Non-North Atlantic	1,110–7,990
Catholic polities—Non-Europe	480–2,910
Islamic polities—Non-OPEC	90–1,200
Polities with major nonliterate religious component, excluding South Africa	90–910
Theravada Buddhist polities	90–490
Hindu polities—India	180

Source: V. Terpstra and K. David, *The Cultural Environment of International Business* (Cincinnati: South-Western, 1985), p. 110.

MAP 6.1   SELECTED MAJOR LANGUAGE GROUPS OF THE WORLD

The languages of the world are quite diverse. This map illustrates major language groups in the world, and shows how widely diverse a geographic area those languages cover. What it does not illustrate, however, is how concentrated those languages are. English, for example, is the first language of some 320 million people. Hindi (Indo-Aryan group), one of the major languages of northern India, is spoken by about the same number of people, but within a significantly smaller geographical area.

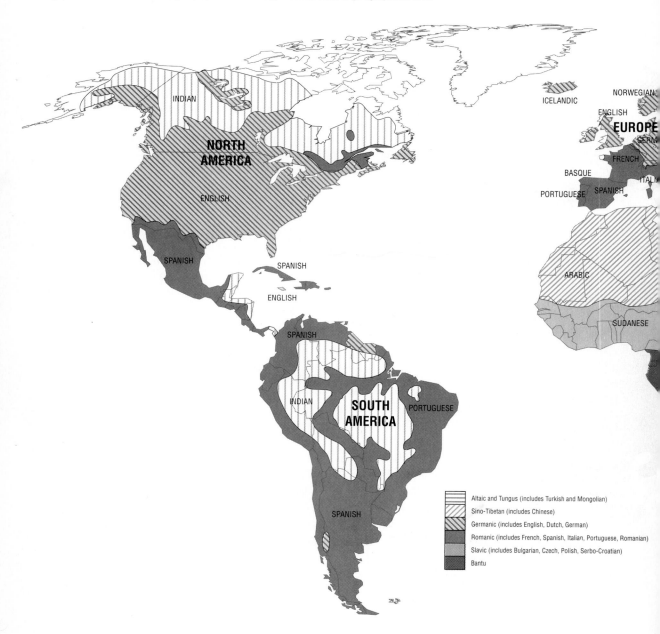

Legend:
- Altaic and Tungus (includes Turkish and Mongolian)
- Sino-Tibetan (includes Chinese)
- Germanic (includes English, Dutch, German)
- Romanic (includes French, Spanish, Italian, Portuguese, Romanian)
- Slavic (includes Bulgarian, Czech, Polish, Serbo-Croatian)
- Bantu

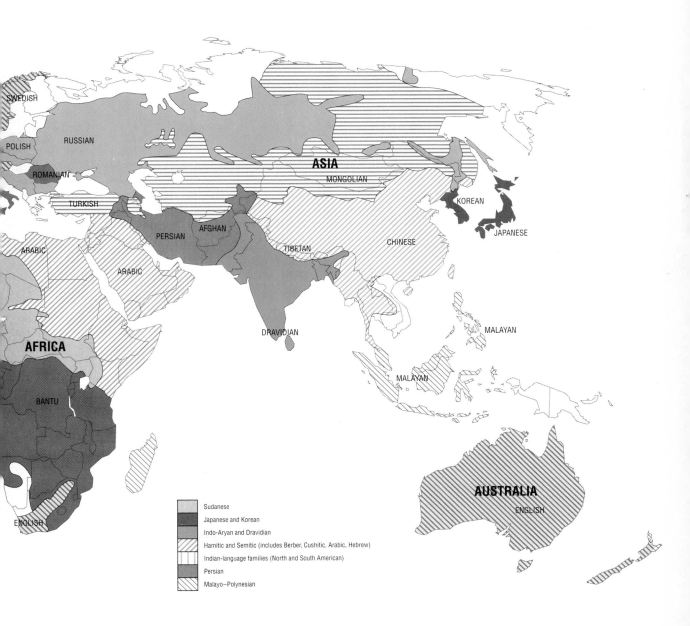

SWEDISH

POLISH

RUSSIAN

ROMANIAN

ASIA

TURKISH

MONGOLIAN

PERSIAN

AFGHAN

KOREAN

ARABIC

TIBETAN

CHINESE

JAPANESE

ARABIC

DRAVIDIAN

MALAYAN

AFRICA

MALAYAN

BANTU

AUSTRALIA

ENGLISH

ENGLISH

	Sudanese
	Japanese and Korean
	Indo-Aryan and Dravidian
	Hamitic and Semitic (includes Berber, Cushitic, Arabic, Hebrew)
	Indian-language families (North and South American)
	Persian
	Malayo–Polynesian

Bridging the language gap can be easier in some situations than in others. In the Netherlands, for example, a very enjoyable evening or party is described as *gezellig*. The same term, which has no English equivalent, can apply to a comfortable house. The existence of a similar term, *gemütlich*, in German means that a German-speaking marketer might have an advantage over someone who speaks neither Dutch nor German in reaching the Dutch-speaking market. Germans would understand the connotation, or cultural meaning, of the Dutch word, whereas others would have to settle for the denotation, or literal translation ("cozy" in English), which omits much of the underlying concept expressed by the word.

From the global marketer's perspective, a complicating factor related to language is that few nations are monolingual. In most nations several dialects are used, and in some nations several languages are used, often reflecting entirely different cultures or subcultures. Switzerland, for instance, has four major language groups: German, French, Italian, and Romansch.[19] Even a single language spoken in more than one nation has differences that may cause problems for a global marketer. For example, in England the word *napkin* means "diaper." Thus, the slogan "Use our napkins for your parties" would produce negative results there.

Education

The educational system, along with the family, passes along the culture.

Culture is learned and shared, a process that takes place largely through the family and the educational system. The **literacy rate** (the proportion of the population that can read and write) and the nature of the educational system affect the development of a culture, the generally accepted rate of change, and the marketing mix that will be most effective for that culture. In Sweden the literacy rate is virtually 100 percent. Its educational system is highly effective in teaching people how to read and write. The educational system, therefore, may be a major avenue for stimulating change in Swedish culture, and Swedish consumers can be reached in ways that require literacy, such as printed materials and advertising. In contrast, in Chad, where the literacy rate is 18 percent,[20] culture is passed along largely through the family and kinship groups, and consumers cannot be reached effectively through print media. Consumers in Chad can also be expected to have a lower tolerance for change than consumers in Sweden.

Aesthetics

Even our preferences in color, music, and art are shaped by our culture.

Colors, forms, shapes, sounds—all that is considered attractive or unattractive in a given culture—constitute the **aesthetics** of a culture. They affect consumers' responses to products and packaging, and they help define what advertising is appropriate in a target market. For example, a bank that wished to enter the Singapore market had to change the color of its logo in order to avoid a cultural association between green and death.[21] Aesthetic preferences may also explain why Japanese men are becoming major consumers of skin-care products, whereas American and Western European men are reluctant to buy such products.[22]

At the same time, cross-cultural markets seem to exist for some products that are strongly associated with aesthetics. Music is especially likely to have cross-cultural appeal. The jazz musician Wynton Marsalis tours the world; for a long time the rock group ABBA was Sweden's leading export; and an Australian entrepreneur signed an exclusive contract to sell the recordings of Moscow-based Molodiya throughout the Asian Pacific Rim.[23]

Material Culture and Living Conditions

The economic success of a culture, and its economic expectations, also affect market viability.

A society's **material culture** is the standard of living or level of economic development it has achieved. It is closely related to the degree of comfort, or **living conditions,** experienced by a society's members, as well as to the amount of leisure available to them. Both material culture and living conditions have a major impact on the cultural viability of a market.

Normally, a low standard of living indicates a low probability of market success for a relatively high-priced good. But a good that has high prestige value because it is produced in a particular country might find a market in a society that views consumption of such goods as a sign of upward mobility. For example, the general standard of living in the Philippines is not high by international standards. But Marlboro cigarettes are popular there, partly due to the high status associated with smoking an American cigarette. The price premium commanded by Marlboro is willingly paid by those who wish to make a social statement about themselves.

Living conditions include the levels of comfort achieved in diet and nutrition, clothing, housing, and health. Differences in the living conditions found in different societies affect the products purchased in those societies. Different food preferences, for example, result in a large market for pâté in France but a smaller one in the United States. Differences in leisure activities result in a large market for golfing equipment in the United States and Japan, but a smaller one in West Germany. Differences in housing standards and styles also affect global marketing activities. The small houses that are typical in Japan dictate home appliances that are smaller than those used in the United States, where houses are larger. American marketers that wish to enter the Japanese housewares market find themselves trying to sell products that are too big for the house in which they are to be used.[24]

Concern with good health and nutrition creates numerous market opportunities. However, it should be kept in mind that different cultures define health differently, and these differences affect the types of products that can be marketed successfully in a given culture. For example, Americans spend about $74 billion a year, or one-third of their total food-store expenditures, on low-calorie foods. This is considerably more, both in total and as a proportion of food purchases, than is spent for such products in any other nation.[25]

BUSINESS PRACTICES AND BEHAVIOR

Business behavior is learned in a culture, as are other forms of social behavior.

Just as culture influences consumption patterns and buyer behavior, it also helps determine accepted business behavior. Not knowing the rules of the game puts any player at a disadvantage; not knowing the rules of the business game means that a foreign competitor is at a disadvantage compared to local businesses. In this section we will discuss a number of cultural elements that affect business practices and behavior—in effect, the business culture.

Business Ethics

Moral standards for business behavior are established by the culture.

Every culture establishes a set of moral standards for business behavior, that is, a code of **business ethics.** This set of standards encompasses a broad range of issues, including what to manufacture, how to compete, what advertising guidelines to follow, and whether to pay extra for certain services. The actions that are considered right or wrong, fair or unfair, in the conduct of business are heavily influenced by the culture in which they take place. Because many ethical issues are based on fundamental—often religious—beliefs, violations of these standards are likely to provoke strong, emotional responses.

A key ethical issue in global marketing is international bribery. Paying large sums of money to highly placed government officials is considered unethical in most countries, and it is often formally defined as illegal (unless it is considered "grease"). Although bribery does occur, when it is discovered it creates embarrassment and often results in the recipient's losing his or her position, or worse. For example, when Lockheed Aircraft paid a large sum to former prime minister Tanaka of Japan, Tanaka was sentenced to 4 years in prison and Lockheed received a great deal of negative publicity, both in Japan and in the United States.[26]

Fees and commissions paid to a firm's foreign representatives for their services are a particular problem—when does a fee (legal) become a bribe (illegal)? One reason for employing a foreign representative is to benefit from his or her contacts with decision makers, especially in a foreign government. If the representative uses part of the fee to bribe government officials, there is little that the firm can do. But under the Foreign Corrupt Practices Act such an action is illegal, and a U.S. firm is held accountable.

Business Manners

Knowing how to behave properly in a business setting depends upon your cultural sensitivity and willingness to learn.

Manners are social codes of conduct. Like personal manners, business manners vary considerably from one culture to another. The business world is full of potential social mistakes. In China, great embarrassment would result if one party to a business relationship failed to bring a gift to the other. Such gifts, which are never opened in front of the giver, are tokens of respect. In Italy, two or three bottles of wine would be an appropriate gift to offer a business colleague, but in France such a gift might be viewed as an insult.

American businesspeople, in particular, find themselves at a disadvantage in other cultures. The American tendency toward informality and "getting right down to work" is considered inappropriate in most other cultures. Europeans, for example, find the American "business breakfast" amusing, if not insulting.

Obviously, a global marketer must be sensitive to cultural influences on business behavior. Before proceeding on a business trip to a foreign country, especially for the first time, the marketer should become familiar with the customs and manners that guide the conduct of business in that country.[27]

Silent Languages

Silent languages must be mastered in order to understand the communication message that is transmitted.

Languages are not only formal and visible (written and spoken) but silent as well.[28] The various silent languages are illustrated in Exhibit 6.2. Each of these languages influences proper business behavior for a specific culture. It is necessary to make a conscious attempt to understand and adjust for silent languages; up to 90 percent of communication, especially in foreign countries, may take place through silent rather than spoken language.[29]

The silent languages that are most important are the languages of time and space, both of which vary widely in different cultures. Indonesians, for example, show respect by arriving "late" for a meeting. This once caused the president of a Dutch company some consternation. Expecting visiting Indonesian guests to be punctual (the Dutch way of showing respect), he was put off by the tardiness of his visitors. Similar misunderstandings can occur over the speed with which a meeting should approach the business topic or how long negotiations should take. For example, trying to force Japanese negotiators to reach

---

EXHIBIT 6.2
SILENT LANGUAGES

The silent languages account for a large amount of communication, so the global marketer must take care to learn them when conducting business in another culture.

Time	Appointments
	Deadlines
	Scheduling of people and events
Space	Size of office
	Location of office
	Furnishings
	Conversation distance
Things	Material possessions
	Interest in latest technology
	Personal connections versus material symbols of status, power, and respect
Friendship	Friends versus self as social insurance for times of stress and emergency
Agreements	Rules of negotiations based on laws, moral practices, or informal customs

Source: E. T. Hall, "The Silent Language in Overseas Business," *Harvard Business Review*, May–June 1960, pp. 87–96.

an early decision is not only difficult but rude; it ignores the need of Japanese team members to reach a consensus before reacting to a proposal.

The concept of spatial language is illustrated by how close to one another people stand or sit. Arabs, for instance, prefer to stand quite close to the person with whom they are speaking—uncomfortably close by North American standards. When an American automatically steps back to a more comfortable distance, he or she inadvertently offends the Arab. Similarly, in some cultures waiting in line means standing close together and jostling toward the front; in others, one is expected to wait one's turn without crowding.

The self-reference criterion creates more difficulty with silent languages than with spoken ones. When one goes to another culture, one expects differences in spoken language and even in some observable behavior. Differences in silent language are much less obvious. Moreover, because silent languages are largely unconscious forms of communication, they have a strong emotional impact.

Much of the difficulty with silent languages has to do with how central the *context*, or setting, is in interpreting communication.[30] Exhibit 6.3 ranks various cultures from the standpoint of context. A "high-context" culture relies heavily on contextual clues to round out communication. In Japanese and Arabic cultures, for example, much information is transmitted through context—through the listener interpreting what is meant to be said, rather than through the actual words spoken. "Low-context" cultures, such as Canada, the United States, and

EXHIBIT 6.3
HIGH-CONTEXT TO
LOW-CONTEXT
CULTURES

This exhibit illustrates how several cultures rate on a scale that ranges from high to low context.

High-context culture

Japanese
Arab
Greek
Spanish
Italian
English
French
American
Scandinavian
German
German–Swiss

Low-context cultures

Source: L. Copeland and L. Griggs, *Going International* (New York: Random House, 1985), p. 107.

Germany, rely more directly on the words themselves; English and German are precise languages with rich and specific vocabularies.

In business communications, a person whose home culture is low-context may have to develop skills in "reading" the environment and listening for unspoken messages. Italian managers, used to a high-context culture, where they look for meaning in what is *not* said, may consider their German counterparts (a low-context culture) "cold," since that culture employs a direct language. In contrast, managers from high-context cultures are trained to examine the entire communication setting for meaning. When such individuals move into a low-context culture, they face the challenge of learning to be precise in their spoken and written messages, so as to avoid misunderstandings. Thus Greeks must adjust to the lower-context American culture to avoid being seen as overly emotional.

Negotiation and Resolution of Disputes

Culture sets the rules for resolving disputes.

Guidelines like those presented in Exhibit 6.4 indicate that the biggest problem facing international negotiators is the lack of a common value system or frame of reference.[31] Russians, for example, negotiate by moving upward through the organizational hierarchy. At each level the negotiator involved must gain a concession of some kind. Sellers who offer major concessions early in this process are likely to lose a lot of money, or they may not make the sale at all. Americans, who are used to making concessions early on and throughout the negotiation process, may find themselves at a disadvantage in negotiating with Russians, who typically make concessions late and reach an agreement at the end of the negotiation process.[32] Fortunately, international business negotiations can be planned and practiced like any other business strategy or skill.[33]

An Indian entrepreneur, Sant Singh Chatwal, believes that part of his success in the United States is due to his cultural background. In India, a relatively high-context culture, patience is considered a virtue and is socially rewarded. Chatwal has found that his patience in negotiating leases for his Bombay Palace restaurant chain is a real advantage.[34]

Like negotiating practices, the processes for recognizing and resolving disputes also vary considerably among cultures. For example, Austrians disagree directly and openly; their ways of resolving disputes are also direct. In contrast, businesspeople in Hong Kong would never disagree directly. They might even say yes when what they mean is maybe or "I don't agree."

Different cultures have developed different methods for resolving disputes. Asians and Europeans are amazed at the American preference for resorting to the legal process. They view going to court as an admission of failure, not as a method of resolving disputes. In more "cooperative" societies, dispute resolution is achieved through discussion. If an impasse is reached, an arbitrator is called in to settle the dispute. Indeed, outside the United States arbitration is not only usual, but it is the preferred method of resolving disputes. (See Exhibit 6.5.)

EXHIBIT 6.4
RULES OF WINNING
FOREIGN
NEGOTIATIONS

To win negotiations the
global marketer must de-
velop cultural and per-
sonal sensitivity.

Before the Negotiations

Rule 1:   Make sure what you are negotiating is negotiable.

Rule 2:   Define what winning means to you.
Be ambitious, but set a realistic walk-away.

Rule 3:   Get the facts.

Rule 4:   Have a strategy for each culture and phase.
Position your proposal in the best light.
Decide whether the negotiation is going to be win-lose or win-win.
Decide on your opening proposal.
Plan to control your concessions.

Rule 5:   Send a winning team.
Don't go alone.
Always have your own interpreter.
Exclude lawyers from the team.
Use a go-between.
Don't change negotiators in midstream.

Rule 6:   Allow yourself plenty of time, and more.
Never tell the other side when you are leaving.

Beginning the Negotiations

Rule 7:   Make the opening scene work for you.
Think about the agenda.
Watch the physical arrangements.
The overture should make music.

Hard Bargaining

Rule 8:   Control information.

Rule 9:   Watch your language.

Rule 10:   Persuasion is an art. Don't paint your argument with the wrong materials.

Rule 11:   Get in stride with the locals.

Rule 12:   Go behind the scenes—where minds are changed.

Rule 13:   Give face.

Rule 14:   Deadlock means neither side wins and both may lose.

Rule 15:   Don't be browbeaten into a bad deal.

Rule 16:   Get your agreements signed before you leave.

Agreements

Rule 17:   Both sides should agree on the significance of what you are signing.

Rule 18:   Be willing to give up cherished notions of the proper contract.

Beyond the Contract

Rule 19:   Discussions are preferable to court settlements.

Rule 20:   Remember—without relationships, you have no deal.

Source: R. Schreffler, "Japan: Targeting a Tough Market," *Distribution*, October 1987, pp. 44–48.

EXHIBIT 6.5
ACTION HIERARCHIES
FOR DISPUTE
RESOLUTION

The resolution of disputes proceeds differently in different cultures. Here, the usual processes in the People's Republic of China and the United States are illustrated.

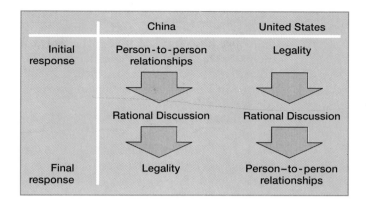

Personal relationships play a more important role in business decision making outside the United States than Americans are used to.

Networking

In many cultures the well-being of family members plays an important role in business decision making. Particularly in a country with a weak or nonexistent social security system, the extended family may share responsibility for the economic well-being of all family members. For example, a U.S. manufacturer of chicken feed found that after establishing a factory in a foreign market it could not sell its product, because the chicken growers preferred to buy from relatives. The manufacturer then established its own chicken farms in order to create a market for the product, but it found that buyers of chickens were also related to the chicken growers. As a result, there was little demand for the U.S. company's chickens.[35]

The impact of family relationships and friendship on business decisions is referred to as **networking.** In an expanded sense, an entire industry is a network of relationships (personal contacts) among the firms involved in production, distribution, and purchase of goods and services.[36] Analyzing an industry as a system of interpersonal relationships—a process known as **network analysis**—can provide insight into business behavior and help identify market opportunities. Understanding the relationships that exist within a network can also help identify ways for the marketer to improve its existing relationships and build new ones.[37]

Work, Achievement, and Wealth

Perspectives on work, achievement, and the possession of wealth depend upon the culture.

Different cultures have different perspectives on work, achievement, and wealth, which are often based on dominant religious values. For example, Asian followers of Confucius do not make a clear-cut distinction between work and play like that contained in the Western ideas of "weekend" and "Sabbath."[38] Such differences are not only reflected in the norms and values of consumers, but they also have an impact on how business is conducted.

A significant factor in a society's perspective on work is the historical importance of agriculture in that society. Countries that are known for a strong work ethic and motivation to succeed may owe these attitudes to an economy based on agriculture. In such societies hard work is less a moral issue than a prerequisite for survival. Even when its economy becomes less dependent on the production of crops, the society may continue to value hard work.[39] This may be true of an entire society or a prominent minority group, such as the Indians in Uganda, who are noted for their achievements in distribution and commerce.

How long one works is only one measure of the value of work in a society, but it does provide a basis for comparison. For example, the average American works 1,800 hours per year and takes 19.6 vacation days; in contrast, the average Japanese works 2,100 hours annually and takes 8.2 vacation days.[40] Germans average about 1,600 hours per year and take much longer vacations (4 to 6 weeks) than their counterparts in either the United States or Japan. Over the years Americans have learned not to schedule major business trips to Europe during July, August, or December, because their European partners or customers are likely to be on vacation during those months. *If It's Tuesday, It Must Be Belgium*, a movie that pokes fun at Americans traveling in Europe, actually reflects the reality of short vacations for most Americans. When the typical two-week paid vacation was first described to one German businessman, he wondered if it was legal to give workers such a short holiday!

Within a culture, attitudes toward work, achievement, and wealth can also vary. In addition, these attitudes, like other cultural elements, change over time. Younger Japanese workers, for instance, believe reward systems should be based on merit rather than seniority, the traditional system for most Japanese companies. They also are more likely to change jobs rather than stay with one company throughout their entire career.[41]

Employer-Employee Relations

Culture sets the tone for the expected relationship between employer and employee, and the proper management of that relationship.

The degree of paternalism that is considered appropriate in employer-employee relations varies from one culture to another. In the United States, employees are often viewed as interchangeable factors of production. In contrast, in a culture with a collective social contract businesses are viewed as providers for and caretakers of their employees: the organization owes the workers employment and should take care of them. Thus, in Malaysia company-provided housing is fairly common. In Austria, corporate executives play a parental role. They are looked up to as figures of authority and are expected to play roles inside and outside the company that reflect their position. For example, they may be expected to play leadership roles in their community or religious groups. Within the company, their role requires that they make business decisions with the best interests of the employees in mind.

Union-management relations can also vary, ranging from antagonistic to cooperative. In Northern Europe, the "social partnership" between workers and management means that workers as well as managers have a sense of responsibility for the well-being of the company. In Japan, it is not uncommon for a firm to have its own "union." This concept differs considerably from the idea of a union in North America, where unions represent all the workers in a particular industry, usually "against" management.

ANALYZING THE CULTURAL ENVIRONMENT

The first step in analyzing the cultural environment is to gather information about the elements of culture and the relationship between culture and the marketing mix. Then one of several possible frameworks for analysis can be applied. This section briefly discusses sources of information and presents two of those frameworks.

Sources of Information about Culture

Global marketers must have facts about a culture, but also know how to interpret those facts.

Exhibit 6.6 lists some of the sources of cultural information available to global marketers. If the marketer is interested in Saudi Arabia, those sources might provide the *factual* information that the population is virtually 100 percent Moslem. But without *interpretative* information about Islamic beliefs and how they influence buyer behavior, the marketer would not be able to conduct a thorough analysis. One company apparently lacked such information when its ads portrayed a refrigerator with the doors open, displaying a ham. Since pork is offensive to Moslems, sales of the company's products suffered.[42]

Obtaining the necessary interpretative information to achieve a thorough understanding of another culture may require a significant investment. One Japanese corporation sent an employee to Spain for a year to study guitar. When asked whether this wasn't a terrible waste of corporate funds, the company president said, "Ah, but you don't understand how important music is to the Spaniards."[43]

There is no substitute for firsthand experience as a source of interpretative knowledge about a culture. However, there are a variety of secondary sources, such as texts, articles, films, and consultants, that can help the marketer obtain

---

EXHIBIT 6.6
SOURCES OF
CULTURAL
INFORMATION

A large variety of cultural information is available to the global marketer.

Country Studies, U.S. Government Printing Office
Country Updates, Overseas Briefing Associates
Information Guide for Doing Business in . . . , Price, Waterhouse
European Customs and Manners, Meadowbrook Books
Foreign Business Practices, U.S. Department of Commerce
Background Notes, U.S. Department of State
Investing, Licensing, and Trading Conditions Abroad, Business International Corporation
Do's and Taboos Around the World, John Wiley and Sons

EXHIBIT 6.7
ADOPTER
CATEGORIES

Products diffuse through
a culture in a manner
similar to the product life-
cycle. Knowing the adop-
ter categories, and their
characteristics, helps the
global marketer develop
better marketing mixes.

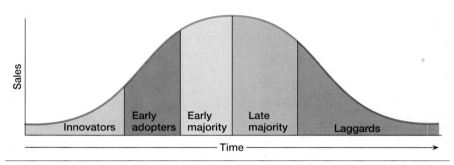

Source: E. M. Rogers, *The Diffusion of Innovations* (New York: Free Press, 1962), p. 76.

relevant information.[44] In addition, firms should train their managers in the techniques of cultural analysis.

The Product Adoption Process

Knowing the character-
istics of buyers permits
more appropriate mar-
keting mixes to be
developed.

One useful framework for analysis is the **product-adoption process.** This model classifies potential buyers (adopters) into five categories: innovators, early adopters, early majority, later majority, and laggards. (See Exhibit 6.7.) It is important to note that buyers may not belong to the same category for every product. Early adopters of stereo equipment will not necessarily be early adopters of high-fashion items.

The value of applying the product-adoption model to cultural analysis is that it forces the marketer to consider the specific characteristics of potential buyers along with cultural influences on them. Early adopters tend to be relatively abstract in thinking and forward-looking in orientation.[45] But early adopters are also influenced by their culture. An early adopter of personal computers in Taiwan does not necessarily have the same characteristics as an early adopter of personal computers in Sweden. Taiwanese culture, for example, is more conservative than Swedish culture, and it emphasizes that the individual should remain part of the group. A standardized marketing campaign aimed at early adopters in those two cultures, therefore, would probably not be successful.

Diffusion of Innovations

Products themselves
influence how quickly
they diffuse in a
market.

Another useful approach is to examine the elements that influence the **diffusion** (acceptance) of an innovative product within a culture. Exhibit 6.8 lists product characteristics that influence diffusion and indicates whether they encourage or inhibit diffusion of innovations. Such information can help global marketers understand the likelihood of cultural acceptance of or resistance to their products.

The value of this approach can be seen in the case of microwave ovens. Microwaves sell well in the United States because they save time. But in most Latin American countries, even if a customer has enough money to buy a micro-

Relative Advantage (encourages)	Degree of product superiority
Trialability (encourages)	Degree to which the product can be tried at low financial, personal, and social risk
Ease of Communication (encourages)	Degree to which relative advantage can be quickly and easily understood
Compatibility (encourages)	Degree to which product use is consistent with current consumption patterns
Complexity (inhibits)	Degree to which the customer finds the product difficult to understand

Source: Based on E. M. Rogers and F. F. Shoemaker, *Communications of Innovations*, 2nd ed. (New York: Free Press, 1971), pp. 22–23.

wave oven, the product is less compatible with cultural norms. In Argentina, for example, the time saved would be the cook's, since the heads of high-income households do not usually do the cooking. Therefore, sales of microwave ovens are likely to be lower in Argentina than in the United States, even among consumers in similar income groups. Knowing this, the marketer might stress energy efficiency in promoting microwave ovens in Latin America.

S U M M A R Y

Culture gives people a sense of who they are, of belonging, of how they should behave, and of what they should be doing. It provides a learned, shared, and interrelated set of symbols, codes, and values that direct and justify human behavior. All human behavior, including market behavior, takes place within a cultural context. Culture establishes acceptable purchasing and product-use patterns for both consumers and businesses. However, when entering foreign markets, marketers frequently fall into the trap of the self-reference criterion, the unconscious application of one's own cultural experience and values to a market in another culture. Even more dangerous than the self-reference criterion is ethnocentrism, the belief that one's own culture is superior to any other.

Each element of culture influences each component of the marketing mix. Promotion, for example, is strongly influenced by language. Product acceptance is affected by culturally based attitudes toward change. And distribution is influenced by social institutions such as kinship ties. Marketing also influences culture, especially by contributing to cultural borrowing and change.

Social organization provides the framework of a culture. It includes virtually every aspect of how people live from day to day, the assignment of social tasks, and how and why people join together to meet their shared needs. The complexity of social organization and the stability of social roles and relationships are related to technological and economic development. In more advanced countries, social relationships tend to be more ambiguous and dynamic. In less-developed nations, in contrast, the task of predicting buyer behavior is primarily a matter of understanding existing social roles.

Major social institutions from the point of view of the global marketer are the family, reference groups, and social classes. Reference groups are groups to which a person looks for guidance regarding norms or rules of behavior; social classes are social categories or status rankings defined by such factors as occupation and education.

Social norms are accepted rules, standards, and models of behavior; values are the deeply held ideas that underlie norms and guide social life. The social contract—the generally accepted relationship between society and the individual—is the foundation of a culture's norms and values. A society's position along the continuum from highly individualistic to highly collective can affect the marketing of many products and services, particularly from the standpoint of promotion. The extent to which change is accepted in a culture affects the speed of product acceptance, and a culture's view of foreigners influences not only product acceptance but also whether international trade can occur at all.

Religion plays a critical role in a product's viability in a given culture. The dominant religious values in a society determine many other cultural norms and values. Another highly significant element of culture is language. Understanding another language not only allows one to conduct business in that language but also provides insight into the social organization and values of those who speak it. Other cultural elements that affect global marketing are the literacy rate, the educational system, aesthetics (what is considered attractive or unattractive), and living conditions.

Culture influences not only consumption patterns but also accepted business behavior. Every culture establishes a code of business ethics. A key ethical issue in global marketing is international bribery. Also significant to global marketers are differences in business manners and the "silent languages" that influence proper business behavior in different cultures.

The biggest problem facing international negotiators is the lack of a common value system or frame of reference. Processes for recognizing and resolving disputes can also vary considerably among cultures.

Various other differences in business practices are important for global marketers. They include the impact of kinship and friendship on business networks; differences in perspectives on work, achievement, and wealth; and the degree of paternalism in employer-employee relations.

A useful framework for analyzing the cultural environment is the product-adoption process, in which potential buyers are classified into five categories: innovators, early adopters, early majority, later majority, and laggards. Applying this model to cultural analysis forces the marketer to consider the specific characteristics of potential buyers along with cultural influences on them. Another useful approach is to examine the elements that influence the diffusion of a product within a culture. Such information can help global marketers understand the likelihood of cultural acceptance of or resistance to their products.

DISCUSSION QUESTIONS

1. Distinguish between the international and global approaches to marketing with respect to the importance they place on the culture of a national market.

2. Discuss and illustrate the two-way relationship between culture and marketing.

3. How important is the family in shaping consumer behavior? Explain.

4. What impact does the social contract have on marketing behavior?

5. How does religion affect market acceptance of a product?

6. Give examples from two different cultures of the impact of aesthetics on the marketing mix.

7. As the global marketing manager of a U.S.-based multinational corporation, you have been told by one of your overseas sales agents that for a "fee" you can make a profitable sale in a certain country. You suspect that the fee is a bribe. What should you do and why?

8. Use a cross-cultural example to illustrate the impact of the various "silent languages" on the marketing mix.

9. How can a marketing manager learn about another culture?

10. Illustrate how product characteristics might affect the diffusion of a new VCR in the United States and England.

CASE

THE UNITED STATES AND EUROPE: HOW FAR APART?

Many business leaders tend to think that the United States and most of Western Europe share a fairly similar culture. Carol Conway, a consultant to food marketers based in the United States and Europe, was on her way to London to advise a food marketing group that firmly believed Europe lags behind U.S. food-industry trends, and what has been popular in the United States will become popular in Europe. Ms. Conway wasn't so sure.

On her last trip from Chicago to Amsterdam, for example, Ms. Conway read an article based on a large-scale research project that included interviews with Dutch and American women who held similar jobs.[1] The research indicated that Dutch and American women vary considerably. For example, when asked about work satisfaction, 55 percent of the American women, but only 8 percent of the Dutch, reported that they wanted to do something else. However, both American and Dutch women told researchers that the work they were doing was different from the work they originally expected to do. The two groups apparently also held different beliefs about job mobility. Of the Americans interviewed, 55 percent reported they planned to leave the company to assume a higher position; no Dutch women did. Dutch women reported that taking on a job with greater responsibility would mean losing the pleasurable part of their job. To Ms. Conway, it seemed that American women elected to pursue a career and money, while the Dutch focused more on "happiness." Perhaps their priorities were reflected in employee turnover rates—35 percent for American companies and 6 percent for Dutch companies.

A Dutch businessman, Pieter Van Der Meer, who ran the import division of a major European brewing company, told Ms. Conway that it is easy to stereotype from such findings, and many Europeans and Americans do. Many Europeans find Americans materialistic, overambitious, and restless. Americans often describe Europeans as complacent and not very serious about work. But Ms. Conway wished to try and set aside a simple interpretation, to consider the larger cultural framework in which these women lived—for example, whether they had been socially trained to seek an identity outside the workplace or to make their career a priority. In that way, she believed she could better understand buyer behavior and provide her clients with more useful advice. After doing further research, she began to organize her report to her English client as follows.

The Work Force

In the United States, there appears to be greater diversity in the work force. In Europe, the majority of the work force consists of heads of household and unmarried men and women. In the United States, married women, students, and recently retired workers add to the work force. In particular, the percentage of married women with a full-time job is much higher in the United States than in Europe. The greater participation of women in the work force has a significant effect on living patterns and family-consumption patterns. For example, about 1 out of every 3 meals is consumed outside the home in the United States, considerably more than in Europe.

Similarly, the percentage of high school and college students who work in Europe is very small compared to in the United States. This trend has also influenced eating habits and the preference for specific consumer goods.

Advertising and Promotion

Ms. Conway had traveled enough in Europe to learn that there are different patterns of advertising there from those in the United States. For example, the frequent European practice of bunching a limited number of advertisements at the beginning and end of TV shows contrasts sharply with the American practice of multiple commercial breaks. And a front-page newspaper discussion of Michael Jackson's role in Pepsi commercials was, from Mr. Van Der Meer's perspective, a uniquely American activity. Europeans—in particular the Dutch—save their front pages for "real news" (the noted exception being the British tabloids). Certainly, the amount of advertising is considerably more in the United States than in Europe, as is the per capita spending on advertising. Further, it seemed to Ms. Conway that American advertising is more direct, even irritatingly persuasive, compared to the more indirect, low-key, informative European approach.

EXHIBIT 6A
OBSERVED LIFE-
STYLE COMPONENTS

	United States	**Europe**
Television	major influence	moderate influence
Education	business-oriented	not business-oriented
Travel abroad	selected groups	common
Mobility	high	low
Life focus	outside home	inside home
Fads	frequent	less frequent
Introvert/Extrovert	extroverts	introverts

Life-style

Since she made six or seven trips to Europe each year, Ms. Conway was able to observe her European counterparts' life-styles firsthand. She summed up some of her observations in a table, to help guide her thinking (Exhibit 6A). Life-style is the product of cultural values as well as the economic environment. It influences the perception of and preference for many products. TV, for example, is watched much more in the United States than in Europe, leading to its having a higher impact on American life-styles. American consumers will more frequently copy what they have seen on TV, such as clothing, hair styles, and cars. Sports heroes also have a much greater influence in the United States, frequently being used in product endorsements, a rare practice in Europe.

Fads seem to develop more often and more quickly in the United States. Wine cooler sales, for example, grew in just a few years to a billion dollar industry. Corona beer, from limited sales in 1985, grew to challenge the leading imported beer, Heineken, in just two years. Shortly thereafter, sales fell sharply. American consumers, by and large, like to try new products (especially if they have low risk) and to be seen doing the latest thing. Europeans are much slower to change their patterns of behavior. Thus brand loyalty is normally much higher in Europe than in the United States.

Case Issue

Ms. Conway's plane prepared to land at Heathrow Airport. She knew that within hours she had to decide what advice to give her British client, who was interested in importing American beer. She also knew that Budweiser beer had been introduced in Britain in 1984, and it was not doing as well as Anheuser Busch had hoped. Its problems in Germany and France were greater still. The question she had to answer, and soon, was what European cultural and social factors were important to her client in considering whether American beer would sell well in Europe.

This case is based on material prepared by Nico Spannenburg, while an executive M.B.A. student at Emory University.

1. See D. Goldbarg and A. Klamer, "U.S. vs. Europe: An Ocean Apart," *Flying Dutchman International*, Summer 1988, pp. 20–23.

NOTES

1. J. Garreau, *The Nine Nations of North America* (Boston: Houghton Mifflin, 1981).

2. D. B. Hamilton, "Institutional Economics and Consumption," *Journal of Economic Issues*, December 1987, p. 1541.

3. P. R. Harris and R. T. Moran, *Managing Cultural Differences*, 2nd ed. (Houston: Gulf Publishing, 1987), p. 12; see also E. T. Hall, *Beyond Culture* (Garden City, N.Y.: Doubleday/Anchor Books, 1976); V. Terpstra and K. David, *The Cultural Environment of International Business*, 2nd ed. (Cincinnati: South-Western, 1985); and L. Copeland and L. Griggs, *Going International* (New York: Random House, 1985).

4. J. B. Ford, W. A. French, and P. Heil, "A Cultural Approach to Market Conflict: Japanese Variations," paper presented at the American Market Association Winter Educators' Conference, San Diego, 1988.

5. O. H. M. Yau, "Chinese Cultural Values and Their Marketing Implications," *Working Paper Series* (Business Research Centre, Hong Kong Baptist College, 1986), pp. 11–15.

6. J. A. Lee, "Cultural Analysis in Overseas Operations," *Harvard Business Review*, March–April 1966, pp. 106–114.

7. D. T. Wilson and A. Ghoneim, "Transferring Organizational Buying Theory Across Cultural Boundaries," in P. W. Turnbull and S. J. Paliwoda, eds., *Research in International Marketing* (London: Croom Helm, 1986), pp. 4–21.

8. D. A. Ricks, *Big Business Blunders: Mistakes in Multinational Marketing* (Homewood, Ill.: Dow Jones-Irwin, 1983), pp. 7–8.

9. Ibid., p. 80.

10. "Banned in Bonn," *Wall Street Journal*, September 10, 1987, p. 1.

11. J. F. Medina, "Modern Material Culture: Effects on Developing Nations' Consumption Patterns," *Academy of International Business Proceedings*, 1987, Academy of International Business, New Orleans, pp. 16–24.

12. "McWorld?," *Business Week*, October 13, 1986, p. 63.

13. J. T. Peach, "Distribution and Economic Progress," *Journal of Economic Issues*, December 1987, p. 1507.

14. J. R. Schiffman, "Drive Against Western Ideas Puzzles Chinese," *Wall Street Journal*, April 9, 1987, p. 28; "China's Student Rebels Are Playing into Deng's Hands," *Business Week*, January 19, 1987, pp. 48–49.

15. R. E. Stanley, *Promotion*, 2nd ed. (Englewood Cliffs, N.J.: Prentice Hall, 1982), p. 29.

16. P. D. White and E. W. Cundiff, "Assessing the Quality of Industrial Products," *Journal of Marketing*, January 1978, pp. 80–86.

17. Religious subgroups within a culture also develop different consumption patterns. See, for example, L. Skenazy, "Marketing to the Converted," *Advertising Age*, November 2, 1987, p. 90.

18. See, for example, Y. Komori, "The Root of Japanese Culture," *The World & I*, January 1986, pp. 222–229; G. D. O'Brien, "The Christian Assault on Capitalism," *Fortune*, December 8, 1986, pp. 181–184; P. Gupte, "An Aga Khan for the 21st Century," *Forbes*, November 17, 1986, pp. 134–142; and R. Cohen, "Clerical Activist," *Wall Street Journal*, August 28, 1986, pp. 1, 16.

19. "Quarta Lingua," *The Economist*, February 27, 1988, p. 46.

20. *Encyclopaedia Britannica: 1987 Book of the Year* (Chicago: Encyclopaedia Britannica, 1987).

21. J. Agnew, "Cultural Differences Probed to Create Product Identity," *Marketing News*, October 24, 1986, p. 22.

22. "A Generation of Wimps?," *Newsweek*, March 29, 1988, p. 141.

23. "Maverick Mogul," *The Bulletin*, March 29, 1988, pp. 57–58.

24. C. F. Keown, "Asian Importers' Perceptions of American Manufacturers," *International Marketing Review*, Winter 1985, p. 49.

25. 5.A Nation of Healthy Worrywarts," *Time*, July 25, 1988, p. 70.

26. Hsin-Min Tong, "International Bribery: Cases Involving Pacific Rim Nations and Recommended Actions," *Academy of International Business Proceedings*, Academy of International Business, New Orleans, 1987, pp. 237–244.

27. Discussions of business etiquette are included in N. L. Braganti and E. Devine, *The Traveller's Guide to European Customs & Manners* (Deephaven, Minn.: Meadowbrook Books, 1984); Copeland and Griggs, op. cit., chap. 8; and Harris and Moran, op. cit.

28. This discussion is based in part on E. T. Hall, "The Silent Language in Overseas Business," *Harvard Business Review*, May–June 1960, pp. 87–96.

29. E. T. Hall and M. R. Hall, *Hidden Differences—Studies in International Communication* (Hamburg: Stern Magazine, 1983), p. 15.

30. E. T. Hall, *Beyond Culture* (Garden City, N.Y.: Doubleday/Anchor Books, 1976).

31. R. Schreffler, "Japan: Targeting a Tough Market," *Distribution*, October 1987, pp. 44–48.

32. Copeland and Griggs, op. cit., pp. 79–80.

33. P. Ghauri, "Guidelines for International Business Negotiations," *International Marketing Review*, Autumn 1986, pp. 72–82; and J. L. Graham, "Across the Negotiating Table from the Japanese," *International Marketing Review*, Autumn 1986, pp. 58–71.

34. P. Gupte, "Inner Patience," *Forbes*, January 26, 1987, pp. 74–75.

35. Ricks, op. cit., p. 120.

36. J. Johanson and L. Gunnar-Mattsson, "International Marketing and Internationalization Processes—A Network Approach," in Turnbull and Paliwoda, op. cit., p. 243.

37. For a more complete discussion of the networking approach to industrial analysis and its implications, see Johanson and Gunnar-Mattsson, op. cit., pp. 234–265.

38. R. B. Oxnam, "Why Asians Succeed Here," *New York Times Magazine*, November 30, 1986, pp. 70–92.

39. For a more complete discussion of the influence of agriculture on Chinese culture, see O. H. M. Yau, "Chinese Cultural Values and Their Marketing Implications," *Working Paper Series* (Business Research Centre, Hong Kong Baptist College, 1986).

40. "The Outlook: Can U.S. and Japan Change Old Habits?," *Wall Street Journal*, November 10, 1986, p. 1.

41. D. Kilburn, "Sun Setting on Japan's Traditions?," *Advertising Age*, January 12, 1987, p. 46.

42. Ricks, op. cit., p. 66.

43. R. Tung, "Japanese Managers—Why Are They Winners?," *International Business Forum Address* (Australian International Business Centre, University of Queensland, 1987), p. 2.

44. See, for example, Harris and Moran, op. cit., pp. 466–476; and C. R. Laurent, "The Changing Nature of Hong Kong Consumer Attitudes," in S. R. Clegg et al., eds., *The Enterprise and Management in East Asia* (Hong Kong: Centre of Asian Studies, University of Hong Kong, 1986), pp. 247–264.

45. E. M. Rogers, *The Diffusion of Innovation* (New York: Free Press, 1962), p. 314.

THE FIRM'S POTENTIAL

INTERNATIONAL INCIDENT

The Rival Japan Respects

"Japan Inc." is the term that many U.S. firms use to describe the Japanese market, because they believe they face unfair competition in Japan. The Japanese government, financial institutions, manufacturers, and buyers join together to keep non-Japanese companies out of the world's second single largest market (120 million consumers). But Motorola has been waging a competitive war there, with products ranging from semiconductors and automotive electronics to pagers and cellular phones. Its goal is "to be the best manufacturer of electronics hardware in the world," according to CEO George Fisher. Introducing a miniaturized cellular phone, with a $2,500 price tag, first in the Japanese market, then following it with a wristwatch pager, Motorola has made significant inroads into the Japanese market. What internal qualities and strengths seem to be behind its success?

Motorola had difficulties in the mid-1980s, when Japanese competitors were beating it not only in Japan, but in the United States also. Motorola realized its approach to planning, executing, and control needed a drastic overhaul. It embraced successful Japanese approaches, such as making market share a primary objective, improving quality, aggressively cutting costs, and increasing research and development in order to be more competitive. Motorola also lobbied the U.S. government to bring pressure on the Japanese government to open up the Japanese market.

Motorola knew that its employees were ultimately responsible for the success or failure of its new global corporate vision. It invested $60 million in 1989 alone to instill the new vision in its 105,000 employees around the world. It also tied promotions, bonuses, and raises to quality improvement, a key issue in its new strategy. Employees responded with improved productivity, new interdepartmental communication systems, and better cooperation among business units.

In short, Motorola read the message from the external environment—become more competitive or fail—loud and clear. But it knew, after an internal audit of its strengths and weaknesses, that it had to alter radically the way it did business. Motorola had to build on its strengths and correct its weaknesses to regain a competitive edge. Its strategy is working. Sales in all of its units have increased, and profits are up significantly. In 1988, Motorola won the Malcolm Baldridge National Quality Award, recognition that it was a global competitor for the 1990s in the United States, Europe, and Japan.

Source: "The Rival Japan Respects," *Business Week*, November 13, 1989, pp. 108–115.

As we have seen so far, a thorough assessment of the external environment includes an overview of opportunities and threats in the market under consideration. But the firm will not be in a position to take advantage of all of the

The firm needs to assess its internal environment and respond to those opportunities where it has the greatest strengths.

opportunities in its environment, nor are all threats equally serious. The marketer must identify the most promising opportunities and the most significant threats for the firm. A detailed analysis of the company's internal environment, of its strengths and weaknesses, will reveal its potential for responding effectively to those opportunities and threats.

As Exhibit 7.1 shows, ideally the company's strengths and the opportunities in the market fit together perfectly (Case 1). For example, the Nigerian government may be interested in attracting communications-equipment industries—which would bring in new technologies, utilize local materials, and allow Nigerians to move quickly into upper-level positions—at the same time that a U.S. supplier seeks to market its know-how in the construction of turnkey plants for communications equipment in developing countries.[1] At times, however, a company's strengths are not relevant to a particular market. For example, the sophisticated distribution know-how of a U.S. producer of frozen foods may not be relevant in a market that lacks a sophisticated transportation infrastructure, such as Hungary (Case 2). On the other hand, even if the Brazilian market for atomic power-generation equipment appears to present a major opportunity for a French manufacturer, the firm will not be able to respond to the opportunity if it lacks technical personnel who speak Portuguese (Case 3). In short, a

EXHIBIT 7.1

THE FIT BETWEEN A COMPANY'S STRENGTHS AND THE OPPORTUNITIES IN A GLOBAL MARKET

Before a company decides to pursue a market opportunity, it needs to determine whether it has the necessary company strengths to turn that opportunity into a viable business. The line that runs from the lower left to the upper right represents an equilibrium of opportunities and strengths. In this example, Case 1 is the best fit.

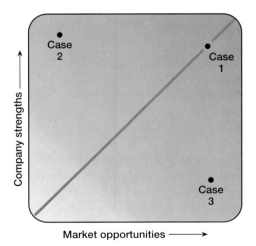

Case 1 = a U.S. turnkey plant supplier for communication equipment and the Nigerian government, which is interested in improving the country's communication infrastructure with locally manufactured equipment

Case 2 = a U.S. producer of frozen foods with sophisticated distribution know-how and the Hungarian market, which lacks a sufficiently reliable transportation system

Case 3 = the Brazilian market for atomic power-generation equipment and a French manufacturer, which lacks technical personnel who speak Portuguese

EXHIBIT 7.2
KEY
CHARACTERISTICS
THAT INFLUENCE A
COMPANY'S
POTENTIAL FOR
SUCCESS IN A
GLOBAL MARKET

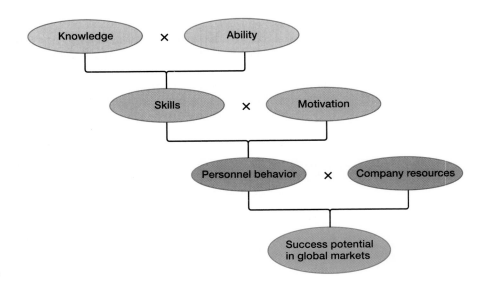

Many factors contribute
to a firm's potential for
success in a global mar-
ket. If any of the neces-
sary first factors (for example, knowledge or
ability) are missing, the
firm cannot make up for
them later. For example,
strong financial re-
sources cannot compen-
sate for personnel who
have very low motivation.

market opportunity cannot be translated into a specific business opportunity
unless it matches the company's strengths. This chapter focuses on the characteristics of the firm that must be examined to assess its potential for global
business.

KEY CHARACTERISTICS OF SUCCESSFUL
GLOBAL BUSINESSES

Companies that do
well globally share
some similar
characteristics.

It is possible to identify some key characteristics of companies that have succeeded in the global arena (see Exhibit 7.2). A company's ability to conduct
business in global markets depends primarily on how closely the skills of its
personnel match the opportunities present in the market. **Skills** are a blend of
superior knowledge and the ability to apply this knowledge appropriately. Managers and employees with distinctive skills may truly set a company apart from
its competitors, who will have a hard time acquiring the skills on short notice.
Other company *resources* that are of major importance for successful globalization
include financial, production, and organizational elements. Both the skills and
resources of a company largely determine its corporate policy, strategy, and
internal structure.

But global success depends on more than skills and resources. It is also
strongly influenced by the *motivation* of company personnel to adjust to new
environments, based on the dominating values and social norms that form the
firm's corporate culture. That is, will the people who work for the company be
motivated to apply their skills globally? This may not be the case, for example,

if the compensation system does not reward foreign assignments, or worse, if it acts as a disincentive in terms of opportunities for promotion.

Personnel behavior includes the interactions occurring inside the firm and between it and its external environment. It can be expressed as the product of skills times the motivation to apply those skills in ways desired by top management. If either personnel skills or motivation is insufficient, the resulting behavior will not lead to achievement of company goals. Overall, the internal factors that determine a company's potential for global success can be described as the product of the company's resources times personnel behavior. If personnel behavior is not globally oriented, or if corporate resources are insufficient, success is unlikely. Thus, when analyzing a firm's global potential, a marketer must look at the "hard facts" (company resources) and the "soft facts" (personnel behavior) within the company.[2] Both should be analyzed in terms of corporate policy (see Chapter 2), the firm's management systems, and its programs and actions[3] (see Exhibit 7.3).

EXHIBIT 7.3
CHECKLIST OF INTERNAL FACTORS THAT INFLUENCE THE FIRM'S POTENTIAL FOR GLOBAL MARKETING

In order to be sure the firm has a strong potential for global success, a manager may wish to perform an audit of the factors in this exhibit.

Corporate Policy	Management Systems	Programs and Actions

Business mission
  Purpose
  Business field
  General objectives
    and priorities
	Leadership
	  Commitment
	  Management style
	  Decision-making
	    processes
	  Incentives
		Marketing
		  Product attractiveness
		  Product competitiveness
		
		Research and Development
		  Product technology

Philosophy
  Rules of internal
    behavior
  Rules of external
    behavior
	Managing organizational
	  change
	
	Organization
	  Structure
	  Lines of
	    communication
	  Integration of
	    functions
		Process technology
		  Rate of innovation
		
		Purchasing
		
		Production
		  Capacity
		  Cost structure
		  Flexibility
		  Productivity

	Information
	  Gathering
	  Using
	
	Planning
	  Process
	  Organization
	  Resource allocation
		Finance
		
		Personnel
		  Availability
		  Attitude
		  Personnel development

	Control
	  Centralization
	  Coordination	

·
ASSESSMENT OF MANAGEMENT SYSTEMS

Several support systems have to be in place, and effectively functioning, in order for a firm to have sufficient internal strengths to respond to market opportunities.

Companies need management systems that support day-to-day business. The most important management systems are leadership, organization, information, planning and resource-allocation, and monitoring systems. A **system** consists of elements (structure) and the relationships among those elements (behavior). A leadership system, for example, includes people in different hierarchical positions (elements) and informal as well as formal interactions (relationships) between them. Because a company itself is an "open" system, its management systems are subject to external influences as well as internal processes. Both lead to marginal but constant change in the management systems. That is, management systems—their elements and relationships—continuously adapt to environmental developments in small steps. Such ongoing changes are not strategically managed, however, and therefore they do not automatically lead to an optimum result for the firm. More important changes in the environment, such as occur when a company globalizes its business, make management intervention necessary.[4] Thus, in evaluating a firm's potential for global marketing, its managers must determine how well the existing management systems will fit the new realities: Will they be able to cope with the more complex environments, what changes may occur without much managerial influence, and what changes will have to be strategically managed?

Leadership

The most critical support system is leadership that is strong and committed to global marketing.

The most important factor determining a company's potential for success is top management's ability and willingness to lead the organization in its global marketing effort. Top management must commit the firm to providing the necessary resources throughout the organization. For example, it must provide support facilities at headquarters, such as a databank or a small staff for the analysis of potential acquisitions. Additional travel budgets must be established. Management must make the needed adaptations in the marketing strategy as well as the marketing mix. The new markets may demand an upgrading of product design and quality. The decision-making process will need to be adapted to the higher complexity of global business. And because it may take longer globally than in the home market to achieve financial success, top management must take a long-range view of financial matters.

Commitment.   If the firm is to succeed in global markets, top management must be committed to achieving and maintaining a global presence. A study of small and medium-sized companies in Finland, West Germany, Japan, South Korea, and South Africa found that companies are significantly more successful in global markets (that is, they have much higher proportions of nondomestic sales) when their top managers have a global perspective.[5] These companies are even more successful than competitors that enjoy advantages in such areas as products, distribution systems, and capital.

The leaders of today's corporations such as Akio Morita, Chairman of Sony, must have a global vision and share that vision with all employees if the firm is to be globally successful.

Moreover, this commitment must be expressed through firm leadership. Through communications as well as actions, management must send clear, consistent signals regarding the priority of global marketing. Only by this means can a corporate culture become global in orientation.[6] In such a culture, globalization of thinking and action becomes an important value for the members of the firm, and behavioral norms that further global activities are positively reinforced.

If they are to have a global perspective, top managers should have experience with more than one culture. Such experience may come from family socialization, education, business experience, or intercultural training.[7]

Management Style. The best management style for leading a firm in its globalization process depends to a large extent on the cultural background of the employees. Successful companies in Western industrial nations tend to have a management style that stresses autonomy and entrepreneurship among the personnel.[8] Formal rules are kept to a minimum, and there is relatively little social distance between employees at different levels of the hierarchy. For example, at IKEA, the global Swedish furniture retailer, nobody wears a tie and employees have the right to disregard the management structure when they feel it is necessary to do so. This management style, however, will work only when there is mutual respect among employees at all levels, responsibilities are accepted by each individual, and there is a high degree of trust between employees and managers.

In other cultures the social and work background is very different. In Japan, for example, the hierarchical structure is very strong, yet open exchange of information on problems concerning the company's business is maintained. Since employees often spend their entire working life in a single company (changing companies is regarded as demeaning), they tend to identify with the company and therefore to be motivated to share their ideas.[9] The success of Japanese companies shows that their management style is well suited for global marketing under social conditions found in Japanese society.

In assessing the firm's potential for global marketing the marketer must evaluate the dominant management style. Is it able to motivate its employees to undertake the additional stress of global business? Will it be flexible enough to account for different norms of leadership behavior in the societies where the company will have employees? Chapter 17 will elaborate on the decisions and actions to be taken if the internal analysis described here indicates a need for change.

Decision-Making Processes.   There is a strong relationship between a company's management style and its decision-making processes. Before entering global markets, management should determine whether its decision-making processes are well-designed, in a way that allows for timely and flexible responses to environmental changes.

Business decisions are riskier and more complex in global markets than in domestic markets. There is more information, but it's less certain. The potential for conflict is increased. For example, in a U.S. bicycle-manufacturing company about to enter the European Community, the marketing manager may enthusiastically state that the EC is booming and will grow further in the coming years. He would try to attract support from all of the firm's functional areas for the new markets. The national U.S. sales manager, however, may worry about production-capacity restrictions. She may try to assure timely delivery to existing clients by interpreting the information concerning EC markets less optimistically.

Under such circumstances speedy and flexible decision-making processes are desirable. But effective decisions also depend on the technical quality of the decisions, the commitment of the individuals involved, and the development of technical and managerial skills, as well as teamwork and cooperation. Japanese companies take more time in making decisions than do U.S. ones, believing it is wiser to arrive at a consensus among decision makers and employees affected by the decision than for a single manager to make fast, solitary decisions.[10] The Japanese know that simply making a decision in response to an environmental stimulus does not result in immediate action (see Exhibit 7.4). The decision must be implemented. If decisions are based on consensus, generally they can be implemented more quickly and the company's response to a changing environment will be much more effective. Firms that are dominated by decision-making processes tailored to single managers may experience short-term success but more frustrations and difficulties in general when they try to globalize their marketing efforts.

Incentives.   Every company has an incentive system to motivate personnel to behave in the ways desired by top management. The system may be formally

EXHIBIT 7.4
REACTIONS OF
COMPANIES TO
EXTERNAL EVENTS

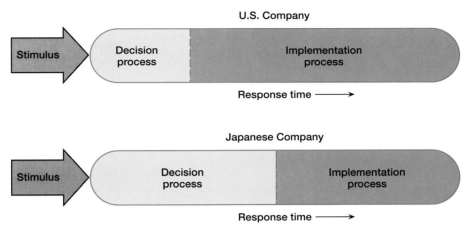

Although the total response time might be similar, companies based in different cultures will still react differently to similar external events. In this exhibit, the U.S. company decides quickly, but takes longer to implement the decision, because employee participation is usually minimized in a fast decision process. The Japanese firm takes considerably longer to decide, but because some agreement was reached among its workers, it is able to implement the decision more quickly.

integrated into the organization's leadership system, or it may be informal, based largely on tradition. Sometimes incentive systems differ from one part of the firm to another. In such cases behavior that is rewarded in one department may be counterproductive to efforts in other departments. For example, if fast and timely delivery of the product is vital to customer satisfaction, an incentive system that rewards the purchasing manager for keeping stock levels to a minimum may be detrimental to the company's overall success. Such built-in contradictions in incentive systems become even more problematic when a company enters global markets. There the purchasing process may, for example, be global and take longer compared to domestic purchasing. At the same time, delivery becomes more complicated and time-consuming. If the old incentive system is kept in place, it may be impossible for the firm to serve global customers within an appropriate time.

Company personnel located in different parts of the world may expect different kinds of incentives. Japanese managers, for example, have budgeted amounts to spend on entertainment after work. German managers prefer fringe benefits like the use of a company car for nonbusiness purposes. A company that is planning to enter global markets must be ready and able to accommodate its incentive system to cultural differences (see Global Dimensions 7.1).

Managing Organizational Change.   When a company globalizes its marketing efforts it will grow. Growth leads to chaos if management systems and personnel do not adapt to each stage of the firm's development. To be successful, the company's leaders must have the skills to develop or redesign continuously the firm's systems and to manage the organizational learning process.

When a company enters new markets, its activities become more complex. In most cases, existing strategies, programs, actions, and management systems will no longer be adequate. For example, existing new product-development procedures may have been sufficient for Japanese car makers as long as they

GLOBAL   DIMENSIONS   7.1

Compensating the Sales Force

If a company is considering global markets and already has a system for motivating salespeople, that system must be evaluated from the standpoint of the requirements of global marketing. For example, a system of bonuses that rewards individual achievement may be appropriate for a Canadian sales force, but it may not be appropriate for salespeople based in Taiwan or Hong Kong. Asian employees tend to favor group rewards and recognition over rewards for individual behavior.

In Japan, job security is an important motivator. There, salespeople are more willing to perform when they are offered security than when they are offered a monetary bonus. In Holland good interpersonal relations are a strong motivator, and employees disapprove of performance-oriented competition. In both countries, sales forces will not be motivated by the same incentive programs that are useful in North America.

When the company is entering a new market, salespeople may need to be compensated differently depending on their nationality. Austrian companies, for example, tend to offer high bonuses to salespeople when they enter a new market. When most potential customers in the market have been reached, the bonuses are reduced. A U.S.-based company might do exactly the opposite. U.S. firms tend to perceive salespeople as entrepreneurs, as self-motivated achievers who want to have more security in the beginning but are interested in receiving larger bonuses after the firm has gained a share of the market.

concentrated on domestic business. But when those companies entered the European market they were confronted with new levels of competition and demand. Instead of concentrating on efficiency and reliability alone, they had to hire European designers to redesign their cars to make a different visual impression.

The long-term success of a company strongly depends on its ability to maintain a constant learning process. For example, if a U.S. firm that manufactures sewing machines enters the Brazilian market, more people in the firm will have to learn about that market. The marketing manager will have to learn about the Brazilians' use of sewing machines, the finance manager will have to become accustomed to new terms of payment, company planners will have to adapt to less information about customers and competitors in the Brazilian market than in the United States, and the shipping department may have to cope with insufficient delivery systems. If the company's leaders are not ready to undergo such learning processes themselves and to change the behavior of personnel when necessary, they may have to rely on outside consultants or refrain from global marketing.

Organization

A firm must have a supportive structure in order for its programs and actions to be successful.

To assess how effective its development and implementation of global strategy, programs, and actions can be, a company must take a close look at its organization, including its structure, lines of communication, and degree of functional integration.

Structure. The firm's organizational structure is crucial for both the development of a global marketing strategy and its implementation. Organizational structure expresses the company's strategic emphasis and its priorities. Manufacturing companies are usually organized around functions (such as marketing, production, finance, and research and development). When the distribution of products is very important the company may be structured regionally (around, for example, the Midwest, Southeast, West, and Southwest). The growing influence of marketing on the success of many firms has led them to restructure their organizations around products (such as detergents, fragrances, and canned food) or customer groups (such as industrial users, professional users, and consumers).

With the broadening of markets that occurs as a result of a global perspective, a new corporate structure may become necessary. For example, an Italian insurance company preparing to serve the entire European Community may find that a product-based structure (such as life, fire, and liability policies), which may have worked very well domestically, will no longer be adequate. Instead, it may have to develop a new structure based on customer groups and regions in order to accommodate differences in life-style and, hence, insurance needs.

The existence or nonexistence of training programs in the firm's structural organization is another important factor to be assessed. A company that conducts training programs on an ongoing basis can adjust to new challenges much faster than competitors that lack such programs. Plessey, a British manufacturer of communication equipment, has installed a training unit to continually develop its sales force; it would have little difficulty in adding a training session for salespeople planning to enter the Indian market. A competitor without any tradition of personnel training would find it more difficult to prepare its salespeople to enter the same market.

Lines of Communication. Fewer levels in a hierarchy result in shorter lines of communication. A company with too many organizational layers between the head office in one country and customer service personnel in another country is likely to experience poor communication. For example, research and development personnel may complain about the lack of firsthand information about market requirements, while sales personnel may feel out of touch with the headquarters staff.

Short lines of communication do not guarantee effective communication, however. Management style plays a major role as well. It is management's responsibility to see that information flows freely in all directions. This is a prerequisite for success in global markets, in which sensitivity to external changes is a key determinant of the company's market position.

Integration of Functions.   Global marketing places many new pressures on the organization. Problems never before encountered must be resolved; a new environment must be mastered. If there is a lack of mutual support and understanding among different parts of the company, effective interaction will not be possible. In global markets even more than in domestic markets, salespeople may promise customers impossible delivery dates; the distribution and delivery systems manager may try to minimize global inventory levels; and production managers may try to optimize use of machinery without regard to delivery requirements.

Without an integrated approach, each function will blame the others when customers complain or sales are lost. It is true that these problems also exist in domestic markets. The point is that they must be resolved before the company attempts to operate in global markets. If they are not, the company will almost inevitably lose the competitive battle to better-managed firms.[11]

Information

Since global marketers deal with many different environments, an information system that gathers, processes, and distributes relevant information to managers is critical for success.

A well-developed information system gathers and processes internal and external information and distributes it among all of the decision makers in the company, as well as interested exchange partners in the external environment. It has to keep members of the company informed about all relevant global developments, such as new EC legislation on national quality standards, and the firm's exchange partners informed about all relevant internal events, such as a new sales manager in Southeast Asia. A company's potential for global marketing is greater when it already has an effective information system for its domestic business. In this section we will discuss the internal aspects of a firm's information system; external aspects (promotion and communication) will be discussed in Chapter 15.

Gathering Information.   Any company gathers information in a more or less systematic way, whether the firm serves domestic or global markets. However, for a global firm the information-gathering system must be formalized. It will have to be much broader and more flexible than is necessary when serving domestic markets. Because of the greater environmental variety, a wider range of information-gathering techniques are needed. In the United States, for example, telephone surveys are a popular and viable marketing-research technique. In other countries, however, they may not be legal, telephone service may be lacking, or people may simply refuse to answer questions on the telephone. Other techniques must be used to gather information (see Chapter 8).

Global marketers must also gather information from a much greater variety of potential sources. The best information may come from salespeople in the

United States, agents in Saudi Arabia, competitors in Spain, or the government in Japan. Global marketers need much creativity concerning new information sources unknown to them, or of little importance in the domestic market. If nobody in the firm has any experience in this regard, it may be useful to hire a consultant to get started.

Finally, a positive working environment within the firm is vital to successful global information gathering. It will not only ease feedback between managers and employees, but it will also encourage experienced employees to stay with the firm longer; the company benefits from increased experience curve effects.[12]

Using Information.   The main purpose of gathering information is to help managers make better decisions. The marketer assessing the firm's potential for globalization has to look at the way information is distributed in the company and how managers make use of it. For example, the globalization of marketing will be hampered if customer information only exists in the minds of salespeople, because there is no system in place to summarize this information, and then to distribute it to marketing, research and development, or production managers. In the complex global environment, any attempt to develop a marketing strategy or to implement consistent product or communication policies will be impossible if the company's management cannot rely on timely and precise customer information from all markets.

A similar problem may arise if relevant information is available to the decision makers but they do not use it. Marketing managers, for example, may think that they know enough about the market without going through all the "paper" on their desks. Research and development managers may believe they know the customers' problems better than the customers do and therefore ignore market information. If such conditions exist, they must be resolved before the company starts to globalize.

Planning

All companies plan. The most successful ones have a well-organized planning system to insure that all employees understand corporate plans and what role they play in helping to carry them out.

A company's planning system involves all of the departments involved in the organization of planning, the planning process itself, and resource-allocation decisions based on the plans. If a firm lacks a planning system, or if its system is designed for the domestic market only, it will be hampered in its efforts to expand globally. The planning system at a British computer-software firm, for example, will have to become much more elaborate if the company establishes subsidiaries in France, Japan, and Canada. Employees from these countries will have to be involved in the planning process. The organization of the firm will become more complex. Resource-allocation decisions will have to take into account potential market developments, as well as the firm's competitive position across markets. Without an adequate planning system it will be almost impossible for the company to develop lasting market relationships, even though single business deals may be executed successfully. But how does a company determine whether its planning system is adequate? It must look at the present planning process, its organization, and its resource-allocation procedures.

Planning Process.   The major purposes of a planning system are to find the right goals and objectives for all parts of the company; to develop strategies, programs, and actions to achieve those goals and objectives; and to allocate the company's resources appropriately. To fulfill these functions, a firm should not rely solely on a budgeting system for planning purposes. Budget figures, even when they are based on careful planning of individual activities, do not necessarily reveal anything about underlying objectives, programs, and actions. If planning is highly budget-driven, centralized coordination of planning is more difficult and synergy among different parts of the company is unlikely to occur (see Exhibit 7.5). This negatively influences top management's ability to effectively manage a global business. The budget for an advertising campaign in Peru, for example, may be based on the Lima manager's budget for last year plus an increase to account for inflation. But even if it is based on Peruvian action plans, the budget may not reflect the company's overall goal if it changed, for example, from gaining a high market share to achieving a high profit on each sale. This should change the way advertising is done in all of the company's markets.

A company with a strategic planning system based on corporate goals and objectives, therefore, is better prepared to enter global markets. Starting from its corporate policy, the firm should develop a core strategy after analyzing the external and internal environments. The company should define its objectives and general policies in areas such as market position and growth, product lines, distribution, communication, personnel, research and development, production, procurement, diversification, cooperation across functional areas, and mergers and acquisitions. Each part of the company should base its own plans on that

---

**EXHIBIT 7.5
PROBLEMS OF
COMPANIES THAT
RELY EXCLUSIVELY
ON A BUDGETING
SYSTEM**

While budgets are important planning devices, overreliance on budget-driven planning means too much attention is paid to numbers, and not enough to the dynamics of global organizations.

Lost opportunities for profit

Meaningless numbers in long-range plans

Unrealistic objectives

Lack of actionable market information

Interfunctional strife

Management frustration

Proliferation of products and markets

Wasted promotional expenditures

Pricing confusion

Growing vulnerability to environmental change

Loss of control over the business

Source: M. H. B. McDonald, "International Marketing Planning," *European Journal of Marketing*, vol. 16, no. 2 (1982), p. 10.

document. Their operational plans and budgets, including programs and actions, timing, responsibilities, and expected results, must reflect the strategy and policies of the company.[13] Departments that have the potential to contribute the most should receive the greatest support.

Organization.   The organization of the planning process will also influence the firm's potential for successful global marketing. If plans only exist in the minds of top management, as is the case in many small and even medium-sized companies, successful globalization will largely depend on chance. Global marketing significantly increases the complexity of the entire business, so a formal planning procedure must be established, with specific responsibilities for its execution assigned to staff members. Dates for the achievement of the different steps in the process have to be set, and planning must be in writing.

Resource Allocation.   In assessing its potential for successful global marketing, the firm must analyze how resources have been allocated in the company so far. In many companies resource allocation is based on experience or intuition. Sometimes it is based on partial analysis (for example, sales volume during recent years); "first come, first serve"; or even "they who shout the loudest get the most." Since it faces a higher level of complexity than a domestic firm, a global company will encounter major problems with such approaches. Intuition allows the manager to recognize "typical" situations, based on past experiences, and to draw the right conclusions in an extremely short time. If the business environment changes in a way not fully understood by the manager, however, the value of his or her experience is sharply diminished. A decision based on domestic experiences may initially lead to satisfactory results, but if the manager ignores changes in the seemingly familiar environment, the quality of the decision over the long term is questionable.

Global resource-allocation decisions have to be based on systematic analysis. To arrive at an optimal allocation of its resources among available business opportunities, the company must segment its existing and potential operations into discrete organizational units known as **strategic business units**. A strategic business unit (SBU) can be defined as a business component that is organized around the customer groups that will be served, the customer needs that will be met, and the products or services that will satisfy those needs. For example, a manufacturer of hair sprays may form three SBUs—one that serves teens who want to be "in," one that serves young professionals between 25 and 35 years old, and a third that serves "settled" people of more than 35 years. Each business unit would have its own brands, communication strategies, and products.

If the company has not been managed via SBUs so far, it will have to identify which existing or potential operations should be distinct business units. SBUs need to be chosen in a way that allows them to be managed independently of other business units without losing the advantages provided by synergy. These advantages can be illustrated by chopsticks. Each single chopstick is useful for pushing things, but together two chopsticks allow an individual to eat a meal.

Thus with synergy, the whole is greater than the sum of its parts. That is, a company that properly manages multiple SBUs has greater success than the individual SBUs would otherwise generate.

A firm can establish SBUs along geographic lines and according to product markets, products, technologies, or other criteria that greatly influence the company or purchase of a product. For example, a global marketer of pet food may establish SBUs based on product markets within specified geographic areas: the cat food market in Latin America, the dog food market in France, and so forth. The resulting units could be further segmented into product lines (for example, Whiskas in Brazil). An alternative would be to define SBUs strictly in terms of product markets (for example, the worldwide market for expensive dog food).

The firm must also be able to determine how its SBUs are distributed in relation to various factors that influence business success (such as political risk, market growth, and competitive position) and to various measures of success (such as profitability, market share, and cash flow). That is, the firm has to be able to do a **portfolio analysis**. A company's portfolio consists of its SBUs. The company will be most successful in the long run if it has a balanced mix of business units, product lines, and products at different stages of maturity, with different cash-flow positions, resource requirements, and technologies in different stages of development.[14] For example, Sony cannot count on its TV sets always selling well and being highly profitable. A portfolio of product lines would spread the market risk (just as a stock portfolio spreads the risk associated with investing in a single stock). If profits decline as its TVs move through the product life-cycle, Sony will need new products to help maintain sales and cash flow. Thus, Sony developed the Walkman, the Watchman, compact discs, and video cameras, investing in them in the expectation that future sales and profits of these products will be strong.

A comparison of business units along three dimensions—strategic importance, economic attractiveness, and competitive position—should be conducted by a potential global marketer in order to assess the potential and necessity for globalization.[15] The **strategic importance** of a business unit increases when that unit's success leads to success for other units. For example, when an SBU achieves a positive corporate identity, technological leadership, or improved competitiveness through higher production volume, it is of greater strategic importance because it can contribute to the success of other units of the firm. The **economic attractiveness** of a business unit depends on such factors as the size and location of its market, its rate of growth, relevant technological developments, financial return relative to the degree of risk involved, and trade barriers and restrictions. Strong markets with low risk and few trade barriers increase the attractiveness of an SBU. The third dimension, **competitive position,** refers to the strengths and weaknesses the business unit has compared to its major competitors. The more strengths it possesses that can be transformed into customer benefits, the more valuable that SBU is to the company.

Resource-allocation decisions should be made within each business unit as well as for the organization as a whole. The resources assigned to product lines, market segments, distribution channels, and functional areas should reflect the overall corporate strategy. For example, a global marketer of men's cologne might decide that its U.S. and Japanese strategic business units are most likely to contribute to the overall objective of being recognized as a marketer of prestigious men's cologne. Those units would receive more financial support than the European units. But within the Japanese unit, distribution channels and product lines that, in the future, are likely to contribute most to overall corporate objectives should receive the greatest support.

The marketing budget should also be based on the elements of the marketing mix, as well as marketing research. The marketing mix in turn should be based on underlying strategy. For example, Toyota's U.S. business unit, whose objective is to be among the market leaders, will probably allocate more of its marketing budget to promotion than the U.S. business unit of a company like Jaguar, whose objective is to pursue a high-status high-price market niche.

Resource allocations should also reflect the strategic importance of different target markets. Most companies are not large enough to serve all possible segments in their domestic market. When they begin entering global markets, it becomes even more necessary to concentrate on the most promising markets. In order to do so, the marketer needs an analytical tool called *portfolio analysis*, which will be discussed in detail in Chapter 9.

Control

Control is the use of any one of several mechanisms to make sure plans are followed.

Planning is not very useful if it is not accompanied by control. In the strict sense of the word, **control** is a process that brings about adherence to a goal or objective through the exertion of power or authority.[16]

Centralization.   Control very often means a strong tendency in companies to centralize power in the hands of a few top managers. This means that a few people make decisions, usually quickly. Top management also understands the implications of these decisions more than if decision making were spread throughout the organization. But a highly **centralized organization** will find a limit to how much power may be maintained at the top management level as it encounters different market conditions and competition in its global markets.

Coordination.   Expansion of the firm's business will depend on management's willingness and ability to allow control by **coordination.** The easiest way of achieving coordination is expanding existing *standardized processes*—such as quality control, cash management, and managerial accounting systems—to foreign markets. However, the marketer has to determine if these systems are appropriate for the new markets. Financial accounting, for example, follows different rules in the United States than in Norway. Further, the systems may not be sophisticated enough to allow effective control of global activities. For example, the firm should be able to identify costs per customer, order, region, and product, as well as costs per geographic and product market.[17] Only if the company can determine its financial status and its profitability in any given market at any given time is it well equipped for global marketing.

Another way to control through coordination is to use **integration,** the building of a tight network of interrelationships among the elements of a social system, such as a business and its partners. If the company has a long-standing tradition of close cooperation with suppliers, distributors, and other exchange partners in the domestic market, it will find it easier to integrate with new partners in attractive foreign markets. The stronger the integration, the less direct control is needed to assure the implementation of strategies and plans.

Finally, the degree of **socialization** of employees within the firm has a major influence on the necessity of direct control over their activities. Socialization is the process of instilling and reinforcing basic values and behavioral norms in members of an organization in a way that leads to a common set of values and accepted rules of behavior. If socialization is strong the employees of the company will act in a predictable manner consistent with the general goals of the firm, even if they are spread out all over the globe. Some of the global success of Japanese companies, for example, stems from the fact that their headquarters can rely on the socialization of the Japanese managers sent abroad. Even without close centralized control they will follow the rules they have learned over the years and their work will be consistent with corporate strategy.

ASSESSMENT OF PROGRAMS AND ACTIONS

All functional areas of a business need to work well together if the company is to be globally successful.

In order to evaluate the firm's potential for success in the most attractive foreign markets, management must determine the current state of its functional areas and their ability to design and carry out successful programs and actions, that is, their ability to effectively implement a globalization strategy. The company's marketing, research and development, purchasing, production, finance, and personnel departments must all function appropriately if the firm is to succeed globally. In this section we will examine what factors should be assessed in each functional area.

Marketing

Developing and delivering products that are superior to competitors' products, and what the market is looking for, is the "bottom line" for the marketing department.

Product Attractiveness.   The central question facing the company is whether its products can be sold in selected nondomestic markets. The organization's size, profitability, and market position are indicators of the resources it has available for investment in new markets, but they do not guarantee success. What is critical is the ability to develop products that, when compared to competitive offerings, will appeal to the target market.

Product Competitiveness.   To get an accurate idea of a product's sales potential in a nondomestic market, the firm must ask: What are the benefits our product provides to customers and are any substitutes available? When the firm has determined the advantages of its product compared to competitive offerings from the customers' point of view, the appropriate balance between standardization and individualization of the marketing mix should be established (see Chapter 2). If the company plans to enter national markets that are quite different from one another, individualization of the marketing mix is called for. But the firm may lack the resources for individualized marketing strategies. In that case it must choose among three options:

1. It may decide not to enter the global market.

2. It may market its product or service globally the same way it markets the product domestically, risking some customer dissatisfaction.

3. It may concentrate on globally offering only those parts of its product or service that have unquestionable competitive advantages.

When opting for the third alternative, which on the surface seems to be the only attractive one, the marketer can analyze the company's current activities by the use of a **value-added chain**.[18] In this approach, a product is viewed as a bundle of related services, and production is viewed as a bundle of processes (see Exhibit 7.6). The company splits its product into individual services and processes, then determines what it does best or better than its competitors. For example, do the greatest strengths of a clothing manufacturer reside in its early determination of attractive market segments, fashionable design, the production of reliable clothes, promotion, the distribution channel, or customer service? Companies that concentrate on offering those parts of the value-added chain that they do best, based on their distinctive skills and accumulated experience,

EXHIBIT 7.6
THE VALUE-ADDED CHAIN

A firm must continually strive for competitive advantages in the marketplace. One place to look for those advantages is in the added-value chain, that is, what the firm does best. For example, a firm may discover that what it does best is research and development. Thus it would concentrate on discovering new products, perhaps even selling them to other companies, as its competitive advantage.

Product	Production
(Bundle of services)	(Bundle of processes)
Entrepreneurial	Information gathering, sorting, or distribution Research and development
Production	Preliminary or prototype development Market testing
Implementation	Market introduction Market development Customer service
Financial	

Source: Adapted from R. D. Robinson, "Some New Competitive Factors in International Marketing," in S. T. Cavusgil, ed., *Advances in International Marketing* (Greenwich, Conn.: JAI Press, 1988), pp. 1–20.

can develop and defend a global advantage over competitors. They may then offer the value-added product to the market at a lower price than competitors' prices. Airlines that offer extremely low prices, but no in-flight service or reservations, have chosen such a strategy, for example.

Production processes, on the other hand, may involve such a high level of expertise and may provide so many customer benefits that higher prices are justified. VAIS, an Austrian company, is one example. It has chosen to globally offer training for managers and workers in new steel mills, or in mills with productivity problems that require additional training. The engineering, financing, management, and maintenance parts of the value-added chain are done by other companies, who are better equipped to provide these services, but are pleased to find a partner who takes over the training function, which requires complex technical, cultural, educational, and managerial know-how. The profit ratios achieved by VAIS are therefore very attractive.

Another approach, **product augmentation,** involves enhancing products so that customers believe their quality justifies a higher price compared to competing products.[19] The product is offered in combination with related services to make it more attractive. An airline, for example, may provide car rentals, hotel reservations, tickets for cultural events, or a 24-hour electronic reservation system, in addition to its flight service.

Research and Development

The technology a firm possesses or can develop is key to its long-term market success.

To determine whether its research and development capacities are appropriate for global markets, the company needs to take an inventory of its technological potential. This potential may take the form of patents, licenses, or copyrights, but it may also involve product or process technology.

Product Technology. Product technology affects customers' perceptions of the benefits offered by the product. "Too little" technology may result in problems for the marketer. For example, a Swiss company that produces leather watch straps wanted to sell them to Japanese watchmakers. The Swiss managers in research and development, as well as production, were convinced their product had the highest levels of tearing and perspiration resistance, as well as color constancy, in the world. All of their customers so far had been satisfied with the specifications of the watch strap. But Japanese watchmakers required much higher technical specifications. For three years the Swiss firm tried to convince potential Japanese customers that the Japanese specifications were exaggerated and had no practical value. During that time the firm did not sell one strap. Only when the Swiss firm understood that its product had to meet customers' expectations, not vice versa, did sales start to grow.

But a company also needs to avoid putting "too much" technology into the product. When a European manufacturer of BTX terminals launched Mupid, it offered the most technologically advanced communications product in the industrialized world. However, Mupid was so complex that nobody was able to take advantage of all of its benefits without training. From a technological point of view, the French Minitel was an inferior product. But customers found it very easy to use. Minitel has been well accepted, whereas Mupid was a flop.

Process Technology. Process technology has a strong impact on a company's cost structure, production flexibility, and the cost per unit produced.

In assessing the production department's potential contribution to success in global markets, the firm should analyze four interrelated characteristics: capacity, cost structure, flexibility, and productivity. Capacity and flexibility influence the company's ability to adapt to changing market demands, as well as to react to the actions of competitors. Cost structure and productivity influence the firm's pricing policies and its reactions to competitors' price changes. Flexibility and cost structure also help determine the company's general marketing strategy. (See Global Dimensions 7.2.)

Rate of Innovation. For both product and process technology, the company's rate of innovation compared to the rate for the industry is of major concern. If the company needs to increase the rate at which it produces innovations for successful globalization, it may undertake any of the following steps:

1. Monitoring trade journals and patent reports, and attending conferences and seminars on relevant technological issues.
2. Entering into agreements with research organizations that give the company access to recent research and the right to bring the resulting innovations to market.
3. Engaging in cooperative research projects with partners that have complementary expertise.
4. Acquiring technologies through licensing.[20]

In general, a global marketer should be able to at least meet the latest standard of technology in its field. If it cannot be among the technological leaders it does not necessarily lack global market potential, but it faces greater difficulty and must choose its target markets with more care. Most South American markets, for example, are not sufficiently technologically developed to use the latest generation of weaving machines. Workers lack the necessary skills, raw materials do not meet the specifications met by materials in highly industrialized markets, maintenance capabilities are lacking, and the machines are too expensive. As a result, there is a large market for simpler machines and secondhand equipment in South America, which can be provided by companies that are not among the technological leaders in the industry.

Purchasing

Previous global purchasing provides an experience curve effect for global marketing.

In general, companies with experience in international or global purchasing are better suited to global marketing. Medium-sized, high-tech U.S. companies, for example, can profit from their experience in purchasing components from Japan, Taiwan, and Korea.[21] They are familiar with the business environment in those

GLOBAL DIMENSIONS 7.2

Entering New Markets

Capacity. A company that is entering a new market must be confident of a minimum number of potential orders. The production department must have enough capacity to handle those orders properly. If additional investment in machinery, equipment, or storage capacity is needed, the timing of market entry is affected. So, too, is the cost per unit produced—it may increase because of higher investment costs, but it may also decrease because of gains in productivity.

Cost Structure. The cost structure of productive facilities strongly influences the strategies a company can pursue. For example, when an automaker like Peugeot increases the number of robots in its plants, the cost per unit produced will decrease as long as robots are more productive than skilled workers. Fixed costs as a share of total costs will increase as variable costs decrease, because of the need for fewer workers.[1] Peugeot would then be in an advantageous competitive position. It could either lower the price of its cars, increase the margin for its dealers, or make higher profits, which could be reinvested to further increase productivity or develop the market.

The marketer should notice, however, that higher fixed costs can have major disadvantages. One is that the company needs a bigger market to be profitable. Therefore, the firm is more vulnerable to negative economic developments in other parts of the world. Peugeot, for example, is vulnerable to economic stagnation in the United States. Additionally, the firm is faced with much higher barriers to leaving a market. In our example, if the car produced by robots is not successful, Peugeot will encounter a financial disaster.

Flexibility. The flexibility of a company's production system determines the speed with which it can make changes in the physical characteristics of a product or its package. BMW has made use of computer-aided manufacturing (CAM) to enable customers to "compose" their own cars. But even greater flexibility is possible. With computer-aided design (CAD), customers and manufacturers can jointly design custom products, which are produced with flexible robots. Note, however, that while the ability to offer such flexibility may be a major competitive advantage, the company must be able to finance the necessary investment.

Productivity. Low production costs may stem from low wages, low taxes, or high productivity.[2] Before management decides to enter a new market it must make sure that the firm's production costs allow for competitive pricing. Manufacturers from highly industrialized countries in Europe and North America encounter problems in this regard compared with producers from East Asia.

---

1. "Peugeot—Alive and Going Global," *New York Times*, March 20, 1988, sec. 3, pp. 1–8.

2. T. Tange, "Trade Frictions and Productivity Performance: Technological, Price, and Cost Competitiveness of Japanese and U.S. Exporters," *Journal of Policy Modeling* 5, no. 3 (1986): 313–333.

For example, German employees only work 30 hours per week in real terms, and Swedish companies have to bear high taxes. Both have to emphasize continually improving productivity to stay competitive in global markets.

However, low costs are not absolutely necessary for a firm to be successful in global markets. If the firm can define a niche, clearly differentiating its products from those of competitors in a way that matches the needs of customers better than other product offerings, it can justify a higher price. In other words, marketing know-how can have a decisive impact on a company's success when the product is equivalent in technological quality to competing products and production costs are higher.[3]

3. K. H. Beckurts, "High-Tech—Mode oder Chance?," *FAZ*, July 27, 1985, p. 11.

countries and know how deals are made there. Their personnel are experienced in dealing with people from other cultures. They know how to negotiate international contracts. It should be easier for such companies to market their products in other countries than for companies that lack such experience.

Finance

The goals of financial management are assuring that the other business functions have enough money to support their activities and managing the financial assets of the corporation.

Financial planning and control are essential to all other operations in the firm. For example, the company must have enough money to buy raw materials or to invest in a marketing campaign. Without appropriate financial management, effective marketing cannot occur. The most important aspect of financial management from the standpoint of potential global marketing is the degree to which top management is willing to make substantial investments that will not yield a return for several years. Thus, Zumtobel AG decided to open sales offices in a number of promising markets, even though it would take up to five years for the investments to become profitable. To take such a long-term view, however, the company must have healthy financial statements, a reasonable debt-to-equity ratio, sufficient cash flow, and consistent growth in revenues and profits.

Global marketing places a greater strain on the firm's financial resources than domestic marketing does. For example, the government of Saudi Arabia charges a nonrefundable fee or bond of up to $100,000 for the right to bid on certain large projects. The firm must either generate the necessary cash flow or be able to finance its global activities from external sources. When the company's financial resources are limited, it must recognize that it cannot enter markets in which financing of activities via bank loans is impossible and cooperation with local business partners is not feasible. A company with a substantial cash flow can choose from a wider array of potential markets. It can afford to look at those markets as investments with different payoff periods and varying potential returns.

Personnel

Ultimately, a firm's potential for global marketing success depends on the number of qualified and motivated employees available to it.[22] If there are not enough such employees, management can try to find qualified employees in both the domestic and international labor markets. In any case the globalization of business means organizational change. That is, employees have to be prepared for change and involvement in an appropriate manner.

Availability.   Skilled employees are a significant factor in a company's ability to enter global markets.[23] Lack of personnel with the necessary language skills and cultural knowledge is often a major obstacle for small and medium-sized firms that wish to market their products in other parts of the world, even when the products are well suited to the potential markets.[24] Many U.S. and some European firms lack personnel with foreign-language skills. Therefore, they tend to select only markets in which they can communicate easily. This is one reason why, for example, Austria conducts 40 percent of its trade with neighboring West Germany. Although this approach is understandable from a practical point of view, it does not necessarily result in optimal market choices.

Another potential constraint is lack of experience in nondomestic markets, coupled with lack of knowledge about how to conduct business in those markets.[25] Finding the initial business contacts, closing a deal, and delivering the product or service may seem to be either insurmountable hurdles or, at the other extreme, without any difficulties, "similar to the home market." Both attitudes are dangerous.

Even when personnel with the necessary skills and experience are available to contact customers and close deals, the problems of providing training, technical assistance, or maintenance services to customers may remain. Intermediaries are often unable to perform these tasks satisfactorily. If the firm does not have qualified personnel to perform these services, it will be forced to refrain from entering markets where the services are necessary.

All of these problems could be overcome by adding new staff with the necessary skills or by engaging outside consultants. But most smaller companies are unwilling to invest in new personnel before they are assured of success in the new market; the risk seems too great. Consultants can help companies enter foreign markets and establish business contacts there, but the company will still lack skilled personnel to conduct business in the new markets on a regular basis.

Attitude.   The attitude of personnel toward the company's plans for globalization is crucial. Training in language and cultural issues can be provided to those who need it. But the company must have enough people who are willing to undergo training if it is to take advantage of global opportunities. For example, in Europe many employees, despite well-developed language skills, are unwilling to leave their own country for an extended period. They are reluctant to exchange a familiar environment for a strange one. Only high salaries can motivate them to spend some time in a foreign market. This attitude acts as a major constraint on the companies' global activities.

The general working climate in the firm also influences its potential for global marketing. If employees have marked prejudices concerning specific markets, or if they are not ready to cooperate with people from other regions, the company may have to refrain from entering such markets. An Indian company with mostly Hindu employees could be forced, for example, not to do any business with Islamic countries in order to avoid conflicts inside the company.

Personnel Development.   The way a company does business must change when it enters global markets. Competition becomes more intense, and all aspects of the business become more complex. To encourage employees to perceive globalization as a chance for them to contribute to a successful future for the company, rather than an overwhelming threat, the company must exhibit great versatility, flexibility, adaptability, and ingenuity, as well as a strong desire to compete. At the same time, cooperation among employees is even more essential.

When all these difficulties are taken into consideration, small and medium-sized companies that lack experience in nondomestic marketing are likely to find that they cannot globalize their business all at once. Rather, they must manage a continuous process of personnel development that can produce the needed number of skilled people and generate a corporate culture that favors global marketing.[26] Managers and employees must be systematically prepared for new tasks in a more complex world. Their problem-solving and innovation potentials have to be developed. Adaptability and flexibility in reasoning and action have to be part of the training program. Leadership skills must be improved. The working climate has to allow for experiments and tolerate mistakes. Providing managers with relevant information should be seen as important as building interfunctional teams and task forces.

It is rare that a smaller organization has the resources to undertake personnel development on such a scale. It will need external consultants, coaches, and training institutions to build up personnel for successful global marketing. But top management, no matter what the size of the firm, should be aware that lasting success in global markets will not be possible without investments in personnel development.

SUMMARY

To take advantage of opportunities in its environment while avoiding potential threats, a company must conduct a thorough analysis of its strengths and weaknesses. Some key characteristics that must be examined are skills, resources, and the readiness of personnel to adjust to new environments.

The most important factor determining a company's potential for success is top management's ability and willingness to lead the organization in a global marketing effort. Management must be committed to achieving and maintaining a global presence, and the management style and decision-making processes must be flexible enough to adapt to changing conditions.

The major systems through which a company is managed are leadership, organization, information, planning, and control. Management style and decision making influence the firm's potential for global success. Incentives must be evaluated from the standpoint of the need to motivate personnel located in different parts of the world. Management must be able to initiate and lead organizational change. The marketer must take a close look at the firm's organization, including its structure, lines of communication, and ability to integrate existing functions into a global framework. The existence of a well-developed information system that keeps members of the company informed about all relevant developments will ease globalization. In planning and control, an important consideration is the ability to modify and expand existing systems. A company with a strategic planning system based on corporate goals and objectives is best prepared to enter global markets. However, planning is not very useful if it is not accompanied by control. The company must determine whether its standardized monitoring systems—such as quality control, finance, and managerial accounting—are appropriate for global markets, how much control can be exerted through integrative measures, and to what degree socialization of personnel can replace control.

The central marketing question facing the company is whether its product can be sold in nondomestic target markets. Two approaches to answering this question are the value-added approach, in which the company concentrates on what it does best, and product augmentation, which involves enhancing products to justify a higher price.

To determine whether its research and development capacities are appropriate for global markets, the company needs to take an inventory of its technological potential. This potential may take the form of patents, licenses, or copyrights, and it may involve product or process technology. The company's rate of innovation compared to the rate for the industry should be considered.

In general, companies with experience in international or global purchasing are better suited to global marketing. In the area of production, the firm should analyze capacity, cost structure, flexibility, and productivity. The most important question about financial management from the standpoint of global marketing is the degree to which top management is committed to backing a global strategy with substantial long-term investments. Finally, the firm must determine whether it has enough qualified and motivated personnel to enter global markets and what measures are needed to develop personnel.

To evaluate all of the factors that influence potential success in global marketing, the marketer will have to gather many pieces of information, put them together, and develop a general but detailed picture of the firm's potential.

DISCUSSION QUESTIONS

1. What specific criteria can a manager use to determine whether a company has the potential to be a successful global marketer?

2. Why is top management's commitment crucial to the firm's success in global marketing endeavors?

3. What organizational and communication issues influence the implementation of a global strategy?

4. How do information, planning and control, and resource allocation affect a company's potential to succeed in the global marketplace?

5. From the standpoint of global marketing, should the firm implement a product standardization strategy or a strategy of differentiation?

6. What role does the company's ability to provide product-related services play in determining its potential for global marketing success?

7. What elements of research and development influence a firm's potential for success in global markets?

8. What role does the cost structure of production play in a company's ability to compete in global markets?

9. "Personnel aren't really important in determining whether we should go into a nondomestic market. After all, we can hire someone in that country." Do you agree or disagree with this statement? Why?

10. Discuss the usefulness of comparing a company with its competitors when assessing its potential for global success.

C A S E

GALVANIK SCHMIDT GMBH

Raimund Schmidt, an MBA student in his second year, was excited. He had assembled a group of fellow students to work on a special study of his parents' company, which he was supposed to take over in a few years. A year previously, his father had decided to invest in a new production technology called the SLOTOLOY Process. This is a chemical-electrical process that protects metal surfaces from corrosion by applying a zinc-nickel alloy. Raimund Schmidt, Sr., had asked for his son's advice on how to fill the new production capacity. The group of MBA students was to develop a marketing strategy for the coming years.

Galvanik Schmidt GmbH was a financially sound family-owned business founded by Raimund, Jr.'s greatgrandfather in 1904. It was located in Fulpmes, a small village near Innsbruck, Austria. Seventeen people were employed by the company, seven of them family members. The company's basic production technology was the application of metal and plastic coating to refined metal surfaces. Sales in 1988 (after adjusting for the value-added tax) were 18 million Austrian shillings, or about 1.5 million U.S. dollars. Because of the high number of family members working in the company, motivation and individual performance were above the industry average. On the other hand, information sharing was limited, and the organizational structure was biased toward the family leaders.

Galvanik Schmidt had only been active in the domestic market. Its three biggest customers accounted for 64 percent of total sales. All other customer shares did not exceed 6 percent. Galvanik Schmidt had done business with two of its biggest customers, Alko Kober and Metallwerk, for 16 years. Both of these customers were internationally involved in just-in-time delivery of spare metal parts for the European automotive industry. Despite the fact that they ran their own galvanic production lines, large car companies like Audi, BMW, Ford, Mercedes, and VW used a number of small suppliers for the same purpose, in order to reduce warehousing costs.

Due to higher quality standards, in 1988 Audi, Porsche, and VW required zinc-nickel plating for every car part that had to be protected from corrosion. Chances were high that most other European car producers would follow their example. As a consequence, the demand among automotive spare part supply firms in Austria, Switzerland, and West Germany for the treatment of their products with the new technology was expected to increase considerably in the early 1990s. Galvanik Schmidt was one of three companies in that region that had a SLOTOLOY license. Schloetter, the owner of the patent, which also provided the needed chemicals, had promised to protect these contractors by refusing to grant further licenses.

Galvanik Schmidt had a very flexible production line. The company refined a range of different metal parts, from tools to ski bindings, trailer couplings, and automotive parts. The only limiting factor was the size of the pieces that could be handled by the machines. So far five machines with a total capacity of 60 metric tons per week had been run in one shift six days per week. The new zinc-nickel production line installed in 1988 had an additional capacity of about 30 metric tons per week. Cost information from Schloetter indicated the need to run the production in two shifts at least five days per week to amortize the investment. To run production at full capacity at least two new workers had to be hired. Raimund Schmidt, Sr., tried not to employ many new people before the development of the market for the SLOTOLOY technology. He relied on having family members run the production lines during weekends when peaks in demand had to be met. The supply of chemicals needed for the production process had been assured through a three-year contract with Schloetter. Schloetter even provided for capacity additions that could be installed in the existing production lines in six months' time if demand developed rapidly.

Pricing

Galvanik Schmidt traditionally priced its products depending on volume. Prices for zinc-plating ranged from 2.8 to 3.5 Austrian shillings per kilo. Galvanik Schmidt faced stiff competition from German producers, whose prices were below 2.8 shillings. The SLOTOLOY process involved nearly double the cost of earlier production technologies. Consequently, Galvanik Schmidt planned to charge 6–7 shillings per kilo. Because of the much better quality achieved by the new process and the small number of competitors in the market, Mr. Schmidt was confident that customers would accept that price. He relied on the fact that the automotive industry imposed zinc-nickel plating on its suppliers and therefore would be ready to pay the additional cost.

Because of the high number of pieces to be treated and their considerable weight, transportation costs represented an important percentage of the final price (15–20 percent for the traditional treatment, 10 percent for the SLO-TOLOY process). In the European automotive industry of the late 1980s, the price competition from Japanese competitors dictated extreme cost-consciousness. The location of suppliers of galvanic treatments, therefore, became a source of potential competitive advantage.

Distribution

The company's management had so far seen no need to develop its own sales force. Customers had found their way to Galvanik Schmidt on their own. They either contacted the Austrian Chamber of Commerce in their search for a supplier, or they learned about the high-quality performance of the company through word of mouth.

The customer shipped the products to be plated to Fulpmes, then picked them up again after treatment. Management concentrated exclusively on the production process, its financing, and its administration. Raimund Schmidt, Jr., was convinced that the additional production capacity available through his father's investment could not be filled fast enough by following the traditional way.

Promotion

As with distribution, Galvanik Schmidt had run no active promotion programs so far. Schloetter, however, was very much interested in quickly spreading the word of its invention among as many potential customers as possible. It had offered to help develop a promotional campaign for the company.

Case Issues

What is Galvanik Schmidt's potential, looking at (a) its strengths versus market opportunities, (b) the key characteristics that influence a company's potential, and (c) its value added?

NOTES

1.   C. Gale, N. H. Borden, Jr., and J.-P. Jeannet, *Cases in International Marketing* (Englewood Cliffs, N.J.: Prentice Hall, 1986).

2. T. J. Peters and R. H. Waterman, Jr., *In Search of Excellence* (New York: Harper & Row, 1982).

3. T. V. Bonoma, *The Marketing Edge: Making Strategies Work* (New York: Free Press, 1985).

4. G. J. B. Probst and U. Ulrich, *Pensée globale et management, Résoudre les problèmes complexes* (Paris: Les Editions D'Organisation, 1989).

5. E. Dichtl, H. G. Koglmayr, and S. Muller, "Die Auslandsorientierung von Fuehrungs-kraeften: Eine Schluesselvariable fuer Exportfoerderung und Exporterfolg," in E. Dichtl and O. Issing, eds., *Exporte als Herausforderung fuer die deutsche Wirtschaft* (Koeln: Gabler, 1984), pp. 429–462.

6. C. L. Suzman and L. H. Wortzel, "Technology Profiles and Export Marketing Strate-gies," *Journal of Business Research* 14 (1984):183–194.

7. S. D. Reid and C. Mayer, "Exporting Behavior and Decision Maker Characteristics," in V. Jones, ed., *Marketing 1980: Toward Excellence in the Eighties*, vol. 1 (Calgary: Admin-istrative Science Association of Canada, 1980), pp. 288–307.

8. Peters and Waterman, op. cit., pp. 200–234.

9. P. Kotler and L. Fahey, "The World's Champion Marketers: The Japanese," *Journal of Business Strategy* 3, no. 1 (1982):10.

10. V. H. Vroom and A. G. Jago, *The New Leadership: Managing Participation in Organizations* (Englewood Cliffs, N.J.: Prentice Hall, 1988).

11. M. McDonald, "International Marketing Planning," *European Journal of Marketing* 16, no. 2 (1982):10.

12. R. D. Robinson, "Some New Competitive Factors in International Marketing," in S. T. Cavusgil, ed., *Advances in International Marketing*, vol. 1 (Greenwich, Conn.: JAI Press, 1986), pp. 1–20.

13. Suzman and Wortzel, op. cit.

14. J. M. H. Dunst, *Portfolio Management* (Berlin: Walter de Gruyter, 1979); G. Specht and K. Michel, "Integrierte Technologie- und Marktplanung mit Innovationsportfolios," *Zeit-schrift feur Betriebswirtschaft* 58, Nr. 4 (1988):502–520.

15. J. M. M. Banham, "The Forgotten Factor in Export Performance," *McKinsey Quarterly*, Winter 1980, pp. 54–57.

16. A. Etzioni, "Organizational Control Structure," in J. G. March, ed., *Handbook of Orga-nizations* (Chicago, Ill.: Rand McNally, 1965), pp. 650–677.

17. P. M. Dunne and H. I. Wolk, "Marketing Cost Analysis: A Modularized Contribution Approach," in S. J. Shapiro and V. H. Kirpalani, eds., *Marketing Effectiveness: Insights from Accounting and Finance* (Boston: Allyn and Bacon, 1984), pp. 390–409.

18. Robinson, op. cit.

19. B. P. Shapiro, *Industrial Product Policy: Managing the Existing Product Line* (Cambridge, Mass.: Marketing Science Institute, 1977), pp. 37–39.

20. R. Ronstadt and R. J. Kramer, "Getting the Most Out of Innovation Abroad," *Harvard Business Review*, March–April 1982, p. 94.

21. "The Long Arm of Small Business," *Business Week*, February 29, 1988, p. 32.

22. H. Mühlbacher and G. Mitterhuber, "Die Internationalisierung der Geschäftstätigkeit österreichischer Unternehmungen," *Journal für Betriebswirtschaft* 33 (1983):103–177.

23. S. Ronen, *Comparative and Multinational Management* (New York: Wiley, 1986), pp. 115–165.

24. S. D. Reid, "Managerial and Firm Influences on Export Behavior," *Journal of the Academy of Marketing Science* 11 (Summer 1983):323–332.

25. Mühlbacher and Mitterhuber, op. cit.

26.   E. Kulhavy, K. Noehmayer, L. Schadenhofer, and H. J. Schelling, "Exportprobleme von Klein- und Mittelbetrieben: Eine empirische Untersuchung," *Marketingstudien*, no. 1 (Linz, Austria: Trauner, 1982).

GLOBAL MARKETING RESEARCH

Face the Sun and Count to Three

In most developing economies, marketing research is complicated considerably by the lack of a sample frame (a list of potential members of the target market). Even an accurate list of the villages and their exact locations doesn't exist. The Ivory Coast, for example, does not have as complete a census as does the United States. Even in the United States, how complete the 1990 census could be was a topic of considerable controversy. But most of the OECD nations have good sample frames.

In a survey in one African nation, researchers were continually frustrated in their attempts to design a sampling process where everyone had an equal chance of being included. There was no census, no complete list of towns, and even in those towns that were recorded, no streets or house numbers. The solution? Those administering the questionnaire were told to go to the western edge of the village when they began in the morning, then to "face the sun and count to three." The third house they came to was their starting place.

Another problem encountered in the same survey was that the survey supervisor was a white American. But the survey target population included many black Africans who lived in remote villages. When the supervisor tried to go along with the interviewers (matched by tribes to make interviewing easier), he found himself the subject of some interest, as no white American had ever before visited the mountain villages. When he was along, the interviews changed into a discussion of politics, ways of life, or beliefs. All of that is, of course, very interesting. But the purpose of the survey was to gather information about villagers' purchases and consumption behavior, not to socialize.

In order to assess the firm's potential for success, a considerable amount of internal and external information is necessary.

Because global market environments are very complex, the marketing analysis needs to include all of the relationships among different parts of the environment. The interpretation of market information has to lead to the right strategic and tactical decisions. To fulfill these expectations top management should establish a **global marketing audit**. The audit should include the firm's internal environments—corporate policy, management systems, programs, and actions relevant to global marketing—as well as external environments that influence the company's global marketing success—the economic, political-legal, and cultural-social environments; the product market; and the industry in which the firm operates.

A global marketing audit starts with the definition of its goals and scope. The key factors that affect market attractiveness and the firm's potential to serve a global market are defined. Before data are gathered, an effective, efficient, and flexible information-gathering procedure should be carefully planned, including what questions to raise, when, and where to find the right information sources. The information analysis and the presentation of results have to be planned as well, in order to have an impact on management decision making.

This chapter focuses on the planning and implementation of the global auditing process. Because most marketing managers will delegate the internal analysis to experts in other functional areas, we will emphasize the external side of the global marketing audit, that is, global marketing research.

DEFINING THE RESEARCH PROBLEM

The most important step in global marketing research is to properly define the problem.

Successful auditing or marketing research requires a systematic and thorough approach. Lack of planning in this area can easily lead the company to the wrong markets or to make bad decisions about the right markets. Such mistakes can be costly and even cause managers to turn away from global opportunities (see Global Dimensions 8.1). Careful planning not only helps prevent research blunders but also ensures that better results are achieved within the firm's budget and time constraints.

Any planned marketing research, domestic or global, begins with definition of the problem the firm is trying to solve. This is by far the most important stage of the research process. The care and accuracy with which this step is carried out largely determines how useful the research results will be. (Exhibit 8.1 presents the elements of this stage.)

In a classic example of poor problem definition in international marketing research, a study conducted by *Reader's Digest* concluded (falsely) that West Germans eat more spaghetti than Italians. The researchers erred in measuring only packaged spaghetti. Italians buy much of their spaghetti in bulk, from local pasta shops, and they consume considerably more spaghetti than West Germans. By defining the problem incorrectly—that is, as the need to measure sales of packaged spaghetti rather than total consumption of spaghetti—the researchers reached a false conclusion.[1]

Before asking questions in marketing research, a global marketer must first carefully define the research problem.

GLOBAL DIMENSIONS 8.1

The Need for Planning

One of the most serious, yet most common, mistakes made in global marketing is to begin studying a promising market without adequate planning. In one such case, an Austrian manufacturer of plumbing fixtures read an American magazine on architecture and concluded that the United States might be a huge market for his products. The only problem, he thought, was to figure out how to sell them "over there." He decided to take a trip to the United States "to study the market." He departed without planning his research effort or identifying potential sources of information. After two weeks of traveling in the United States, struggling to find out where to go and whom to talk to, he had spent his entire marketing-research budget for two years without making a single valuable contact.

After spending several nights in American hotels, the manufacturer was more convinced than ever that the United States represented a high-potential market for his products. But he had been able to gather only superficial information about potential customers, distribution channels, pricing, and the like. When he complained to a fellow member of a local business organization about the "disappointing outcome" of his expensive and time-consuming trip, he learned to his surprise of the existence of Austrian trade delegations in four U.S. cities. That resource alone would have provided better information free of charge than what the entrepreneur was able to gather himself. His lack of planning had been costly indeed.

As we can see from this example, the marketer needs some preliminary information about global markets, such as the relevant decision makers, business habits, or consumption patterns, to be able to define the research problem properly. Without such information, the problem will be treated as in the domestic market. To gather preliminary information about potential markets, the marketer may read professional journals or talk with managers of other companies that serve the targeted market. Suppliers located in that market are another cheap source of valuable information.

It may also be helpful to visit major trade fairs or exhibits for the company's product in the market region to be researched. Major trade fairs include ISPO (for sporting goods) in Munich, Germany; the New York International Gift Fair; the International Fair in Frankfurt, Germany (the biggest fair in the world for consumer goods, with over 4,400 participating firms from 60 or so countries); and the Hanover Fair in Germany, which is the biggest fair in the world for industrial goods. They provide the marketer with numerous opportunities to observe and talk with competitors, suppliers, distributors, and customers; to gather brochures, catalogs, reports, reference lists, and technical specifications; and to participate in cocktail parties and experts' talks and presentations. Information on trade fairs and exhibits can be obtained through local Chambers of Commerce and local embassies.[2]

complex — why?   #

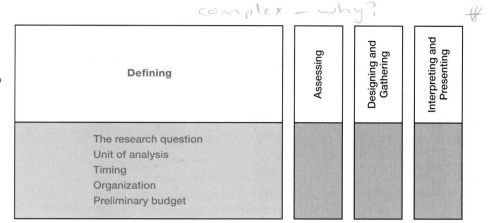

EXHIBIT 8.1
DEFINING THE
RESEARCH PROBLEM

Of greatest importance to
conducting good global
marketing research is
proper definition of the
research problem. Al-
though it may sound sim-
ple, most errors that oc-
cur in global marketing
research are due to im-
proper, often hurried,
problem definition.

Defining	Assessing	Designing and Gathering	Interpreting and Presenting

The research question
Unit of analysis
Timing
Organization
Preliminary budget

Effective problem definition may require the participation of the firm's decision makers as well as that of research specialists. The team approach has the added value of keeping key individuals informed and involved in solving the research problem and eventually using the findings.

To define the problem fully and accurately, the research team must address not only the general content of the problem, but also specific elements. This has to be done in writing. A useful way to document the thinking involved in defining the problem is to develop a **research brief** or preliminary proposal to be submitted to management for approval. The research brief states the research

This trade fair in Guang-
zhou (Canton), China
may look peaceful in the
exhibit hall, but it attracts
tens of thousands of visitors, about half of them
overseas Chinese, to look
at Chinese-made industri-
al equipment.

problem, the objectives of the research (the benefits that will be realized), and the potential costs of making a decision without the information to be obtained from the research. The brief also defines the unit of analysis, the timing of the research, who will be responsible for the project, and a preliminary budget. This document serves as a framework for the research project and also provides a basis for deciding whether to proceed with the research.

The Research Question

The problem needs to be restated as a research question; this helps define what information is needed in the research process.

The research problem should be defined as research questions. The information needed to answer each question varies with the type of question being asked. In global marketing, research findings are used to help make strategic as well as tactical marketing decisions. **Strategic decisions** are mainly concerned with the allocation of scarce resources over more than one product or geographical market. They should ensure the overall success of the firm instead of local optimization.

Market-development decisions concern where to invest, where to hold a competitive position, and where to retreat from. A small producer of highly specialized glass-treatment machinery, for example, may not have enough cash flow to finance research and development while maintaining a presence in every potential market. The market research questions that have to be answered are, for example: Which markets are more attractive than others? In what sequence should they be entered? What specific treatment do they need? How much emphasis should be put on the penetration of one of these markets before entering the next? **Market-clustering decisions** concern whether there is a chance to form clusters of similar product markets, independent of national boundaries, that allow a standardization of the marketing mix or if individualization has to take place (see Chapter 3).

Finally, marketing research has to help the firm's management define how to position the firm itself or one of its product lines in the global target markets. For example, a tour operator such as Waggon-Lits in Brussels, will not leave the decision of how to position the company and its product lines in each country to the local managers. Because the firm's customers may be in contact with a number of different offices, it is very important that they act uniformly. Market research will provide information about the strategies of local, regional, and global competitors to help Waggon-Lits develop a competitive and consistent global image.

Tactical decisions relate to the marketing mix for a particular product-market or a special target segment. The different expectations of different customer groups may mean that the product must be adapted in different ways for these markets. Marketing research can also supply information on the usual terms of delivery and payment, the price of competing or substitute offers, appropriate outlets, and the availability of advertising media in each market.

The important point to keep in mind is that research questions should reflect the nature of the marketing problem to be solved. If the problem is a strategic one, the questions that the research attempts to answer must be framed in strategic terms, not as tactical questions.

Unit of Analysis

The researcher needs to define the sources of information that will be gathered.

The **unit of analysis** is the smallest source of information that will be used to answer the research question. For example, a research project that aims to compare total consumption patterns for a product in two countries uses the country as the unit of analysis. However, if the goal is to measure specific brand preferences within each country, the unit of analysis might be the household.

Traditionally, the country has been the most common unit of analysis for international marketing research. The advantage of this approach lies in the fact that most information available on the environment (cultural, economic, and political) is organized by country. In addition, it is still common for the sales force, the internal sales department, or the firm's subsidiaries to be organized according to national boundaries.

Although this approach is convenient, it is not always effective. Its chief disadvantage is that data describing a whole country give an impression of homogeneity that may mask considerable diversity. Italy, for example, consists of the highly industrialized, wealthy north and less-developed, relatively poor, rural south. These two areas have differences in income distribution (although rich and poor people are found in both areas, there are more poor people in the south); marketing infrastructures; and, to a lesser extent, culture.

Research projects that use country data for purposes of comparison often fail to discover the best business opportunities. Such opportunities are more likely to be recognized if the unit of analysis is based on a product-market perspective. A product market is composed of organizations or individuals. Units of analysis may be, for example, firms, buying centers, households, or individuals. Product markets face similar problems, seek similar benefits, or display similar response patterns, but they do not necessarily share the same nationality. By starting with a product-market perspective, the marketer gains the advantage of being able to compare target segments regardless of size and geographic boundaries and to cluster them into homogeneous global markets.

The major disadvantage of using a product-market perspective to define the unit of analysis lies in subjective influences in defining product-market boundaries. The perspectives and ambitions of the marketer have a significant impact on the research design and findings. For example, if a manufacturer of downhill skis defines its market as wealthy, experienced skiers in the Alpine regions of Europe who ski for fun, the research project to discover their purchasing behavior will be very different from a project with a similar research problem, where the manufacturer defines its product market as all the people in the western industrialized nations who like to spend their leisure time in winter doing outdoor sports. The impossibility of an objective definition of product-market boundaries should not discourage researchers from using that perspective, however. It simply emphasizes the need to clearly define the problem underlying the research project.

Because the costs of data collection often rise as the size of the unit of analysis is reduced, it is important that researchers be clear about the level of detail needed. An easy trap to fall into, especially in a global context, is assuming that more information is needed, in more detail, than is really necessary. There-fore, careful choice of the unit of analysis, depending on the content of the research question (for example, whether it is strategic or tactical), is particularly important.

A practical way of choosing the unit of analysis may be to follow a stepwise procedure. This starts with an exact definition of the potential global product market to be served. Then the most attractive geographic areas are determined (see Chapter 3), and finally the adequate unit of analysis for the product market in those areas is chosen. For example, a Dutch manufacturer of durable plastic pipes for use in building construction may want to explore global product mar-kets. But the firm may not be large enough to simultaneously expand from one geographic market to all potential markets. To cope with such limitations, it should focus on product markets for plastic construction supplies in a carefully selected geographic area, such as Scandinavia, and take a closer look at construc-tion-supply wholesalers there.

Timing

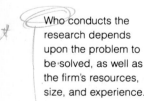

Global marketing research usually takes more time than domes-tic research. To make sure the information is available when it is needed, the timing of the research needs to be carefully planned.

Timing is an especially sensitive issue in the development of a research brief. Thorough global research projects often take more time than many firms believe they can afford. Before embarking on a full-scale research project, it is important to determine the latest possible date on which the results of the research could contribute to decision making. Similarly, it is important to determine the latest date on which one might begin the research process in order to produce results based on the most recent information available. These two factors obviously pose a dilemma. The marketing researcher will have to find a reasonable com-promise that relies on thorough planning, paired with personal experience.

Organization

Who conducts the research depends upon the problem to be solved, as well as the firm's resources, size, and experience.

The assignment of responsibility for a research project depends not only on the specific problem to be explored but also on the size, resources, and experience of the firm. Research for strategic purposes is usually conducted by members of the firm. The export manager, a marketing researcher, or a business-unit manager, for example, could take over the direction of the project. Small firms and those with little international experience may prefer to consult with experts outside the firm.

If a company plans to become active in a region where it has no experience and to assign a new manager to the region, the firm should assign the research responsibilities for this new market area to the chosen manager. Knowing that strategy, programs, and actions will be based on the findings of the research project, the manager will be much more motivated to produce reliable and relevant information than a marketing research specialist who is less involved.

In global *industrial* marketing most of the research for tactical decisions will also be done by members of the company. They have the technical expertise needed for research concerning their products, which is not usually available from external organizations. In addition, the number of distribution-channel members, potential customers, and important competitors is rather restricted in many industrial product markets. Little or no field organization is needed for data gathering, therefore.

In global marketing of *consumer products and services*, only a few companies have enough personnel and specialized knowledge to conduct marketing research projects for tactical purposes in an effective and efficient manner. They may be able to define the specifications for the research design. But in most cases they do not have a field organization to run interviews on an international level, or they are not familiar enough with local environments and languages to avoid misunderstandings and misinterpretations. They rely on external marketing-research organizations, therefore. What choices they have, and related advantages and disadvantages, will be discussed later in this chapter.

Preliminary Budget

A tentative budget should be drawn up based on the research questions, a preliminary understanding of what information is needed and at what level of detail, and a consensus about timing, organization, and what the firm's management is willing and able to spend. This is only a **preliminary budget.** Assuming that the proposal goes forward and the project moves into the next stage, a more detailed budget and a full research design should be developed to guide the remainder of the project.

ASSESSING INFORMATION NEEDS AND AVAILABILITY

The second major step in global marketing research is to state the scope of the research problem and assess the availability of information within and outside the firm.

A **research brief** is seldom specific enough to serve as a detailed research plan. In its statement of what kind of information is needed, the proposal points to the second stage of the research process: assessing information needs and availability (see Exhibit 8.2). This requires that the researchers define more clearly the dimensions of the research problem. The list of those dimensions allows researchers to find out what information is available inside the company and what information must be gathered from external sources. It also provides a substantial amount of information to be used in developing the research design and final budget.

Dimensions of the Research Problem

In global marketing the specific dimensions of a research problem depend on the research objectives, product markets, geographic areas of interest, and targeted market segments. Exhibit 8.3 illustrates the dimensions of a research prob-

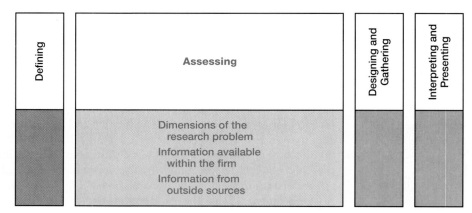

EXHIBIT 8.2
ASSESSING
INFORMATION NEEDS
AND AVAILABILITY

The second major step in global marketing research involves finding out how broad the research problem is, what internal and external information exists, and what information must be gathered.

lem that were defined by a European manufacturer of eyeglass frames interested in entering the fast-developing South Korean market. Note that this outline only focuses on one country; other geographic areas might be included, and target segments within each would probably be identified. Different research dimensions for each segment may result. The researcher can use the list of dimensions as a checklist, which will be further refined during the research process. Its first use is to identify information available within the firm.

Information Available Within the Firm

Before looking elsewhere, the researcher should determine what data are available within the firm. The value and scope of such information vary with the firm's size, experience, and policies.

Statistics. Relevant information can often be derived from accounting records, especially sales and cost figures. The most valuable internal statistical data for marketing purposes are summarized in Exhibit 8.4. Internal statistics can help the marketing manager judge the effectiveness of various strategies and tactics. The eyeglass-frame manufacturer described earlier, for example, may examine data on orders, sales, and profits or losses for exports to other markets and conclude how large the market volume and market share would have to be in South Korea to be profitable. In order to overcome comparability problems caused by different rules of bookkeeping and cost accounting as well as tax legislation in various countries, globally operating firms must apply standardized systems that are used exclusively for internal purposes.

Portfolio Analysis. More advanced companies will possess more sophisticated control systems. An important one for global marketers is a portfolio analysis system. Researchers can use portfolio analysis when addressing a strategic research

EXHIBIT 8.3
SPECIFIC
DIMENSIONS FOR
ASSESSING THE
SOUTH KOREAN
MARKET FOR
EYEGLASS FRAMES

The dimensions of a re-
search problem may be
quite wide and require
gathering considerable
amounts of internal and
external information.

Environment	Political/legal	Role of government
		Political stability
		International
		  trade policy
		Trademark protection
			Restrictions on
			  capital flows
			Price regulations
			Restrictions on
			  ownership
			Regulation of
			  competition

	Cultural/social	Business ethics
		Negotiation
		  customs
		Networks
		Resolution of
		  disputes
		Social structure
			Norms and values
			Attitudes towards
			  foreign products
			Aesthetics
			Consumption patterns

	Economic	Growth of GNP
		Rate of inflation
		Balance of trade and
		  payments
		Currency and
		  banking
			Population
			  development
			Communication
			  systems
			Transportation
			  systems

Product market	Structure	Potential Volume	Imports/exports Development

	Consumers	Buying power
		Buying and usage
		  behavior
		Product-specific
		  physiological
		  characteristics
			Life-styles
			Preferences

	Intermediaries	Number Reliability Margins expected	Size Buying habits
	Competition	Number Market shares Apparent strategies Product lines Price levels	Size Profitability Positioning Distribution policy Promotion policy

EXHIBIT 8.4
INTERNAL STATISTICS
FOR MARKETING
RESEARCH

The amount of internal
statistics that either exist
or need to be gathered
for a global marketing-research project can be
considerable.

Order statistics

Offers made

Orders accepted (by delivery time)

Cancellations of orders (including reasons why)

Order structure (size of orders, costs per order, number and size of orders per
  customer and per salesperson)

Sales statistics

Sales (pieces, value)		Market segment
Average prices		Channel of distribution
Price cuts/bonuses	per	Sales area
Terms of payment		Product (line)
Promotion costs		Customer

Profit and loss statistics

Profit and loss structure		Product (line)
(including absolute and relative	per	Customer
contributions to gross margin)		Sales area
		Channel of distribution
		Market segment

problem, such as the selection of a new market. Product-portfolio management
is discussed further in Chapter 9. However, portfolio analysis is also useful as
a source of internal information. For example, comparing different nations as
elements of a portfolio may help the company realize it is slow to enter new
geographic markets compared to its competition.

Data Banks.   Some firms, in particular smaller ones and those whose interest
in global marketing is relatively recent, may have internal data for only a limited
market area. In more experienced and sophisticated firms with more complex
information and control systems, up-to-date **data banks** may already exist. They
will contain not only the results of portfolio analysis but also information on
market development, as well as customer and competitor behavior, based on
reports from salespeople, subsidiary managers, distributors, or professional
journals. Findings from other research projects that are relevant for the research
problem at hand may also be available in the data bank.

Information from Outside Sources

Having obtained internal data, the researcher may need to obtain additional
information from external sources. The question is how to obtain this infor-

mation at a reasonable cost and in a timely manner. As Chapter 3 discussed, there are basically two ways of obtaining data from sources outside the firm: primary research and secondary research.

For reasons of cost, time, and problems in data collection, firms often attempt to satisfy their information needs by using **secondary research.** This approach provides information quickly and cheaply, but it is less precise than primary research because the data have already been collected and analyzed for purposes that differ from the firm's research objectives. Such data can be used to reduce the amount of information that must be obtained through primary research, thereby reducing the amount of time and money needed to complete the project. Most research problems can be addressed through secondary research, but require **primary research** for precision at the end of the research process. The next section presents a two-step approach to research design, beginning with secondary analysis and following up where necessary with primary studies (see Exhibit 8.5). The characteristics and difficulties of both approaches in carrying out global marketing research are also discussed.

SECONDARY RESEARCH

Research should begin with an examination of already available (secondary) information.

Secondary data sources are most valuable in assessing the attractiveness of markets about which management has little knowledge. They are regularly used to identify geographical or product markets that merit in-depth consideration and to monitor changes in the global environment. Secondary data enable the researcher to evaluate the risk associated with operating in a specific market, to determine the likely costs of alternative modes of operation and different marketing strategies, and to forecast the probable returns associated with operating in the market under study.

EXHIBIT 8.5
DESIGNING THE
RESEARCH: STEP 1

The research design may involve secondary or primary research or, often, some combination of both.

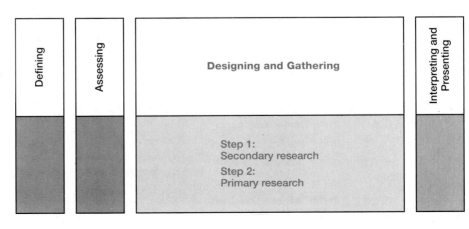

Defining | Assessing | Designing and Gathering | Interpreting and Presenting

Step 1:
Secondary research
Step 2:
Primary research

Statistics

The cheapest sources of secondary data are census and other statistical reports published by government agencies and by specialized agencies such as trade associations, chambers of commerce, research institutes, and banks.

Production Statistics.   Production statistics on product categories are available for all industrialized countries. Together with other statistics they help the marketing researcher to estimate market volume, the degree of saturation, and the level of local production. Production statistics are published with varying frequency, from monthly, as in western industrialized nations, to every few years, as in some of the COMECON countries. In using production statistics for market research the marketer has to be careful, because:

1. *Not all production facilities are included in the statistics; frequently, small firms are not included.* If the industry the marketer is interested in is characterized by a multitude of small family businesses, as is the case with the European textile industry, production statistics would lead to erroneous conclusions.

2. *The way products are classified may vary from one country to the other.* It is important, therefore, to thoroughly study the product lists accompanying production statistics or to ask for specific information at the office that publishes them.

3. *The product categories may contain a different number of products.* Smaller countries often use broader product categories than do big ones. TV sets, for example, are a category of their own in some countries, whereas in others they belong to the consumer electronics category.

4. *An industry may contain only a few producers, whose data are not published for competitive reasons.* For example, when an industry in an EC market is controlled by very few companies no production data are published, because they would provide too much information to foreign competitors.

5. *The value of the products in the statistics may have been calculated in different ways.* Some of the calculations contain only the production costs; others include sales or value-added taxes; and others consider market prices.

6. *The structure of the statistics may follow different international trade codes.* (See Exhibit 8.6.) The marketing researcher used to a particular domestic code may be misled.

EXHIBIT 8.6
INTERNATIONAL
TRADE CODES FOR
THE CLASSIFICATION
OF PRODUCTS

As a marketer moves across nations, even the way secondary data is put into categories, such as trade codes, will vary.

SIC	Standard International Classification
SITC	Standard International Trade Classification
BTN	Brussels Tariff Nomenclature
NIMEXE	Harmonized nomenclature of international trade of EC members
ETNVT	Product classification of COMECON countries

Consumption Statistics.   Statistics on a country's consumption of consumer products are usually organized according to the major purpose of consumption or usage. For example, in the furniture category the statistics may be grouped into living room, bedroom, kitchen, and so on. Unfortunately, such statistics exist only for the highly industrialized nations.

Import-Export Statistics.   Import and export statistics contain data on the volume, value, and destination of a country's imports and exports. They allow insights into the global flow of products and services. The major geographic markets for a specific product, as well as the most competitive areas in a global product market, can be determined. The statistics show the degree of saturation of demand through local versus nondomestic production. Therefore, they are the single most valuable source of information for a preliminary evaluation of a country's market attractiveness. But, as with production statistics, there are some problems with import and export statistics that a researcher should keep in mind:

1.   *Different product classification codes are used from one country to another.*

2.   *Exports and imports are valued differently.* Exports are usually valued without international freight or insurance costs added at the export harbor, for example. (For an explanation of differences in valuations, see Chapter 14.)

3.   *The statistics are published at different intervals.* The data will therefore vary considerably in timeliness.

4.   *The data are sometimes unreliable.* In researching small or economically less-developed markets the marketer may find the import data published by their administrations to be unreliable. The export statistics of the most developed industrialized nations generally provide more reliable information on imports in those markets.

Other Statistics.   Tax statistics for industrialized countries, in particular sales and value-added tax statistics, are organized by industry and product categories. They allow the assessment of the number and size of potential customers, intermediaries, and competitors. Other statistics, such as construction, transportation, and agricultural statistics, are not only of interest to marketers in these fields, they also provide information on a country's stage of industrial development, its general economic situation, and its infrastructure.

Information Sources

The most valuable source of information for U.S.-based firms is the U.S. Department of Commerce. Its Global Market Surveys furnish detailed information on, for example, market shares, product use, repeat-purchase rates, and competitive activities in key markets for selected products. For other countries, specialists known as **country desks** can provide the latest governmental import-export statistics for their country.

Through the embassies and consulates of other governments, firms can gain access to a wide variety of references on business conditions and opportunities. Often a staff member, such as a commercial attaché, commercial officer, or economic secretary, is available to provide specialized assistance. They have access to data banks, names of firms interested in business contacts, industry publications, address books, and telephone books. From these sources information can be gathered on market conditions, potential intermediaries, and competitors. Schedules of international promotion programs are also available; they provide perspective on which industries are particularly important to the respective governments.

Some countries have governmental commercial delegations in the researcher's country of interest. U.S. companies interested in doing business in Holland or Japan, for example, can contact the Dutch Trade Commission or JETRO (Japanese External Trade Organization) for valuable secondary information. These organizations, plus trade organizations sponsored by industries in the country of interest, also help companies to establish direct contacts with potential partners. In addition to government agencies, other organizations regularly compile and publish reports that are useful in global marketing research. Exhibit 8.7 illustrates some of these sources.

Chambers of commerce and trade commissions regularly ask consultants to study particular markets. (Addresses of chambers of commerce and trade commissions can be found in address or telephone books.) Unfortunately, they usually concentrate on one country market. A global product-market perspective is missing. When using industry reports from such sources, the market researcher must keep in mind that in many countries there is no obligation to belong to a trade commission. The data only cover the members of the organization, therefore.

A number of research institutes, such as the Institut für Weltwirtschaft of the University of Kiel and the Institut für Wirtschaftsforschung in Hamburg,

EXHIBIT 8.7
SELECTED REPORTS
PUBLISHED BY
INTERNATIONAL
ORGANIZATIONS

Valuable reports (secondary data) are available from a variety of international organizations.

Organization	Publication
United Nations	Statistical Yearbook, Yearbook of International Trade Statistics, Handbook of Industrial Statistics, Demographic Yearbook
United Nations International Development Organization	Trade by Commodities
OECD	Country Reports
International Monetary Fund and EC	Analytical overviews of international trade
World Bank	World Tables, World Development Report

Germany, regularly publish reports on global economic topics. Market research companies and information services offer purchasing-power maps, analyses of the economic structure of specific regions, reports on the development of an entire industry, and information concerning the financial reliability of potential customers and intermediaries. The foreign-business departments in banks have information on market risks, terms of payment, and transportation and insurance problems in different countries.

The fastest way to collect secondary data is through electronic data banks. More than 3,000 data banks are available for on-line use, and their number is growing steadily. Examples include COMEXT-EUROSTAT, a time series of import/export data from the European Community, and NIKKEI Economic, a source of economic statistics on Japan. Approximately 75 percent of the data banks are located in the United States, another 20 percent are in Europe, and the remaining 5 percent are in other parts of the world. Although most data banks charge fees for accessing the data, these costs are minimal compared to what a firm would have to spend to collect the information on its own. A carefully planned on-line search can reduce data-collection costs even further. Exhibit 8.8 contains a list of economic data banks that are of special interest to marketing researchers.

Industry journals contain information on market development, new products, and competitors. Newspapers like the *Wall Street Journal*, the *Economist*, *Frankfurter Allgemeine Zeitung*, *Neue Zürcher Zeitung*, *Asiaweek*, and *Le Monde* offer detailed analyses of environmental factors as well as specific features of national and product markets. Public libraries often contain nontechnical but nonetheless valuable sources, such as country yearbooks, economic atlases, and tourist guidebooks.

Finally, personal contacts with domestic suppliers of complementary services or products can be very helpful in the interpretation of information about environmental influences, specific business behaviors, consumption patterns, competitors, and potential intermediaries. Contacts with companies with subsidiaries in the target country may provide similar information.

Survey Techniques

A wide variety of survey techniques exist to capture verbal and/or visual inputs.

The marketing researcher can choose between verbal and visual surveys, or a combination of the two, depending on the research problem, the units of analysis, and the advantages and disadvantages of each technique.

Mail surveys can be effectively used in many industrial marketing-research projects. The costs of administering a mail survey appear to be low on a per-unit basis. But, in addition to problems that are well known from domestic surveys (such as varying levels of literacy), in a global context there are additional limitations on this approach. Motivation to respond may be even lower than in the domestic market, and mail surveys may suffer from inadequate or unreliable postal services. In some African countries, for example, mail delivery is so unreliable that mail surveys are useless. In India, the postal service claims to deliver mail anywhere in the country within two days, but recipients may not

EXHIBIT 8.8
EXAMPLES OF
ECONOMIC DATA
BANKS

Due to the explosion of
data bases and electron-
ic communication sys-
tems to share them, glob-
al marketing researchers
can access secondary
data more easily.

Name	Supplier	Content	Number of Documents
ABI/Inform	BRS, Data-Star, Dialog	Reference of articles in 500 business magazines	300,000
BI Forecasts	Dialog, IP-Sharp	Economic-development forecasts for 35 countries	—
BI Time Series	DIALOG, IP-Sharp	Economic indicators for 130 countries	—
BUNDESBANK	IP-Sharp, DRI Europe	Statistical publications of the German Federal Bank	13,000 (time series)
CBD	DIALOG	Publications of the U.S. Dept. of Commerce	1 million
CNC	GSI-ECO	Time series of financial information on France	1,300
COMEXT-EUROSTAT	CISI	Time series of import/export statistics on EC countries	3 million
CURRENCY	IP-Sharp	Daily currency-exchange rates	449 (time series)
Dun & Bradstreet	DIALOG	Data on U.S. firms and major non-U.S. corporations	2.5 million
Direction of Trade	IP-Sharp, DRI Europe	Import/export statistics on 130 IMF countries	121,000 (time series)
EK-BDI	GENIOS	Product information for Germany	220,000
EKOL	KODA (Kompass)	Information on European companies	300,000
Electronic Yellow Pages	DIALOG	Information on U.S. companies	8 million
FIND/SUP	DIALOG	Market studies	10,000
ICC Directory	DIALOG, Data-Star	Information on companies in Great Britain	1 million
IFS	IP-Sharp, DRI Europe	IMF statistics	57,000 (time series)
Industry Data Sources	Dialog, Data-Star	Market studies, economic publications	120,000
ITIS	DRI Europe	Import/export statistics for OECD	7 million (time series)
Japan Economic Daily	Dow Jones	Information on Japanese economy	—

(Continued)

EXHIBIT 8.8 (*Continued*)

Name	Supplier	Content	Number of Documents
Kompass Sweden	Data Arkiv	Information on Swedish companies	40,000
LDC	DRI Europe	Economic data on Africa, Asia, Australia, Latin America	—
NIKKEI Economic	DRI Europe	Economic data on Japan	15,000 (time series)
PROGNOS	Prognos AG	Forecast data for 36 countries	10,000 (time series)
PTS F&S Indexes	DIALOG, Data Star	Reference of articles in 2,500 business magazines	3 million
SCAN-A-BID	Data Star	Development projects in developing countries	—
TELEFIRM	G-CAM	Information on French companies	380,000

Source: Adapted from *Handbuch der Wirtschaftsdatenbanken*, Munich, Verlag Hoppenstedt, 1986.

be able to read the questionnaire because of language differences—there are fifteen major languages in India!

Telephone surveys, like mail surveys, can be effectively used in global industrial marketing research and sometimes in consumer research. Almost all firms have telephones, and relevant respondents can be identified by means of a few preliminary questions. Multiregional studies can be conducted from a single location, saving time and money and increasing the response rate, because of the higher motivation to respond to international telephone calls.[3] The main drawback of telephone surveys in industrial marketing research is the anonymity of the interviewer. Respondents may be concerned about revealing information that competitors could use, or reluctant to respond fully because of work pressures. As a result, only a limited amount of information may be obtained.

Limited ownership of private telephones in many areas of the world restricts the feasibility of telephone surveys for consumer research, except among the most affluent consumer groups. Moreover, in many cultural contexts, such as Latin America, there is a strong reluctance to respond to strangers and respondents may be unaccustomed to lengthy telephone conversations.

Computer-aided surveys may be useful in conducting specialized research on consumer behavior. This approach is limited to urban areas in highly developed countries where people are familiar with keypads or keyboards and video screens. Automated interviews, in which respondents answer questions posed on the computer screen, produce lower error rates and fewer biases than other survey techniques. Visual aids make them easy to use, and the computer can register the response time of interviewees as well as the responses themselves.[4]

Personal interviewing is the most expensive survey method, but it is also the most cost-effective. This is because high response rates, a flexible interview situation, and the ability to address complex issues all result in higher-quality data. In areas where postal services are poor, illiteracy rates are high, and telephones are not available, personal interviews are mandatory. However, in some cultures interviewers may encounter suspicion; for example, in Latin America they may be perceived as tax inspectors. Thus, care must be taken in the selection of interviewers. The social class and language of the interviewer and the target group should be matched.

Reliability

A major problem with secondary data is determining how accurate it is.

To establish the comparability and usefulness of secondary data, the researcher must locate the original sources. In addition, the researcher must make sure that the data-collection and analysis procedures that were used in producing the secondary data meet the standards of the current project. In other words, using someone else's sloppily collected information will not save money and time; in the long run, the information will have to be collected again in a more effective manner.

Timeliness is another factor that must be considered; the data may be too old to be relevant for the current research problem. This would be the case, for example, when a marketer interested in Belgium finds census data that is seven years old, and an informative country report that is five years old. Demographic and economic changes may have changed important parts of the relevant product market in the meantime.

Secondary data are not fully comparable if:[5]

1. *The criteria used for grouping data into statistical categories are different.* For example, an area classified as urban in Japan has at least 50,000 inhabitants, whereas in Sweden and Norway the same term means an area with a population over 200.

2. *The categories in the statistics to be compared have been given different widths.* For example, occupational statistics in the United States may use different age categories than the same statistics in Italy.

3. *The categories are defined too broadly.* For example, if a marketer of ball bearings for ski lifts wants to determine market volume in France, production and import-export statistics won't help if the statistics only contain a category for all metal parts in ski-lift equipment.

4. *The data come from different units of analysis.* Two data sets about the projected markets for computer-paper forms in Switzerland and Spain, for example, would not be comparable if the first data set came from domestic manufacturers and the second from a survey of users.

Decisions on Further Research

After the firm has gathered and analyzed secondary data, it must decide whether further research is necessary. It may turn out, for example, that the research problem has to be redefined in light of newly gained insights. The marketing researcher may also use the data and the list of research issues to determine what additional information has to be gathered. Consider again the example of the European eyeglass-frame manufacturer. Based on secondary data, the firm may have decided that the South Korean market is attractive. But it may still need to know more about the life-styles and preferences of South Korean consumers, as well as their attitudes toward foreign products. It may also want to find out more about potential intermediaries and the marketing strategies of competitors in the South Korean market. These kinds of information can seldom be obtained in any other way than through primary research.

The decision whether to go on to primary research or not will be based on estimates of how much research is still needed and what it will cost to obtain the desired information. If, for example, secondary data account for 75 percent of the information needed by management at 10 percent of the estimated research budget, the remaining 25 percent of information may not be worth the additional expense required to obtain it. In most cases, however, the marketing researcher will not be able to avoid gathering information through primary research, in order to fine-tune the firm's marketing mix.

PRIMARY RESEARCH

Although primary research provides the most specific information about the research problem, it is more costly and requires more time to conduct than secondary research.

As noted earlier, **primary research** promises the most specific and targeted information possible for a given research problem. But it is also costly and time-consuming. Researchers used to studying domestic environments may face new problems. For example, statistical data for a reliable sampling frame may be missing. There may be the need to translate questionnaires into different languages. Moreover, in many parts of the world there are no service organizations to assist in the collection of data.

Because of such problems, careful planning of a primary research project for a global market is particularly important. Different types of research designs (exploratory for aid in problem definition and initial insights, descriptive for examining patterns of market behavior, and causal for determining what stimulus leads to what behavior) may be used to help the marketing researcher answer the questions of market behavior: what, when, by whom, and how much. The research plan must specify the objectives and scope of the study as well as what techniques will be used for data collection, analysis, and interpretation. On the basis of this plan, a budget and schedule for carrying out the research can be established, and personal responsibilities for different parts of the project can be assigned (see Exhibit 8.9).

EXHIBIT 8.9
DESIGNING THE
RESEARCH: STEP 2

Research often involves a
second step, primary
research.

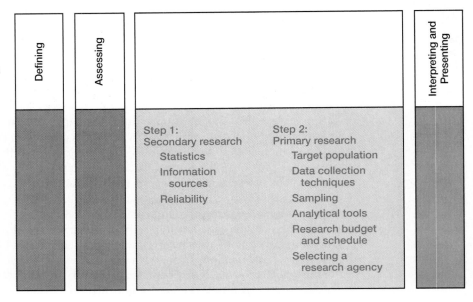

Target Population

Primary research
focuses on the target
population.

The appropriate **target population** for a research study depends on what the researchers are trying to learn and what is likely to be the best source of this information. Researchers then have to choose the best information sources from the defined units of analysis. For example, researchers who want to learn about the attitudes and expectations of intermediaries who handle high-technology communications equipment will try to obtain data from wholesalers, retailers, and even independent sales representatives in that industry. The marketer of an expensive consumer product may try to get information directly from affluent consumers in a number of countries. A marketer of machine tools will be mostly interested in decision makers such as purchasing specialists, production managers, technical directors, and top management.

Depending on management and decision-making styles, the right choice of the target population may be different from one geographical market to another. In consumer product marketing the relevant target population may also change from one country to another. In the United States and Western Europe, for example, family car purchases are strongly influenced by women. Therefore, they are part of the target population if consumer preferences for different cars are to be determined. In Saudi Arabia, religious guidelines and a patriarchal family structure do not permit the inclusion of women in the target population for research on car purchases.

Sometimes the firm may want to obtain information from more than one target population. For example, a vacation destination in Switzerland will be interested in its image with both travel agents and travelers. The researcher will

MAP 8.1   INTERNATIONAL RESEARCH HOT SPOTS

Research company executives were asked to identify the nations where they did the most business in 1989. Thus, the countries are ranked by order of importance in terms of level of business activity. The U.K. and Germany, for example, were the busiest markets.

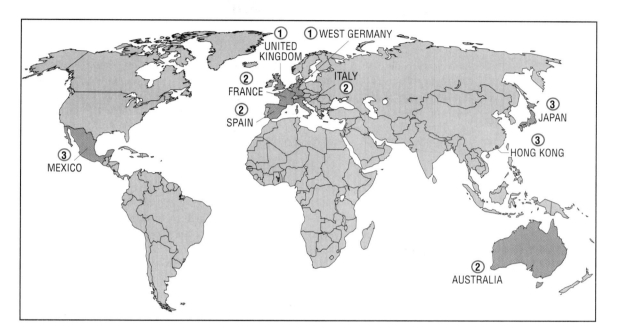

also have to decide if information on a topic has to be gathered in all potential markets and from all the potential partners, or if research findings from one area are representative for others. However, even if the budget is restricted and the markets under consideration seem to be similar, as would be the case for the Scandinavian markets, for example, researchers have to be careful in making generalizations. A Finn would not appreciate being classified as being similar to a Swede.

Data-Collection Techniques

A careful choice of how best to collect information from the target population is made.

Once researchers have determined the best potential sources of information, they must select the most appropriate method for collecting the data. The best data-collection technique is a function of what has to be found, who has to be contacted, the size of the sample, and how the members of the sample can be reached. There are basically three ways to get information from primary sources: observation, experiments, and surveys.

Observation.   Observation is a means of collecting information without asking questions. A French manufacturer of sun-roofs, for example, can hire an agency to observe the advertising campaigns of its three most important competitors in all of the EC markets. It can also gather information on potential intermediaries in the Italian market by observing the number of customers they have, their business behavior, and their service capacity at the Ravenna trade fair.

The biggest advantage of observation is that it is not obtrusive.[6] It is most appropriate when direct methods (experiments and surveys) might affect the way subjects behave or respond. Another advantage is less danger of researchers' imposing a cultural frame of reference on the units of analysis than there is with, for example, standardized questionnaires. The problem associated with observation, however, especially in a global context, is that the observer must understand what he or she is seeing well enough to interpret it. (Global Dimensions 8.2 illustrates the danger of cultural bias in observation experiments.)

Experiments.   The second means of gathering primary data is through experiments that test the potential impact of a given marketing decision. A supplier of international travel tours, for example, might test a new arrangement with an airline carrier on a limited number of destinations to project how the target market will respond to the offer. Theoretically, experimental techniques can be applied to all markets. A manufacturer of plants for burning toxic waste may even build a plant at its own expense, for example, to prove the promised benefits and to test the reactions of potential customers and environmentalist groups. Marketers of consumer products sometimes choose a smaller national market as a test arena for their products before they decide on entering a bigger market. A manufacturer of leather clothes in Istanbul, Turkey, for example, may choose Austria as a test market for its marketing strategy, before taking the risk to enter the much bigger German market.

Although in theory experimental techniques are applicable to all markets, in global marketing it is often difficult to control the experiment's reliability. Ideally, a global researcher has two experimental groups: one in which the experimental variable is manipulated while all other variables are held constant, and another in which no variables change at all. The researcher can then measure the impact of the experimental variable. Such conditions are even more rare in global research than in domestic test marketing. The difficulty is magnified when experiments are attempted in different cultures. In addition, researchers may confront technical problems. For example, it may be impossible to compare the effects of the same advertising approaches in two geographical markets because of media differences and the inability to control for the behavior of competitors. Even laboratory tests cannot rule out certain cultural elements.[7] For example, cultural differences in attitudes toward authority affect perceptions of spokespeople in different countries.

Surveys.   A third means of gathering primary data is to ask questions directly. Survey research is conducted for the purpose of gathering information that is

GLOBAL DIMENSIONS 8.2

Bias in Observation

A North American food-packaging expert scanning the European environment for new opportunities might notice that Dutch grocers stock milk in containers no larger than one liter. She might conclude that Dutch households do not consume enough milk to warrant the use of larger containers, such as the half-gallon and gallon jugs that are widespread in North America. However, upon seeing several shoppers purchase two liters at a time, she might conclude that there is a market for larger containers in the Netherlands.

Neither of these conclusions would accurately reflect the milk consumption and shopping habits of Dutch families. Dutch consumers place a high value on freshness, shop every day (often by bicycle), and own small refrigerators. These factors combine to make one-liter cartons and bottles highly suitable for the Dutch market.

difficult or impossible to collect in any other way, such as the attitudes, knowledge, and behavior of respondents. How structured the survey should be depends on the amount of knowledge the researchers already have about the target population and the product market under study. Basically, the less that is known, the more important it is to use an open-ended approach to data collection. Exploratory or pilot studies are very useful in identifying issues that can be addressed later in more structured surveys.[8] On the other hand, when there is considerable knowledge about the research issues, a highly standardized and structured approach is more suitable.

The greatest challenge in conducting survey research in a global context is to obtain valid, comparable, and reliable data.[9] Researchers must check the validity of each variable measured in the different geographical areas. That is, they must make sure that the survey instrument really measures what it is intended to. Without validity over the markets to be compared, similarities or differences in the gathered data could be due to the research design, rather than market differences.

Even if validity is assured, comparability or equivalency of findings is a concern. When comparing product markets in different countries to each other in order to find opportunities to standardize parts of the marketing mix, comparability of the data has to be assured. Comparability should be established for the research process as well as for content. For example, the questions used in data collection and interviewees' responses to these questions must have the same meaning in the markets to be compared. And the respondents must interpret the questions and their own responses in the same way. There may be culturally based emotional differences in the meaning of a question that lead to incomparable responses between people from different countries. The content, phrasing, and presentation of the question may result in different responses (for example, "to be outstanding" means "not to stand out" in China).

To obtain comparable results, it may be necessary to use different approaches in different areas.[10] For example, energy-saving household behavior may need to be measured in different ways in the United States and Norway. In the United States, people who are highly motivated to save household energy may install insulating materials in the walls, floors, and attics of their homes. But in Norway, where heating costs have traditionally been higher, homes may be insulated as a matter of course. There, a high level of energy-saving behavior might be represented by the purchase of an energy-efficient heating system. Under such conditions, the use of a standardized data-collection form would result in astonishment or little understanding from respondents in one of the countries. New statistical methods for dealing with comparability problems are being developed. However, they are still in the formative stage, and researchers should continue to seek expert opinions concerning the concept they are trying to measure in each nation.

Besides the question of comparability of data from different environments, the problem of potential miscommunication between researcher and respondent is particularly prominent in global marketing research. On the one hand, the data-collection form has to be translated into other languages and dialects in a way that exactly transmits the intended content. This may be difficult with new technical terms, which may not even exist in the other language. Even if the translation is perfect, the researcher may find that respondents in the countries under consideration have different levels of education. For the respondents in one country it may be appropriate to formulate a question in an abstract, verbal manner. But for the respondents in another country the same question may have to be communicated through visual means. The marketing researcher, therefore, must understand even slight cultural differences between countries and target groups. More than with domestic research, careful pretesting of global data-collection methods is necessary.

Sampling

When the data-collection technique has been established, the researchers must decide how to go about selecting particular respondents for observation, experimentation, or surveying.

Sampling Frame.   A **sampling frame** is a list from which elements of the target population can be identified. Researchers in western industrial nations can choose among a variety of reliable sampling frames—mailing lists, telephone books, voter registration lists, motor vehicle registration lists, the International Business and Company Yearbook, and so forth. In many developing countries, however, there are few reliable sampling frames for either industrial or consumer target markets. Census data may not be available or recent enough to use. (India, for example, does not have an accurate count of its total population.) The reliability of the few lists that are available may be limited by such problems as unusual

The members of the target population to be included in primary research are selected through sampling.

housing situations (such as people living on boats or out in the open), rapid changes in small-business ownership, and a high proportion of family-owned businesses. These problems not only make it difficult to compare markets but can actually prevent researchers from reaching sources of information. Under such conditions different sampling techniques may be needed to obtain representative samples.[11]

Sampling Techniques.   The method used to select potential respondents from a sampling frame is the **sampling technique.** With a reliable sampling frame, the researcher can choose a **probability sample**, in which each member of the population has a known chance of being drawn into the sample. When detailed sampling frames are not available, the global marketer may use a **cluster sample**. For example, the city of Bombay, India, might be divided into equal-sized units or neighborhoods. A random sample of these units would then be drawn. Within these clusters, every member or every household would be included in the survey.

Probability samples are more elegant from a theoretical point of view. The absence of a reliable sampling frame and other practical reasons, however, often lead global market researchers to draw a nonprobability sample. A **convenience sample** allows the researcher to choose respondents who are readily available, such as people in a marketplace in Indonesia or production managers in Bolivian companies. **Judgment samples** are often used for global industrial marketing research. With this technique the researcher chooses "experts" on "typical" representatives of a product or country market.

Because of their sensitivity to many sources of bias—such as high nonresponse rates, unreliable sampling frames, and interviewer influences—the reliability of different sampling techniques varies with the market environments. It is not reasonable, therefore, to apply one standard technique independent of research areas and product markets. An intelligent adaptation of the sampling technique to the specific circumstances encountered in the markets will largely improve response rates, the quality of the data, and the price/benefit relationship of the research project.

Sample Size.   The quality of research results depends not only on the instrument used to collect data and the sampling technique employed, but also on the size of the sample. There are both technical and practical issues associated with sample size. Sample size is partly a function of the diversity in the population to be sampled.[12] In areas where the population to be surveyed is not well known, the degree of variability may be difficult to determine. For example, there are no census data for Bombay. To allow for possibly high variability among households in Bombay a larger sample would be required. In such instances exploratory studies with small samples may help researchers gain a better understanding of the population to be studied.

On the practical side, since most research budgets are fixed, trade-offs must be made among the number of areas that can be studied, the size of the sample in each area, and the amount of data collected from each respondent.

Even where larger samples are appropriate, their cost may be considerably reduced by using a multistage sampling technique. Such an approach was used by a European manufacturer of cast-metal parts when it studied the feasibility of enlarging its mold-construction department to serve all potential users of industrial molds in Germany, Switzerland, Italy, and Austria. In the first stage, a probability sample of potential customers was drawn from addresses provided by trade commissions. Telephone calls were used to find out which companies and which individuals within these companies should be included in the second stage. The individuals identified in this way were mailed questionnaires designed to gather additional information about potential customers. The responses to the questionnaires were used to identify a third sample of individuals who were interviewed personally, to get more details about how to successfully approach new customers.

Such a stepwise sampling procedure keeps the costs of research lower than those associated with one-step projects. On the other hand, it takes more time to be implemented and the errors committed at each stage accumulate over the duration of the project. Unfortunately, there is no general recipe for how to draw perfect samples in global marketing research. The size and structure of research projects depend on the firm's information needs, the characteristics of the target market, and the research budget.

Analytical Plan

The data analysis plan, to tell the researcher what has been learned, is an important part of the research design.

An important part of the research design is the plan for analyzing the data. This involves determining what data are needed for what purpose, as well as what tools will be used in their analysis. For example, if the research is designed to find out how consumers in Canada and Mexico respond to one packaging design compared to another, the **analysis plan** must include a way to group and compare the responses of consumers to each design. Specifically, the plan has to specify if the researchers want to compare the average response of users of one design with the average response of users of the other design for each country, or if they want to identify groups of consumers in both countries for whom brand recognition is important. The statistical techniques to be used will depend on this decision. By answering these kinds of questions in the research design before data gathering has started, researchers ensure that information will be collected in an appropriate manner and that irrelevant and unnecessary (and therefore costly) information will not be sought. The tools used to analyze the data collected in global marketing research do not differ from those used in domestic research.[13]

Research Budget and Schedule

The cost of each activity included in the project must be estimated. If the firm has a fixed research budget, the project must be designed to meet the constraints imposed by that budget. If the budget is based on the costs of the planned

Estimation of research budgets and schedules in global marketing research is complicated by different costs in different nations.

activities, the marketing researcher should compare these costs with the profit the company may lose if management makes poor decisions because of the lack of information.

Estimating a budget for global marketing research can be difficult. The costs of doing comparable studies vary in different countries, even in the same part of the world. (Exhibit 8.10 shows the price variation for quantitative and qualitative studies in EC countries.) For this reason, many researchers (and marketing managers) may prefer to establish the project budget in stages and review expenditures at the end of each stage. When this approach is used, the stages need to be outlined in the research brief.

EXHIBIT 8.10   PRICES OF MARKETING RESEARCH STUDIES IN THE EUROPEAN COMMUNITY

The price of a marketing-research project can vary greatly depending on the country in which it is conducted. In this exhibit, the average price in the European Community is indexed to 100, and each country is compared to that average. Thus, Germany is 29 percent more expensive than the average EC price, while Greece is 45 percent less expensive.

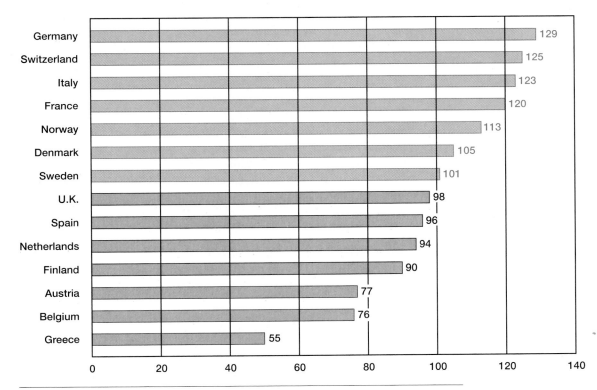

Source: S. Shalofsky, "What Price Market Research? The ESOMAR Survey of Market Research Prices in Europe," *Marketing and Research Today,* May 1989, pp. 67–80.

Rank	Organization, Location	Research only revenues* ($ mill.)	Number of countries (subsid.)
1	Nielsen, Northbrook, Ill.	$765.0	27
2	IMS International, New York & London	297.6	64
3	Pergamon/AGB, London	195.0	21
4	SAMI/Burke, Cincinnati	170.0	2
5	Arbitron Ratings Co., New York	155.0	1
6	Information Resources, Chicago	105.5	1
7	GfK Group, Nuremberg	102.0	11
8	Research International, London	93.1	14
9	Infratest, Munich	66.8	6
10	Video Research, Tokyo	65.8	1
11	WESTAT, Rockville, Md.	61.3	1
12	MRB Group, New York	61.1	5
13	M/A/R/C, Irving, Texas	50.3	1
14	Cecodis, Chambourcy, France	45.0	2
15	Maritz Marketing Research, St. Louis	38.0	1
16	Market Facts, Chicago	37.4	2
17	Social Research Institute, Tokyo	32.5	1
18	SRI Research Center, Lincoln, Neb.	32.0	1
19	NOP Market Research, London	29.7	2
20	Elrick & Lavidge, Chicago	28.8	1
21	Audit & Surveys, New York	28.5	1
22	Taylor Nelson/MaS Group, Epson, Surrey	28.0	2
23	The NPD Group, Port Washington, N.Y.	25.7	1
24	IHA Group, Hergiswil, Switzerland	25.4	1
25	MIL Research Group, London	24.5	3

Source: Jack Honomichl survey for *Advertising Age* (December 5, 1988, pp. 5–18).
Notes: *Revenues. These are, as best can be determined, 1987 research-only revenues (turnover) for calendar 1987 plus revenues for any acquisitions made during 1988 so far. Some of these organizations have higher total revenues when non-research activities are included, as is explained in the company profiles. Because of currency fluctuations during 1987, some foreign based companies' figures are approximations.

Listing activities on which budgets are based also serves to help schedule the project and control its implementation. Global marketing research projects are usually complex, taking place across many nations and using agencies that have a variety of skills and capabilities. In order to ensure that the job is done within the budget and on schedule, the activities list is used as a planning tool for these projects.

Selecting a Research Agency

The research agency may be chosen on the basis of geography, industry, or whether the agency has a global network.

When considering hiring an outside organization to carry out a research project, management has three alternatives among which it may choose. These exist in all of the developed countries and in many developing ones. First, there are research agencies based in the geographic area of interest. They have expertise on the local environment, as well as the ability to cope with problems of language and concept translation. The difficulties associated with using such agencies include finding reliable ones and coordinating their activities.

The second alternative is to select a research firm that specializes in the industry in question. Such firms are more likely to understand the research issues related to that industry and may have experience in carrying out studies in many different parts of the world.

Happily for many managers, globalization has had an impact on market research agencies as well as on other business services. (For example, see Exhibit 8.11.) The needs of customers who do business on a global level have led some agencies to sign multilateral cooperative agreements, thereby building worldwide chains of research agencies, such as U.S.-based International Research Associates (for a European-based example, see Exhibit 8.12), or to merge on a global level. For example, by merging with Dun & Bradstreet, A. C. Nielsen has become the largest market research firm in the world. Thus, a third option is to contract with a well-known, reliable global research agency or chain of cooperating agencies to manage the entire project. Such companies rely on branch offices and associated agencies in all of the developed countries and most of the developing ones, but the customer deals with only one office, located in the home country.

Exhibit 8.13 presents a checklist for evaluating market research agencies. But even with the help of outside experts, marketers may have difficulty carrying out primary research in some parts of the world.[14] In developing countries in Asia and Africa there are relatively few market research organizations. Even in Latin American countries consumer surveys are available only for urban areas. In addition, it may be difficult to establish a field research staff with enough training to produce reliable interviews. The cheapest and most effective way of getting information in such cases may be to design the research around secondary data and add interviews of carefully selected experts in the markets of interest.[15] The marketer may visit each market to verify the interpretation of secondary data and the insights gained from expert interviews.

EXHIBIT 8.12
RESEARCH WITHIN
THE EUROPEAN
COMMUNITY

Even though the Europe-
an Community is moving
toward a united market,
there are still strong national and regional differences in buyer behavior.
One of the biggest mar-
keting-research chal-
lenges in the European
Community, as this ad il-
lustrates, is how to un-
derstand these differ-
ences in order to make
better marketing
decisions.

Will we change our habits when our borders disappear?

*Will the Portuguese
start wearing Lederhosen?*

*Is the bowler hat going
to be a French phenomenon?*

*Will the Danish
take to sidewalk cafés?*

*Will the Dutch apply
themselves to mountain climbing?*

*Will we finally have
a European Soccer League?*

*Is Dallas going to be
Europe's favorite TV program?*

*Will the Italians
take to cricket?*

*Will the Germans get
addicted to Bordeaux wines?*

*Will jeu de boules
conquer the Greek Islands?*

*Will the British continue to
drive at the wrong side of the road?*

When consumer habits change, we will be the first to know. And we will be only too happy
to share our knowledge with you. Contact your local IRIS agency for any research requirement.

International Research InstituteS

I R I S

Source: IRIS advertisement in *Marketing and Research Today*, May 1989, p. 384.

EXHIBIT 8.13
CHECKLIST FOR
EVALUATING MARKET
RESEARCH AGENCIES

The quality of the marketing-research project is heavily influenced by the quality of the agency used to conduct the research. This exhibit provides a checklist of the criteria a manager should use in evaluating the suitability of a particular research agency.

1. Technical and marketing know-how, including capability in the content and methods of the proposed research.

2. Use of experts in special areas (e.g., psychologists, sociologists, statisticians).

3. Client references for similar research problems or product markets.

4. Client references concerning the application of similar research techniques.

5. Careful selection, training, and supervision (including quality control) of interviewers and other agency staff.

6. Appropriate and accurate methods of data collection and analysis.

7. Demonstrated quality (content and style) of project reports and presentations.

8. Control of price and financial procedures, including cost calculation and billing methods.

INTERPRETATION AND PRESENTATION OF RESULTS

Exhibit 8.14 illustrates the final stage of the global marketing-research process. The data that have been collected and analyzed must be interpreted and presented in a form that will help improve management decisions.

Interpretation

The final step in global marketing research is to interpret the results; that is, What has management learned?

The interpretation of research results requires a healthy skepticism because of the potential for errors in data collection and analysis, especially when data have been collected under varying circumstances.[16] For example, there may be substantial biases in the answers to attitude questions because of cultural differences. In some societies it is quite common to openly express one's opinion; in others, however, understatement is more common or people are reluctant to express their attitudes to strangers. If researchers want to compare the answers given to the same questions in two such different environments they need to correct for biases due to the typical response styles of the interviewees. This can be achieved by normalizing or standardizing the gathered data. When a questionnaire scale is standardized, for example, the mean answer for each respondent is set to zero, and differences from that answer are expressed in terms of standard deviations. Normalization occurs when the differences are expressed in terms of deviation from the country's means.

The interpretation of data gathered on an international level demands a high level of cultural understanding. In global market research there is the constant danger of selective perception due to cultural biases. This problem can derail an otherwise well-designed and well-executed research project. The prob-

EXHIBIT 8.14
INTERPRETING AND
PRESENTING THE
RESULTS

The final step in the global marketing-research process is the interpretation and presentation of results.

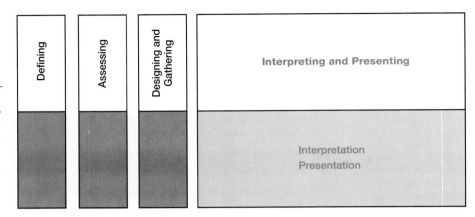

ability of correctly interpreting data can be improved by ensuring that at least one person who interprets the data from a particular region is well acquainted with the culture and business customs of that region.

Presentation

Research results should be presented according to who is receiving the results and how the information will be used.

The findings of a research project are a "product" that, like any other product, deserves its own marketing strategy. The findings should be presented in a fashion that meets the needs of different "customers" within the company. Because there are many different customers of research findings, with different degrees of technical and cultural expertise, it is almost always necessary to prepare both a written report and oral briefings. The purpose of the research report is to explain to those who did not participate in the research exactly what problem was studied, how it was studied, what the results were, and how the researchers believe the results should be interpreted. The report should make a case for using the results of the research.

The report should also be easy to understand. An extremely detailed and precise report is not best under all circumstances. Strategic and tactical decisions need different degrees of detail in information. Furthermore, high-level managers shy away from long reports. They prefer short summaries of the most important facts, backed by verbal and visual presentations where the managers can ask supplementary questions of special interest to them. On the other hand, product managers often need very detailed market information for their tactical decisions.

The shared commitment developed through a team approach to preparing the research brief can be reinforced through proper presentation of the findings. A preliminary presentation of the findings can be made to the team that helped generate the research brief. They can be asked for suggestions regarding revision or expansion of the findings. After the recommended changes have been made, the team may be willing to "sponsor" the reporting of the research to the rest of the organization. This approach can result in a sense of shared ownership of the research. It can be especially important when the results of the research indicate a need for changes in the way the organization conducts business.

MANAGING GLOBAL MARKETING RESEARCH

Organizing for Research

The question of whether research should be centralized or decentralized applies to global research as well.

The way a firm organizes its research reflects its overall structure. For example, highly centralized companies are likely to centralize their marketing research, particularly strategic research activities. On the other hand, firms that decentralize management decision making, especially those that delegate tactical decision making to local organizations, are likely to have decentralized marketing research.

The advantages of decentralized marketing research are more intimate knowledge of markets, greater appreciation of differences among markets, and the potential for greater control over the implementation of research. Potential disadvantages include ineffective communication with the home company and lack of comparability of information gathered in different research projects. To overcome such difficulties, central coordination is useful to ensure agreement on research objectives. However, as in any other marketing activity, central coordination of research leads to higher costs and more delays.

A small firm is unlikely to have a formal marketing-research department. Usually only one or a few people are responsible for research and are part of another unit, perhaps the marketing department. For larger projects, therefore, such firms have to rely on outside agencies and experts.

Budgeting for Research

Determining which unit of the company will have to pay for the research is an important control decision.

In order to control expenses and the efficiency of the firm's marketing-research activities, it is necessary to determine which unit within the company will bear the expense of the research. If the information is to be used to support strategic decision making, the costs may be assumed by top management or the appropriate business unit. If the firm is organized according to a product-management system or by region, the corresponding units may have to bear some of the cost of the study, especially if the findings are to be used in making tactical decisions. A marketing-research unit that operates as a separate cost or profit center that supports all of the firm's marketing-research efforts may have its own budget.

Marketing Information System

Because of the multitude of information sources and the great variety of information available at many different levels of detail, global marketing research is best carried out not on a study-by-study basis but in an integrated fashion, with a marketing information system. Efficient and effective data collection and analysis can be assured only when research activities are directed by a central coordinating unit that has available to it all of the data that are routinely collected for the purpose of supporting marketing decisions. Such a system not only permits managers to carry out a single research study, but it also makes it possible to track major changes in the firm's marketing environments over time. Chapter 18 will elaborate on how to manage a global marketing information system.

SUMMARY

To be able to systematically assess global market opportunities and to evaluate them from the perspective of the firm's strengths and weaknesses, top management should establish a global-marketing audit. The audit should cover the firm's internal environments, that is, the parts of corporate policy and the firm's management systems, programs, and actions that are relevant to global marketing, as well as parts of the external environments that influence the company's global marketing success.

A global-marketing audit starts with the definition of its goals and size. The key factors that have to be analyzed to assess the most attractive markets and the firm's potential to serve a global market were defined in the preceding chapters. Before data on these factors is gathered, the information-gathering procedure should be carefully planned.

Marketing-research projects start with definition of the research problem. While sometimes neglected, this is the most important step in the research process. The care and accuracy with which the research question is specified, the unit of analysis determined, the timing and organization of the project laid out, and a preliminary budget set up largely determines how useful the research results will be. Therefore, a research brief containing all of these elements is prepared in writing and submitted to management for approval.

The second stage of the research process is assessing information needs and availability. In this stage the researchers must outline all the dimensions of the research problem. This outline is used to identify information that might be available within the firm and then to determine what information needs must be met from outside sources.

If external sources are needed, the researchers should first attempt to solve the research problem through the use of secondary sources, such as statistics published by government agencies or other specialized institutions. Secondary data, which are inexpensive and often easy to obtain, are regularly used to identify product markets that merit in-depth consideration and to monitor changes in the global environment. However, the reliability of secondary data must be confirmed.

If secondary research cannot provide enough information to solve the research problem, the firm may decide to carry out primary research. This will mostly be the case when precise data are needed for tactical decisions in an attractive market. Primary research starts with a definition of the target population. Then the most appropriate method for collecting the data has to be selected.

Marketing researchers can choose among observational, experimental, and survey techniques.

In most global research projects some kind of sampling will have to take place. That is, the researchers will select a representative subset of the target population. With a reliable sampling frame, they can choose an appropriate probability sample. In its absence, convenience or judgment samples will have to be accepted. Such a sample will not necessarily be representative, but it may be more cost-effective than a probability sample.

To determine the final research budget, the cost of each activity included in the project must be estimated. The list of activities needed for budget estimation can also be used for preparing and monitoring the research schedule. If the firm has a fixed research budget, the project must be designed in such a way as to meet the constraints imposed by that budget.

In many cases the company may decide to hire a research agency to carry out the project. Research agencies may be based in the geographic area of interest, they may specialize in the industry in question, or they may be global agencies with branch offices or partners in all of the developed countries and in most developing ones.

The data that have been collected and analyzed must be interpreted and presented in a way that is most useful to decision makers. When preparing the written report and oral presentation, researchers should keep in mind that the findings of a research project are a "product" that should be "packaged" and communicated in a fashion that meets the needs of different "consumers" within the company.

The way a company organizes its marketing audit, that is its internal and external research efforts, reflects its overall structure. Highly centralized companies are likely to centralize their marketing audit and hire external consultants to do the work. Firms that decentralize management decision making are likely to have a decentralized marketing audit, conducted by members of the company. Because of the multitude of information sources inside and outside the firm and the great variety of information available at many different levels of detail, a global marketing audit is best carried out in an integrated fashion using a marketing information system.

DISCUSSION QUESTIONS

1. How does global marketing research differ from domestic marketing research?

2. How does the unit of analysis affect the results of marketing research?

3. "A global marketing-research project must have the latest in-depth market data to be of any value to a marketing decision maker." Do you agree or disagree with this statement? Why?

4. How can information available within the firm help in a global marketing-research project?

5. When should primary research be conducted?

6. What are some of the problems associated with using secondary data in global marketing research?

7. Why is it important to determine the target population before conducting primary research?

8. What special problems may be encountered in obtaining a sampling frame for global marketing research?

9. What types of agencies may be employed to conduct a global marketing-research project? What trade-offs are associated with each type?

10. What is a global marketing information system?

CASE

MARKETING RESEARCH ON TOURISM FOR DUTCH AND AUSTRALIAN FARMS

Sharon Smith, vice-president for research at InterTourist Inc., had a unique research request on her desk. InterTourist had been in business since 1976, providing research studies and marketing consulting services for organizations that served the tourist industry. One of her recent clients had been a major European airline. It was interested in Americans' images of various countries to which they flew. After InterTourist developed a "country-of-destination" profile, the airline was better able to develop a marketing campaign and promotional materials, which increased the number of tourists who chose that airline for their European trips.

One of InterTourist's steady customers, Globally Unique Travel, asked Ms. Smith to evaluate the interest among American tourists in Dutch and Australian farm holidays. Globally Unique Travel had long been known in the travel industry for its expensive and, as its name implied, unique travel packages for the more experienced and wealthy American traveler. One of its agents, who had extensive experience in both Holland and Australia, was sure that Americans would be interested in a farm travel package. He had kept up with changes in the American environment and believed there were several that might contribute to the success of this venture. Americans were increasingly interested in living healthier lives, getting "back to basics," and pursuing travel activities that were "out of the ordinary."

Dutch farms were thought to be of interest because they were small, family-run, convenient to cities, picturesque, and in many places similar in appearance to the ones seen in the paintings of the "Old Dutch Masters," such as Rembrandt. The farms near Amsterdam, already a popular American tourist destination and a common gateway to Western Europe, were especially charming. Further, due to the Dutch educational system, in almost every Dutch farmhouse at least one member of the family spoke English.

Australian farms were quite different. They tended to be large, "even by Texas standards," as Globally Unique Travel's vice-president for tour development said. Australian farms (or properties) were usually of mixed use, often combining the raising of large herds of cattle or sheep with grain crops. These farms offered a greater variety of outdoor activities than did the Dutch farms, ranging from riding the herds to long trail rides to look at the wildlife.

Farm tourism had long been popular in Europe, and it was growing in popularity in Australia. In both areas, government agencies helped farmers learn more about the services they needed to provide in order to make their farms more comfortable for tourists. Especially in Europe, government agencies also provided promotional support to increase demand for farm visits. In both areas, farm tourism was seen as a benefit for farmers (an income supplement) and a healthy change from standard activities for tourists.

However, it was a fairly new idea to develop the American market for farm holidays in either Holland or Australia. Although similar activities, such as dude ranches, were popular in the United States, as yet overseas farm holidays were not very popular. Globally Unique Tours was interested in determining whether or not a viable American market for such a product might exist. Ms. Smith knew that some research on the topic had already been conducted in Holland and Australia. One such survey had identified the following market segments: families, naturalists, excitement seekers, farm-life seekers, and outdoor enthusiasts. Research in Europe had found that most farm-holiday goers had taken a farm vacation before, and about 60 percent had children under 16 years of age. In both surveys, the "farm-life seekers" segment was the largest single segment, although not by much; they tended to be older, without children, and while they wanted to experience farm life, they did not want to "get their hands dirty."

CASE ISSUES

1. What basic issues face Ms. Smith in responding to this research request?

2. What unique international dimensions do you see that might cause difficulties in implementing such a research project?

Source: Some of the research reported in this case is adapted from P. Geale, "Farm Tourism," in P. Graham (ed.), *Readings and Cases in Marketing* (Sydney: Prentice Hall, 1988).

NOTES

1. D. A. Ricks, *Big Business Blunders: Mistakes in Multinational Marketing* (Homewood, Ill.: Irwin, 1983), p. 137.

2. For further discussion of the role of trade fairs in marketing research, see J. Whitelock, *"International Exhibits as a Source of Competitor Information: A Neglected Tool of Marketing Research,"* working paper, Department of Business and Management Studies, University of Salford, Spring 1988.

3. L. England and P. Arnold, "Telephone, Mail and Other Techniques," in R. M. Worcester and J. Downham, op. cit., pp. 245–272.

4. W. Kroeber-Riel and B. Neibecker, "Elektronische Datenerhebung Computergestützte Interviewsysteme," in Forschungsgruppe Konsum und Verhalten, ed., *Innovative Marktforschung* (Würzburg-Wien: Physica Verlag, 1983), pp. 193–208.

5. R. Bartos, "International Demographic Data? Incomparable!," *Marketing and Research Today*, November 1989, pp. 205–212.

6. W. G. Coonran, *Planning and Analysis of Observational Studies* (New York: Wiley, 1983).

7. J. Rothman, "Experimental Designs and Models," in R. M. Worcester and J. Downham, eds., *Consumer Market Research Handbook*, 3rd ed. (Amsterdam: North Holland, 1986), pp. 57–83.

8. J-Ch. Chebat and J. Picard, "The Prenotification of Respondents in Mailed Questionnaire Surveys as a Source of Simple Bias," *International Journal of Research in Marketing* 1, no. 3 (1984):235–239; J. Hornik, "Comparative Effectiveness of Four Models of Telephone Prenotification on Refusals to a Mail Questionnaire," in H. Larson and S. Heede, eds., *Proceedings of the European Academy for Advanced Research in Marketing* (Copenhagen: European Marketing Academy, Brussels, Belgium, 1981), pp. 7–96.

9. For further discussion of reliability and validity in marketing research, see G. A. Churchill, Jr., *Marketing Research—Methodological Foundations*, 4th ed. (Hinsdale, Ill.: Dryden Press, 1987), pp. 382–389.

10. D. Mitchell, "A European Researcher's View of European Business Marketing—Some Observations and Tips," *Business Marketing*, April 1984, pp. 70–76.

11. S. P. Douglas and C. S. Craig, *International Marketing Research* (Englewood Cliffs, N.J.: Prentice-Hall, 1983), pp. 207–211.

12. For a good discussion of technical issues related to sample size, see Churchill, op. cit., pp. 477–496.

13. D. R. Lehmann, *Marketing Research and Analysis*, 2nd ed. (Homewood, Ill.: Irwin, 1985), pp. 365–420.

14. M. Fox, "Guanxi Is Everything," *Advertising Age*, November 2, 1987, pp. S12, S14.

15. J. K. Johansson and I. Nonaka, "Market Research the Japanese Way," *Harvard Business Review*, May–June 1987, pp. 16–22.

16. W. A. Belson, *Validity in Survey Research* (Aldershot Gower, 1986), pp. 423–543.

BUILDING

THE FIRM IS MOTIVATED TO ENTER GLOBAL MARketing (Part One) and has assessed its global market opportunities (Part Two). Now, in order to be successful, it must build a global marketing strategy and design a product mix to carry through that strategy. Part Three will describe these efforts.

First, a marketing strategy is designed that is consistent with overall corporate strategy, as discussed in Chapter 9. Decisions will be made at two levels: (1) the firm's portfolio strategy—product and national market choices—and (2) its competitive market strategy—how the firm plans to meet competitive firms. (Although the firm is pursuing product-markets of like customers—possibly across nations—it still must take national similarities and differences into account when considering specific marketing mix decisions and designs.

Next, the global marketer must make decisions as to how to position the firm so that it will occupy a unique place in the mind of customers, and how best to enter a foreign, national market (Chapter 10). The total product is, of course, what a customer buys. Therefore three chapters in this section discuss how to build the best product mix that will satisfy the problems and needs of customers while helping to meet the objectives of the organization. Chapter 11 focuses on consumer products, those that are purchased for relatively immediate consumption, usually directly by consumers. The global marketing of industrial products, those that are purchased for reuse, is discussed in Chapter 12. Chapter 13 is concerned with services. As products, services have unique characteristics. They are also of increasing importance in international trade and therefore deserve special attention by global marketers.

BASIC STRATEGIC DECISIONS

General Motors

General Motors. The name brings a huge company to mind for car buyers—the maker of Chevrolet, Pontiac, Buick, Oldsmobile, and Cadillac. It is one of the largest U.S. corporations, with 1989 sales of about 3.4 million cars per year, about 35 percent of the U.S. car market. But the times and the automobile industry have changed things considerably for GM. Japanese, Korean, West German, Italian, French, Swedish, and Yugoslavian competitors have entered the U.S. car market very successfully. GM's 35 percent market share in 1989, for example, is down from 45 percent in the early 1980s.

In response to the globalization of the automobile industry, GM has been moving toward a global orientation itself. It has built a global portfolio and been particularly successful in Western Europe, the world's largest passenger car market (35 percent larger than the U.S. market, with a growth rate twice that of the U.S. rate expected throughout the 1990s). Although GM's Western European sales are on the order of 1.5 million cars per year, European sales account for about half of GM's profit. In effect, GM is using European product markets to subsidize investment in the United States.

But the 1990s will see increased competition in Western Europe, and Eastern Europe as well, so GM's top priority there is to slash costs, becoming a cost-efficient competitor in the lower-priced car market. For example, it has gone to three production shifts in its Spanish factory, running it around the clock in order to move down the experience curve. With such an approach, GM has been able to produce well-styled, reliable cars that are offered to the market at a price lower than the competition.

Additionally, GM is expanding its product lines. For example it purchased a half interest in Saab, the Swedish car maker, in order to have a stronger product line in the luxury car market. In Eastern Europe, it has expanded into new geographic markets, forming a strategic alliance with RABA, a state-owned Hungarian company, to produce 15,000 small Kadett cars a year for sale to the Eastern European market. GM's future competitive strategy seems to be based on these three positions: cost leadership, extension of the product line, and the pursuit of new geographic markets.

Source: Adapted from "GM Europe: How to Get Something Right," *New York Times*, February 4, 1990, pp. 3–1 and 3–6.

Before the basic strategy is chosen, the firm must do internal and external analyses.

When the firm has completed its analysis of the external environment, management has an overview of potential opportunities and threats. An assessment of the firm's potential compared to its competitors should be conducted at the same time, leading to an understanding of internal strengths and weaknesses.

Management can then proceed to determine the firm's competitive advantages. It will use this analysis as a basis for making strategic decisions—deciding upon the optimal extent of its global activity, its global portfolio strategy, and its competitive market strategy. In this chapter we provide an overview of how to identify competitive advantages, what factors to account for in planning a global core strategy, and how to schedule global expansion.

ASSESSMENT OF COMPETITIVE ADVANTAGES

After identifying the firm's strengths, management must decide whether they translate into competitive advantages.

Having identified the current state of internal characteristics that determine the firm's chances of success in global markets, we need to ask what criteria should be used in evaluating these characteristics. How do we know if they will enhance or diminish the firm's chances to succeed globally? A U.S. marketer of electronic devices for measuring gas pressure, for example, may have found out that her firm's debt-to-equity ratio is 23 percent, that some of the firm's personnel have experience in Latin America, and that the firm has enough production flexibility to accommodate specific customer needs. But what does this tell her about the firm's ability to successfully enter the French market? There are three possibilities for how she may proceed with her evaluation: historical criteria, normative judgments, and how the firm compares with its most important competitors.

Historical Criteria

Past experience is a useful guide as to whether the firm's competitive advantages will be useful in other markets.

To use historical criteria is to rely on past experience. In the ever-changing environment of global markets, past experience is likely to be quickly outdated. Moreover, most companies do not have a history of global activity. Even if historical criteria exist, it is dangerous to generalize from one geographic market to another. Nestle, for example, knows from its U.S. experience that a big budget for national consumer advertising is very important for getting enough shelf space in supermarkets all over the country. But will that also be true in Japan? It may be much more important there to use networking skills, that is, to build up personal relationships, to obtain the desired shelf space.

Normative Judgments

Normative judgments—that is, evaluations of how things *should* be—may rely on rules of thumb or the opinion of experienced consultants.

A firm may also assess its competitive advantages through general guidelines or experienced consultants.

Rules of Thumb. **Rules of thumb** are based on experience. In the United States, for example, advertisers expect that potential customers must be exposed to an ad six or seven times before they will be able to recall it. Informal rules such as this may work in a familiar, stable domestic market environment, where management has enough experience to formulate such rules. In global marketing, however, it is more difficult to develop rules that can be applied to different markets. Rules of thumb that have been developed in one national market are seldom applicable in another. For example, if it takes an advertising budget of 3–5 percent of sales to reach a particular market-share objective in the United States, the same percentage may result in overspending in Norway.

Consultants' Opinions.   An experienced consultant may have extensive knowledge based on work with numerous and diverse companies. Such an individual is in a good position to determine whether the firm's characteristics are consistent with the requirements of global marketing. However, it is rare to find a consultant who specializes in the firm's business; moreover, consultants do not have to assume responsibility for the decisions they suggest. A further difficulty arises from the difference between what the company *should* do and what it *can* do. For example, a consultant might recommend that 25 percent of the firm's personnel be laid off in order to make the firm price competitive in world markets. If the firm is based in a country like West Germany, such an action may be regarded as socially unacceptable, hence, something the firm cannot do.

Competitive Advantages

To gain the most insight into the value of corporate strengths, a competitive analysis should be performed.

The best way to evaluate a firm's ability to successfully enter a new market is a comparison between its own characteristics and those of its most important competitors in the market relative to the needs and expectations of the (potential) customers as well as other exchange partners there. For this purpose the results of all of the external and internal analyses (Chapters 4–8) have to be brought together (see Exhibit 9.1).

Potential strengths and weaknesses were identified (Chapter 7). They lead to a list of distinctive competencies the firm can rely on in the development of a strategy. Apple Computer, for example, is well known for its superior know-how in the development of user-friendly computers. It has built its globally successful strategy on this distinctive competence. The firm should also determine the most important environmental elements that present a threat or opportunity to the firm. These lead to a list of factors that are critical for success. For example, it may be critical for a French producer of steel construction parts who wants to start a joint venture in Poland to be able to establish firm relationships with members of the supply system, such as steel mills and transportation companies, in order to ensure timely distribution.

By matching its distinctive competencies with the critical success factors in the market under consideration the company can identify its **competitive advantages**. Competitive advantages are corporate competencies that are demanded by the market and that competitors cannot easily match, except at high cost and/or over an extended period. They are strongest when they are unique to the firm, that is, when they cannot be easily duplicated. The long-term business relationships Austrian companies have built up with Hungarian firms, for exam-

EXHIBIT 9.1
DETERMINATION OF A
FIRM'S COMPETITIVE
ADVANTAGES

To determine a firm's
competitive advantages,
the marketing manager
combines internal analy-
sis, competitor analysis,
and external analysis in
the process illustrated
here.

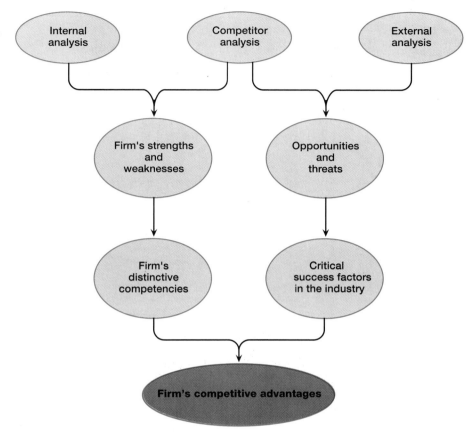

ple, give Austrian companies a competitive advantage over U.S. companies in obtaining joint-venture contracts with Hungarian firms.

Sometimes a company does not have a particular competitive advantage on which to build a strategy. In such cases it may undertake a strategy of exploiting small differences between itself and its competitors. Such differentiation may take the form of providing creative solutions to previously unsolved problems, applying new technologies, or developing customer benefits that are not currently offered. For example, Kodak developed a disposable camera with a wide-angle lens. Its rationale was that tourists often need a wide-angle lens while on vacation (to take a picture of the Colosseum in Rome or Niagara Falls, for example). While most people are not willing to invest in the cost of a wide-angle lens, they will do so if it is part of a low-cost camera that is disposed of when the film is developed.

Being successful in business is due in part to following your own corporate strategy, not letting your competitor establish how business is to be conducted.

"Vince! Just trample him!…He's drawing you into his kind of fight!"

THE GLOBAL CORE STRATEGY

After determining its competitive advantages, the firm should develop a core strategy.

The firm's competitive advantages are the foundations for its global strategy (see Exhibit 9.2). A **strategy** is "the way a firm seeks to compete in its chosen product market to achieve some specified goals."[1] The **core strategy** broadly defines the company's competitive posture, providing guidance regarding what it will do and imposing constraints by delineating what it will not do (see an example in Exhibit 9.3). It outlines how the company will reach its goals and objectives. It also specifies the direction in which the company will develop in the future. For example, the firm may decide to become a cost leader, such as the Yugoslavian producer of ELAN skis; a specialist in one or more market niches, such as Gucci; a technological leader, such as Motorola; or a "me too" follower, like most of the producers of PC clones in southeast Asia. To develop any one of these strategies, management must closely examine the firm's competitive advantages in the markets to be served.

As illustrated in Exhibit 9.2, where the relative strengths of a company are well matched to factors critical for market success, the global core strategy should build on those strengths. A global leader in the production of technologically advanced textile machines, for example, should concentrate its mar-

EXHIBIT 9.2
MATCHING
DISTINCTIVE
COMPETENCIES WITH
CRITICAL SUCCESS
FACTORS IN
INDUSTRY

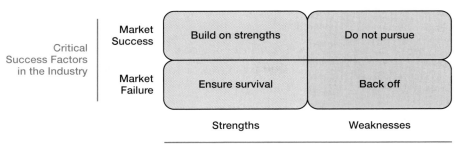

A firm should build its strategy on its strengths and critical success factors in the industry.

keting activities on the most developed industrial markets in the world. Where opportunities exist but the company is relatively weak compared to its competitors, the firm should not pursue those opportunities. The North American market for ski-lift equipment, for example, may look promising to an Italian producer of passenger cars, but it should refrain from investing money in this market if it finds out that competitors are in a better cost position, because they have production facilities in place. When a factor of potential failure in the market can be countered by a distinctive strength, the strategy should be to try to ensure survival. BMW, for example, may counter its difficulties in building a satisfactory distribution system in Japan by exploiting the attractiveness of its cars. On the other hand, if the company's weaknesses are such that it cannot counter a threat in a given market, it should not pursue that market.

Regardless of the specific match between the firm's strengths/weaknesses and market opportunities/threats, competitive advantages must be evident to intermediaries as well as final customers. A global company may derive

EXHIBIT 9.3
THE GLOBAL CORE
STRATEGY OF A
EUROPEAN TURNKEY
PLANT SUPPLIER

A company's core strategy helps define its competitive position, guides managers in taking and avoiding actions, and specifies the company's future direction.

1. Defend global market share.
2. Increase the return on investment by increasing product specialization and perfecting quality control.
3. Focus on existing product markets instead of further diversification.
4. Standardize systems, components, parts, and projects as much as possible. Accommodate local needs when decisive for a contract.
5. Attack competitors frontally in our established business domains.
6. Cooperate when know-how and market share can be gained more cheaply and quickly that way.
7. Base product innovation exclusively on the company's existing strengths.

competitive advantages from qualities that are not shared by domestic firms, such as:

- Efficiencies of global scale and volume
- Transfer of experience, ideas, and successful concepts
- Global reputation
- Transfer of resources between business units spread globally
- Exploitation of local advantages
- Ability to provide global services[2]

The global scale of business can lead to significant gains in production efficiency and sales volume that can be transformed into customer benefits. Global efficiencies of scale allowed Asian manufacturers of VCRs, for example, to make and sell their products at lower prices than was possible for U.S. manufacturers serving only the domestic market. As a consequence, U.S. manufacturers no longer produce VCRs.

A global company is also able to transfer experience, ideas, and successful concepts from one national market to another. McDonald's country managers in Europe, for example, regularly meet to compare notes on products and promotional ideas and to discuss whether they might be appropriate in specific markets.

Moreover, global companies often have a stronger global reputation than can be achieved by domestic companies. As travel and communication across national boundaries increase, this potential is likely to grow. To take just one example, McDonald's, which is active in many national markets, enjoys a higher reputation for product quality in Australia than does the domestic Hungry Jack, an affiliate of Burger King, which was unable to use its better-known name in Australia because of registration problems.

A further competitive advantage may stem from the ability of global marketers to transfer resources between business units in different parts of the world. These resources might include personnel (such as experienced marketing managers), financial resources (global organizations usually have a lower capital cost than domestic firms), and superior market information.

One might expect that global marketers are less well situated than local firms to exploit local advantages, such as closeness to the market and knowing distributors on a personal basis. However, domestic marketers, especially those located in small national markets, often are underfinanced, lacking in well-qualified management, and not highly competitive in nature. The additional resources available to global marketers, coupled with a more aggressive market orientation, may make them better prepared to seek out and exploit local advantages.

Finally, global marketers have the ability to provide global services. Increasingly, customers in industrial and consumer markets are looking for more complete products, including pre- and post-sale services. In particular, services that can be delivered through technology (such as international investment) may be performed more efficiently or more fully by global marketers.

The decisions that must be made in developing a global core strategy concern the extent of the firm's global activity, the optimal allocation of its resources, and its competitive behavior. They are discussed in more detail in the following sections.

EXTENT OF GLOBAL ACTIVITY

The core strategy should include the extent to which the firm wishes to be involved in global business.

The core strategy incorporates top management's decision regarding the extent to which the firm will engage in global activity. This decision is influenced by the relative size of the domestic market compared to nondomestic markets. As we discussed in Chapter 1, managers living in big countries, like the United States, do not see as much need to globalize their business as do managers in smaller countries, like The Netherlands. This may turn out to be a mistake, however, when competitors first concentrate on the rest of the global product market and then start competing in the large national market when they have accumulated enough experience.

The competitive situation in domestic and nondomestic markets is distinct. If competition is strong in the domestic market, management may look for relief in foreign markets, where the need for its product or service may be satisfied to a lesser extent. On the other hand, intensive local competition may consume most of the company's resources, so that globalization is not feasible.

The extent to which competitors engage in global activity must be known. The globalization of an industry is a gradual process that results in basic changes in the firm's environment. For example, French manufacturers of refrigerators, used to competing with local rivals, have suddenly been confronted by two large Italian competitors, Zanussi and Candy, which operate throughout Europe. As a result of changes like this, a firm may lose total market share. The British computer firm ICL, another example, is in a global industry. It has a high local market share, but other competitors have a higher return on investment, because their global shares are higher, allowing them to invest in lower-cost production technology.[3]

If a company's major competitors are all active on a global scale, as is the case in the commercial aircraft and watch industries, geographic market restriction may turn out to be fatal. On the other hand, in an industry such as the furniture industry, where most business is done locally, the example of IKEA shows that a global business perspective also can be very successful.

The company's resources and competitive advantages are critical to the extent of global activity. Competitive advantages are not only the foundation of a successful global strategy, they also restrict the range of markets in which the firm can compete effectively. In the example presented in Exhibit 9.3, the core strategy includes a competitive advantage in product quality. This has the effect of decreasing the number of potential markets, because markets in which customers are not concerned with superior quality are excluded.

The firm should match the extent of its global activity to its distinctive competencies and critical success factors in the target markets. It must keep in mind, however, that competitors that lack certain competencies may be able to acquire them through merger, acquisition, or cooperative agreements.

GLOBAL PORTFOLIO ANALYSIS

The firm should analyze its business-unit portfolio at different levels to seek ways to manage the potentially positive relationships among those levels.

The development of a global portfolio strategy is based upon a **global portfolio analysis**, which provides an overview of how the firm has allocated its resources so far. It starts at the corporate level, where the firm may have a portfolio of different business units; proceeds to the strategic business unit level, where each SBU may consist of a couple of product lines; then goes down to the product-line level, where each product line can be regarded as a portfolio of products. The analysis of a global portfolio is more complex than domestic portfolio analysis, because it must provide for additional units of analysis. At the *corporate level*, geographic and product markets, as well as available technologies, must be considered. At the *strategic business unit level*, different market-entry alternatives and specific market segments, in addition to the SBU's product lines, must be analyzed. And at the *product-line level*, different marketing strategies for different products must be evaluated. The results of all these analyses are interrelated (see Exhibit 9.4) and should be interpreted simultaneously.[4]

If, for example, the product market of interest is women's shoes, the corporate-level analysis would consider whether a high level of technology (such as complete automation) or a low level (hand assembly) should be used to produce the shoes. In addition, barriers to entry in specific geographic markets would be considered. At the SBU level, the market segments and product lines would have to be consistent (for example, high-fashion shoes for wealthy consumers), and this would affect the choice of market-entry techniques. And, of course, the product mix and marketing strategies would be influenced by all of these factors (as described in Global Dimensions 9.1).

Global portfolio analysis provides information related to an SBU's or a product line's position within the portfolio. External factors, such as the transferability of funds earned in different regions of the world,[5] may influence the optimal combination of SBUs. Portfolio analysis can indicate whether business units that are supposed to generate cash flow to support units in newly entered markets do this in regions from where funds can be freely transferred to areas where they are needed, or if the funds have to be reinvested in the local business where they are generated (see Exhibit 9.5). For example, if a U.S. company has cash cows in Latin America, but is not allowed to transfer funds from Latin America to its star business units in Europe, the global business strategy will be handicapped.

The results of portfolio analysis can be used to determine whether the company has acted quickly enough to seize opportunities in new geographic

EXHIBIT 9.4
INTERRELATIONS OF
PORTFOLIO
CATEGORIES

Portfolio planning and implementation must take into account the influences different levels (corporate, strategic, business unit, and product line) have upon corporate choices, such as product markets, product lines, and marketing strategies. Essentially, each level and dimension within a level impacts the level below it.

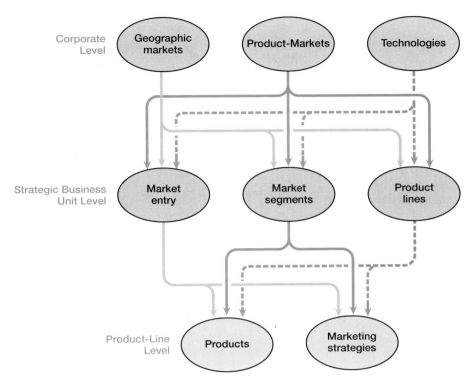

areas or whether it has allowed competitors to establish strong positions before it entered new markets. The existing portfolio of markets served can also be compared to regional and global opportunities, so that management can determine whether the company is overcommitted in slow-growing markets, leaving high-growth markets untapped. For example, in Exhibit 9.6 Denmark represents a market that needs more attention.

Portfolio analysis can take political and legal factors into consideration. It can, for example, consider profitability in relation to political risk. A highly profitable market can be threatened by political unrest, religious upheavals, or restrictive laws concerning business. For example, trade between the United States and the Republic of South Africa, although profitable, is less attractive due to apartheid, taxation policies, currency exchange-rate fluctuations, and so forth (see Exhibit 9.7).[6]

Portfolio analysis is also used to help a firm allocate resources and select among strategies for future business activity.

No company has unlimited financial or personnel resources. In the light of the portfolio analysis and the competitive advantages detected with respect to potential markets, management must decide whether to increase the extent of the firm's global activity and how to allocate resources to specific geographic and product markets. For example, BASF, a large German manufacturer of

EXHIBIT 9.5
PORTFOLIO
COMBINING MARKET
ATTRACTIVENESS/
COMPETITIVE
POSITION ANALYSIS
WITH INTERNATIONAL
TRANSFERABILITY OF
FUNDS

Portfolio analysis is used
in this exhibit to help the
firm analyze the relationship between its prod-
ucts' strengths and its
ability to transfer funds,
by major geographic
area. For example, its
"stars" and "problem children" are in the United
States and Europe, where
it can transfer funds. But
its "dogs" are generally in
areas with low fund transferability. This may not
matter with "dogs," be-
cause they don't gener-
ate positive cash flow.
But firms depend
on"cash cows" to fund fu-
ture growth. For this company, the inability to
transfer funds from its
"cash cows" in Latin
America and Europe
means it faces severe
funding limitations.

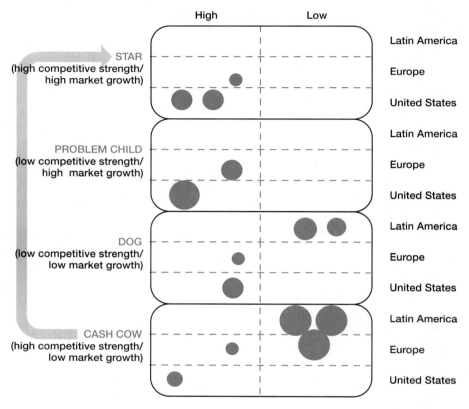

International Transferability of Funds

Note: Circle sizes are proportional to potential business-unit size in sales.

Source: J. C. Leontiades, *Multinational Corporate Strategy: Planning for World Markets* (Lexington, Mass.: Lexington Books, 1985), p. 48.

chemicals and related products, has reduced its Latin American operations and intensified its investments in South Korea, India, and Indonesia.[7] Additionally, a global firm must allocate resources among technologies; for example, Should current production facilities be expanded, or should new plants with newer equipment be built? Chrysler has decided to build a production facility for their new generation of cars near Graz, Austria, for example, in order to be fully competitive in the European markets.

   Global portfolio strategy boils down to a decision about how dispersed the firm's resources will be. A wrong decision will result in an inappropriate concentration of resources, creating a competitive disadvantage. Serving too broad a range of product markets may lead to a loss of overall competence, since

EXHIBIT 9.6
GLOBAL MARKET
ATTRACTIVENESS/
COMPETITIVE
POSITION PORTFOLIO

Portfolio analysis can be
used to determine market
priorities. In this exhibit,
the firm has mapped the
attractiveness of national
markets compared to the
firm's competitive posi-
tion. Thus France is its
best market, but Den-
mark merits attention be-
cause it is large in size.
However, the firm's com-
petitive position in Den-
mark is only fair.

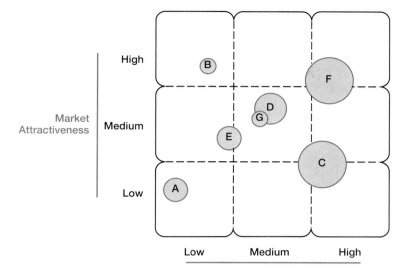

Note: Circle sizes are proportional to potential business-unit size in sales: Letters represent country
markets: A = Austria, B = Belgium, C = Canada, D = Denmark,E = Spain, F = France, G = Greece.

EXHIBIT 9.7
POLITICAL RISK/
PROFITABILITY
PORTFOLIO

The future profitability of
a business unit can be
mapped against an issue
that affects profitability—
in this example, political
risk.

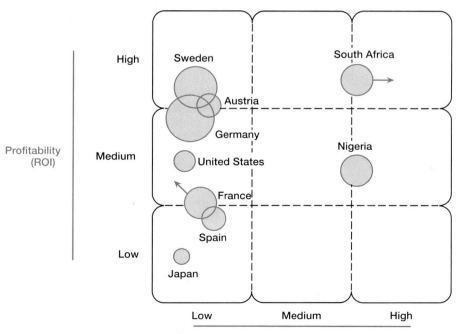

Note: Circle sizes are proportional to potential business-unit sales.
Arrows indicate the direction of change in business-unit position in the past three years.

GLOBAL DIMENSIONS 9.1

The Different Levels and Dimensions of Portfolio Analysis

Portfolio analyses at three levels (corporate, business unit, product line) help identify the various marketing strategies and tactics that need to be implemented. Such analyses can also address issues such as where to locate production or whether to specialize. For example, at the corporate level a manufacturer of shoes might decide to specialize in low technology (hand assembly), in order to create expensive "designer" shoes. This decision would be complemented by efforts to market the shoes to wealthy, status-conscious women throughout the Triad markets.

At the strategic business unit level, the preferred market-entry technique might be exporting, which would permit close quality control over production. The target market would be offered five lines of shoes, designed by leading fashion designers.

At the product-line level, tactics would have to be developed to achieve the desired positioning. This would include the development of advertising to reinforce the prestigious image, appropriate pricing, and distribution through a select number of fashionable stores. The product mix each season may include one top model, to attract consumers to the rest of the products, which would be changed twice a year.

---

resources will be spread too thinly among research and development, engineering and customer service, or sales force training and support.

But underestimating the size of a geographic market compared to what markets have been served so far may result in too little resource allocation. Thus, some European companies, such as VW, have failed in the U.S. market largely because of underspending. Their dealer and service systems were not dense enough to seem reliable to potential customers. Their promotion budgets did not produce enough national visibility to make the firm a real contender. On the other hand, limiting the company's activities to a small number of geographic markets, like the neighboring EC countries, may result in overspending of resources. This is particularly true when competitors do the same thing. As a result these markets will be characterized by high competitive pressure. Serving too narrow a product market can also have adverse consequences. For example, when Porsche Design took over the marketing of its prestige sunglasses in the United States from Carrera, a company that previously had sold them as part of a broader product line, it discovered to its dismay that its product market was too narrow to cover the costs of distribution.

In developing a portfolio strategy, the marketer can choose among four general alternatives: product-market penetration, geographic expansion, product-market development, and diversification (see Exhibit 9.8).

EXHIBIT 9.8
PORTFOLIO-
STRATEGY OPTIONS

Whether a firm is involved
in an existing or new market, with existing or new
products, helps define
which portfolio-strategy
the firm should follow.

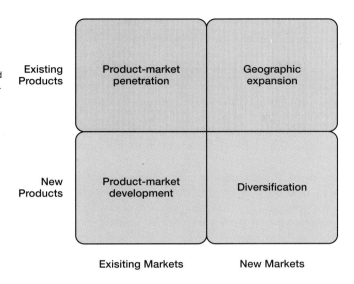

Source: Adapted from H. I. Ansoff, "Strategies for Diversification," *Harvard Business Review*, September–October 1957, pp. 113–124.

Product-Market Penetration

The highest degree of resource concentration occurs when the firm decides to penetrate a product market in a limited number of geographic areas that it already serves. This results in production and marketing experience curve effects, which permit the firm to lower prices and increase quality at the same time. The result is increasingly loyal customers.

Markets that are in an early stage of development require a greater investment of resources. When, for example, Philips first introduced compact disks, a large budget was necessary to train sales personnel both within the company and in stores that would sell the new product, and to communicate the benefits of the new technology to customers through advertising and promotion campaigns. If the market has high growth potential, such an investment is justified, because it will establish a strong competitive position before other firms enter the market.

This strategy makes possible the use of several different tactics, including **product-line stretching, product proliferation,** and **product improvement.** These can be illustrated by the case of Japanese companies operating in the United States and Europe, as follows.[8]

Product-Line Stretching.   Beginning with a small segment of the market that it has successfully served in the past, the company gradually adds new items to the existing product line in order to reach a broader market. Japanese car producers, for example, started their market penetration in Europe with inexpensive, middle-sized cars. From there they first stretched their product line to small cars, then started offering bigger and stronger cars. Their latest move has been to challenge European competitors with luxury and sports car models.

Product Proliferation.   The company introduces as many different models or product types as possible at each point in the product line. Casio, for example, introduced a variety of hand calculators, with different functions, features, and designs. The same tactic has been used with watches.

Product Improvement.   The company continually augments the capabilities and reliability of its products, extends warranties and services related to the products, and is quick to apply improved technologies. An example of a company following such a strategy is Komatsu, the most important competitor of Caterpillar in the market for earth-moving and construction equipment.

Product-market penetration involves a trade-off: the more the firm limits the number of geographic markets that it serves, the more opportunities it gives competitors to build up their presence in other markets. Japanese companies, for instance, strengthened their competitive positions in southeast Asia and Latin America before entering the U.S. market. They were not challenged in these markets by U.S. competitors, who were focused on European markets.[9]

Geographic Expansion

Expanding operations to new geographic areas is most appropriate when the firm is a relatively small one that has developed an innovative product for which patents offer little protection, when the advantage of the product can be matched by competition in a fairly short time, when important competitors are opening up new markets, or when opportunities in new markets will be available for only a short time. These characteristics are often found in high-tech industries like computer technology and advanced circuit technology.[10] The speed with which new computer chips, for example, can be matched by competitors means that they are marketed globally as quickly as possible to take advantage of product superiority as long as possible.

Geographic expansion also becomes necessary when intense price competition in slow-growing markets leads to diminishing profit margins. To achieve higher sales volume, the company introduces its products in markets where few product modifications are required. Geographic expansion is especially appropriate if the life-cycles of the company's products in different markets are similar, as is often the case in developed economies, including the newly industrialized countries, such as South Korea and Taiwan.[11]

A company is not obliged to sell its innovative products in its current markets before entering new ones. If other markets are better suited to the new product, the firm should start there. For example, a Japanese firm exported its color TV sets to the United States five years before it introduced them at home;

its managers did not believe that the Japanese market was ready for the new product.[12]

Product-Market Development

Another strategy is to allocate the company's resources to a limited number of geographic areas and focus its operations on the development of new product markets in these areas. This approach is appropriate if the company is well established in its geographic markets and lacks the ability or knowledge to adapt to a new environment. It is most appropriate when the geographic markets have matured and the new product markets are fast growing.

VOEST-Alpine Industrial Services, an Austrian company that originally specialized in personnel training at steel mills, provides a good example. Its competitive advantage is in the marketing of its training skills to the governments of less-developed countries. Instead of moving to other countries, where strong competitors may reside, to achieve growth, it chose to provide training for other industries, such as paper and pulp mills, in national markets where it had already established a presence.

Diversification

If new product markets in new geographic areas generate a high return on investment and have high growth potential, diversification may be an attractive strategy. There are two dangers associated with this strategy, however. First, entering a new product market in a new geographic area is risky,[13] especially when it involves a technology that is new to the firm. The new business is likely to have few aspects in common with existing operations, so the firm will benefit very little from synergy. Second, even if the company is able to overcome this problem, competitors may choose a more focused resource-allocation strategy and dominate markets in which the firm is weak.

COMPETITIVE MARKET STRATEGY

In implementing its portfolio strategy, the firm must choose among high-share, planned modification, niche, confrontation, cooperation, and innovation strategies.

To implement its portfolio strategy, the company must choose a **competitive market strategy**, that is, certain behaviors or actions in the market, to ensure success. Depending on whether the company's competitive advantages are mainly based on its efficiency and effectiveness, compared to competitors, or a close relationship with customers, the firm can choose among basic strategies that are global variations of well-known domestic strategies—cost-leadership, differentiation, and focus. Depending on its resources, its market power compared to that of major competitors, and opportunities and threats in the external environments, the company can emphasize confrontation with competitors or cooperation strategies. Finally, it should formulate strategies concerning innovation.

Basic Strategies

Global High-Share Strategy.   A large, dominant firm has sufficient personnel, technology, and capital resources to follow **global high-share strategy.** Examples of such firms include IBM, Matsushita, Philips, Siemens, and Hyundai. In these firms all functional areas make maximum use of economies of scale and accumulated experience. To implement this strategy, the firm must have achieved a large market share and a high degree of product standardization. Its operations—and its image—must be global. The firm's products should be at the forefront of technological development, even if the firm is not a technological pioneer. To achieve cost reductions, the firm seeks partnerships and cooperative ventures. These partnerships permit the firm to enter more markets, spreading costs and providing access to technology and management expertise that would otherwise not be available.

In many cases, the implementation of a uniform global strategy will be impeded by tariffs, quotas, financial controls, local content requirements, or government incentives for local firms. Therefore, a general strategy is designed so that it can be modified to suit local conditions when necessary.[14] For example, HILTI's general strategy involves offering high-quality, high-priced drilling devices with the latest technology throughout the world. HILTI is determined to be the market leader in quality, price, and technology in each of the markets it serves. However, its prices, product characteristics, service level, and promotion strategy are not entirely standardized. Local HILTI managers are given clear strategic guidelines, but those guidelines are flexible enough to permit local adaptations when necessary.

Local High-Share Strategy.   Large but nondominant firms need to develop a **local high-share strategy**, which avoids direct competition with dominant global competitors. They usually opt for strategic differentiation. This may be achieved by formulating competitive strategies on a domestic basis, taking advantage of distinct competencies in specific national markets. Such companies rely on national barriers to entry—such as banking laws in the United States that prevent foreign banks from providing retail banking services (services to consumers) and government preferences for purchasing from national companies (for example, Air Italia, run by the Italian government, buys from Airbus Industries, which is a joint venture of several European governments, including Italy)—and other advantages, including specific knowledge of conditions in a country, customer preferences for local firms, or flexibility in responding to changing local conditions.

Global Niche Strategy.   Nondominant firms, whether large or small, may choose a **global niche strategy.** This approach involves focusing on a specialty product that is relatively insensitive to price competition, such as NutraSweet, leading to higher volumes and lower costs per unit. This is a focused strategy; the firm caters to special market needs, concentrating its resources in a narrow field where it has a distinct competitive advantage. Such a firm can dominate the competition in its chosen market segment.[15] The strategy may rely on a product (as in the case of Monsanto chemicals), on technology or environmental knowledge (as with VOEST Alpine Intertrading, which provides trading advice and assistance to inexperienced companies that want to do business with less-developed countries), or on a certain customer group (Dainichi Kiko, a Japanese robot manufacturer, concentrates on small customers that lack in-house robotized production system development capabilities).[16]

Confrontation Strategies

A firm with local and global competitors in its product markets may choose among a variety of confrontation strategies. These include flanking, frontal attack, encirclement, and bypassing.

Flanking. **Flanking** is a focused strategy that is often chosen by companies that do not have the resources to attack a large competitor head-on. With **geographic flanking**, the firm chooses geographic areas in which major competitors are weak or nonexistent and offers products that are similar to those that competitors sell in comparable product markets elsewhere. With **segmented flanking**, the firm enters a product market that is not served by major competitors or in which customers are dissatisfied. Dr. Pepper, for example, flanks Coca-Cola and Pepsi. Companies use flanking to build a position that will permit direct competition in another product market later on. The success of segmented flanking depends on the company's ability to identify shifts in the market that will allow it to enter and develop a particular segment faster than potential competitors. The segment must be large enough to repay the effort, but not so large that it attracts strong competitors.

Both forms of flanking assume that competitors will not take notice of the firm's actions or see any reason to intervene in its chosen markets. Success can be achieved more easily when the entire market is growing rapidly; under such conditions competitors do not fight for sales volume in every market niche and dominant firms in the market do not consider the new entrant a major threat to their position.

Frontal Attack. **Frontal-attack** strategies are appropriate for large companies with substantial resources and a significant competitive advantage. There are four types of frontal-attack strategies.

In a **pure frontal attack**, the firm targets the same customers in the same geographic markets as its major competitors, in an attempt to outperform them. When the company limits its attack to a specific customer group and tries to win these customers away from the competition, it is applying a **limited frontal attack** strategy. A U.S.beer manufacturer, for example, might compete against German breweries for exclusive supply contracts with top restaurants in major German cities. This strategy requires a great deal of attention to the specific needs of the targeted customers, in order to convince them of the superior benefits to be derived from the product.

A **price-based frontal attack** relies on product features that are similar to those of competitors, offered at a significantly lower price. This strategy was used by Toshiba when it pursued a higher market share in the medical-equipment market. It works only when price is not viewed as indicative of quality and competitors are unable or unwilling to lower their prices further. The company must be willing to cross-subsidize its efforts or be a cost leader. (A cost leader uses technology, production, management, and marketing improvements to lower costs faster than the competition. Thus it can maintain a cost advantage over the competition, charging lower prices in the market, yet still maintain profits.)

A **value-based frontal attack** relies on product differentiation through characteristics other than price. The nature of the difference is determined by the company's creativity, competencies, and resources. The firm may use a competitive advantage in research and development, for example, to constantly improve its products. One such firm is the plastics division of Allied Corporation, which starts with a rather simple, basic product and adapts it for different applications. In general, a value-based frontal attack can succeed only when customers and intermediaries in the distribution system perceive the firm's product as more attractive than competitors' offerings.

Encirclement.　With **market encirclement**, the firm tries to attack its major competitor in as many ways as possible. It offers different product lines to customers in almost every segment in the entire market. The company applies product-line stretching and product proliferation simultaneously, as Seiko has done in the watch market. Because the firm can satisfy all or most of the needs of potential customers in the given product category, intermediaries have less need to associate with other suppliers. Encirclement requires that the firm spend large amounts of resources over a long enough period to gain sufficient market share to repay the large investment necessary to implement an encirclement strategy. If this strategy is to succeed, competitors should be unable or unwilling to invest large amounts of resources to defend their markets. This may not be the case if the global marketer encounters dominant competitors. Therefore, it is necessary to conduct an in-depth analysis of the entire market before attempting an encirclement strategy.

Bypassing.　Relatively small companies that are unable to confront major competitors in the global marketplace may choose a bypassing strategy. They can either satisfy customer needs in existing markets that are not served in a comparable manner by any competitor, or enter geographic markets for existing products that no important competitor has yet served. In both cases the company needs adequate marketing experience and know-how.

In the first case, **product bypassing**, the firm may develop an entirely new version of its traditional product or service, thereby opening up a new market with little competition. For example, Crown Cork & Seal designed and sold packaging equipment specifically tailored to customer needs.[17] Previously the company and its competitors had offered only packaging materials. The combination of materials and equipment gave Crown a distinct competitive advantage. In the second case, **geographic bypassing**, the firm may concentrate on minor markets. Small firms that face strong competition in developed economies may seek opportunities in less-developed countries. Although such markets may be difficult to enter, once established the firm may secure a quasi-exclusive position in the market. Thus, Merloni Refrigerators has signed a government procurement contract to meet the total need for refrigerators in a small, less-developed country.

Cooperation Strategies

Small and medium-sized companies that wish to become global marketers often possess the required technical know-how, but lack the financial and personnel resources, to operate in many markets simultaneously. Under such circumstances, it is very difficult to enter global markets without cooperating with other companies that operate in these markets. Through cooperation, such as the use of a strategic alliance, the company can supplement its strengths with those of partners. The firm may even cooperate with competitors, as in the case of the strategic alliance between Toyota and General Motors, or with suppliers and distributors.

Compaq Computer of Houston, Texas, has used the latter approach. In 1982 Compaq did not exist; five years later it reported sales of $1.2 billion. Its success has been largely due to close connections with component makers, which supply the latest technology; software houses, which guarantee that new operating systems and programs work well on Compaq's equipment; and dealers, which give Compaq's products more shelf space.[18]

Innovation Strategies

Technology Leader versus Follower.   The global company must decide whether it should be a technology leader or follower in its industry. This decision is influenced by management's attitude toward risk and the firm's resources, current market position, and orientation toward innovation. Technology leaders can normally charge higher prices for their products. They tend to enjoy customer loyalty. In addition, they can influence the direction of technological development, set industry standards, and profit from experience curve effects. Thus Boeing has tried to maintain its lead in the global aircraft industry for large airplanes. To maintain a leadership position the company must develop and implement new technologies or acquire them through licensing, strategic partnerships, or mergers. Japanese companies often buy the rights to use technologies that have been developed by companies in other advanced economies.

Toyota and General Motors have entered a joint venture, building Toyota Corollas and Chevrolet Novas at the same plant in Fremont, California. GM gains production technology, and Toyota gains market access and marketing expertise.

They then improve the basic technology until they reach a level of experience and know-how that allows them to take the lead in technology development.[19]

A technology follower may also be in a position to set standards and influence the technological development of the industry. For this to occur, the firm must be a significant force in the market, as is IBM in the personal computer market. Technology followers may be able to avoid the mistakes made by leaders. They also have lower research and development costs (in effect, lowering fixed costs) and therefore may be able to match the leaders' low costs. Merck, a producer of pharmaceutical products, successfully pursues a follower strategy. A large firm operating in many different markets where it faces primarily local competition, it can use its global distribution network to quickly introduce the products, services, or ideas of its more innovative, but localized, competitors.[20]

Product versus Process Innovation.   The firm must decide whether to emphasize product innovation (changing the product) or process innovation (changing the way the product is produced). Product innovation involves making the product more useful (portable VCRs, for example, assist in industrial selling), adding new services (for example, banking by phone), or challenging the total product assortment. In mature product markets, where rates of product innovation are low and cost pressures are high, process innovation can be a significant means of lowering costs.[21] In some cases, product and process innovation are pursued simultaneously. When Hirsch, a leading manufacturer of leather watch straps, decided to develop a new line of plastic straps, it also had to develop the necessary production processes, including specialized machine tools.

When production costs are high because of high labor costs (sometimes even after automation, as in Germany), a company that does not want to transfer production to low-wage countries may concentrate on product innovation for special market segments. In doing so, it may have to give up large parts of the market (if its products are priced too high for most customers) or it may find new markets in which a lower level of product technology (and, hence, a lower price) is better suited to customers' needs. For example, Dornier, a German manufacturer of weaving machines, found that its products were too sophisticated for most Latin American customers. It therefore entered the secondhand machinery market, adapting used machines for those customers.

Even intensified product innovation may not protect the firm against situations in which high-tech, high-quality products become the industry standard. In such cases the company must turn to new product markets, provide new customer benefits, or develop new technologies to regain a competitive advantage. An example of this approach is Daimler-Benz, the producer of Mercedes automobiles. In order to enter new product markets, the firm has acquired companies like MSS, which specializes in aviation, related electronics, and military equipment. As a result, Daimler-Benz has become one of the leading suppliers of military aviation products in Europe.

Rate of Product Innovation. A company's rate of product innovation is heavily influenced by traditions in the home market and the basic values of domestic customers, as well as those of the company's personnel. German automakers, for example, prefer not to change their models too often, not only in order to communicate an image of reliable quality and craftsmanship, but also to let their products develop a strong visual image in the minds of their relatively conservative customers. This strategy is an advantage in European markets. In the United States and eastern Asia, in contrast, customers are interested in continual product innovation. There, the quality of a company's offerings is judged partly on the basis of the firm's rate of product innovation.

One way of overcoming this problem is to split the world market into customer segments on the basis of innovation orientation and develop different strategies for each segment. In many cases, however, this approach entails higher costs than marketing to a unified market. Another solution is to offer changes in many different product features. Computer-aided production planning and production flexibility can enable customers to design individualized products. In the case of cars, for example, the customer can specify such features as color, power, and "options."

SCHEDULING OF GLOBAL EXPANSION

The choice of market-entry strategy and the timing of that strategy demand careful consideration.

Few companies can enter all potentially viable markets at once. Depending on their resources and the nature of the competition they face in the new markets, they will choose different competitive strategies and an appropriate schedule for market entry. The schedule can be based on a strategy of concentric expansion, platform expansion, or focused expansion.

Concentric Expansion

Many small companies use **concentric expansion,**[22] in which the company
starts from a strong competitive position in its home market and enters neighboring markets first, gradually expanding its marketing activities from those
markets to their respective neighbors. A Norwegian firm, for example, might
enter Sweden, Finland, and Denmark before attempting to expand to Germany.
(See Map 9.1.) Resources are allocated to well-defined product markets. The
company continually seeks to increase its penetration of the markets it is currently serving and gradually develops superior competitive advantages in these
markets. The main problem with this approach is that neighboring markets are
not necessarily the most attractive ones. Moreover, competitors can gain a dominant position in other markets before the company reaches them. In addition,
the firm may develop a false sense of security, underestimating the difficulties
of entering new markets simply because they are familiar.

Platform Expansion

In technologically advanced industries like computers, machine tools, and consumer electronics, a company must quickly attain a sizable share of the global
market in order to remain competitive.[23] Companies in such industries may

GLOBAL DIMENSIONS 9.2

The Sogo Shosha

The *sogo shosha*, the Japanese term for general trading companies, were founded over a hundred years ago, when Japan became more involved in international trade. In the beginning, they took care of paperwork, provided financial assistance for exports and imports, and assisted in transportation and storage. Essentially, they helped import raw materials for Japanese manufacturers, and then helped export finished products. Their role grew to include manufacturing, marketing and sales, assumption of risk, and raw materials processing. They matured into global trading countries of such size that the sixteen largest *sogo shosha* today control about 55 percent of Japan's exports and 65 percent of its imports.

The *sogo shosha* must adapt to today's competitive global environment. Banks are becoming more involved in trade financing, for example. Manufacturers are taking over marketing functions, especially in larger markets, and high-technology products are more often supported by the company itself than a middleman. The *sogo shosha* have responded by moving in the direction of manufacturing, increasing their own direct foreign investment. And, as Japan becomes more of a globally oriented nation, investing internationally and even undertaking a more important political role, as opposed to an export-oriented nation, the *sogo shosha* will probably undertake the roles and operations of a global firm (resources, manufacturing, and marketing) themselves.

Sources: Adapted from "Sogo Shosha," *The Banker*, January 1984, pp. 78–84; M. Kotabe, "Changing Roles of the Sogo Shosha, the Manufacturing Firms, and the MITI in the Context of the Japanese 'Trade or Die' Mentality," *Columbia Journal of World Business*, Fall 1984, pp. 33–42; and P. Kotler, L. Fahey, and S. Jatusripitak, *The New Competition* (Englewood Cliffs, N.J.: Prentice Hall, 1985), pp. 29–30, 205–206.

choose a **platform expansion strategy.** This approach involves starting out in the technologically advanced Triad markets and then expanding to other markets.[24] Thus, IBM uses its U.S., Canadian, Japanese, and EC markets as platforms from which it enters other markets in South America, Asia, and Europe. This strategy may seem to be appropriate only for large companies, but smaller firms can also use it, either by building a network of cooperative partners or by utilizing the services of a global trading house, like the Japanese *sogo shosha*. (See Global Dimensions 9.2.)

Focused Expansion

Companies of any size operating in an industry in which physical distances are relatively unimportant (such as small consumer goods or large industrial products) may choose a **focused expansion strategy.** In this approach, the marketer examines the most promising markets, regardless of location, enter[...] attractive ones and avoiding the less attractive ones. This approach [...] bined with a platform expansion strategy. Thus, when a U.S. manufa[...] movable gas barbecues decided to enter the attractive German market, it also decided to expand from there to the neighboring German-speaking markets (Austria, Switzerland, northern Italy), in order to take advantage of the possibility of synergy.

Timing

Decisions have to be reconsidered periodically and adapted to changes in external and internal environments. They must be precisely timed for maximum success. An appropriate schedule for market entry has to be chosen, depending on the company's resources and the nature of its competition. Strategy should include commitment to long-term goals. Management should not withdraw immediately if success cannot be achieved in a short time. Global marketing, to a large extent, is a learning process. Only if a reasonable amount of time has passed by without success should management withdraw from a market.

SUMMARY

In this chapter we have discussed how a firm that desires to globalize its business develops its general strategy. Companies beginning global marketing activities have to determine which markets to enter and how to enter them. Firms already established in the global market should consider reallocating their resources and management time and effort across geographical and product markets.

Strategy must be closely linked to the company's mission and major objectives, as well as how it is willing to behave in the competitive arena. Before a strategy can be developed, the marketer must analyze the relevant external environments, as well as the firm's potential to cope with resulting opportunities and threats. The comparison between this potential and competitors' skills and resources leads to a list of distinctive competencies the firm can rely on in the development of its strategy. By matching its distinctive competencies with critical success factors for the markets under consideration, the company can identify its competitive advantages.

The firm's competitive advantages are the foundations for its global strategy. The core strategy broadly defines the company's competitive posture, providing guidance as to what it will and will not do. It incorporates top management's desires regarding the extent to which the firm will engage in global activity. The firm should carefully match the extent of its global activity with its competitive advantages.

No company has unlimited financial or personnel resources. It therefore must make choices in allocating its resources to specific geographic and product markets, as well as technologies. In developing a global portfolio strategy management decides whether to extend the firm's global activity and how many resources to allocate to what endeavor.

A competitive market strategy defines behavior or actions in the market to achieve market success. It includes the basic decision of whether to go for a high global market share, planned modification, or a global niche, as well as the mixture of confrontation and cooperation with competitors and other exchange partners in the market. Because of the growing importance of technology, the competitive market strategy should also include the firm's innovation policy.

Once the global portfolio, competitive strategy, and time schedule have been determined, the marketer must decide how individual business units should operate in the chosen geographic and product markets. A specific entry strategy—concentric, platform, or focused expansion—must be developed for each new market, along with an optimal marketing mix.

DISCUSSION QUESTIONS

1. What is the role of the firm's core strategy in determining its global marketing strategy?

2. What are the basic steps in portfolio planning?

3. What factors influence the importance of a strategic business unit to the global organization?

4. Is global portfolio analysis more or less complex than domestic portfolio analysis? Why?

5. What are the four basic strategies that a firm may employ in managing its portfolio? What are the main advantages of each strategy?

6. What strategies are available to the firm that wishes to penetrate a current market further?

7. How does globalization of markets, suppliers, and competition affect a firm's general strategy?

8. Describe how a small company in the automobile industry might follow a global niche strategy to survive when faced with larger global competitors offering lower prices.

9. When are confrontation strategies appropriate, and what factors determine which strategic option should be used?

10. What determines whether a firm should be a technology leader or follower? What determines whether it should emphasize product versus process innovation?

11. How can a focused expansion strategy be combined with a platform expansion strategy?

C A S E

NESTLÉ: GLOBAL MARKETER

The food industry is globalizing! In the Triad, a growing market of single consumers and dual-career couples dine on gourmet frozen dishes designed to be prepared in a microwave oven. Coffee is increasing in popularity in Japan, and U.S.-style frozen dinners are a hit in Europe. To develop new food products to match social and demographic changes, companies must spend more on research and development. And, increasingly, to gain a return on their investment companies need wide distribution, heavily backed by advertising, in chain stores all over the world.

With plants in more than 60 countries, Nestlé would appear to be in an excellent position to take advantage of the globalization of the food industry. It has already established a major market presence in the United States, and it is rapidly expanding its activities in the European Community. With a wide variety of food products sold around the world, Nestlé is especially noted for Nescafé, the world's first instant coffee. In total, Nestlé produces 200 types of instant coffee, earning over $600 million on sales of $4.7 billion, more than 25 percent of its operating profits. And its Lean Cuisine frozen dinners have achieved strong market success in the United States, Britain, and France. (In Britain, a dozen Lean Cuisine dinners have been designed to appeal to British tastes, including Kashmiri chicken curry.)

Nestlé has recovered nicely from the recent infant formula boycott. Helmut Maucher, who became Nestlé's chief executive in 1982, met with boycott leaders and accepted World Health Organization demands that Nestlé stop advertising infant formula and distributing free samples. Former Senator Edmund Muskie headed a commission that monitored Nestlé's compliance with the agreement. Since then, Nestlé's share of the Third World infant formula market has been maintained, even without advertising.

Nestlé has traditionally taken a long-term view of its markets. Years of losses may be accepted in order to create a market. The entry of Lean Cuisine into Britain, for example, required a sizeable investment in a frozen-food plant. Nestlé was willing to tolerate four years of heavy losses, even importing spaghetti bolognese and paying customs duties, in order to gain the market position it wanted. Now it holds a 33 percent share of the frozen dinner market in Britain, and it is profitable there.

Nestlé's expansion policy is illustrated by its strategic alliance with Rowntree, a British candy maker. During a bidding war between Suchard, a Swiss rival, and Nestlé, Maucher suggested the winning strategy of shifting all responsibility for planning marketing strategy and product development to Rowntree. As he said, "We needed the single-mindedness of people who think about chocolate 24 hours a day." Other Nestlé alliances and acquisitions indicate that advertising and research and development funds will be increased at Rowntree as will

Nestlé's traditional hands-off management style. As Carnation's president, Tim Crull, describes it, "If things are going well, I never hear from Maucher."

Case Issues

1. Refer to the text, where it lists a global company's competitive advantages (in the section "The Global Core Strategy"). Which of these benefits does Nestlé enjoy, and how does that give it a competitive advantage in the global marketplace?

2. Which general strategy, global high share, local high share, global niche, or planned modification, does Nestlé seem to follow, and why?

NOTES

1. P. Kotler, L. Fahey, and S. Jatusripitak, *The New Competition: Meeting the Marketing Challenge from the Far East* (Englewood Cliffs, N.J.: Prentice Hall, 1985), p. 245.

2. J. C. Leontiades, *Multinational Corporate Strategy: Planning for World Markets* (Lexington, Mass.: Lexington Books, 1985), p. 51.

3. *Ibid.*, p. 53.

4. K. Segler, *Basisstrategien im Internationalen Marketing* (Frankfurt: Campus Verlag, 1986), pp. 104–144.

5. Leontiades, op. cit., p. 47.

6. Leontiades, op. cit., p. 45.

7. G. Specht and W. W. Zirngiebel, "Technologieorientierte Wettbewerbsstrategien," *Marketing ZfP* 3 (1985):161–172.

8. Kotler, Fahey, and Jatusripitak, op. cit., pp. 104–110.

9. Leontiades, op. cit., p. 176.

10. B. Mascarenhas, "International Strategies of Non-Dominant Firms," *Journal of International Business Studies*, Spring 1986, p. 19.

11. K. Ohmae, *Triad Power* (New York: Free Press, 1985).

12. Y. Tsurumi, "Japanese Multinational Firms," *Journal of World Trade Law*, January–February 1973, p. 78.

13. R. G. Cooper, "The Performance Impact of Product Innovation Strategies," *European Journal of Marketing* 19, no. 5 (1984).

14. M. Colvin, R. Heeler, and J. Thorpe, "Developing International Advertising Strategy," *Journal of Marketing* 44, no. 4 (1980):73.

15. F. W. Webster, Jr., "Marketing Strategy in a Slow Growth Economy," *California Management Review* 28, no. 3 (1986):95–97.

16. Mascarenhas, op. cit., p. 19.

17. Mascarenhas, op. cit., p. 20.

18. "The World's Fastest-Growing Company," *The Economist*, March 19, 1988, p. 67f.

19. "Mazda Gains a Market by Staying," *New York Times*, July 15, 1982, p. F-8.

20.   Mascarenhas, op. cit., p. 21.

21.   W. J. Abernathy and J. M. Utterback, "Patterns of Industrial Innovation," *Technology Review*, July 1978, pp. 40–47.

22.   H. Mühlbacher and G. Mitterhuber, "Die Internationalisierung der Geschäftstmtigkeit osterreichischer Unternehmungen," *Journal für Betriebswirtschaft* 33, no. 2 (1983):103–117.

23.   R. Abravanel, "Shaping Effective Responses to the Globalization Challenge," in Riccardo Varaldo, ed., *International Marketing Cooperation* (Pisa: Ets Editrice, 1987), pp. 35–92.

24.   Ohmae, op. cit., p. 144.

POSITIONING AND MARKET ENTRY

Who Made This Car?

"World cars"—designed, manufactured, and marketed through cooperative agreements among car companies from many countries—are actually here. More than twenty-five major car and truck companies worldwide have joined together in over 300 strategic partnerships. Even GM, Ford, and Chrysler have agreed to conduct research together on materials that would produce stronger cars.

The Ford Probe and the Mazda MX-6 are even made in the same plant. Ford and Nissan have a joint venture where Nissan-designed minivans are produced and sold under both the Ford and Nissan brand names. Pontiac LeMans was engineered by Opel (GM's West German subsidiary) and is built by Daewoo in South Korea. Chrysler plans to make minivans with Renault, allowing Renault to begin manufacturing in Europe. In fact, consumers would be hard-pressed to identify which car is made where.

What is behind all of these strategic partnerships? No company can afford to design, build, and market a complete line of cars—which car makers want to offer to satisfy customers. In the United States, for example, close to 600 car and truck models are in competition. Cooperation allows car companies to enter more markets, faster, cheaper, with a broader product line than if they tried it alone. Indeed, such strategic partnerships are the only economically viable way for car companies to remain globally competitive in the 1990s.

Source: "Driving Toward a World Car?," *Newsweek*, May 1, 1989, pp. 48–49.

Once the marketer has identified the markets to be served and chosen an appropriate competitive strategy, it must decide how to conduct business in particular geographic or product markets. It must choose an entry strategy and develop an appropriate marketing mix for each market. A prerequisite for these decisions is positioning, or determining a specific market position for the company's product.

Positioning decisions, which flow from other corporate decisions, help determine the best way for the firm to enter a market and what the marketing mix should be.

Exhibit 10.1 illustrates how the positioning decision fits with the analysis performed by the company, and the decisions they reached, as discussed earlier. Clearly, these decisions are not independent—they affect each other. Exhibit 10.1 also illustrates the influence of the positioning decision on market-entry and marketing-mix decisions. For example, if the firm is entering a mass market that crosses several national boundaries, it must determine its competitive advantages relative to other firms operating in that market. If these advantages are based on technology (for example, the firm's production costs are lower than competitors' because it has advanced robot-aided manufacturing processes), this factor will play an important role in portfolio and market strategy.

EXHIBIT 10.1
POSITIONING AND
MARKETING-ENTRY
DECISIONS—THEIR
PLACE IN GLOBAL
DECISION MAKING

After assessing external
environments and the
firm's potential in those
environments, the firm
must make decisions as
to how best to respond to
the available options.
These decisions (market
choice, basic decisions,
and differentiation) determine how the firm should
position itself in the product market and which
market-entry technique is
best for a given national
market.

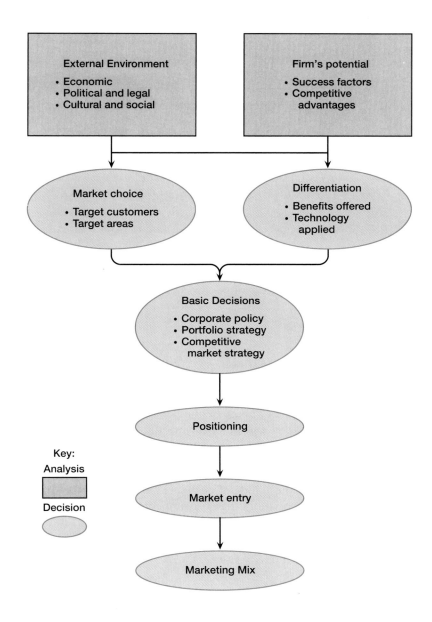

POSITIONING

Developing a **positioning strategy** involves determining the desired image of
the product in the minds of potential customers.[1] The marketer takes a position
relative to competitors: it explains why its product is better than or distinct from

GLOBAL DIMENSIONS 10.1

Global Positioning by Canon

In introducing one of its new cameras, Canon followed a different positioning strategy in two major markets, although the camera was physically similar in each market. The camera was positioned differently through different promotion, pricing, and distribution policies. In particular, the use of different advertising campaigns allowed Canon to enjoy economies of scale in producing the camera while positioning the product to suit the preferences of consumers in the target markets.

In the United States, the new camera was positioned as "foolproof"—the camera you can always count on to take good pictures. Many U.S. consumers were tired of expensive 35mm cameras that require constant adjustment to ensure good photographs. Canon emphasized that its camera would be easier to use than competing products, yet would still produce excellent photographs. In contrast, in Japan consumers were looking for the most modern camera available. There, the camera was positioned as the leader in state-of-the-art photography.

others. For example, in the U.S. market Porsche automobiles are positioned as sophisticated, well-engineered status symbols. Hyundais, in contrast, are positioned as affordable, dependable transportation. In other words, a positioning strategy chooses a bundle of benefits that is attractive to customers in the target market and distinguishes the product or company from its competitors. Positioning thus serves to establish a reason to buy a particular product. (For an example of global positioning, see Global Dimensions 10.1.) Firms use **positioning analysis** to determine whether the desired position has been established in the minds of customers and whether the firm is achieving this goal more successfully than its competitors.

MARKET ENTRY

Positioning, of course, occurs within a target market. Thus, the marketer must choose a market-entry technique that is consistent with the desired product position, and develop a marketing mix that communicates and supports that position. For example, to support its market position in the United States Porsche works through its subsidiary, Porsche U.S., to coordinate dealer selection, advertising campaigns, special sales events, pricing strategies, and postsale service. Porsche must use a market-entry strategy that entails a high degree of risk and a high level of management involvement in order to maintain maximum control over marketing activities.

EXHIBIT 10.2
GUIDELINES FOR
SUCCESSFUL
MARKET ENTRY

U.S.-based corporations
that compete well against
foreign rivals in global
markets seem to follow
some of the same guide-
lines for successful mar-
ket entry. The three major
guidelines for global success are illustrated here.

1. Be patient.	Entering a market other than the domestic one, where the company is experienced, requires more patience and pre-entry analysis than does entering an additional domestic market.
2. Structure operations to fit the market.	Potential local partners, the distribution system, trade restrictions, and other industry and market variables must be thoroughly considered before deciding on market entry.
3. Be flexible in product and marketing design.	Unique conditions require adaptation.

Source: Adapted from K. Labich, "America's International Winners," *Fortune*, April 14, 1986, pp. 34–46.

When growers of Chinese gooseberries were planning to enter the U.S. market, one of the first decisions they faced was the choice of an appropriate market-entry technique. At the time Chinese gooseberries were grown mainly in New Zealand, and the growers could not shift production to the United States. Chinese gooseberries are fragile and must receive special handling as they move through the distribution channel. After carefully considering these and other factors, the growers chose to employ an import agent to direct the marketing of Chinese gooseberries in the United States. Among other things, the agent is credited with giving the fruit the more appealing name of *kiwi*.

In attempting to maintain the firm's competitive position, managers often consider the potential benefits of entering a foreign market.[2] Federal Express provides a good example. Its managers view foreign expansion as a necessary part of maintaining the company's market leadership position in the United States. Even though the firm has not made money in the short run, it believes overseas expansion is necessary to support its customers as they expand globally.[3] For managers faced with the decision of how best to enter a foreign market, some choices are relatively easy to make (for example, the host government may grant access only through joint ventures). Others, however, may be quite difficult, especially when the range of choices is extensive. Some general guidelines for selecting a market-entry technique are presented in Exhibit 10.2.

This chapter addresses the decisions a firm must make when it is considering a new market. A range of alternatives—from exporting to establishing a foreign subsidiary—and the advantages and disadvantages of each are discussed from the perspective of the global marketing manager. The chapter concludes with a discussion of strategic partnerships, or alliances with suppliers and competitors that are designed to help the firm obtain the maximum benefit from global opportunities.

MAKING THE MARKET-ENTRY DECISION

The firm must choose from a wide variety of market-entry options, each with its own set of benefits and costs.

Each market under consideration may require a different market-entry technique, and each technique entails a different combination of risks and rewards. In deciding which technique is most appropriate for a given market, the global marketing manager should consider both external and internal factors, which are discussed later in the chapter. In this section we present two basic approaches to making the market-entry decision.

Decisions related to market entry are closely tied to the firm's broader decisions—especially its positioning strategy— and to information gathered by the firm in conducting an opportunity assessment. One approach to making these decisions is to begin with an assessment of corporate strategy and to evaluate alternative market-entry techniques in terms of their potential contribution to that strategy. For example, when a basic corporate strategy is to minimize financial risk, market-entry techniques that entail minimal capital involvement would be preferable. Exhibit 10.3 illustrates how direct and indirect forms of market entry are related to risk and control for both the home and host organizations. A firm that seeks to minimize its own risk would automatically limit itself to the options on the left-hand side of the figure.

This approach is uncomplicated and easy to carry out; however, it often produces less than optimal results. A second approach is to begin by evaluating

EXHIBIT 10.3
ALTERNATIVE
MARKET-ENTRY
TECHNIQUES:
INVOLVEMENT, RISK,
AND CONTROL

As the home organization becomes more involved in marketing and production in another country, it shifts risk and control away from the host to the home organization. For example, Company A is involved in marketing only—its risk and control are low, and the host partner has higher risk and control. Company B, involved in marketing and production with extensive capital, has assumed higher risks to gain greater control in the foreign market.

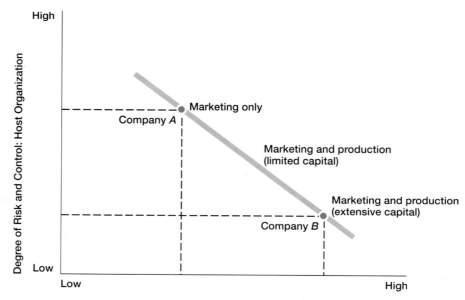

all possible market-entry techniques from the standpoint of all relevant decision criteria, selecting the one that is likely to be most effective. The marketing manager does not make a final decision until all available information has been considered. In effect, this approach forces the manager to continually reevaluate criteria and options. Although it requires more market information, it usually results in a better decision.[4] In the remainder of the chapter, therefore, we assume that this approach will be used in making market-entry decisions.

ALTERNATIVE MARKET-ENTRY TECHNIQUES

When Timberland Company, a U.S.-based marketer of outdoor shoes, was deciding how to enter the Japanese market, it considered options ranging from using a Japanese trading company (thereby passing along some risk and control) to operating its own retail stores (thereby maintaining more control but also increasing the level of risk).[5] As illustrated in Exhibit 10.4, Timberland had many options among which to choose. Market-entry options can be classified along two dimensions: whether they are direct or indirect and whether they involve marketing or both marketing and production. Each technique involves trade-offs between market control and degree of risk. These trade-offs are illustrated in Exhibit 10.5.

EXHIBIT 10.4
MARKET-ENTRY
ALTERNATIVES

Market-entry techniques can be classified according to whether they require indirect or direct involvement on the part of the firm, and whether they involve marketing activities only or both marketing and production. Note that a direct entry strategy for marketing and production has to involve extensive capital, while indirect market entry never involves extensive capital.

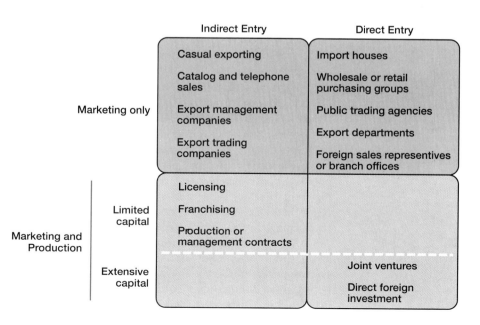

	Indirect Entry	Direct Entry
Marketing only	Casual exporting Catalog and telephone sales Export management companies Export trading companies	Import houses Wholesale or retail purchasing groups Public trading agencies Export departments Foreign sales representatives or branch offices
Marketing and Production — Limited capital	Licensing Franchising Production or management contracts	
Marketing and Production — Extensive capital		Joint ventures Direct foreign investment

EXHIBIT 10.5
MARKET-ENTRY
TRADE-OFFS

The market-entry alterna-
tives involve different
trade-offs.

	Indirect Entry	Direct Entry
Marketing only	Limited involvement in marketing	Daily involvement in marketing
Marketing and production	Limited involvement in marketing	Daily involvement in marketing
	Limited capital risk	Extensive capital risk
	Limited involvement in production	Daily involvement in production

Indirect Entry, Marketing Only

Indirect market-entry
techniques are low in
risk, but they also limit
the firm's control over
marketing activities in
the host market.

The market-entry technique that offers the lowest level of risk and the least market control to an expanding firm is indirect entry involving marketing functions only. There are several variations on this approach. For example, if a U.S. business receives an unsolicited order from a customer in Spain and responds to the request on a one-time basis, it is engaging in **casual exporting**. However, just as risk is minimized in this approach, so too is opportunity. If the exporting firm does not follow up the contact with a sustained marketing effort, it is unlikely to gain future sales.

Catalog and telephone sales may be pursued on either a casual or a continuing basis. In either case, risk is limited to the costs of distributing the catalogs in foreign markets. Consumer goods are frequently sold in this way. For example, a specialist in Scottish foods based in Edinburgh uses a catalog to sell products to upscale markets in the United States. Similarly, a Swiss producer of electronic measuring devices sells spare parts to the European market through catalogs.

Export management companies function like external export departments. The export management company assumes most or all of the company's risk of market entry. Often such companies perform all the services necessary to sell the exporter's product in a foreign market. A popular arrangement is for the export management company to buy the product from the manufacturer; however, some companies perform an agency role and do not take title to the goods. Export management companies vary in other ways, too. They handle different product lines, and the completeness of the service provided varies. Regardless of these differences, they are all located in the same country as the producing firm and provide a relatively risk-free means of entering foreign markets.

An **export trading company** is one that not only buys products or acts as an export agent but also imports, invests, manufactures, and engages in **countertrading** (the trading of goods for other goods, instead of money). Perhaps the best-known export trading companies are the *sogo shosha* of Japan. As discussed in Chapter 9, their worldwide operations, combined with an information network that provides market knowledge and links to capital resources throughout the world, make them major trading organizations in a great many markets. A recent trend for *sogo shosha* is to reach beyond their traditional functions and become involved in direct investment: for example, Mitsui, the fourth-largest exporter of grain from the United States, considered buying established U.S. food businesses like Sara Lee.[6]

Export trading companies may operate in several national markets and handle a variety of products, or they may specialize in a single industry or market. In the United States, the ability of small and medium-sized firms to export their products was given a boost by the Export Trading Company Act of 1982, which was designed to facilitate the establishment of export trading companies. This act modified antitrust legislation to allow participation in joint ventures, particularly those with export potential. In addition, banks were encouraged to become more directly involved in such exporting organizations. To date, however, the impact of this legislation has been less than expected.[7]

Direct Entry, Marketing Only

When a company becomes directly involved in the marketing of its products in another nation, it gains additional control but it must also be willing to assume greater risks.

Direct entry involving only marketing occurs when the firm becomes directly involved in marketing its products in the host market. In general, this approach represents a stronger commitment to global markets than indirect approaches do. It also entails greater risk for the firm, because it requires that more corporate resources be invested outside the home country. But the results are often well worth the risk. An Australian firm using this approach was able to achieve profits in foreign markets that were twice as high as its domestic profits.[8]

Perhaps the simplest form of direct, marketing-only entry is selling to an **import house**. An import house, based in the host country, provides marketing services through which products are sold to consumers. The home organization need only sell its products to the import house. Because control passes to the import house, the home company loses the ability to determine how its products are marketed in the host country. But this loss of control is offset by a lower level of risk.

In a similar manner, the sale may be made to a **wholesale** or **retail purchasing group**. Normally, wholesale purchasing groups serve a limited buying group within the host country. For example, the Independent Grocers Association in the United States might buy salmon from a Norwegian marketer for distribution to member supermarkets.

In centrally controlled markets consumer and industrial products are often sold to a **public trading agency**. For example, until recently firms entering the CMEA markets in Eastern Europe had to sell their products to a state trading company, as discussed in Chapter 3. The agency, not the ultimate buyer, is the customer. It resells the product to the consumer.

Expansion into international markets often begins with the establishment of an **export department**. This is not actually a form of market entry; rather, it is an internal response to the need or desire to move into new markets. Located within the home organization, the export department is responsible for international sales and possibly shipping, advertising, credit evaluation, and other activities related to operating in foreign markets. Export departments are organized either by geographic area (such as European sales) or product category (such as world sales of construction equipment). Their chief disadvantage is their domestic base; the firm cannot react quickly enough or obtain enough information about trends in international markets.

One way to improve the organization's ability to react to market trends while maintaining a relatively low level of risk is to use foreign sales representatives or branch offices. **Sales representatives** are usually not employees of the home organization; rather they are independent sales agents working on a commission basis. They may act as a foreign sales department for the home organization. A well-run system of sales representatives can provide the foundation for a successful long-term export program.[9]

Branch offices, on the other hand, are normally staffed by employees of the home organization, who are compensated on a salary or salary-plus-commission basis. One advantage of this option is that in addition to performing the sales function, branch office staff may perform other marketing functions, such as customer service. They also participate in the home organization's planning of its international marketing efforts.

A company may start with a sales representative or branch office and, as the market grows and the company gains experience, establish more extensive operations in the host market.

The same advantages and disadvantages of using salary versus commission, or some combination of the two, exist internationally as for domestic marketing. Generally, when selling is the individual's primary job, commissions are preferred. But when additional activities (such as gathering customer information or extensive post-sales service) are important, salaries and salary-plus-commission compensation are more popular. However, there are some markets where a commission-only approach is not useful. In highly collective societies (Asian or Arabic, for example) individual efforts and rewards (especially high commissions for the best sales representatives) may not be culturally appropriate. In other cultures, commissions may be interpreted as a signal that the firm is not committed to the employees and is prepared to get rid of them as soon as they fail to perform. So cultural norms should be considered when deciding how to pay sales representatives or branch office employees.

Indirect Entry, Marketing and Production

The firm may choose an indirect entry method that combines marketing and production elements, but involves limited capital risks.

There are three indirect market-entry techniques that involve production with limited capital involvement: licensing, franchising, and production or management contracts. For organizations that want to rapidly establish a market presence with limited capital risk, licensing and franchising are especially popular.

Industrial property rights, including rights to technology, patents, processes, and trademarks (registered brand names), may be licensed to an organization in the host market. Licensing is frequently combined with a joint venture. An example is the arrangement of San Miguel, a Philippine beer brewer, with Mt. Everest Breweries of Nepal to produce and market San Miguel beer in Nepal.[10] A manufacturing firm that wants to enter a series of foreign markets quickly may license its technology to partners in those markets. Or a trademark holder like the Disney Company may license a trademark—say, Mickey Mouse—to several companies in foreign markets, thereby permitting the production and marketing of Mickey Mouse products in those markets. The capital risk associated with licensing is relatively low. At the same time, the home organization must retain some measure of control to ensure that quality standards are maintained and the corporate or brand image remains positive.

Licensing may embrace all forms of industrial property; **franchising,** in contrast, is usually limited to trademarks. The reasons for franchising are similar to those for licensing—the organization wants to enter a foreign market with a limited degree of risk. An advantage of franchising compared to licensing is that it strikes a balance between adapting the marketing mix to local conditions and maintaining high standards in international markets. The franchising organization tends to be more directly involved in the development and control of the marketing mix, while the franchisee is more directly involved in the execution of that strategy in the host market. Italy-based Benetton, for example, franchises retail outlets in many countries, including the United States. While Benetton produces its clothes in Italy, its franchisees feed valuable market information to the home organization through a computer network. The franchisees also execute local advertising and sales-promotion activities designed specifically for their markets.

Franchising permits rapid market expansion with relatively little capital risk (the franchisee invests some of its own capital). But because the franchisee is directly involved in running the business, franchising offers less control by the home organization than would be possible if it owned the foreign organization. Indeed, sometimes control must be reclaimed by the home organization. For example, McDonald's has had a stormy relationship with some of its franchisees in France, due to concerns about the maintenance of corporate standards. On the other hand, franchising has allowed McDonald's to expand rapidly and profitably. Of the firm's $14 billion in sales to date, 25 percent is due to franchisee activity in forty-seven foreign markets.[11]

A **production** or **management contract** allows the firm to be involved either in the manufacture of a product or in the management of an enterprise in a foreign market. Such contracts are sometimes entered into as a result of the expropriation of a company or industry by the host-country government. The former investors in the enterprise may be asked to continue to manage the business after it has been nationalized, and in this way they may recover some of their losses.

Increasingly, companies are actively seeking production or management contracts in foreign markets. Turnkey operations often include a production or management contract that stipulates that the home organization will continue to manage the operation for a specific period at a specified fee. Energy corporations like Aramco provide technology, skills, and experience to countries in the Middle East that have oil fields but lack the management capacity to develop them.[12]

Direct Entry, Marketing and Production

The market-entry options with the highest degree of control, and the highest level of risk to the firm, are those which permit direct entry with marketing and production activity, as well as extensive capital investment.

In many developing countries, direct entry into the market requires production with extensive capital involvement. In fact, many industrial and service projects in such countries are based on the **turnkey concept,** in which the home organization agrees to enhance the host country's ability to provide certain products and services in the future. This is especially true in areas that affect the host nation's infrastructure—transportation, communication, power plants, and even military systems.

As capital involvement increases, the level of risk and the need for control by the home firm also increase. Yet many companies are still willing to share control in order to share or diversify risk. One frequently used market-entry technique that shares both risk and control is the **joint venture.** A partnership between host- and home-country firms is formed, usually resulting in the creation of a third firm. A joint venture often combines the market knowledge and skills of the host-country firm with the production or technical skills of the home-country firm. For example, Honeywell has entered into a joint venture in the Soviet Union in which it will construct automated manufacturing plants; this sort of technology transfer is at the heart of many joint ventures involving production. Host-country partners in a joint venture usually bring other critical resources to the partnership, such as low labor costs or access to scarce natural resources.[13]

The desirability of joint ventures is often tempered by factors in the external environment, especially the legal and political environment. In China, for example, the process of establishing a joint venture is so complex that would-be partners must weigh the potential advantages against the effort and cost associated with getting started. (See Exhibit 10.6.)

The selection of an appropriate partner is critical to the success of a joint venture. If the partners do not understand each other well, the venture may be a disaster. In one such case an American firm entered into a joint venture with an Asian company. They planned a large, simultaneously run promotional effort that never materialized because each company assumed that the other would coordinate and pay for all promotional activities. The venture was eventually terminated.[14] Partners are usually chosen on a case-by-case, or market-by-market, basis. When a corporation pursues such alliances as part of its overall strategy, they are referred to as **strategic partnerships.** Strategic partnerships are discussed more fully later in the chapter.

For companies with sufficient capital that want to maintain high levels of control and believe certain markets will be large enough to justify the capital expenditure, **direct foreign investment** may be a viable market-entry strategy; the company may make a direct acquisition or merger in the host market, provide venture capital to a firm serving the market, or establish a subsidiary. It has been suggested, for example, that the management, financial, and distribution risks of entering the Japanese market are so high that the preferred entry technique is acquisition of a Japanese company.[15] Certainly acquisition is a major route to the U.S. market and the rapidly expanding European Community. Acquisition is an appropriate strategy in both, because of their large size and diversity. The marketing skills of a host-country company are likely to be more highly developed than those of a foreign company just entering the market; therefore, acquisition enables the foreign company to move along the experience curve more quickly. Moreover, during the late 1980s the lower value of the U.S. dollar relative to other currencies meant that it was cheaper for a foreign firm to purchase a U.S. company than it had been earlier in the decade.[16]

Another approach that enables the firm to remain in contact with the target market is **venture capital**. In such a case, a company, bank, or investment firm provides capital to an innovative firm that is developing a new product or approach to a market. These high-risk companies normally find it difficult to attract a sufficient amount of capital from traditional sources. Making such an investment gives the funding corporation a "window" on the market; it keeps informed on research and development through its links to innovative firms, yet avoids full commitment to those firms, thereby reducing overall risk.

Establishing a **subsidiary** usually means hiring host-country employees. Limited capital participation may be offered to host-country investors. But both risk and control are retained primarily by the home company. IBM in Japan, Nestlé in Australia, and Toyota in the United States are but a few companies that have taken this approach.

Foreign companies engaging in direct foreign investment not only face higher capital risks, but they may also be subject to protectionist policies, and more backlash than either domestic companies or joint ventures.[17] Large-scale foreign investment is controversial in most countries. Restrictive laws governing such investment are becoming increasingly common in developed countries, as well as in developing ones.

DECISION CRITERIA

In making the market-entry decision global marketers must review multiple criteria, ranging from macroenvironmental issues to firm-specific issues.

The criteria on which a firm bases its decisions about market-entry technique may be classified into six categories: macroenvironments, industry conditions, market considerations, product considerations, financial considerations, and issues specific to the firm. As with the various market-entry techniques, there are several subcategories within each of these categories. (See Exhibit 10.7.) The most effective decisions are based on a careful review of all applicable criteria.

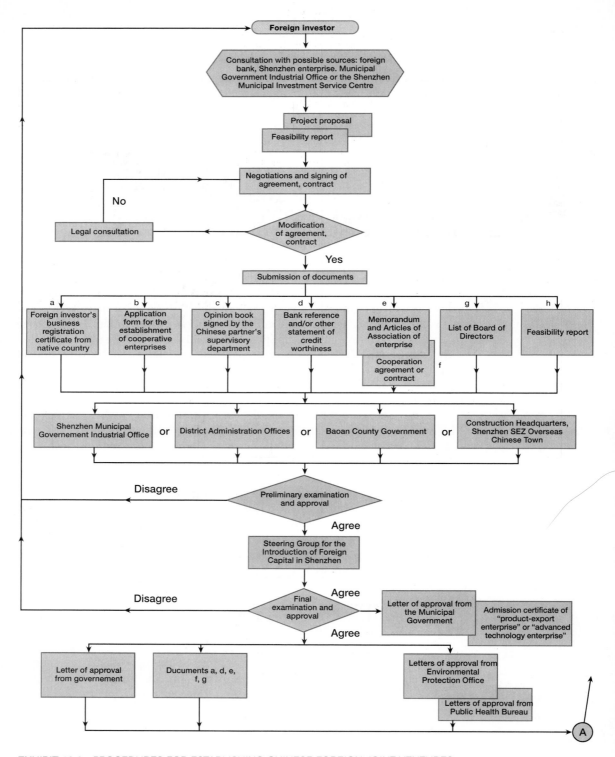

EXHIBIT 10.6 PROCEDURES FOR ESTABLISHING CHINESE-FOREIGN JOINT VENTURES

Establishing a joint venture is frequently difficult. This is particularly true for centrally planned economies, such as China, as this diagram illustrates.

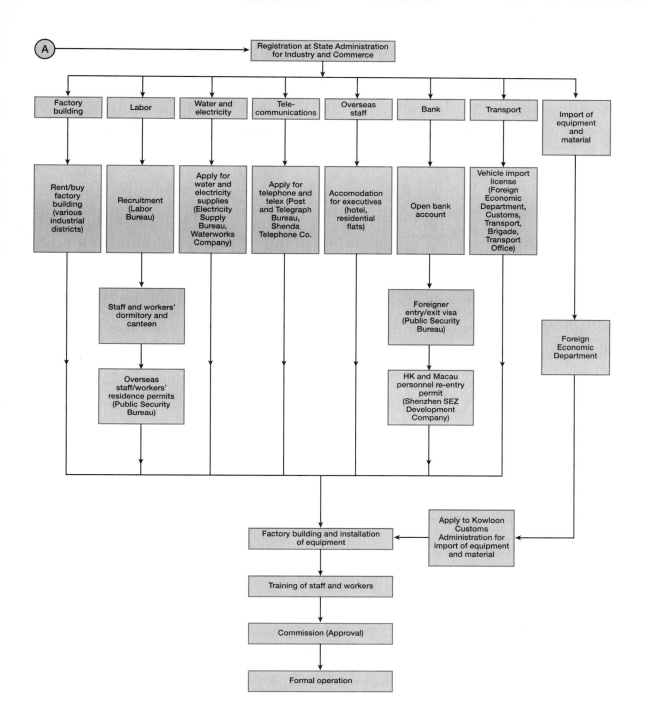

Source: Adapted from *Shenzhen Industrial Investment Guide* by Takugin, as illustrated in *China Trader*, vol. X, issue no. 5, 1987, pp. 70–71, 74–75.

Criteria	Element
Macro Environments	Economic
	Political and legal
	Cultural and social
Industry	Competition
	Market volume
Market	Influence and power
	Distance
	Technological development
	Resource supply and control
	Infrastructure
	Distribution
	Information
Product	Product characteristics
	Service intensity
	Product usage
	Product life-cycle
Financial Considerations	Acceptable risk and required capital
	Costs
	Currency risks
Firm	Mission and goals
	Sales objectives
	Nonfinancial resources
	Competitive strategy
	Experience

Macroenvironments

Market-entry choice is
affected by what level
of risk a firm wishes to
assume and what level
of control it believes is
necessary to assure
that the marketing mix
is properly
implemented.

Macroenvironments affect the selection of a market-entry technique by eliminating some options and making others more viable. *Economic considerations*, such
as limited buying power in the target market, may suggest entry techniques that
minimize capital risk. For example, in Chad, an African nation where per capita
income is $135 per year, foreign firms generally prefer to export their products
or sell them to wholesale or retail purchasing groups rather than establish subsidiaries there. In their view, the level of economic activity in Chad is too low
to justify direct investment.

Similarly, *political conditions* influence both the choice and the success of a
market-entry technique. As noted earlier, if a U.S. company wishes to enter a
COMECON market it usually has to undertake some form of joint venture in
order to obtain permission to do business there. Pepsi, for instance, entered into

a joint venture with a Soviet public trading organization (FTO) to sell Pepsi in hard-currency stores* in the Soviet Union. The recent easing of political tension between the United States and the Soviet Union has led several other U.S. companies to establish joint ventures with such organizations.[18] Positive political relations between two nations, such as those between Australia and the United States, permit a broader range of market-entry choices. In fact, the United States is the foremost foreign investor in Australia.[19]

Legal restrictions strongly influence the choice of a market-entry technique. Such restrictions may be motivated by political concerns, as when a host country requires local participation in any business conducted by a foreign company, thereby limiting the choice to a joint venture. **Trade restrictions** control or limit trade within a nation. India, for example, has very strict restrictions on imports of automobiles, including low import quotas and a high tariff on each vehicle. A European marketer of automobiles that wishes to enter this market would probably choose exporting over other forms of market entry. Trade may be so restricted that firms are prevented from entering the market at all; U.S. advertising agencies, for example, have been denied any role other than non-equity affiliation in Korea.[20] When trade restrictions are eased, a wider array of market-entry options is available. Trade restrictions in Japan were eased in 1985. For example, foreign firms no longer have to submit products that meet their own safety tests to the Japanese testing bureau. As a result, foreign companies can enter Japanese markets more quickly than before.[21] Sometimes high trade restrictions in an otherwise attractive market make direct foreign investment the most appropriate entry technique. In the United States, for example, increased protectionism, coupled with the devalued dollar and a sizeable market, have resulted in increased direct foreign investment by Asian and European manufacturers.

Legal restrictions may also take the form of government involvement in business operations. For example, when France began to denationalize major industries, U.S. firms increased their level of direct investment in France, because they felt more comfortable with an economy in which the private sector plays the dominant role.[22]

Another macroenvironment that influences the choice of a market-entry technique is the *cultural environment*. A society that is characterized by a high level of ethnocentrism is probably best entered through a management contract, licensing, or a joint venture. Korean firms that want to enter the Japanese market are more likely to succeed when they take this approach. In contrast, Japanese electronic firms entering the United States are probably better off maintaining their home-country identity. Because American consumers believe that Japanese manufacturers produce higher-quality products, a joint venture incorporating the Japanese name or even direct foreign investment probably makes the most sense.

---

*Hard-currency stores are those in which products must be paid for in a currency other than rubles or other COMECON currencies. Pepsi receives vodka in return, which it resells at a profit.

Industry Conditions

Industry conditions in
different nations vary,
affecting the market-
entry technique that is
best for a given nation.

Competition influences not only the attractiveness of a market but also the choice of a market-entry technique. The global marketing manager must think about the competition in broad terms—size, intensity, relative market share, rate of growth, and technological sophistication. Each of these aspects of competition affects market entry in different ways. For example, foreign companies entering the car market in the United States face intense competition. In this situation it is more effective to "buy" market share through affiliation with a firm that is already in the market than to enter the market alone and build market share slowly. Renault used this approach when it affiliated with American Motors after years of trying unsuccessfully to penetrate the market on its own.

Market volume can also influence the choice of a market-entry technique. In large markets, especially those with strong growth rates, direct foreign investment is more easily justified than in small markets with low or negative growth rates. One of the reasons U.S. and Japanese companies have made major investments in Europe is that the European Community represents an even larger market than the United States. Without the economic integration provided by the European Community, national markets in Europe would be less attractive and would be entered by less financially risky methods, such as exporting.[23] Some firms can find high-volume markets outside the Triad markets. The excess production capacity of companies operating in developed economies may be used to make products for the rapidly growing populations of developing countries. Global marketers should not forget that developing economies may become major markets in the future.[24]

Market Considerations

Several dimensions of
the market itself must
be evaluated in choos-
ing a market-entry
technique.

The nature of the market, as well as the need and ability to influence it, affect the choice of a market-entry technique. If the company wishes to *influence* the market and is unable to do so from its home base, direct marketing and production entry techniques are called for. Thus, IBM established a subsidiary in Japan to enter the computer market there, so that it could influence the marketing of its products in Japan.

The *distance* between the home organization and the target market can also affect market entry. A U.S.-based company entering the New Zealand market would probably use some form of direct entry. Given the distance between the two countries, some 8,000 miles, an indirect market-entry technique, such as casual exporting or an export management company, would pass all control to the host-country organization. If the company were to have any control at all, it would have to arrange for more direct involvement (for example, through its own sales office). Recently the impact of distance has been reduced by advances in telecommunications. Phone calls, telexes, and fax messages are conveyed as easily between the United States and New Zealand as they are within either country. Nevertheless, distance still creates a gap in face-to-face communication, and this may affect the choice of a market-entry technique.

These open pit mines in Chile provide employment for Chileans, but most of the value-added from copper comes from its processing and manufacturing, which occurs in other countries.

The level of *technological development* in a market also influences the selection of a market-entry technique. When entering a technologically sophisticated market like Sweden, a firm that manufactures computer hardware may be able to transfer its technology directly into the market. This might be done without capital involvement, through a licensing arrangement between the manufacturer and a Swedish firm. In a market with a lower level of technological sophistication, direct production with capital involvement may be necessary, to ensure appropriate use of the technology. In Argentina, for example, a direct, marketing-only technique (such as a sales office) or even an indirect, marketing-only technique (such as an export management company) might be used for the same computer hardware. However, if the product is a highly sophisticated one that cannot be obtained elsewhere, such as a Cray computer, the host country might allow the company to export to the market while requiring that companies with less technologically sophisticated products enter into joint ventures.[25] This approach is used by China, which is trying to upgrade its technology.

Resource supply and control requirements also influence market-entry decisions. A company that wants to be vertically integrated from raw materials through distribution should probably use a direct production entry technique. Copper companies in Chile, for example, want to control copper mining, extraction, and processing into a semifinished product. They therefore invest directly in mining, smelting, and processing activities.

A nation's *infrastructure* can act as either a resource or a constraint. A French coffee company developing a plantation in central Africa will probably have to use a market-entry technique that entails capital involvement. It will probably need to build roads to ship its product to urban centers. It may also have to build its own electrical power plants and house its employees. But when entering the European market the same company could use an indirect technique or a direct, marketing-only strategy, because the infrastructure there is more highly developed.

Distribution channels and objectives require local partnerships when the distribution system is complex and resistant to change, as is the case, for example, in Japan. Direct investment in distribution systems may be necessary when marketing objectives cannot be met using existing distribution systems.[26] For example, when entering a less economically developed market the firm may need to establish new distribution channels. This might be appropriate, for instance, in the case of food products, which usually pass through several wholesalers and retailers before reaching consumers. A firm that wants to lower distribution costs might establish a more efficient channel. The most appropriate market-entry technique would probably be one involving direct investment. When entering a market in which the distribution system is sophisticated and accepts new entrants easily, as is the case in Hong Kong, an indirect entry technique may be used. A Dutch company that exports VHT milk (which is processed at very high temperatures, so that it does not need to be refrigerated before the container is opened) to Hong Kong has achieved a substantial market share by selling to two supermarket chains that together control some 70 percent of the market.

Because of its close link to market influence and control, the availability of *information* is an important factor in market-entry decisions. When in-depth market information is necessary but difficult to obtain, the best strategy is a direct, marketing-only entry technique or direct marketing and production with capital involvement. In both of these cases a local partner is needed, either because it possesses the necessary information or because it is better able to gather the information than a foreign organization would be. For example, a Canadian firm entering the Malaysian market for food products would be well advised to form a joint venture with a Malaysian partner. Food preferences are quite different in Malaysia than in Canada, and a local partner could provide the information necessary for successful product adaptation. At the same time, because market information is not as readily available in Malaysia as in Canada, a local partner may be the only viable source of the needed information. (For a discussion of factual versus interpretive market knowledge, see Global Dimensions 10.2.)

Product Considerations

Just as product characteristics affect market acceptance of the product, they also influence market-entry decisions.

Numerous *product characteristics* influence both the rate of diffusion in a market (see Chapter 7) and the choice of a market-entry technique. The greater the market's resistance to a product, the greater the need for a market-entry technique that gives the organization direct control. Microwave ovens, for example, have met with fairly strong resistance in Puerto Rico and England, due to cooking habits and social norms that are not consistent with the benefits provided by the product. Microwave-oven manufacturers must undertake appropriate marketing efforts to reposition the product as consistent with social values to succeed in these markets. There is less need for direct control by the home organization when the product is likely to diffuse rapidly through the market, such as Gummy Bears, which are made in Germany and exported to the United States.

The greater the level of *service* needed to support a product, both before and after the sale, the more the preferred market-entry technique will be one

GLOBAL DIMENSIONS 10.2

Market Entry and Market Knowledge

Factual knowledge, which is the knowledge usually possessed by managers who live and work outside of a particular national market, may lead to a different view of the optimal means of entering that market than would the interpretive knowledge that can be gained from living and working within the market. For example, one study showed that foreign managers in Japan consider their main market-entry problems to be competition, recruitment of Japanese managers, and marketing. In contrast, when asked to describe the problems they would face in entering Japanese markets, managers in Germany referred to institutional barriers, such as tariffs and regulations.

The latter view is likely to result in the choice of a direct market-entry method, such as a joint venture or a strategic alliance, as a means of reducing the risk to the home-country organization. Of course, this would also result in minimal control by the home organization. On the other hand, if competition, personnel, and marketing are viewed as the main problems, a market-entry technique that permits greater control will probably be chosen. The study also found that managers working in the Japanese market preferred direct foreign investment, willingly accepting higher risk in return for greater control and profit potential.

Source: H. Simon, "Entry Barriers and Entry Strategies in the Japanese Market," in K. Moller and M. Paltschik, eds., *Contemporary Research in Marketing*, Vol. 1 (European Marketing Academy, Helsinki, 1986), pp. 321–322.

that entails direct product involvement.* Caterpillar Inc., for example, is committed to worldwide service excellence. This requires direct marketing and production involvement in every market the company enters. Independent dealerships, branch offices, parts warehouses, joint ventures, and foreign subsidiaries, enable the organization to maintain service quality. In the consumer market, Japan's Daimaru department store chain is entering the Australian market through direct foreign investment. The company predicts that its high levels of customer service, especially its packaging and wrapping of products, will give it a competitive edge and may even force other Australian department stores to change their approach.[27]

Product usage affects the degree of control needed in particular markets. For industrial markets, entry techniques involving direct marketing or production (often with capital involvement) are required. For example, an advertising

---

*The necessary services might include warehousing, repair or warranty programs, spare parts, promotional support, technical training, product-update programs, or superior customer service.

U.S. construction companies and products are now in a global business. Caterpillar provides products and services to customers throughout the world, and competes against other global construction equipment companies.

agency that wishes to serve major global corporations must be directly involved in the markets its clients seek to reach. Saatchi & Saatchi Advertising, based in England, has undertaken a series of multinational joint ventures and acquisitions in an effort to offer a better product (more efficient and effective advertising) to corporate clients throughout the world.

Just as the marketing mix changes at each phase of the *product life-cycle*, market-entry techniques also change. For products in the introductory phase of the life-cycle, indirect market-entry techniques may be appropriate.* But high-growth products often require direct market-entry approaches. In such cases the home organization usually wants to manage the marketing of the product. Thus, Hyundai wanted to manage the marketing of its automobiles in the United States. Companies with products in the mature phase often extend the direct approach followed during the growth phase, so that the product will maintain its market position and profit margin as long as possible. After Hyundai successfully penetrated the U.S. market for inexpensive cars, it proceeded to reposition the company and its product line, "trading up" customers to more expensive models during the maturity phase. During the decline phase the firm may switch back to an indirect approach, decreasing the degree of risk as sales fall.

Financial Considerations

Acceptable financial risk and capital requirements influence which form of market entry is best.

The degree of financial *risk* that the corporation is willing to accept, together with the amount of *capital* required to finance market entry, is often central to the market-entry decision. Acceptable levels of financial risk are determined

---

*On the other hand, if the market is very attractive and the product is new, it may be much easier to invest directly in the early stages, gain product and brand awareness, and thereby gain market share quickly while raising barriers to entry by competitors. Japanese and Korean firms, in particular, employ this approach.

largely by corporate strategy. For companies with low tolerance for financial risk and limited capital, indirect production entry is more attractive than direct production entry, and indirect, marketing-only entry may be preferred. Franchising is popular because they share financial risk with host-country firms. The global expansion undertaken by companies like McDonald's, Benetton, Domino's, Ford, and Toyota would not be possible if the home organization had to provide all the necessary capital.

Similarly, the higher the financial *costs* of market entry (for example, expensive marketing campaigns or high capital requirements for plant and equipment), the more likely the organization is to enter into a joint venture or strategic partnership rather than establish a wholly owned subsidiary.

Small companies, for example, may find that the only way to enter a major market that requires extensive marketing support (in the United States, for example, supporting a national consumer brand costs $20–$30 million a year) is to sell through an export trading company. The export trading company may be able to bundle together several products that may be profitably sold as a group. Or the home organization may wish to sell to an import house or a wholesale purchasing group in the host market, which performs similar services.

Currency risks increase the degree of risk associated with direct marketing and production entry techniques. For example, a profit margin of 10 percent of gross sales can be eliminated by an 11 percent currency devaluation. (It would be increased, of course, if the exchange rate were to shift the other way.) Market entry by means of direct production permits the firm to avoid rapid changes in exchange rates through reinvesting profits until they may be transferred out at an appropriate exchange rate. A blocked currency (one that is not freely traded), like that of the Soviet Union, usually requires the use of countertrade to indirectly transfer profits to the home organization. (See Chapter 16.) Countertrade is often aided by a joint-venture arrangement, as in the Pepsi example.

Issues Specific to the Firm

Firms with varying goals, objectives, strategies, and international experience will choose different market-entry techniques, even for similar products in the same national markets.

A company whose corporate goal is to be number one or two in every market it serves would probably choose a direct market-entry technique. This is an example of how the *corporate mission and goals* affect market-entry decisions. When a company is the market leader, it usually needs to achieve the greatest possible control over the marketing of its products in foreign countries. Thus, IBM enters foreign markets through joint ventures or direct foreign investment. Firms that view international sales as an "extra," on the other hand, are more likely to select an indirect market-entry technique.

The firm's *sales objectives* also influence its market-entry strategy. High sales or market-share objectives demand a major presence in the market; at the very least, a corporate sales office is required. In such situations the company is likely to establish a joint venture or a subsidiary. A firm that wants to test a market or start a long-term sales-growth trend can use an exporting approach or sales representatives. When the firm has become familiar with the market and wishes to increase its control, it can move toward higher-risk forms of market entry, like direct foreign investment. Garrett Automotive, for example, originally entered the Japanese market as a U.S.-owned sales and warehouse operation. Following a plan calling for slow, careful growth, the company developed its Japanese operation into a wholly owned plant (direct production with capital involvement); currently it holds a 25 percent share of the market with sales of $20–$25 million.[28]

The firm's *nonfinancial resources*, such as personnel, strong management, and planning or control systems, also affect its market-entry decisions. Without properly trained and experienced personnel, for example, an organization is well advised to avoid high-risk, high-control entry strategies. Indeed, human resources can be critical to the success of a global corporation.[29] Coca-Cola's global success during the 1980s was due in part to the perspectives contributed by a Cuban-born chief executive officer and an Egyptian chief financial officer. A small company without extensive nonfinancial resources may still be successful in foreign markets. An indirect strategy, such as using an export management company or selling directly to an import house, allows the company to use external personnel with the necessary skills and experience.

The firm's *competitive strategy* (see Chapter 9) may dictate certain entry techniques. Nestlé, with 98 percent of its sales outside its home market of Switzerland, has a philosophy of decentralization of responsibility. It therefore markets global brands like Quik, Nescafé, and Carnation through autonomous subsidiaries in major markets.[30] Small U.S. firms often define their competitive strategy in terms of the U.S. market; they lack an export orientation.[31] This means that they also lack the ability to respond to global opportunities. At most, they might engage in indirect market-entry techniques, such as casual exporting. A small company in Switzerland, on the other hand, may believe that its survival depends on regular exporting; it may therefore undertake a direct market-entry strategy.

The firm's level of *experience* is related to the degree of risk it is willing to accept. A firm that is entering its first foreign market is at the beginning of the marketing experience curve. A firm that has been involved in foreign markets for years is usually willing to accept higher levels of risk, because it has progressed along the experience curve and is better able to manage risk. Frequently a firm that is entering foreign markets for the first time uses a market that it perceives to be similar to its home market as a bridge, waiting until it has gained a comfortable level of international experience before entering a more dissimilar market. Swedish companies, for example, often enter the U.K. market before moving into the U.S. market. And Japanese companies often enter Australian markets before attempting to enter the U.S. market. *Bridging* is similar to a **market roll-out campaign**, in which the company uses its experience in a particular market segment to gain a competitive advantage in similar segments.

STRATEGIC PARTNERSHIPS

Today's global firm is increasingly involved in strategic partnerships—alliances with customers, suppliers, even competitors—to improve their chances of success in a market.

In today's competitive global marketing environment, an important corporate survival strategy is emerging. More than just a market-entry option, **strategic partnerships** (or **strategic alliances**) are corporate alliances between organizations, often former competitors, in which the combined strengths of the partners permit each to perform better in global markets.[32] Sometimes the strategic partner is a supplier or distributor.

Strategic partnerships are a type of cooperative strategy. They are more extensive than joint ventures and are usually used in mature economies, with the goal of ensuring long-term competitiveness. One or both partners contribute marketing knowledge and skills, production technology, manufacturing competence, and access to distribution channels. Economies of scale and experience-curve effects can be gained more quickly and efficiently through a strategic partnership than through the efforts of a single firm. In addition, the research and development investment needed to remain competitive on a global scale may be beyond the financial resources of a single organization, but become feasible

MAP 10.1
WHERE THE
VENTURES ARE

As East Europe continues to change its political and economic methods of operation, joint ventures have become a highly popular method of market entry. This map illustrates registered Western joint ventures in Eastern Europe as of March 1990.

[1]As of Aug. 8, 1989   [2]Letters of intent

through the establishment of a strategic partnership. Overall, strategic partnerships are a corporate response to the changing political, technological, and economic realities of the global marketplace.[33]

Numerous examples of strategic partnerships exist. AT&T and Olivetti have formed a strategic partnership that brings AT&T's computers to Europe and Olivetti's typewriters to the United States.[34] In fact, Olivetti is involved in a series of strategic alliances, cooperating with firms based in the United States, Japan, and Germany. It believes that the way to remain independent is to cooperate. This apparent contradiction is explained by the fact that, given global competition and the cost of resources, no single organization can generate enough cash flow to operate independently on a global scale. Alliances make it possible to obtain resources and share experience with partners, rather than be acquired by another organization.

GM and Toyota have formed a much publicized strategic partnership to manufacture and market a new car in the United States. This arrangement may co-opt what might have been a long-term move by Toyota into the U.S. market at the expense of GM's sales. Caterpillar Tractor has formed a strategic partnership with Mitsubishi in Japan in order to compete more directly with Komatsu.[35] And, as mentioned earlier, firms that want to gain access to markets in China, the Soviet Union, and several Eastern European countries may have to establish strategic partnerships with foreign trade organizations. In the late 1980s, when China made strategic partnerships more attractive, Western companies invested more than $6 billion in China.[36]

Although only about 250 companies account for fully 80 percent of U.S. exports, strategic partnerships are not necessarily restricted to major corporations.[37] For small and medium-sized firms that would like to take advantage of global market opportunities, the skills needed to ensure competitiveness through strategic partnerships—for example, patience in negotiating with foreign partners—are similar.

As with any corporate strategy, there are risks associated with strategic partnerships. Often failure to foresee differences in corporate cultures may place the partnership at risk.[38] Other problems occur when the partnership pushes one, if not both, of the new partners into areas in which it has no previous experience.[39] Still another problem with establishing a strategic partnership, a joint venture, or even a licensing arrangement is the cost of a one-way flow of technology. If guarantees are not established and strictly enforced, an organization might share technology only to find that it faces additional competition from its supposed partner.[40] For example, some observers believe that U.S. companies that enter into strategic partnerships with Japanese corporations are likely to transfer technology to future competitors.[41]

Strategic partnerships must have shared and mutually understood objectives if they are to succeed.[42] Partners that seek short-term profits will have problems with partners that are more concerned with long-term gains in market share. Similarly, organizations that are looking for marketing assistance may have difficulties with partners that prefer technical solutions.[43]

Success in a strategic partnership occurs when each partner brings to the alliance a strength that the other partner lacks. Thus, GM contributes marketing and distribution skills, while Toyota brings manufacturing and management strengths to their strategic partnership. In other cases, such as strategic alliances between middle-sized firms, one partner may produce the product while the other sells it under its own name.

The strategic partners must understand and trust each other. U.S. executives, in particular, seem impatient with international standards. In the United States "time is money," but in China "time is eternity."[44] Other attributes of successful strategic partnerships include respect for cultural differences, careful study of the market, sharing equity, and maintaining a dialogue between the partners.[45]

In sum, strategic partnerships are both a response and a stimulus to globalization. Firms of any size should consider establishing such partnerships to enter markets, gain access to distribution systems, maintain technological and manufacturing competence, gain access to scarce resources and skills, monitor the activities of competitors, keep abreast of technological development, and gain economies of scale and experience curve effects, all of which serve to enhance the firm's global competitiveness.

S U M M A R Y

Before entering a foreign market, the firm must position its product. The positioning strategy consists of making the corporation or its product distinct and important in customers' minds. A company positions itself relative to competitors, always bearing in mind its basic corporate policy, portfolio strategy, and competitive strategy.

The marketer must select a market-entry strategy that is consistent with its desired position in the target market, and develop a marketing mix that communicates and supports that position. Market-entry options range from casual exporting to direct foreign investment. Each option entails a different combination of risks and rewards, and each market under consideration may require a different market-entry technique.

One approach to making market-entry decisions is to begin with an assessment of corporate strategy and to evaluate alternative market-entry techniques in terms of their potential contribution to that strategy. A second approach is to evaluate all possible market-entry techniques from the standpoint of all relevant decision criteria, selecting the one that is likely to be most effective. Although it requires more market information, this approach usually results in better decisions.

Market-entry alternatives can be classified along two dimensions: whether they are direct or indirect approaches and whether they involve only marketing or both marketing and production. Each market-entry technique involves trade-offs between market control and degree of risk. The technique that offers the lowest level of risk and the least market control is indirect entry involving marketing functions only. There are several variations on this general approach, including casual exporting, catalog and telephone sales, export management companies, and export trading companies.

Direct entry involving only marketing occurs when the home organization directly markets its products in the host market. This may be done by selling directly to an import house or to a wholesale or retail purchasing group. In centrally controlled markets products are often sold to a public trading agency. Another alternative is for the home organization to establish an export department for international sales. The company may also use foreign sales representatives or branch offices.

There are three indirect market-entry techniques that involve production with limited capital involvement: licensing, franchising, and production or management contracts. Industrial property rights, including rights to technology, may be licensed to an organization in the host market. Whereas licensing may embrace all forms of industrial property, franchising is usually limited to trademarks. Franchising also offers less control by the home organization. A production or management contract allows the home organization to be involved either in the manufacture of a product or in the management of an enterprise in a foreign market.

In many developing countries direct entry into the market requires production and extensive capital involvement. A frequently used market-entry technique that shares both risk and control is the joint venture. Joint ventures are usually entered into on a case-by-case basis. When a corporation pursues such alliances as part of its overall strategy, they are referred to as strategic partnerships. Another approach is direct foreign investment, either by making a direct acquisition in the host market or by establishing a subsidiary there.

Among the criteria that should be considered when deciding to enter a new market are its macroenvironments. Economic considerations, such as limited buying power, may require entry techniques that minimize capital risk. The political situation can influence both the choice and the success of a market-entry technique. Legal restrictions play an especially important role in market-entry decisions. And trade restrictions may be so severe that firms are prevented from entering the market at all. Cultural conditions, such as a high level of ethnocentrism, also affect the choice of a market-entry technique.

Industry conditions that determine the choice of a market-entry technique include competition in the target market and market volume. The nature of the market, as well as the home organization's need and ability to influence it, must also be considered. Key factors include the distance between the home organization and the target market, the level of technological development in the market, resource supply and control requirements, the host nation's infrastructure, distribution channels and objectives, and the availability of information. Product issues that affect the choice of a market-entry technique include the degree of resistance to the product, the level of service needed to support the product,

product usage, and the product life-cycle. Financial considerations include the degree of financial risk that the corporation is willing to accept, the amount of capital required to finance market entry, and currency risks. Finally, issues specific to the firm must be considered in developing a market-entry strategy, including the firm's corporate mission and goals, sales objectives, nonfinancial resources, competitive strategy, and level of experience.

In today's competitive global marketing environment, strategic partnerships have become an important corporate survival strategy. Such partnerships are alliances between a firm and another organization, often a former competitor, in which the combined strengths of the partners permit each to perform better in global markets. Such partnerships can be formed by organizations of any size, provided that they have the necessary skills and resources. Strategic partnerships must have shared and mutually understood objectives, and they are most likely to succeed when each partner brings to the alliance a strength that the other partner lacks.

DISCUSSION QUESTIONS

1. What trade-offs are involved in selecting a direct market-entry technique over an indirect one?

2. What trade-offs are involved in deciding to enter a market with marketing functions only or to enter it with marketing and production functions?

3. Explain how the legal, cultural, or economic environment might affect market-entry decisions.

4. Explain how the nature of an industry influences market-entry decisions.

5. What characteristics of a firm have important implications for market-entry decisions?

6. How does the nature of the product affect market-entry decisions?

7. Under what conditions is it necessary to produce a product in a foreign market? When might this approach be desirable, if not required?

8. What conditions favor direct foreign investment as a market-entry strategy?

9. What are the pros and cons of establishing a joint venture? Under what conditions might a joint venture be most appropriate?

10. Discuss bridging as a market-entry and extension strategy. What macroenvironmental factors, if any, are likely to encourage bridging?

11. How does the existing infrastructure in a market influence the choice of a market-entry technique?

12. Discuss the risks and opportunities presented by strategic partnerships. Under what conditions are such partnerships likely to be successful?

C A S E

WORLDWIDE BEARINGS

Worldwide Bearings is one of the world's largest suppliers of plastic bearings and rollers used in escalators. The headquarters and major plant are located in Sweden, with sales subsidiaries and small plants in Switzerland and Western Germany. Worldwide's market share in Europe and the United States was 36 percent as of 1989, an increase from 26 percent in 1988. Demand for bearings and rollers, both for new escalators and replacements, is expected to grow over the next 5 years at an average rate of 3 percent per year.

The greatest international marketing challenge currently facing Worldwide is entering the Japanese market. Top management has made this market a major priority, with a goal of achieving a market share of 30 percent in 6 years. The Japanese market has been growing rapidly, faster than the world average, and is expected to continue to do so until the year 2000. It represents about 30 percent of the global market. Worldwide has five competitors in Japan, two of which control 60 percent of the market.

Worldwide's bearings and rollers are used in conveyer systems to provide optimal sliding and reduce unwanted movement and noise. Worldwide produces four different types of bearings and rollers, depending upon use. It has a strong reputation in the European and U.S. markets, due to its high-quality products. Other competitive distinctions include a wide range of products (Worldwide is one of the few producers of both roller ball and slide bearings, offering more flexibility to its customers) and a low price, achieved through economies of scale. Worldwide's competitors in Japan offer their products at $5–$8; Worldwide's Japanese products could be priced at $2.00. Technically, there is little difference between the products.

To improve its knowledge of the Japanese escalator market, Worldwide conducted secondary and primary research. Analysis of secondary data provided the following description of the Japanese market. Japanese buyers and companies focus on long-term commitments between suppliers and buyers. Japan's escalator market, therefore, is stable, with few competitors. Problems in developing a long-term relationship include cultural differences and communication; these problems are generally viewed as an important market-entry barrier. Reliable delivery and high quality, with guaranteed long performance, are extremely important in Japan. Marketing research indicates that of all the variables involved in the purchasing process, product quality is rated highest.

Case Issues

1.   What form of market entry would you recommend for Worldwide Bearings, and why?

2.   What are the most important factors Worldwide's marketing strategy should focus on for Japan?

N O T E S

1. For a more complete discussion of product positioning, see Y. J. Wind, *Product Policy: Concepts, Methods, and Strategy* (Reading, Mass.: Addison-Wesley, 1982), chap. 4.

2. S. Rabino and J. Zif, "How to Counter the Onslaught of Imports," *Journal of Business Strategy*, Summer 1987, pp. 58–64.

3. M. Geewax, "Federal Express to Expand Its Overseas Delivery Service," *Atlanta Constitution*, March 31, 1988, p. C-2.

4. For a more complete discussion of this subject, see J. Jacoby et al., "New Directions in Behavioral Process Research: Implications for Social Psychology," *Journal of Experimental Social Psychology* 23 (1987):146–175; J. R. Bailey and A. D. Shulman, "The Effects of Response Mode and Personal Relevance on Information Search Strategies," paper presented at the 95th meeting of the American Psychological Association, New York, 1987; J. R. Bailey et al., "Response Mode and Personal Relevance as Moderators of the Attitude-Behavior Relationship," working paper (Washington University, 1987), p. 6.

5. J. S. Hill, "Japan Is Next for Timberland," *Advertising Age*, October 27, 1986, p. 62.

6. "Changing Menu," *Wall Street Journal*, November 18, 1986, pp. 1, 27.

7. See D. C. Bello and N. C. Williamson, "The American Export Trading Company: Designing a New International Marketing Institution," *Journal of Marketing*, Fall 1985, pp. 60–69; and M. R. Czinkota, "The Business Response to the Export Trading Company Act of 1982," *Columbia Journal of World Business*, Fall 1984, pp. 65–71.

8. L. D'Angelo, "Export Profits Support New Austrade Drive," *Business Review Weekly*, March 31, 1988, p. 59.

9. S. W. Damon, "Establishing a Foreign Distributor and Agent Network," *Business America*, June 25, 1984, pp. 12–13.

10. J. Galang, "Successful Brew," *Far East Economic Review*, February 18, 1988, p. 6.

11. "McDonald's Milestone a Big, Meaty Moment," *Atlanta Constitution*, April 8, 1988, p. 32; "McWorld," *Business Week*, October 13, 1986, pp. 78–86; and S. Greenhouse, "McDonald's Tries Paris, Again," *New York Times*, June 12, 1988, pp. F-1, F-14, F-16.

12. F. Gluck, "Global Competition in the 1980s," *Journal of Business Strategy*, Spring 1983, p. 23.

13. K. K. Wiegner, "How to Mix Sake and Tequila," *Forbes*, March 23, 1987, pp. 48–51; see also G. H. Rott, "A Business Plan for a Joint Venture in Japan," in P. D. Grub et al., eds., *East Asia Dimensions of International Business* (Englewood Cliffs, N.J.: Prentice Hall International, 1982), pp. 175–201.

14. D. A. Ricks, *Big Business Blunders* (New York: Irwin, 1983), pp. 49–50.

15. "If You Can't Beat 'Em, Buy 'Em: Takeovers Arrive in Japan," *Business Week*, September 29, 1986, pp. 80–82; "Invading Japan," *Wall Street Journal*, October 16, 1986, pp. 1, 29; and J. C. Abegglen and G. Stalk, "The Role of Foreign Companies in Japanese Acquisitions," *Journal of Business Strategy*, Spring 1984, pp. 3–10.

16. "Europe Goes on a Shopping Spree in the States," *Business Week*, October 27, 1986, pp. 54–55; "Japan's Bigger and Bolder Forays into the U.S.," *Business Week*, November 7, 1986, pp. 80–81; and T. F. O'Boyle, "German Companies Seek More U.S. Assets," *Wall Street Journal*, October 7, 1986, p. 36.

17. See, for example, A. Stewart and R. MacDonald, "Japanese Takeaway," *Business Review Weekly*, March 31, 1988, pp. 46–53; and E. A. Finn, Jr., "Achtung! Achtung! Die Japaner Kommen!," *Forbes*, November 3, 1986, p. 96.

18. "Ivan Starts Learning the Capitalist Ropes," *Business Week*, November 2, 1987, p. 154; "U.S. Companies Study Ventures in Soviet Union," *Wall Street Journal*, March 5, 1987,

p. 1; and "Fast Food Is Coming, Fast Food Is Coming," *Business Week*, December 1, 1986, p. 50.

19. Australian Bureau of Statistics, *Australian Bureau of Statistics Year Book*, 1986, p. 618.

20. "Korea's Barrier to Entry," *Advertising Age*, November 17, 1986, p. 17.

21. Government of Japan, *Open to the World: Japan's Action Program for Easy Access to Its Markets*, August 1985.

22. P. Revzin, "French Denationalization Lures U.S. Firms," *Wall Street Journal*, October 24, 1986, p. 34.

23. M. Specht, "Portugal Luring Major Marketers and Shops," *Advertising Age*, October 21, 1985, p. 58.

24. R. I. Kirkland, Jr., "Entering a New Age of Boundless Competition," *Fortune*, March 14, 1988, pp. 40–48; and P. Kotler and N. Dhokalia, "Building a Bridge to Third World Markets," *Business Week*, October 13, 1986, p. 24.

25. K. Bertrand, "China Trade: More Than Joint Ventures," *Business Marketing*, November 1986, p. 20.

26. See E. Anderson and A. T. Coughlan, "International Market Entry and Expansion via Independent or Integrated Channels of Distribution," *Journal of Marketing*, January 1987, pp. 71–82.

27. "Daimaru Set to Shake Up Retail Giants," *Courier Mail*, April 19, 1988, p. 27.

28. G. Bronson, "Just in Time—American Style," *Forbes*, March 9, 1987, pp. 132–134.

29. J. F. Bolt, "Global Competitors: Some Criteria for Success," *Business Horizons*, January–February 1988, pp. 34–41.

30. N. Shoebridge, "Nestlé Brews Up a Quiet Revolution," *Business Review Weekly*, March 31, 1988, pp. 20–23.

31. "U.S. Exporters That Aren't American," *Business Week*, February 29, 1988, p. 39.

32. S. C. Jain, "Perspectives on International Strategic Alliances," working paper, University of Connecticut, 1986; and F. J. Contractor, "International Business: An Alternative View," *International Marketing Review*, Spring 1986, pp. 74–85.

33. "How Business Is Creating Europe Inc.," *Business Week*, September 7, 1987, pp. 40–41.

34. S. Solomon, "More Rabbits, Please, Signor De Benedetti," *Forbes*, March 9, 1987, pp. 114–118.

35. T. Hout, M. E. Porter, and E. Rudden, "How Global Companies Win Out," *Harvard Business Review*, September–October 1982, pp. 98–108; see also J. T. Sims, "Japanese Market Entry Strategy at Work: Komatsu vs. Caterpillar," *International Marketing Review*, Autumn 1986, pp. 21–32.

36. F. Barringer, "To Russia, for Partners and Profits," *New York Times*, April 10, 1988, pp. 1-F, 13-F; and "The Reformers Say: Let a Thousand Businesses Bloom," *Business Week International*, April 11, 1988, pp. 36–37.

37. See C. F. Valentine, "Pro: Don't Leave Exports to Big Firms," *USA Today*, December 10, 1987, p. 4B; and "Most U.S. Companies Are Innocents Abroad," *Business Week*, November 16, 1987, pp. 168–177.

38. L. Berton, "Mixed Marriage," *Wall Street Journal*, April 22, 1987, pp. 1, 27.

39. "A Solid Gold Record Deal," *Business Week*, November 30, 1987, p. 36.

40. S. Prokesch, "Stopping the High-Tech Giveaway," *New York Times*, March 22, 1987, sec. 3, pp. 1, 8; and M. Beauchamp, "Use a Long Spoon," *Forbes*, December 15, 1986, p. 122.

41.   P. Kotler, L. Fahey, and S. Jatusripitak, *The New Competition* (Englewood Cliffs, N.J.: Prentice Hall, 1985), p. 219.

42.   R. Abravanel, "Shaping Effective Responses to the Globalization Challenge," in R. Varaldo (ed.), *International Marketing Cooperation Conference Proceedings*, Pisa, 1986, p. 50.

43.   Solomon, op. cit., p. 114.

44.   A. Kupfer, "How to Be a Global Manager," *Fortune*, March 14, 1988, p. 63.

45.   R. Tung, "Japanese Managers: Why Are They Winners?," International Business Forum Address, Graduate School of Management, University of Queensland, Australia, July 15, 1987.

11

GLOBAL MARKETING OF CONSUMER PRODUCTS

Mrs. Olsen Goes Global

Coffee, Mrs. Olsen's favorite beverage, is consumed all over the world. But as a drink and as part of the culture, it varies considerably. If you walk into an American restaurant and order a cup of coffee, you get a very different drink than in Finland (one of the largest coffee consumers in the world on a per capita basis) or Japan. If you order a cup of coffee in Japan, you must choose the type of bean, the degree to which the bean is roasted, the quantity of beans, and the exact temperature of the water. In Italy, you may hear someone say "spotted, tepid coffee in a glass without foam." There, consumers may debate whether coffee should be served in a glass or cup, and if in a cup, porcelain or not.

Coffee, of course, starts with a bean. Most coffee comes from the economically less-developed nations of Brazil, Colombia, the Ivory Coast, Indonesia, El Salvador, Uganda, Mexico, and Guatemala. But the primary users (and importers) of coffee are the Triad markets. Within the Triad, four zones of coffee consumers exist: (a) the United States and Canada, (b) Japan, (c) the United Kingdom, and (d) Germany, France, Italy, and The Netherlands. Each of these varies somewhat in terms of coffee consumption habits and flavor preferences. U.S. and Canadian consumers, for example, prefer a lighter roast than do Europeans, and import a lower-quality bean than Japan or Europe.

The marketing mix for any product must be carefully planned, whether the product is physical or nonphysical, consumer or industrial, domestic or global. The core of the marketing mix is a set of benefits that satisfies the customer. The other elements of the marketing mix—price, place, and promotion—must be planned as well, but they cannot compensate for a product that does not satisfy the customer.

WHAT IS A PRODUCT?

All products have tangible and intangible elements.

Every product combines tangible (physical) and intangible (nonphysical) attributes. Even a **good** (a physical product) has intangible elements, and a **service**, which is by definition intangible, has some tangible elements. It is critical to remember that customers may be attracted to a product by both tangible and intangible elements. Coca-Cola, for example, is more than just a soft drink. In several languages, "Coke Is It." This slogan recognizes that Coke is not only a physical good but also refreshment, enjoyment, even entertainment, all of which are intangible attributes but are part of the total product.

Products are not limited to goods or services. They also include ideas, people, and organizations. For example, social issues such as population control

Coca-Cola strives for "one sight, one sound" in its global marketing efforts, demonstrated here by labels for the U.S. and China.

can be marketed in an attempt to change people's ideas about family-planning practices. Political campaigns market people as products; the French presidential race between François Mitterand and Jacques Chirac used some of the same advertising and promotion techniques as the U.S. presidential campaign of Michael Dukakis and George Bush. Even organizations can be viewed as products. Charitable groups like the American Cancer Society and UNICEF use marketing techniques for everything from fund raising to research on how to better serve clients.

Chapters 11–13 focus on three groups of products: consumer, industrial, and services, respectively. Consumer and industrial products differ mainly in terms of the purposes for which they are purchased: consumer products are purchased for consumption, industrial ones for reuse. Services may be directed either to consumers or to industrial users; they differ from physical goods in that they are mainly intangible.

This chapter first discusses consumer behavior and how it influences the global marketer. The next section looks at global dimensions of products and product design. The management of global products is analyzed, as well as packaging, labeling, and branding. The impact of consumerism on global marketing is also discussed. The chapter concludes with an examination of the impact of the product on the marketing mix.

CONSUMER BEHAVIOR

Understanding the global consumer is the first step toward developing an appropriate global marketing mix.

At the heart of the controversy over standardized versus individualized marketing mixes is the question of whether there is such a thing as a "global consumer." As the global marketing manager seeks opportunities for standardization, the focus on consumer behavior becomes critical. It is always necessary to understand the consumer in order to develop the best marketing mix for a product.[1] McDonald's, for example, understands that its customers want high-quality, reliable, fast food at a competitive price—regardless of the country in which they live. The many factors that influence consumer behavior combine

MAP 11.1   CONSUMER PROFILES

Although Western Europe is integrating economically, the tastes, preferences, and life-styles of members of different nations will still be considerably different. This map illustrates how four major Western European nations have considerable differences in the dominant life-style segment of each nation.

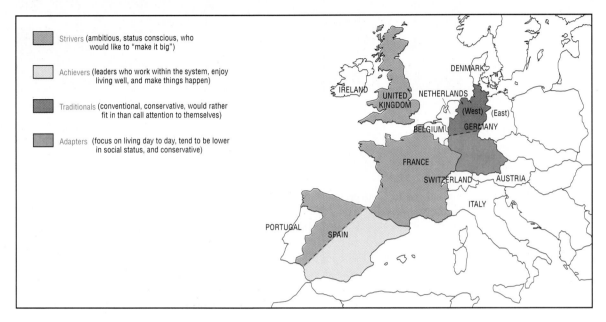

Strivers (ambitious, status conscious, who
        would like to "make it big")

Achievers (leaders who work within the system, enjoy
        living well, and make things happen)

Traditionals (conventional, conservative, would rather
        fit in than call attention to themselves)

Adapters (focus on living day to day, tend to be lower
        in social status, and conservative)

in unique ways to shape the behavior of consumers in different market segments. Within a particular product market, however, consumer behavior is relatively consistent—even when that segment exists in more than one culture.

Behavior and Motivation

Consumers are motivated by rational and emotional motives. These motives may be different in different markets, even for the same product.

A consumer motive is the reason a person buys a particular product. Consumer motivation is a complex phenomenon that is influenced by many cultural and individual variables. However, consumer motivations can be divided into two basic groups: rational and emotional.[2] Exhibit 11.1 illustrates rational motives.

Rational motives involve deliberate reasoning. Almost every consumer decision is based on rational as well as emotional motives. Even a simple, inexpensive purchase like a candy bar has an economic dimension: How much change does the consumer have handy? Each rational motive has to be understood within the context of the economy, the political/legal system, and the culture in which the market is located. Low price, for example, increases in importance as the *relative price* of the product increases. In low-income countries the price

EXHIBIT 11.1
RATIONAL MOTIVES

Consumer motives play a part in the purchase decision. Rational motives are basically economically motivated. Emotional motives relate to an individual's feelings.

Quality	The desire for products that provide superior, long-term benefits.
Price	The desire to buy at a low price, saving money for other purchases.
Life-cycle	The desire for the product to have a long life.
Performance	The desire to have a predictable, reliable product.
Use	The desire for a product that is easy to use.

Source: Adapted from R. E. Stanley, *Promotion*, 2nd ed. (Englewood Cliffs, N.J.: Prentice Hall, 1982), pp. 42–44.

of a telephone may be so high in relative terms that it is a luxury item. In the United States, most households define a telephone as a necessity, partly because of its low relative price.

Emotional motives, in contrast, do not involve much deliberate analysis. They are based on the individual's needs and wants. Given sufficient economic resources, emotional motives usually become more important, especially for high-involvement products (those relating to important values or life-styles). The Romanian-built Olcit automobile, for example, may not be seen as a viable alternative by upper-income Americans, despite its price of $3,980, because an automobile is a fairly high ego-involvement purchase for these consumers.[3]

Most consumer purchases are a result of unique combinations of motives. For example, automobile purchases are almost always based partly on price considerations. But within a given price range, emotional motives usually influence the consumer's decision more than price. Any given market segment may represent a unique combination of purchase motives as well. Thus, global marketers may find that purchase motives are the most useful segmentation variable when numerous national markets are under consideration. Porsche, for example, is able to sell its automobile to consumers in many countries in spite of its high price. A Porsche costs $60,000 in the United States, $79,000 in Australia, and $80,000 in Japan—yet in all three markets the price is justified in the buyer's mind by the high emotional satisfaction of owning a Porsche.[4]

Trends in Consumer Behavior

Aging, youth, and singleness are among the consumer trends that are shared across national boundaries.

Some similar trends in consumer behavior are emerging in the Triad markets and in many developing countries. (See Exhibit 11.2.) When these trends converge, the result is a more global market. An example of how these trends affect demand for specific products can be seen in the effects of the aging of the population in most markets. As consumers grow older, their behavior changes, both individually and collectively. Older consumers with enough income travel more than when they were young. Thus, the travel industry in Japan has grown dramatically since the mid-1980s. In addition, older consumers often have lower saving rates, because they live on their past savings during their retirement years.

EXHIBIT 11.2
CONSUMER TRENDS:
IMPLICATION FOR
GLOBALIZATION

Especially in the Triad, several major consumer trends share characteristics across national markets, which has important implications for global marketers.

Trend	Implication
Aging	Lower savings affect the supply of world capital.
	Products must be redesigned to take physical changes into account.
	Increased demand for health care and retirement services and products.
	Marketing mixes need adjustment to account for different media, economic, and access dimensions.
Youth	Youth within nations have access to, and greater control of, money.
	Youth markets across nations are more similar than youth and mature markets within nations.
	Global products and standardized marketing mixes may be appropriate.
Singleness	Deferred marriage results in more households with higher discretionary income than that for traditional multiple-person households.
	Increased demand for "single-sized" products.
	More women working outside the home.
	Increased demand for services serving singles.
Other trends	Increased tourism.
	Smaller families.
	Two-career households.
	Increased exposure to varied products from nontraditional suppliers.
	Increased discretionary income, more travel.

This change affects not only consumption but also the amount of capital available in the society. The point is that consumer trends must be continually monitored by the global marketing manager.[5]

Product Acceptance

Customers buy perceived product benefits—or solutions to problems.

As students of marketing know, consumers buy product *benefits*, not product *features*. The relationship between the benefits provided and the cost of obtaining those benefits determines whether a purchase will be made. As long as perceived benefits are greater than perceived costs, consumers will buy the product. A marketing manager can overcome resistance to a product by changing the perceived balance between benefits and costs. Several product characteristics influence consumer acceptance (a cultural variable), as discussed in Chapter 6. Increasing the consumer's ranking of the product on any characteristic that encourages acceptance, or decreasing it on characteristics that discourage acceptance, has the same effect as increasing (or decreasing) perceived benefits. The more important a particular motive is to consumers, the more they seek products that provide benefits that enable them to satisfy that motive.

If a product provides few perceived benefits, the marketing manager can change the marketing mix to increase the level of benefits offered to the consumer. An alternative approach is to stress a benefit to which the consumer attaches particular importance. For example, home-delivered pizza is a successful product in the United States, largely due to the importance consumers attach to convenience. To sell more pizza in the United States, the marketer might make the product even more convenient, perhaps by combining it with delivery of another product, such as home videos. In Belgium, home delivery of food is not as popular as it is in the United States, because consumers there place less emphasis on saving time. For a home-delivery pizza business to be successful in Belgium, it might have to stress the freshness of the product or appeal to consumers' curiosity about a new idea—home delivery.

CONSUMER PRODUCT MANAGEMENT: A GLOBAL VIEW

The Total Product

A product is more than its features or characteristics; it includes nonphysical elements, such as status.

Marketing managers must keep in mind the fact that a product is more than the sum of its physical characteristics. A consumer buys the **total product**, a combination of tangible and intangible attributes that may satisfy the consumer's needs and wants. Major elements of the total product are the core or basic product, packaging, brand, image, credit, installation, delivery, warranties, and after-sale service.[6] Each of these elements can be used as a competitive tool, increasing the level of perceived benefits relative to the cost of the product. Offering better credit terms, for example, may attract consumers with limited economic resources, especially in less-developed countries. Free or quick delivery of the product may make it more attractive to consumers with limited transportation resources; such consumers are found in many cities in Triad markets. Warranties may serve as a major marketing tool, positioning the product as superior in quality. After-sale service may also provide a marketing advantage by distinguishing the company from its competitors. BMW, for instance, built a warehouse near Tokyo to guarantee delivery of spare parts within 24 hours, a move that helped it capture 25 percent of the imported-car market in Japan.[7]

Offering warranties and after-sale service is more difficult on a global scale than domestically. Differences between legal systems affect the nature of the warranties that can be offered. Competitive practices and the level of technology also influence the firm's ability to offer certain kinds of warranties and service. Global marketing managers must decide what type of warranty or level of service will enable the firm to be competitive, in accordance with legal and cultural considerations in a given market, yet they must not commit the organization to a level of performance that is not realistically possible. Sometimes it may be necessary to delegate warranty or service performance to a third party in the host country, a strategy that runs the risk of reduced customer satisfaction. In such situations the manager may consider entering into a strategic partnership, in which case there is a higher likelihood that warranty and service activities will be carried out to the satisfaction of customers.

New Product Development

Many product ideas must be generated before even one achieves market success.

The product-development process described in this section (see Exhibit 11.3) can be applied to consumer, industrial, and service products. It is included here to provide an overview of the product- and marketing-planning process.

A product may be new to the organization, to the host market, or to the entire global market. The artificial sweetener Nutrasweet, for example, was new both to the company and to the market when it was introduced. More commonly, a "new" product has already been marketed by the company in another market but is new to the host market. For example, Georgia Coffee, a coffee-flavored noncarbonated drink marketed by Coca-Cola that has long been popular in Japan, was introduced as a new product in Australia in the late 1980s.

New product successes are relatively infrequent. In the United States only 2 out of 10 new products succeed, while in Japan the success rate is 2 out of 100.[8] These low success rates point to the importance of improving the product development and introduction process, especially given the ever increasing cost of developing products.

EXHIBIT 11.3
NEW PRODUCT-
DEVELOPMENT
STAGES

In order to have one new product be successful in the marketplace, many new product ideas must be generated. After ideas have been developed, they go through the various stages of the product-development process, until one product is successful in the marketplace.

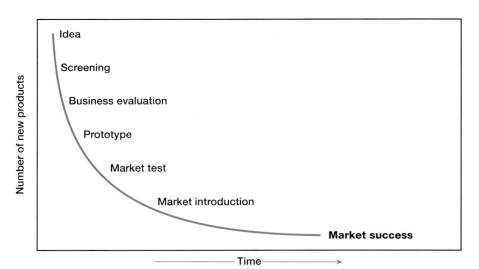

Several new product ideas are necessary for each new product that succeeds in the marketplace. These ideas may be developed as products for the domestic market in general, as products aimed at specific domestic markets, as global products with planned modifications for different national markets, or as standardized global products. Increasingly, marketers seek product ideas that are either fully global (that is, standard) or readily modified for different markets. Other criteria that need to be considered include how well the product fits with overall corporate objectives and capabilities.

Each new product should be subjected to a **business evaluation**, an analysis of demand, costs, and profit potential. Demand, of course, is influenced by economic, political/legal, and cultural considerations. For example, little pancakes called *poffertjes* are popular in Holland. A franchiser that attempted to establish a chain of *poffertjes* restaurants in the United States would be faced with cultural resistance in terms of different food preferences. In addition to estimating demand, the business evaluation estimates production, transportation, marketing, and other costs. These are combined with sales estimates (demand-plus-price projections) to establish a **break-even point**. This is the point at which costs equal revenue (and the firm is not making or losing money). Global Dimensions 11.1 illustrates a break-even analysis.

The next step in new product development is creating a **prototype**, a working model or sample of the product.[9] (A service can also be prototyped, as a trial demonstration.) During this step the production, engineering, and marketing departments work together. Earlier assumptions regarding the cost and feasibility of production can be verified at this time.

After the prototype has been developed, the product should be *tested*, preferably in a market situation. The value of a test market is that it provides information about consumer reactions and enables managers to identify appropriate marketing strategies. For these reasons, global firms frequently use the most representative test market they can find, despite the problems involved in global marketing research (see Chapter 8). Holland and Belgium, for example, are often used as a European test market. Experience has shown that the results from a test in these two countries provide information that is applicable to Western Europe in general and more than worth the cost of the test. If the test-market results are promising, the firm will consider introducing the product to the intended market. At this point the global marketing manager must not only choose the appropriate market-entry technique but also design the marketing mix for the product.

Product Design

Quite simply, better-designed products are more successful in the marketplace.

An organization that designs a better product can gain a distinct competitive advantage. Product design affects the product's attractiveness, usefulness, and acceptability, as well as production costs. The objective is to design a product that is more attractive to consumers and can be manufactured at a lower cost

Break-Even Analysis: Domestic Product vs. Preplanned Modification

This simplified example illustrates the advantages inherent in product ideas that incorporate preplanned modification, compared to domestic products. Demand is represented by total revenue (TR_1); in our example, each unit costs \$20. The total cost for domestic products is represented by TC_1. The break-even point is 5 units, where $TR_1 = TC_1$. If the organization can offer a product with preplanned modification, the total cost will be lower, represented by TC_2. (Marginal costs are distributed over a wider set of markets.) If the product continues to sell for \$20, the firm's break-even point at TC_2 is 4 units. If the firm can sell 5 units at \$20, it will increase its profit by the area in the shaded part of the graph. If it prefers, it can lower its price to \$18, indicated by the dotted revenue line (TR_2), which returns it to a break-even sales figure of 5 units (at TC_2).

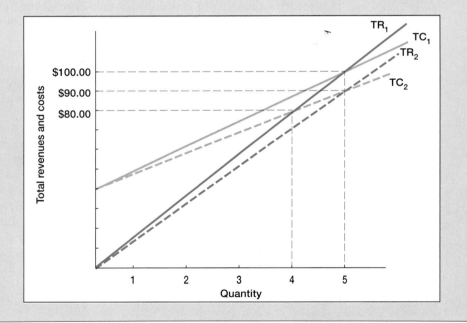

than competitors' products. For example, IBM redesigned its Proprinter to make it not only more visually pleasing and attractive to consumers but also cheaper to manufacture, because the number of parts was reduced by 65 percent and assembly time by 90 percent.[10]

Factors that influence market acceptance of a product design include color, form, shape, size, application, and use. In different national markets these fac-

GLOBAL DIMENSIONS 11.2

Product Design

Globally there seem to be different "schools" of product design. The "new American" school, for example, tends to emphasize ease of use and simplicity of design. The "Memphis" school in Milan uses pastels exclusively. German design is often minimalist and rational. These varying approaches to product design are a resource available to global managers. They can choose from a variety of design approaches around the globe to achieve superior product attractiveness and function and to lower production costs. In this manner, a global manager can achieve an experience curve effect from product design.

Source: "Smart Design: Quality Is the New Style," *Business Week*, April 11, 1988, pp. 80–86; and "Special Report on Design," *Adweek*, October 6, 1986, pp. D.R. 3–D.R. 32.

tors are complicated by cultural differences in tastes and preferences. Sears Roebuck, for example, found that it had to redesign its refrigerators for the Japanese market so that they would fit into smaller spaces and run more quietly to accommodate smaller homes with thinner walls.[11] Global Dimensions 11.2 illustrates some of the different approaches to product design that are necessary because of differences among national markets.

Another product-design consideration has to do with the type of economy in which the product is to be marketed. In general, products require more adaptation when they are sold in a developing country than when they are destined for consumers in a developed country. For example, Singer developed a foot-powered sewing machine for sale in less-developed African nations, where reliable power is not available. Moreover, within a developing country more product redesign will be necessary if the market is a rural one rather than urban.[12] The impact of macroenvironmental factors on product design is illustrated in Exhibit 11.4.

Portfolio Management

Global marketing managers must decide what new products to develop, what combinations of products to sell to which markets, and how to manage those products.

In addition to developing new products, the global marketing manager must decide what combination of products will be offered in a given market and how they should be managed. Offering different versions of what is basically the same product (that is, a product line) permits the company to offer a variety of products to consumers in a single market segment or in several market segments. For example, Queensland Uniform Foods sells over twenty flavors of milk in Australia. Lime-flavored milk appeals more to children, while coffee-flavored milk appeals mostly to adults. The company gains considerable production econ-

MAP 11.2 GLOBAL DIET ADEQUACY

Although the world produces enough food to feed everybody, it is not available where it is needed.
Distribution problems, price fluctuations, and weather patterns combine to frustrate attempts to provide
everyone on the globe with an adequate diet.

Calories per head per day

Greater than 3,000

2,400 – 3,000

0 – 2,400

no reliable data

average daily protein consumption
per head per day less than 45 gm

UNION OF SOVIET SOCIALIST REPUBLICS

MONGOLIA

N. KOREA
S. KOREA
JAPAN

TURKEY
CYPRUS
LEBANON
ISRAEL
JORDAN
SYRIA
IRAQ
IRAN
AFGHANISTAN
PAKISTAN
KUWAIT
CHINA
BHUTAN
NEPAL
TAIWAN

IBYA
EGYPT
QATAR
SAUDI
ARABIA
UAE
OMAN
INDIA
BURMA
LAOS
HONG KONG

HAD
SUDAN
YEMEN
S. YEMEN
DJIBOUTI
BANGLADESH
THAILAND
VIETNAM
PHILIPPINES

NTRAL AFRICAN
REPUBLIC
ETHIOPIA
SRI LANKA
KAMPUCHEA
BRUNEI
MALAYSIA

ZAIRE
UGANDA
KENYA
SOMALIA

RWANDA
BURUNDI
TANZANIA
SINGAPORE
PAPUA
NEW GUINEA

OLA
MALAWI
INDONESIA

ZAMBIA
MOZAMBIQUE
E. TIMOR

IBIA
ZIMBABWE
MADAGASCAR

BOTSWANA
AUSTRALIA

S. AFRICA
SWAZILAND
LESOTHO

NEW ZEALAND

351

EXHIBIT 11.4
PRODUCT-DESIGN
IMPLICATIONS OF
ENVIRONMENTAL
FACTORS IN LESS
ECONOMICALLY
DEVELOPED NATIONS

Environmental factors,
in developed and less-
developed nations, have
a considerable impact
upon product design.
High labor costs, for ex-
ample, lead to automa-
tion, and low income lev-
els often lead to lower
product quality, in order
to offer lower prices.

Environmental factors	Product-design implications
Level of technical skills	Product simplification
Level of labor costs	Automation or manualization of the product
Level of literacy	Remarking and simplification of the product
Level of income	Quality and price change
Level of interest rates	Quality and price change (investment in quality may not be financially desirable)
Level of maintenance	Change in tolerances
Climate	Product adaptation
Isolation	Product simplification and reliability improvement (heavy repair difficult and expensive)
Standards	Recalibration and resizing of the product
Availability of other products	Greater or lesser product integration
Availability of materials	Change in product structure and fuel
Power availability	Resizing and automation or manualization of the product
Special conditions	Product redesign or invention

Source: Adapted from D. Robinson, "The Challenge of the Underdeveloped National Markets," *Journal of Marketing*, October 1961, p. 22.

omies from producing many versions of milk, since the marginal costs of changing flavors are insignificant.

A useful approach to building a product portfolio is illustrated in Exhibit 11.5. This approach involves two main criteria. The first, **market attractiveness**, is a function of market growth, degree of competition, relative market size, and corporate competencies. The second criterion, **product strength**, is based on market share, profitability, and degree of compatibility with the market's needs. One product portfolio can be developed for the company's own products and another for its competitor's products. Sales, or contribution to profits, can be indicated by the size of the circle representing each national market.

Product-portfolio analysis offers managers a systematic way to examine what products to offer and what level of support they should have.

Company *B* in Exhibit 11.5 has a strong market in the United States featuring high growth, market share, and profits. Company *A* believes that the United States could be an important market for its products, but it does not have a viable product for that market. If it wants to be more successful in the United States, it will have to become more aggressive. In that case Company *B* can counterattack, perhaps by dropping its price in order to make profit margins in the U.S. market less attractive.

By examining the relative positions of various markets through portfolio analysis, Company *B* may identify other strategies that could be employed, instead of a price war in one of its most profitable markets. It may choose to counterattack in Japan, where it is relatively strong. Company *A* may not be

EXHIBIT 11.5
PRODUCT-PORTFOLIO
ANALYSIS

Product portfolios help
firms analyze product
strength compared to
market attractiveness on
a nation-by-nation basis.

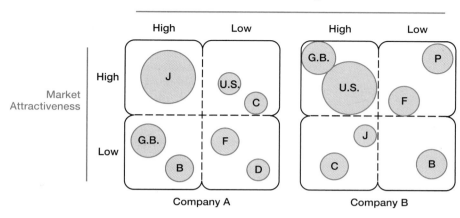

J = Japan, G.B. = Great Britain, C = Canada, B = Brazil, D = Denmark,
U.S. = United States, F = France, P = Peru

Source: Adapted from J. C. Larreche, "The International Product-Market Portfolio," AMA Educators' Proceedings, American Marketing Association, Chicago, 1978, p. 277.

able to afford to engage in a profit war in Japan at the same time that it attempts to develop the U.S. market. Company *B* could also use its strong market position in Great Britain to subsidize its counterattack in Japan. This strategy would allow it to continue to reinvest profits from the U.S. market to improve its position there still more.

An important part of
the product manager's
job is to decide which
products to delete from
the product line.

Firms must plan and execute product-deletion as well as product-introduction strategies. Normally a product with a low relative market share in a low-growth market is a cash drain on the organization. The company might be justified in carrying a promising product that requires a current investment that is higher than current returns for a while, but it should not continue to market products whose performance cannot reasonably be expected to improve.

In a global setting, other factors enter into the product-deletion decision. As a result of strategic partnerships as well as mergers and acquisitions, companies are carrying broader product lines in global markets than in domestic ones. Spreading management skills over more products and markets may result in overextension and less than optimal product management. Global corporations are increasingly likely to prune their product lines, keeping the winners. In this way they can gain greater experience curve effects through more careful management. In addition, product deletion reduces inventory carrying and transportation costs, as well as currency exposure risks, thereby improving profit potential.

Ultimately, the product must pass the test of market acceptance (see Global Dimensions 11.3). Even the best advertising, the lowest prices, and the most intensive distribution cannot overcome a product that is not perceived by consumers as satisfying their needs. The French, for example, don't have a need to eat cereal for breakfast. Since the late 1970s Kellogg's has been unsuccessfully trying to get French consumers to try an American-style breakfast. It has found that some 30 percent of French adults skip breakfast, others have café au lait and a croissant, or some other bread (perhaps with a chocolate spread), for breakfast.[13]

Product Standardization\

Standardization of the global marketing mix usually begins with the product.

The first step in standardizing the marketing mix is usually standardizing the product. This is because *if* standardization is a viable marketing strategy, it is easiest and most efficient to begin closest to the the point of manufacture. Elements of the marketing mix that must be performed at the point of exchange, or very close to the market (such as distribution and pricing), are more difficult to standardize than product and promotion strategies.[14]

A standardized product strategy requires the development of a single product that is acceptable in as many markets as possible. Large experience curve effects may be realized through the standardization of products, or focusing product design and manufacture on basic human needs or motives that cross national boundaries. These experience curve effects, as well as economies of scale, enable the company to offer the product at a lower price. Thus, Honda of Japan was able to market a small motorcycle to the U.S. market that appealed to a basic need (transportation) at a much lower price than Harley-Davidson's. By satisfying an economic motive, Honda took sales and market share away from Harley-Davidson, which had followed a domestic product strategy.[15]

Country-of-Origin Effects

An association between the product and a country with a reputation for high quality can aid sales.

Consumers sometimes assign value to a product on the basis of where it is made. This is known as a **country-of-origin effect.**[16] Because consumers everywhere increasingly demand high-quality products at competitive prices, country-of-origin effects can sometimes be overcome by quality and price.[17]

Some nations' products have such a strong image of quality that products made in another country may be given names that take advantage of that image. For example, Ghurka luggage, which is made in Norwalk, Connecticut, was given that name to convey an image of "indestructibility and English history."[18] The image of quality has become so strongly associated with Japanese products that one British marketer of products that are assembled at locations throughout the world (but not in Japan) chose the brand name Matsui and adopted the slogan "Japanese Technology Made Perfect." In a court ruling, the company was ordered to drop the slogan but allowed to keep the name.[19]

A significant increase in nationalistic sentiment is occurring in France, Japan, the United States, Australia, Argentina, and many other markets throughout

GLOBAL DIMENSIONS 11.3

Product-Management Implications of Macroenvironmental Changes

Macroenvironmental changes, such as political instability and economic upheaval, in a national market can cause corporations to reevaluate their product portfolio. Tax-law changes or increased tariffs may cause a product to be unprofitable in some markets. New Zealand's butter exports to England, for example, have declined due to increased tariff protection since England joined the European Community. Companies have even been forced to eliminate products from their product line as lower market demand, due to macroenvironmental changes, has made them unprofitable. Competitors may introduce a new product that severely affects the demand for another corporation's products. The personal computer market, for example, is in constant turmoil, with new technology frequently making older models outdated. The older machines must often be eliminated, because replacement markets for them cannot be found.

the world. Marketers have attempted to build on this trend and persuade consumers to buy products "made in our country." The "Crafted with Pride in the USA" campaign, for example, is a response to the nation's negative balance of trade and the rapid increase in foreign investment there.[20] In entering nations like these, the marketing manager should consider licensing, franchising, a joint venture, or a strategic partnership. These approaches give the host-country organization a higher profile and keep the public exposure of the home country to a minimum.

The Product Life-Cycle

The product life-cycle model can be used to explain why firms become involved in global marketing.

The **product life-cycle model** (see Exhibit 11.6) is useful in explaining **market-extension strategies.** One of the most frequently employed means of extending the product life-cycle is entering new markets, especially those that are culturally similar to current markets, on the assumption that the product is likely to be accepted there. In the past, for example, U.S. firms often introduced new products into markets in Great Britain, Canada, and Australia.[21] This rather simplistic approach can be very successful with consumer products,[22] and when production costs can be sharply reduced, results in lower prices to consumers. But it cannot fully explain the success of global competitors like Phillips or Toyota. As we saw in Chapter 2, successful application of this strategy requires that the product be in the same stage of the product life-cycle in different national markets. Moreover, the strategy is less likely to produce positive results in the future. As global competition increases, firms that wish to maintain a globally competitive product portfolio must consider introducing products simultaneously (or nearly so) in different national markets. This is increasingly necessary

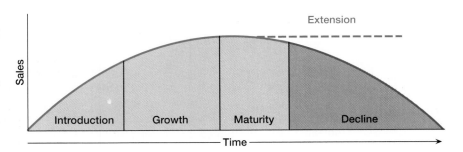

in order to maintain an edge over the competition and to spread high research
and development costs over a wider market base.

PACKAGING AND LABELING

The Functions of Packaging

Especially for consum-
er goods, the package
and label are an im-
portant part of the
product.

Because the package is the last point at which the marketer has a chance to
influence the purchase decision, it can play a powerful role in promoting the
product. Consumer reactions to packaging and labeling are highly subject to
influence by macroenvironmental variables, such as cultural norms. An experiment measuring consumers' reactions to packaging in Hong Kong and the United
States, for example, found that reactions to floral designs on soap packages
differed considerably.[23] Consumers in Hong Kong tended to give such designs
a low value, whereas Americans associated the same designs with feminine
products of neutral value. Packages that are the wrong color, such as a black
cigarette package in Hong Kong, or the wrong size, such as a 2-liter soft-drink
bottle in Holland, can have a negative influence on sales. Multiple packs, which
are designed to increase sales because of added convenience, are also affected
by cultural elements. A U.S. manufacturer exporting golf balls to Japan packaged the balls in groups of four. However, when the Japanese word for four is
said aloud, it sounds like the word for death. Products grouped in fours, therefore, don't sell well in Japan.[24]

Packaging provides protection, a function that is often overshadowed, for
consumer goods, by the promotion function. Still, protection is necessary for
successful marketing. Products that are destined for consumers in very wet areas
need packages that withstand humidity. Goods destined for consumers in mountainous areas must be packaged carefully for transport over rough terrain.

Packaging can also result in greater convenience for consumers and intermediaries. For example, a shipping container that is easier to open makes the

wholesaler's bulk-breaking job easier. At the consumer level, packages that are easy to open and reseal are an additional benefit.

Intermediaries, Shippers, and Government Policy

Intermediaries in the distribution channel and shippers influence packaging and labeling decisions.

Even in Triad markets, intermediaries, shippers, and government policies and regulations must be taken into account. The complex distribution channels found in Japan may demand different packaging than that typical in the United States. Air shipment may require different types of protective packaging than shipment by boat.

As noted earlier, making packages more convenient for intermediaries can contribute to a product's success. The size and shape of the package are important to shippers as well. In India, for example, intermediaries and shippers usually handle products by hand, not by machine. Products that are packaged in too large or heavy a container will be difficult to move through the distribution channel. Also, if the shipping containers are too large, the wholesaler will have no choice but to break them down for reshipment or storage, thereby increasing the risk of damage to the product. Retailers' needs too must be considered. Products must be of a suitable size and quantity to be manageable (and affordable) for the retailer.

Legal constraints imposed by governments must also be kept in mind. Aim toothpaste had to change its package in Australia (after spending $5 million on a promotional campaign) because it was ruled to be too similar to that of a competitor.[25] The way ingredients are listed and the manner in which promotional material is presented on labels are regulated differently in different national markets. Cigarette labels, for example, include statements ranging from Japan's rather mild warning, "Don't smoke too much," to Oman's much stronger statement, "Smoking is a major cause of cancer, lung disease, and diseases of the heart and arteries."[26]

BRANDING

The brand name and its relationship to the rest of the product line have an important impact on sales.

Companies should develop brands only after they have considered the costs of developing a brand image relative to the benefits. For example, most consumer goods require repeat purchases to generate the greatest profit, in which case high brand loyalty would be worth engendering through promotion and distribution efforts. But for some products, such as inexpensive drinking glasses, the consumer is not likely to make enough repeat purchases to justify the cost of developing brand loyalty.

When a company decides to develop a brand, the brand name and image become part of the total product. By providing status, a brand name can even command a price premium, thus helping to insulate the marketer against low-priced competitors. Sales of Mercedes-Benz automobiles, for example, were affected less by the introduction of Yugos than were sales of Chevrolet Novas. A marketer can also segment markets by offering different versions of the product in various markets under different brand names. General Motors has pursued this strategy for years, offering different brands (Chevrolet, Pontiac, Buick, Oldsmobile, Cadillac) to different customer groups.

Product introduction is more efficient when the new product is introduced under a popular brand "umbrella." It is easier, for example, for Campbell or Knorr to add a new soup flavor than for another company to enter the soup market. Branding also offers advantages to consumers. In a typical Triad supermarket 10,000 or more items are offered for sale. The guide to quality provided by brands is an aid to consumers shopping in such stores. In fact, in areas where brands are not highly developed, shopping normally takes much more time, because consumers must compare products for quality every time they shop.[27]

> Because global marketers seek global options, they have a wider variety of choices in brand decisions than their nonglobal competitors.

A company that wishes to develop a global brand has several options. One is to develop a **local brand**, one that is specific to a given national market. For cultural, linguistic, legal, and other reasons, this may be a suitable option for many companies. Soupline, for example, is a leading laundry detergent in France. This brand name would not be suitable in the U.S. market, where it would have very different social connotations. Local brands are especially appropriate when a market analysis indicates that the differences between national markets are much greater than the similarities.

Another option is to develop **regional brands**, or brands that are used in more than one national market. For many consumer products the use of a regional brand can result in high returns, due to improved coordination and control. For example, in Austria, Germany, and the German-speaking part of Switzerland, which together account for some 85 million consumers, it is appropriate to use the same brand name and strategy throughout the region. In these markets there is much sharing of media and cross-national travel.

Global corporations like Honda (Japan), Coca-Cola (the United States), and Phillips (Holland) often use a **global brand**; that is, they use the same brand in all the national markets they serve. The greatest economies of scale and experience curve effects, of course, can be realized through the use of global brands. But a global brand is not necessarily the best choice for every product. Organizational and environmental conditions must be appropriate to support a global product.

CONSUMERISM AND GLOBAL MARKETING

> Especially in the Triad, consumerism is rising, presenting the global marketer with challenges and opportunities.

Consumerism is the protection of consumer well-being through legal, moral, and economic pressures on business.[28] The level of consumerism varies considerably from one nation to another. Some societies, such as Sweden, have a national agency that brings the consumer's perspective to proposed legislation,

Environmental action groups like Greenpeace are increasingly active around the world, making consumers aware of the environmental impact associated with purchasing various products.

business negotiations, and even economic policy. In the United States, consumerism is represented by federal and state government agencies and by private organizations like Common Cause.

In most developing nations the level of consumerism tends to be low, for two reasons: (1) demand is greater than supply, so producers don't have to pay as much attention to consumers, and (2) consumer complaints are less acceptable from a cultural standpoint. For example, the fatalism that is characteristic of Hindu beliefs has retarded the progress of consumerism in India. Public complaints about products are rare even when the product is clearly defective.

Global marketers should view consumerism as an opportunity, not a threat. Consumerism is often associated with markets with high discretionary income, a strong signal that customers are not satisfied with current product offerings. Whenever a marketer can identify an unmet need and satisfy that need, the probability of market success is increased. Recently, the "green" (environmental) movement has coupled consumerism with political activity. In almost every Triad market, consumers are changing their purchasing patterns to take environmental concerns into account.

A low level of consumerism does not necessarily mean that consumers are satisfied. Not having a ready outlet for complaints or the ability to choose among alternative products may result in low reported levels of consumerism. But underlying dissatisfaction, which can be discovered through research, is a signal that consumers would be brand loyal if a suitable product were offered. Chinese consumers, for example, usually do not complain even when they are dissatisfied. But once they find a suitable and reliable brand, they are very brand loyal.[29]

IMPACT ON THE GLOBAL MARKETING MIX

Since the product is the key to market acceptance, the implications of product-management decisions for the rest of the marketing mix must be understood.

The product is the key element of the global marketing mix. Consumer products must satisfy a consumer need or buying motive if the marketing mix is to be successful. In the remainder of this section we briefly describe the impact of the product on other elements of the global marketing mix.

Price

The higher the perceived quality of the product, the more freedom the marketer has in setting prices. Similarly, if the product is perceived as delivering superior benefits or satisfying buyers' motives better than competing products, the marketing manager has greater flexibility in pricing. The product also influences pricing through costs. It normally costs more to produce higher-quality products. The marketing manager must be sure the added quality will be perceived by consumers before setting a higher price on the product. A domestic product will often have higher per-unit production costs than a standardized global product, due to the lack of economies of scale. This means that in the long run domestic products will become less competitive from a pricing standpoint.

Place

Whether the product is an impulse, convenience, shopping, or specialty good affects the choice of a distribution strategy. Shopping goods, which are sought out by consumers, need different levels of distribution support than convenience goods. Convenience goods require extensive distribution, because they must be available when and where the consumer happens to want them. Distribution is so important to the success of a product, and so difficult to achieve in some highly competitive markets, that Benetton, Toys R Us, and Laura Ashley create their own distribution outlets when they enter new markets. They are not just creating global brands, they are creating "world brand/places."[30]

Promotion

The most effective way to promote a product is to communicate its benefits to the target market. The better the fit between consumer desires and product benefits, the easier the promotional task. The potential for standardized promotion is directly affected by the product strategy. Local brands usually require individualized promotion, while global brands can often be supported by standardized promotion. This means that product strategy affects costs and profit potential not only directly, but also indirectly, through the product's influence on promotional strategy.

The optimal combination of promotional elements depends on the total product offering. When a brand has a strong image, a strong advertising campaign is needed to sustain that image. Products that offer superior performance need not only advertising (to inform the market of their superiority) but also sales promotions, such as demonstrations or samples, to prove the marketer's claims. Products that demand special care by intermediaries (such as flowers, which are fragile, or food products that spoil quickly) may require more personal selling to distribution-channel members.   ∎

S U M M A R Y

Products include goods, services, ideas, people, and organizations. Every product combines tangible and intangible attributes. Together, these attributes create the total product that is sought by customers.

Consumer motivations can be divided into two basic groups: rational and emotional. Most consumer purchases are a result of unique combinations of both types of motives. Within a particular product market, consumer behavior is relatively consistent, even when the segment exists in more than one culture. Similar trends in consumer behavior are emerging in many markets throughout the world, leading toward increasingly global market segments.

Each element of the total product—the core product, packaging, brand, image, and so on—can be used as a competitive tool. However, offering warranties and after-sale service is more difficult on a global scale than domestically. In some situations the global marketer may consider entering into a strategic partnership to provide these elements of the total product.

Most products that are new to a market have already been marketed by the company in another market. New product successes are relatively infrequent; several new product ideas are necessary for each new product that succeeds in the marketplace. Each new product should be subjected to a business evaluation—an analysis of demand, costs, and profit potential. Then a prototype may be developed, and the product may be introduced in a test market.

A well-designed product can create a distinct competitive advantage. Among the factors influencing market acceptance of a product design are color, form, shape, size, application, and use. Also significant are cultural differences in tastes and preferences, as well as the type of economy in which the product is to be marketed.

A key decision facing any company is what combination of products to offer and what kind of support to give to each product. Portfolio analysis considers two main criteria: market attractiveness and product strength. By examining the relative positions of various products, the company may identify the most appropriate strategy for a given market.

When standardization of the marketing mix is advisable, the first step is to standardize the product. This entails focusing product design on basic human needs or motives that cross national boundaries. Large experience curve effects may be realized in this way. Another product factor that influences acceptance is that consumers sometimes assign value to a product based on its country of origin. This tendency may be overcome by strategies based on quality and price. Whether a product may be extended to another market may be examined with the product life-cycle model. For products with low production costs, an extension strategy may be viable, but the product must be in the same stage of the product life-cycle in the markets the company wishes to enter. Toward the end of the product's life-cycle, firms must plan and execute product-deletion as well as product-introduction strategies. Overextension is especially likely in global markets, making it important for corporations to prune their product lines. In the long run every product must pass the test of market acceptance.

Packaging and labeling deserve special attention in global marketing. The package is the last point at which the marketer has a chance to influence the purchase decision. The appearance of the package and label must be compatible with the tastes and preferences of consumers in the target market. The package also provides protection and convenience. Marketing intermediaries, shippers, and government policies and regulations must be considered when packaging and labeling decisions are being made.

When a company decides to develop a brand, the brand name and image become part of the total product. Product introduction is more efficient when the new product is introduced under a popular brand "umbrella." The company may develop local, regional, or global brands.

Global marketing is affected by the level of consumerism, or efforts to protect consumer well-being, in various nations. The level of consumerism tends to be low in developing nations. In contrast, consumerism is prevalent in markets with high discretionary income.

The product is the key element of the global marketing mix. The higher the perceived quality of the product, the more freedom the marketer has in setting prices. The nature of the product affects the choice of a distribution strategy. And the better the fit between consumer desires and product benefits, the easier the promotional task.

DISCUSSION QUESTIONS

1. Discuss the basic differences between consumer and industrial products and between goods and services. Is a ballpoint pen a consumer product or an industrial product? Why?

2. "As consumers become more alike, marketing managers do not have to pay as much attention to consumer behavior as they did in the past." Do you agree with this statement? Why or why not?

3. Identify two current consumer trends. Illustrate each trend in at least two countries, and indicate its implications.

4. How does the product-development process in a global firm differ from the product-development process in a firm with a domestic orientation?

5. Develop a global product portfolio for a company with which you are familiar. Which national markets might represent growth opportunities for your firm? Why?

6. Interview ten of your friends or classmates to see if a country-of-origin effect exists for consumer products such as automobiles, shoes, television sets, and key chains.

7. Describe a package or label of a product manufactured or sold in a country other than the United States. How does it resemble or differ from packages or labels from U.S. products?

8. What kinds of products lend themselves best to global brands? What are some problems in the development of a global brand?

9. Identify an issue related to consumerism and compare two countries in terms of that issue. What differences and similarities do you find?

10. Briefly discuss the impact of the product on the other elements of the marketing mix.

C A S E

BENETTON

The "united colors of Benetton" is an advertising slogan, and a product line, familiar around the world. Luciano Benetton, the founder of the Benetton fashion stores, believed that fashion preferences were similar among similar groups of people around the world. In particular, young people, especially women between the ages of 18 and 22, were interested in colorful, cheerful knitwear at affordable prices. Employing a franchise system with extensive market coverage, Benetton built a European clothing empire. A common thread ran among his shops. In every nation, they were fun and fashionable, but they also made a statement about their customers' values, including conservation, world peace, and environmentalism.

The company started small, in the Venetian region of Italy. At first it sold sweaters directly to retailers, but it soon set up its own store. The store was very successful, and with other entrepreneurs the franchise system was adopted to gain wider access to the market. After building a strong system in Italy, Benetton entered Paris in the early 1970s. Beginning with that store's success, strong and rapid growth was achieved throughout Europe.

In 1981, Benetton decided to enter the U.S. market. Recently some U.S. franchises have encountered difficulties, due to saturation of the market, but they were initially highly successful. Currently Benetton seems to be retrenching in the United States. It has reduced the number of stores in some areas, as well as the number of brand names, putting all of its products under the Benetton name, in Benetton stores. Due to a 35 percent import tax, the company was forced to price its products at a higher range in the United States than in other markets. To compensate, Benetton has recently opened a U.S.-based manufacturing plant.

Although now a global company, Benetton has stayed with its original strategy—to market mass-produced, medium-priced clothes that move with the trends, yet maintain a classic quality. This strategy appeals, in Benetton's view, to the whole world. Benetton's ads also reflect idealism and pacifism, which many young people share. In 1983–1984 the "Benetton—all the colors in the world" campaign was developed. This slogan had a double meaning, reflecting the company's philosophy. Not only did Benetton clothing have a variety of colors, but so too did the people wearing those clothes. The "united colors of Benetton" campaign was begun in 1985. This campaign referred to the uniting of vibrant colors in Benetton clothing, and to the uniting of different-colored people and different cultures. These ads, run in magazines throughout the world, show groups or pairs of people from different countries holding hands.

These campaigns and products have proven to be successful in Eastern bloc countries such as Yugoslavia and Hungary as well. In these countries, however, one needs "hard" or Western currency to make a purchase in a Benetton store. Therefore the customer base is limited, and the stores are regarded as high-priced and exclusive. Still, when a store opened in Prague in 1985, there was a line of people down the street—despite the fact that there had been no advertising.

Benetton has created a worldwide network of stores, linking people in over sixty nations, a nearly unparalleled success. As *The New Yorker* noted, "It is worth remembering that Benetton, all but unknown in most places less than a decade ago, now owns one of the world's most recognized brand names, as familiar as Coca-Cola and Reebok."

Case Issues

1. What strategic segment of consumers has Benetton appealed to, and why is that segment similar across national boundaries?

2. In addition to developing an excellent product, well promoted and priced, what other marketing activities did Benetton undertake that contributed to its success?

Sources: A. Dunkin, W. C. Symonds, T. Mason, and K. Denevy, "Why Some Benetton Shopkeepers Are Losing Their Shirts," *Business Week*, March 14, 1988, pp. 78–79; P. Fuhrman, "Benetton Learns to Darn," *Forbes*, October 3, 1988, pp. 122–126; and A. Lee, "Profiles: Being Everywhere," *The New Yorker*, November 10, 1986, pp. 52–74.

NOTES

1. For a discussion of Japanese consumer behavior and its implications for the marketing mix, see J. K. Johansson, "Japanese Consumers: What Foreign Marketers Should Know," *International Marketing Review*, Summer 1986, pp. 37–43.

2. R. E. Stanley, *Promotion*, 2nd ed. (Englewood Cliffs, N.J.: Prentice Hall, 1982), pp. 42–44.

3. D. D. Buss, "Mahindra, Oltcit, and More: New Wave of Car Imports Set to Hit U.S. Market," *Wall Street Journal*, February 6, 1987, p. 23.

4. The Australian price for the Porsche 944 Automatic as of May 1988 was $105,114. At A $.75 = U.S. $1.00, this is equivalent to U.S. $79,000.

5. "Hottest Products 1987," *Adweek*, November 2, 1987, p. H.P. 19.

6. P. Kotler, *Principles of Marketing*, 2nd ed. (Englewood Cliffs, N.J.: Prentice Hall, 1983), p. 247.

7. "Beating America to the Punch," *International Management*, March 1988, p. 32; "Japanese Yen for the BMW Grows," *Atlanta Journal*, June 7, 1987, p. 73; and D. Darlin, "Foreign Car Firms Make Inroads in Japan," *Wall Street Journal*, August 19, 1986, p. 32.

8. "Marketing Exec Focuses on Failure," *Daily Herald* (Arlington Heights, Ill.), October 26, 1987, sec. 4, p. 3.

9. See J. R. Hauser and D. Clausing, "The House of Quality," *Harvard Business Review*, May–June 1988, pp. 63–73.

10. "Smart Design: Quality Is the New Style," *Business Week*, April 11, 1988, p. 83.

11. D. A. Ricks, *Big Business Blunders: Mistakes in Multinational Marketing* (Homewood, Ill.: Irwin, 1983), p. 26.

12. J. S. Hill and R. R. Still, "Effects of Urbanization on Multinational Product Planning: Markets in Lesser-Developed Countries," *Columbia Journal of World Business*, Summer 1984, pp. 62–67.

13. P. Revzin, "While Americans Take to Croissants, Kellogg Pushes Cornflakes on France," *Wall Street Journal*, November 11, 1986, p. 40.

14. M. E. Porter, "The Strategic Role of International Marketing," *Journal of Consumer Marketing*, Spring 1986, pp. 17–21.

15. P. Kotler and L. Fahey, "The World's Champion Marketers: The Japanese," *Journal of Business Strategy*, Summer 1982, p. 7.

16. J. K. Johansson and H. B. Thoreli, "International Product Positioning," *Journal of International Business Studies*, Fall 1985, pp. 57–76.

17. See K. G. Dickerson, "Consumers Rate U.S. Clothes Higher Than Imports," *Marketing News*, November 7, 1986, p. 30; and T. Levitt, "The Globalization of Markets," *Harvard Business Review*, May–June 1983, pp. 92–102.

18. "The Not-So-Ugly Americans," *Forbes*, December 1, 1986, p. 214.

19. S. Lohr, "Made in Japan or Not: That Is the Question," *New York Times*, April 3, 1988, p. 1.

20. "Draping Old Glory Around Just About Everything," *Business Week*, October 27, 1986, pp. 66–68.

21. W. H. Davidson, "Market Similarity and Market Selection: Implications for International Marketing Strategy," *Journal of Business Research* 11 (1983):439–456; W. H. Davidson and R. Harrigan, "Key Decisions in International Marketing: Introducing New Products Abroad," *Columbia Journal of World Business*, Winter 1977, pp. 15–23.

22. M. van Mesdag, "Winging It in Foreign Markets," *Harvard Business Review*, January–February 1987, pp. 71–74; and Ricks, op. cit., pp. 28–29.

23. J. Knutsen, S. Thrasher, and Y. Kathawala, "The Impact of Culture Upon Package Perception: An Experiment in Hong Kong and the United States," *International Journal of Management*, June 1988, pp. 117–124.

24. Ibid.

25. Ricks, op. cit., p. 34.

26. "An Unhealthy Trade Surplus," *Asiaweek*, April 29, 1988, p. 48; and J. S. Hill and R. R. Still, "Adapting Products to LDC Tastes," *Harvard Business Review*, March–April 1984, p. 95.

27. L. D. Dahringer and M. T. Hilger, "Alienation and Market Systems Development: Lessons for the Multinational Marketer," *Economic and Political Weekly, Review of Management* (Bombay, India), February 27, 1987, pp. 23–26.

28. D. W. Cravens and G. E. Hills, "Consumerism: A Perspective for Business," *Business Horizons*, August 1970, p. 21.

29. O. Yau, "Chinese Cultural Values and Their Marketing Implications," *Working Paper Series* (Business Research Centre, Hong Kong Baptist College, 1986), p. 16.

30. "Foreign Marketers Are Placing Products on Their Own Shelves," *Marketing News*, March 13, 1987, p. 12; and E. E. Toll, "German 'R' Us," *Advertising Age*, November 9, 1987, p. 56.

GLOBAL MARKETING OF INDUSTRIAL PRODUCTS

INTERNATIONAL INCIDENT

Global Construction

It may seem that the construction industry would be difficult to globalize. And in many ways it is, because of expensive building equipment; local laws and regulations concerning safety, labor, and ownership; and a strong "buy national" view on the part of those paying for the construction. But recently firms based in Korea, The Netherlands, the United States, and Japan, in particular, have been active around the world. For example, a $138 million project for a hotel and conference hall in Yokohama is being constructed by a joint venture between U.S. and Japanese companies.

The $489 billion Japanese construction market (as of 1988) has always been difficult for foreign firms to enter. U.S. companies were awarded contracts there worth $7 million in 1988. That same year, in the $403 billion U.S. market, Japanese companies gained contracts of more than $2.2 billion. Many U.S. builders claim that the Japanese system is rigged to keep foreigners out. But only seven U.S. companies had applied for construction licenses as of 1988. These companies all entered successful strategic alliances with Japanese partners. In the United States, most Japanese companies are also involved with a local (U.S.-based) partner. For example, Palos Verdes, a suburb of Los Angeles, will see 150 single-family homes built by such an agreement, each selling for between $1.2 million and $1.6 million. As markets are increasingly opened, industrial markets that were once highly protected and difficult to compete in internationally, such as construction, present the global industrial firm with new opportunities, greater risks, and potentially greater rewards.

Sources: "U.S. Contractors Finally Break Ground in Tokyo," *Business Week*, April 3, 1989, p. 56; and K. Shocket, "The Japanese Don Hard Hats for a New U.S. Role," *New York Times*, July 9, 1989, pp. 6–29.

Just as consumer products have certain unique characteristics from the standpoint of global marketing, so do industrial products. Purchasing decisions for industrial products are similar to those for consumer products; that is, both emotional and rational motives are involved. However, because industrial buying behavior tends to be more influenced by rational motives, the marketing mix for such products will differ from that for typical consumer products. This chapter examines the distinctive dimensions of global industrial products and buying behavior, as well as the nature of marketing management for these products. A section on marketing to governments is included in light of the important role played by governments as buyers of industrial products.

. . . .

GLOBAL DIMENSIONS OF INDUSTRIAL PRODUCTS

Any product can be an industrial product. Advertising services, supplies, raw materials, and consumer products for immediate resale are just a few types of industrial products. A frequently used classification scheme for industrial products includes the following categories: construction; light and heavy equipment; components and subassemblies; raw materials; processed materials; maintenance, repair, and operating supplies; and manufacturing and management services.[1]

Industrial products have several characteristics that distinguish them from consumer products. These dimensions must be taken into account in analyzing industrial buying behavior and developing a marketing mix for an industrial product. The special dimensions of industrial products can be divided into two groups: those related to the nature of industrial demand and those related to the nature of industrial customers.

Industrial Demand

> Intent of purchase (for reuse) is what defines a product as industrial.

The primary distinguishing characteristic of industrial products is that they are purchased for **reuse** in creating other products. Whether the product is a typewriter, a mainframe computer, or even an entire plant, all industrial products will be used in the production or offering of some other product. The product itself may be identical to a consumer product; a typewriter, for example, may be purchased as either a consumer good (to be used by the final customer) or an industrial product (to be used in an office). What differs is the intent behind the purchase, not the product itself. This is an important distinction. It means that a marketer like Olivetti or IBM must develop different marketing campaigns to sell typewriters to consumers and industrial buyers.

> Industrial demand is derived and reciprocal, and it has higher volume and is more concentrated than consumer demand.

Industrial demand is also *derived* demand: it is ultimately derived from consumer demand for particular products. Thus, a German manufacturer of industrial robots used by U.S. companies in the production of automobiles will sell more robots when demand for automobiles is higher. Because industrial demand is derived, the demand for industrial products tends to fluctuate more widely than the demand for consumer products. For example, automakers like Ford use forecasts of consumer demand for cars in making decisions regarding purchases of industrial goods. If Ford and its competitors all forecast a long-term increase in the demand for cars, they will all want to buy industrial products at the same time. This will cause the demand for robots, steel, tires, glass, and so forth to increase sharply.[2] On the other hand, if all the major automakers forecast a decrease in consumer demand for automobiles, they will cut back on their purchases of industrial goods and use the supplies they have on hand. This will sharply decrease the demand for automobile-related industrial products.

In addition to being derived, industrial demand is often **reciprocal**. That is, two companies sell to and buy from each other at the same time. For example, the decision to purchase an industrial robot may depend in part on the seller's willingness to purchase a product, such as part of the electronic control mechanism used in the production of robots, from the buyer or from an affiliate of the buyer. Global strategic partnerships increase the likelihood that reciprocal demand will be a factor in international industrial purchasing decisions. A U.S. company buying Japanese-made robots, for instance, may expect that the Japanese seller will purchase steel from an affiliated company of the U.S. firm, based in the European Community.

Another important dimension of industrial demand is the *high volume* of that demand. While a household may buy one or two boxes of paper clips a year, the U.S. government buys millions of dollars' worth of paper clips every year. A home computer system may cost a few thousand dollars, but a small business may buy three or four such systems, and a large business may buy a computing system worth several million dollars.

For the marketer of industrial products, high-volume demand also means **concentrated demand**. Industrial marketers can focus their marketing campaigns on specific buyers. Aircraft manufacturers, such as Airbus and McDonnell-Douglas, for example, need to address their marketing efforts to relatively few customers. As global mergers and acquisitions become more frequent, industrial demand will become even more concentrated. Global industrial marketers will experience a higher volume of demand per customer, and that demand will be concentrated among a smaller number of customers. As the level of demand per customer increases, industrial suppliers may find that they lack sufficient productive capacity to produce the higher volume demanded. To meet the needs of customers, they will increasingly turn to strategic partnerships to increase their productive capacity.

Industrial Customers

The concentration of industrial demand is linked to a relatively limited number of customers in many industrial markets. In some markets, however, concentration effects are lacking and the number of customers is quite large. Food wholesalers and retailers exist in large numbers in India, for example. At the other extreme, in Australia three supermarket chains handle some 80 percent of the total sales volume of food products. Although food is a consumer product, it is sold by food marketers to wholesalers and retailers, who resell it to consumers. This means that in Australia a small number of customers (wholesalers and retailers) have more power over the marketing process than do customers in India. For expensive industrial products, such as large computer systems and airplanes, there tend to be fewer customers than for inexpensive products like office supplies.

Industrial customers, especially in large companies, are frequently organized into **buying committees** or groups. As the price, volume, or importance of a purchase increases, increasing numbers of buyers are likely to be involved. For example, a U.S. automaker purchasing a Japanese industrial robot would probably use a team approach in making the purchase decision. The team might include representatives from various departments, such as production, labor management, finance, engineering, and purchasing. Together they would weigh organizational objectives and the product's potential contribution to achieving those objectives against the cost of the product and the features of competing products.[3]

The personal objectives and attitudes of the various members of the purchasing team are likely to affect the team's final decision. For example, the team member from the labor management department might be strongly opposed to increased mechanization of the production process, anticipating that workers would react negatively. The team member from the engineering department might prefer German robots. Or there might be a power struggle among all the members of the group to determine who will have the greatest impact on the purchase decision.

As the number of people involved in the buying decision increases, and as personal objectives become more important, the marketer must pay more attention to multiple roles. The possible roles involved in a buying committee include initiator, decider, influencer, purchaser, gatekeeper, and user.[4] As the size of the organization and the importance of the buying decision increase, these roles are increasingly likely to be played by different individuals within the organization. In a smaller company, they may be played by a single person or, at most, a few people.

Formal buying roles include the following:

- Initiator: A person who makes the initial request for the product; for example, a machine operator who notifies a supervisor that a machine is not working properly due to old age, or a vice-president of production who wants to purchase new machines that are more efficient.

- Decider: An individual or, frequently, entire buying committee that formally decides which product to buy.

- Influencer: A person or organization that has an impact upon the buying decision. This may be a machine operator, service organization, financial office (which may be concerned about the cost of a machine or the costs of operating the machine), labor union (which may fear layoffs if new machines are purchased), and so forth.

- Gatekeeper: A person who controls access to individuals on the buying committee. For an executive on the committee this may be a secretary; for a worker it may be a supervisor.

- User: A person who uses the product; for example, a machine operator.

- Purchaser: A person who agrees to the purchase and makes an arrangement with the seller concerning terms of sale, delivery, price, and other exchange specifics. For a large organization, purchasers are frequently part of a formal purchasing department.

EXHIBIT 12.1
INDUSTRIAL
CUSTOMERS: ROLES,
OBJECTIVES, AND
CULTURES

The multiperson-multi-
department purchasing
situation that marketers of
industrial products face is
complex, due to the many
roles and objectives that
are involved. For a global
marketer, the situation is
even more difficult, be-
cause those people will
not necessarily share the
same individual or corpo-
rate culture.

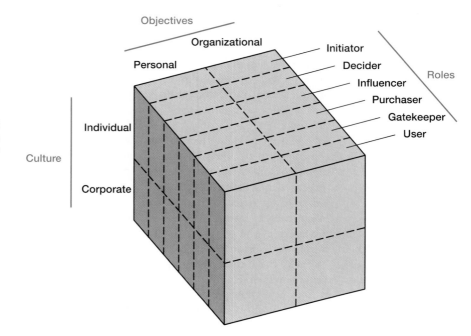

The interactions that occur in a multiple-purchaser situation obviously
will be more complex than those that occur in a single-person buying situation.
Industrial marketers therefore must develop more complex and flexible marketing mixes for multiple-purchaser buying situations. One frequently used approach
is to create a team sales force that matches the buying group. A marketer of
industrial robots, for example, might create a sales team that includes people
with the technical and managerial know-how to address the objectives and concerns that arise in a multidepartmental buying situation. In general, including
technical specialists on the selling team improves the likelihood that a potential
buyer will be interested in purchasing a technical product.[5]

In a global industrial buying situation, the problem of multiple roles may
be complicated still further. In addition to having potentially different personal
and corporate objectives, role players may come from different cultures or be
located in different countries. A marketer selling to Procter & Gamble's European operation, based in Geneva, may face a buying group whose members are
American, Swiss, Irish, and Taiwanese. Although the negotiations would be
conducted in English, the cultural background and objectives of each member
would result in a complex matrix of roles, objectives, and cultures. (See Exhibit
12.1.)

Negotiations, in fact, can create numerous problems in industrial markets.
A businessperson's approach to negotiations is strongly influenced by his or her
culture.[6] Chinese buyers in one survey, for example, rated U.S. sellers lower

EXHIBIT 12.2
STANDARD
INDUSTRIAL
CLASSIFICATION
CODES

The United States has classified industrial sectors into Standard Industrial Classification codes to help organize secondary data that are available for market, competitor, and customer analysis.

Two-digit classification	Industry
10-09	Agriculture, forestry, fishing
10-14	Mining
15-17	Construction
20-39	Manufacturing
40-49	Transportation and other public utilities
50-59	Wholesale and retail trade
60-67	Finance, insurance, and real estate
70-89	Services
91-97	Government: federal, state, local, international
99	Other

than sellers from Japan and Hong Kong on effort and patience. Since these two characteristics are essential for success in selling to Chinese customers, this possible cultural difference may help explain why U.S. firms do not do as much business in China as Japanese or Hong Kong firms.[7] In short, while patience and extensive negotiations are critical to success in industrial marketing in general,[8] success in negotiations between people from different cultures may be as much a function of their ability to establish communication as whether or not the business proposition is attractive.[9]

Industrial customers can be classified in several different ways, and the categories used tend to differ in different national markets. In the United States, the Standard Industrial Classification (SIC) codes are used to organize and present statistical information about businesses of all kinds. Businesses are divided into groups and subgroups on the basis of the products sold and the manner in which they operate, resulting in ten major categories. (See Exhibit 12.2.) For each group and subgroup, information can be obtained about sales volume, number of organizations, and number of people employed. Such information can be useful to industrial marketers who want to analyze opportunities in U.S. markets and identify potentially viable sectors for a particular product.

INDUSTRIAL BUYER BEHAVIOR

Industrial buyer behavior tends to be more rational than consumer behavior, but motives vary considerably according to the buying situation.

Like consumer behavior, industrial buyer behavior varies considerably, depending on the purchase being considered and the buyer's economic, political and legal, and cultural environments. The marketing manager needs to understand the motives of industrial buyers for the same reason that it is necessary to understand the motives of consumers: such understanding permits the development of a superior marketing mix. The same sets of emotional and rational motives are found in both industrial and consumer markets. However, there are considerable differences in which motives are dominant and the ways in which they affect the purchase decision. The elements that are unique to industrial markets are discussed here.

A Global Marketplace

More global and stan-
dardized marketing is
found in the industrial
marketplace than for
consumer products.

In general, the industrial marketplace is more global than the consumer marketplace. The criteria for industrial products, such as performance capabilities, reliable delivery, and price, tend to be fairly consistent across national boundaries. Purchasing agents and buying teams are judged by the extent to which their decisions contribute to the accomplishment of the company's objectives. Although there are some differences among industrial buyers in different nations, the fact that all corporations need to remain competitive and profitable creates similar priorities among industrial buyers throughout the world.

In addition to the increasingly global nature of industrial marketing, the relative ease with which technology and skills can be transferred among geographic markets has led to a realignment of market leadership in industrial markets.[10] For example, Indian students with science and engineering degrees from Western universities have returned to India and found employment in software development companies; as a consequence, these companies have become more competitive in the global software market.[11]

Another factor in industrial marketing is the trend toward large-scale operations and expensive research and development activities. Firms are under continual pressure to lower their prices in industrial markets. In order to do so, they must achieve greater economies of scale and learning curve effects. One way to accomplish this is to operate on a global scale. In effect, the demand for high-quality industrial goods at lower prices reinforces the trend toward global marketing.[12]

Buying Situations

Industrial buying situa-
tions vary by how
unique they are.

Buying situations can be classified according to their frequency. If the buying situation is unique, such as a one-time purchase of an expensive capital good, it is classified as **extensive problem solving**. The rules and procedures guiding the buying process are developed as that process unfolds. There are few, if any, initial preferences regarding a particular supplier.

Situations that are classified as **limited problem solving** are characterized by partially structured buying procedures and rules. Supplier preferences may exist to some extent. Industrial products that are purchased under these conditions tend to be of considerable technical or financial importance to the buyer, in product categories in which the buyer has already gained some experience.

Routinized purchase behavior occurs when products are purchased on an ongoing basis and buying procedures and rules are well developed. Supplier preferences are usually well established. Standardized materials and supplies, such as computer paper, often fall into this category.[13]

Behavior and Motivation

As noted earlier, the same sets of emotional and rational motives guide the behavior of consumer and industrial buyers. The difference, of course, is that industrial buyers are generally more likely to be motivated by rational motives than by emotional ones. Economy, for example, is a primary motivation for many industrial purchases. However, the advantage of low price may be offset by disadvantages, such as unreliable supply. One survey of Japanese buyers showed they were more concerned with reliability than with cost.[14] Reliability of supply is especially important in international marketing, because products are often shipped over long distances and subject to greater physical risk than products in a domestic market.

Personal objectives often play a role in industrial buying as well. These are emotional motives. A newly hired purchasing manager, for example, may be very concerned about job security. This could cause him or her to follow the low-risk strategy of repurchasing from dependable current suppliers.

Country-of-origin effects are a well-documented feature of industrial markets. Such effects may occur even when technical specifications are identical.[15] Although such effects may be based on prior experiences of low quality or poor performance, they are usually stereotypes without a rational basis.

Combinations of motives are common in industrial as well as consumer markets.[16] Within these combinations in industrial markets, however, rational motives are more important, especially in the case of expensive products such as capital equipment. Like consumers, industrial purchasers buy total products to satisfy a collection of needs and wants. But for an industrial purchaser the product is a solution to a business problem—a way of achieving rational goals such as improving productivity on the shop floor, lowering costs by purchasing less expensive supplies, or using new technology to produce a superior product.

A marketing manager selling to industrial buyers must understand the combination of motives affecting the buying decision. In this respect it is useful to examine an industrial buying decision model. Such models may vary for different products, cultures, and organizations, but the one presented in Exhibit 12.3 illustrates steps that are common to many industrial buying decisions. For a routine purchase, such as office supplies, need recognition may occur when someone notices that supplies are running low. In the case of a more capital-intensive good, such as a powerful computer system, the need may become apparent when staff members recognize that they cannot get adequate marketing information using the existing system. The model shows how the buyer first recognizes a need, then determines product specifications, then searches for information and evaluates suppliers, and finally generates a purchase order. In this model, feedback occurs through performance evaluation.

For a global industrial-marketing manager, the model is somewhat more complex. For example, a potential buyer in a foreign country may have a low level of technological expertise and hence may not recognize a new product as providing a superior solution to a business problem. If a problem is defined strictly in terms of an old technology, products embodying a new technology

EXHIBIT 12.3
INDUSTRIAL BUYING
DECISION MODEL

The industrial-buying process is complex and varies each time. But most authorities agree that the basic steps illustrated in this exhibit describe that decision.

Source: D. W. Cravens and R. B. Woodruff, *Marketing* (Reading, Mass.: Addison-Wesley, 1986), pp. 163–168. For an examination of the generalizability of a similar model across the United States and Europe, see A. G. Woodside and E. J. Wilson, "Supplier Choice Strategies in Industrialized Nations," *International Marketing Review*, Winter 1985, pp. 75–79.

may not be considered. Thus, if a textile plant in Hong Kong defines its business problem as needing a faster weaving machine, it will not consider purchasing an automated system. In such cases the seller needs to help the buyer realize that the problem is not merely buying a faster machine but remaining competitive in the global marketplace.

Trends in Industrial Markets

Globally, industrial markets are responding to increased international competition in similar ways.

A major trend in industrial markets is a strong movement toward **integration** (when control of two organizations merges), both vertical and horizontal. Through integration, businesses hope to gain economies of scale, access to sources of raw materials, control over distribution, access to new markets, and diversification (in order to spread risk among more units). The current trend toward integration differs from previous trends, however, in the increasing use of strategic partnerships with current or potential competitors. To give just one example, Metallgesellschaft AG of Western Germany, Teck Corporation and Cominco (Canada), MIM Holdings (Australia), and Asarco (United States) are involved in an alliance that has the potential to influence the prices of base metals, like zinc and copper, worldwide.[17]

Another trend in industrial markets is an increasing tendency toward rationalization and concentration. **Rationalization** refers to the change that occurs within an industry to compensate for some form of imbalance, such as external competitive pressures or the need to achieve greater economies of scale. **Concentration** refers to the degree to which all or most of the sales volume in an industry is accounted for by a small number of firms. As the need for economies of scale increases, smaller organizations either merge with others or become less competitive. Ultimately, some are forced out of business. In an industry that is experiencing these pressures, a "shakeout" is said to occur as some companies combine resources and others leave the industry. This is simply another way of saying that rationalization is taking place. The outcome is a more concentrated industry—one with fewer, larger companies. The airline industry has recently undergone this process in the United States, and it is under way in the European Community as well.

INDUSTRIAL PRODUCT MANAGEMENT: A GLOBAL VIEW

The process of product management is similar whether the product is a consumer or industrial good or a service. However, there are some elements that are unique to the global management of industrial products. They are discussed in this section.

New Product Development

For both consumer and industrial markets, the firm has product-development options depending upon its market orientation and product idea.

The global firm has four basic options in developing and planning consumer or industrial products. It may develop products for specific national markets, numerous products for numerous national markets, global products with planned modifications for different national markets, or standardized global products. (See Exhibit 12.4.) In industrial markets, the global marketer has more opportunities to develop standardized products or products with planned modifications for specific markets. Industrial customers' motives tend to be more similar among national markets than consumers' motives.

Certainly, cultural variations, such as different negotiating customs, need to be taken into account in developing the product and marketing mix. But the relative similarity of buyer motives means that a more standardized product, and often a more standardized marketing mix, can be successful in industrial markets. GE Medical Systems, for example, found that in marketing high-technology diagnostic systems to doctors in Europe it could adapt materials and programs that had been successful in the United States.[18]

The development of new products for industrial markets consists of the same steps as the development of consumer products. However, research and development costs are much higher in industrial markets, particularly in high-technology areas like computers and automated production systems. As a result, the possibility of product failure carries with it a much higher financial risk for

EXHIBIT 12.4
PRODUCT-
DEVELOPMENT
OPTIONS

A firm's product ideas and market orientation determine what product-development option it will pursue. As a firm moves from a national to a standard global product, it gains from marketing experience curve effects.

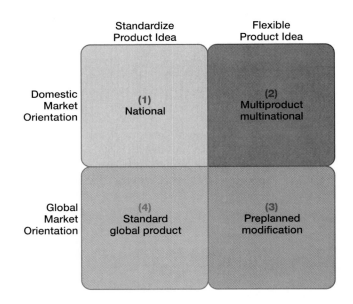

the company. The screening and business-evaluation steps of new-product development, therefore, are more rigorous than is true for many consumer goods. In addition, prototype development is more expensive for most industrial products. A working model of a new steel-producing technology is a costly undertaking.

For some industrial products, a market test may not be possible. In a highly concentrated industry a market test is in effect a market introduction. However, before introducing an industrial product globally, the marketer might well introduce it in a single national market to get an idea of its potential.

Product Life-Cycles

Product life-cycles are usually longer for industrial than for consumer products, due to the high cost of industrial product development and the need to recapture those costs.

The tools of marketing management are similar for industrial and consumer product markets.[19] However, often there are fewer, more powerful competitors in industrial markets. This is because of the high costs of entering most industrial product markets, due to extensive development costs and high manufacturing plant and equipment costs. Concentration means that if there is a clear market leader, price competition is rare. Instead, the market leader sets the effective market price and weaker competitors follow suit.

However, aggressive price competition may be a means of entering a global market and taking market share away from entrenched competitors. In other words, a market that appears to be unattractive, due to strong competition, may become attractive if the firm can enter the market with lower-priced products. Low price is especially attractive to the market when it is combined with high quality. This was the case, for example, in the heavy-construction industry when Komatsu battled Caterpillar.[20]

Product life-cycles are usually longer for industrial products than for consumer products, especially for construction equipment, component parts, raw materials, and maintenance services. Fads and fashion changes, which tend to shorten product life-cycles, are less common for industrial products than they are for most consumer products. Also, the higher levels of investment required for many industrial goods necessitate a longer product life-cycle, so that the firm can recover the costs of research and development.

However, as global competition increases and new technologies are developed, industrial product life-cycles are becoming shorter. Companies with new or improved products are introducing them quickly, in order to gain a competitive edge. As a result, older products may have shorter than anticipated life-cycles.[21] If industrial marketers plan product modifications in advance, however, they can change the product at a relatively low cost. The "new" product can then be introduced into other national markets, in effect extending the product life-cycle. The firm must devote more attention to research and development to generate new products that will enable it to remain competitive.

Portfolio Management

In today's increasingly competitive industrial markets, careful product management is crucial. The trend toward rationalization and concentration can be expected to lead to greater experience curve effects and economies of scale. The savings accruing from these effects can be either reinvested in new product development or passed along to industrial buyers in the form of lower prices. Products that generate a negative cash flow are more likely to be eliminated in today's environment, because companies usually cannot afford to maintain a money-losing product in the hope that it will "turn around." Another factor affecting product portfolios is the development of increasingly specialized technologies in the Triad and the newly industrialized countries.[22]

Warranties, Service, and Parts

Warranties, service, and access to parts are important features of consumer goods, but they are critical elements of industrial products. Rational motives, such as continuity of supply or enhancement of earnings, are heavily influenced by a strong warranty, service, or spare-parts program. Cybex has focused on this aspect of the total product, providing a strong international sales and service staff for its fitness systems, which match Nautilus-like equipment with computers to analyze back pain.[23]

Macroenvironmental Influences

By and large, cultural factors such as religious beliefs have less influence on the marketing of industrial products than on consumer product marketing. (A major exception is cultural differences in negotiating practices.) As noted earlier, rational

While some macroenvironments, such as culture, tend to influence global industrial marketing less than consumer marketing, political and legal macroenvironments may be more important.

motives are more similar from one nation or culture to another than emotional motives. Because rational motives are more important in industrial markets than consumer markets, cultural dimensions are correspondingly less significant.

In contrast, political and legal dimensions may be more important in industrial markets. This is particularly true in the case of products with high political visibility. For example, large airplanes are manufactured by relatively few corporations. In the European Community, Airbus (a joint venture among France, Spain, Germany, and the United Kingdom) makes a plane that is more likely to be purchased by airlines in those countries than planes made by competing firms. (The same argument holds, of course, for Boeing and Lockheed in the United States.) Airbus's competitive edge, combined with an excellent product and aggressive marketing, has enabled it to gain 20 percent of the aircraft market, which was formerly dominated by U.S. manufacturers.[24]

Product liability is a legal problem that affects industrial as well as consumer marketers. For example, overseas marketers that wish to enter U.S. markets may find that strict product-liability laws act as a barrier to entry. In fact, the impact of these laws is so great that some manufacturers are abandoning U.S. markets.[25] For example, manufacturers of small private aircraft have found that U.S. product-liability laws are so strict that they cannot afford the insurance they need. Rather than risk bankruptcy as a result of an expensive lawsuit, they have chosen to leave the market.

Product Design

Cultural tastes such as color preferences play a smaller role in the marketing of most industrial products than in the marketing of consumer goods. Office equipment may be selected partly on the basis of cultural tastes and preferences, but such concerns do not extend to capital-intensive plant and equipment.

For global industrial products, the single most important design element is quality.

As noted earlier, product standardization is often feasible in industrial markets. As a result, the design of industrial products usually focuses on reducing manufacturing costs and increasing product reliability. Attention to such details as number of parts, ease of assembly, and strict tolerances has enabled Japanese firms to dramatically improve the quality of both consumer and industrial products.[26] Quality is the single most important dimension of industrial product design.[27] Industrial products are reused; they become part of the buyer's manufacturing process. They must be of consistent quality so that the buyer can predict how they will contribute to the manufacturing operation.

A major problem facing global industrial marketers is the lack of uniform standards. For example, although the metric system of measurement is used in most nations, in the United States the traditional English system (inches, pounds, and so on) remains in use. Manufacturers of industrial equipment must therefore produce both metric and nonmetric versions of their products, which increases the average cost per unit. In addition, electric currents differ in different nations (for example, 110 volts in the United States and 220 volts in many other nations), with important consequences for the design of electric motors.

Airbus uses component parts manufactured throughout the European Community. Here, part of the main body manufactured in Germany is prepared for shipment to the assembly plant in Toulouse, France.

Most industrial customers prefer products that meet common technological standards. This enables them to purchase products from different suppliers. It also permits the interchanging and linking together of products made by different manufacturers. For example, if there were a single standard for computing operations an office would have no difficulty linking together Apple, IBM, and Olivetti systems. When there are widely accepted standards it is easier for marketers to enter certain product markets. In the case of computers, a new producer could make a single product to meet the global standard, instead of several to match different operating systems in different markets. The design of internal-combustion engines is affected by differences among gasoline and diesel fuel products in different nations. Other industries, such as chemicals, telecommunications, steel, and pharmaceuticals, must also be concerned with standards. Often they enter into industry-wide agreements on a specific set of standards.[28]

MARKETING TO GOVERNMENTS

Governments are particularly important industrial buyers, due to their large purchases.

Governments are major buyers of goods and services. Government spending for defense, for example, totals about $30 billion per year.[29] Although governments are often required to purchase from suppliers in their own nation, there are still numerous opportunities for globally oriented corporations.[30] Not all nations have the manufacturing capability to meet all the needs of their governments; some needs have to be met by companies based in other nations. Companies can also enter into strategic partnerships with companies in other countries in order to gain access to the market for governmental purchases in those

MAP 12.1
DEFENSE SPENDING

Defense spending as a percentage
of government spending

Greater than 15

10–15

5–10

0–5

No available data

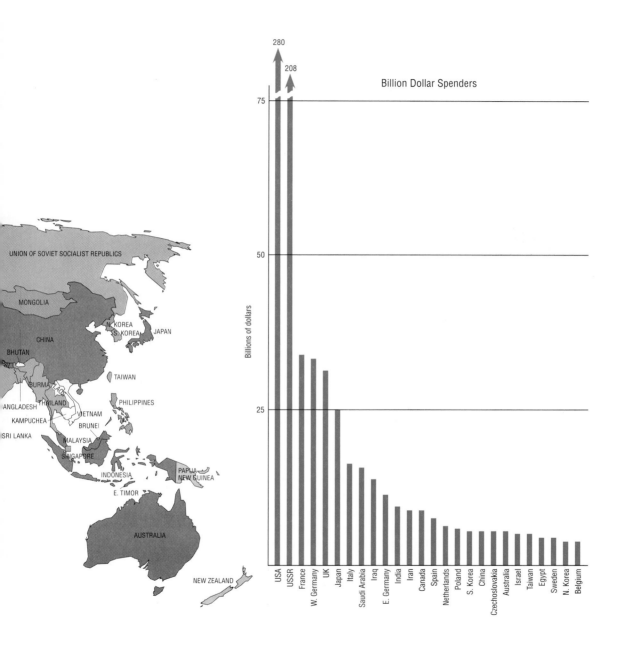

countries. For example, only Brazilian companies are permitted to sell small computers to the Brazilian government. A U.S. firm wishing to enter that market could form an alliance with a Brazilian firm.[31]

Governmental spending represents a high proportion of the economic activity in some countries, especially developing countries and those with centrally controlled economies. As noted earlier, until recently even consumer goods entered Russia through central governmental buying agencies, and hence were in effect an industrial sale. In view of the importance of government purchases in particular industries, global industrial marketers should carefully consider the possibility of marketing to governments and be familiar with the unique elements of governmental markets.

Centrally Controlled Economies

Governments with centrally controlled economies are customers for consumer as well as industrial products.

Governments in centrally controlled economies have consistently represented a significant industrial market. Although entry into COMECON markets (the USSR and most of Eastern Europe) is becoming less dependent on the ability to conduct business with a state trading agency, governments in other centrally controlled economies, such as Cuba, Vietnam, North Korea, and China, continue to purchase consumer goods for redistribution and to obtain inputs for production.

Many economically developing countries have economies that are heavily influenced, if not directly controlled, by their governments. There, too, marketers of consumer goods may find that they must sell their products to the government for resale to consumers. Marketers of industrial products must also sell their products to the government. In the early 1980s, for example, Kuwait had contracts with multinational corporations totaling over $7 billion.[32]

Government Sectors

Governments buy for a wide variety of needs, ranging from tourism to defense.

Industrial sectors in which governments are active purchasers can be classified in several ways. One way is shown in Exhibit 12.5, which illustrates the wide variety of sectors in which governments make purchases. *Defense* and *public protection* are among the most important responsibilities of governments. National, regional, and local governments often buy goods and services to aid in fulfilling these functions. Such purchases include not only weapons and armament but also office equipment and supplies, consulting services, buildings, and computer and communication systems. In key basic industries, such as steel, oil, cement, and coal, industrial marketers may supply governments with everything from raw materials to entire plants. This is especially true in centrally controlled economies.

Tourism is a rapidly growing industry throughout the world, and governments often support tourism in an attempt to attract foreign funds, generate jobs, and increase economic well-being. Particularly in countries that are only now developing their tourist industry, there will be growing demand for hotel-

EXHIBIT 12.5
GOVERNMENT
PURCHASES:
INDUSTRIAL SECTORS

Governments are major
buyers in the industrial
market. This exhibit lists
the major sectors where
they actively purchase
goods and services.

Defense and public protection

Industry: oil, coal, chemicals, steel, cement

Tourism

Infrastructures: communication, transportation, energy

Health care

Education

Consumer goods (in centrally controlled economies)

management services; airplanes and airports; boats, trains, and other means of transportation; educational services; and promotional services, among others. The island of Grenada provides an example of a country that is beginning to develop support systems for tourism, to take advantage of the island's natural beauty.[33]

Governments may also offer opportunities to industrial marketers of goods and services related to *infrastructures*. Properly functioning, reliable communication, transportation, and energy systems are needed in all societies. Developed nations often need to enhance existing systems, while developing nations need assistance in constructing basic infrastructures. Construction companies, manufacturers of construction equipment, engineering firms, trucking companies, and power utilities are but a few types of industrial marketers that may find opportunities in this sector. The Turkish government, for example, requested bids from foreign companies to build a $200 million highway.[34] Aussat, a satellite communications corporation based in Australia, sells its products to a government-operated television station and Australia's Department of Aviation. Australia's international communications company, OTC, is increasing its business with developing Asian countries at a rate of about 40 percent per year.[35]

Health care also presents opportunities for industrial marketers. Health care goods and services purchased by governmental buyers range from medical supplies and equipment to educational programs and sometimes entire hospitals. England currently spends 6 percent of its gross domestic product on its national health service.[36] As the average age of the world population increases, even more opportunities should become available to marketers of health care products. One such opportunity is the sale of computer systems that permit specialists to evaluate CAT scans and electrocardiograms transmitted from facilities in other nations.[37]

Governments also purchase goods and services related to *education*, including books, supplies, and the services of teachers and administrators. Recently the country of Oman spent $135 million to build its first university.[38] Many nations today are attempting to improve the technological standing of their major industries. Therefore, the market for technological and business education should be very strong in the immediate future. For example, in the United States MBA programs that include foreign study are becoming increasingly popular. Similar programs are being developed elsewhere in the world, often with government assistance.[39]

Levels of Government

Just as government policies may influence marketing at more than one level (see Chapter 5), governments at different levels—national, regional, and local—are involved in purchasing. While national governments are the largest potential market, governments at all three levels are active purchasers for most of the industrial sectors listed in Exhibit 12.5. A variety of products may be marketed, including equipment, supplies, and training. Defense and public safety, for example, is a potential market at all three levels in many countries: the national government provides an army and a navy; regional governments provide state police services; and local governments provide police departments.

From the standpoint of industrial marketing, the distinctions between levels of government are largely ones of scale and market access. The U.S. government is likely to buy in much larger quantities than the state of Nevada, which in turn would probably make larger purchases than the town of Reno. However, large cities may control large budgets. The city of Belfast, Ireland, spends $18 million annually on leisure services and park facilities alone.[40]

In general, the smaller the scope of a government, the more localized the organizations that influence the purchase decision. For example, the town of Poplar Bluff, Missouri, may buy supplies for its police force from a local merchant. The government of Botswana, on the other hand, may consider proposals from marketers in other nations.

Unique Aspects of Marketing to Governments

Marketing to governments has certain unique features. One, which was just discussed, is the issue of market access. Global marketers may find that some form of strategic partnership is necessary to gain access to local and regional government markets. Even for national markets, a strategic partnership or foreign direct investment may be necessary to overcome a climate of nationalism or a "buy national" policy. Of course, if there is a limited number of suppliers of a particular good, such as submarines, it is not necessary to establish a "presence" in the host country. Even when a significant national presence is not necessary, an appropriate corporate presence is. Thus, Lockheed lobbied energetically to gain the support of influential politicians in Japan, a country that does not manufacture large airplanes. The danger in this area lies in identifying and maintaining the distinction between influence and bribery. Lockheed reportedly overstepped the line between the two, creating legal problems both for the company and for the Japanese prime minister, who was subsequently sentenced to a prison term.[41]

Formal bidding requirements are much more common in marketing to governments than in other industrial markets. For certain purchases, such as office equipment and other operating supplies, or more complex products such as rocket parts, the government may be required to accept the lowest bid that meets a particular set of qualifications. Corporations that wish to compete in these markets must develop strong skills in cost estimation and maintain strict control over costs throughout the life of the contract. In addition, they must be knowledgeable regarding potential competitors and their bidding strategies.

Strategic partnerships, joint ventures, or other types of alliances with governments may be required in some government markets, especially those that are centrally controlled. The government-controlled trading organizations in the Soviet Union, for example, have traditionally been involved in sales of industrial and consumer goods. In developing nations, the government may wish to be included in business arrangements, often requiring sellers to reinvest some of the value of the contract in the host nation. Boeing, for example, sold a defense system to Saudi Arabia on the understanding that 35 percent of the technical value of the contract would be invested in projects that would aid in the transfer of technology to Saudi Arabia.[42]

Developing countries and state-controlled economies may also require countertrade arrangements, that is, exchanges of products for other products. For example, about half of the trade between Eastern Europe and developing countries is conducted through countertrade.[43] Countertrade permits governments that lack large amounts of foreign currencies to extend their trading activities and increase their exports. However, while countertrade may open up markets that would otherwise be closed to global marketers, it must be engaged in carefully to ensure that the products received can be resold at a profit that covers not only the original product's profit potential but the costs of engaging in the countertrade agreement as well. Changes in such factors as manufacturing or transportation costs can dramatically change the attractiveness of a countertrade proposal.[44]

IMPACT ON THE GLOBAL MARKETING MIX

In the industrial marketing mix, the product is the key element, because industrial buyers tend to be less influenced by emotional motives than buyers of consumer products. Industrial buyers are concerned with how much the product costs and how well it performs. Nonphysical dimensions of the product, such as the brand name or image, are less important. (See Global Dimensions 12.1.)

Price

Competitive pricing is especially important in industrial marketing. Although some companies (such as IBM) are able to develop a corporate or brand image that gives them some flexibility in pricing, due to customer perceptions of superior product quality, most industrial products are highly price-sensitive. Raw

GLOBAL DIMENSION 12.1

Industrial Sales to Japan: The U.S. Telecommunications Experience

Technology and good timing seem to be critical to success in marketing to the Japanese. Sales to Japan of U.S. telecommunications equipment grew from $194 million in 1984 to $226 million in 1985. High technology, product design, patience, persistence, long-term commitment, and flexibility were essential to this success. Deregulation of the Japanese market helped open the way, but even more important were the aggressive marketing programs, headed by Japanese strategic partners, of companies such as Hughes Communications.

Source: Adapted from K. Betrand, "Marketing to the Land of the Rising Yen," *Business Marketing*, October 1986, pp. 77–86.

materials illustrate this point. Similar grades of sand or coal are essentially commodities, products that do not differ from one supplier to another and are purchased strictly on the basis of price. For such products, the global marketing manager must discover aspects of the total product (such as superior sales service) or the entire marketing mix (such as more reliable delivery) that will prevent potential buyers from classifying the product as a commodity.

Place

Place is relatively unimportant for industrial products, except when reliable, cost-efficient distribution adds value to the product. Distributors of industrial goods are concerned largely with the physical storage and distribution of the goods; they are less concerned with in-store product displays or providing retail support. An important exception, of course, is consumer goods purchased for resale by wholesalers and retailers. For these industrial purchases, place concerns are the same as they are for all consumer goods.

Promotion

To communicate the benefits of industrial products to potential customers, marketing managers rely heavily on personal selling. Although advertising is used, as are sales promotions and public relations, these elements of the promotional mix usually function to support the sales force. It might appear that personal selling is less amenable to standardization than advertising. However, many industrial products, including raw materials and technologically sophisticated products, are marketed to an increasingly concentrated set of industrial buyers, so personal selling may be standardized to some extent. For example, a concentrated set of customers interested in supercomputers could be served by a single sales force. The sales force, including engineers and other specialists, would be able to address concerns such as technical specifications, speed, and reliability whether the buyer was located in New York, Taipei, Milan, Caracas, or Cairo.

For global industrial marketing managers, the country-of-origin effect may be either an advantage or a disadvantage. When faced with a negative country-of-origin image, the marketer may wish to enter into some form of alliance in order to achieve a more positive image. This could be done, for example, by licensing the company's technology to a company based in a nation with a positive country-of-origin image. On the other hand, a positive country-of-origin image can be incorporated into an international positioning strategy.[45] For example, if machines made in Western Germany are widely regarded as incorporating state-of-the-art technology while machines made in Peru have a negative image, it will be easier for a German marketer to position its product as a high-quality, high-priced item than it will be for a Peruvian marketer, even if the products are technically similar. ∎

SUMMARY

Industrial products include construction; light and heavy equipment; components and subassemblies; raw materials; processed materials; maintenance, repair, and operating supplies; and manufacturing and management services. In marketing these products it is important to be aware of the special characteristics of industrial demand and industrial customers.

Industrial products are purchased for use in creating other products, and the demand for such products is ultimately derived from consumer demand. As a result, the demand for industrial products tends to fluctuate more widely than the demand for consumer products. Industrial demand is often reciprocal: two companies may sell to and buy from each other at the same time. Also, industrial products tend to be sold in large quantities to relatively few customers, enabling industrial marketers to focus their marketing campaigns on specific buyers.

Industrial customers are frequently organized into buying committees or groups. The personal objectives and attitudes of the various members of such a group are likely to affect the purchase decision. When many people are involved in the buying decision, the marketer must pay attention to multiple roles (initiator, decider, influencer, gatekeeper, user, purchaser); such situations also require complex and flexible marketing mixes. In global marketing situations, cultural differences must also be taken into consideration.

Some aspects of buyer behavior are unique to industrial markets. In general, the industrial marketplace is more global than the consumer marketplace;

product criteria tend to be fairly consistent across national boundaries. Other important factors are the relative ease with which technology and skills can be transferred among geographic markets and the trend toward large-scale operations and expensive research and development activities.

Industrial buying situations can be classified according to their frequency. A one-time purchase of an expensive capital good is classified as extensive problem solving. Limited problem solving involves products that are of considerable technical or financial importance to the buyer and in product categories in which the buyer already has some experience. Routinized response behavior occurs when products are purchased on an ongoing basis.

Industrial buyers are generally more likely to be motivated by rational motives than by emotional ones. Economy is a primary motivation in many industrial purchases. However, emotional motives, sometimes due to country-of-origin effects, are not lacking in industrial purchasing.

A major current trend in industrial markets is a strong movement toward integration, both vertical and horizontal. Another trend is rationalization and concentration. Rationalization refers to the change that occurs within an industry to compensate for some form of disequilibrium. Concentration refers to the degree to which all or most of the sales volume in an industry is accounted for by a small number of large firms.

Since the needs of industrial customers tend to be more similar among national markets than those of consumers, a more standardized product, and sometimes a more standardized marketing mix, can be achieved. The development of new products for industrial markets consists of the same steps as the development of consumer products, but research and development costs are much higher. However, product life-cycles are often longer for industrial products than for consumer products, enabling the firm to recover these costs.

In today's increasingly competitive industrial markets, careful product management is crucial. The savings accruing from experience curve effects and economies of scale need to be either reinvested in new product development or passed along to industrial buyers in the form of lower prices. Products that generate a negative cash flow are more likely to be eliminated.

Warranties, service, and access to parts are critical elements of industrial products. Cultural factors (other than differences in negotiating practices) have less influence on the marketing of industrial products than on consumer product marketing. Political dimensions may be more important, especially for products with high political visibility. Legal problems that affect industrial as well as consumer products include product liability issues.

The design of industrial products usually focuses on reducing manufacturing costs and increasing product reliability. Cultural tastes, such as color preferences, play a smaller role. The single most important dimension of industrial product design is quality.

A major problem facing global industrial marketers is the lack of uniform standards throughout the world. Most industrial customers prefer products that meet common international standards. This enables them to purchase products from different suppliers with the knowledge that they are technologically interchangeable.

Governments are major buyers of goods and services. Especially in developing countries and centrally controlled economies, governmental spending may represent a high proportion of the economic activity in a country. Industrial sectors in which governments are active purchasers include defense and public protection, basic industries such as steel and oil, tourism, infrastructures, health care, and education. When state trading organizations are involved, the entire transaction takes place between the seller and the buyers representing the state agency.

Governments at different levels—national, regional, and local—are involved in purchasing. From the standpoint of industrial marketing, the distinctions between levels are largely ones of scale and market access. Some form of strategic partnership may be necessary to gain access to local and regional government markets and to national markets with a "buy national" policy. Formal bidding requirements are much more common in marketing to governments than in other industrial markets.

In the industrial marketing mix, the product itself is the key element. Competitive pricing is also important. Place is relatively unimportant, except in situations in which on-time, reliable, cost-efficient distribution adds value to the product. In the area of promotion, industrial marketing managers rely heavily on personal selling.

DISCUSSION QUESTIONS

1. How does demand for industrial goods differ from demand for consumer goods? What are the implications of those differences for global marketing?

2. Comment on the following statement: "All of the members of a particular buying group share similar corporate objectives; this makes the industrial marketer's task easier."

3. How does the process of becoming a global marketer differ for industrial and consumer marketers?

4. How important are warranties, service, and parts in the global marketing of industrial products?

5. What issues of product design are of special concern to the global industrial marketing manager?

6. In what situations are government markets particularly important to industrial marketers?

7. Comment on the following statement: "Due to the political views of COMECON countries, U.S. firms should not sell products to those governments."

HOBBS-ADAMS ENGINEERING COMPANY

In December 1983, Mr. Hobbs and Mr. Adams, the president and the CEO of the Hobbs-Adams Engineering Company, respectively, were reviewing the company's efforts to expand sales of its peanut-harvesting machinery in Senegal. Both men had a keen interest in opening new markets around the world. They had been involved in the past with Indonesia, India, and Egypt. They planned to gain a foothold in West Africa, a region endowed with groundnuts (peanuts), next. Their strategy was to access this region through Senegal.

The Peanut Industry

The peanut is grown throughout the world. In Africa, Asia, and South America, commercial peanut production dates back to the 1700s. There were some commercial peanut farms in the United States in the 1700s and early 1800s, although these were small, located primarily in the southeastern United States. After the Civil War, increased demand for peanuts led to expansion of the industry. Today, there are seven main peanut-producing states in the United States. According to estimates made by the U.S. Department of Agriculture in February 1986, "Seven states accounted for approximately 98% of all peanuts grown in the U.S.: Georgia grows about 47% of all peanuts, followed by Alabama (15%), North Carolina (11%), Texas (10%), Virginia (7%), Florida (5%), and Oklahoma (4%)." Georgia has consistently maintained its standing as the leading producer. (See Exhibit 12.A.)

By the late 1940s, the demand for peanuts had increased tremendously in the United States. The invention of labor-saving equipment for planting, harvesting, and processing peanuts had led to a greater supply of peanuts. The increased production of peanuts encouraged people to explore various ways of using the product for food. Peanut oil, roasted peanuts, peanut butter, and the use of peanuts in many confections made peanuts a multimillion-dollar industry. (See Exhibit 12.B.)

Between 1970 and 1983, the average annual production of peanuts worldwide had been about 18.5 million metric tons. In 1983 the major producers of peanuts were the United States, India, Brazil, Nigeria, Gambia, Sudan, and Senegal. The annual production of peanuts in the United States was about 1,974 metric tons.

In 1981 Senegal produced 587,000 metric tons of peanuts, 300 times the average production in the United States. Peanut production in Senegal, however, has not been stable. In 1979 Senegal exported $150 million in peanuts. In 1981 peanut exports dipped to $27 million. Then in 1983 the exports rose to $110 million. According to Saleh (*Foreign Agriculture*, September 18, 1979, p. 7), the fluctuation can be attributed to declining demand for peanuts and peanut products. Increased competition from other snack products has led to a static market for peanuts, making producers reluctant to put more farmland under cultivation.

EXHIBIT 12.A   U.S. PEANUT PRODUCTION BY STATE

State	Area Harvested (1,000 acres)			Yield (pounds)			Production[1] (1,000 pounds)		
	1983	*1984*	*1985*	*1983*	*1984*	*1985*	*1983*	*1984*	*1985*
Alabama	180.0	219.0	200.0	2,525	2,960	3,000	464,600	648,660	600,000
Florida	60.0	77.0	72.0	2,780	3,200	3,000	166,800	246,400	216,000
Georgia	562.0	640.0	595.0	2,790	3,375	3,240	1,567,380	2,160,000	1,927,800
New Mexico	11.0	14.5	13.0	2,330	3,220	2,400	25,630	32,190	31,200
North Carolina	147.0	155.0	154.0	2,165	2,900	2,935	318,266	149,500	451,990
Oklahoma	91.0	91.0	81.0	1,940	2,077	2,100	176,640	189,000	170,100
South Carolina	12.5	14.5	12.0	2,000	2,700	2,850	25,000	39,160	34,200
Texas	215.0	223.0	240.0	1,685	1,665	1,800	362,275	371,295	432,000
Virginia	95.0	95.0	95.0	2,090	2,780	2,930	198,660	269,660	278,350
Total United States	1,373.5	1,531.0	1,462.0	2,399	2,378	2,333	3,295,630	4,405,745	4,141,640

Source: Crop Reporting Board, SRS, USDA, February 1986.
1. Estimates comprise quota and nonquota peanuts.

Hobbs-Adams

The Hobbs-Adams Engineering Company was founded in early 1963 as a partnership between Oliver K. Hobbs and his brother-in-law, J. Carlie Adams. Mr. Hobbs had worked for many years in selling, manufacturing, and designing farm machinery, and the two partners were convinced that Mr. Hobbs' many ideas for new machines could form the basis for a successful manufacturing business. Through Mr. Hobbs' engineering efforts, Mr. Adams' marketing efforts, and the hard work of their excellent employees, Hobbs-Adams has enjoyed solid growth and success. Today it has three major machinery lines: peanut harvesting and processing machinery; tree-bark processing, bagging, and pelletizing machinery; and irrigation machinery. In the United States, Hobbs-Adams is a leading name in traveler irrigation systems. It received the "E" and "E-Star" Awards from the U.S. Department of Commerce because of its pioneering activity in the export of peanut harvesting and processing machinery. It also received the Virginia Exporter of the Year Award. Headquartered in Suffolk, Virginia, it has a branch at Albany, Georgia.

Hobbs-Adams has sold its peanut machinery in more than forty countries. The most successful peanut harvesting machinery ever produced by the company is the Hobbs Model 511. (See Exhibit 12.C.) This machine was designed

EXHIBIT 12.B   PEANUTS, SHELLED: U.S. EXPORT BY COUNTRY OF DESTINATION[1]
MARKETING YEARS 1979/80 – 1984/85 (in metric tons)

	1979/80	1980/81	1981/82	1982/83	1983/84	1984/85[2]
Greece[3]	—	—	—	6	10	80
Belgium-Luxembourg	1,085	583	4,190	1,736	1,182	2,843
Denmark	16	—	—	17	—	33
France	90,399	45,963	13,050	27,276	29,295	24,859
Federal Republic of Germany	11,540	2,946	2,426	3,119	3,868	7,699
Ireland	337	—	—	—	—	—
Italy	1,792	7,694	2,422	171	365	1,400
Netherlands	34,548	14,822	26,734	23,898	42,234	49,738
United Kingdom	37,160	11,347	28,884	42,823	47,621	58,028
Total EC	176,877	83,855	77,706	99,045	124,575	144,680
Canada	57,688	25,056	38,497	51,029	56,686	51,284
Japan	28,631	10,663	14,766	24,916	24,608	26,757
Mexico	602	2,335	249	—	27	1,984
Norway	1,960	637	825	2,514	1,728	3,587
Panama	149	4	56	101	143	105
Poland	—	—	—	—	—	—
Portugal	—	—	16	—	16	—
Spain	8,800	1,888	3,709	5,286	4,832	3,743
Sweden	939	378	601	1,064	1,690	1,205
Switzerland	23,135	9,676	2,291	7,742	4,888	2,938
Trinidad-Tobago	1,668	1,093	1,743	1,991	1,952	1,784
Venezuela	258	81	593	21	100	—
Other	10,603	5,373	9,745	4,636	6,542	19,784[4]
Total	311,310	141,039	150,797	198,345	227,787	257,851

Source: U.S. Department of Commerce, September 1985.

Note: Figures computed from unrounded data.

1. Beginning in January 1979 includes peanuts shelled for oil stock and peanuts not shelled for oil stock.

2. Preliminary.

3. Greece became a member of the European Community in January 1981.

4. Other includes 11,087 metric tons of exports to Nigeria.

for peanuts that have been cured. It has been marketed successfully in the United States, where it is quite suitable for U.S. peanut farmlands. It has also received international acclaim, because of its high quality. Most peanut producers all over the world prefer the Hobbs Model 511 over the similar Brazilian machine, because of its durability and Hobbs-Adams' demonstrated interest in the export market. Unlike many U.S. corporations, which use European agents to promote

EXHIBIT 12.C   PEANUTS, UNSHELLED: U.S. EXPORTS BY COUNTRY OF DESTINATION
MARKETING YEARS 1979/80 – 1984/85 (in metric tons)

	1979/80	1980/81	1981/82	1982/83	1983/84	1984/85[1]
Greece[2]	11	7	1	8	—	37
Belgium-Luxembourg	295	141	403	228	126	835
France	1,919	1,812	2,704	867	601	1,888
Federal Republic of Germany	2,120	450	5,148	2,070	2,780	4,771
Italy	6,185	2,035	6,631	4,331	2,509	7,357
Netherlands	839	863	3,205	3,652	1,231	3,275
United Kingdom	2,015	611	3,540	1,607	757	1,657
Denmark	—	78	16	—	—	—
Ireland	—	—	—	36	18	—
Total EC	13,384	5,997	21,668	12,799	8,022	19,820
Bahamas	27	10	32	29	7	1
Canada	5,923	4,854	4,349	4,734	6,017	6,172
Japan	708	1,041	268	—	60	145
Switzerland	4,692	363	3,677	2,091	1,714	1,557
Venezuela	296	357	125	11	21	—
Other	4,368	2,379	5,172	3,615	2,080	5,376
Total	29,398	15,001	35,291	23,279	17,921	33,071

Source: U.S. Department of Commerce, September 1985.

Note: Figures computed from unrounded data.

1. Preliminary.
2. Greece became a member of the European Community in January 1981.

their products overseas, Hobbs-Adams has sent its own representatives from Suffolk, Virginia, to every country that has shown interest in the 511.

Automation in the Farming Industry

The focus of most technological innovations has been on large-scale industrialized operations where the processes of basic and applied research, engineering, production, and marketing all take place through a series of progressions within the industry. This phenomenon can be attributed to intense competition in the U.S. market, in which manufacturers are forced to constantly search for better ways to satisfy the needs of their customers. The availability of investment capital also plays a part in technological innovations. Consequently, technological discoveries seem to follow each other in a kind of sequence—one discovery leads to another.

A major factor that contributed to the development of farm machinery in industrialized countries was the size of farmlands. In the United States, peanut farms are large, some with more than 100 acres of cultivated peanut farmland.

In 1960 there were nearly 4 million farms in the United States, with an average of 297 acres per farm. By 1971 the number of farms fell to 2.9 million, with an average of 389 acres per farm. Farms of more than 1,000 acres accounted for 54 percent of all farmland in 1969. The use of complex harvesting machines is, understandably, feasible in this environment, in which the machines can roll from acre to acre without hindrance.

The second reason why industrialized countries developed farm machinery was the decreasing number of workers in the farming industry. It became essential to replace farm workers with farm machines. In the United States, farm manpower fell from 7.5 million in 1960 to 4.7 million in 1970, a drop of 37 percent. However, during the same period the index of farm output (1967 = 100) rose from 90 to 111, a gain of 23 percent. This growth was made possible by the improvement in farm output per man-hour. Undoubtedly, the increased use of farm machinery accounted for much of this growth.

A different farming environment prevails in most developing countries, however. Farms, whether for peanut farming or not, are small, and there is a surplus of farm workers. Cultivation methods are very simple. The traditional hoe is generally used, and during the harvest farm workers manually pick the peanuts.

Religious beliefs and practices govern the manner in which the Senegalese grow and reap their crops. The farming cycle is divided into different periods. For example, the period in which the crop is harvested is always followed by a festival that ushers in the new year. None of the harvested crop will be eaten by any member of the local community until a rite has been conducted to propitiate the sacred powers believed to be active in the generation, growth, and reaping of crops. This phenomenon is common to most agrarian societies that place emphasis on the use of human labor in planting and reaping crops. Machines of any type, which tend to deprive the people of their agricultural rites, are opposed.

Case Issues

1. The Senegalese market has been disappointing in terms of sales so far. What would have caused slow sales there, when the 511 was so successful in other countries?

2. What changes should the company consider in its marketing mix?

3. What factors are critical for success in the Senegalese market?

This is an adaptation of a case written by Ayuba J. Sarki, Hampton University. It is intended to be a basis for class discussion rather than to illustrate either effective or ineffective business management. Preparation of the case was assisted by a U.S. Department of Education Grant #GOO8540859. Copyright © 1987 by Hampton University.

NOTES

1. See F. E. Webster, Jr., *Industrial Marketing Strategy*, 2nd ed. (New York: Wiley, 1984), p. 5.

2. See, for example, "A Shopping Spree Starts Turning Japan Around," *Business Week*, August 17, 1987, pp. 50–51.

3. For an analysis of the importance of the stage of the buying process and departmental involvement, see P. M. Banting, D. Ford, et al., "Generalizations from a Cross-National Study of the Industrial Buying Process," *International Marketing Review*, Winter 1985, pp. 64–74.

4. T. V. Bonoma, "Major Sales: Who Really Does the Buying?," *Harvard Business Review*, May–June 1982, p. 113.

5. See R. D. Dewar and J. E. Dutton, "The Adoption of Radical and Incremental Innovations: An Empirical Analysis," *Management Science*, November 1986, pp. 1422–1433.

6. A. M. Whitehill, "America's Trade Deficit: The Human Problems," *Business Horizons*, January–February 1988, pp. 18–23.

7. C. D. McCullough and C. N. Chao, "China's Perception of Its Trading Partners: The United States, West Germany, Japan, Hong Kong," *Proceedings, Academy of International Business Conference*, Douglas Lamont (ed.), Academy of International Business, James Madison University (1987), pp. 13–15.

8. D. Burstein, "Sun's Eastern Enlightenment," *High-Tech Marketing*, March 1986, pp. 14–21.

9. See L. Copeland and L. Griggs, *Going International* (New York: Random House, 1985), pp. 72–98; P. Ghauri, "Guidelines for International Business Negotiations," *International Marketing Review*, Autumn 1986, pp. 72–82; P. R. and R. T. Moran, *Managing Cultural Differences*, 2nd ed. (Houston: Gulf Publishing, 1987), pp. 54–73; and P. Wright, "Doing Business in Islamic Markets," *Harvard Business Review*, January–February 1981, pp. 34–40.

10. See J. A. McKinney and K. A. Rowley, "Trends in U.S. High Technology Trade: 1965–1982," *Columbia Journal of World Business*, Summer 1985, pp. 69–81; and R. N. Noyce and A. W. Wolff, "High-Tech Trade in the 1980s: The International Challenge and the U.S. Response," *Issues in Science and Technology*, Spring 1986, pp. 61–79.

11. R. I. Kirkland, Jr., "Entering a New Age of Boundless Competition," *Fortune*, March 14, 1988, p. 42.

12. R. Abravanel, "Shaping Effective Responses to the Globalization Challenge," in R. Varaldo, ed., *International Marketing Cooperation Conference Proceedings* (Pisa, Italy; 1988), pp. 35–92.

13. K. E. K. Moller, "Buying Behavior of Industrial Components: Inductive Approach for Descriptive Model Building," in P. W. Turnbull and S. J. Paliwoda, eds., *Research in International Marketing* (Breckenman, Kent: Croom Helm, 1986), pp. 79–133.

14. G. H. Rott, "Japan's Trade Surplus: A U.S. Failure," in P. D. Grub, T. C. Huat, et al., eds., *East Asia Dimensions of International Business* (Englewood Cliffs, N.J.: Prentice Hall International, 1982), p. 105.

15. P. D. White and E. W. Cundiff, "Assessing the Quality of Industrial Products," *Journal of Marketing*, January 1978, pp. 80–86.

16. For further discussion of the role of economic factors and the influence of organizational know-how, see F. F. Abu-Ismail, "Modeling the Dimensions of Innovation, Adoption and Diffusion in Foreign Markets," *International Management Review* 22 (1982–1983):54–64.

17. T. Dunca, "MIM's Global Alliance," *Business Review Weekly*, April 29, 1988, p. 52.

18. T. Keane, "How GE Medical Systems Coordinates Sophisticated International Promotion," *Business Marketing*, October 1983, pp. 118–120.

19. For a more complete discussion of portfolio planning, see W. A. Dymsza, "Global Strategic Planning: A Model and Recent Developments," *Journal of International Business Studies*, Fall 1984, pp. 169–183.

20. T. Hout, M. E. Porter, and E. Rudden, "How Global Companies Win Out," *Harvard Business Review*, September–October 1982, p. 103.

21. For a discussion of the impact of the adoption of new technology combined with the substitution effect, see J. A. Norton and F. M. Bass, "A Diffusion Theory Model of Adoption and Substitution for Successive Generations of High-Technology Products," *Management Science*, September 1987, pp. 1069–1086.

22. R. Ronstadt and R. J. Kramer, "Internationalizing Industrial Innovation," *Journal of Business Strategy*, Winter 1983, pp. 3–15.

23. "The Little Guys Are Making It Big Overseas," *Business Week*, February 12, 1989, p. 94.

24. "Airbus Hits U.S. Planemakers Where It Hurts—At Home," *Business Week*, October 20, 1986, p. 34; and "Airbus Industrie—A Better Way to Fly," *The Economist*, April 16, 1988, pp. 74–77.

25. See, for example, "The Marketing Strategy of U.S. Commuter Aircraft Manufacturers: Product Liability the Cause, Market Abandonment the Effect," *Proceedings: Academy of International Business Conference* (1987), pp. 319–323.

26. "U.S. Manufacturers Learn the Hard Lesson of Simplicity," *Business Week*, February 29, 1988, pp. 50–51.

27. For a discussion of how loss of quality has made U.S. firms less competitive internationally, see Rott, op. cit., pp. 100–110.

28. "Centre Helps Business Meet Overseas Standards," *Business Review Weekly*, April 29, 1988, pp. 132, 135.

29. A. R. Dowd, "How U.S. Arms Dealers," *Fortune*, February 16, 1987, pp. 58–68.

30. See, for example, "Exporter's Guide to Australian Commonwealth Government Purchasing," *Export News* (Department of Trade and Industry), Australia, April 1986, pp. 19–23.

31. "How Brazil Is Barreling into the Big Time," *Business Week*, August 11, 1986, pp. 38–40.

32. For a more complete discussion of the opportunities and challenges involved in marketing to developing economies, see M. Luqmani, G. Habib, and S. Kassem, "Marketing to LDC Governments," *International Marketing Review*, Spring 1988, pp. 56–67.

33. "America's Adopted Island in the Sun," *Forbes*, November 3, 1986, pp. 216–222.

34. Luqmani, Habib, and Kassem, op. cit., p. 5.

35. "Aussat Begins to Offer Specialized Services," *Business Review Weekly*, April 29, 1988, pp. 129, 132; and "OTC Stakes Its Claim on Overseas Contracts," *Business Review Weekly*, April 29, 1988, p. 138.

36. "Health Spending: A Model for the Mainland," *The Economist*, March 26, 1988, p. 52.

37. "Now Latin American MDs Can Get Second Opinions—In Miami," *Business Week*, February 29, 1988, p. 62.

38. G. F. Seib, "Born Yesterday: Oman Finally Has a College of Its Own," *Wall Street Journal*, November 10, 1986, pp. 1, 16.

39. "Harvard in Jakarta," *Asiaweek*, April 29, 1988, p. 52.

40. "Local Government: City Hollow," *The Economist*, March 26, 1988, p. 53.

41.   H.-M. Tong, "International Bribery: Cases Involving Pacific Rim Nations and Recommended Actions," *Proceedings, Academy of International Business Conference* (1987), pp. 237–244.

42.   Luqmani, Habib, and Kassem, op. cit., p. 62.

43.   *Ibid.*, p. 58.

44.   D. F. Hefler, "Global Sourcing: Offshore Investment Strategy for the 1980s," *Journal of Business Strategy*, Summer 1981, pp. 7–12.

45.   M. F. Bradley, "Developing Communication Strategies for Foreign Market Entry," in P. W. Turnbull and S. J. Paliwoda, eds., *Research in International Marketing* (Breckenman, Kent: Croom Helm, 1986), pp. 35–60.

GLOBAL MARKETING OF SERVICES

INTERNATIONAL INCIDENT

"EC—Phone Home"

Telecommunications is one of the industries benefiting the most from the single economic EC market that will arrive in 1992. Europe, in fact, is on a "telephone binge." By the year 2000, telecommunications is projected to grow from about 3 percent of the EC gross domestic product to 7 percent. And the rate of growth of spending on equipment and services will grow by 9 percent a year throughout the 1990s, more than double the U.S. rate.

Deregulation of the postal, telephone, and telegraph (PTT) authorities, until recently state-owned, and the lowering of technical and regulatory barriers have begun to open the EC borders to international companies. In their rush to catch up with the latest technologies, governments and corporations throughout Europe are spending billions of dollars. Major European telecommunication companies (Siemens of Germany, Italtel of Italy, L. M. Ericsson of Sweden, and Alcatel of France) are busy pursuing strategic alliances and acquisitions to gain a foothold throughout the European Community. U.S. firms have been similarly busy. AT&T, for example, was awarded a $30 billion contract to update the Italian telephone system with its partner, Italtel.

The demand for services is even higher than that for equipment. Data services, such as credit card verification, are projected to increase from $8 billion in 1988 to $21 billion in 1994. Mobile phones are also growing in popularity. While 1 European in 200 has a mobile phone, roughly half that of the United States, demand for mobile phones is expected to increase more than fourfold by the mid-1990s. Scandinavia and Britain seem to be especially high growth markets. Britain has the lowest prices for phones in the world, because phone retailers share revenues from phone calls. This aggressive retailing has attracted 650,000 subscribers in Britain, compared to 450,000 on the continent outside Scandinavia.

Adapted from S. Tully, "Europe Goes on a Telephone Binge," *Fortune*, August 2, 1989, pp. 107–110.

Services are an important economic activity within, and increasingly between, nations.

Services are an increasingly important component of the economy of most countries in the world today. In industrial nations, for example, an average of about 60 percent of gross domestic product comes from services. In middle-income countries the average is about 50 percent, while in low-income countries almost one-third of GDP can be attributed to services.[1] Although data from socialist countries are more difficult to obtain and analyze (because of reporting and accounting differences), it appears that in these countries an average of almost 30 percent of GDP is derived from services.[2] In general, the higher a country's per capita income, the larger its service sector is likely to be. The major countries that are involved in trading direct services are listed in Exhibit 13.1.

EXHIBIT 13.1   WORLD SERVICES TRADE

World trade in services is of considerable importance to all nations. The United States, in particular, is interested in the global marketing of services, because it enjoys a positive balance (exports greater than imports) in its services account.

	Total Exports (USSB)	Total Imports (USSB)	Net Services (USSB)	Imports as % of Total World Imports	Exports as % of Total World Exports
United States	138.7	120.5	18.2	16.3	21.5
France	54.5	47.7	6.8	6.5	8.5
United Kingdom	47.2	37.8	9.4	5.1	7.3
West Germany	45.7	50.7	−5.1	6.9	7.1
Japan	41.2	48.7	−7.6	6.6	6.4
Belgium-Luxembourg	30.3	28.4	1.9	3.8	4.7
Italy	25.6	23.6	2.0	3.2	4.0
Netherlands	23.2	22.9	0.3	3.1	3.6
Saudi Arabia	17.2	44.1	−26.9	6.0	2.7
Switzerland	17.2	10.1	7.0	1.4	2.7
Spain	13.7	8.6	5.1	1.2	2.1
Canada	12.1	27.1	−15.0	3.7	1.9
Austria	10.9	8.1	2.8	1.1	1.7
Singapore	9.2	5.7	3.5	0.8	1.4
Norway	8.6	10.0	−1.3	1.4	1.3
Mexico	8.1	17.1	−9.0	2.3	1.3
Sweden	7.9	10.4	−2.5	1.4	1.2
Australia	5.2	12.1	−6.9	1.6	0.8
Brazil	3.1	16.0	−12.9	2.2	0.5
Argentina	1.8	8.1	−6.3	1.1	0.3

Source: K. Tucker and M. Sundberg, *International Trade in Services: The ASEAN Australian Experience* (London: Routledge Publishing, 1988), Table 2.4.

Services account for between 20 and 30 percent of world trade, with an estimated growth rate of up to 20 percent.[3] (Discrepancies in estimates of total world trade arise from problems in measuring services as they move across national boundaries.) Recently, GATT talks were expanded to include ways to make the international trading of services more efficient.[4] These trends signal an increase in the role of services in world trade.

It is important to consider the marketing of services in a global context separately from that of consumer and industrial goods, for several reasons. First, services are continuing to increase in significance within national economies. Second, the opportunities for worldwide growth are considerable, especially in banking and finance, computer software, telecommunications, tourism, transportation, and insurance.[5] Third, the barriers to trade in services are somewhat different from those that affect the marketing of goods. Finally, certain dimensions of services as products affect the ways in which they can be marketed globally.

This chapter examines the global marketing of services by first explaining the special dimensions of services and how the marketing of services differs from the marketing of goods. The role of services in the world economy is discussed, as well as the classification of service industries and trends in those industries. Unique aspects of the marketing of services across national boundaries are explored, and the associated problems and opportunities are analyzed. The chapter concludes with a discussion of the impact of services on the global marketing mix.

THE NATURE OF SERVICES

The more a product is intangible, the more it becomes a service rather than a good.

As we have seen, every product is a combination of physical (tangible) and nonphysical (intangible) attributes. (See Exhibit 13.2.) Products that are primarily intangible are classified as services. Exhibit 13.3 lists industries that are based predominantly on services. (There is no international standard for measuring the contribution of services to GNP. This makes it difficult to compare data from different nations. For a discussion of this problem, see "Pick a Number, Any Number," *International Management*, May 1988, p. 45.)

The major difference between goods and services is that goods are produced, while services are performed.[6] In addition, services are activities, not things, and the production and consumption of a service are more or less simultaneous.[7] Services possess other characteristics that suggest certain marketing approaches, which in turn lead to particular marketing strategies, that differ from those for goods.[8] Among these characteristics are four that are widely accepted: intangibility, heterogeneity, inseparability, and perishability.[9] (See Exhibit 13.4.)

Services are, by definition, primarily *intangible*. This means that they cannot be stored or transported in the same ways as tangible goods. It also means that it is more difficult to protect services through industrial property rights. For example, business software systems, such as the programs written to run a bank's automatic teller machines, are more difficult to legally protect than the computer hardware used in the same system.

One problem arising from the difficulties in storing, transporting, and protecting services is enabling customers to assess the quality of the service. Firms that provide global legal or consulting services, for example, must create a physical environment (such as well-dressed employees based in a prestigious office building) that provides tangible evidence of quality.

Because services cannot be independently stored or transported, service providers must deal directly with service customers. In fact, a service is consumed at the same time that it is produced—the two are *inseparable*. This makes it difficult to mass-produce services, and indirect channels of distribution are

EXHIBIT 13.2
PRODUCTS:
TANGIBLE TO
INTANGIBLE

All products are made up
of tangible and intangible
elements. A balanced
product is one that con-
sists of equal amounts of
tangible and intangible
elements. Products that
are mostly intangible are
classified as services.

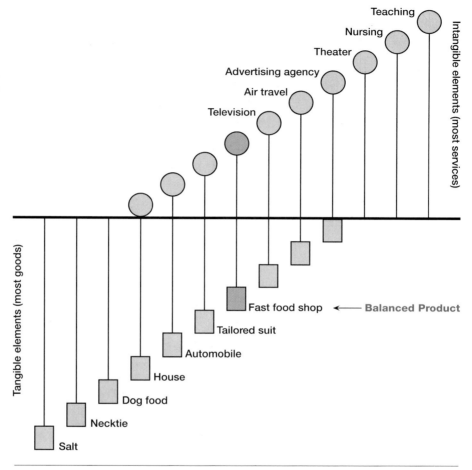

Source: Adapted from G. L. Shostack, "How to Design a Service," *European Journal of Marketing* 16,
no. 1 (1982):52.

EXHIBIT 13.3
SERVICE INDUSTRIES

Classification is more difficult for services than for
goods, due to the lack of
readily agreed upon cat-
egories. This exhibit illustrates the most commonly
used categories
internationally.

Wholesale and retail trade

Restaurants and hotels

Transportation, storage

Communications

Finance, insurance, real estate, and business services

Public administration, defense

Community and personal services (including entertainment and recreational services)

Source: Adapted from The International Labour Office and the Organization for Economic Cooperation and Development, as reported in K. Tucker, G. Seow, and M. Sundberg, "Services in
ASEAN-Australia Trade," *ASEAN-Australia Economic Papers* no. 2 (ASEAN-Australia Joint Research Project, Kuala Lumpur and Canberra, 1983), p. 9.

Unique Service Features	Resulting Marketing Problems
Intangibility	Services cannot be protected through patents.
	Services cannot be readily displayed or communicated.
	Prices are difficult to set.
Inseparability	The consumer is involved in production.
	Other consumers are involved in production.
	Centralized mass production of services is difficult.
Heterogeneity	Standardization and quality control are difficult to achieve.
Perishability	Services cannot be inventoried.

Source: V. A. Zeitham, A. Parasuramon, and L. L. Berry, "Problems and Strategies in Services Marketing," *Journal of Marketing*, Spring 1985, p. 35.

rare in service marketing. Although agents may assist in title transfer, as when travel agents sell international airline tickets, the actual service (for example, transportation from Chicago to Brussels) is provided directly to the customer by the airline company. Indirect channels like travel agencies may serve as a means of access to the service, but to obtain the service itself the buyer must go to a location where the service is provided (O'Hare Airport, in our example). Moreover, customers' conclusions about the quality of the service will be based on the nature of the service provider, since the two are inseparable. This is why airlines invest heavily in training their customer-contact personnel.

The *heterogeneous* nature of services means that a service is virtually unique each time it is produced and consumed. Thus, for example, every tour of India is different from any other such tour. Since it is difficult to standardize services, it is also difficult to produce them in large quantities and to control their quality. The heterogeneous nature of services is even more pronounced on a global level than domestically. A visit to a dentist in Denver is likely to be quite different from a visit to a dentist in Bogotá, Colombia.

Marketers can choose between two ways of dealing with the problem of heterogeneity. One is to standardize the service as much as possible; for example, through the creation of service packages. Home landscaping services, for example, are sometimes sold in packages that include basic lawn or garden treatments that vary according to the season. Another standardization approach is to provide personnel with intensive training and make each element of the service provided as specific as possible. Thus, McDonald's assigns a specific job to each member of the service team. This results in less variation than would occur if every member of the team performed all parts of the service. The second way to deal with heterogeneity is to customize the service for each customer. Rather than providing prepackaged bus tours, for example, a travel firm might offer a car and assistance in planning an itinerary to each traveler, according to his or her needs and preferences.

Because services must be used at the time that they are produced, and hence cannot be carried in inventory, they are *perishable*. If an airplane takes off from Chicago to Brussels with only 60 percent of its seats filled, the airline has lost the opportunity to make money on the unused seats. Because of perishability, the marketing manager must devise a way to deal with fluctuating demand. (In the case of the airline, after the flight takes off demand drops to zero.) Discounts for off-season flights, lower fares for advance purchases, and discounted tickets for resale by travel agents are all examples of efforts to counteract fluctuations in demand.

The same service can be sold to either the industrial or consumer market, just like goods.

Like goods, services are marketed both to industrial buyers and to consumers. In fact, the same service can be provided in both markets. For example, a doctor may provide services directly to a patient, receiving payment from that patient (a consumer sale), or be employed by a corporation to provide medical care for its employees (an industrial sale). Governments also buy medical services. The government may employ doctors directly, through an agency like the U.S. Navy, or it may influence medical services through regulation, as in the case of the Medicare system, which sets treatment standards and reimbursement rates.

The motivations for purchasing a service are the same as those for purchasing goods. They vary, of course, according to whether the purchase is being made in an industrial or a consumer market. As mentioned before, a distinctive feature of services is that their quality is difficult to judge. This is partly because they are intangible and heterogeneous. Most service marketers, therefore, have to provide tangible cues and physical symbols that communicate a positive image for their product. India's tourism advertising, for example, often includes pictures of the Taj Mahal, an enduring monument, as the symbol of India. This is an attempt to provide a tangible, visual representation of tourism and travel in India. By providing such cues and symbols, the marketer can appeal to emotional motives as well as rational ones.

SERVICES IN THE GLOBAL ECONOMY

Services are increasingly important in the global economy, but they are more difficult to measure and record than goods.

It is difficult to measure the contribution of services to the global economy because of differences in reporting systems and classifications of services. This problem is compounded by the fact that some services are direct while others are indirect.[10]

Direct services are separate from physical goods and are traded directly between nations. Examples include financial services, insurance and consulting services, and tourism. If a management consulting firm based in Great Britain obtains a contract with an Egyptian firm, the fees paid are recorded as a service transaction in the balance of payments of both nations.

Indirect services are associated with a physical good. When NEC exports a computer, for example, part of the value of the product lies in the pre- and post-sale services provided as part of the total product. Although these services can stand alone, the transaction is recorded as a product exchange in reports of exports and imports.[11] Other examples of indirect services include packaging, transportation, and some consulting and financial services.

Indirect services are not recorded separately in national income accounts and do not appear in reports of exports and imports. This means that the importance of services in world trade is understated. Thus, to give just one example, Thailand's exports of indirect services are probably equivalent to about one-third of its recorded direct-service exports.[12]

Services and Economic Development

Services may contribute to a nation's economic development by providing basic infrastructures and employment.

Traditionally, it has been argued that services are "nonproductive" and hence constitute a drain on the economic development of a nation. More recently, some experts have taken the position that certain essential services, such as a communications infrastructure, must be in place before significant economic development can be achieved. At least one analysis concluded that the remarkable economic growth that has occurred recently in such countries as Japan, Singapore, Hong Kong, Taiwan, and the Republic of Korea can be attributed to the availability of key services such as communications, financial markets, and transportation.[13]

Services also contribute to economic development by absorbing labor. For example, as agricultural workers leave farms as a result of the mechanization of agriculture, the labor-intensive service sector of the economy can provide them with jobs more readily than the less labor-intensive manufacturing sector. Moreover, some small service organizations can be established with little expense. Starting a business as a street peddler requires considerably less capital than starting even the smallest of manufacturing firms. Thus, a healthy service sector can absorb more unemployed workers, contributing to the general health of the economy.

Trends in Service Markets

As economies in which services are highly important, such as the United States, continue to develop, they increasingly look beyond their borders for new markets. The trend toward increased trade in services will naturally lead to an increase in the global marketing of services. For example, the United States has a large, well-educated labor force, giving it a comparative advantage in technically complex, high value-added services like computing, information services, and telecommunications.[14] (A high value-added service is one that has a high price or is very profitable because of the value it provides to consumers.) The U.S. economy therefore has increasingly focused on providing these services in both domestic and foreign markets, while the production of other goods and services has been shifed to countries with lower labor costs. It should be noted, however, that trade in services is not fully explained by some nations' comparative advantages. An organization's superior management team, advanced technology, or positive image might give it the competitive edge necessary to sell a service internationally.[15]

Another reason that services are increasing in importance is the tendency of multinational corporations to offer services as their primary product lines.[16] Organizations that specialize in providing highly technical services, for example, are finding that they must invest in training (the service firm's version of research and development) at increasing rates in order to remain competitive. Just as marketers of consumer and industrial goods need larger markets to justify such expenditures, so too do service companies.[17] (For an illustration of service-market expansion, see Global Dimensions 13.1.)

Governments are increasingly interested in services, partly for the reasons of comparative advantage just discussed. A major concern of governments is gaining greater control over their economies. Multinational companies operate beyond the control of any single country—a fact that is especially true in the case of service organizations. Governments are concerned that the operations of MNCs—for example, in telecommunications or information transmittal—may endanger national security. Another concern is protection of fledgling industries,

MAP 13.1 GLOBAL SERVICE CORPORATION

Of the world's 1000 largest corporations, measured by market value of their stock, 194 are service corporations. This map shows the national base of those service corporations, and how many are based in each nation.

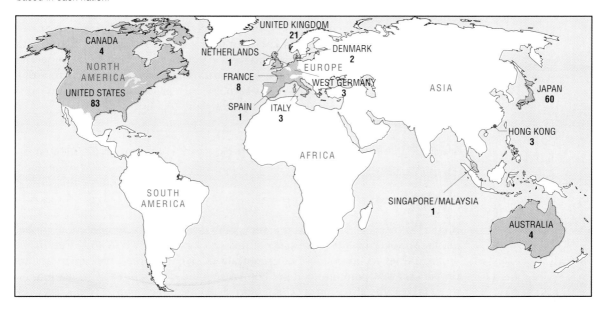

The Airline Industry

Governmental policies have a significant impact on service marketing. For example, since the United States deregulated the airline industry, foreign airlines have prospered, offering a wider variety of international travel services to businesspeople and tourists. But U.S. carriers have found themselves mired in conflict with the government, as well as with foreign airlines, as they have attempted to hold onto their share of international air travel.

International air rights (the right to fly from one country to another) are covered by bilateral agreements between nations. From the perspective of U.S. airlines, deregulation has hindered their efforts to expand in international markets as much as it has helped. For example, in 1987 KLM, of which the government of The Netherlands owns a 38.3 percent share, received permission to fly between Amsterdam and Orlando, Florida. In return, U.S. carriers received permission to serve Rotterdam and Maastricht, two minor destinations in Holland. However, KLM controls over 80 percent of air travel between the United States and Holland. And people traveling from Amsterdam to Rotterdam or Maastricht are likely to travel by train. From the U.S. airlines' point of view, a major international competitor had been granted access to the U.S. market, while the gains by U.S. carriers were negligible.

British Airways has become particularly skilled at playing the international expansion game. It serves seventeen airports in the United States, more than any other foreign carrier. Using aggressive advertising and offering excellent service as the centerpiece of its business strategy, British Airways has avoided competing solely on the basis of price. By these means it has succeeded in carving out lucrative niches in the international air-travel market. Its CEO believes that service constitutes a competitive advantage, saying, "It never ceases to amaze me that the U.S. carriers think they can get away with standards that are not much better than in their domestic market." After investing heavily in upgrading service quality and marketing aggressively to older Americans with high disposable income, British Airways has seen its share of passenger traffic between the United Kingdom and the United States grow to 34 percent.

Source: J. M. Feldman, "The Dilemma of 'Open Skies,'" *New York Times*, April 2, 1989, pp. 31, 32, 69.

such as computer software, until they gain the capability to operate in global markets. Governments are also major markets for services, providing significant opportunities for global service organizations. At the same time, governments provide services, often in competition with domestic or global organizations.

Generally, as nations become more developed in economic terms, services increase in importance as a proportion of GNP. In the OECD nations services

As the world develops economically, services should become even more important.

already play a larger economic role than manufacturing, agriculture, or mining. As other nations develop, their economies also can be expected to become more service oriented. This is happening, for example, in the newly industrialized countries, like Taiwan, Hong Kong, and Malaysia.[18]

As services become more important to national economies, they are likely to play a greater global role as well. Although directly traded services have increased only slightly faster than directly traded merchandise, they may have more potential for growth in the future. The competitive battles of the future are likely to take place in service markets.[19] In an information age, services like computer systems, software, telecommunications, education, advertising, and consulting have the greatest growth potential.[20] A global corporation like Phillips must have current, accurate information that can be communicated throughout the organization, across national boundaries, whenever and wherever management needs it. This creates a need for a variety of information-related services. Other services, such as advertising agencies, must also expand to serve global clients.

Service organizations are finding that they can benefit from experience curve effects through global expansion. Insurance companies, for instance, are entering foreign markets. Some U.S. companies used their experience with a variety of types of life insurance policies to design policies that are new to Korean customers. Korean consumers are responding favorably to these new products, giving the U.S. firms a competitive edge.

Investment services are also becoming more global in scope. Management consulting firms are finding that their clients, which increasingly operate in global markets, need global services. Education, too, is increasingly a global product—Malaysia, for example, had some 65,000 students studying overseas in the mid-1980s.[21]

As barriers to market entry are eliminated for services as well as merchandise, service industries have more opportunities to expand globally. For such growth to be dramatic, however, both tariff and nontariff barriers must be lowered significantly. Recently this subject has been introduced for discussion under the GATT agreement, which traditionally has not addressed service-related issues. (See the appendix to this chapter for a further discussion of efforts to reduce barriers to trade in services.)

SERVICE SECTORS: A MARKET ANALYSIS

The analysis of global market potential for services can be approached from several perspectives. It is useful, for example, to bear in mind that the same service can be marketed to industrial, consumer, or government customers. Global marketing managers should analyze markets from the standpoint of both industry sectors and country sectors; otherwise the resulting perspective on these markets is likely to be incomplete or misleading. Because there are so many service sectors, the tourism industry will be used to illustrate the industry-sector analysis.[22]

Industry Sectors

An industry-sector analysis is performed to predict the future product needs (services or goods) of the sector.

Tourism is bought and sold both formally and informally by industry, consumers, and governments. Governments often "sell" tourism through promotional efforts designed to build demand for travel to a particular country. Industrial groups purchase tourism as a means of bringing personnel together for meetings and conferences. They may also sell tourism for particular areas. And, of course, individuals travel both alone and in groups, and spend money on tourist services. Informal tourism services can be illustrated by the New Delhi taxi driver who offers to serve as your guide around the city the next day.

A characteristic of tourism as a product is that it may provide unique elements, such as the Grand Canyon or the Taj Mahal, with similar benefits (for example, food and lodging). That is, a country's comparative advantage in tourism may be based on service elements that go beyond its natural assets. For example, tourism to China had increased dramatically, due partly to the relaxation of restrictions on visas and partly to the recent construction of a number of world-class hotels. Now tourists can enjoy the beauty of China with the level of comfort they expect. Thus, a country's comparative advantage in tourism may be based not only on natural assets but also on such factors as its infrastructure, its level of technological advancement, and the ease of obtaining a visa.

Tourism can make an important contribution to a country's income. Singapore, for example, earns over 2 percent of its gross domestic product from tourism, and more than 5 percent of its labor force is employed either directly or indirectly in the tourism industry. However, tourism can also act as a drain on a country's resources. It may require higher imports of certain products than

Marketing services such as tourism in China depend not only on unique attractions like the Great Wall, but also on external environments. The Tienanmen Square incident in 1989, for example, resulted in a sharp decline in western tourists to China.

would be required for domestic use, or even imports of products that are not used domestically at all. For example, restaurant owners on the Gold Coast in Australia, an area similar to Miami, Florida, have found that they must import *sake* for Japanese tourists. Hotels there have even imported special furnishings to satisfy Japanese tastes. Singapore's imports of such products offset about 31 percent of its earnings from tourism.[23]

As international travel becomes easier, faster, and less expensive, the tourism industry can be expected to grow at a faster rate. For example, the number of Japanese traveling as tourists outside Japan increased by 554 percent between 1950 and 1985.[24]

Within the tourism industry there are several types of service providers. Among these, lodging is probably the most important in terms of total expenditures. Food and food services make up the second most important category. Local transportation is of particular importance in large countries like the United States and Canada. Sightseeing fees and related expenditures normally account for the smallest percentage of tourism revenues.

Country Sectors

Country-sector analysis looks at the need for a product within a specific nation.

Another way to analyze the market for services is to consider the service sectors of specific national economies. Malaysia's economy, for example, tends to expand and contract along with the prices of oil exports. But over the past twenty years Malaysia has made substantial progress toward becoming a middle-income industrialized nation. During this time the service sector has grown at a rate 12 percent faster than the rate of growth of the industrial sector; in fact, services accounted for 55 percent of GDP in the early 1980s.[25]

These facts suggest that Malaysia may be an attractive market for global service providers. To determine the viability of this potential market, the global marketing manager would need to look more closely at the composition of the service sector. In Malaysia nearly one-third of the service sector consists of government-provided social, police, and defense services. The demand for other kinds of services, such as transportation and communication, is affected by rising labor costs, which have the effect of increasing the prices of these services. The net effect is a decrease in the rate of growth of these services.

An analysis based on country sectors must determine whether the country will welcome and support the organization's marketing efforts. In the case of services, such characteristics as inseparability may make them more politically sensitive than most goods. For example, a U.S. firm providing consulting services to the oil industry will not be as welcome in Iran as a French firm providing the same services. Moreover, the lowering of trade barriers for services is a politically charged issue in most countries. Services are politically sensitive because they are labor intensive; loss of sales to a foreign competitor may have a significant impact on local employment. In addition, some service industries, such as insurance, banking, and other financial services, are headed by business leaders who have a major influence on the country's political system. These leaders naturally protest when lower trade barriers are proposed. For such reasons, a marketing manager evaluating a particular national market for services must conduct a thorough macroenvironmental analysis before arriving at a conclusion about market viability.

If a global market for services is to be considered attractive, both the industry sector and the country sector analyses must arrive at favorable conclusions. If either analysis indicates a lack of potential, the global marketer would be well advised to search out alternative product markets.

The Informal Sector

The informal sector is examined to see how marketing plans may be affected by unofficial economic activity.

The **informal sector**, the part of a national economy that operates outside the officially regulated structure of business activities, may provide numerous services that compete with those of established businesses. Also known as "the **grey market**," in some cases it is quite large—that of OECD countries has been estimated as equivalent to 8.75 percent of GNP,[26] and in developing countries the informal sector accounts for an average of 50 percent of the urban labor force.[27] Due to the low costs of entering many service businesses, governments may tolerate or even encourage a relatively inefficient informal sector as long as it generates jobs. Thus, a wholesale or retail organization that attempts to enter a foreign market may be denied entry, without explanation, because it represents a threat to the labor-intensive informal sector.

Countries in which a high percentage of the service sector is informal pose a problem for global service marketers even when they are allowed to enter markets in those countries. If the wages accepted by workers in the informal sector are lower than those paid in the formal sector, the global marketer may face higher costs and be priced out of the market. For example, if street vendors accept a wage of 75 cents a day, as they do in some developing countries, a supermarket chain that has to pay its employees $3.50 a day as a result of governmental regulation will be at a severe disadvantage in marketing food products. On the other hand, global service marketers may be quite successful in these counries, because global organizations are usually able to provide superior services at a lower price than local competitors.

Because of their small size, informal service providers are able to customize their services more readily than a global marketer, which is more likely to standardize its services to the extent possible. The marketing manager must determine whether customers will accept a standardized service or will prefer the customized services available in the informal sector.

. . . .

Global marketers of services must take the unique features of services into account when designing the marketing mix.

CHALLENGES TO GLOBAL SERVICE MARKETERS

The basic principles of marketing management for services apply both domestically and globally. However, because of the impact of macroenvironmental differences, tariff and nontariff barriers, geographic distance, and other constraints on the international trading of services, it is worthwhile to examine the unique dimensions of the global marketing of services.

Macroenvironmental Factors

All of the macroenvironmental dimensions discussed in Chapters 4–6 have an impact on the international trading of services as well as goods. Language, for example, may constitute a nontariff barrier to trade in consulting services. And business customs, especially norms of negotiation, come into play as much for international service transactions as they do in the trading of goods.

Cultural factors, such as the tastes and preferences of consumer and industrial buyers, tend to vary from one nation to another. In the case of services, it can be argued that because of their inseparable nature, services are affected by cultural dimensions even more than goods are. For example, hairstyles in France are likely to differ considerably from those that are popular in Oman. A global marketer of hair salons would have to develop specific services for each of these markets.

However, given the diversity found within any given service sector, service organizations may also find opportunities for planned modification or even a standardized product. For example, Kentucky Fried Chicken is equally committed to high-quality food and service in the United States and Japan. The stores in both countries look similar, but in Japan the recipe is altered slightly to accommodate Japanese taste preferences. In addition, fish is added to the menu. Before a new outlet is opened, a Shinto priest is asked to bless the new store, and nearby tradespeople are invited to the opening ceremony.

Trade Barriers

Services usually face more trade barriers, especially nontariff barriers, than goods do.

Barriers to the global marketing of services tend to be more restrictive than barriers to the marketing of goods, largely because of the close cultural links between a country and the services it offers.[28] Banking, insurance, telecommunications, and aviation tend to face more trade barriers than other service industries. For example, in the early 1980s organizations attempting to market services in EC countries encountered an average of twenty-two barriers per country, mostly in the industries just listed.[29]

Barriers to trade in services include both tariff and nontariff barriers, which are summarized in Exhibit 13.5. For purposes of illustration we will discuss only one nontariff barrier, scarce factors of production, in this section. The other barriers are equally important, however, and Exhibit 13.5 should be studied carefully.

Scarce factors of production present a challenge to global service marketers,[30] partly because services are inseparable. Thus, they normally are labor-intensive, requiring a competent provider interacting directly with the customer. Surgery cannot be performed without a surgeon, nor can a first-class tourist resort be operated without well-trained, experienced personnel. For these reasons, the demand for services often increases faster than an organization's ability to meet

EXHIBIT 13.5
BARRIERS TO
INTERNATIONAL
MARKETING OF
SERVICES

Just as services have
unique product features,
they face unique interna-
tional marketing barriers.
In particular, because
services are performed
roughly at the same time
they are consumed, ser-
vice marketers must deal
with a long list of nontariff
barriers.

Type	Example	Impact
Tariff	Tax on imported advertising	Discrimination against foreign agencies
	Tax on service contracts	Prices of international service providers higher than domestic providers' prices
	Higher fees for university students from outside the country	Decrease in foreign-student enrollment
Non-tariff		
Bilateral and multilateral country agreements	GATT multilateral lowering of barriers	Increased international market potential and competition
	U.S.-Korean insurance	Lowering of barriers to entry for U.S. companies
Buy-national policies	Purchase by U.S. government of training services only from U.S. companies	Discrimination against foreign suppliers
Prohibitions on employment of foreigners	Priority given to Canadian citizens for jobs in Canada	May prevent suppliers from going to buyers
Distance	International business education	Economies of bringing supplier to buyer, buyer to supplier, or both moving to a third location
Direct government competition	Indonesian monopoly on telecommunications	Must market services to government
Scarce factors of production	Lack of trained medical workers in Biafra	Limits production of services
Restrictions on service buyers or sellers	Limited number of tourists allowed to visit North Korea	Limits growth of the restricted industry

the demand. Therefore, the selection of appropriate partners for joint ventures, franchising, licensing, or strategic partnerships is even more critical for service organizations than it is for marketers of goods. For example, the value of tourist services includes not only the destination but also all the goods and services that enhance its attractiveness and thus are part of the total product. Satisfactory restaurants, hotels, travel facilities, transportation, and trained personnel must be available. Developing countries, though they may be blessed with great natural tourist attractions, often find it difficult to provide the capital and training necessary to build a tourism support system. For this reason, joint ventures and strategic partnerships are common in the tourist industries of developing countries. The host country contributes the natural tourist attraction and personnel, and the foreign partner contributes capital and expertise for building hotels, training their staff, and marketing to tourists.

One way to get around barriers to trade in services is to include services with physical goods (also called **embodying**). This makes possible the import or export of services along with merchandise, for which trade barriers are lower. For example, a buy-national policy might require that stand-alone warranties be purchased only from domestic companies. But a warranty that is part of a total product might not be subject to the buy-national policy. A global marketer, therefore, might provide the warranty service as part of the total product (and price), thereby exporting the service.

Mobility of Services

Among the special characteristics of services, inseparability and perishability have the greatest effect on the global marketing of services. These characteristics present a challenge to the marketing manager by determining the extent to which the producer and/or buyer of the service must be mobile. Exhibit 13.6 presents a classification of services on the basis of mobility. By examining the extent to which a service must be performed in a specific location, the marketing manager may determine the category in which that service fits best. Each category carries with it certain implications regarding how that type of service can best be managed. (Note that a change in technology or access to markets might shift a service from one category to another.)

The classification of services is determined in part by the need for a physical facility for performing the service. Open-heart surgery, for instance, requires a hospital with expensive equipment. Physical facilities for providing services do not necessarily require a large capital investment. Tourists are attracted to the Grand Canyon by its natural beauty; the state of Arizona does not have to make a major investment to attract them.

An international transaction may occur without any movement by either the supplier or the receiver of the service (category 1). An example is the exporting of services by the producer to a buyer in another country. An architect's design, for instance, might be produced in the United States and exported to Belgium. However, because of the inseparable nature of most services, very few services fall into this category. Most global trade in services requires mobility on the part of either the producer or the buyer or both.[31]

In some situations (category 2) the buyer must go to the supplier of the service. Tourism, for example, requires that the tourist travel to the provider of the service. When a service is inseparable from its provider, the marketing manager must inform buyers of the availability of the service and persuade them that its benefits make it worthwhile for the buyer to move to the location where it is provided. Thus, India's travel industry must convince tourists that what they will see and experience in India is worth the time and money they will spend to travel there.

EXHIBIT 13.6
CLASSIFICATION OF
MOBILITY IN SERVICE
EXCHANGE

As the focus of the buyer
and seller changes from
domestic to international,
their mobility must also
shift if exchange (sale
and purchase) is to
occur.

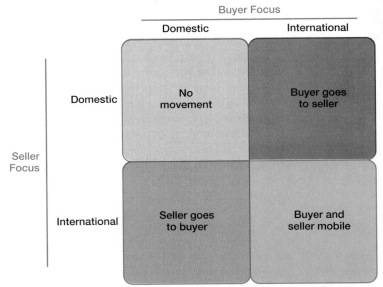

Source: Adapted from G. P. Sampson and R. H. Snape, "Identifying the Issues in Trade in Services," *The World Economy* (London: Trade Policy Research Centre, 1985), pp. 171–182.

Category 3 consists of services that are taken to the customer. Although management consultants, for example, are based in offices that their clients may visit, consultants frequently provide their services at the client's place of business. When such consultation occurs in another country, it is a global service. (Such a service is illustrated in Global Dimensions 13.2.)

Finally, for some services both the buyer and the supplier must be mobile (category 4). For example, the International Management Center, located in Budapest, provides management training in locations that may be home to neither the students (buyers) nor professors (providers). Similarly, doctors and patients may both move to a hospital for surgical procedures. The hospital may be located near the doctor or the patient, or at some distance from both.

The Role of Technology

Technology has proven
effective in surmounting barriers to the
international trade of
services.

New technologies have had a major impact on global marketing, particularly as an aid in the design and delivery of services, and as a means of circumventing barriers to trade.[32] Advanced communications and computer technologies have effectively eliminated distance as a barrier to trade in financial and other services. Using satellite transmission, traders in equity or capital markets can instantaneously transfer funds from one country to another. Global technological links also enable stockbrokers and other investment advisors to trade stocks and bonds in markets around the world. International banking services are also provided by means of global computer and communications systems.

GLOBAL DIMENSIONS 13.2

Egon Zehnder International

Business services of all types may be provided by global corporations, including management consulting firms. Such firms are usually staffed with personnel from the home country, but they can usually apply a similar approach in serving their clients, regardless of location. Egon Zehnder, for example, uses similar approaches to consulting problems and a standard business philosophy with all of its customers, whether they are based in Tokyo, Geneva, or New York.

Egon Zehnder is among the fastest-growing global executive search firms. Founded in 1964 in Zurich, it now employs 115 consultants of 23 different nationalities, who are based in 24 offices in 18 different countries. Instead of defining itself as an employment agency, the firm views itself as a consultant to top management. It works directly with presidents and CEOs to identify the client's management personnel needs, and it uses its worldwide network to identify the best candidates for those positions. Its employees throughout the world adhere to the same strict professional and ethical standards. By maintaining such standards and forming long-term partnerships with clients, the firm has been able to achieve a growth rate of about 35 percent per year.

Another use of technology to circumvent trade barriers is to transfer intellectual property rights. A given technology (itself a service) can be readily transferred to another nation in situations in which it is difficult to trade products that incorporate that technology. A licensing agreement, for example, can transfer to another nation the capacity to produce products that depend on a particular technology. Thus, an advertising agency that controls a superior computer program to assist in media buying decisions could license the program to a firm in another nation, even if the agency is barred from operating in that nation. Technology transfer is a substitute for direct import of the service.

SUCCESSFUL GLOBAL SERVICE MARKETING

Global service firms may achieve success by making the service unique, customizing the service, implementing a superior management system, or providing superior quality.

Educational services, entertainment, medical care, fast food, and business services are only a few examples of services that have been marketed profitably in foreign countries.[33] In the case of entertainment, as of this writing, *The Phantom of the Opera* was playing in London, New York, and Tokyo, and *Cats* had been produced in sixteen countries.[34]

Multinational transportation firms like Delta Airlines and British Caledonian, advertising agencies like Dentsu and Ogilvy & Mather, and entertainment providers from Bruce Springsteen to Luciano Pavarotti all provide services in a variety of national markets. Yet, as we have seen, the global marketing of services presents special problems arising from the nature of service products.

Bruce Springsteen, an entertainment or service "product," enjoys world-wide popularity.

Uniqueness

The more unique the supplier of the service, the more global potential the service offers. Given adequate support systems, a unique service will attract customers from around the world. People come from everywhere to see the Taj Mahal and the Grand Canyon. Similarly, the Beatles, though often copied, were never duplicated. Their unique style of entertainment was marketed to customers worldwide through concerts, tapes, radio, and records.

Customization

Because services are heterogeneous, they can be customized. Customers with sufficient disposable income will either seek out the service that most closely matches the desired benefits or pay enough to attract the service to them. To obtain the finest in high-fashion clothing, for example, wealthy shoppers may fly to Paris to buy dresses designed for them by Yves St. Laurent. (St. Laurent's designing services are also embodied in dresses sold through leading retailers throughout the world.) Or a hairdresser with an international reputation may be flown to the homes of rich clients to help them prepare for important occasions.

Of course, marketing managers can make services more attractive to potential customers through the creation of unique packages. Such a strategy might include providing strong pre- and post-sale services.[35] For example, construction equipment purchases require complete service support, usually at the construction site, after the purchase.

Superior Quality

Higher quality at a competitive price always gives the firm an advantage, whether the product is a good or a service. This is particularly true in countries where domestic firms have been slow to invest in improved quality. Thus, Domino's has successfully entered European markets because domestic pizza shops provide undependable home delivery, if they offer it at all. Similarly, Japanese department stores are succeeding in other national markets partly because their managers are dedicated to providing superior service to customers.[36]

Superior Management Systems

Superior management systems may enable the firm to transfer a service to another national market. The fastest-growing market-entry technique for services is franchising. The advantage of franchising for service marketers is that it combines relevant local knowledge with control systems that ensure consistent quality. Hyatt Hotels, for example, has management contracts in countries throughout the world because of its ability to provide standardized, high-quality services to business travelers and tourists.

IMPACT ON THE GLOBAL MARKETING MIX

Price

Because a service is
intangible, insepara-
ble, heterogeneous,
and perishable, the
marketing mix
becomes part of the
service—playing a
crucial role in shaping
the total product.

Because a service is intangible, its price is greatly affected by customers' perceptions.[37] For example, a haircut obtained on the Champs-Élysées in Paris costs more than one obtained on Broadway in Cape Girardeau, Missouri. Part of the reason for the higher price is the customer's perception that the prestigious address and stylish decor of the French hair salon reflect a higher-quality service. This relationship holds true for both domestically and globally marketed services.

Indeed, in some industries a service provided by a foreign corporation may be able to charge a higher price because of the country-of-origin effect. If a French hairdresser opens a salon in Fresno, for example, he may be able to charge more than a local hairdresser, due to the superior image of French hair styling. The country-of-origin effect can also operate in the opposite direction, of course.

The extent to which a service is labor intensive also affects its price. In fact, a location in a low-wage country can provide a competitive advantage for a global service marketer. Thus, Korean firms have been very successful in the international construction industry in part because of the lower wages and higher productivity of Korean workers.[38]

Place

Technological advances are opening up new distribution options for global services. Automated teller machines (ATMs), for example, enable financial institutions to provide many of their services to customers in a greater variety of locations and at more convenient times. ATMs also illustrate the use of technology to circumvent restrictions on trading hours or union work rules. This technology can be applied on a multinational scale. There is no technical obstacle to providing ATMs throughout the European Community, thereby allowing a customer vacationing in Copenhagen to draw funds from her bank account in Rome. Worldwide linkages are also possible—American Express is an example of an organization that provides services to cardholders throughout the world, regardless of location. Without technological support, the perishability of services would make it impossible to distribute them globally.

Because services cannot be transported or stored in the same way that goods can, and because of the barriers to trade in services, global service marketers often engage in direct foreign investment. This technique not only assures market entry but also enhances quality control in sectors such as business services,[39] while reducing the costs of transporting services. Thus, U.S.-based multinational corporations manufacture and sell nearly three times as much abroad as they export from the United States. Because of the numerous market and production constraints on global service marketing, most of these companies serve global markets primarily through local sales by foreign affiliates.[40]

Promotion

A high-quality image is generated largely through promotion. Customers need symbols or cues to the quality of a service. A French hairdresser opening a salon in Fresno would probably choose a French name, decorate the salon in a French style, and perhaps offer French champagne to waiting customers. These symbols have little to do with the nature of the hair styling received by the salon's customers, but they have a lot to do with their perception of the service provided.

Promotion becomes, in effect, part of the total product. Thus, a trip to India consists partly of the anticipation built up by reading advertisements, looking at pictures, and evaluating information in travel brochures. The role of promotion as part of the total product is especially significant in the case of services, because they do not have a physical form and hence are highly dependent on promotion.   ∎

S U M M A R Y

The major difference between goods and services is that goods are produced, while services are performed. Because services are largely intangible, they cannot be stored and transported in the same ways as tangible goods. In addition, the production and consumption of a service are more or less simultaneous—

the two are inseparable. This means that services are inseparable and perishable. Marketers can deal with the heterogeneous nature of services (that is, a service is virtually unique each time it is produced and consumed) in two ways. They can standardize the service as much as possible, by creating service packages or providing intensive training for personnel, or they can make each element of the service as unique as possible. The perishability of services means that they cannot be carried in inventory, and the marketing manager must devise a way to deal with fluctuating demand.

Like goods, services are marketed both to industrial buyers and to consumers; in fact, the same service can be provided in both markets. The motivations for purchasing services are the same as those for purchasing goods, but they vary according to whether the purchase is being made in an industrial or a consumer market.

Some services are direct whereas others are indirect. Direct services are separate from goods and traded directly between nations. Indirect services are associated with goods, and they are not recorded separately in national income accounts.

Services are an increasingly important component of the economy of most countries and account for a large and fast-growing percentage of world trade. As service-based economies develop, they increasingly look beyond their borders for new markets. Another reason for the growing importance of trade in services is the tendency of multinational corporations to offer services as their primary product lines. Governments, which serve as major markets for services, are also increasingly interested in providing services.

Certain essential services, such as a communications infrastructure, must be in place before significant economic development can be achieved. Services also contribute to economic development by absorbing labor. Generally, as nations develop economically, services increase in importance as a proportion of gross national product. As services become more important to national economies, they are likely to play a greater global role as well. For this to occur, however, barriers to trade in services must be lowered significantly.

Global marketing managers should analyze the world market from the standpoint of both industry sectors and country sectors. They should also keep in mind that the informal sector—the part of a national economy that operates outside the formal structure of business activities—may provide numerous services that compete with those of established businesses.

Services are more difficult to market globally than physical goods. The difficulties of standardizing the production process and achieving economies of scale mean that global service marketers are less likely to be successful in penetrating foreign markets through aggressive pricing strategies. However, the experience curve effects of coordination and concentration may be achieved by well-run organizations. Other obstacles to global service marketing include macroenvironmental factors, trade barriers, and possibly the need for producer and/or buyer mobility (depending in part on the need for a physical facility for performing the service).

New technologies, like computer and communication systems, have helped global service marketers meet these challenges. Unique services, customized products, superior management systems, and superior quality also contribute to successful global service marketing.

Because a service is intangible, its price is greatly affected by customers' perceptions. The extent to which a service is labor intensive also affects its price. Place is less of a constraint on service marketing, because technological advances are opening up new distribution options for global services. The primary role of promotion is to create a perception of quality. Promotion thus becomes part of the total product.

DISCUSSION QUESTIONS

1. What are the four basic characteristics of services? How does each affect marketing strategy?

2. How does the labor-intensive nature of services affect their global marketing?

3. What are some ways by which a marketing manager might attempt to smooth out the demand for a particular service?

4. What is the implication of excess supply in services?

5. Why is control over demand especially important in the marketing of services?

6. Describe two barriers to global trade in services and discuss ways of overcoming them.

7. In what ways does the service sector contribute to a nation's economic development?

8. Why and how do cultural factors have a special impact on the global marketing of services?

9. How have technological advances helped promote the global marketing of services?

10. Identify and discuss the aspects of services that are likely to lead to success in their global marketing.

CASE

SWAPPING DEBT FOR EDUCATION: A PROPOSAL TO FITZE UNIVERSITY

Only 50,000 American college students study in foreign countries each year (most of them attend schools in Western Europe), yet over 350,000 foreign students study in the United States each year. This lack of balance in direct exposure to other cultures means that the future business people in other countries know more about the U.S. market than Americans know about overseas markets. The need to improve U.S. competitiveness in the world market, combined with the need to deal more directly with mounting Third World debt, led the dean of the Fitze University Business School to develop an imaginative proposal entitled "Improving U.S. Competitiveness: Swapping Debt for Education." The proposal, which the dean submitted to Fitze University's president, is outlined below.

The United States is losing its position as a primary force in international trade, partly because its business leaders do not understand the language, customs, and business practices of other nations. In order to help resolve this imbalance, it is proposed that Fitze University become involved in a debt-for-education plan. Under such a plan, banks or corporations holding Third World debt, in particular those holding debt of the "Baker-15" countries, would donate a portion of that debt to support the education of American students in those countries. Both the U.S. Department of Commerce and the IRS have endorsed this concept. While many of the "Baker-15" countries potentially have more favorable rates for the purchase of debt (such as Peru, at $0.06 per dollar at this time),* this proposal recommends Mexico (at $0.55 per dollar) for its proximity, its historically close ties with the United States and its precedent in entertaining novel forms of debt/equity swaps in the past.

A Proposal for the Establishment of a Fitze-Mexico Campus

A program has been underway for two years to increase the emphasis on international trade in the curriculum of the Fitze University Business School. This proposal recommends the establishment in Mexico of a satellite campus of the Business School, at which students would be instructed in international trade in general, Latin American trade in particular, and the languages, social customs, and business practices of Latin America and the rest of the world.

The facilities for a Fitze-Mexico campus (classrooms, dorms, and offices and housing for the faculty and staff) could be obtained either through new construction or the purchase and renovation of an existing structure, such as a small school or hotel. In the beginning, five credit courses would be offered each semester, with four taught by Fitze professors and one by a visiting professor, preferably from Mexico. Additional courses could be added later.

All MBA candidates concentrating in international trade would be required to attend Fitze-Mexico for at least one semester. Attendance would be optional for other MBAs. Consideration should be given to offering some core BBA courses (such as accounting), to open the campus to undergraduates. Students from Mexico and other Latin American countries should be encouraged to attend, with local students receiving significant scholarships (for the sake of good relations with the people and government of Mexico).

Ideally, the Business School would solicit and receive from either a local bank or a money-center bank a given sum of Mexican debt. The IRS has ruled

---

*The debt of many Third World countries can be purchased on the open market at a discount; a loan to Peru of $1,000,000 book value, for example, could be purchased for $60,000.

that the market value of such donations can be written off as a charitable contribution, with the difference between market value and face value written off as a loss, resulting in a 100 percent write-off of the donated debt. However, it should be noted that an outright sale of such debt at a discount, with a write-off of the loss, would leave the bank in a better financial position. The Mexican government presumably would redeem the debt at a reduced rate in pesos, to be used for the benefit of Fitze-Mexico. While there is no current precedent for such a swap, in the past Mexico has shown a propensity for novel approaches to reduce its debt, redeeming debt at 70 percent to 90 percent of face value, depending on the contracted application of the funds. (At 70 percent, the immediate return on debt purchased at $0.55 per dollar would be approximately 27 percent.)

The establishment of a foreign branch would provide immediate prestige to the Fitze University Business School. While exchange programs are common, facilities that are owned 100 percent are comparatively rare. The concentration on international studies would contribute to making Fitze a national center for business education, with the attending recognition and upgrading of its student body and faculty.

If the required debt is donated by a bank or corporation, the immediate financial benefits are readily apparent. U.S. banks currently hold an estimated $71 billion in Mexican debt alone, making the donation of $1–2 million not out of the question (especially considering the quantity of debt already written off). A $1 million donation at a (low) 70 percent redemption rate would yield approximately $1,270,000 in working capital for Fitze-Mexico.

However, let us assume for the moment that no donor for the debt can be found, and it would have to be purchased at full market value. Let us also assume the Mexican government agreed to redeem the debt at 70 percent of face value. This still would provide, as already mentioned, a return of about 27 percent over the actual cost of the debt. The negative side of this would be the usual contingency that most funds remain in Mexico. The positive side is that the funds to purchase the debt would be generated through the normal payment of tuition by students, while expenses incurred for the services provided in Mexico would be considerably less than they would be for comparable services in the United States, and they would be paid for with the discounted pesos. According to one professor familiar with U.S. study-abroad programs, the average monthly cost of maintaining an American student in a Third World country is about $500. At Fitze-Mexico campus housing alone would become a significant profit center.

Further, many of the Business School's current expenses could be shifted to Fitze-Mexico. Faculty, for instance, could legitimately be paid through the swapped debt. A $40,000 salary paid for with exchanged pesos would cost approximately $31,500. Also, an agreement could probably be reached with the Mexican government to allow Fitze-Mexico to reimburse Fitze University for many costs incurred in the United States on behalf of the Mexican school, such as recruiting students and processing paperwork. Students from Mexico and other countries in nondegree programs at Fitze-Mexico without scholarships would be an added source of revenue, which at present cannot be tapped by the Business School. Finally, the transference of a number of students and professors from the main campus to Mexico would make it possible to increase student enrollment without increasing class size at home, while freeing office space for new faculty and thus avoiding further renovation or expansion of the current facilities.

Banks prefer to sell their debt, even at reduced rates, than to donate it for the tax write-off. However, local area banks seem more open to the idea than money-center banks, perhaps because they are more eager to get out of the foreign loan business and/or because they have closer ties with the community of which the university is a part. Local banks holding Mexican debt, as well as money-center banks with which faculty members have inside contacts, should be contacted on the subject. As an alternative to outright donations, purchase of debt at below-market rates could be considered. Finally, cash donations could be solicited from companies with overseas interests, to purchase debt to finance Fitze-Mexico. Various incentives could be included with the requests, such as a "funded seat" for company employees at the Business School (instead of an endowed chair for a professor).

Case Issues

1. What are the benefits to students who would be enrolled in such a program?

2. Refer to Exhibit 13.6. How would you classify such an international education program? What international marketing management implications does this classification have?

3. What negative considerations have not been considered in the proposal?

4. If the proposal is approved and the Mexican government approached, what social and political issues should be considered and how should they be approached? How could these be used to advance the proposal?

Source: This case was adapted from a case by R.A. Heisler, Emory Business School, Atlanta, GA USA.

NOTES

1. K. Tucker, G. Seow, and M. Sundberg, *Services in ASEAN-Australian Trade*, ASEAN-Australia Economic Papers no. 2 (Kuala Lumpur and Canberra: ASEAN-Australia Joint Research Project, 1983), p. 7.

2. R. K. Shelp, *Beyond Industrialization: Ascendancy of the Global Service Economy* (New York: Praeger, 1981).

3. J. D. Aronson and P. F. Cowhey, *Trade in Services: A Case for Open Markets* (Washington, D.C.: American Enterprise Institute, 1984), p. 1; and K. Tucker and M. Sundberg, *International Trade in Services: The ASEAN-Australian Experience* (London: Routledge, 1988), pp. 17–26, 38.

4.   For a thorough discussion of GATT and trade in services, see Aronson and Cowhey, op. cit., chap. 3.

5.   An example of evolving competitive advantage for banking services is the case of Hungary, now the leading provider of "safe" bank accounts. See "Hot Money Haven," *Fortune*, November 10, 1988, p. 8. For a detailed analysis of the future of international banking, see "International Banking—Survival of the Fittest," *The Economist*, March 26, 1988, pp. 6–76. For a discussion of the global potential for software and computer services, see L. Arossa, "Software and Computer Services," *OECD Observer* (Paris), April-May 1988, pp. 13–16.

6.   A. M. Rushton and D. J. Carson, "The Marketing of Services: Managing the Intangibles," *European Journal of Marketing* 19, no. 3 (1985):22.

7.   C. Gronross, "An Applied Service Marketing Theory," *European Journal of Marketing* 16, no. 7 (1982):31.

8.   See R. P. Fisk and P. S. Tansuhaj, *Services Marketing: An Annotated Bibliography* (Chicago: American Marketing Association, 1985).

9.   For a more thorough discussion of service characteristics and service marketing management, see V. Zeithaml, A. Parasuraman, and L. L. Berry, "Problems and Strategies in Services Marketing," *Journal of Marketing*, Spring 1985, pp. 33–46; and C. H. Lovelock, "Classifying Services to Gain Strategic Marketing Insights," *Journal of Marketing*, Summer 1983, pp. 9–20.

10.   For further discussion of this distinction, see K. A. Tucker, *Traded Services in the World Economy*, Working Paper no. 16 (Canberra: Bureau of Industry Economics, 1981).

11.   For an illustration of the embedding that occurs in the computer industry, see "Current Status and Future Trends of the Computer Industry in Japan," in Centre of International Co-Operation for Computerization, *Continuing Process of Computerization in Japan 1986–1987*, Tokyo, 1988, pp. 1–27.

12.   Tucker and Sundberg, op. cit., pp. 10, 21.

13.   See D. I. Riddle, *Service-Led Growth: The Role of the Service Sector in World Development* (New York: Praeger, 1986).

14.   Rachel McCullouch, *International Competition in Services*, Working Paper no. 2235 (Cambridge, Mass.: National Bureau of Economic Research, 1987), p. 25.

15.   See A. V. Deardorff, *Comparative Advantage and International Trade and Investment in Services*, paper presented at the Third Annual Workshop on U.S.-Canadian Relations, 1984.

16.   J. J. Boddewyn, M. B. Halbrich, and A. C. Perry, "Service Multinationals: Conceptualization, Measurement, and Theory," *Journal of International Business Studies*, Fall 1986, pp. 41–57.

17.   J. H. Dunning and M. McQueen, "The Eclectic Theory of Multinational Enterprise and the International Hotel Industry," in A. M. Rugman, ed., *New Theories of the Multinational Enterprise* (New York: St. Martin's Press, 1987), p. 103.

18.   See D. I. Riddle and M. H. Sours, "Service-Led Growth in the Pacific Basin," in W. C. Kim and P. K. Y. Young, eds., *The Pacific Challenge in International Business* (Ann Arbor, Mich.: U.M.I. Research Press, 1987), p. 226.

19.   Tucker and Sundberg, op. cit., p. 38; and P. K. Y. Young and W. C. Kim, "The Challenge of the Pacific Century," in W. C. Kim and P. K. Y. Young, eds., *The Pacific Challenge in International Business* (Ann Arbor, Mich.: U.M.I. Research Press, 1987), p. 11.

20.   See, for example, A. C. Gross, "The Information Vending Machine," *Business Horizons*, January–February 1988, pp. 24–33; Arossa, op. cit., pp. 13–16; and R. S. Greenberger, "East Meets Est: The Soviets Discover Werner Erhard," *Wall Street Journal*, December 3, 1986, pp. 1, 20.

21. Tucker and Sundberg, op. cit., p. 72.

22. For a more thorough discussion of industry sectors, structure, and trade performance, see Tucker and Sundberg, op. cit., chap. 4, on which the discussion of tourism as an international service sector is based.

23. The illustration in this and the following section is based on Tucker and Sundberg, op. cit., pp. 129–130.

24. "Tourists to and from Japan on Increase," *Business JAPAN*, July 1987, p. 45.

25. Riddle and Sours, op. cit., p. 237.

26. H. Weck-Hannemann and B. S. Frey, "Measuring the Shadow Economy: The Case of Switzerland," in W. Gaertner and A. Wenig, eds., *The Economics of the Shadow Economy* (Springer-Verlag, 1985), p. 100.

27. S. V. Sethuraman, ed., *The Urban Informal Sector in Developing Countries: Employment, Poverty, and Environment* (Geneva: International Labour Office, 1981), p. 8.

28. "Services Also Feeling Sting of Global Barriers," *Marketing News*, February 13, 1987, p. 1; see also Tucker, Seow, and Sundberg, op. cit.

29. P. E. Fong and M. Sundberg, "ASEAN-EEC Trade in Services: An Overview," in J. Waelbroeck, P. Praet, and H. C. Rieger, eds., *ASEAN-EEC Trade in Services* (Kuala-Lumpur, ISEAS, ASEAN Economic Research Unit, 1985), pp. 48–49.

30. "Conference: Services in World Trade," *Bulletin of Industry Economics* no. 4 (Canberra: Australian Government Publishing Service, 1988), p. 40.

31. McCullouch, op. cit., p. 21.

32. For a discussion of the impact of technology on banking, see Y. B. Quinn, "The Development of International Business by Australian Banks," *Australian Banker*, April 1988, pp. 42–45; see also K. Tucker, "Traded Services, Regulated Markets and Technological Change," in J. F. Brotchie, P. Hall, and P. W. Newton, eds., *The Spatial Impact of Technological Change* (London: Croom Helm, 1987), pp. 104–107.

33. See, for example, S. Fisher, "Law Firms Lured by Asia Business Boom," *Business Review Weekly*, April 29, 1988, p. 110.

34. "The Phantom in the Dark," *The Bulletin*, March 8, 1988, pp. 78–79.

35. A. C. Samli and R. Kosenko, "Support Service Is the Key for Technology Transfer to China," *Industrial Marketing Management*, April 1982, p. 95.

36. P. Wilson, "Daimaru Set to Shake Up Retail Giants," *The Courier-Mail* (Brisbane), April 19, 1988, p. 27.

37. Implications for the global management of service marketing are discussed in A. M. Rushton and D. J. Carson, "The Marketing of Services: Managing the Intangibles," *European Journal of Marketing* 19, no. 3 (1985):29–33.

38. K. David, "International Competitiveness in Construction and Computer Software: The Case of South Korea and India," in W. Kim and P. K. Y. Young, eds., *The Pacific Challenge in International Business* (Ann Arbor, Mich.: U.M.I. Research Press, 1987), pp. 245–284.

39. Boddewyn, Halbrich, and Perry, op. cit., p. 53.

40. McCullouch, op. cit., p. 2; and "Help Wanted from the Multinationals," *Business Week*, February 29, 1988, p. 36.

GATT AND SERVICES

Starting in the 1980s, there has been growing pressure to include services in the GATT framework. The Uruguay round of discussions considered a U.S. proposal for the "immediate and progressive liberalization" of trade in more than 100 service sectors. Developing countries have tended to oppose such an expansion, fearing that their fledgling service industries would be eliminated by foreign competition if barriers to service trade were lowered. These countries also take the position that developed countries would benefit from freer trade in services without providing any assistance to developing economies. Other critics argue that the United States dominates the world market in services, so it would be the chief beneficiary of lower barriers to trade in services.[1]

Some critics believe that it is premature to put services on the GATT agenda, in view of the unreliable data on international trade in services. At least one analyst has found that the types of service exports that are most likely to increase if trade barriers are lowered would result in only a modest increase in total U.S. exports. However, one reason for including services within the GATT framework is that some services are embodied in goods (indirect services). Barriers to trade in services act as nontariff barriers to international trade in goods.[2]

Despite current barriers, most industrialized nations are already major exporters and importers of services; the same is true of many developing nations. Trading in services is expected to increase. For developing economies, shifting technologies and competitive advantages might actually work to their advantage if barriers to trade in services are reduced. India, for example, has a large supply of well-qualified engineers. This resource, coupled with relatively low labor costs, is being applied effectively to service industries like computer software and telecommunications.

International air transport and shipping are governed by international conventions and agreements, and telecommunications are covered by regulations that address technical issues. In general, these agreements do not deal with barriers to trade. If there is to be a systematic, worldwide approach to the issue of barriers to trade in services, it will probably have to be carried out through GATT.

For trade in services to be brought within the GATT framework, a number of GATT articles and codes must be modified.[3] For example, under "most-favored-nation" guidelines, concessions to one trading partner are extended to all signers of GATT. It may be necessary to apply this code to services on a conditional basis, in order to protect the new service industries of developing nations. Another GATT code, "national treatment," requires that imported products, once they have entered the country, must be treated in the same way as the products of domestic firms. Currently, international banks are allowed to enter the U.S. market but are not allowed to engage in consumer or "retail" banking. If the national treatment rule were applied to services, foreign firms with an established presence in the United States might have an advantage over firms that seek to enter the U.S. market.

Another important GATT principle is "barriers at the border." The idea behind this principle is that when barriers are imposed on trade in goods, they should be imposed at the nation's borders. But most obstacles to trade in services are independent of national borders. Moreover, it is more difficult to identify, measure, and classify services than goods. Thus, this aspect of GATT may not be applicable to services.

In sum, given the general movement of the world economy toward increased integration and freer trade, it can be expected that the GATT framework will be expanded to include services, although the discussions required to accomplish this are likely to be complex and extensive.

NOTES

1. "Freeing Services," *The Economist*, October 28, 1989, pp. 19–76; for a review of the arguments presented by developing countries, see J. Bhagwati, "International Transactions in Services from a Developing Country Perspective," paper presented at the World Bank Symposium on Developing Countries' Interests and International Transactions in Services, 1987; see also R. K. Shelp, "Trade in Services," *Foreign Policy*, Winter 1986–1987, pp. 64–84.

2. R. McCullouch, "International Competition in Services," Working Paper no. 2235 (Cambridge, Mass.: National Bureau of Economic Research, 1987), pp. 11–12.

3. This section is based on J. D. Aronson and P. F. Cowhey, *Trade in Services: A Case for Open Markets* (Washington, D.C.: American Enterprise Institute, 1984), pp. 24–29.

IMPLEMENTING

AFTER THE FIRM BUILDS A GLOBAL MARKETING strategy and designs a product mix (Part Three) it must implement those marketing decisions, as we will see in Part Four. Implementation consists of building and executing tactics in the remaining elements of the marketing mix: distribution, communication, and price.

Distribution, or place, is the subject of Chapter 14. This chapter focuses on how to ensure that the product is in the right place at the right time, so that market exchange can occur. The global distribution process demands attention not only to the physical movement of a good, such as by ship or plane, but also to the varying macroenvironments discussed earlier in this text, in terms of how they affect distribution policies and channels.

Communication, or promotion, between the organization and its various publics, is the topic of Chapter 15. As one might expect, international promotion has many hazards for the unwary marketer. Environments such as culture, law, or economics have a major impact on what is suitable in an international promotional campaign and what is doomed to fail. Even the existence of familiar marketing communication techniques or media varies considerably across national boundaries. Promotion—in particular, advertising—is also one of the most visible elements of the marketing mix and thus subject to the most criticism. But the opportunities for pursuing a global approach to international promotion are considerable, and may present the firm with significant experience curve effects.

The final chapter in this section, Chapter 16, focuses on an important concern for international marketers: how to set a price that will help sell the product at a sufficient profit. Here again, international marketers face a wider set of issues than domestic marketers face. This chapter examines those issues, and discusses some of the different approaches an organization may take in establishing that key element in any marketing mix: the economic and non-economic price the customer must pay in exchange for a product.

GLOBAL DISTRIBUTION

"Pilot to Cabin Crew—Have the Cattle Fasten Their Seatbelts; We're Ready for Take Off"

Boeing 747 aircraft are longer than the distance of the Wright brothers' first flight in Kitty Hawk, North Carolina. Designed to carry hundreds of passengers, or tons of freight, they are technological breakthroughs that perhaps represent the tremendous changes in global distribution over recent years better than anything else.

The price of fresh beef was so high in Japan at one time, for example, that a 747 could be filled with cattle in Des Moines, Iowa, and flown to Tokyo at a profit. At another point, Porsche automobiles were flown from Germany to their dealers in the United States, as were daily shipments of car parts from other manufacturers. The list of goods that have been moved from one nation to another in 747s is quite long. Even with the higher cost of air freight, compared to sea freight, some high-value goods, for which inventory-carrying costs are also high, can be delivered at a lower cost through air freight.

Now 747s are also used to deliver services globally. For example, express delivery services, available in almost every developed country, use 747s to deliver letters and packages to other nations within a few days. Service providers and buyers—including students, consultants, tourists, and entertainers—fly around the world by the thousands either to buy services or deliver their own services to buyers.

Transportation technologies have improved from reed rafts through huge ships that even specialize in the products they transport (oil, sheep, or cars). Air travel has become faster and less expensive. Satellites and undersea cables provide global communication links among suppliers, buyers, and markets. As technology has permitted more efficient delivery of goods and services, the ability to conduct international trade has improved at the same time.

Before the sale of a good or service can actually be completed, the global marketer must have a global distribution system in place.

Every company must manage **distribution**, or the flow of products to final customers. In some cases distribution is relatively straightforward, as illustrated in Global Dimensions 14.1. The examples presented there may seem strange to readers who are familiar with distribution in highly developed countries, but they clearly show that any company's distribution system has two major components: (a) **distribution channels**, that is, the means by which goods are distributed, and (b) the tools and facilities that bridge the physical distance between the company and its customers. The company's **distribution system**, therefore, consists of all the people and organizations involved in transferring the good or service from the producer to the customer, including agents, dealers, wholesalers, and retailers, as well as all the tools and facilities used to carry out this process.

Two Simple Ways of Organizing Distribution

In the past, a brewery in Iraq put bottles filled with beer into cases, placed the cases on pallets, and transported them from the end of the production line to the fence surrounding the company's property. There, customers were waiting impatiently to purchase the product. They climbed to the top of the fence, where the cases were lifted up to them and the price was paid. The firm's distribution system consisted of a forklift and its driver.

A whiskey-bottling company in Nigeria has developed a different technique for bridging the physical and psychological distance between its production facilities and its customers. When its warehouse is full of bottles of whiskey, the company stops production. Employees, who had been engaged exclusively in filling the bottles, are then sent out to sell the whiskey to customers until the warehouse is empty again.

This chapter examines various types of distribution channels and discusses the advantages and disadvantages they offer to global marketers. Various market-entry alternatives, such as exporting or investment in sales offices, are not specifically considered here, as they were discussed in Chapter 10.

A global distribution system shares many characteristics with a domestic one. Both, for example, must make the product available to potential customers, help inform them about product benefits, manage distribution partner relationships, and be suited to the company's competitive position and overall marketing objectives. However, designing a global system is more complicated because it must take into account different geographic areas, the varying expectations of distribution partners, and the macroenvironments already discussed in previous chapters. This chapter addresses such factors and others that help determine the best distribution system for goods and services for a global marketing effort.

GLOBAL DISTRIBUTION POLICY

To design a distribution system that will prove effective, a company first needs a clearly defined distribution policy.

Many small and medium-sized companies are so overwhelmed by the complexity of global distribution that they simply conform to existing company procedures (which are likely to be inappropriate for international markets) or take advantage only of opportunities that arise by chance.[1] Even multinational corporations often leave specific distribution decisions to their local offices. In both cases there is a clear need to establish a global distribution policy.

A global distribution policy should reflect the company's overall goals and objectives in a set of specific distribution guidelines. Those guidelines help

Supermarkets in developed economies, such as this one in the U.S. (left), are a sharp contrast to the distribution system found in developing economies like India (right).

determine how much money and personnel will be committed to achieving a desired level of coverage in each market. The global distribution policy should also set market share, sales volume, and profit margin goals for each region, taking into account market-entry alternatives, the desired level of company involvement in the distribution system, and the desirability of ownership of intermediaries. These decisions significantly affect the level of market control achieved by the company and the quality of marketing in the targeted areas.

The desired level of market coverage has to be determined in light of the company's general competitive posture, its long-term market potential and expected return on investment, its financial strength, the positioning of strategic business units and products, and the geographic location of product markets. For example, mass-production companies and manufacturers of specialty items need different distribution policies. The mass-production company wants **intensive distribution**—that is, to be represented in as many outlets as possible. Coca-Cola is an example of a product that is distributed in this way. The producer of specialty items, on the other hand, may choose **selective** or **exclusive distribution.** It may severely limit the number of partners in the distribution channel, cooperating, for example, only with channel partners that are well suited to the product's intended positioning. Patek Philip, a Swiss producer of expensive watches, chooses a single renowned specialty shop in every large city to sell its products.

ALTERNATIVE DISTRIBUTION SYSTEMS

Goods may be distributed either directly or indirectly, depending on the product, market, and available distribution alternatives.

In general, there are two ways to distribute goods: directly to the final customer or indirectly through a more complex system that employs intermediaries. Producers of industrial goods often sell directly to their customers, using an internal sales force to initiate and maintain business relationships. Most manufacturers of consumer goods, on the other hand, sell to wholesalers or large retailers, which sell to other wholesalers and smaller retailers, which in turn sell to the final customer. In either case, distribution often becomes more complex when national boundaries are crossed. This section describes both direct (integrated) and indirect (independent or company-bound) distribution systems.

Integrated Distribution

A firm interested in maximizing its control of the distribution function would choose an integrated system.

In an **integrated distribution system** the company's own employees generate sales, administer orders, and deliver products or services. The distribution system is integrated because employees, whatever their title or function within the company, are the agents of distribution. Several variables determine which employees are most directly involved in generating sales; they include the company's size, the size of the potential market, the importance of customer services, the complexity of the product, and the means by which customers are contacted.

Large turnkey plant projects, for example, are normally negotiated by employees, but the final negotiations and the signing of the contract are done by top management, because they often involve high-level government customers or top managers in the purchasing organization. At the other extreme, salespeople will handle the entire selling process if their customers are simply purchasing agents. The salespeople may report directly to the company's home office, but often visit customers in foreign markets; or they may operate out of subsidiaries or sales offices in different geographic areas. HILTI, a leading manufacturer of drilling equipment, for example, is dedicated to direct selling. Salespeople throughout the world operate from what the company calls "market organizations," that is, regional sales and service offices.

Marketers can also sell goods or services directly to the final customer through manufacturer-owned stores or showrooms, or by means of mail-order, telephone, or electronic marketing. (See Global Dimensions 14.2.) For example, sales clerks may use the telephone or a computer to establish and maintain contact with customers.

Independent and Company-Bound Distribution

Firms with company-bound or independent distribution systems use intermediaries to get their products to their customers.

Independent distribution systems are not directly controlled by the organization. The company uses intermediaries to establish contact with the final customers. In domestic as well as global marketing, there are basically two types of intermediaries: agents and merchants.

Agents (in domestic marketing they are often called **manufacturers' representatives**) fully represent the company (also called **the principal**) in a particular market. They operate in the name of the principal, but they do not take title to the products being distributed, nor do they bear any economic risks.

Merchants, in contrast, do take title to the goods, which they buy, handle, and sell on their own account. In domestic marketing, they are commonly referred to as **distributors** or **wholesalers**. Through merchants' activities, time, place, finance, and service utilities are added to the product bundle.

Special Forms of Integrated Distribution

A system of stores owned by the manufacturer is a type of distribution channel that is usually available only to financially strong companies. This approach may also be used when all other distribution channels are blocked or when the company's marketing strategy is based on direct contact with the final customer.

Mail-order selling is a distribution system that is becoming increasingly important in global marketing. A number of specialized companies operate internationally; they include Great Universal Stores, headquartered in England, and Quelle Versand, headquartered in Germany. Manufacturers of high-tech industrial products sometimes use this approach. For example, Wild-Leitz, a Liechtenstein-based company specializing in opto-electronics, sends catalogs to customers to sell standard products and spare parts.

Telephone selling, or telephone marketing, can be used in two ways. Potential customers may be called to generate leads for the field salesforce. Or existing customers may be called to sell products, promote new services, and collect information.

Electronic markets exist for both consumer and industrial goods and services in the most developed economies. These computer-based systems provide customers with product offers and information, service, and billing with the help of a video screen and a printer. One such system, Videotext, is an interactive information service that allows users to request product or company information from a central data bank, which contains information supplied by participating companies, and to order products or services.

Companies that use intermediaries but largely control them are said to have **company-bound distribution systems**. A more complete discussion of the types of intermediaries that global marketers use is provided in the appendix to this chapter. In most cases the intermediaries in a distribution channel are a mixture of the types described.

Integrated versus Independent Distribution

An integrated system provides several advantages for the company.

The following conditions favor an integrated distribution system:

- Specialized product or product use knowledge
- A high level of service requirements
- A highly differentiated product
- The product is closely related to the company's principal business

For example, with complex products such as IBM mainframe computers, marketing success depends on specialized product or application knowledge. With automobile marketers, a high level of service is necessary, especially after the sale. Specialty steels are examples of products that are highly differentiated or unique from competitors' products. In each of these cases, the firm is likely to select an integrated distribution system,[2] because only company employees may be able to acquire the know-how that is necessary to adequately serve customers, or only they can ensure close contact with customers and aggressive sales support when the product is very important to the company's principal business.

An integrated distribution system, or channel, facilitates corporate control and motivation of channel members. A channel member who is a company employee can readily monitor distribution activities and use the authority of the company to influence the behavior of distribution personnel.[3] For an integrated distribution system to be successful, the company must know what customers expect in terms of delivery time, product modifications, personal contact, and the like. Then it must ensure that it hires personnel who are willing and able to meet those expectations.[4]

An integrated distribution system has drawbacks as well as advantages. Legal restrictions on foreign investment may prevent marketers from using such a system. But the major disadvantage of integrated distribution is its high cost. Sales managers and salespeople must be hired and trained. The sales organization is likely to lose money during the first few years in a new market, because sales volume will not be sufficient to cover overhead costs. For these reasons, most companies that are expanding into foreign markets at least initially choose a company-bound or independent distribution system. Also, when a company competes in a mature product category, direct competition by similar products is likely to be strong. Low costs and prices are crucial to success. In such a situation most companies use nonintegrated distribution.[5] The tendency to choose independent distribution partners is reinforced by sociocultural differences between domestic and nondomestic markets. Such a choice may be reasonable, because transferring title to an independent channel member also transfers risk.

From the customer's perspective, however, an independent distribution system may be entirely wrong. The use of independent distributors reduces the company's opportunities to become familiar with the specific characteristics of the new market, thereby limiting its ability to offer a product that meets the market's needs. Independent distributors may also be a problem because they have considerable freedom to establish local marketing policies. Moreover, independent distributors' loyalty to the manufacturer is likely to be limited, because they may carry a wide range of products, from different manufacturers, and they naturally will favor those that yield the greatest sales and profits. To overcome these problems, some firms only work with distributors who will focus exclusively on their product lines. This can only be done, however, if the product line is broad enough to generate sufficient sales volume for the distributor, and the profit margins are attractive.

In general, companies tend to develop a global distribution system that reflects their domestic distribution channels. For example, Tissot, a Swiss marketer of watches, may have a strategy of appealing to a mass market interested in high quality, using as many jewelry stores—which are numerous in Switzerland—as possible. Often a similar distribution system does not exist in another

Warner-Lambert, the marketer of Schick razors, Trident and Chiclets gum, and pharmaceutical products, has succeeded in Japan by using distinct distribution systems for each set of product lines. Schick razors and blades are sold through the Hatori trading organization, which in turn sells Schick products through independent wholesalers that provide considerable service to retailers. The result is Schick's 70 percent share of the market in Japan for stainless-steel razor blades.

When Warner-Lambert tried a similar system for its chewing gum, it failed. Not satisfied with the wholesalers' efforts, Lambert tried to bypass them. This change made wholesalers mad and retailers suspicious about a company switching business tactics. Warner-Lambert then successfully used its own salesforce to obtain orders from retailers and passed the orders back to the wholesalers, resulting in a 17 percent share of the Japanese gum market.

Warner-Lambert has been manufacturing pharmaceutical products in Japan since 1960, and selling them directly to large drug companies there. Warner-Lambert's gelatin capsules have achieved a 40 percent share of this market, largely because its high level of quality control has won the loyalty of a few large customers.

Source: Based on "Corporate Performance," *Fortune*, April 14, 1986.

national market, however. In such situations management must determine whether a different distribution channel can be used without departing radically from the overall corporate strategy. For example, an Italian manufacturer of high-fashion, high-priced knitwear considering a new market may find that there are not enough prestigious specialty shops in that market. To achieve sufficient market coverage, the company must look for other outlets. If appropriate alternatives cannot be found, the firm might decide not to enter the market, or it might enter it under a different brand name. Companies that are successful in global markets generally rely on a mix of different, more or less integrated distribution channels. For an example, see Global Dimensions 14.3.

GLOBAL CHANNEL EVALUATION

Making the appropriate choice among the distribution options available in foreign markets requires an understanding of the ways in which each might contribute to the goals and objectives of the distribution policy. The marketer must consider a range of factors and develop a set of selection criteria, a process that is discussed in this section.

Customer Characteristics

Customer characteristics are the first criteria to consider in evaluating which channel is best for the firm in a given market.

An evaluation of distribution methods for a particular geographic area must consider the number of potential customers and their location, purchasing power, and specific needs. For example, in analyzing the U.S. market a European manufacturer of furniture fittings would find a considerable concentration of furniture manufacturers in North Carolina and South Carolina. It therefore would be likely to choose either an integrated distribution system with a sales office in the Carolinas or an intermediary that is familiar with the major customers and handles complementary product lines.

The purchasing habits of potential customers also affect distribution decisions. Dannon yogurt is distributed differently in the United States, Asia, and Europe because of the different purchasing habits of customers in those areas. In France and Germany, Dannon uses self-service discount stores with spacious fresh-food areas and large assortments of general merchandise. These stores, which occupy as much as 250,000 square feet of space and have up to 100 checkout counters, serve as major outlets for dairy products. However, it would be impossible for Dannon to rely on such outlets in Hong Kong, where 83 percent of the homemakers shop once a day and buy most of their food either in a street market or an urban shopping mall.[6] The main reason for these differences is variations in the cultural and economic environments.[7] Turkish consumers, for example, prefer fresh products that have just been harvested, while Saudis require that poultry and meat be slaughtered in accordance with the Islamic practice of *Sharia*; in both countries supermarkets are unpopular.[8] Supermarkets are also relatively unpopular in India, where most people are unable to afford cars or refrigerators.

Intermediary Characteristics

Analyzing the strengths and weaknesses of intermediaries is important when choosing a distribution channel.

Functions. Any evaluation of potential distribution partners in a foreign market must be based on an analysis of the responsibilities, or functions, of both the distributing agents and the company itself. (See Exhibit 14.1). The same title may imply different responsibilities, depending on the location. Therefore, it is necessary to find out what an intermediary's title actually means in each market. It is necessary to determine the extent to which an intermediary can take over the physical handling of goods. This is especially important for companies with little or no nondomestic experience. In addition, intermediaries can assist in promoting and selling the product, as well as providing services to local customers. They can help build and maintain the goodwill of government agencies and members of the local community. Finally, intermediaries often take over part of the financing and bear some of the risk of the distribution process.

Structure. The structure of a distribution channel is characterized by the number of product lines carried, the number and types of intermediaries in the channel, and the relationships (or networks) among manufacturers, channel

EXHIBIT 14.1
FUNCTIONS
POTENTIALLY
PERFORMED BY
MIDDLEMEN

Middlemen perform four basic functions. Each of the functions has subfunctions, which would still need to be performed even if the middlemen were eliminated from the distribution channel.

Physical handling of products

Importing the product

Arranging for customs clearance

Providing warehousing facilities

Maintaining a certain inventory level

Performing break-bulk operations

Adapting parts of the product to local needs

Assembling parts

Performing or overseeing delivery

Promotion, sales, and service activities

Obtaining and maintaining a certain level of sales effort

Service levels

Existing customers

Management of business relationships

Building and holding good will of business-community members

Building and maintaining the necessary relationships with governmental agencies

Financing and risk taking

Providing foreign payment exchange

Financing the distribution process

Assuming certain business risks

members, and government agencies. The **length of a distribution channel** is characterized by the number of levels and types of intermediaries in the channel. As a rule of thumb, the more economically developed a country, the shorter the distribution channels in that country. In Europe, for example, there is a trend toward the formation of voluntary chains of retailers sponsored by wholesalers like Intersport. A similar trend toward the vertical integration of wholesalers is occurring in Japan.[9]

As the Japanese system shows, however, a country's level of economic development is not the only factor that determines the length of distribution channels. High population density may create a shortage of storage space, which in turn requires low levels of inventory and frequent deliveries. This situation results in more intermediaries in the distribution channel. Thus, "Papa-Mama" stores in Japan account for 56 percent of retail sales, compared to 3 percent in the United States and 5 percent in Europe. In addition, the ratio of wholesalers to retailers is four times higher in Japan than in the United States.[10]

The **width of a distribution channel** is determined by the number of each type of intermediary in the channel. The larger the number of similar

intermediaries in a market, the greater the width of the channel and, consequently, the higher the level of competition. High channel width should make
it easier for a marketer to find adequate distribution partners.

Intermediaries carry different numbers and assortments of product lines.
For example, the Japanese *sogo shosha* import and export products ranging from
consumer electronics to steel. They are also involved in financing, banking, and
other services associated with those products. The global marketing manager
should be aware that intermediaries handling broad product lines are interested
mainly in mass markets. If a conflict of interest arises between the marketer's
product and those of other manufacturers, a *sogo shosha* will put more energy
into distributing the products of manufacturers with which it has a long-estab-
lished relationship or in which it holds a financial interest.[11]

Networks.   A company that seeks to establish a distribution channel in a new
market must deal with an existing network of relationships. Because the network
is already functioning with products, sellers, and buyers, a variety of problems
may arise. If, for example, the producer of a competitive product is related to
the wholesalers or retailers, or owns the channels, entry is made more difficult.
Governments may control access to the channels, in order to control which
goods are marketed. Or access may be allowed to one part of the channel, but
effectively barred through regulation or practice from another level, which of
course limits the channel's usefulness to the marketer. It is imperative, therefore,
that the marketer understand the structure of the existing network.

Channel ownership by local competitors can be a major problem for new
firms entering the market. For example, in Japan most of the wholesalers of
household electrical appliances are owned by only four manufacturers. A similar
situation exists for other products; in 1982 approximately 70 percent of all electronics retailers were tightly controlled by Matsushita, Hitachi, and Toshiba,
while the six largest producers of cosmetics controlled 70 percent of all cosmetics
retailers.[12] But changes are occurring. Retailers are including new brands in
their assortments, and new distribution channels, such as party and door-to-
door selling, are developing.

Distribution channels may be blocked because competitors have well-
established product lines and exclusive contracts with existing channel members.
This is the case in some European beer markets, for example. Competitors also
may have divided the market—and, hence, **channel power,** the ability to control activity within the channel—among them by forming cartels. Powerful
trade associations may have lobbied successfully to restrict channel alternatives
or to close them to new entrants. Thus, many European countries protect the
owners of small shops by regulating the placement of stores. In Sweden, for
instance, town planners decide on the location of retail outlets, so that thinly
populated areas, as well as elderly and handicapped customers, will be served.

A marketer faced with these kinds of obstacles can find ways to get around
them. One possibility is to choose an innovative distribution channel. Fran-

chising and mail-order and electronic marketing are among the possible alternatives to traditional channels. In one case, Italian refrigerator manufacturers began selling their products through discount stores and mail-order businesses in Germany at a time when their German competitors were selling their own products exclusively through specialty stores and department stores. By the time the German manufacturers recognized the threat, the Italians had already captured a considerable share of the market.

The marketer can also look for ways to diversify channels. One way is to find distribution partners that want to broaden their product lines with complementary products. That was Sony's goal when it established its "life-style shops" in Japan, for example. It is also possible to team up with other wholesalers or retailers that have been excluded from the distribution networks. In addition, new channels are always being created—supermarket or department store chains, for instance, or groups of hotels and restaurants—providing new distribution opportunities. It may also be possible to "piggyback" onto a new market by using a distribution channel established by a friendly company located in the firm's home market. To facilitate its entry into the U.S. market, a Swiss producer of high-fashion sun glasses, for example, could use the distribution channel, consisting of a number of wholesalers and jewelry stores established by a cooperating manufacturer of watches.

Other means of circumventing obstacles to market entry include offering higher margins to channel members than are offered by competitors, special bonuses, or other kinds of financial incentives. However, U.S. companies must be careful not to violate the Foreign Corrupt Practices Act, which prohibits specific types of payments that facilitate business activity in international markets.[13]

A company may also consider buying equity in an intermediary. In Japan, banks are used for this purpose, because they are closely linked with the large industry groups through joint ownership and serving as board directors. With their assistance a foreign company can gain an equity share in a Japanese intermediary; in most cases a 10 percent share will enable the company to become part of an existing distribution network.

Power Relationships.   The distribution of power between producers and intermediaries varies from one country to another and from one product market to another. (See, for example, Exhibit 14.2.) These power relationships affect the marketer's ability to control the implementation of distribution strategies at each level of the channel. In France, for example, the seven largest retail agents for supermarkets control more than 80 percent of the market. Since a limited number of retailers effectively control access to supermarkets, they have enormous power over producers' strategies. Producers and marketers, for example, may have to provide special programs and support fees before the retailer will agree to stock their product. Such funds would not, therefore, be available to spend on consumer advertising.

EXHIBIT 14.2
POWER
RELATIONSHIPS IN
JAPANESE CHANNELS
OF DISTRIBUTION

The power relationships
that exist in Japanese
distribution channels de-
pend on the degree of
brand loyalty and the
consumption rate. For ex-
ample, TV sets have high
brand loyalty and a low
consumption rate. They
fall into the category
where major producers
act as "channel cap-
tains." *Diverse power
structure* means that no
single distribution chan-
nel exists; thus control of
the channel is difficult for
producers or
intermediaries.

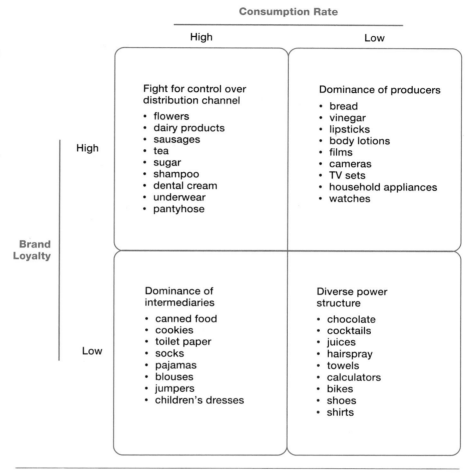

	Consumption Rate	
	High	**Low**
High (Brand Loyalty)	**Fight for control over distribution channel** • flowers • dairy products • sausages • tea • sugar • shampoo • dental cream • underwear • pantyhose	**Dominance of producers** • bread • vinegar • lipsticks • body lotions • films • cameras • TV sets • household appliances • watches
Low	**Dominance of intermediaries** • canned food • cookies • toilet paper • socks • pajamas • blouses • jumpers • children's dresses	**Diverse power structure** • chocolate • cocktails • juices • hairspray • towels • calculators • bikes • shoes • shirts

Source: Adapted from M. Tamura, "Distribution and Marketing in Japan," in H. Simon, ed., *Marketfold in Japan* (Wiesbaden, Germany: Gabler, 1988), p. 273.

SELECTION OF CHANNEL MEMBERS

The process of selecting distribution-channel members starts with the development of a list of potential candidates, using information obtained from secondary sources. Then the candidates are asked whether they are interested in
acting as intermediaries for the company. Those that express interest are interviewed, and the interviews are used as a basis for the selection of appropriate
distribution partners.

Selection Criteria

After selection criteria
are determined, chan-
nel members are
selected to match the
ideal as closely as
possible.

Ideally, an intermediary will resemble the most effective members of the company's existing distribution channels. The following criteria are useful in selecting channel members:

- Control of activities within channel
- Capital required and costs to be covered
- Adequate coverage of the market
- Compatibility between firm and channel member
- Continuity of functions provided by channel member
- Distance between firm and channel member

Because no single candidate is likely to meet all of the firm's criteria, the marketer will probably have to make trade-offs among the characteristics of various potential distribution partners. Two of the criteria important in the selection of intermediaries—costs and distance—are discussed below.

Costs.   Two kinds of costs are important in implementing a distribution channel: the capital costs of establishing the channel and the costs of maintaining it. Maintaining costs include the direct costs of the firm's integrated distribution channels plus margins, markups, commissions, and other forms of compensation to channel members, whether integrated or independent. In addition, the costs of the management systems needed to manage the distribution channels have to be considered. These costs will vary over the life of a distribution relationship.

Distance.   The distance between a marketer and a potential channel member has five dimensions: geographic, social, cultural, technological, and temporal.[14] (See Exhibit 14.3.) Geographic distance is the physical distance separating the two partners. Social distance stems from lack of familiarity with the partner's

EXHIBIT 14.3
EXAMPLES OF THE
DISTANCES BETWEEN
MARKETERS AND
DISTRIBUTION-
CHANNEL MEMBERS

The global marketer and
channel members must
bridge various types of
distances in order to
have a close working
relationship.

Distance	Example
Geographic	San Francisco to Seoul
Social	In France August is largely a vacation month
Cultural	Profit is a primary motivator in the United States; loyalty is a primary motivator in Japan.
Technological	Exports from Chad are perceived as inferior to exports from West Germany
Temporal	The length of time between order placement and delivery (now, thanks to telecommunication systems such as fax machines, this distance is reduced).

operating methods. Cultural distance reflects differences in values, norms, and behavior. Technological distance is described in terms of the competitiveness, compatibility, and quality of product lines currently carried by potential intermediaries, as well as differences in product experience and process technologies. Temporal distance is measured by the length of time between placement of an order and delivery of the product. The shorter the distance between manufacturer and potential distribution partner, the better the candidate.

Finding Intermediaries

To find the best intermediary, the firm must become directly involved in the search process.

In most cases, a company that wishes to enter a foreign market should take an active role in selecting intermediaries. Although contacts with intermediaries can arise from unsolicited orders or contacts at trade shows, the firm would be well advised to follow a series of systematic steps in investigating potential distribution partners. Those steps are described below.

Secondary Information Sources.   The first step is to locate secondary sources of information about intermediaries. The marketer should investigate these sources before traveling to other geographic areas to gather firsthand information. Sources of information about potential distribution-channel members are listed in Exhibit 14.4. The U.S. government will supply specific information for a small fee; the relevant agencies are listed in Exhibit 14.5.

An important source of information is intermediaries used by competitors. They are already familiar with the product and the market, and they have an established organization to deal with potential customers. However, there are risks associated with using intermediaries that are serving competitors. First, if an intermediary does not change its alliance, it may provide competitors with information about the firm's product line. Second, the intermediary may accept a new product line and maintain the competitor's line simply to drive the new line out of the market. And third, the intermediary may negotiate with a new competitor at any time. For these reasons, it may be safer to choose intermediaries that handle complementary products. They have an established organization and contact with potential customers, together with the necessary technical proficiency and knowledge of the local market.

On-Site Visits.   An on-site visit is the best way to determine a potential partner's requirements and establish an effective working relationship.[15] Interviewing final customers in the target market is also an excellent means to find a good channel partner. It helps the marketer discover which distribution channels are preferred and why.[16] The marketer may also learn the names of appropriate intermediaries in this way.

Evaluation.   Using the information gathered from secondary sources and on-site visits, the global marketer creates a short list of appropriate candidates. Before entering into a contract with any candidate, the marketer should obtain

EXHIBIT 14.4
SOURCES OF
INFORMATION ON
POTENTIAL
DISTRIBUTION-
CHANNEL MEMBERS

This exhibit illustrates the
information sources a
marketer can consult
when evaluating potential
distribution-channel
members.

Governmental agencies

Trade organizations in the host country

Local chamber of commerce

Home-country trade representatives in the host country

Banks

Related companies (customers, agencies, carriers)

Own sales force

Listings of industry members

Industry or trade journals and magazines

Trade fairs

Answers to advertisements, direct mail, and personal correspondence

Independent consultants

Listings of industry members can be found in telephone directories (yellow-page section) and trade directories. They normally are organized by geographical criteria and product categories. Very often they are incomplete and out of date, however, with new and small intermediaries missing.

Advertisements in trade journals and newspapers soliciting representation are more direct approaches to the problem. Advertisements have the disadvantage that their response rate is generally small, and they often attract the weakest and most unreliable potential intermediaries.

Direct mail and *personal correspondence* can be addressed to names on a mailing list derived from directories or government sources, such as the U.S. government's Foreign Traders Index.

Trade fairs can be used to look for intermediaries and analyze their business behavior in action.

additional information on its business conduct and credit reliability from such sources as banks, carriers, consultants, and trade organizations. (See Exhibit 14.4.)

Selection.   The marketer then sends selected candidates a letter inquiring about their interest in becoming a member of the company's distribution channel. The letter should contain an extensive description of the products to be carried, an explanation of the firm's general marketing policy and strategy, and a statement of its specific goals in the intermediary's market. The interested intermediary should be asked to describe the market from its point of view; the description should include major customers and competitors, an estimate of the firm's potential market share and sales volume within a specified period, and the marketing strategy necessary to achieve those objectives.

The Contract.   The contract must be drawn up and reviewed in detail before being signed. Because of differences in legal regulations between different coun-

New Product Information Service (NPIS)
Provides global publicity for new U.S. products
Trade Opportunities Program (TOP)
Matches middlemen interests indicated by the U.S. company with product searches of
  nondomestic buyers
Foreign Traders Index (FTI)
Contains data on more than 150,000 potential middlemen, as well as final customers
  from 143 countries
Agent/Distributor Service (ADS)
Contacts up to six middlemen prospects in the countries designated by the firm and
  determines their interest in corresponding with the firm
World Traders Data Report (WTDR)
Provides general narrative reports on the reliability of the potential middlemen
  indicated by the firm, as well as a profile of their existing product line(s)

tries, the global marketer should seek the advice of a legal specialist in the
intermediary's market. For example, the contract-termination conditions, including
just causes of termination (such as deceit, fraud, damage to the other party's
interests, or failure to comply with contractual obligations), must be spelled out
carefully.

Even with explicit contract specifications, termination of a contract is time-
consuming, often expensive, and in some cases impossible. In Japan, for example, terminating a contract with a business partner means breaking a strong
commitment; it can be very difficult to find another partner. In most European
countries, termination, even with just cause, will cost the firm the equivalent
of a year's commission as compensation for the intermediary's efforts to build
market share. Thus, it is imperative that the marketer conduct an extremely
thorough investigation before signing a contract with a distribution partner.

MANAGING CHANNEL RELATIONSHIPS

Careful management of relationships with intermediaries is critical to success in
global marketing. Distribution can be viewed as an exchange system that incorporates many interdependent organizations, each with its own objectives. Only
when the transactions satisfy the needs of both partners will the relationship
between them remain stable and marketing objectives be achieved.

Organization

In order for the distri-
bution channel to func-
tion properly, an orga-
nizational structure
must be in place to
help manage channel
relationships.

The company must develop an appropriate organizational structure to manage
channel relationships. These relationships can be quite complex; personal contacts between a supplier's and an intermediary's staff may span several levels of

the organization and involve employees in the company's sales, service, design, manufacturing, and quality-control departments. Channel relationships therefore represent a considerable investment of human resources in information exchange, negotiations, transfer of technical knowledge, and social bonding.[17] The company must take care not to allocate too great a share of organizational resources to domestic distribution partners and the most cooperative intermediaries at the expense of building satisfactory relationships with more distant and difficult ones. (Organization is discussed further in Chapter 17.)

Motivation

The intermediary must be able to make money by handling the product; otherwise it will have little interest in maintaining a relationship with the supplier. Higher margins, larger commissions, or more advantageous credit terms have traditionally served as ways of motivating distribution partners. However, these inducements are less important to channel members than the amount they derive from the selling process. Therefore, a global marketer that does not want to sacrifice profits should offer the usual margin percentages and, at the same time, help intermediaries increase the turnover of products through intensive promotion and/or sell the product at a higher average price by providing a more attractive and better-positioned product line.

Assistance to intermediaries in the form of personnel training, technical assistance, special product displays, and advertising and public relations materials may increase the intermediary's selling effectiveness. Some companies even provide sales personnel to assist retailers. In Japan, for example, many department store salespeople are paid by wholesalers rather than by the retailer.

Communication

Global distribution channels require intensive communication to ensure that the activities of channel members conform to the company's global strategy. Communication efforts may be personal (visits, telephone calls, or telexes) or impersonal (as in periodic corporate newsletters or magazines). International and regional meetings can also be used for transmitting product information, planning, or simply exchanging experiences.

Visits play an important role in reinforcing the personal bonds between distribution partners. So do personnel exchanges. These techniques may be used to resolve problems before they escalate and damage trust. For this reason, Honda USA's Japanese managers decided to spend up to 50 percent of their working time visiting and talking with distributors and dealers in the United States.

Control

Visits can also serve a control function without being obtrusive. Isao Makino, president of Toyota's U.S. sales subsidiary from 1975 to 1983 (a difficult period for the company), visited every Toyota dealer in the United States at least once a year.

To control the activities of channel members and avoid conflict, the marketer must ensure that its corporate objectives are clearly communicated to intermediaries. Performance standards based on those objectives may include sales volume per product or product line within a specified period; inventory level; market share; and number of accounts per sales territory. Communication objectives are influenced by the promotional efforts of channel members; those efforts, therefore, must be assessed from the standpoint of their contribution to the desired global corporate identity as well as their contribution to the intermediary's objectives. This assessment should be conducted jointly to avoid differences in interpretation.

GLOBAL PHYSICAL DISTRIBUTION

The role of physical distribution is to make sure the product is where it should be, when it should be.

Physical distribution includes customer service, inventory management, warehousing, storage, shipping and receiving, transportation, and all associated documentation. The physical distribution of products and services is increasingly recognized as an important strategic tool in global marketing. Such factors as rapid delivery and reliable sources of supply often outweigh competitive pricing in the struggle for customers.[18]

The distribution manager, working within the framework of the company's basic strategy, must be concerned with the optimal combination of costs for the global movement of goods. This means that the physical-distribution process must be administered in such a way as to minimize total costs while providing a satisfactory level of customer service. Low inventory levels entail the risk of providing less than satisfactory customer service. Better service may require improved storage and transport facilities. The decision maker must take such trade-offs into consideration in attempting to achieve the company's goals.

Customer Service

Customer service expectations may have an impact on channel design and management decisions.

The level of customer service provided by a global marketer in nondomestic markets tends to be lower than that provided in its domestic market, because of factors like geographic distance, errors in transmitting and filling orders, inadequate packaging and preparation for shipment, transportation problems, and delays in clearing customs. Time in transit can vary significantly from one shipment to the next because different carriers may be involved, multiple transfers of goods may be necessary, and numerous national boundaries may have to be crossed.

However, it is possible to maintain a level of customer service in global markets that is as high as or even higher than the level maintained in domestic markets. In particular, a global marketer can achieve an advantage in customer service when the company establishes its own distribution facilities in foreign markets or when existing distribution systems in those markets work faster than those in the domestic market.[19] Some manufacturers establish plants in non-domestic markets in order to achieve a more predictable distribution schedule.

Service delivery is also affected by differences in available infrastructures. Automatic teller machines are popular in the United States and are used to deliver many kinds of banking services. But in most parts of Europe the machines are limited to cash dispersion. And in most parts of Africa such a distribution system for banking services does not exist.

It is not advisable for a global marketer to attempt to maintain the same level of customer service in all markets. Like product quality, the quality of customer service is a subjective phenomenon that depends on customers' perceptions. Therefore, the company may specify a general service level in qualitative terms, adapting its physical-distribution system to the local service requirements in each market.

Packaging

The following factors influence the packaging of goods for global distribution.

- Handling necessity and ease
- Damage during transportation
- Climate
- Pilferage
- Customers' requirements
- Freight rates
- Customs duties
- Communication

While it may seem that packaging's most important role is to help sell the product, packaging must play several roles and make many contributions if global marketing is to be successful.

The U.S. Carriage of Goods by Sea Act makes the shipper responsible for appropriate packaging to protect products from damage. The marketer therefore must pay special attention to handling characteristics in package design. The development of containers is playing a major role globally in fulfilling the protective function of packaging. Containers make it possible to keep the weight of the actual package relatively low. At the same time, the container protects the product against climatic influences, damage during transit, and pilferage. In general, protection is even more necessary in international shipping than in most domestic markets.

To keep freight costs down, the marketer must use transportation equipment and warehouses as efficiently as possible. This may require adaptations in package design. For example, high stacks of products in containers or warehouses can be used only when the package is constructed so as to resist pressure.

The following example illustrates the importance of appropriate packaging. A Western European manufacturer sent four truckloads of plastic extruders to Iran, using the pallets (wooden platforms on which several extruders are loaded together) that are normally used in its domestic market. Shortly after the arrival of the merchandise, the marketer received a telex from the customer's bank stating that 90 percent of the cargo was damaged or did not work. A group of service engineers sent to find out the cause discovered that the customer had neither a forklift nor a crane to use in unloading the trucks. The workers had simply pushed the pallets to the side of the truck and let them fall to the floor; thus the product on the pallet also fell on the floor.

Transportation

The choice of a transportation method depends on the availability of transportation, total costs, and global distribution objectives.

The global marketer must evaluate the existing transportation infrastructures in the geographic areas it wishes to serve. These will differ from one country to another, as will the forms of transportation services available and their cost. U.S. retailers, for example, rely heavily on trucking services to deliver goods to retailers, whereas in some areas of India, goods are delivered in carts drawn by animals or humans.

The choice among the basic transportation modes—surface, water, and air—depends on total costs, transit time, reliability (including loss and damage rates as well as punctuality), and the level of customer service required in a specific market. The marketer should bear in mind that transportation costs may influence the competitiveness of a product in a particular market, especially when the price per unit of weight is low (as in the case of concrete). But for high-value products with high inventory-carrying costs, such as large computers, the total costs of distribution will be lower if a faster, though more expensive, mode of transportation like air freight is used.

Transit time determines the level of inventory required in the markets to which goods are being transported. For perishable and seasonal products, and especially for fashion goods, this can be a decisive factor in successful marketing. Fresh flowers exported to the United States from Colombia, Israel, and The Netherlands, for example, are highly perishable and therefore are flown to wholesale markets in the United States each day.

The reliability of transportation affects the level of "safety" inventory that must be maintained. It is especially important when marketing success depends on precise delivery dates and when a high unit price makes damage or loss very expensive.

The most important mode of transportation in global marketing is by *water*. Exhibit 14.6 presents an overview of the types of vessels available and the services provided. Water transport is advantageous when markets are characterized by extensive coastlines and heavily populated coastal regions. For example, about half of Australia's population is located in the crescent between Brisbane and Adelaide, which is readily accessible by ocean freight.

On the other hand, water transportation requires an extensive transpor-

EXHIBIT 14.6
TYPES OF WATER
TRANSPORT VESSELS
AND SERVICES
PROVIDED

Different vessels and
their shipping routes vary
considerably, and must
be accounted for in a
global distribution
decision.

Cargo liners
Carry general cargo over predetermined routes with scheduled times of departure and
   arrival

Bulk carriers
Offer contractual services over extended periods of time or for individual voyages

Tramp vessels
Scheduled on demand on irregular routes

Container ships
Transport containers of standard sizes on regular routes

Break-bulk ships
Traditionally designed ships with their own cranes and cargo-handling equipment
   (particularly well suited for small ports in LCDs)

Ro/Ro ships
Allow trucks to deposit their containers in the cargo space

Lighter-aboard ships (LASH)
Store barges by crane and lower them at the point of destination

Source: Adapted from H. P. Gray, "International Transportation," in I. Walter and T. Murray, eds.,
Handbook of International Business (New York: John Wiley & Sons, 1982), pp. 11.3–11.18.

tation infrastructure to move goods from the ship to the customer. Port facilities
in less-developed countries often lack the equipment to handle modern vessels.
Even countries with large ports may have an inadequate internal transportation
system, with the result that cargos may remain on vessels or docks for weeks or
even months before they can be transported to their final destinations.

   Rail transportation is important in countries where roads are poor or railroad
companies are heavily subsidized by the government. All of southeastern Africa,
for example, depends on a single railroad line leading from the coast of Mozambique to the mineral-rich inland countries. This line is so important to the
economy of the area that the industrialized nations agreed to contribute significantly to the costs of its reconstruction after it was destroyed by rebels during
a political coup.

   Truck transportation can overcome the problems of inefficient or overloaded
port facilities and the lack of adequate railroad lines. For example, Swedish
machinery and Austrian fruit juices are trucked to Saudi Arabia, where even
the truck may be sold (because it is more economical than supporting an empty
return trip) after having discharged its load. Because of the flexibility of truck
transportation, this mode of transport is becoming increasingly popular in Europe.
Each day 5,000 trucks use the Brenner Autobahn between Munich and the
industrial centers of northern Italy.

   Planned restrictions on truck shipping in the European Community—a
result of pollution and noise—have led to the development of mixed transportation modes using roll-on/roll-off cars or special rail containers. The containers
are loaded at the shipper's facilities, set on trucks going to the nearest rail terminal, and then loaded onto trains which go as near as possible to their desti-

nation. There they are picked up by other trucks to be transported to their final destination. Once the goods have been loaded into the containers, no other handling is required along the entire route.

Shipment by *air* reduces transportation time and the need to maintain a large inventory. In many cases air freight, despite its higher cost, is necessary for successful marketing. For example, Rosenbauer, a European marketer of fire engines, guarantees delivery of essential spare parts within 48 hours. Between 1983 and 1986 Porsche cars sold in the United States were shipped by air. Demand for the product was strong during those years, and profit margins were high enough to justify use of this faster, though more expensive, means of transport.

For air transportation to be efficient, good ground support services are vital. Such services tend to be more expensive than the services offered at truck terminals. In addition, in some regions theft and pilferage pose serious problems. The global marketer should ask an international carrier for advice before selecting this transportation mode.

Warehousing and Storage

A product must be shipped and warehoused in its journey from manufacturer to customer.

A company can develop its own warehousing, storage, and transportation facilities, or these functions can be performed by the firm's intermediaries or by specialized companies. Products can be stored at different levels of the distribution channel—at sales offices in various markets, with foreign freight forwarders, or with merchants. The marketer must decide how many warehouses to use and where to locate them.

Location of Warehouses. In most industrialized countries, modern warehouse facilities are readily available. Specialists like Kuehne & Nagel in Europe offer customs brokerage, freight forwarding, insurance, packaging, labeling, and transportation services, in addition to warehousing. Similar services are provided by specialist firms in the United States. In Japan, in contrast, there are few public warehouses, and demand for those that are available is high, resulting in high costs. In less-developed countries, storage facilities are often limited or not available at all. The product may have to be stored in its package or container unprotected, in the open—a possibility that must be considered in designing the package.

Decisions about the location of warehouses may be influenced by the availability of government subsidies, tax breaks, or tariff protection. However, such advantages might be offset by controls on exports or imports, fluctuations in exchange rates, insufficient infrastructure, or restrictions on inventory levels due to government policies trying to control hoarding. Thus, the distribution manager should look at the total picture before making a decision.

Foreign Trade Zones. **Foreign trade zones (FTZs)** offer interesting opportunities for global shippers. FTZs are special areas within a country to which companies may ship products for storage, bulk breaking, labeling, assembling,

EXHIBIT 14.7
BENEFITS OF
SHIPPING FROM FTZs

Products can be assembled, processed, and stored in foreign trade zones.

Increased working capital

Exemption from paying duties on labor and overhead costs incurred in the FTZ

Lower insurance costs

Savings of duties on goods rejected, damaged, or scrapped

Opportunity to stockpile products when quotas are filled or market conditions are suboptimal

Reexportation without complicated paperwork

Source: "Foreign Trade Zones: What's in It for the Shipper?," *Distribution*, March 1980, pp. 44–47.

refining, repackaging, and the like without paying customs duties or taxes.[20] Only when the products leave the FTZ to be sold elsewhere in the country do they become subject to local tariffs or taxes. The benefits derived from using FTZs are listed in Exhibit 14.7.

Inventory Management. When it takes a long time to transport products from the company to its intermediaries or customers, and when delays during transport are frequent, the company may have large quantities of products in transit at any given time. Global marketers must keep more inventory "in the pipeline" than domestic marketers generally do. As a result, more working capital is invested in inventory, capital costs are higher, and there are more accounts receivable. Inventory control is particularly important under such conditions.

Global distribution managers should consider centrally coordinated inventory management, in which a computer data bank is used to monitor the volume and value of products in transit or stocked in various warehouses. Because products are not sold at the same rate in every national market, an item that is urgently needed in one place may not be selling in another. When computer monitoring is used, fashion products like knitwear or sunglasses, for example, can be shipped directly between two national markets rather than indirectly via the home country.

For products that must be delivered on very short notice, inventory must be stocked at locations near the final customers. For products with longer order cycles, more centralized inventory stocks can be maintained. It is important, however, to consider the purchase patterns of final customers. Not only do the frequency and volume of purchases differ in different markets, but seasonal fluctuations and irregular demand (such as in the fashion industry or for innovative products) complicate the task of the distribution manager.

Inventory policies may differ according to the extent of the company's control over the distribution channels in its various markets. Integrated channels may be fully stocked during periods of high inflation or unfavorable exchange rates, but independent channels will set their own policies. The latter can be influenced by discounts based on order size, order time and frequency, or other characteristics, depending on the firm's objectives. For example, a marketer may offer one free case of the product if the channel member orders ten. Or, if the buying firm changes from ordering every six months to every three months, the seller may reward that change with a lower price.

A centrally coordinated inventory-management policy is also difficult to enforce when distribution channels are company-bound. A distributor's idea of an optimal inventory level is usually based on their market, sales level, and capital needs. But the manufacturer is quite likely to want the distributor to carry a larger inventory, to minimize production and shipping costs. In order to balance these different points of view, the manufacturer needs to establish strong relationships with its distributors.

Documentation.   The distribution of products in global markets is complicated by the need for extensive documentation. If the documents are not filled out properly, the shipment is delayed, the customer does not receive the product on time, and the seller will not be paid promptly. The most frequently required documents are listed below.

- **Export declaration**
  A form serving the statistical purposes of export administration agencies
- **Bill of lading**
  A document in which the carrier acknowledges receipt of goods from the shipper; serves as evidence of title
- **Commercial invoice**
  A statement or bill of the goods sold, describing the transaction in detail
- **Certificate of origin**
  A document specifying the exact origin of the product; needed for specifying the applicable tariff

In addition to these, export licenses may be required for politically sensitive goods, such as electronic measurement devices. The marketer may also have to fill out a "shipper's declaration of dangerous goods" or obtain an insurance certificate. A consular invoice may be necessary in the country of destination. And many LDCs require foreign-exchange licenses (these enable the shipper to collect the price of the goods in hard currency) and import licenses.

Most of the documents required for global distribution are coordinated through the U.S. Standard Master for International Trade, a master list of documents that improves the flow of international trade by having trading partners use the same documents. However, small and medium-sized companies should seek the assistance of a specialist if they do business in a number of countries or have a large number of items in their product lines.[21] Not only must the necessary documents be filled out, but they must be processed accurately. Errors can cause delayed shipments, higher inventory costs, additional handling and shipping charges, customer dissatisfaction, and penalties and financial losses. In addition, customs procedures, restrictions, and requirements differ from one country to another.

EXHIBIT 14.8
SERVICES PROVIDED
BY FOREIGN FREIGHT
FORWARDERS

The many activities re-
quired to ship a good
from one nation to anoth-
er are frequently provid-
ed by independent com-
panies, freight
forwarders. Without these
independent companies,
small and medium-sized
businesses in particular
would find it difficult (if
not impossible) to be in-
volved in global
marketing.

Preparation of export declarations required by the local government

Booking of cargo space

Transportation from the firm's premises to the indicated destination

Preparation and processing of airway bills and bills of lading

Preparation of consular documents in the language of the country to which the goods are shipped

Provision for certification of receipt of goods

Provision for warehouse storage

Provision for insurance upon request

Preparation of shipping documents and sending them to banks, shippers, or consignees as directed

Source: J. R. Stock and D. M. Lambert, "Physical Distribution Management in International Marketing," *International Marketing Review*, Autumn 1983, p. 37f.

Facilitating Agencies.   The most frequently used facilitating agencies are customhouse brokers and foreign freight forwarders. A **customhouse broker** serves as an agent for exporters and importers of goods, performing two essential functions: facilitating the movement of products through customs and handling the documentation accompanying international shipments. A **foreign freight forwarder** provides a broader range of services, including coordination and assistance in all phases of shipment from the company's plant to its markets. (See Exhibit 14.8.)

IMPACT ON THE MARKETING MIX

Distribution has a major impact on the other elements of the marketing mix. The distribution channel becomes part of the total product and influences the product design and packaging. For example, mass-market customers engage in self-service at the point of purchase (such as a large supermarket). In such cases the product design must be simple and the package must convey a strong message to the customer. The package must also be designed to protect the product on the store shelf. Such a package will be quite different from one that must protect the product during a three-month ocean crossing. Branding decisions are also influenced by the channel that is used. When channel members provide little or no personal selling, the brand must be quickly recognizable.

Pricing, too, is influenced by distribution decisions. For example, longer distribution channels tend to result in higher prices. The "quality" of a chosen channel strongly influences the possible market price. It is difficult, for example, to charge a premium price for products distributed through discount department stores. The terms of sale also make a difference. More sophisticated buyers and sellers want to control the transaction for as long as possible, because if sellers can lower transportation costs, for example, they make additional profits by setting the price at the buyer's door. If the buyer sets the price at the seller's door, the buyer must pay freight, but in effect may have a lower total price if the buyer is able to lower transportation costs. Finally, channel control affects terms of payment. A firm selling to an integrated channel member can offer more liberal credit terms, because in most cases it is assuming less risk. A seller with a strong position in an independent channel can dictate more favorable terms of payment, such as payment in advance or an irrevocable letter of credit.

Channel decisions also influence sales promotion. The potential for joint advertising and promotional activities depends largely on the nature of the channel members. In fact, marketers may use joint promotional activities to build stronger channel relationships. In addition, the "quality" of the channel affects the image the marketer is able to convey through its promotional campaigns. It is difficult, for example, to convey a youthful, modern image via a channel dominated by small, old-fashioned, poorly decorated retail stores.

Finally, the distribution channel affects the marketer's opportunities for personal contact and communication with customers. An important role of channels for industrial products and prestige consumer goods is to provide positive personal contact between the marketer and the customer. Thus, the impression conveyed by channel members is very important to the successful marketing of these products. ∎

SUMMARY

Global distribution is a critical step in successful international marketing. If the product cannot be delivered to the market, sales will not occur regardless of the value of the product, the price charged, or the persuasiveness of promotion. Whether the channel is direct or indirect, the global marketing manager has a major challenge in matching a global distribution system to the firm's objectives and competitive position, and in managing relationships within its distribution system.

The manager must choose a channel that will reach customers and take their characteristics into account. The potential channel members themselves, the functions they perform, and their structure and networking ability must also be evaluated. Managers do so through the application of several selection criteria, including costs and the multiple types of distance (geographic, social, cultural, technological, and temporal). Finding the best intermediaries may require research, not dissimilar to the marketing-research process described earlier.

Managing channel relationships across multiple nations and cultures can prove quite challenging to the international manager. Motives for handling the product may vary, for example. Communication and control systems must be established to enable all channel members to share information and understand how each member contributes to success.

The physical-distribution process involves getting the product to the customer, including documentation. Due to the physical distance involved, international marketers must pay special attention to global physical distribution in order to assure that high levels of customer service are maintained. Packaging, in addition to its promotional role, must be carefully considered in making international distribution decisions. Due to longer channels, shipping methods of varying sophistication, freight costs, and the way products are physically handled, the range of international packaging issues is usually broader than for domestic distribution. Transportation alternatives are usually evaluated on the basis of total distribution costs. Evaluations of warehousing and storage alternatives are based on the need to be close to the market, inventory and distribution costs, and political and legal considerations.

DISCUSSION QUESTIONS

1. Why is global distribution more difficult than domestic distribution, even if the functions performed by a channel of distribution are similar in both situations?

2. What are the advantages and disadvantages of using an integrated distribution system?

3. How do the characteristics of the final customer affect the evaluation of global channel options?

4. What influences the length of a distribution channel in a national market, and how does that impact global channel evaluation?

5. Why are intermediary networks of importance to the global marketer, and how should they be managed?

6. How does distance influence channel-member selection?

7. What are the advantages and risks to a marketer of discussing a possible partnership with an intermediary who already handles a competitor's product?

8. Describe the process of finalizing the relationship between a marketer and an intermediary.

9. What are the major elements in managing global channel relationships, and what is one potential problem for each that marketing managers must be prepared to overcome?

10. How does global physical distribution differ from global channel management?

11. Who should carry out global warehousing and storage, and what elements influence that decision?

C A S E

STROTHER'S SHOES: BUILDING A DISTRIBUTION CHANNEL

Strother's Shoes, the company reported on in Chapter 4, has decided to explore the Indian market. It has contacted a local wholesaler in Bombay, which has access to most of the independent shoe retailers in India. Erin Strother, the president of Strother's Shoes, has asked Joe May, the vice-president for international marketing, to report to her on the distribution issues her company will face in exporting shoes to India.

Joe has already found that independent shoe retailers account for about 60 percent of the retail shoe sales in urban areas in India (company-owned stores account for the other 40 percent), but the independents handle about 90 percent of the shoe sales in rural areas. Of course, shoe sales are much less in rural areas than in urban areas, due to the poorer population. There is already considerable competition in the shoe market in India. Many small and local producers make several styles and types of shoes. But Joe has found that Strother's Shoes are much better in quality than most shoes in the market. There are some Indian manufacturers who compete in the high-quality market (mostly urban), but no imported shoes are very important there yet. Joe is sure this represents a strong opportunity for Strother's Shoes.

From what Joe has been able to find out about the physical distribution process, shipping is preferable to air freight, because the shoes wouldn't perish on a long voyage, and the cost of air freight is so high that it would make the shoes too expensive. Strother's Shoes would first need to get the shoes on a ship out of New York and ship them to India, probably Bombay. Due to the limited working capital of shoe wholesalers in India, Strother's Shoes would have to pay for the shipping and carry the inventory on its books until the shoes were received in the wholesaler's warehouse. Once the shoes cleared customs, the wholesaler could pick them up. The wholesaler would warehouse and then ship them to other independent wholesalers or independent retailers as orders were received. The Bombay wholesaler's salesforce covers most of the market, selling directly to other wholesalers (who order in smaller lots than the Bombay wholesaler, but greater lots than any single retailer) as well as retailers in the fifteen largest Indian cities.

Joe has found that retailers in general are considerably smaller in size and sales volume in India than in the United States. The average store in an urban area serves a specific neighborhood, as most customers do not have their own means of transportation, which would permit them to go to stores outside their own neighborhood. Another difference in India is that self-service is not as popular in its stores as in the United States. In India, it is much more common, especially in smaller stores, for a clerk to wait on the customer, for another clerk to make out the bill, and for perhaps a third to package the goods for the customer.

Strother's Shoes is committed to the Indian market, which it believes will be profitable in the long run, in spite of the competition. Strother's Shoes has already been granted a license to export shoes to India, and it has held an initial conversation with the Bombay wholesaler. Before making a final decision, however, Erin Strother wants Joe to completely analyze the global distribution issues which would be important to Strother's Shoes.

Case Issues

1. Which type of channel system has Strother's Shoes chosen to use, and why? Is it the best choice?

2. What channel characteristics should Strother's Shoes use in evaluating a possible business relationship with the Bombay wholesaler?

3. What major channel-management issues will arise for Strother's Shoes, and how should they be managed?

NOTES

1. J. P. Valla, "The Development of Marketing Networks and the Internationalization Process," paper presented at the Second IMP Research Seminar on International Marketing, Uppsala, 1985.

2. E. Anderson, "The Salesperson as Outside Agent or Employee: A Transaction Cost Analysis," *Marketing Science*, Summer 1985, pp. 234–254; A. T. Coughlan, "Competition and Cooperation in Marketing Channel Choice: Theory and Application," *Marketing Science*, Summer 1985, pp. 110–129; and W. H. Davidson and D. G. McFetridge, "Key Characteristics in the Choice of International Technology Transfer Mode," *Journal of International Business Studies*, Summer 1985, pp. 5–21.

3. E. Anderson and A. T. Coughlan, "International Market Entry and Expansion via Independent or Integrated Channels of Distribution," *Journal of Marketing*, January 1987, pp. 71–82.

4. S. J. Paliwoda and N. Vardar, "The Relationship with Foreign Suppliers in Industrial Purchases: A Study of British Importers," paper presented at the Third International IMP Research Seminar on International Marketing, Lyon, 1986.

5. G. L. Lilien, "Advisor Two: Modeling the Marketing Mix Decision for Industrial Products," *Management Science*, February 1979, pp. 191–204.

6. S. Ho and H. Lau, "Development of Supermarket Technology: The Incomplete Transfer Phenomenon," *International Marketing Review*, Spring 1988, pp. 20–30.

7. E. Kumcu and M. E. Kumcu, "Determinants of Food Retailing in Developing Economies: The Case of Turkey," *Journal of Macromarketing*, Fall 1987, pp. 26–40.

8. E. Kaynak, "Global Spread of Supermarkets: Some Experiences from Turkey," in E. Kaynak, ed., *Global Perspectives in Marketing* (New York: Praeger, 1985); and U. Yavas and S. Tuncalp, "Perceived Risk in Grocery Outlet Selection: A Case Study in Saudi Arabia," *European Journal of Marketing*, 1984, pp. 13–25.

9. M. Tamura, "Distribution and Marketing in Japan," in H. Simon, ed. *Marketfold in Japan* (Wiesbaden, Germany: Gabler, 1988), pp. 257–281.

10. D. Darlin, "Shelf-Control: 'Papa-Mama' Stores in Japan Wield Power to Hold Back Imports," *Wall Street Journal*, November 14, 1988, p. 1.

11. D. E. Vaubel, "Methoden des Markteintritts in Japan," in H. Simon, ed., *Marketfold in Japan* (Wiesbaden, Germany: Gabler, 1988), pp. 75–98.

12. Tamura, op. cit., p. 269.

13. S. Reid and J. McGoldrick, "Greasing the Foreign Channel Mechanism," in *1982 Educators' Conference Proceedings: An Assessment of Marketing Thought & Practice*, B. Walker, ed., Series no. 48, (Chicago: AMA, 1982), pp. 318–321.

14. D. Ford, "Buyer/Seller Relationships in International Industrial Markets," *Industrial Marketing Management*, May 1984, pp. 101–112.

15. D. Cook and D. Shipley, "The Search for and Selection of Overseas Distributors: An Explorative Study," paper presented at the Annual Conference of the European Marketing Academy, Bradford, England, 1988.

16. L. D. Dahringer and M. T. Hilger, "A Comparative Study of Public Food Marketing as Viewed by Consumers in Mexico and India," *Journal of Macromarketing*, Spring 1985, pp. 69–79.

17. M. T. Cunningham, "Interaction, Networks and Competitiveness in Industrial Markets," paper presented at the European-American Symposium on World-Wide Market Place for Technology-Based Products, Enschede, 1987.

18. See "Just-in-Time Report," *Traffic Management*, September 1988, pp. 41–56.

19. M. Ikeda, "The Process of Physical Distribution in Japan," *Transportation and Distribution Management* 14, no. 1 (1974), p. 41.

20. F. Robles and G. C. Hozier, Jr., "Understanding Foreign Trade Zones," *International Marketing Review*, Summer 1986, pp. 44–54.

21. S. Reid and L. Burlingame, "Documentation and Logistics Issues in Exporting Firms," V. Kothari, D. R. Arnold, T. Cauvusgil, J. D. Lindquist, J. Nathan, and S. Reid, eds., *Developments in Marketing Science*, vol. V (New Orleans: Academy of Marketing Science, 1982), pp. 221–225.

TYPES OF INTERMEDIARIES

Representatives

A **representative** establishes and maintains relationships with prospective and existing customers in a specified geographic area on behalf of the principal. Representatives do not take physical possession of the product, do not arrange for its shipping or handling, and do not take any credit, market, or exchange risk. A representative does arrange sales between the manufacturer and buyers. The representative must pass all legal documents to the principal for approval and cannot sign them on behalf of the principal. In a continuing relationship the representative may handle only the principal's product lines and complementary lines of other firms. Compensation is in the form of a commission.

Brokers and Factors

Brokers and factors are independent agents. They can legally bind the principal to a contract and expose it to risk without taking any risk themselves. **Brokers** are independent individuals or organizations that bring together prospective buyers and sellers to facilitate sales. They often deal in commodities and food products, handling large volumes of merchandise. Normally this is not a continuing relationship and exclusivity is not expected.

Factors, many of which are banks, perform all normal brokerage functions plus financing. They may finance goods at various stages of the value-added chain. Factors serve to relieve both the seller and buyer of credit risk. The noncontinuing relationship between the principal and the factor is also nonexclusive; that is, a factor can serve other sellers as well. Brokers and factors are paid a fee by the seller for services provided.

Distributors

A **distributor** has a formalized, continuing relationship with the manufacturer, with exclusive sales rights for a specified geographic area. Distributors take title to (buy) the products they sell to other merchants (wholesalers or retailers) or to industrial customers. Close cooperation between the manufacturer and distributor gives the principal more control over prices, promotional activities, inventory, and service policies than it has when it sells products to a wholesaler.

Dealers

Dealers have the same function as retailers. But, in addition, they have the same type of continuing relationship with suppliers that distributors have. The major difference between dealers and distributors is that dealers sell the principal's goods directly to final customers. Sometimes the principal holds an equity share in the dealer's business. In such situations the principal has considerable control over the relationship and the dealer provides the principal with a great deal of market information. In most cases dealers have exclusive selling rights for the manufacturer's products in a specified area and the principal is the dealer's only supplier. Most automobile manufacturers use dealers as their intermediaries. Dealers are also common in the marketing of industrial goods.

Franchising

Franchising is a special kind of dealership agreement that is well suited to companies with innovative products and fully developed marketing strategies, but insufficient capital to implement those strategies. A **franchisee** is an individual or organization that is granted the right to conduct business under the franchiser's trade name. The franchiser assists the franchisee in locating, equipping, and designing the business premises. In most cases franchisees must closely follow the terms of contractual agreements regarding how business is to be conducted. The franchiser is paid a fee or royalties as compensation for fulfilling such functions as management assistance and training and global marketing.

Global franchising has become increasingly popular in a number of industries in which standardized services or brand names are especially important to customers. Fashion franchises like Benetton, Rodier, Champion, and Escada are found in most developed countries. Fast-food franchises—like McDonald's, Kentucky Fried Chicken, Wienerwald, and Wimpy's—and hotel franchises—like Novotel, Holiday Inn, and the Hilton—are also found throughout the world.

Importers

Importers fulfill the same functions as distributors but generally do not have exclusive territorial rights. They may be either wholesalers or retailers, and they may handle the products of many suppliers, sometimes even competing product lines. As a result, the principal has limited control.

Distributors, dealers, and importers do not receive direct compensation; their profit is the margin between the buying and selling prices of the products they carry, minus their costs. The margins or discounts offered to merchants vary greatly from one country to another. They depend on the level of competition in a given market, the level of service offered by the intermediary, geographic distance, sales volume, purchasing power, efficiency, and tradition.

GLOBAL PROMOTION

"You Speak English?" or "Top Agro-mate"

Language and translations cause considerable problems for international marketers (such as export of the German candy bar "Zit" to the United States). Even countries that speak the "same" language don't. England, the United States, and Australia, for example, all speak English. But an Englishman looking for a "panel beater" (automobile repair shop) would be frustrated in the United States. Or an Australian asking you if you enjoy "footie" (Australian football) might be misunderstood in the U.S.

Too often, businesspeople in countries that share a language assume they speak the same language, and they aren't prepared for communication difficulties as a result. One Australian businesswoman who has traveled to the United States several times still has trouble with the frequently used American term "regular." Americans use the term to mean normal, or acceptable: for example, "regular coffee" (versus caffeine-free). In Australia, it is not used in this way. The closest Australian equivalent to "regular guy," for example, would be "mate."

When businesspeople travel to another country that does not share their language, they usually are aware of the possibility of communication difficulties. They use a translator, speak slowly, avoid slang, and in general alter their communication behavior to improve their chances of being understood. But between nations that share a language, a more subtle but nevertheless important problem exists—the *unknown* traps of the "same" language.

The most important communication rule to remember is that it really isn't all English. British, Australian, and American English have developed differently. Another example is to "table a motion"; in the United States it means to postpone discussion; in England it means to begin discussion. President Bush's baseball terms—"stay at home," for example—don't quite mean the same thing in England. The Aussies love abbreviations ("medico" for medical doctors, "agro" for aggravation, or "avro" for afternoon), which are difficult for Americans to follow. Witness the following headline: "Aussie Medicos Warning—Mozzies Over the Top Agro." (Translation: "Australian Doctors Warn—Mosquitos May Cause Considerable Aggravation") Thus, it is as important when speaking the "same" language as it is when speaking "different" languages not to use slang or speak too quickly.

Promotion is the organization's tool for communicating with its publics.

The objective of promotion is to influence the receiver of a message to behave in a particular manner. Sometimes the desired behavior is a shift in attitude. For example, the government of Saudi Arabia may hire a public relations firm in Washington, D.C., to lobby Congress for the passage of specific bills. In business, the desired behavior is often the purchase of a particular product.

No matter what the objective of the communication effort, the need to appreciate cultural differences is fundamental. This is especially true of global promotion campaigns. In fact, marketing errors are the leading cause of global business difficulties, and a significant proportion of such difficulties are due to the marketer's failure to adjust promotional efforts to accommodate differences in language, laws, social customs, and other cultural factors.[1] Thus, the airline advertisement that offered "rendezvous lounges" to traveling businesspeople created problems in Brazil, since that phrase means "rooms for love making" when translated into Portuguese.

This chapter discusses promotion as a form of communication and examines its uses and limits in global markets. It also discusses the major tools in the promotional mix: advertising, public relations, personal selling, and sales promotions from a global perspective.

PROMOTION AS COMMUNICATION

Communication is the transmission of information from a source to a receiver. The information may be passed along either intentionally or unintentionally. An example of the latter is that differences in accepted norms of behavior lead many Nigerians to believe that Americans talk too much and ask for too much detailed information. In Nigeria such behavior indicates a weak character and suggests that the individual represents an organization that is not entirely reputable.

Communication Publics

Firms communicate with a wide variety of publics.

Customers are only one of the communication publics of a firm. A global organization communicates with a variety of publics through different promotional mixes. The various types of communication publics, possible communication objectives, and promotional tools and tactics that may be used to achieve those objectives are illustrated in Exhibit 15.1.

An example of an unusual promotional tactic is Magna's sponsorship of chairs for professors of international business. This tactic is part of a promotional mix designed to generate favorable attitudes toward the firm, a Canadian automotive parts manufacturer. It is aimed at one of the firm's communication publics, the general public. Other publics would require different blends of communication or promotional elements.

The Communication Model

No matter what the communication objective, the basic communication model is the same.

Regardless of the objective or the tactics used, the basic communication model is the same for all publics. Exhibit 15.2 presents this model. The *sender* of the communication, usually a company, *encodes* an idea, image, or information into symbols, words, or pictures that constitute a *message*. The message is then sent

EXHIBIT 15.1   COMMUNICATION BETWEEN A FIRM AND ITS PUBLICS

An organization must manage a wide variety of communications between itself and a number of publics. Communication objectives and the appropriate promotional tools and tactics vary depending on
the specific public.

Public	Possible Communication Objective	Appropriate Promotional Tool	Examples of Promotional Tactics
General public	Obtain favorable attitude	Public relations; image advertising	Guided tours for students; "Gee. No, GTE"
Government	Obtain fair or favorable treatment by decision makers	Public relations; lobbying	Lobbying of U.S. government agencies by Japanese companies
Suppliers (finance and production)	Obtain financial or other resources at favorable rates	Public relations; image advertising	Briefings for securities analysts; "The Name Is Nissan"
Customers	Improve sales	Advertising; public relations; personal selling; sales promotions	"Coke Is It"; films for use in schools; sales call by IBM salesperson; phone-in trivia contests
Employees	Improve morale; increase productivity	Public relations; promotions; image advertising	Employee magazine; sales contests; "I've been working on the railroad"
Media	Obtain favorable coverage	Public relations	Press releases; media briefings; corporate spokesperson
Stockholders	Improve investment climate	Public relations	Stockholder meetings; annual reports
Industry	Maintain desired levels of competition	Public relations	Lobbying for legislation to protect competition
Intermediaries	Obtain favorable distribution to improve sales	Advertising; public relations; personal selling; sales promotions	Advertising in trade publications; meetings for wholesalers and retailers; sales call by representative of pharmaceutical company; sales contests

through a *channel* to the *receiver* or public that is the target of the message. The
receiver then *decodes* (gives meaning to) the message and provides *feedback* (a
reaction to the message). The model is the same for any communication. Procter
& Gamble's effort to convince German consumers to buy Ariel detergent is
more complex and expensive than an informal chat between friends, but it
involves the same processes.

The communication process can encounter a variety of barriers when the
sender of the message is in one culture (for example, Ford Motor Company in

EXHIBIT 15.2
A COMMUNICATION
MODEL

Global marketers must
not only understand the
basic communication
model, but they must also
be sure that the frames of
reference overlap, in or-
der to make sure that the
correct message is
communicated.

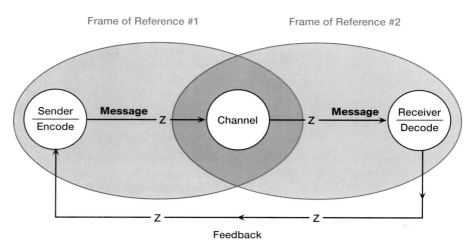

Z = Barrier to communication ("noise")

Detroit, Michigan) and the receiver is in another (potential automobile buyers in France). A message that was encoded in one culture may not "work" in another. To give another example, Singer was thinking of using blue as the background color in outdoor advertising in an Arab market. It avoided a major mistake when a local representative revealed that in Arab society the color blue represents death.

Establishing a *common frame of reference* is the key to effective communication. As illustrated in Exhibit 15.2, the sender of the message is responsible for understanding the frame of reference of the communication target (receiver). In other words, the marketer must "speak the language" of the receiver. This includes formal language, of course. Such an understanding might have prevented the use of the slogan "highly rated" to advertise automobiles in Venezuela, where this phrase was interpreted as meaning "highly overrated." But effective communication also includes the informal or "silent" languages of space, time, possessions, friendship, and agreement.[2] Understanding and managing differences in these dimensions is particularly important for effective global communication. The Dutch concept of space, for example, is very different from the American concept, due to the higher population density in Holland. Dutch businesspeople report being uncomfortable in American social and business settings because Americans like to sit "too far apart." When Americans do business in Holland, they feel uncomfortably crowded. In both cases, it is important to understand and make adjustments for the silent language of space.

Many elements, such as the availability of advertising media, affect the channel through which a message is conveyed. Even climate may have an impact, as can be seen in the experience of a company that used billboards in the Middle East. In that area billboards often last less than two weeks. The impact of the severe climate was underestimated in the company's promotion budget.

A reaction on the part of the communication public (such as a purchase or an attitude shift) is called **feedback**. Naturally, the global marketer wants positive feedback. Purchases of a product constitute positive feedback that can be measured by sales; a favorable shift in the attitudes of members of a government regulatory agency is positive feedback that can be detected by an opinion survey.

Major Obstacles to Communication

Most global communication problems occur when the firm does not fully understand the similarities and differences across nations.

Both the rate and costs of communication failures are higher for global firms than domestic ones. Misperceptions of the similarities and differences among markets lead to three major difficulties. The first is *inability to reach the target market* with the message. For example, TV advertising may not be legal. In many countries there is a lack of suitable media.

A second major problem is that even when the target market can be reached, the *message may not be understood* the way the sender intended it to be understood. Not only does language present a problem (as in the case of Chevrolet's Nova, which means "no go" in spoken Spanish), but the various types of informal language can cause difficulties as well. Cultural differences also affect the decoding of the message. A German ad for soap featuring a nude or partly nude model would violate the cultural norms of decency that prevail in India. It would communicate the message that the product or promoter is somewhat immoral—not the ad's intended message.

The third major difficulty occurs when the target audience is reached, understanding is achieved, and yet *action is not motivated*. This problem frequently results from lack of understanding or appreciation of the product. As discussed earlier, the sender of a message must share a frame of reference with the receiver for effective communication to occur. This applies to the language used in the promotion as well as the product benefits described. It even extends to the question of whether an equivalent product concept exists in the target market. If a U.S. marketer of personal-care products attempted to convince French consumers that foot odor is a serious problem and that they should buy a product that eliminates it, the response might be "those crazy Americans" rather than interest in the product. French consumers are not as concerned about body odors as Americans are.

Personal and Nonpersonal Information Sources

As a buyer moves closer to making a purchase, the sources of information that are most important change.

Another factor that must be considered in establishing a global promotion strategy is the potential buyer's sources of information. In making a purchase decision, a potential customer usually goes through a series of steps that may be viewed as distinct stages of buyer behavior. One of the most popular models of buyer behavior is known as AIDA, for *attention, interest, desire,* and *action*. This model is useful to marketers, because as the buyer goes through these various

EXHIBIT 15.3
RELATIVE
IMPORTANCE OF
PERSONAL AND
NONPERSONAL
SOURCES OF
INFORMATION

As a buyer moves
through various stages of
behavior, the relative importance of any source of
information changes;
thus the optimal promo-
tion mix changes.

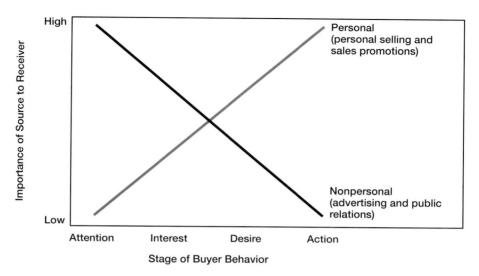

stages, changes occur in the relative importance of personal and nonpersonal sources of information, as shown in Exhibit 15.3. The marketer should plan the use of promotional tools accordingly. For example, a buyer who is first considering purchasing a product is interested primarily in gathering information about it. Information is most effectively passed along to such a buyer through nonpersonal sources (advertising or public relations). Thus, McDonald's introduced a new salad in its German restaurants by using extensive advertising to inform consumers that the product was available.

As the buyer moves through the decision process, nonpersonal sources of information help create a state of mind that may predispose him or her toward purchase. As the actual purchase decision is approached, however, personal information sources become more effective. For example, when a buyer is close to choosing between a BMW and a Honda, he or she will visit a showroom, talk to sales personnel, and take a test drive, whether the purchase is being made in St. Louis or Taipei.

Distinctive Features of Global Promotion

There are both similarities and differences among national markets. **Global promoters** concentrate on the similarities. But a major problem can develop when promotional programs are based on perceived similarities that are actually superficial. Campbell Soup had this experience in the British market, where canned soups are as popular as they are in the United States. Although consumer tastes in the two markets are similar and British consumers routinely purchase canned soup, Campbell overlooked the absence of canned condensed soups in the British market. Condensed soup not only was new to British consumers but

Global Advertising at Revlon

Revlon tries to consider all 130 countries in which it sells cosmetics when developing an advertising campaign. After consolidating its domestic and international advertising divisions into "one world marketing group," Revlon is trying to upgrade its U.S. image, while avoiding duplication of costs.

Creating campaigns that work everywhere still requires attention to local market attitudes and needs. Mexican managers, for example, wanted a younger Charlie model, because the Mexican market for that perfume is somewhat younger than in other countries. Because Revlon generally uses the same model to advertise a particular product worldwide, headquarters had to decide whether it could accommodate the request, without tampering with Charlie's sophisticated image. The decision was yes.

Thus, after its local marketing offices have met Revlon's global priorities, they may with headquarters approval promote a cosmetic specifically for their markets. In this way, global strategies are kept on track, but local managers have some leeway to adapt to local market situations.

---

looked like a poor buy. When a can of Campbell's condensed soup was placed on a grocery shelf next to a can of uncondensed soup, it looked as if the customer who chose the condensed soup would buy a smaller amount for about the same price. Sales suffered considerably until Campbell recognized the cause of the problem and began an informational advertising campaign to explain the difference. Correcting such assumptions can be a costly process, however.

Individualization versus standardization debates apply to promotion just as they do to the entire marketing mix.

The debate about whether to individualize or standardize the marketing mix (see Chapter 2) applies to the promotion mix. (See Global Dimensions 15.1.) Those in favor of a standardized promotion mix argue that only minor and necessary adjustments should be made when entering a new market. Others emphasize that the success of a promotional program in a global environment requires **cultural empathy** (the ability to identify with different cultures) and the *willingness* and *ability* to adjust to market differences. Pepsodent found that a promotional theme stressing white teeth was not effective in Asian markets where teeth stained by chewing betel nuts are a symbol of high social status. For those markets, the company had to develop an individualized promotional campaign. On the other hand, the manufacturer of Swatch watches uses the same ad in close to twenty countries, thereby lowering its advertising production costs and presenting a consistent brand image in all of its international markets.

Experience curve effects can be extensive in global promotion. For example, Playtex's standardized global advertising campaign to promote the WOW bra in twelve countries achieved significant cost savings: a TV commercial that was used in all of the targeted countries was produced for $250,000. The average cost for producing a single commercial in the United States is almost half that amount.[3]

Limitations on Global Promotion

National market differences must be understood, in order to avoid serious promotional blunders.

The types of promotion that are useful or even permitted in a global promotional campaign vary considerably from one country to another. Marketers often approach a promotion problem from an egocentric perspective, that is, in the belief that their way of doing things is the best and, therefore what works at home will work elsewhere. But what actually works depends on the characteristics of target markets. The use of direct-mail brochures, for example, works well for many consumer products in the United States, but this approach may not be effective in Chad because of low literacy rates. There are several other restrictions besides literacy (and education) that have a critical impact on the design of an optimal promotional mix for global markets. These are listed in Exhibit 15.4, together with a description of how each element affects one of the tools of the promotional mix. In reality, each limitation affects all of the promotional tools.[4] But these brief examples show how important it is for a global promoter to know the limitations and adjust to them.

Legal and Tax Considerations.   A commercial that was popular in the United States showed a German car being driven very fast while a rock group sang "Little GTO" in German in the background. But in Germany there are legal restrictions on the use of foreign words. There an ad can be run in English for a raincoat made in England, but not for one made in Germany. Tax laws affect the cost of promotion as well as the choice of media. For example, France has proposed taxing advertising on commercial television and radio (thereby increasing the cost of advertising) in order to provide revenue for public stations that do not accept advertising.

Symbols.   **Symbols** are abstract characters that represent ideas, feelings, and other aspects of a culture. Snakes symbolize danger in Sweden. In Korea they represent wisdom. A Korean company that uses a snake as its corporate symbol should expect some difficulty with its public image when entering the Swedish market.

Tradition.   What has traditionally been viewed as "appropriate" behavior plays a strong role in the way a promotional campaign is received. In Japan, for example, women have not been strongly represented in salesforces or upper management. Ads or brochures depicting women in these roles would lack credibility in Japan.

Values and Norms.   **Values** and **norms** (a society's underlying set of beliefs about acceptable behavior) affect promotion in several ways. One effect has to do with the structure of achievement rewards for the salesforce. Individual achievement is highly valued in the United States, whereas in Japan group achievement is more highly valued. In Japan an award for achievement, even if it is largely earned by one individual, is presented to and shared by that person's work group.

Language. Linguistic limitations on global promotion range from the risk of using outdated slang to that of making embarrassing and costly translation errors. One firm, advertising in Quebec, claimed that its laundry detergent was particularly well suited for the really dirty parts of the wash—*les parties de sale*. It was quite embarrassed when it discovered (after a rapid decline in sales) that this phrase is comparable to the American slang expression "private parts."

EXHIBIT 15.4
EXAMPLES OF
LIMITATIONS ON
GLOBAL PROMOTION

Although each limitation might influence each element of the promotional mix, this exhibit illustrates the variety of issues a global marketer will have to be concerned with in designing the best promotional mix.

Limitation	Promotional Tool	Examples	Countries
Legal and tax	Advertising	Advertising for weight-reduction products is not allowed	Finland
Symbols	Packaging	The color red represents masculinity or death	England, Turkey
Tradition	Advertising	A couple discussing mouthwash and bad breath is considered inappropriate	Thailand
Language	All	"Skinababe" baby soap; a dress shop urging customers to "come in and have a fix"	United States, Japan
Literacy	Advertising	Direct-mail campaigns	Chad
Subcultures	Media	Billboards in two or more languages	Belgium, India, Hong Kong
Costs	All	Smaller markets mean higher per capita production costs; salesforce support costs include housing and dependent education	Denmark, Saudi Arabia
National control	Advertising	Impact of advertising campaigns on national culture	France, Mexico
Values and norms	All	Children should not be the direct objects of promotion as they lack experience to make proper judgments	Sweden

(Continued)

EXHIBIT 15.4 *(Continued)*

TV-Advertising Restrictions in Various Countries

Australia: Cigarettes, slimming products

Brazil: Cigarettes, alcohol until 9 P.M.

Canada: Drugs, use of cartoons in advertising to children, cigarettes

Chile: Toothpaste, aspirin

France: Investments and savings, use of cartoons in advertising to children, margarine, slimming products

Japan: Cosmetics, exercise plans, investments, use of cartoon characters in advertising to children, use of athletes to promote vitamined beverages

New Zealand: Health claims related to foods and drugs, contraceptives, politics

Norway: Actual use of the product by the endorser, use of celebrities

Spain: Detergents, tobacco, hard drinks

Sweden: Use of fictitious characters to endorse products

Switzerland: Alcohol, drugs, tobacco, politics, religion, use of actors to represent consumers

U.S.: Use of endorsers with real expertise, tobacco, fortune tellers

Literacy. The proportion of the population that can read and write also affects promotion, especially advertising. In countries with low literacy rates, such as India, movies, posters, billboards, and other visual media are very important. In fact, in India more advertising is done through the cinema than through any other medium.

Subcultures. Cultural differences can exist within as well as between nations. **Subcultures** are groups of people who share a common religion, ethnic origin, or other characteristic that distinguishes the group from the larger culture. The presence of subcultures affects media options and requirements. For example, in The Netherlands major newspapers appeal to Protestant, Roman Catholic, or nonreligious groups. In the United States, radio programming is often designed to appeal to specific ethnic and regional subcultures.

Costs. A global promotional campaign is frequently more expensive than a domestic one, especially on a per capita basis. In addition to higher per capita production costs when the market base is small, as in several countries, additional costs may be incurred due to translations and rewrites, lack of cost-effective media, and the larger amount of management time needed to make sure a campaign is executed properly in several national markets.

National Control. Promotion is the most visible of all the elements of the marketing mix. It attracts attention not only from consumers but also from governments, which act through legal policies, and from international organizations that wish to influence global promotion. An example of the latter is the

World Health Organization, which has established a voluntary code of ethics to guide marketers in the promotion and distribution of powdered baby formula. The code recommends that governments ban advertising of powdered formula and encourage breast feeding. It also recommends limitations on other forms of promotion, such as the distribution of free samples of powdered formula to new mothers in hospital settings. Arguments for the code center on the inability of many buyers to use such products correctly or to detect deception in the way they are promoted.

The Promotional Mix

The four tools in an organization's **promotional mix** are advertising, public relations, personal selling, and sales promotions. Advertising and public relations are nonpersonal forms of communication, while personal selling and sales promotions are more personalized. Each element of the mix is useful in different ways and for different purposes. Properly combined and managed, these tools can help an organization achieve its communication objectives with a specific exchange partner. To facilitate the discussion of promotional tools, we begin with a brief definition of each.

Advertising is any nonpersonal presentation, through any medium, that is paid for by an identifiable sponsor. Thus, PepsiCo's television commercial based on a scene from the movie "Top Gun," in which a fighter pilot rolls his plane over to get a drink of Pepsi, is an example of advertising. So is Coca-Cola's use of traveling sound trucks in Africa, where other media are scarce.

In **public relations**, another nonpersonal form of communication, the organization conveys messages to various publics or exchange partners to create a favorable image of the organization. Japanese companies, for example, employ over 300 lobbyists to present their interests to the U.S. Congress.

Personal selling involves direct communication between a seller and a buyer. For example, an Austrian company employs a Swiss citizen living in Zurich to call on sales prospects in the Far East, New Zealand, and Australia.

Sales promotions include a wide variety of techniques meant to stimulate a short-term response by the exchange partner. Examples include special events, coupons, contests, and other personalized forms of communication. Discounts are frequently used in sales promotions. Lever Brothers, for example, might offer its intermediaries (wholesalers and retailers) short-term discounts to induce them to stock more soap.

GLOBAL ADVERTISING

Advertising, as the most visible and controversial promotional element, must be especially sensitive to cultural differences.

Advertising is the most visible and often the most controversial form of promotion, especially in a global context. In fact, many of the problems that are frequently encountered in a global communication campaign pertain to media planning and analysis. Lack of cultural understanding is the source of most global advertising problems. As fundamental as cultural empathy is, managers overlook it surprisingly often. Even managers who would not dream of pursuing a domestic market without first conducting an in-depth analysis of that market often assume that domestic advertising is directly transferable to foreign markets. To cite just one example, a German manufacturer of automatic doors for train cars used the word *wagon* in its French sales literature. Unfortunately, *wagon* refers to freight cars, for which the French didn't see the need for automatic doors. The appropriate word would have been *voiture*.

Advertising's Changing Role

The appropriate role of advertising within the promotional mix varies among national markets.

The development of global markets is causing a shift in the role of advertising. Although advertising often plays a leading role in promotional mixes used in Triad markets, in other global markets advertising does not always carry the lead role. A promotion manager must always evaluate the cost/benefit ratio of advertising compared to other elements of the promotional mix. If advertising facilities are not well developed or media are not readily available, then even if advertising would be "best" from a strategic point of view, it may not be the best choice compared to other alternatives.

It is often difficult for American marketers to assign advertising a less important role than that given to other promotional tools. In the United States advertising tends to be at the heart of the promotional mix, especially for consumer goods, partly because advertisers have extensive support from advertising agencies and the media. (See Exhibit 15.5.) They may spend between $10 and $20 million annually to promote a consumer product, a figure that many Europeans and Asians find astonishing. (For examples of worldwide advertising activity, see Exhibit 15.6.)

Advertising Agencies

At the same time that the role of advertising is shifting, the global market for the services of advertising agencies is quickly growing. Some advertising agencies have been involved in international business for a long time. For example,

EXHIBIT 15.5
WORLDWIDE AD
SPENDING: TV,
RADIO, AND PRINT

Worldwide ad spending increased throughout the late 1980s, with higher growth outside the Triad markets.

Region	1987 ($000,000)	1988 ($000,000)	1988 % Change	1989 ($000,000)	1989 % Change
North America	$74,484	$80,785	+8.5%	$86,248	+6.8%
Europe	$42,326	$46,914	+10.8	$51,521	+9.8
Asia/Pacific	$28,957	$31,443	+8.6	$34,176	+8.7
Latin America	$ 2,980	$ 3,254	+9.2	$ 3,514	+8.0
Africa/Middle East	$ 1,162	$ 1,269	+9.2	$ 1,371	+8.0

Source: Saatchi & Saatchi estimates.

EXHIBIT 15.6 UNILEVER RANKED NO. 1 IN NON-U.S. ADVERTISING

As this exhibit illustrates, advertising is a big business throughout the world.

Rank	Advertiser	Headquarters	Primary business	Non-U.S. spending ($000)	U.S spending ($000)	Worldwide spending ($000)	Non-U.S. as % of worldwide
1	Unilever NV/PLC	Rotterdam/London	Soaps	$1,207,509	$ 607,500	$1,815,009	66.5%
2	Procter & Gamble	Cincinnati	Soaps	932,724	1,506,900	2,439,624	38.2
3	Nestlé SA	Vevey, Switzerland	Food	600,586	573,800	1,174,386	51.1
4	Renault SA	Paris	Automotive	370,056	NA	370,056	100.0
5	Matsushita Electric Industrial Co.	Osaka, Japan	Electronics	365,252	61,754	427,007	85.5
6	Fiat SpA	Turin, Italy	Automotive	354,568	458*	355,026	99.9
7	Mars	McLean, Va.	Food	352,983	339,700	692,683	51.0
8	Kao	Tokyo	Soaps	344,233	12,022*	356,255	96.6
9	Nissan	Tokyo	Automotive	333,215	224,900	558,115	59.7
10	Toyota	Toyota City, Japan	Automotive	322,598	272,900	595,498	54.2
11	Henkel	Düsseldorf	Soaps	318,647	NA	318,647	100.0
12	Philip Morris	New York	Food	318,065	2,058,200	2,376,265	13.4
13	Peugeot SA	Paris	Automotive	292,341	24,342*	316,683	92.3
14	General Motors	Detroit	Automotive	274,061	1,294,000	1,568,061	17.5
15	Honda	Tokyo	Automotive	272,599	243,300	515,899	52.8
16	Mitsubishi	Tokyo	Automotive	266,256	68,931	335,187	79.4
17	Hitachi	Tokyo	Electronics	257,620	14,069*	271,689	94.8
18	Colgate-Palmolive	New York	Soaps	253,532	306,600	560,132	45.3
19	Coca-Cola	Atlanta	Food	236,603	385,100	621,703	38.1
20	Ford	Dearborn, Mich.	Automotive	234,914	569,800	804,714	29.2

Source: Adapted from *Advertising Age*, December 4, 1989, p. S-2.

EXHIBIT 15.7
TOP TEN AGENCIES
WORLDWIDE

As global advertising agencies follow their global clients, form strategic partnerships, and undergo mergers and acquisitions, they become global corporations in their own right.

Rank	Agency	Worldwide gross income	% change
1	Dentsu Inc.	$1,316.4	11.9
2	Saatchi & Saatchi Advertising Worldwide	890.0	20.2
3	Young & Rubicam	865.4	14.2
4	Backer Spielvogel Bates Worldwide	759.8	10.2
5	McCann-Erickson Worldwide	715.5	8.9
6	Ogilvy & Mather Worldwide	699.7	10.1
7	BBDO Worldwide	656.6	12.1
8	J. Walter Thompson Co.	626.4	12.0
9	Lintas: Worldwide	593.3	10.4
10	Hakuhodo Inc.	585.5	12.1

Notes: Dollars are in millions.
Source: Adapted from *Advertising Age*, March 29, 1990, p. S-1.

Advertising agencies, like other suppliers of business services, have been globalizing along with their customers.

the J. Walter Thompson Agency, based in the United States, established international connections in 1899. More recently, global advertising agencies, such as Saatchi & Saatchi of England, have been involved in aggressive campaigns to reach a worldwide market. As their clients pay more attention to global markets, agencies must grow in order to serve their clients. Today, as a result, all major advertising agencies operate internationally. The largest single advertising agency in the world is Dentsu, based in Japan. The group claimed total billings in 1989 of over $1.3 billion. (See Exhibit 15.7.)

The massive size of global agencies presents some problems for advertisers. Clients are often concerned about conflicts of interest that might arise when formerly independent agencies merge into a mega-agency. Procter & Gamble, for example, does not want any subgroup within its advertising agency to handle any competitor's brands. In the face of large corporate and agency mergers and increased global competition, the potential for conflicts of interest increases. Thus, in the late 1980s, Saatchi & Saatchi gained $310 million in client billings as a result of acquisitions. However, its losses due to client departures, including those caused by conflicts of interest, amounted to $462 million.[5]

Agencies based in less-developed countries vary considerably in their competencies and in their approaches to markets. For example, most of the advertising generated by agencies in less-developed countries is persuasive in nature, rather than informative. Such agencies also focus largely on advertising alone rather than providing services like marketing research and public relations. In some less-developed countries, such as Peru, managers of advertising agencies complain that businesses underuse agencies and that their advertising is less effective as a result.[6]

Agency-client relationships also vary considerably in different national markets. In many cultures relationships with agencies are viewed as long-term personal ties, not simply as contracts that may be broken whenever the client or the agency is displeased. In the United States, it is not difficult to change agencies. But McDonald's, for example, found that changing agencies in Brazil not only is difficult but can be harmful to the company's image. When the company switched to a new agency, its former agency generated a great deal of negative publicity, calling McDonald's "paramilitary" and claiming that it had lost money because of the company's actions.

In some countries there are legal restrictions on agency-client relationships. Korea, for example, bars foreign agencies from the country. In response, agencies like Ogilvy and Mather have developed "technical consultant" agreements with Korean agencies. These agreements enable the Korean agencies to serve their clients more fully. They also permit greater coordination of the advertising used in Korea (the second-largest advertising market in Asia) with that used in the rest of Asia.

Media Issues

Global media selection is more difficult than domestic, due to more choices and lack of experience of marketers.

Inexperience and more diverse media choices make global media planning a challenging task. Triad marketers entering other markets are confronted by a relative lack of media and data, higher production costs, and the inability to benefit from economies of scale. Four specific media problems must be managed by global advertisers: availability, cost, frequency and reach, and verification.

Availability.   In mid-1982, for the first time, radio ads were legally broadcast by private radio stations in Belgium. But government-controlled radio and television networks still refuse to broadcast ads. In Australia a quite different problem presents itself: media are available, but only if ads have been produced in Australia or with Australian actors. Faced with the lack of media, advertisers must be willing to try new options (such as advertising in movie theaters) or develop what is for other markets somewhat unusual (sound trucks or even sails on ships).

Sometimes the problem is too many media choices rather than too few. A nationwide advertising campaign using newspapers in India would require the purchase of space in about a hundred major papers. The advertiser would face problems of scheduling and possible overlap, and it could still miss a considerable portion of the target market. In Japan there are three national newspapers that would provide adequate market coverage. However, access could be limited by the Dentsu agency's purchase of 30 to 50 percent of the advertising space and the papers' possible refusal to expand to accommodate additional advertising. Another problem of availability has to do with the timing of media purchases; in South Africa, for example, television time must be purchased one year in advance.

One response to the problem of media availability is the growth of global media. (See Exhibit 15.8). For certain markets, such as some industrial markets and upscale consumer goods markets, newspapers and magazines are providing international editions. *The Wall Street Journal*, for example, publishes American, Asian, and European editions. Magazines like *Newsweek* and the German *Wirtschaftwoche* provide international editions. Satellite broadcasting of television programs and ads is also developing into an international medium, especially in Western Europe. The Music Box (similar to MTV in the United States) is seen in over 5 million of the 40 million households in Western Europe, and Europe TV reaches 3.5 million homes. As of this writing, about twenty satellite stations are available.[7]

Cost.   Global advertising is further complicated by cost considerations. Translations are expensive, and the cost of rewriting an ad in culturally acceptable terms may be high. Inefficient production facilities, which must be used on a market-by-market basis, also increase the cost per exposure. And due to the fragmented nature of media in some markets, as well as the lack of media that can be used in a precise manner to reach specific target markets, global advertising frequently involves higher percentages of wasted circulation. Advertising costs vary considerably from one market to another. For example, the cost of reaching 1,000 readers in European countries ranges from $1.58 in Belgium to $5.91 in Italy.[8] Whenever possible, media space should be purchased by buyers who are familiar with the targeted national market. It is not unusual for a seller of media space to charge an advertiser from another country more than a local advertiser for the same space.

Advertisers can lower their costs by reusing visual presentations and changing only the text or soundtrack to satisfy local needs. But that strategy by itself may not be enough. Visual or nonverbal cues in the presentation will be interpreted differently by members of different cultures and may result in unintended communication effects. For example, when an American underarm spray was sold in Europe, a woman was shown applying the product to a shaved underarm. In Italy the product did not sell well until the marketer found out that in that culture women who shave their underarms are held in low regard. After the company developed a new presentation using a model who had not shaved her underarm, sales increased.

Frequency and Reach.   Another problem with advertising in some national markets is the inability to generate sufficient frequency and reach. Media vary considerably in their ability to contact the target market as often as the advertiser would like (frequency). One expert claims that "lack of frequency of [global] advertising is the single most common cause of program failure."[9]

Exposure of an ad to the largest possible target market (reach) must be achieved through a combination of media. For example, television if used by itself would not reach enough of the target market for sports cars in Holland.

EXHIBIT 15.8   ADVERTISING AGE'S 1989 GLOBAL MEDIA LINEUP

As markets become increasingly global, so too, do the newspapers and magazines that serve those markets, as is illustrated in this exhibit.

Title/ publishers/ headquarters	Paid North American circulation/ % chg*	Paid foreign circulation by region/ % chg*	Worldwide circulation/ % chg*	b&w pg cost/ 4/c pg cost in 1989	Global cpm b&w pg in 1989	Top worldwide advertisers in 1989
Financial Times of London Financial Times London	20,760 10.8%	Europe: 257,133 (1.1%) Middle East/Africa: 3,369 (1.0%) Asia/Pacific: 3,800 (0.4%) Latin America: 302 49.5% Caribbean: 415 (43.5%)	285,779 (0.3%)	$ 34,944 $ 56,100	$122.28	British Airways British Gas Toshiba Daimler-Benz Renault
International Herald Tribune New York Times & Washington Post Neuilly, France	4,754 16.7%	Europe: 133,343 0.1% Middle East/Africa: 6,809 (16.5%) Asia/Pacific: 34,953 10.0% Latin America: 2,334 13.3%	182,193 3.0%	$ 39,432 $ 74,920	$216.43	Republic Bank of N.Y. Lufthansa Airlines Thai Airlines AT&T Carrera
People's Daily Gao Di Beijing	52,000 NA	Europe: 15,000 NA Middle East/Africa: 7,000 NA Asia/Pacific: 63,000 NA Latin America: 13,000 NA China: 3,850,000 NA	4,000,000 NA	105 NA	$ 0.26	Panasonic Sharp Electronics Sanyo Boeing Toyota
USA Today Gannett Arlington, Va.	1,755,000 6.4%	Europe: 40,100 17.7% Asia/Pacific: 13,000 8.2%	1,808,100 6.6%	$ 52,113 $ 69,083	$ 28.82	AT&T TWA Stouffer Hotels Thai Airlines American Airlines
Wall Street Journal Dow Jones New York	1,835,714 (1.8%)	Europe: 44,758 3.7% Asia/Pacific: 37,093 4.2%	1,917,564 (1.6%)	$117,394 NA	$ 61.22	American Express IBM Merrill Lynch AT&T General Motors

Publication / Publisher / City	Circulation (% change)	Regional breakdown	Circulation (% change)	b/w & 4/c rates	cpm	Major advertisers
Business Week McGraw-Hill New York	900,989 1.0%	Europe: 46,331 5.8% Middle East/Africa: 7,470 15.3% Asia/Pacific: 28,527 12.2% Latin America: 21,410 7.3%	1,004,727 1.7%	$ 41,895 $ 63,680	$ 41.70	AT&T General Motors IBM Digital Canon
The Economist The Economist Newspaper London	161,166 13.0%	Europe: 158,716 7.1% Middle East/Africa: 13,502 (1.4%) Asia/Pacific: 41,056 7.6% Latin America: 6,484 3.4%	380,924 9.1%	$ 9,000	$ 23.63	Singapore Airlines Lufthansa Airlines Bank of America Nynex Morgan Guaranty Trust
Newsweek Newsweek New York	3,288,453 (0.8%)	Atlantic: 310,293 2.8% Asia: 209,432 0.8% Latin America: 55,471 2.3% Australia: 109,200 0.1%[7]	3,972,849 (0.4%)	$ 95,615 $156,100	$ 24.07	Singapore Airlines Rothmans International Rolex Thai Airlines KLM
Paris Match International Publications Filipacchi Paris	35,045 (11.6%)	Europe: 136,506 (3.0%) Middle East/Africa: 34,022 (9.1%) Asia/Pacific: 1,979 3.6% Latin America: 3,434 (20.6%) Other: 25,182 29.5%	236,167 0.0%	$ 8,561 $ 12,532	$ 36.25	Philip Morris B.A.T. Tobacco S.M.H. Group Peugeot Citroen
Time Time New York	4,746,417 (6.7%)	Europe: 441,147 0.7% Middle East/Africa: 72,397 (6.4%) Asia/Pacific: 422,000 6.8% Latin America: 88,000 0.0%	5,769,961 (5.2%)	$144,741 $225,680	$ 25.00	Singapore Airlines Rothmans International Philip Morris Daimler-Benz IBM
National Geographic National Geographic Society Washington	9,456,510 1.7%	Europe: 723,356 11.1% Middle East/Africa: 67,776 6.4% Pacific: 382,357 8.1% Latin America: 98,515 3.9%	10,728,514 2.6%	$136,725 $180,480	$ 12.74	Canon Iberia Airlines Spanish Tourist Board Olympus Optical Mazda
Reader's Digest Reader's Digest Association Pleasantville, N.Y.	18,280,470 (1.5%)	Atlantic: 7,190,342 (0.3%) Asia/Pacific: 1,728,995 5.7% Latin America: 1,203,570 2.1%	28,403,377 (0.7%)	$254,170 $340,275	$ 9.12	Franklin Mint Nestlé SA Unilever NV NV Philips Kraft

Source: Adapted from *Advertising Age*, December 4, 1989, p. S-4.

Note: Percentage change from previous year: b/w = black and white; 4/c = full color; cpm = cost per thousand readers.

The marketer would also need to place advertisements in newspapers, magazines, radio, or other media to contact the target group.

When attempting to generate sufficient reach, the advertiser must choose among three levels of media: national, regional, and international. *National* media are those whose reach is limited to one country. *Regional* media cover more than one country (for example, part of a continent). *International* media, which have the widest reach of all, cover several regions.

When an advertiser is faced with a lack of appropriate media to reach its target market, it may purchase a wider variety of media. But this tactic often spreads the advertising budget too thin, thereby sacrificing frequency. This is particularly true when the marketer is introducing a product into several countries at the same time. In situations in which reach is likely to be achieved at the expense of frequency, it is preferable to introduce the product into one country or region at a time.

Verification.   A final problem with global advertising media is the relative lack of data to verify whether the promised reach has been achieved or, in the worst case, whether the ad has been run at all. Few monitoring agencies like Nielsen, which provides ratings for television programs in the United States, exist outside the United States, Japan, and the European Community. Moreover, it is estimated that in some nations as much as 25 percent of the commercial advertising that is paid for is never broadcast or published. Newspapers and magazines are especially difficult to monitor. And in most cases outside major markets, reliable descriptive data on the receivers of broadcast or print advertising are virtually nonexistent. If ratings or circulation figures do exist, they may be measured differently in different markets, making it difficult to compare data from various markets.

This situation is further complicated by *spillover*, or exposure of the ad to markets in more than one country. A household in France, for example, may see advertisements designed for the French-speaking Swiss and Belgian markets. Under such conditions it is difficult to obtain data on actual reach and frequency. Such a situation argues for using the same communication mix when possible. Of course, the possibility of words having multiple meanings in different languages must be taken into account. As satellite television broadcasting grows in importance, this problem will become more common.

Global marketers have responded to these challenges in a variety of ways, ranging from establishing associations to campaign for reliable data to establishing their own media, whose effectiveness they can verify more accurately. For example, in India, free entertainment is provided to draw a crowd, and products are sold directly to the audience in the same way that patent-medicine shows operated in frontier communities in the United States. This may sound less reliable than employing an advertising agency's media department to negotiate long-term media purchases. But where problems of availability, cost, frequency and reach, and verification are encountered, marketers must be willing to experiment with alternative media mixes.

Media Options

Each media option has unique global opportunities as well as limitations that must be kept in mind when designing a global advertising strategy. This section discusses each major advertising medium from a global perspective.

Newspapers.   As a global advertising medium, newspapers vary considerably in usefulness. Due to the wide variety of newspapers and the low literacy rates in some markets, it is often difficult to generate sufficient levels of frequency and reach through newspapers. In some markets, the main advantage of newspapers—a short lead time between submission and publication of the ad—does not exist. In other markets, verification is a particular problem.

Newspapers can suffer from poor production facilities, especially in less-developed countries. Visual representations of the product may dissolve into unappealing smudges. Because of their limited production facilities, newspapers are limited in the number of pages they can print. As a result, they may sell more advertising than they can fit into the paper, deciding which ads to run with a lottery or even not to run some.

Magazines.   Internationally, magazines represent a smaller portion of the media mix than they do in the Triad markets. If the target market consists of relatively affluent people in less-developed countries, magazines are a viable option. And, of course, for global industrial markets, specialty markets, and general consumer markets in media-rich countries, magazine ads are quite valuable.

Radio.   Government controls and even bans on radio advertising are the norm rather than the exception around the world. Verification of data on radio audiences is also a problem outside the Triad markets. But radio-audience involvement is generally high, due to the relative importance of radio as a communications medium in less-developed countries. In these countries it is not unusual for radio to be one of the few media, if not the only one, to which a sizeable portion of the population is exposed. When radio broadcasting is available in such a market, it serves as a personal medium, with high listening rates.

Television.   In highly developed economies, television is usually an extremely important advertising medium. However, in most countries in the European Community there are limitations on the number and length of television commercials that may be broadcast. In these markets commercials are normally broadcast in blocks between shows, not within the shows themselves. The blocks often begin and end with audio and visual cues indicating that ads are being aired. In contrast, American and Japanese television advertising has a different problem: too many commercials are shown. The resulting clutter inhibits communication. In less-developed countries, television commercials are extremely limited and are purchased more as a defensive strategy (so that competitors won't gain more exposure) than as part of an active strategy for effective communication.

Direct Marketing in Japan

As the yen increases against other national currencies, global mail-order companies are doing a booming business in Japan. For example, foreign catalogue centers at Japanese department stores let San Francisco's Sharper Image and Germany's Otto Versand sell to Japanese consumers as well as those in their own country. Overall, mail-order sales are expected to increase in Japan by 10 to 20 percent a year throughout the 1990s. Telemarketing is also growing quickly in Japan; it increased close to 50 percent throughout the 1980s. And direct mail, other than catalogues, is increasing some 20 percent per year, as is business-to-business direct marketing.

One advantage to direct marketing in these ways is that foreign companies don't have to build new distribution systems. But postal rates are high, credit cards are not widely used in Japan, and toll-free phone service is expensive to provide to overseas customers.

Source: Based on T. Holden, "The Japanese Go on a Mail-Order Shopping Spree," *Business Week*, September 7, 1987; and "Direct Marketing World Survey," *Direct Marketing*, April 1987, p. 36.

The amount of exposure to television varies greatly. The average number of hours watched per person is dramatically lower in most countries than in the United States. For example, in the United States the average person watches almost eight hours of television per day, compared to two hours in Europe.

Specialty Advertising.   "Something of value that serves as a vehicle for advertising" is an apt description of specialty advertising, whether it is a pen distributed by an insurance company in Illinois or a paper fan given to customers at an ice cream store in India. Specialty advertising options range from very inexpensive items, such as matchbook covers, to original works of art. Sometimes it is difficult to decide which option to use. There are literally tens of thousands of possibilities. Popular in many nations, especially those with developed economies, specialty advertising appeals to potential buyers because they feel that they are getting something for nothing.

Direct Mail.   The key advantage of direct mail is its ability to present an advertising message to high-potential customers. Actually obtaining this advantage, however, depends on having access to a well-developed, targeted mailing list. (See Global Dimensions 15.2.) It also depends on high literacy rates and dependable postal services. These requirements mean that direct mail is not appropriate for a large number of markets. In some African nations, for example, it takes longer to send a letter to another city within the country than to send one overseas. India, on the other hand, boasts that a letter mailed in India will reach any destination in the country within three days. This means that global advertisers should give serious consideration to sending direct mail to educated consumers in India, but they should avoid it in some African markets.

Outdoor Advertising.   Billboards and other outdoor advertising are of considerable importance in markets where the literacy rate is low and advertisers wish to project an image or increase the visibility of their brand or product. Even though customers may not be able to read the brand name, they may recognize it as one they have seen advertised, and they may be more inclined to buy the product. Some advertisers have found that hiring people to walk around with sandwich boards is effective in urban markets, where the novelty of this form of advertising generates curiosity among pedestrians. In economically developed economies, outdoor advertising can achieve high frequency rates by being placed along heavily traveled commuter routes, where it will serve as a steady reminder of the availability of the product.

Transit Advertising.   Transit advertising is done on or in mass transit vehicles or terminals. Mass transit is very important in countries where private transportation is too expensive. The captive audience exposed to transit advertising may be subject to several repetitions per day. In many markets, advertising on a variety of transit vehicles may be useful. For example, trucks and minicabs (which are not usually used for transit advertising in Triad markets) may be used as moving billboards.

Swiss watchmakers, when faced with intense competition from watchmakers in Asia, used transit advertising to convince residents of Hong Kong that Swiss watch parts make a better timepiece.

Electronic Advertising.   This is a media option that is growing in importance. It is sometimes used to support personal-selling activities. For example, pharmaceutical firms such as Pfizer[10] have adopted interactive videodiscs to support their salespeople when they call on hospitals, physicians, and pharmacists. Even the store directory at Printemps, a well-known Paris department store, is offered in a touch-screen format.

Telemarketing, or the use of telephones for marketing, is used in both industrial and consumer markets to increase sales. Of course, it can only be used in markets with reliable telephone systems—these can be found in Triad markets but are rarer in developing economies.

Selling directly through television is an electronic option that originated in the United States and is expanding into Western Europe. Another option is electronic catalogs. In France, the telephone company has distributed electronic terminals that display products, which consumers can then order directly from the sellers by telephone.

Cinema.   Cinema commercials are gaining in popularity in developed countries. Many U.S. movie theaters, for example, advertise not only coming attractions and popcorn but also local services and products. The cinema is also an important media option in countries where media alternatives are limited and literacy rates are low. Because of its low cost, large numbers of consumers use the cinema as a major form of recreation. This medium reaches even more people when cinema shows travel from village to village.

GLOBAL PUBLIC RELATIONS

Public relations are managed to achieve the most positive image possible.

A business must communicate with customers, financial suppliers, employees, and governments at all levels, to illustrate just a few of the relevant publics. (See Exhibit 15.9.) The ability to influence these publics is very important. The more favorably the financial community views the company, for example, the lower the interest rate the company may be charged when it borrows money, and the faster a stock offering may be sold.

Public relations includes publicity, plant tours, stockholders' meetings, and any other activity the organization undertakes to convey a positive image. For example, in the mid-1970s, in response to the fuel crisis (due to large increases in petroleum prices), oil companies like Mobil turned away from product advertising and undertook extensive public relations campaigns to counter charges that they were exploiting customers. The oil companies wanted to make sure customers and government regulators knew their side of the story and would not attempt to penalize them.

Publicity generates "free" exposure in the print and broadcast media, because the organization does not pay for the media time or space. But obtaining publicity requires the use of staff or an outside agency, and that costs money. A

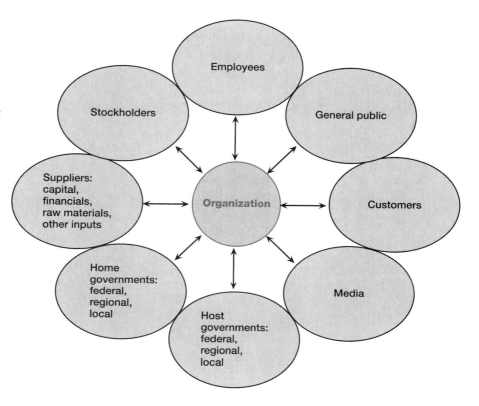

large problem with publicity is that because it is "free," the organization gives up some control of what is said about the organization or product, how it is said, and where it is said.

Most industrial and consumer buyers are somewhat skeptical of advertisements. They know that advertising is an attempt to influence them, and that a great deal of effort goes into making sure the message is "right." On the other hand, buyers are more likely to believe publicity, because know it cannot be influenced as directly. This makes positive publicity a valuable asset. (See Global Dimensions 15.3.)

If the general public relations campaign is successful, the other elements of the promotional mix have an easier task.

However, because the organization cannot directly control publicity, its communication with any public cannot be limited to this tool alone. For one thing, publicity can sometimes be negative, as Union Carbide discovered in the aftermath of the tragic accident at its plant in Bhopal, India, in which thousands of people were killed or injured. Usually an organization has even less control over global publicity than it has over domestic publicity. Few corporations are so powerful that they can control their image in host-country media.

When a company enters a foreign market, it can use properly translated product news releases, feature articles, and other published information, or it

Positive Public Relations

Positive public relations should generate positive publicity, so that the organization and its products are more readily accepted by customers as well as by the societies in which it operates. Thus, Mobil sponsors art projects throughout the world. While it performs a valuable public service, Mobil also generates positive publicity. Its actions are based partly on the recognition that people are more likely to deal with companies that they consider "good citizens."

It is relatively easy to generate positive global publicity when the target of the publicity is an identifiable group of people who are in a position to affect the organization's operations. Editors and journalists from the broadcast and print media, for example, may be targeted for special attention because they influence the news about a company that is released to the public. In smaller countries or those with limited media, editors and journalists are a fairly small target. Another likely target for a publicity campaign consists of government regulatory agencies. If they have a positive view of the company, it may be easier for the company to conduct business. Currently, for instance, Japanese companies like Toyota and Sony are very concerned that the huge U.S. trade deficit will result in tariffs and other protectionist policies. They have initiated public relations campaigns—including press releases, lobbying, and general publicity—to convince journalists, regulators, and the public that protectionist policies are not the best solution to the trade deficit.

can develop new, market-specific materials. Manufacturers of computers and other high-tech products may find it easier to use materials developed for their domestic markets than would manufacturers of consumer goods. The use of standardized technical language in industry journals means that existing promotional materials for high-tech products are often directly transferable to another market. It is much more difficult to translate the shortened (often slang) expressions used in promoting consumer goods and services.

Public relations activities complement other promotional tools by establishing an environment of credibility in which those tools can be used more effectively. For example, French wines often command a premium in other national markets because of the favorable image cultivated by French wine makers. But publicity can also work in the other direction, as was noted before. For example, imports of Italian wines to the United States decreased after it was reported that Italian wine was polluted with methyl alcohol, which can be harmful or even fatal if ingested. Even though no polluted wine ever entered the United States, sales of Italian wines there declined by 30 percent and have yet to recover fully.

GLOBAL PERSONAL SELLING

The flexibility of personal selling is its greatest asset, but its higher costs must be justified by communication needs.

Personal selling is the most effective way to sell anything. The greatest advantage of personal selling is its flexibility. If a potential customer objects to the product or conditions of sale, the salesperson can modify the message on the spot. But individualized communication costs money. On a per-contact basis, personal selling is the most expensive of all the promotional tools. Hence, it is usually used in situations in which flexibility is required and high per-contact costs can be justified. Marketers of industrial products, especially capital goods such as computer systems or entire plants (which may cost millions of dollars), rely heavily on personal selling. In consumer markets personal selling is used more selectively; it is used, for example, in the sale of furniture and automobiles.

Types of Personal-Selling Activities

There are four basic types of selling activity that help define who should be selected for that task.

There are four basic types of domestic and global selling. **Creative selling** is the process of establishing contacts, locating distributors, and filling orders. It requires a thorough knowledge of formal and informal communication processes. Salespeople working in a foreign market usually have difficulty with creative selling, because they do not have a thorough understanding of the host-country environment.[11] Establishing contacts, in particular, requires considerable knowledge about proper conduct. For example, in Moslem societies religion plays an important role in determining when business is done and how. Hiring local sales representatives usually works better in foreign markets than using home-country reps.

Missionary selling, a form of creative selling, involves building and maintaining close and mutually advantageous relationships with intermediaries. Drug companies like Organon Pharmaceutical, a Dutch multinational corporation, use missionary salespeople to communicate with organizations and individuals that handle their products. They often establish friendly long-term relationships with doctors, druggists, and retailers (helping druggists, for example, set up point-of-purchase displays) and develop training programs for the intermediary's salesforce. Again, local sales representatives are normally used.

Technical selling emphasizes technical knowledge of the firm's products. For example, a multinational bank that wants to be able to transfer information from any branch in the world to any other needs to be served by a salesperson with technical knowledge of computer systems, not necessarily one who understands how consumers behave in different national markets. In such situations, the organization can hire salespeople who understand clients' needs and match them with the seller's products, regardless of the salesperson's nationality.

Selling to ultimate consumers includes a wide variety of activities. Department store clerks sell to the ultimate consumer, as do salespeople who work at fairs, caravans, trading centers, or central markets, and even from door to door. Not surprisingly, residents of the host country are normally most effective at this type of selling.

Types of Salesforces

A firm must first decide whether to use an **indirect salesforce** (which the firm does not directly employ or control) or a **direct salesforce** (which it does directly employ). This decision is based on the same concerns (cost, control, the ability to reach the market) in global and domestic markets. Once the decision to hire a direct salesforce is reached, the composition of the salesforce must be addressed. The salesforce may be composed of expatriate, national, or cosmopolitan personnel.

Expatriate personnel are employed by a corporation in a country other than their home country. An Italian citizen who works for Olivetti in Spain is an expatriate. As world trade has increased and global marketing groups have been formed, the proportion of expatriate employees has declined. Expatriates are expensive over the long run—they cost an average of 200 percent over base salary, they often have problems of personal adjustment, and it takes a long time for them to fully appreciate a foreign market. However, sometimes a company entering a high-growth market needs time to develop a host-country salesforce, and finds that expatriates are a good investment.

Nationals are sales employees who are based in their home country. An Australian citizen who sells the construction services of Hollandsche Beton Maatschappij in Australia is a national. There is a definite trend toward using nationals in global business. Many nations, particularly those with less-developed economies, are increasingly putting pressure on corporations to employ nationals. Moreover, as educational systems and training opportunities improve, more qualified national personnel are becoming available. Because of their lower total cost compared to expatriate salesforces, national salesforces are more attractive for industrial as well as consumer markets. The overwhelming argument in favor of nationals, however, is their superior understanding of the market and their ability to work within its cultural and social norms while pursuing the company's objectives.

Cosmopolitan employees are citizens of one country who are employed by a corporation based in a second country and are working in a third country. A Spanish engineer who works in Portugal for Philips is a cosmopolitan. Large multinational corporations frequently hire cosmopolitan employees, often at the sales-management or product-management level as well as at the salesforce level. The increase in world trade has led to an increase in the availability and use of cosmopolitan employees. This trend has been reinforced by the development of educational programs, such as master's degree programs in international business studies offered by management schools in Europe, North America, and Asia.

Special Issues in Global Selling

Implementing personal-selling strategies on a global scale requires that the marketer pay attention to some special issues. For example, bargaining is viewed and carried out differently from one culture to another. Americans, in particular, seem to have difficulty adapting to different bargaining methods. Several successful Japanese businesspeople have said that all they had to do to gain a price concession from an American was remain silent. Sooner or later, the American would reduce the price just to break the silence.

Another issue is whether a sales technique that has been used effectively in one market will be effective in another. In their hurry to close a deal, Americans seem rude to many Europeans. Yet Europeans often underestimate the amount of time a contract negotiation will take in China.

Finally, there is the problem of side payments, sometimes referred to as bribes, bonuses, or "greasing the wheel." In some business environments such payments seem to be a necessary part of doing business. For example, the clearance of products through customs may be facilitated by a side payment. But many countries and companies view this as bribery and either punish it or refuse to engage in the practice.

Managing the Global Salesforce

Because the salesforce is in direct contact with customers, it must be carefully managed in order to carry out the best promotional mix.

How a firm manages its salesforce is critical to the success or failure of a global marketing strategy. A firm initially entering a foreign market frequently relies on an export or import house; it sells its products directly to that organization, which then sells the products in the new market. Through the intermediary, the firm ties into an already established salesforce and does not have to go through the difficult and expensive process of developing its own salesforce for the new market. But firms that want to be more involved in the market and gain greater control over the promotion process must establish and manage a global salesforce.

Recruitment and Selection.   For many years the leading criterion for selecting host-country sales personnel was the ability to speak the home-country language. Thus, U.S. firms recruited Arab salespeople, sales managers, and marketing managers by first screening them on the basis of their ability to speak English. Although communication between salespeople and management is essential, it is not clear that language ability is the best indicator of the employee's potential for long-term success, even though it may be the easiest standard to apply. Certain personal characteristics, such as maturity, adaptability, and motivation, are much more important than language skills.

An employee who accepts an assignment in a foreign country often faces high personal costs. Foremost among these, and the ones over which management has the least control, are those that pertain to the employee's family. Spouses are often unhappy about moving to another country, partly due to limitations on their own career opportunities. Most countries issue a work permit to the corporate employee but make it considerably more difficult for the employee's spouse to obtain a work permit. Children also worry about living in a foreign land. They must leave familiar surroundings and friends to attend a new school, sometimes in a foreign language. Music lessons, sports activities, and other hobbies and interests that are important to them may be interrupted. The pressures on family relationships brought about by living in a strange culture add to the strain on the employee. Japanese corporations have found that employees designated to work in the United States have serious reservations about the American educational system and the ability of their children to become reintegrated into Japanese society upon their return. Relocation difficulties can represent a major cost to corporations if they result in early return from overseas assignments or ineffective sales performance, in addition to costly relocation programs. (See Global Dimensions 15.4.)

Some employees may refuse overseas assignments because of the fear, common among expatriates, that they will be forgotten if they stay away from the home office for several years. An upward-moving manager for a large U.S. advertising agency reported that he turned down a two-year overseas assignment, with a higher salary and more responsibility, because he was "afraid to be gone that long."

Training.   Increasingly, corporations are realizing that their international personnel at all levels need specialized training in how to perform effectively in a foreign environment. Most global corporations have extensive training programs in product benefits and selling techniques. Nippon Electronic Corporation (NEC), a Japanese computer company with $15 billion in annual sales, goes far beyond the norm; its 162 courses help employees prepare for foreign assignments in a wide variety of ways. One NEC course for salespeople helps them polish their language skills. Another familiarizes them with the business customs of foreign markets and trains them in negotiating skills.[12]

Motivation and Compensation.   Understanding what motivates people is critical to successful salesforce management. Economic rewards, such as bonuses, are the most effective motivators in North America. But in Northern Europe, where personal income tax rates may reach 70 percent, noneconomic motivators work better. In Japan, sales representatives place greater emphasis on collective achievement.

Caterpillar uses an international working vacation to motivate and train outstanding sales personnel. The best Caterpillar salesperson from each country is invited, together with his or her spouse, to Marbella, Spain, for a vacation combined with further training. This approach appears to be more effective overall than a straight economic reward.

GLOBAL SALES PROMOTIONS

All sales-promotion techniques share the objectives of stimulating interest in purchasing the product.

Sales promotions are short-term promotional activities that gain attention, stimulate interest, and provide motivation. Sales promotions are effective in many different cultures and markets, but they must be used carefully to ensure that they are acceptable in cultural, economic, social, and legal terms. (See Exhibit 15.10.)

Expatriate Salesforces:
A Tough Life in the United States

Most Americans think, quite naturally, of expatriates as being Americans living abroad. But as foreign investment and business activity increases in the United States, so too do the number of foreign businesspeople living there. They face the same basic problems adjusting to another culture that Americans do when going abroad.

For example, an Asian or European expatriate in the United States is isolated from the home culture and (usually) language. The expatriate's family has to adapt to new living conditions, schools, and social systems. One expatriate's wife was shocked when, alone one evening, she opened the door to her home to be confronted by people in face paint and strange clothing, celebrating Halloween. Of more serious concern to the nearly 200,000 Japanese business executives living in the United States is whether their children will get the education necessary to prepare them for the notoriously difficult entrance examinations at Japanese universities.

In general, employees' families are not prepared for foreign assignments as extensively as the employees themselves are. Despite the fact that such training is good "people policy" and makes strong economic sense, many corporations assume that a half-day seminar of general information will suffice to prepare families for foreign assignments. One four-hour seminar, which excluded children, claimed to prepare U.S. families for a two-year assignment in Saudi Arabia. The Saudi religious environment and its implications for behavior, including how executives' spouses could expect to be treated socially, were "covered" in a 15-minute talk by an American national who had never been to Saudi Arabia or had any specific training in Saudi customs. In sharp contrast is a three-day course for NEC executives' wives. The course prepares them for the difficulties of living in the United States by offering language training, information about social customs, and even tips on how to shop successfully in American supermarkets.

Source: Based in part on B. O'Reilly, "Japan's Uneasy U.S. Managers," *Fortune*, April 25, 1988, pp. 10–14.

Sales-Promotion Techniques

A wide variety of sales-promotion techniques are in use throughout the world, but each of them can be placed in one of three basic categories. (See Exhibit 15.11.) The first consists of promotions that *reduce the price* of the product in some way. Coupons, discount promotions, and trade allowances offer a price

EXHIBIT 15.10
AN INTERNATIONAL
VIEW OF SELECTED
SALES-PROMOTION
METHODS

Sales-promotion tech-
niques can be used
across nations, but the
global marketer must be
sensitive to the impact
different environments
have on how well the
techniques work.

Coupons

Require literacy and some sophistication on part of retailers and consumers

Require well-developed backward channels to handle redemption

For new product introductions, usually require well-developed print media

Social status perceptions affect effectiveness

Contests and sweepstakes

Cross-national use complex due to differing legal requirements

Prize choice should vary to match target-market tastes

Likely to be less effective where mass media coverage is poor

Require some sophistication on part of retailers

Price-offs

Likely to be ineffective in environments where prices are subject to bargaining

Require some sophistication on part of retailers

Subject to trade misuse

Stamps

Ineffective where target market is not amenable to delayed gratification

Unfeasible in unstable economic conditions (for both manufacturer and target market)

Handling and redemption both require fairly stable and sophisticated channels

In, on, and near packs

Do not require literacy

Do not require extensive mass media support

Do require secure distribution channels and some control over channel members

May require packaging adaptation depending on level of channel development

Source: Adapted from R. Foxman, P. S. Tansuhaj, and J. K. Wong, "Evaluating Cross-National Sales Promotion Strategy: An Audit Approach," *International Marketing Review*, Winter 1988, p. 11.

reduction at the time of purchase. Rebates reduce the price under certain conditions following sale. In the United States, 300 billion coupons are distributed to consumers each year via the print media, direct mail, and product packages.

Another type of sales promotion technique *adds value* to a product or adds to the perceived value of the product. Bonus packs; free samples; in, on, and near packs (coupons attached to or near the product); and premiums all add value to a product. Wine marketers in Belgium sometimes offer samples at small local markets; candy is often sold in free "decorator" containers in the United States, especially at holiday times; the Albert Heijn grocery chain in the Netherlands sells savings stamps based on the total amount of a customer's purchases. Contests and sweepstakes offer "something for nothing," which has universal appeal. British newspapers, for instance, "give away" thousands of pounds daily in Bingo and other contests that may be entered by readers.[13]

Sales-promotion techniques that *provide information* are especially important in marketing highly technical products. Product demonstrations, displays, special events, and trade shows and exhibitions are often used in combination with other sales-promotion techniques and other elements of the marketing mix. For convenience, displays such as those used by L'Eggs, the pantyhose company, not only provide information but aid in inventory control and storage.

Targets of Sales Promotions

Sales-promotion activities may be directed at one or more of three types of targets. **Customer promotions** are directed toward industrial or consumer buyers. A Lever Brothers detergent coupon, for example, is aimed at consumers. A **staff promotion** is designed to stimulate a particular response among employees or an external salesforce. A sales contest run by a Volvo dealer, in which the most outstanding member of the salesforce is rewarded with a free automobile, is an example of a staff promotion. Intermediaries can be targets of sales promotions, too. The Miller Brewing Company might use a contest to increase sales of its products to wholesalers by tying contest entry to larger orders.

Objectives of Sales Promotions

All sales-promotion techniques have the goal of stimulating sales. They achieve this objective in several ways. (The multiple objectives are listed in Exhibit 15.11. The most common are discussed here.) Techniques aimed at customers frequently are designed to stimulate a trial purchase. When other elements of the promotional mix, such as advertising, have captured a customer's attention, sales promotions can motivate the customer to try a product by reducing the risk involved. The wine marketers that offer free samples in small Belgian markets know that consumers are more likely to buy their products when they have had an opportunity to taste them before buying. Other sales-promotion techniques are designed to convert trial users into regular users or to induce repeat purchase. Premium programs, such as the Delta Frequent Flyer program, are an example. Two-for-one bonus packs of toothbrushes are another.

Sales promotions can also be designed to build distribution (and increase orders). Trade allowances can persuade distributors to order larger quantities of a product or to provide more shelf or display space. They are especially effective in highly competitive markets or when no single manufacturer has a dominant share of the market. Samples and contests are used to induce both the salesforce and intermediaries to increase orders. Trade shows, exhibitions, and other special events are designed to build distribution by meeting the information needs of target audiences.

Technique	Objective	Target	Key Issues
Reduce price			
Coupons	Encourage trial or repeat purchase	Consumers	Channel capacity
Trade allowances	Build distribution; increase orders	Intermediaries	Legal constraints; channel power
Price-offs	Encourage repeat purchase	Consumers	Pricing laws
Add to value or perceived value			
Samples	Encourage trial purchase; build distribution; increase orders	Consumers; intermediaries; staff	High cost
In, on, and near packs	Increase perception of value	Consumers	Space limitations; service norms; impact on price
Self-liquidating premiums	Encourage trial or repeat purchase; extend image; reinforce advertising	Consumers	Relate to product
Continuity premiums	Reward users; encourage repeat purchase	Consumers	Channel capacity; value of premium
Bonus packs	Increase perception of value; convert trier into user	Consumers	Space limitations; service norms
Contests and sweepstakes	Encourage trial purchase; draw attention to other promotional messages	Consumers; intermediaries; staff	High cost; lack of mass trial; legal constraints
Provide information			
Displays	Draw attention to product; provide information	Intermediaries; consumers	Must combine with other techniques

(Continued)

EXHIBIT 15.11   (*Continued*)

Technique	Objective	Target	Key Issues
Special events	Draw attention to product; provide information	Intermediaries; staff	High cost
Trade shows and exhibitions	Create presence in target's mind	Intermediaries; staff	High cost; usually for industrial or durable goods
Product demonstrations	Allow consumers to evaluate product without risk; build distribution	Consumers intermediaries	High cost

Factors in the Choice of Sales-Promotion Techniques

Like other promotional-mix elements, sales promotions must be evaluated in terms of national market factors.

Several factors affect decisions about which sales-promotion techniques to use. Some of these factors are universal and must be taken into account regardless of the culture in which the organization is operating. Other factors are culturally based and therefore have special significance for international marketers.

Costs.   The cost considerations associated with a sales-promotion campaign include not only an estimate of the total outlay but some idea of what contribution the outlay would make toward increasing sales. For example, free samples are a much more costly means of attracting new customers than cents-off coupons. But when a product benefit, such as good taste, is most easily communicated through trial use, the expense of samples may be necessary to promote the product adequately.

Cost factors also arise in considering the use of contests and sweepstakes. Contests are considerably less expensive to administer than sweepstakes. In the United States, a contest costs about $3 per thousand entrants, whereas a sweepstakes costs about $350 per thousand entrants. Although these techniques increase the amount of attention paid to product ads and serve to reinforce the product's image, one of their limitations is lack of ability to stimulate mass trial of the product. In the United States, where they are most popular, only about 20 percent of the population generally sends in entries to contests or sweepstakes. And some 76 percent of those entries are accompanied by copies of the entry form rather than by proofs of purchase.

Channel Capacity.   The willingness and ability of distributors, wholesalers, and retailers to accommodate the special requirements of sales promotions is another important issue. Cents-off coupons, for example, must be handled and processed by retailers. In Northern Europe coupons are not as popular as they are in the United States because retailers resent the cost and time required to process them.

Bonus packs and premiums may require flexibility in storage and shelf space so that oversized and oddly shaped products can be accommodated. Trade allowances that involve the provision of marketing services must take into account such factors as the size of the store. Indian retailers rejected one promoter's banners and point-of-purchase displays because they were simply too large to fit in their small stores.

Channel power.   The position of channel members relative to one another is another factor that affects the choice of sales promotion techniques. When a single manufacturer has a high degree of channel power, trade allowances typically are not used; the distributor either buys from that manufacturer or not at all. When a large distributor or retail organization, such as Woolworth's in Australia or Albert Heijn in The Netherlands, has substantial channel power, it can demand large trade allowances or threaten to buy from another manufacturer.

Legal Constraints.   The use of some sales-promotion techniques may be constrained by the laws in specific nations. Laws against price discrimination may prevent the use of price-offs, for example. Legal issues constitute the largest implementation problem in the case of contests and sweepstakes. In the United States, for example, a sweepstakes that requires proof of purchase is considered an illegal form of gambling. Similar laws in other countries constrain the use of these techniques. (See Exhibit 15.12.)

Taxes also affect the choice of promotion techniques. In Sweden liquor products are subject to high sales taxes, which raise the price to the consumer. A costly sales promotion, such as a commemorative decanter, would be unattractive if it were to raise the price of an already expensive product beyond a level that consumers find acceptable.

Norms.   The degree to which a sales-promotion technique is consistent with or violates cultural or service norms is a factor to be considered carefully in each target market. Point-of-purchase displays work well in situations where self-service is the norm. But by placing the product within reach of the customer, such displays violate the service norms of small shopkeepers in many areas of the world. For example, in a country in which coffee is typically sold in small stores where the shopkeeper grinds the coffee beans, resistance to ground coffee, even with a free coffee cup attached, is likely to be high and may lead to channel conflict or cause premiums to be ignored by wholesalers and retailers.

Business norms should also be considered. For example, trade shows and exhibits have become the norm for selling industrial goods, because of the difficulty of displaying and demonstrating industrial products to potential customers. These centralized markets include the Leipziger Messe, which is viewed as the gateway to Eastern Europe for industrial goods, and the annual Bobbin

Promotion	U.K.	Spain	Germany	France	Italy
In-pack premiums	●	●	○	▲	●
Multiple-purchase offers	●	●	▲	●	●
Extra product	●	●	▲	●	●
Free product	●	●	●	●	●
Mail-in offers	●	●	○	●	●
Purchase-with-purchase	●	●	○	●	●
Cross-promotions	●	●	○	●	●
Contests	●	●	▲	●	●
Self-liquidating premiums	●	●	●	●	●
Sweepstakes	▲	▲	○	▲	▲
Money-off coupons	●	●	○	●	▲
Next-purchase coupons	●	●	○	●	▲
Cash rebates	●	●	▲	●	○
In-store demos	●	●	●	●	●

● Permitted   ○ Not permitted   ▲ May be permitted

Source: *Advertising Age*, August 7, 1989, p. 45.

Show in Atlanta, Georgia, which provides a market for everything in the sewn-goods industry, from new packaging ideas to computerized pattern-cutting machinery.

In recent decades the use of large shows and exhibits aimed at retail markets has grown. The Consumer Electronics Show, held in Chicago each year, successfully applies the ideas and strategies of industrial trade shows to consumer audiences. At the show, consumers have an opportunity to see and try new products; perhaps more important, manufacturers have an opportunity to observe consumer responses to new products and product lines.

MAP 15.1   SALES PROMOTION IN EUROPE: A MAZE OF REGULATION

Even though the EC'92 movement resulted in a more standard legal environment for global marketers, laws still vary with respect to promotional activities. Running the same sales promotion campaign, for example, is not necessarily possible in every country, given varying legal restrictions.

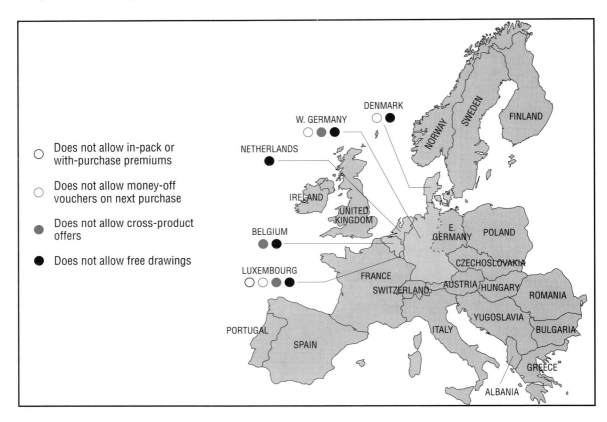

IMPACT ON THE MARKETING MIX

As the most visible element of the marketing mix, promotion is especially vulnerable to misinterpretation and misuse. Advertising, public relations, personal selling, and sales promotions are all highly subject to cultural, legal, and economic constraints that vary considerably in different national markets. Therefore, they demand special attention in the development of a global marketing mix.

Product

In many ways promotion becomes part of the product, especially for consumer goods. Whether a consumer buys Revlon cosmetics in Boston or Paris, she is purchasing the promise of beauty, not just a tube of chemicals. The perception that using Revlon cosmetics will make the consumer more beautiful is largely a result of a promotional campaign. An image of the product conveyed through promotion has thus become part of the product. To a certain extent this is true even for industrial goods. High-technology products that are promoted as manufactured in Germany sell better than products with the same technical specifications that are identified as manufactured in Brazil.[14]

It is often necessary to modify the promotional mix when marketing in different national markets because of cultural variations. This works against product standardization. From a total-product viewpoint, a consumer in Norway who buys a laundry detergent that is chemically similar to one sold in Malaysia may actually be buying a different product if the detergent is promoted differently. In such situations gains from the production-experience curve are maximized, but the organization does not benefit from the marketing-experience curve.

Price

Because the promotional mix affects the total product and because promotion affects the product's perceived value in the buyer's mind, it directly affects the price of the product. High-quality or high-status products like Jaguar automobiles command higher prices.

To the extent that promotional activities can be standardized, prices may be lower; when promotion has to be tailored to a particular market, it contributes to higher prices. Global corporations want to reach a level of market demand at which production economies will allow them to charge lower prices. In a large market, promotion is needed to boost market demand to a point at which those economies may be realized. One of the best examples of what can occur in a large market fueled by aggressive competition can be found in the market for small computers. Partly in response to strong promotional campaigns, the demand for small computers has increased, resulting in lower prices.

But in smaller, dissimilar markets increased promotion may result in higher prices, because the associated costs cannot be offset by increased demand. In such cases the level of demand will not be high enough to permit experience-curve effects or economies of production and marketing sufficient to offset the increased promotional expenses. Lower demand and higher costs will lead to higher prices, thereby decreasing demand even more.

Distribution

International promotion also affects distribution, especially channel control and relationships with intermediaries. In any market a firm may find it useful to develop a "pull" campaign in order to stimulate demand. This type of campaign temporarily bypasses the distribution channel and communicates directly with buyers about the value of the product. Such a strategy assumes that the channel member will become convinced that buyers want the product and will stock it.

However, given the difficulty of reaching buyers in foreign markets, global promotion is often characterized by a "push" approach. This type of campaign convinces channel members to stock the product and then promotes it to consumers. In Pakistan, for instance, low literacy rates and the lack of mass media in remote places mean that marketers of food products must develop strong, long-lasting relationships with intermediaries. Their promotional mix will follow a "push" strategy, containing more personal selling, public relations, and sales promotions for intermediaries than advertising directed at consumers.

The types of promotion used, the product, and the desired price level affect the choice of a distribution channel. Thus, when British Sterling after-shave cologne was introduced in the United States, it was priced at a premium, promoted with romantic themes, and distributed through jewelry stores. In contrast, in the Philippines Marlboro cigarettes are popularly priced, promoted for everyday use, and distributed extensively (even sold singly by street vendors).

SUMMARY

Communication is the transmission of information from a source to a receiver. In the case of business organizations, communication occurs through promotion. A global organization communicates with a variety of publics through different promotional mixes.

In the basic communication model, the sender of the communication encodes an idea, image, or information into symbols, words, or pictures that constitute a message. The message is then sent through a channel to the receiver that is the target of the message. The receiver decodes the message and provides feedback, or a reaction to the message.

Effective business communication occurs when the exchange partner receives the message the way the sending organization intends it to be received. Establishing a common frame of reference is the key to effective communication. Obstacles to communication include the inability to reach the target market with the message, the possibility that the message may not be understood the way the sender intended it to be understood, and the inability to motivate action by members of the target audience. Limitations on global promotion include legal and tax considerations, differences in the meanings of symbols and in traditions, differences in values and norms, language barriers, low literacy rates, differences among subcultures, cost factors, and standards set by international organizations.

Advertising is the most visible and often the most controversial form of promotion, although it may not be the central element of the promotional mix in foreign markets. Effective advertising requires a thorough understanding of the target market. The global market for the services of advertising agencies is growing fast, a trend that poses some problems for advertisers. Conflicts of interest may arise when formerly independent agencies merge, and agencies based in less-developed countries vary greatly in their competencies. Global advertisers must deal with four specific media problems: availability, cost, frequency and reach, and verification.

Public relations is the management of the images an organization projects to its publics. One public relations tool, publicity, consists of free exposure in print or broadcast media. Positive publicity is a valuable asset, but an organization cannot always control the nature of the publicity it receives. This is particularly true in the case of global publicity.

Personal selling involves direct communication between a seller and a buyer. Four basic types of activities are found in global selling: creative selling, or establishing contacts, locating distributors, and filling orders; missionary selling, or building relationships with intermediaries; technical selling, or communicating technical knowledge about the firm's products; and selling to ultimate consumers.

A salesforce may be indirect or direct. Expatriate personnel are employed by a corporation in a country other than their home country. Nationals are sales employees who are based in their home country. Cosmopolitan employees are citizens of one country who are employed by a corporation based in a second country and are working in a third country. Management of the salesforce is critical to the success of a global marketing strategy. Special considerations include the recruitment and selection, training, and motivation and compensation of sales personnel.

Sales promotions fall into three basic categories: those that reduce the price of the product in some way; those that add value or perceived value to the product; and those that provide information. Among the factors that must be considered in the choice of sales-promotion techniques are costs, channel capacity, channel power, legal constraints, and the cultural norms of the target market.

Promotion affects all the other elements of the marketing mix. In many ways it becomes part of the product, especially for consumer goods. It also directly affects the price of the product and its distribution. Global marketers should remember that promotion is the most visible element of the marketing mix and hence is most vulnerable to misinterpretation and misuse.

DISCUSSION QUESTIONS

1. What is the difference between domestic and global promotion?

2. What "languages" must an organization speak in order to achieve effective communication?

3. Illustrate at least one limitation on global promotions in the United States that has an impact on organizations based in other countries.

4. What is the cause of most problems encountered in global advertising? Give an illustration.

5. The media problems traditionally faced by global advertisers are disappearing. Do you agree or disagree, and why?

6. Why is transit advertising by and large more popular outside the Triad markets than within them?

7. How important is global public relations, compared to domestic?

8. Assume you are a promotional manager for a global marketer of highly technical robots that aid manufacturing. What are your choices in terms of salesforce composition? What is your likely choice, and why?

9. Assume you are an American sales manager. Of all of the steps in managing global salesforces (recruitment and selection, training, and motivation and compensation), which would you focus on most to improve sales? Why?

10. Why are sales promotions more popular in the United States than in many other nations?

C A S E

GLOBAL PROMOTION

"The problem, you see, is that American and Japanese tourists don't think about coming to Denmark when they start planning their vacations." At least that was the opinion of the Director of Tourism Marketing for the Danish Tourism Bureau. And recent research supported his view. "Country of Destination" profiles developed by InterTourist Inc., a research firm specializing in research in the international tourism market, had just been completed for several European and American airlines that served the Danish market.

According to the surveys, Japanese and Americans who thought about traveling to Europe thought first about the "major" European nations: Germany, England, and France. But smaller European nations such as Belgium, Finland, or Denmark were not as well known, therefore less frequently mentioned as "likely to visit." In the survey, only 10 percent of Americans and 5 percent of Japanese surveyed said they would be "slightly or more" interested in a trip to Denmark. When asked about France, 40% of Americans and 50% of Japanese indicated an interest.

Making the promotion and marketing problem more complicated for the Danish Tourism Bureau was that Eastern Europe had been gaining rapidly in popularity as a tourist destination. Poland and Hungary, for example, were reported to be of interest by 30 percent and 15 percent of Americans and Japanese, respectively. In other words, Denmark was not well known by potential tourists, nor seen as a first priority vacation spot compared to most West or East European nations.

Naturally, this situation did not please the Danish Tourism Bureau. As a governmental body, one of their major responsibilities was to increase the number of tourists who came to Denmark, and to increase their length of stay. America and Japan were important markets in the tourism industry. Overall, Japanese and American tourism to Europe had been growing about 5 to 7 percent per year over the last five years. The Japanese growth rate was even higher than the American one. But tourist traffic to Denmark had been increasing only by 2–3 percent.

Over the past several years, the Bureau had worked with advertising agencies based in New York and Tokyo. Each had developed, under the guidance of the Bureau, an advertising campaign for potential tourists, as well as a smaller campaign that promoted Denmark to travel agents. Magazines and newspapers were the most important media in both markets. Brochures were mailed to travel agents as well to anyone who called requesting information. No sales promotions had been used.

The government minister in charge of tourism, however, had become convinced that more could be done in terms of a global promotion campaign. Although funds were limited, she had asked the Bureau to design a new, more complete promotional campaign that would increase the number of American and Japanese tourists who visited Denmark.

Case Issues

1. How would you describe the type of tourist who would be likely to visit Denmark?

2. What would you recommend be included in a promotional campaign to appeal to this target market?

3. What differences, if any, would you recommend for the Japanese and American market, and why?

NOTES

1. The global business mistakes discussed in this section are based in part on D. A. Ricks, *Big Business Blunders* (Homewood, Ill.: Irwin, 1983).

2. E. T. Hall, "The Silent Language in Overseas Business," *Harvard Business Review*, May–June 1960, pp. 87–96.

3. "Playtex Kicks Off a One-Ad-Fits-All Campaign," *Business Week*, December 16, 1985, pp. 48–49.

4. For a more complete discussion of the limitations on global promotion, see C. L. Bovee and W. F. Arens, *Contemporary Advertising* (Homewood, Ill.: Irwin, 1982); D. M. Peebles and J. K. Ryans, Jr., *Management of International Advertising—A Marketing Approach* (Boston: Allyn and Bacon, 1984), chap. 9; J. B. Neelankavil and A. B. Stridsberg, *Advertising Self-Regulation: A Global Perspective* (New York: Hastings House, 1980); and J. J. Boddewyn, "International Advertisers Face Government Hurdles," *Marketing News*, May 8, 1987, p. 21.

5. *International Werburg*, December 1, 1986, p. 9.

6. See E. Kaynak, *Marketing in the Third World* (New York: Praeger, 1982), chap. 5.

7. *International Werburg*, December 2, 1986, p. 7.

8. P. R. Cateora, *International Marketing*, 6th ed. (Homewood, Ill.: Irwin, 1987), p. 432.

9. R. F. Roth, *International Marketing Communications* (Chicago: Crain Books, 1982), chap. 14.

10. *Business Week*, September 7, 1987, p. 108.

11. For other examples and a fuller discussion of the importance of informal communication in the international promotional process, see E. Hall, "The Silent Language in Overseas Business," *Harvard Business Review*, May–June 1980, pp. 87–96

12. "Prior Adjustment—Japanese Executives Going Overseas Take Anti-Shock Courses," *Wall Street Journal*, January 12, 1987, pp. 1, 18.

13. "The Gimmick, the Gift, and the Giveaway," *Direct Marketing*, October 1986, p. 58.

14. P. D. White and E. W. Cundiff, "Assessing the Quality of Industrial Products," *Journal of Marketing*, January 1978, pp. 80–86.

GLOBAL PRICING

INTERNATIONAL INCIDENT

"A Pepsi and a Sub to Go Please"

Pepsi has been selling its products to the USSR for many years. Generally, it has traded soft drinks for vodka, a "countertrade" agreement. Recently, however, the Soviets proposed a trade where soft-drink syrup from Pepsi would be paid for with subs—obsolete Soviet submarines. The Soviets apparently believed Pepsi might turn the submarines into a chain of floating restaurants. In fact, Pepsi took the deal, but instead of turning the subs into restaurants, it sold them for scrap.

This countertrade agreement (trading goods for goods instead of for money) illustrates a pricing challenge facing today's global marketer. If Pepsi had not agreed to the deal, it may have lost a sale. But the exchange ratio of soft-drink syrup for obsolete submarines is more difficult to determine than an economic price. Pepsi had to calculate an exchange ratio where it would make a profit on the transaction, taking into account how long it would take to resell the subs.

Countertrade has a long history in international trade. Manhattan Island, for example, was sold in such an agreement to settlers from Europe. Today more than 100,000 U.S. companies are engaged in more than $20 million worth of countertrade agreements. Ralston-Purina, for example, had an excess inventory of canned salmon and tuna. It sold the overstock to a countertrade specialist, who in turn privately labeled the product as a cat food. And Sears is active in several countries with its own countertrade operation in order to sell its products in markets that are low on foreign funds.

Nations, in fact, may prefer countertrade to monetary transactions as a matter of policy. Nigeria, for example, trades crude oil with many nations in return for tires, paper, steel, automobile parts, gasoline, and vegetable oil, among other products. Other nations, such as Turkey, strongly encourage countertrade in their attempts to manage negative balance of trade accounts or in reaction to large national debts. Whatever the motivation, countertrade accounts for roughly one-third of world trade, and it is likely to grow in importance.

Sources: "Pepsi and a Sub," *Newsweek*, August 21, 1989, p. 3; L. G. Reiling, "Countertrade Revives 'Dead Goods'," *Marketing News*, August 29, 1986, p. 1; and S. C. Okoroafa, "Determinants of LDC Mandated Countertrade," *International Marketing Review*, Winter 1988, pp. 16–24.

> The pricing decision is probably the most difficult marketing-mix decision a global marketer has to make.

Many marketers operating on a global level mention pricing when asked for the most difficult decision in their company's marketing mix. They attribute that difficulty to the increasing level of global competition from firms with different production costs, taxation systems, labor regulations, or other business environments. Low growth in markets also contributes to the price-setting prob-

Pepsi has sold success-
fully in the USSR since
the early 1970s.   ·

lem. So do different locations on the experience curve due to the varying size
of home markets.

When talking about prices most marketers think in terms of monetary
returns. From a customer's perspective, however, the price of a good or service
is the sum of all monetary and nonmonetary assets the customer has to exchange
(or "spend") in order to obtain the good or service. As the balance of exchange
discussed in Chapter 2 illustrated, customers may perceive that many "costs"
are associated with the product. Some of them cannot be influenced by the
global marketer. Some are part of the product design; others are due to the
distribution system the marketer has chosen or the positioning of the product
offer.

But pricing decisions still need to be made, including the basic price of a
product; the price structure of the entire product line; the system of rebates,
discounts, and refunds the firm will offer in exchange for specific actions; the
terms of sale under which a contract is entered; and the terms of payment.
Because of their importance in nondomestic marketing, this chapter gives special
attention to nonmonetary and partial monetary exchanges. Countertrade is of
growing importance in a global business environment characterized by enhanced
competition between industrialized and newly industrialized economies, as well
as the hard currency shortages and huge trade imbalances of centrally controlled
and developing countries. Intracompany or transfer pricing will be discussed in
Chapter 18.

GLOBAL PRICING POLICY

A firm's pricing policy needs to be an extension of its overall strategy.

The intended strategic position of the company as well as the positioning of its product lines and individual products are the basis for all pricing decisions. The *pricing policy* should restate corporate objectives relevant to individual pricing decisions. It should include expected profit margins, returns on investment, and market shares. It should also include the pricing strategy, such as quick penetration of markets through low prices; skimming of high margins in market niches where the company has a significant competitive advantage; maintaining competitive positions in saturated markets; or concentrating on a market niche which requires a high-priced product versus covering the entire product category-market. The company policy concerning rebates, refunds, and discounts given to customers should be stated. The terms of sale available to the salespeople in their struggle for getting orders, and the terms of payment to be used in specific markets, should also be stated. These terms should be chosen according to company expectations, knowledge of the customers, and the acceptable level of financial risk.

Global pricing decisions are much more difficult to standardize than are global product decisions or promotion activities. Competitors in various countries have different cost structures, resulting in different prices. Taxes, duties, government regulations, and political influences vary, as does the purchase power of the target markets. The distribution channels are of different lengths, and distribution-channel members expect margins specific to their markets.

Standard Pricing

Standard pricing policies represent a standardized element of the global marketing mix.

With a **standard pricing policy,** the marketer charges the same base price for a product in every product market served. A company, for example, may set the price to wholesalers for its fountain pens at $25.00 each in all markets. The customer either has to pay for freight, insurance, and duties directly, or the company adds a specific amount to the base price.

This is the simplest policy for a company to administer. The task of setting the product price according to the firm's position on the experience curve is also simplified. That is, the price can be set with reference to the company's projected unit costs. But standard pricing is also the least customer-oriented pricing policy, and it does not respond to competitive and environmental factors specific to each market. Products may end up overpriced, or even underpriced. Optimal positioning as well as maximum profitability are achieved only by chance.

Standard Formula Pricing

With **standard formula pricing,** the company calculates the price for a product following the same formula in all markets around the world. There are different ways to establish this formula. One formula is **full-cost pricing.** It consists of

A firm may choose to standardize the formula it uses to set its prices, rather than set the same price in all markets.

taking the full-cost price calculated for the product (production plus marketing, etc.) in the domestic market and adding the additional costs resulting from international transportation, taxes, tariffs, distribution, and promotion. Often this alternative results in prices too high to be competitive in nondomestic markets.

Therefore, a **direct-cost-plus-contribution-margin formula** may be chosen. The production cost of the product is taken as the basis and additional costs due to the nondomestic marketing process plus a desired profit margin are added. Because of the complexity of the global marketing process, however, additional indirect administrative and marketing costs may arise without being included in the formula. This method, therefore, may lead to prices that do not cover all the costs incurred by the company.

A **differential formula** or **relevant cost formula** is the most useful formula in making pricing decisions. It includes all the incremental costs resulting from a nondomestic business opportunity that would not be incurred otherwise and adds them to the production cost. The manager then compares those costs with the additional revenues from the sale. If a suitable profit results, the price is set.

The biggest disadvantage of all these formulas is the resulting loss in company flexibility to react to differing or changing circumstances in the markets. A given strategic goal, such as high penetration of all served markets, may not be achieved due to the nonflexible nature of the company's pricing policy.

Price Adaptation

Price adaptation, where a price is set in each market, is the most individualized approach to global price setting.

Price adaptation as a global policy means that prices for the company's products are determined in a decentralized manner, according to the local managers' perceptions of the various markets. This policy allows extremely flexible reactions to market and competitive developments. But it has some major disadvantages. First, local pricing increases the difficulty of developing a global strategic position. For example, a pen priced at $15.00 (wholesale) in Italy but $32.00 in Norway represents two different market positions—one more prestigious than the other. Second, if the price differences between markets become too big there is a danger of *parallel imports*, or **grey markets** (basically, an import by an unauthorized party). When this occurs, channel members located in low-price markets not under the strict control of the firm may resell the product to market areas with significantly higher prices. In our example, an Italian intermediary could sell the pen to a Norwegian intermediary for $20.00. The Italian would make $5.00, and the Norwegian could resell the pen at a lower price and still make a profit. Depending on the legal regulations in the countries involved, this can be relatively easy to stop. But in the EC countries, for example, parallel imports cannot be prohibited. Distribution channels that are not at all consistent with the firm's strategic positioning can easily get certain products. Perfume, for example, that has been promoted as highly sophisticated and prestigious may suddenly be found in discount stores. The grey-market outlets profit from the marketing efforts of the company, but often they do not provide the same level of customer service that the approved intermediaries do. Those intermediaries, of course, complain about the unexpected competition. Because customers do not draw a distinction between regular channels of distribution and grey markets, such a development is usually detrimental to the overall business of the company.

Strategic Pricing

Frequently, a global marketing organization will set a standard minimum price, but allow local managers to set the actual market price.

The absolute minimum of price standardization necessary to attain a competitive position can be achieved through **price lines** (or **price patterns**) set by the home office. Price lines set the company's prices relative to competitors'. They are followed in each market, but regional or local management can accommodate local costs, customer-income levels, distribution margin requirements, and competition. Price lines also allow adaptation of prices to the changing market-saturation levels that accompany different stages in the product-life cycle.

Price differentiation among geographic markets can be achieved without hampering the company's overall pricing strategy. HILTI, one of the leading manufacturers of drilling devices in the world, follows a global high-price strategy based on superior quality and direct distribution. Its products are more expensive than those of all competitors wherever they are sold. Nevertheless, HILTI's prices in Japan are only 55 percent of European prices over all its product lines, because of necessary adaptation to local price levels.

Strategic pricing requires central coordination of pricing decisions. The people responsible for local pricing decisions not only have to follow the price lines, but they also have to report to the company headquarters their decisions concerning specific prices. The specialists in the home office, having a general overview of the company's prices and the prices of relevant competitors, will then accept the suggested prices or negotiate with the local managers to come to a mutually acceptable solution.

FACTORS THAT INFLUENCE PRICES

The marketing manager often has limited control over what price will be charged for the firm's products.

In certain cases the marketer has little influence on the price that can be obtained for a product. The mechanisms of supply and demand dictate the price for largely undifferentiated products (such as wheat, copper, coffee, cement, flour, and crude oil) that are marketed in large quantities on international commodity exchanges. Also, when a government is the customer or the marketer is confronted with strongly restrictive governmental regulations, the company often has only one alternative: accept the price or lose the customer's business.

However, most manufactured products and many services offer the opportunity of price setting. The marketer analyzes all relevant costs, the market environment, and the governmental influences; sets the price based on these analyses; and then manages price escalation.

Costs

The price floor is determined by the costs of producing and marketing the product.

Costs determine the product's lower price limit. In the long run they have to be fully covered for the business to survive. In global pricing decisions, the same basic cost factors apply as in domestic pricing. There are some additional costs, however, that can strongly influence the minimum price of a product when sold in another country.

The costs of doing business such as information gathering, travel expenses, and support of employees are usually considerably higher in global than in domestic marketing. The longer the distribution channel, the higher the sum of margins and allowances added for middlemen will be. (See Exhibit 16.1.) Additional packaging and labelling, transportation, and inventory-financing costs, as

EXHIBIT 16.1
THE COST IMPACT OF
DISTRIBUTION
CHANNEL LENGTH

International marketers face longer distribution channels, which has a price escalation effect. This exhibit illustrates a typical three-member domestic channel and a typical five-member international channel. Assuming each channel member adds 50 percent to its price to cover costs, taxes, and its own profits, the impact on the retail price is considerable.

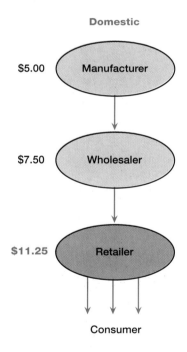

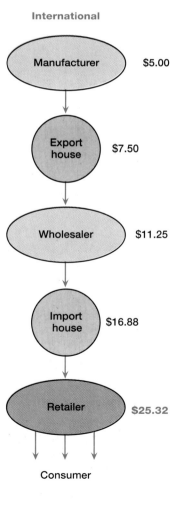

well as additional insurance against damage or loss, also increase the price. Regardless of whether they are absorbed by the marketer or passed on to the customer, taxes, tariffs, and administrative fees (for documents, for example) add to global costs as well. Turnover taxes (in Japan and other countries) and value-added taxes (most popular in Europe) vary between 2 and 32 per cent.

The Market

In a free-market system the price is partly set by the market itself.

Market factors that affect the prices of goods and services are customers, competitors, business groups, and the economic environment. The attractiveness of a product to the target *customers* determines its real value, that is, the theoretical price ceiling in a given market. This price level will be decreased in many cases by the limited purchasing power of customers (especially in LDCs). When prices are negotiated between business partners (for example, marketers and governmental agencies), the final price also depends on their negotiation skills.[1]

Competition has the tendency to lower prices, to a point that may become dangerous to the existence of the firm. The prices of competitive products and customer satisfaction with those products strongly influence what customers are willing to pay for the global marketer's product.

Companies may try to limit competition by forming one or more *business groups*. Industry associations, for example, gather information about market developments and transactions. They may represent their members in negotiations with governments or unions, as is the case in most European countries. Loose groups of competitors may agree on general rules of fair competition. Cartels may set prices (as does OPEC), allocate market areas (as in the Austrian beer market), establish sales volumes (as in the paper industry in some countries), or even constitute a selling unit that distributes profits to the members at the end of the year. The global marketer has to evaluate the market power of such groups and sometimes join them, when the legal regulations at home and in the local market are appropriate. When the chances of winning are high, some firms choose to fight them.

Of all the *economic conditions* discussed in Chapter 4, income distribution, growth rates, exchange rates, and inflation have the strongest impacts on pricing decisions. The income distribution of a geographical market affects the prices at which different groups of customers can afford the company's products. Growth rates are an index of market maturity. Fast-growing, young product markets allow more freedom for pricing decisions than mature, stagnant markets, where price competition is fierce.

The influence of exchange rates on prices is illustrated by fluctuations in the value of the U.S. dollar in Germany in 1980–1988. The dollar was exchanged for 1.8 DM in 1980, went up to a value of more than 3 DM in 1984, but went down again to nearly 1.5 DM in 1988. This means that prices for U.S. products headed for Germany first rose nearly 100 percent, and then were cut in half in less than 4 years. Managing such fluctuations will be discussed in detail in Chapter 18.

High inflation requires periodic price adjustments to cover rising costs. Because inflation rates are not the same in different geographical markets, the global marketer is confronted with a sometimes complex puzzle of possible price changes and risks. If inflation is high in the country of production, the firm may not be able to adjust prices as necessary, and it may thus be forced to absorb increases in input prices. If inflation is high in the customer's country, the feasibility of increasing prices will depend on the reaction of customers,[2] government controls, and the additional costs of changing price tags, reprogramming cash registers, and other activities related to price changes. If payment from a customer located in an inflationary market is expected to be delayed (which would lower the real price paid), the inflation rate should be considered in price negotiations.

Government

In many markets, especially centrally controlled ones, governmental activities ranging from subsidies to price controls will influence the price.

Government activities and regulations also influence prices. The effects of exchange-rate and balance-of-payment policies have already been discussed in Chapter 4, and they will be further discussed in Chapter 18. Governments may also impose **price controls** on specific products. These may be price floors, price ceilings, restrictions on price changes, or maximum profit margins. In some European nations, for example, retailers are forbidden to sell products below the price they paid for them, and standard-quality bread, milk, sugar, and flour have regulated prices that retailers may not increase. In the early 1980s, all price changes were forbidden by the French government for a certain amount of time to support its struggle against inflation. More recently, for certain products the Norwegian government has set maximum margins that may not be undercut by competitors.[3]

Government subsidies can help lower prices to increase marketers' global competitiveness. Such subsidies often depend on the power of lobby groups and other noneconomic developments. The U.S. government, for example, is an ardent fighter against subsidies that decrease prices and distort competition in the iron and steel industries. But it heavily subsidizes farmers, allowing them to export grains at prices that cannot be matched by farmers in developing countries.

Frequently, exports of government-subsidized products are viewed in the importing country as dumping, as was discussed in Chapter 4. In these situations, domestic competitors put pressure on their governments to impose a countervailing tariff to make the imported product equivalent in price to the domestically produced one.

Price Escalation

Perhaps the biggest pricing difficulty facing the global marketing manager is price escalation.

The result of all of these costs and factors may be *price escalation*. Exhibit 16.2 contains an example of how the costs of an exported product from manufacture to delivery to the first channel member, are calculated. Marketing costs and

MAP 16.1 ECONOMIC STRENGTH

The economic environment of the target market is of prime importance in setting a product's price. This map illustrates national income levels (as indicated by per capita GDP), which helps the global marketer identify those markets of relative wealth, which might support a higher priced product.

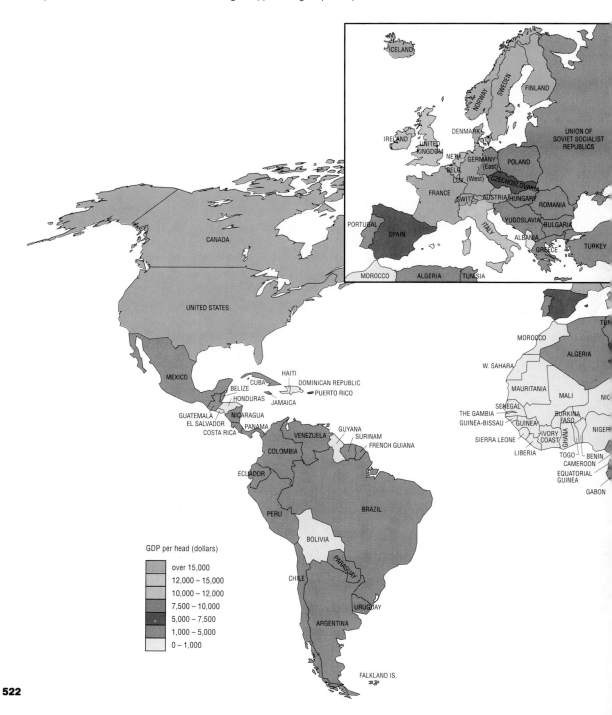

GDP per head (dollars)

over 15,000
12,000 – 15,000
10,000 – 12,000
7,500 – 10,000
5,000 – 7,500
1,000 – 5,000
0 – 1,000

UNION OF SOVIET SOCIALIST REPUBLICS

TURKEY
CYPRUS
LEBANON
ISRAEL
SYRIA
JORDAN
IRAQ
KUWAIT
IRAN
AFGHANISTAN
PAKISTAN

IBYA
EGYPT
QATAR
UAE
SAUDI
ARABIA
OMAN
YEMEN
S. YEMEN
DJIBOUTI

HAD
SUDAN
ETHIOPIA
SOMALIA
NTRAL AFRICAN
REPUBLIC
ZAIRE
UGANDA
KENYA
RWANDA
BURUNDI
TANZANIA
MALAWI
OLA
ZAMBIA
ZIMBABWE
MOZAMBIQUE
MADAGASCAR
IBIA
BOTSWANA
S. AFRICA
SWAZILAND
LESOTHO

MONGOLIA
N. KOREA
S. KOREA
JAPAN
CHINA
NEPAL
BHUTAN
INDIA
BURMA
BANGLADESH
LAOS
TAIWAN
HONG KONG
THAILAND
VIETNAM
PHILIPPINES
SRI LANKA
KAMPUCHEA
BRUNEI
MALAYSIA
SINGAPORE
INDONESIA
E. TIMOR
PAPUA
NEW GUINEA

AUSTRALIA

NEW ZEALAND

523

EXHIBIT 16.2
AN EXAMPLE OF THE
PRICE CALCULATION
FOR AN EXPORTED
PRODUCT

In order to export a product, many functions must be performed. Each, of course, must be paid for. This exhibit illustrates how the price to the importer (the price "delivered, duty paid") grows from the full cost of manufacturing.

Production cost	$10.00
+ Profit margin (10%)	1.00
Price "ex works"	$11.00
+ Transportation	.50
+ Transport insurance	.05
+ Freight-forwarding fee	.02
+ Handling costs	.02
Price "FOR/FOT"	$11.59
+ Cost of shipment to boarder	.20
+ Export support fee	.03
+ Export administration fees	.01
Price "delivered at frontier"	$11.83
+ Cost of shipment to port of departure	.05
Price "freight carriage" (and insurance), port of departure	$11.88
+ Port costs	.04
Price "free on board," port of departure	$11.92
+ Cost of documents	.01
+ Cost of bill of lading	.01
+ Sea freight	.15
Price "C&F," port of destination	$12.09
+ Freight insurance FPA (free particular average)	.06
Price "cost, insurance, freight," port of destination	$12.15
= Price "ex ship," port of destination	
+ Port costs	.10
Price "ex quai" (duties on buyer's account)	$12.25
+ Import duties	1.10
Price "ex quai," port of destination	$13.35
+ Transportation costs	.70
+ Freight-forwarder costs	.25
+ Transportation insurance	.15
Price "delivered, duty paid"	$14.45

taxes in the local market have to be added to derive the final customer price. Considering all the additions to the domestic price "ex works" (at the point of production), it is understandable that the consumer price for a U.S.-manufactured product sold in Japan may be double the price charged in the domestic market.

In many cases, price-escalation effects will prohibit the marketer from successfully entering new geographical markets. However, there are several approaches to counteract the problem, as is demonstrated by consumer products sold overseas with a lower price than the domestic price (such as Italian wine and shoes sold in the United States).

The firm may choose to enter markets that are in an early stage of the product's life-cycle, and are therefore less resistant to higher prices. It may position the product (or product line) so that it does not directly compete with less-expensive competitors. An innovative shortening of the distribution channel, without decreasing the level of customer service, may also reduce costs. This is particularly important when a cumulative turnover tax has to be paid.

Product modifications, such as shipping components to be assembled in the target market, may change the tariff rate. Cars exported to Brazil, for example, once rated a lower tariff when the tires were not mounted on them until after their arrival at the docks. The modification may also consist of replacing costly materials and features with less expensive ones, if the change does not negatively influence the value to the customer.

Assembly of components, production of parts, or production of the entire product either locally or in a third, low-wage country are other possible ways to counteract price escalation. European companies, for example, may find it necessary to produce goods for the U.S. market in an Asian country.

A way to reduce the impact of higher prices on customer demand is to lease the product. This is a particularly attractive approach for international marketers of industrial goods, like machine tools, transportation vehicles, or industrial robots. It not only helps overcome the short term negative effect of a high price, but it may also help to lessen the problems of insufficient hard currency or costs of product-maintenance personnel. In fact, the ability to lease, or to provide credit at low interest rates, is a significant marketing tool for today's global competitor.

A final solution is to lower the net price. This can be achieved by constantly increasing the company's productivity, then gaining economies of scale. But it can also be done for a short span of time by diminishing the profit margin. Or the firm can charge only part of the costs. Most or all of the product's R&D (research and development) costs, for example, can be charged to the home market. This approach has to be considered with prudence, however. It not only directly influences the company's profit margin, but it may also lead to the filing of dumping charges by local competitors.

The final price for a product should not be set before the business partners negotiate the terms of sale and the terms of payment. These terms are discussed in the next two sections.

TERMS OF SALE

The delivery of goods or services has to be thoroughly negotiated and regulated in the contract of sale between the business partners. The contractual conditions of the sale are called the **terms of sale.** Major difficulties in their negotiation may arise from a lack of knowledge about international shipment and distribution. Very often the business partners do not know much about the trade cus-

EXHIBIT 16.3   ABBREVIATIONS AND TRANSLATIONS OF INCOTERMS

Incoterms, although standardized, have different translations, which the global marketer may need to know in order to manage the terms of sale.

Incoterms	English	German	French	Italian
EXW	Ex Works	Ab Werk	A L'Usine	Franco Fabrica
FOR	FOR/FOT	FOR/FOT	Franco Wagon	Franco Vagone
FOB	FOB	FOB	FOB	Franco a Bordo
FAS	FAS	FAS	FAS	Franco Sottobordo
DCP	Freight Carriage } Paid to	Frachtfrei	Fret } Payé Port } Jusqu'a	Nolo } Pagato Porto }
CIP	Freight Carriage and Insurance } Paid to	Frachtfrei Versichert	Fret } Payé Port } Assurance Comprise Jusqu'a	Nolo/Porto Ed } Pagato Assicurazione }
CFR	C&F	C&F	C&F	Costo e Nolo
CIF	CIF	CIF	CAF	Costo, Assicurazione e Nolo
DDP	Delivered Duty Paid	Geliefert Verzollt	Rendu Droits Aquittés	Reso Sdoganato

Source: International Chamber of Commerce, *brochure no. 350*, Paris, 1980.

To receive the correct amount of payment, the global marketer must pay attention to the terms of sale and other contract conditions related to the price.

toms in the other country. Different interpretations of terms already agreed upon are a source of continuous trouble. Uncertainty about which country's laws will be applicable to the contract adds to the difficulties.

To help avoid such problems, standard terms of sale have been developed in international trade over the years. These were precisely phrased by the International Chamber of Commerce (located in Paris). Referred to as **Incoterms,** their wide usage today is due to international acceptance of their interpretation of the terms of sale most often applied in global marketing.[4]

The Incoterms contain fourteen types of trade terms.[5] They are listed in Exhibit 16.3 in English, German, French, and Italian, together with their abbreviations. The Incoterms regulate the forms of shipment, the location and point in time of loss and damage risk transfer from the supplier to the customer, as well as the repatriation of costs of shipment between the business partners, and the obligations of the buyer and seller concerning the export, transit, and import of the merchandise. Even when the two parties to the contract agree on the Incoterms, care must be taken to make sure they are in complete agreement on the specifics. For example, FOB (free on board) might be interpreted by a buyer in Peru as meaning the factory in Vermont, not the New York port. The buyer might refuse to pay for the transportation costs between Vermont and New York, potentially eliminating the Vermont firm's profit and causing ill will between the two parties. The most commonly used terms are discussed in Exhibit 16.3.

Ex works (EXW) signifies the term of sale most advantageous to the seller. It puts all the obligations of shipment, including documentation for export, transit, and import, on the buyer. The buyer also bears the risk of merchandise damage or loss as soon as the goods leave the premises of the seller. The global marketer should be aware, however, that this term may increase the "perceived costs," including the psychological price the customer has to pay, to the point where they are greater than the "perceived benefits." A substantial number of business opportunities may be lost to competitors who choose terms of sale more convenient to customers.

Free along ship (FAS) obligates the seller to deliver the merchandise to the vessel and port specified in the sales contract (for example "FAS, Los Angeles"). The costs of packaging, shipment, and documentation until the merchandise has been unloaded in the port of departure are the seller's responsibility. The risk of damage or loss is transferred when the products are unloaded.

Free on rail/free on truck (FOR/FOT) is similar to FAS. It includes rail and truck transportation, and loading the merchandise onto the train or truck is the seller's responsibility.

Under the terms **free on board** (FOB) or **free on board airport** (FOA), the seller has to deliver the merchandise on board the transport vessel indicated by the buyer at the shipping point (for example, "FOA, Chicago") and time specified in the sales contract. The seller has to provide all the necessary export documents and bear all the costs of packaging, shipment, and documentation. In addition, the seller bears the risk of damage or loss until the merchandise has been loaded, but not beyond.

It is important to note that FAS and FOB, although often used interchangeably, are not the same. Normally, the seller on FOB shipments and the buyer on FAS shipments pay those charges. Using the wrong term may place the charges for loading the goods onto the ship (usually 10–15% of the cost of ocean freight) in dispute.

Under the term **freight, carriage paid to** (DCP) the seller has to pay all the costs of packaging, shipment, and documentation until the merchandise is handed over to the first freight forwarder at the location and time specified in the contract. The risk of merchandise damage or loss is transferred to the buyer at the same point in time. This term can be applied to all kinds of transportation, including multiform shipment and container and ro-ro (roll-on, roll-off) transportation. When these conditions are enlarged to include the seller's obligation to insure the merchandise against damage and loss during shipment, it is called **freight, carriage, and insurance paid to** (CIP).

Under **cost and freight** (C&F), the seller has to cover the costs of packaging, shipment, and documentation until the goods are unloaded in the port indicated in the sales contract. The risk of merchandise damage or loss is transferred to the buyer when the goods have actually passed over the vessel's side in the port of destination. **Cost, insurance, freight** (CIF) is similar to C&F, but it obligates the seller to insure the merchandise against damage and loss during shipment.

Changes in distribution technology have revolutionized world trade. An artist's sketch of a "roll on/roll off" trailership and a photo of a containership from China being unloaded both illustrate how new approaches to shipping speed the distribution of goods around the world.

Disagreements arise under these terms with respect to the point at which the damage occurred, affecting who is responsible. For example, if the goods were damaged in shipment the shipper is responsible. But if the goods were defective at the time of shipment, the seller is responsible. In either case, the buyer is left with damaged goods. For a further discussion of potential problems when using C&F and CIF terms, see Global Dimensions 16.1.

Delivered duty paid (DDP) puts the entire burden of the costs and risk involved in the international shipment of goods on the seller. The products must be delivered to the buyer's premises as stipulated in the sales contract. DDP is generally viewed as the least viable term. It requires considerable experience in international shipment on the part of the marketer, even when an international freight forwarder is used. In most cases, therefore, some other term of sale will be used by the business partners, leaving part of the obligations to the buyer.

Today, sophisticated companies are using terms of sale (and the related shipping costs) as a source of profit. The Japanese and Australians, for example, typically try to purchase on an "ex works" basis so that they can control all the costs themselves. They prefer to sell on a C&F or DDP basis. Controlling more aspects of the sale can make the seller more competitive, because more than the price of the product can be manipulated. Assume, for example, that the standard rate for shipping a ton of lead from Missouri to Brussels is $200. If a company can find a way to get the product to Brussels for $100, it could quote "C&F, Brussels" and bill $150 for transportation. It would not only have a $50 price advantage over the competition, but it would also make an extra $50 on the sale.

Terms of Trade: C&F/CIF

Suppose that a bakery based in Atlanta, Georgia, is modernizing and wants to sell its old ovens. A buyer in Japan is found for the ovens. The bakery ships the ovens on a "C&F, Yokohama" basis (the buyer designated the port). For payment, they agree on shipping under a letter of credit, payable against a clean set of on-board bills of lading, from Savannah. The "C&F, Yokohama" price covered by the confirmed, irrevocable letter of credit is $100,000.

The vessel carrying the ovens departs on March 25th. The bakery recognizes that the sooner it gets its money in the bank, the better. It goes to the steamship agency on the 26th, picking up the clean set of on-board bills of lading, and then goes directly to the bank to negotiate the letter of credit. By the time the vessel arrives in Yokohama, the money is safely in the bakery's bank.

But the buyer discovers a few days after the ovens arrive that all of the handles are broken off. The costs to repair them amount to about $10,000, which the buyer asks the bakery to pay. The bakery, however, argues that the ovens were carefully packed, and that the damage occurred in shipment or during unpacking in Japan. C&F terms transfer the risk of damage or loss to the customer when the goods are unloaded. The Japanese buyer claims the damage occurred before that point; the bakery argues it occurred after that point.

There would be no problem if CIF had been used, making the damage the insurance company's problem. But, the Japanese firm did not insure, as they would have to with CIF, because it believed the seller to be the party at risk, so it could avoid paying expensive insurance. The bakery refuses to negotiate, there's no insurance company to pay the $10,000, so the Japanese client hires an Atlanta lawyer and sues.

The lesson is that, in addition to defining C&F in the terms of sale, it is critical that one of the parties, the one at greatest probability of risk, buy insurance. Just because it is the other party's "obligation" does not mean that both parties are not at risk. The cost of the insurance, of course, affects the price that is paid.

METHODS OF PAYMENT

To be paid quickly and appropriately, the global marketer must set proper terms of payment.

Methods of payment, often the result of a sales-negotiation process, state the means of payment for the goods or services to be delivered.[6] Every marketer wants to get paid as quickly as possible and according to the invoice. Customers want to obtain the merchandise as ordered. A smooth process of exchange is in the interest of both parties, therefore. But many potential payment disputes can disturb the process, especially in global marketing.

Factors Affecting Choice

The most important determinant of payment terms is the risk anticipated by the business partners in the transactional process. An obvious risk concerns *business-partner reliability*, or the level of trust and the strength of the relationship between the two business partners. Sales subsidiaries normally get their merchandise on an open-account basis. But most U.S. companies will not deliver anything to Colombian customers, for example, without having received an irrevocable letter of credit due to the higher risks.

Another risk factor is the *distance* between the partners. Distance influences the duration and complication of shipment. It can also reduce the safety and quality of the product. *Institutional risk* results from political or social instability in one or both of the partners' home countries (see Chapter 5). *Currency risk* results from fluctuating exchange rates (see Chapter 18), which strongly affect the price of the merchandise and the potential profit. *Financial risk* results from lack of knowledge about the buyer's financial strength or weakness.

The *nature of the merchandise* also influences the choice of payment methods. If a German firm purchases tobacco from Egypt, for example, it will not pay the invoiced amount before having inspected the quality of the merchandise. On the other hand, a Swedish supplier of heavy weapons may not start to deliver arms to Zaire before getting paid an advance of one-third of the entire contract's value.

Also, the *industry standards* and *degree of competition* may affect the choice of methods of payment. Companies that are in a highly competitive industry (such as the computer industry) or are mass marketers of consumer goods may have to accept a higher-risk payment form in order to offer a competitive pricing option to their customers.

Other determinants of payment terms include the *market strength* and *negotiation skills* of each of the business partners, and the degree of the marketer's *customer orientation*. The methods of payment not only regulate the way goods or services are to be exchanged, but they also represent a financial tool that can be effectively used in a competitive marketing program. Chapter 18 will elaborate on this.

Alternative Methods of Payment

The method of payment affects the true price of the product.

Exhibit 16.4 gives an overview of the parties potentially involved in global payment procedures and their relationships. In addition to the primary business partners, most often their banks will be involved. National regulations and international agreements also affect payment procedures and have to be followed. Third parties—for example, investors who buy the financial arrangement (similar to the idea of factoring account receivables) or government-run export banks providing guarantees—may enter the picture. Depending upon the parties involved, and the factors that affect choice, the specific method of payment will be selected.

EXHIBIT 16.4
THE PARTIES
INVOLVED IN AN
INTERNATIONAL
PAYMENT
PROCEDURE

To ensure that the exporter gets paid by the im-
porter, many parties must
be involved, and many
activities must be
completed.

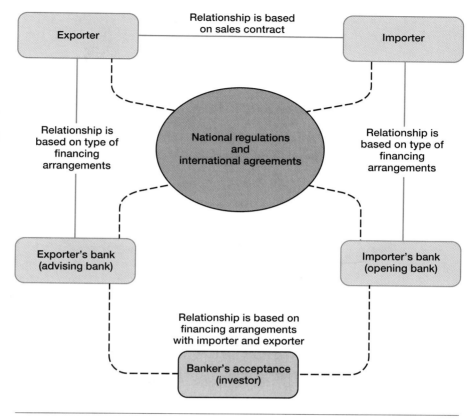

Source: M. Eng, "Trade Financing," in I. Walter and T. Murray, eds., *Handbook of International Business* (New York: John Wiley & Sons, 1982), p. 13.7.

The alternative methods of payment available to the global marketer reach from high-credit, high-risk, customer-oriented methods to low-credit, low-risk, producer-oriented methods. These are discussed in the following section.

Consignment. When a **consignment** contract exists, the marketer or con-signor delivers the products to the customer but retains the title to them until the customer has sold them to a third party or has consumed/used them and paid the marketer. For example, BASF, a German marketer of special chemicals, may have a contract with a customer in France under which the barrels con-taining the chemicals are stored at the customer's premises, but remain BASF's property until they enter the production process. The consignee is assured of having the needed volume of merchandise at each point in the production process and in many cases does not have to pay taxes or duties before using the products. Efficient use of consignment requires that the marketer be able to control the volume of both the merchandise in stock and consigned merchandise. The major problem with consignment is that the marketer assumes part of the financing of the customer's inventory and absorbs a high credit risk.

Open Accounts. This is the payment method most often used in domestic marketing. It offers full credit terms to the customer. Because of the high risk involved in **open accounts** in global marketing, this alternative is mostly used between production and sales units of globally operating companies or in cases where long-lasting, reliable business relationships exist.

In Europe many business deals have to be made on an open-account basis, because customers will not accept any other payment method. But even in the European Community, open accounts are risky. Italian customers have a reputation for being extremely slow in paying their open accounts. In such cases it is up to the marketer to gather precise information on the credit reliability of a new customer before signing a contract.

Drafts. A **draft** for payment is an order written by a seller requesting the buyer to pay a specified amount of money at a specified time. After shipping the goods to the customer, the marketer presents the draft to its bank and documents that the goods specified in the contract were sent to the customer. The bank, in turn, forwards the draft and documents to the bank of the customer for collection. This way the customer is guaranteed that the merchandise has been shipped as stated in the contract before it is paid for. The marketer gains security in that the documents are not handed over to the customer before the customer has accepted the draft and the merchandise is paid for.

Basically, there are three different kinds of drafts, which can be negotiated and included in the contract. On presentation of a **sight draft** the marketer has to be paid immediately. With a **time draft,** payment must be made within a specified time period, usually 30, 60, 90, 120, or 180 days. **Deferred payment** means that the marketer is paid by a specific date fixed in the contract.

Deferred payment may be negotiated when the merchandise has to pass governmental examination before it is allowed to enter the country, as is the case with food and drugs exported to the United States. If the marketer needs to be paid before the fixed time has elapsed, the draft can be sold in a financial market or to the customer's bank at a discount.

The two most popular forms of drafts are the **document against payment draft (D/P)**, based on a sight draft, and the **document against acceptance draft (D/A)**, based on a time draft. Upon receipt of payment from the customer, the bank proceeds as indicated by the marketer. The documents are handed over to the customer and the funds are remitted to the marketer's bank. This bank, in turn, makes them available to the firm. Costs incurred by the marketer for the draft method of payment are approximately 2 percent of the dollar sales volume.

Letters of Credit. A **letter of credit (L/C)** is a written obligation from a bank made at the request of the customer to honor a marketer's drafts or other demands for payment upon compliance with conditions specified in the document. Exhibit

EXHIBIT 16.5
THE LETTER-OF-
CREDIT PROCESS

Letters of credit, which
reduce international com-
mercial risk, must be
managed through a se-
ries of steps and involve
a variety of organizations.

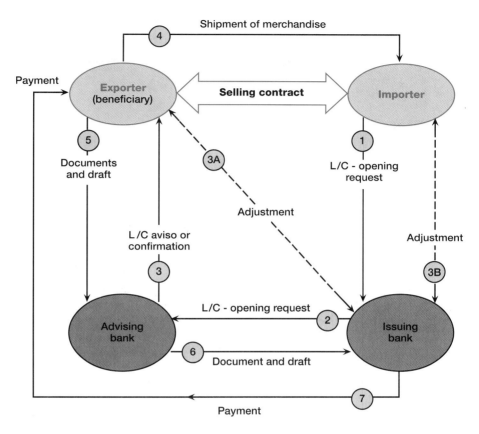

The most important
credit-related docu-
ment for the global
marketer is the letter of
credit.

16.5 depicts the entire process. For example, if a Canadian manufacturer of snowmobiles signs a contract with a Finnish customer requiring a letter of credit, the Finnish buyer will ask its bank to prepare a letter of credit in favor of the Canadian supplier. If that bank (the *issuing bank*) is ready to assume responsibility for payment, it will contact the marketer's bank in Canada. This bank (the *advising bank*) can either confirm the letter of credit or not, forwarding the letter of credit to the snowmobile manufacturer.

After receiving the letter of credit, the marketer should carefully review all the points listed in Exhibit 16.6. If there are any discrepancies between the contents of the letter of credit and the sales contract the marketer should ask the issuing bank and/or the customer for adjustment. It is important to do this before shipping the merchandise, because even an extremely small difference between the contents of the letter of credit and the shipment documents may result in refusal of payment by the issuing bank. For example, the Finnish bank may refuse to meet its obligations because one letter in one word in the documents of the Canadian supplier is different than in the letter of credit.

1. The name and address must be correct.

2. The credit amount must be sufficient to cover the shipment agreed on in the sales contract, especially if freight and insurance charges are to be paid by the exporter.

3. The required documents must be obtainable and in accordance with the sales contract.

4. The points of shipment and destination of the merchandise must be correctly stated.

5. The shipping date must allow sufficient time to dispatch the goods from the supplier's warehouse to the shipping point.

6. The expiration of the credit must allow sufficient time for the presentation of the draft and required documents at the banking office where the credit expires.

7. The description of the merchandise and any specifications must agree with the terms of sale.

After shipping the merchandise, the Canadian marketer (the *beneficiary*) presents all needed documents and a draft to the advising Canadian bank. The bank reviews and forwards them to the issuing Finnish bank. This bank will closely examine the documents and the draft. If it confirms the information in the letter of credit, the marketer will be paid according to the type of draft, and the customer will receive title to the merchandise.

Depending on the decisions of the two banks involved, the letter of credit may take different forms. The issuing bank may *irrevocably* commit itself to pay the marketer's draft. If the bank keeps its freedom to amend or cancel the credit at any time, the letter of credit is *revocable*. In practice this form of letter of credit is not common, because it does not provide any security to the marketer and, therefore, does not justify the cost of the procedure. Exhibit 16.7 gives an overview of how risk related to letters of credit can be transferred by the marketer.

Irrevocable letters of credit may be confirmed by the advising bank or not. If an irrevocable letter of credit is unconfirmed, the advising bank is not obliged to pay the draft. The advising bank will not confirm a letter of credit when the issuing bank (perhaps because of its political/economic environment) represents a credit risk. Most banks located in industrialized countries issue lists of countries for which they are not ready to confirm letters of credit.

Letters of credit must be closely checked for forgeries, which have become more and more sophisticated. For example, the only mistake in a faked letter of credit from Nigeria was that the trunk of the elephant in the bank logo pointed to the left instead of to the right.

Most marketers dealing with unknown customer banks will try to get a confirmed, irrevocable letter of credit. This is the most secure payment method, after cash in advance. It assures that the marketer will be paid by the advising bank, provided all conditions stated in the letter of credit are met, even if the issuing bank will not honor the draft for any reason.

EXHIBIT 16.7 RISK TRANSFER FOR LETTERS OF CREDIT

There may be commercial risk even with a letter of credit. This exhibit illustrates how that risk can be managed—for example, it can be transferred to a third party, such as a bank or government agency that provides insurance.

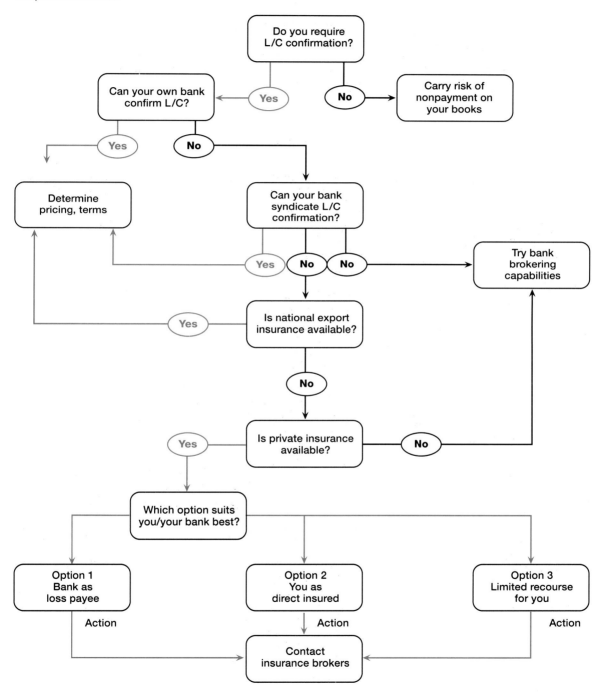

When goods are shipped to a customer on a continuing basis, a **revolving letter of credit** may be issued. In other words, the letter of credit applies to the sale of multiple shipments over an extended period of time. **Back-to-back letters of credit** occur when an intermediary uses an irrevocable letter of credit to ask the advising bank to open a similar letter of credit in favor of the ultimate supplier of the merchandise. A small European trading house may, for example, possess an irrevocable letter of credit for a shipment of electric generators, manufactured by General Electric in the United States, to Iraq. Because of the small size of the trading house, GE may not be ready to do business without an irrevocable letter of credit from the trading house. The trader, therefore, may ask its bank to issue the letter of credit in favor of GE, offering the Iraqi irrevocable letter of credit as security.

The costs of a letter of credit can approach 3 percent of the sales value shown in the invoice. Despite this high cost in comparison to an open account, the marketer will choose to rely on a letter of credit if the customer represents an unknown credit risk; if the foreign-exchange regulations of the customer's country do not allow simple, direct payments; or if transportation costs are high.

Payment in Advance.   **Payment in advance** is the most attractive method of payment for the marketer, generating revenue before goods are shipped or services are provided. The customer bears all risks and, in effect, helps finance production of the goods or services. The payment can be made by the customer, its bank, or the marketer's bank at the time the order is placed with the marketer.

Payment in advance is rarely encountered in global marketing. It may be used when the market position of the supplier is very strong and the customer's credit rating is unsatisfactory or unknown. For example, when China opened up its trading policy with Western nations, it offered payment in advance for training, by European specialists, of managers at industrial plants.

Partial payment in advance may be negotiated when the size of the order is so large that it overwhelms the supplier's financing capability. For example, customer-specific engineering and/or production involves enormous working capital. When the construction of a steel mill for the site of Ahwaz in southwestern Iran was negotiated between an Iranian delegation and a European steel mill, the Iranians offered one-third of the project's anticipated dollar volume as payment in advance to indicate their willingness and ability to finance the huge project.

. . . .

COUNTERTRADE

In today's global marketplace, payment for products is increasingly nonmonetary.

Under certain circumstances, described in the following section, the customer may prefer **countertrade**. This has been defined as "a commercial transaction in which provisions are made, in one or a series of related contracts, for payment by deliveries of goods and/or services in addition to, or in place of, financial settlement."[7]

Some 10–30 percent of international trade involves countertrade, and the trend is growing.[8] Up to 1970, it was mainly COMECON and other centrally controlled economies, like Albania and Yugoslavia, that proposed countertrade agreements, usually to firms located in industrialized countries. The number of countries interested in countertrade has steadily expanded since then. Today not only is east-west business characterized by countertrade, but north-south business (between industrialized and developing countries) and a growing amount of south-south business (between LDCs) are too. For example, approximately 50 percent of the trade between Eastern Europe and the developing countries is conducted through countertrade. Even highly industrialized economies (such as Australia, Austria, Belgium, Canada, The Netherlands, New Zealand, Norway, Sweden, and the United Kingdom) have joined the ranks of countries that use countertrade arrangements for certain kinds of transactions. In addition to trading companies that specialize in countertrade, approximately half of the Fortune 500 companies were involved in countertrade transactions in the mid-1980s.[9] And 92 multinational manufacturing firms reported having in-house countertrade operations in the late 1980s.[10]

Barter

Over the years many different forms of countertrade have developed. Three different kinds of barter found in global business as discussed in this section. Three other forms of countertrade are discussed in the following section.

Barter is the exchange of goods or services without transfers of money in a short time frame, generally one year or less, formalized in one contract. All the other forms of countertrade are based on two or more separate contracts. They include full or partial monetary compensation, and the contracts are generally for periods longer than one year.

In **classic barter** both parties function as buyers and sellers in a mutual exchange of products with offsetting values. The exchanged products may be industrial goods, consumer goods, services, or commodities. Bangladesh, for example, has classic-barter agreements with COMECON countries, such as Bulgaria, and other LDCs, such as Pakistan. It trades agricultural commodities, textiles, hides, and paper products for industrial equipment, machinery, chemicals, fertilizers, metals, and medicines.[11] Another example is the Malaysian-owned rubber trading company, Sime Darby, which exchanged cocoa beans delivered by Mexican tire manufacturers for Malaysian rubber.[12] Classic barter is relatively rare in global marketing.

Closed-end barter differs from classic barter in that one of the business partners already has a buyer at hand for the products to be traded before the contract is signed. Most often it will be the partner located in the more economically developed area. Closed-end barter very much diminishes the risk associated with barter.

Clearing-account barter is based on bilateral clearing agreements between governments, as was discussed in Chapter 3. For years it was largely practiced between COMECON members and LDCs. It is increasingly common between

LDCs, but as COMECON members unblock their currencies, barter may become less popular for them.

Other Forms of Countertrade

Compensation arrangements, used for industrial projects, involve technology or capital transfer from industrialized to developing and/or centrally controlled economies. When plant equipment or turnkey plants are sold to firms in those countries, their governments may sign the contract only if the suppliers are willing to take back the products manufactured by that equipment over an extended period of time (5–10 years) as part of the payment. For example, Dunbee-Combex-Marx, a British toy manufacturer, and China agreed that the firm would furnish toy-making machinery and molds to China in return for a 50 percent cash downpayment and 50 percent of the toys made in the Chinese factory.[13] Such contracts are also called **buyback arrangements.**

Counterpurchase is an indirect form of compensation trading. It is characterized by buying and selling agreements that are basically independent from each other. They are either partially or totally paid in cash or in bank credit. Counterpurchase is a form of countertrade, because the supplier in a business deal signs a second contract agreeing to buy products, defined within broad categories, from the customer within a period of time that ranges from 1 to 5 years.

A special case of counterpurchase is the establishment of **evidence accounts.** These usually occur when an exporter or a trading company in an industrialized country signs a counter-purchase contract with the government of a developing country. In an **"umbrella" trade agreement** the two parties arrange that two-way trade between the firm—as well as other businesses designated by it—and firms in the developing country be partially or fully balanced over a specified period of time, typically 1 to 5 years. In one such deal, a trading company agreed to buy a large amount of crude oil at OPEC prices and use the country's bank credit stemming from that deal to pay Western companies, in hard currency, for their delivery of industrial as well as consumer products to customers in that country.

Offsets are most common in sizable weapon delivery contracts between a supplying firm and a government. They usually combine domestic-content, coproduction, and technology-transfer requirements with long-term counter-purchase arrangements. The marketer is confronted with a (governmental) customer who is ready to sign a contract only if the marketer agrees to counter-purchase goods from the customer country, transfer technological know-how by producing components and equipment in the buyer's country, subcontract compatible components to local manufacturers, or meet other conditions. In 1980 the Canadian government announced, for example, that in exchange for a $2.3 billion purchase of McDonnell-Douglas F-18 fighter aircraft, Canadian firms would participate in the production of aircraft components; receive the necessary advanced manufacturing technologies; obtain expertise in solar energy, cryogenics, health care, and processing of agricultural products; and receive market-development assistance for Canadian exports and tourism.[14]

Company and Government Motives

Government initiatives concerning countertrade vary. They range from incentives to the imposition of such agreements as a condition of doing business. Mexico has imposed export-performance requirements on imports and investment, and Brazil has imposed domestic-content requirements on imports and local industrial projects. Global Dimensions 16.2 illustrates the countertrade policies of several other nations and their effect on the countries' international trade. EC nations officially are neutral concerning private companies' decisions, but most have created public services to advise firms or actively promote countertrade.

The reasons for the increase of countertrade in LDCs are found in the countries' economic-development difficulties. Many LDCs experience severe financial bottlenecks due to a combination of credit cuts, balance-of-payment problems, sluggish exports, and high debts with U.S., European, and Japanese banks. These conditions have left most developing countries with few alternatives other than countertrade to acquire badly needed capital goods and services. As about 40 percent of industrialized nations' trade is done with LDCs, this is of tremendous importance to firms from those nations.[15]

A second major reason for countertrade agreements is the chronic shortage of hard currency in most centrally controlled economies and LDCs.[16] They need equipment and technology from highly industrialized markets to enhance their economic development and global competitiveness, but they lack economic resources. Countertrade is often the only way they can obtain those resources.

The lack of globally competitive industrial skills is another reason some countries engage in countertrade. Most selling problems in centrally controlled economies and LDCs occur due to their low level of familiarity with basic marketing activities. They do not have enough experience in building a global distribution system, packaging, design, promotion, and after-sale services.[17] Many industrial exports from these countries are not due to active marketing by the manufacturer, but result from the purchasing activities of companies from developed countries. Those companies bring in product and process technology and management know-how, and they use the less-developed country's raw material and cheap labor, but they may not transfer much of their technology.

Another reason for countertrade is that it opens markets to products that would not be bought otherwise, because of existing global overcapacities or insufficient quality or promotion. Consumer goods from China, for example, may not have found their way to the U.S. consumer without China's requirement that U.S. companies accept countertrade items. Machinery from Romania would also probably not be sold to Western buyers without the imposition of countertrade agreements through the Romanian government.

GLOBAL DIMENSIONS 16.2

Selected Governments and Countertrade Policies

Country	Policy
Australia	*Offset.* Recommends 30-percent-and-up domestic participation for purchases funded by government; applies to equipment and services.
New Zealand	*Offset.* Government purchases over NZ$ 2 million require export of locally produced goods or domestic content in manufacturing. Purchases of professional services require 30 percent local labor participation.
Israel	*Offset.* Over $100,000 in government purchases requires offset purchases, usually 25 percent of the contract value. Local content offset preferred to local participation.
Indonesia	*Counterpurchase.* Foreign suppliers to government must buy equivalent amounts of nonpetroleum goods. 50 percent of the transaction value must be deposited beforehand in an Indonesian bank.
United States	*Dual policy.* Opposes government-mandated counterpurchase agreements. Supports private initiatives; passed Export Trading Company Act, which liberalized banks' role in export trading companies; and extended exemption from antitrust law to trading-firms members.
West Germany	*Supportive.* Provides support through national trade associations.
France	*Supportive.* Countertrade supported by Ministry of Foreign Trade, national trade and industry groups, and banks. While the government is not directly involved, the association provides information for French exporters, identifies trading companies of importers willing to participate, and advises government authorities on desired policy initiatives.

Source: Adapted from P. Verzariu, *Countertrade, Barter, and Offsets: New Strategies for Profit in International Trade* (New York: Mcgraw-Hill, 1985), pp. 16, 38–39; J. Wills, L. Jacobs, and A. Palia, "Countertrade: The Asia Pacific Dimension," *International Marketing Review*, Summer 1986, pp. 20–21; and K. Hicks, "Exports Prove Tough Ground But Banks Say Field Will Mature," *American Banker*, September 21, 1984, pp. 21–23.

A fifth reason for countertrade is the restrictive production regulations of cartels, which have led to overcapacity in some countries' commodity production. The relatively low production quota for crude oil for OPEC members in the second half of the 1980s led some of them to use their overproduction in countertrade offers to industrialized countries at official OPEC prices. Trading firms in those countries accepted the relatively high prices as a means to open up the oil producers' markets to Western products.

EXHIBIT 16.8   REASONS FOR NOT ENGAGING IN COUNTERTRADE

The research reported in this exhibit reveals the concerns international marketers have about becoming involved in countertrade.

Response	International Firms			Domestic Firms		
	No. of Responses	(%)	Rank*	No. of Responses	(%)	Rank*
Firm has no in-house use for goods offered by customers	110	77	1	124	64	1
Difficult to resell goods offered by customers	106	75	2	110	56	2
General increase in uncertainty	91	64	3	90	46	3
Complex negotiations	99	70	4	100	51	6
Time-consuming negotiations	97	68	5	103	53	4
Overpricing problems	88	62	6	93	48	5
Increases costs	88	62	7	91	47	7
Firm does not know enough about it	89	63	8	91	47	8
Brokerage costs and facilities needed	88	62	9	85	44	9
Customer's negotiating strength	78	55	10	76	39	11
Customer becomes potential competitor	64	45	11	74	38	10
Other	20	14		54	28	

Source: C. W. Neale and D. Shipley, "Effects of Countertrade—Divergent Perceptions Between Practitioners and Non-Participants," *Journal of Management Studies*, January 1988, p. 66.
*Importance of response.

Finally, there may also be political reasons for countertrade. Iran, for example, circumvented officially restricted relationships with some of the major Western countries by signing countertrade contracts with international trading houses for crude oil and chemicals in return for all kinds of industrial and even consumer goods. Those trading houses, not constrained by any similar political restrictions, were able to deliver the products from sources otherwise not officially available to Iran.

Concerns about Countertrade

Most companies located in Western industrialized economies have not entered the countertrade business with much enthusiasm. Exhibit 16.8 shows the results of an empirical investigation of British companies' reasons for not engaging in countertrade. Their two major concerns are that the company may have no in-house use for the traded goods, or it may encounter difficulties in reselling them to third parties. This may be due to the type of compensating goods offered by the partners, or possibly their low quality. But it may also be due to a lack of sufficiently trained people in the British companies.

A Canadian company that exported steel rails to Indonesia was required to take back an equivalent value of Indonesian products from a list containing alternatives such as palm oil, coffee, timber, and rattan furniture.[18] Coca-Cola, in one of its first countertrade deals, found itself stuck with substandard Chinese honey that could not be sold for two years.[19]

Another major concern expressed by the British companies is the uncertainty and complexity of a countertrade deal. Information from the countertrade partners regarding prices, product quality, and proprietary issues may be hard to get. A firm dealing with an indebted country may find out, for example, that banks and/or the IMF have prior claims on the goods offered as part of the countertrade agreement.[20] Legal and contractual issues can be difficult to deal with.

There is the further problem of setting exchange ratios for the goods to be traded. Government instability, red tape, and inefficiency add to the complications. Other concerns include increased costs, overpricing, negotiation problems, and the possibility of strengthening potential competitors.

Countertrade Opportunities

Despite these difficulties and constraints, countertrade can be regarded as a possible source of additional service for customers who have exchange problems, rather than as a burden. As Global Dimensions 16.3 shows, countertrade can be a major competitive marketing tool vis-à-vis other firms that may not feel comfortable with such deals. It allows the firm to take advantage of local tariff laws that may be stricter for traditional imports than for countertrade goods. It can also be used to open markets and gain favorable recognition from local bureaucrats, an important asset later on.[21]

Traded consumer goods are sometimes difficult to sell, but products like Russian fashions, Hungarian salami, Polish vodka, and Czechoslovakian crystal have proven to be very attractive products for resale. McDonnell-Douglas agreed, for example, to promote Yugoslavian goods and tourism in exchange for cash purchases of its DC-9, DC-10, and MD-80 commercial airliners. The Yugoslavian Trading Company has an office in McDonnell-Douglas's Los Angeles–area plant, selling hams, wine, vacation trips, power-transmission lines, and other products and services.[22]

Countertrade is a way of developing a market despite credit difficulties, exchange problems, and currency controls. It increases the company's sales volume, allows fuller use of the firm's productive capacity, and it may even provide a source of economically attractive inputs in the firm's production process.[23]

GLOBAL DIMENSIONS 16.3

Countertrade as a Competitive Tool

General Electric has successfully used countertrade as a competitive tool, helping it to beat out competition for business around the world. William Evonsky,
GE's manager of advanced trade development, has reported that using barter
helped GE save a deal the company had made to build turbine generators for
nuclear-energy generation in Romania. When the country got into a cash-flow
squeeze, GE agreed to accept $75 million (one-half of the total contract) worth
of Romanian industrial products, including railroad cars and ship containers.
GE later won a second contract over competitors for nuclear-energy equipment
worth $165 million, in part due to its flexibility in accepting barter in the first
contract.

Source: H. Eason, "Barter Boom," *Nation's Business*, March 1985, p. 24.

IMPACT ON THE MARKETING MIX

The pricing strategy strongly interacts with decisions concerning the company's
product policy, distribution system, and promotional goals and efforts. The
buyer may use the price of the product or service to judge its quality, its attractiveness to others, and its general value. That is, in the absence of other cues,
especially when the customer has little experience with the product, price will
be used as an indicator of the product's technical and social reliability. Thus
price may be a major communication tool for the global marketer.

Price can also be used to compete, through a better price-value relationship. When the product quality and design is at least as attractive as that of
competitors, the price may nevertheless be set at a lower level to gain market
entrance and penetration. The success of Japanese cameras, automobiles, motorcycles, and audio and video products in the United States and Europe is a
striking example of the concerted use of such a strategy.

Price also interacts with distribution. High-fashion, high-prestige, and
high-quality products, which have correspondingly high prices, are not sold
through discount outlets. Marketers of these products carefully choose the right
distribution channels. On the other hand, if the existing distribution infrastructure in a geographical market is complicated, with long distribution channels, the price will automatically be higher than in markets with short distribution channels. If a given price is essential for the company's market success,
its management will try to establish control over the entire distribution process.
The choice of distribution system will follow from this requirement. ■

SUMMARY

Proper pricing of goods and services is key to the success of a global company. Although a firm should have a global pricing policy, the actual price charged in the marketplace is influenced by many different factors, several of which the firm may influence in a limited way. Calculation of that price—whether standard formula, price adaptation, or strategically set—must take these factors into account.

The major factors of influence include the cost of the good, which determines the lower price limit, and market demand, which sets the upper price limit. The final price usually lies between the two and depends upon the company's pricing policy, competition, and actions of local governments.

In order to avoid direct price competition and to have a broader range of pricing alternatives, the global marketer must handle the terms of sale and methods of payment in a sophisticated manner. Incoterms are used in an attempt to minimize confusion from using a variety of terms to describe the same conditions of the sale. The methods of payment selected are affected by several factors: most importantly, the merchandise itself, the risks associated with the sale, and industrial and competitive practices. Alternative terms of sale and methods of payment must be chosen to make the firm's product more attractive to customers and to increase corporate profits.

When economic or political factors inhibit the exchange of goods or services strictly for money, various forms of countertrade can be employed. Barter is normally a short-term, one-time, countertrade contract. Other forms of countertrade that are for longer periods of time, or multiple contracts such as buyback or counterpurchase, permit a more permanent relationship between buyer and seller without necessarily involving money. Companies usually engage in countertrade in order to enter markets that are otherwise blocked to them by governments that are trying to manage severe financial constraints. These deals are so important that no global company can afford to overlook countertrade in the future.

DISCUSSION QUESTIONS

1. Why is pricing probably the most difficult element in the global marketing mix to manage?

2. Which is the best global pricing policy for a corporation: standard, standard formula, price adaptation, or strategic pricing? Why?

3. "Because a price is the market's perception of the product's value, costs really don't matter, especially in international marketing. Another less price-sensitive market can always be found." Do you agree or disagree with that statement, and why?

4. How do governmental policies affect the international pricing decision?

5. Which of the terms of sale is of greatest advantage to the global marketer? Which results in the greatest risk being retained by the global marketer? Explain.

6. What factors affect the choice of terms of payment, and what is their effect?

7. When and why would you recommend that a global marketer use an open account as the method of payment?

8. What role does a letter of credit play in global marketing?

9. Will countertrade increase or decrease in importance in the future, and why?

10. Describe how pricing affects the other elements of the global marketing mix: place (distribution), product, and promotion.

C A S E

OLIVER DRILLING: GLOBAL PRICING ISSUES

John Oliver, founder and president of Oliver Drilling Products, Inc., of Kansas City, Missouri, had an international pricing problem. Through an agent who represented the company on an ongoing basis in Finland, he was surprised to find out that a Russian coal mine was interested in ordering $3 million worth of drilling equipment for use in medium-sized coal mines. Mr. Oliver was justly proud of his equipment, which was developed especially by Oliver Drilling for smaller mines. Oliver Drilling's products helped other machines drill faster, and at a lower cost, than competitors' equipment. This, of course, saved its customers money over the long run compared to competitive equipment. Oliver Drilling was a world leader in its market segment and although premium-priced in all of its markets, it offered excellent value.

Oliver Drilling had been in business for 20 years, and in the past 5 years it had built up a strong export business, to some 40 percent of its $32 million in annual sales. In fact, 75 percent of the growth in sales over the past 5 years had come from overseas sales. Oliver Drilling used an agency with three representatives in Western Europe, one in Australia, one in Taiwan, and two in Latin America. The agents were paid on a commission basis. Service for the products was provided through local independent service contractors, which so far had provided Oliver Drilling's clients with excellent service in all markets.

But Oliver Drilling had never exported before to an Eastern European nation. It was experienced, as was its bank in Kansas City, in various export terms of payment and terms of sale. It generally shipped "FAS, New York" to European customers and "FAS, Long Beach" to Asian customers. In both cases, about 20 percent of its exports (those for long-term customers) were sold on an open-account basis (after a 25 percent downpayment). Other customers were offered a time draft of 60 days. But the bulk of first-time sales had always been through a confirmed, irrevocable letter of credit.

Oliver Drilling's bank in Kansas City, however, was not willing to confirm a letter of credit for a Russian central trading organization. It advised Oliver Drilling to obtain payment in advance. While Mr. Oliver thought that was a good idea, his Finnish agent insisted that some other terms would have to be offered, especially because a German competitor and a Korean competitor were also interested in the sale. Their machines were not quite as good as Oliver Drilling's, but better terms of sale or payment have been known to influence such deals before.

The buyer, a central trading organization in Russia, was waiting to hear from Oliver Drilling before contacting the competition, although it would not wait for long. The buyer until now had always insisted on countertrade when dealing with U.S. companies. Although Oliver Drilling had no experience with countertrade, a countertrade specialist in St. Louis, which had an excellent reputation, was more than willing to help Oliver Drilling with the transaction. It would serve as a broker for the transaction, helping Oliver Drilling to sell the coal that the central trading company proposed to trade for Oliver Drilling's machines. Mr. Oliver knew little about countertrade, but was willing to consider it if there was long-term potential for additional sales. On that point, the Finnish agent was not certain.

Mr. Oliver was interested in getting this sale. He thought it might prove useful in exploring whether the entire Eastern European market might be opening up. But he did not want to undercut his market position as the provider of high-quality, high-priced equipment in other foreign markets. The sale would be made through his Finnish agent, who, he feared, might tell the other European agents if the Russian deal were completed at a big discount off normal prices.

The U.S. government was not an obstacle to going ahead with the deal. The drilling equipment was not considered vital for national security, so no special export license was required. In fact, the easing of political tensions between the United States and the USSR meant that the U.S. government was encouraging U.S. firms to become active in trading with the USSR.

Case Issues

1. Should Oliver Drilling become involved in countertrade? Why or why not?

2. If it does not undertake countertrade, what should the terms of sale and terms of payment be?

3. What global pricing issues should Mr. Oliver keep in mind in making his decisions?

NOTES

1. N. C. G. Campbell, J. L. Graham, A. Jolibert, and H. G. Meissner, "Marketing Negotiations in France, Germany, the United Kingdom, and the United States," *Journal of Marketing*, April 1988, pp. 49–62.

2. D. M. Johnson, "The Impact of Hyperinflation on the Purchasing Habits of Consumers: The Case of Brazil," paper presented at the 13th Annual Macro Marketing Conference, San Jose, 1988.

3. For more examples of price control see V. H. Frank, "Living with Price Control Abroad," *Harvard Business Review*, March–April 1984, pp. 137–142.

4. Following the countries of western Europe and all the industrialized COMECON countries, in 1980 the seven most important U.S. trade organizations (American Importers Association, U.S. Chamber of Commerce, Council on International Banking, National Association of Councils on International Banking, National Foreign Trade Council, National Committee on International Trade Documentation, U.S. Council of the International Chamber of Commerce) have suggested using the Incoterms instead of the U.S. definitions applied so far.

5. International Chamber of Commerce, brochure no. 350, Paris, 1980.

6. This section is largely based on: M. Eng, "Trade Financing," in I. Walter and T. Murray, eds., *Handbook of International Business* (New York: John Wiley & Sons, 1982); and J. C. D. Zahn, E. Eberding, and D. Ehrlich, *Zahlung und Sahlungssicherung im Aussenhandel* (Berlin: Walter de Gruyter, 1986).

7. U.N. Economic Commission for Europe, "Countertrade Practices in the Region," *TRADE/R 385*, November 1979.

8. H. Eason, "Barter Boom," *Nation's Business*, March 1985, p. 20; H. Marschner, "Counter Trade: Ein Instrument für neue Markte?," *Absatzwirtschaft*, April 1988, p. 68; J. W. Dizard, "The Explosion of International Barter," *Fortune*, February 1983, pp. 88–95; and I. A. Ronkainen, "Special Issue on Export/Import Strategies: An Introduction," *Journal of Business Research* 12, 1984, pp. 137–140.

9. A. E. Fishman, "By Bartering, Dealers Avoid Laying Out Cash for Goods," *Merchandising*, August 1984, pp. 93–96.

10. L. G. Reiling, "Countertrade Revives 'Dead Goods,'" *Marketing News*, August 29, 1986, p. 22.

11. P. Verzariu, *Countertrade, Barter, and Offsets: New Strategies for Profit in International Trade* (New York: McGraw-Hill, 1985), p. 26.

12. G. Banks, "The Economics and Politics of Countertrade," *World Economics*, June 1983, pp. 159–182.

13. W. W. Kassaye, "Countertrade Prospects and Dilemma for Small Businesses," *American Journal of Small Business*, Winter 1985, pp. 17–24.

14. P. Verzariu, op. cit., p. 44.

15. D. Ford et al., "Managing Export Development Between Industrialized and Developing Countries," in P. J. Rosson and S. D. Reid, eds., *Managing Export Entry and Expansion: Concepts and Practice* (New York: Praeger, 1987), pp. 71–90.

16. J. G. Kaikati, "The Reincarnation of Barter Trade as a Marketing Tool," *Journal of Marketing*, April 1976, pp. 17–24.

17. I. P. Akaah and E. A. Riordan, "Applicability of Marketing Knowhow in the Third World," *International Marketing Review*, Spring 1988, pp. 41–55.

18. D. Goldfield, "Countertrade: New Ways of Selling to the Third World," *International Perspectives*, March–April 1984, pp. 19–22.

19. E. G. Martin and T. E. Ricks, "Countertrade Grows As Cash-Short Nations Seek Marketing Help," *Wall Street Journal*, March 13, 1985, pp. 1, 30.

20. J. Wills, L. Jacobs, and A. Palia, "Countertrade: The Asia-Pacific Dimension," *International Marketing Review*, Summer 1986, p. 25.

21.   G. Banks, "The Economics and Politics of Countertrade," *World Economy*, June 1983, p. 169.

22.   H. Eason, op. cit., p. 24.

23.   R. Mirus and B. Yeung, "Economic Incentives for Countertrade," *Journal of International Business Studies*, Fall 1986, pp. 27–39.

FIVE

MANAGING THE GLOBAL MARKETING PROCESS

So FAR WE HAVE LOOKED AT GLOBAL MARketing from the perspectives of the underlying business philosophy (Chapters 1 and 2) and the activities necessary to take a firm's marketing global (Chapters 3 to 16). Successful global marketing, however, depends on more than a basic orientation, a careful analysis of potential markets, an exact determination of competitive advantages, and a future-oriented decision on the proper strategies for positioning and market entry. The implementation of a sophisticated global marketing mix also strongly relies on the presence of two well-functioning infrastructures inside the company: management systems and financing.

A variety of management systems must be in place to manage a global approach to marketing. The elements of a firm's management systems are shaped by its organizational structure. The management processes that occur within this structure are leadership, information, planning, and control. They are discussed in Chapter 17, together with the organizational structure on which they are based.

Financing from a marketing manager's point of view, may be a resource or a constraint for the globally oriented firm. Chapter 18 examines how a firm's financial policy, programs, and activities can contribute to worldwide marketing success. Finally, Chapter 19 looks at the future of global marketing in a rapidly changing world.

GLOBAL MANAGEMENT SYSTEMS

INTERNATIONAL INCIDENT

Bata Shoes

Bata Shoes is a global corporation. It produces and sells shoes over a wide range of styles and prices, advertising in over 100 languages. With more than 85,000 employees worldwide, and sales of over $2 billion, this Canada-based corporation can truly claim to be fulfilling its global potential.

Thomas Bata emigrated from Czechoslovakia to Canada, bringing with him a strong international orientation learned from his father, the founder of Bata. Applying his manufacturing skills and political awareness, he built Bata into the world's largest shoe manufacturer and seller. This took his skills, corporate financial resources, and an organization that rewarded its employees for pursuing new markets, even if seemingly risky.

For example, in the mid-1980s Bata built a plant in Upper Volta. This nation (since renamed Burkina Faso) has an average per capita income of $85 per year. Bata still thought it represented a potential market. The plant produces a shoe that retails for $2.50. Plant employees are paid an average of $5.00 per week. While the seemingly low wage is controversial, Bata has created jobs, at wages that allow for a reasonable standard of living.

Bata has built a corporate culture of excitement and dedication to serving international markets through a socialization process. That is, Bata managers have been trained, motivated, and rewarded to think and behave globally. Perhaps what is most impressive about Bata is its control system. As just one example, the top managers meet daily in their headquarters to review where other key personnel are around the world that day, and when and where they are going next. In that session, they also review political, social, legal, or economic activities or changes that are going on in various national markets, to see what the potential business impacts might be. In other words, the managers share a culture of responding to international business challenges, through global production and marketing.

A company functions as a system with inputs (such as people and raw materials). It processes those inputs (produces goods and services), and it has outputs (such as products and societal impacts).

From a systems perspective, a company can be defined as an open socio-economic system. Such a system is characterized as exchanging scarce and valued resources with its environments. A business firm carries out its exchanges through different functions, such as procurement, production, marketing, and finance. To effectively and efficiently coordinate those functions, the company needs management systems. These systems have to be gradually adapted to the level of a firm's globalization.

When Grass AG, one of the leading manufacturers of furniture fittings in the world, created a production company in the United States and sales companies in Canada, Great Britain, France, and Italy, it found out that centralized planning and control did not lead to the expected results. It therefore founded a holding company, which acts as a coordinating agency. As a result, the firm's information systems became much more important. The existing leadership system also had to be adapted to the different motivations of managers and employees in the various countries.[1]

The design of management systems depends on various factors, to be described in the following section. The rest of the chapter focuses on the specific problems with managements systems the marketer may encounter during the process of globalization and some possible solutions. These systems include leadership, organization, information, planning, and control.

FACTORS OF INFLUENCE

The shape of a company's management systems depends on the external environments with which important exchange processes occur, as well as the company's resources (such as discussed in Chapter 8), culture, and corporate strategy. A company's management systems are not only influenced by such factors, but the factors are also influenced by management systems. For example, a company's incentive system is influenced by the structure of taxes. But if many companies cannot hire new employees due to high payroll taxes, a change in government policy may occur to increase the employment rate or to improve the quality of new personnel.

External Environments

Management systems must match corporate strengths to the relevant external environments.

The most successful business firms are characterized by management systems that match the specific requirements of their external environments, either through proper adaptation to external demands or superior business definition based on the existing management systems.[2] On the other hand, a company that has a competitive advantage in its information system should choose product markets where superior information is a key success factor. A good fit between environments and management systems helps to reduce the uncertainty inherent in global marketing. Uncertainty may stem from the complexity, variability, or interrelationships of the environments in which the company operates.

The more complex the company's environments, the more diverse its organizational structure and management processes have to be. If a U.S. pizza-delivery firm decides to extend its business to the EC markets, the complexity of its environments will increase. For example, it will have to develop a planning system that takes national differences in taxation into account.

The greater the rate of fluctuation in the firm's environments, the more flexible and adaptable an organization must be. Higher flexibility often requires a less formal organizational structure and decentralized management processes. For example, Compaq, a computer firm in Houston, emphasizes group decision making and minimizes hierarchical structures to better respond to the dynamics of the firm's environments.

As Chapter 1 pointed out, the interrelationships among global environments are steadily growing. Management systems have to be able to cope with this development, increasingly interlinking different parts on a global basis. An information system, for example, may need to contain on-line connections with all of the sales offices to allow simultaneous stock management of products around the globe, thereby reducing the danger of parallel imports.

Corporate Culture

One of the cultures a global marketer must work in is the culture of the corporation itself.

A global marketer is confronted with varying cultures and subcultures that underlie the behavior of consumers, competitors, suppliers, and other exchange partners. In addition, a firm develops and is characterized by its own corporate culture, which influences decisions just as powerfully as external environments do.[3] It strives to attain goals, it has formal and informal groups, and it is composed of a multitude of individuals with different personal backgrounds.

Corporate culture is the sum of values shared by the members of a company and the rules of behavior (social norms) they follow. That is, it represents a general frame of reference that the members of the organization use to interpret events and facts in the company's environments. Corporate culture results in observable behavior among employees, traditions, rituals, stories told about past events, and specialized language.[4] High-tech firms, for example, use a different vocabulary in their everyday work than do financial firms.

The strongest impact on a firm's management systems results from the values shared by the dominant group in the organization. In most cases this is top management. In some countries, including most EC nations, representatives of unions, financiers, and government may belong to the group that dominates the company. The dominant group formally or informally develops a philosophy on how to run the business (see Chapter 2) and the company's "rules of the game."[5]

The firm's existing management systems are an expression of this philosophy. IKEA, for example, has two basic ideas in its corporate philosophy: equality among employees and the danger of corporate bureaucracy. While this provides a positive climate for internal communication among employees at all levels, it also results in managers resisting formal planning and control systems.

Because the members of a firm belong to formal and informal groups with potentially different goals and values, they may also follow different norms of behavior. That is, subcultures exist within the company. A global marketer may be confronted with additional subcultures inside the company due to the different national backgrounds of its employees. These varying subcultures affect acceptance of management systems. A planning system may, for example, be well understood in the United States and in Europe, whereas in the Middle East and in Latin America it may be a source of continual conflicts because planning is done quite differently in those regions.

Corporate Strategy

The corporation's strategy partially defines its internal and external environments.

Corporate strategy determines in general terms how business is conducted. Managers' strategic choices flow from their perceptions of environmental conditions, including market characteristics, such as the number, size, distribution, and power of buyers and sellers; barriers to market entry and exit; the specific characteristics of (potential) customer demand; and competitors' advantages. By correctly matching strategy to both external and internal environments, a firm can increase its efficiency of resource use, and its profits.

External and internal environments are partially defined, in turn, by the chosen strategy. The choice of product market, for example, defines the market size and restricts the number of competitors and relevant consumers. For example, if the product market is defined as sweatbands for European women who ski, the size of the market is different than if it is defined as sweatbands for European women involved in sports. Internally, strategy influences the optimal organizational structure, as well as the information, planning, and control systems. For example, a highly standardized marketing strategy requires highly centralized control, but it may also require a planning system that permits flexible implementation of the basic strategy in local units.

The members of an organization will only support strategic goals when motivation and incentives are consistent with the goals. The company's decision-making process has to account for potential conflicts and inflexibility toward achieving strategic goals, and manage organizational change accordingly. The managers of a local unit, for example, are likely to be most interested in maximizing short-term profits if their pay is based on the unit's quarterly profits. This may conflict with a corporate goal of maximizing market penetration or having a balanced portfolio of product lines. Top management at Alfa-Laval's filtration profit center, for example, had major difficulties convincing its local marketing organizations to introduce the new Ultra Filtration system, because it required sales engineers to undergo extensive training, which kept them from generating profits with established products.

- -
LEADERSHIP

Proper leadership styles vary across cultures.

Leadership affects employee motivation (see Chapter 8) and, therefore, the entire outcome of global business efforts. Due to differences in values, attitudes toward authority and achievement, motivation, risk taking, and the learning process, the patterns of appropriate leadership vary across cultures.

Indian and Australian managers, for example, attach more importance to employee welfare than to the goal of profit maximization. Obedience and conformity are more consistently emphasized by Indian managers than by their U.S. and Australian counterparts.[6] French managers tend to deemphasize peer

Without leadership from the very top of the corporation, the firm will not achieve its international marketing objective.

"As if we all knew where we're going."

relationships, whereas the Dutch find them very important. The Japanese are committed to group decisions; Latin Americans are not.[7]

Cognitive processes influence how people from different cultures construct social reality. Exhibit 17.1 shows alternative approaches to reality found in Western societies versus Oriental societies. For different perceptions of reality, the firm uses different processes and tools to motivate employees, make decisions, prevent or resolve conflicts, and manage organizational change. For example, in Japanese companies a decision will not be made until all the employees involved have had a chance to express their views and a solution is found that enables them not to be socially disregarded. In U.S. firms, on the other hand, top management may decide to release personnel when sales are down, without paying any attention to what it may mean to them socially.

Motivation

The global firm has to determine the conditions that seem likely to increase employees' willingness and ability to cooperate. Managers and other personnel must understand and accept their role in the implementation process. It may be necessary, therefore, to include lower-level managers along with top managers early in the process of strategy development, assigning them different roles and levels of influence and creating commitment to the results. Managers, in turn,

EXHIBIT 17.1
CULTURAL
PARADIGMS IN
WESTERN VERSUS
ORIENTAL SOCIETIES

Western and Oriental so-
cieties have very different
cultures. These differ-
ences must be taken into
account when designing
management systems.

	Western	**Oriental**
Conceptualization of time	Single flow	Multiple Flows
Self-sanction mechanism	Guilt (individualistic)	Shame (social)
Science	Traditional "cause-and-effect" model	Interwoven relationships
Cosmology	Predetermined universe	Self-generating and self-organizing universe
Ideology	Authoritarian	Cooperative
Philosophy	Universalism	Network
Ethics	Competitive	Symbiotic
Decision process	Dictatorship, majority rule, or consensus	Elimination of individual hardship
Logic	Deductive axiomatic	Complementary
Perception	Categorical	Contextual
Knowledge	One truth. If people are informed, they will agree.	Multiple truths. People must learn and consider different views.
Analysis	Preset categories for all situations	Changeable categories depending on the situation

Source: Adapted from S. Ronen, *Comparative and Multinational Management* (New York: John Wiley & Sons, 1986), pp. 211ff.

are responsible for communicating the basic strategic directions to their personnel and to involve them in the development of objectives, programs, and actions
for local implementation.

Managers must be willing, and motivated, to implement international marketing activities. To do this, they must have freedom of action as well as some
control of the marketing budget. This will permit them to respond to local
demand and competition. In order to do so, they must be motivated to carry
out such programs and inclined to undertake such tasks.[8] Motivating managers
to implement marketing plans is part of the responsibility of human-resource
management, which provides a large number of tools that help managers be
successful.[9]

Role Models. A positive motivation among employees can often be achieved
through managers serving as role models. People learn much of their behavior
through imitation. If leaders consistently demonstrate behavior that can be related
to business and personal success, many of their employees will try to imitate
them. For example, if the top managers in a company regularly visit customers
to stay in contact with the market, the firm's product managers and R&D managers will have to go regularly into the field, too.

Reinforcement.   Reinforcement is another important motivator. Performances that help the company achieve its goals should be rewarded through appropriate compensation packages and job assignments.[10] The global firm faces the difficult task of developing a consistent compensation system and performance-appraisal system that can be accepted by all the personnel from a variety of cultures. U.S. managers, for example, are used to one bonus per year and promotions based on achievement. Their Japanese counterparts receive bonuses at least twice a year, and whether they are promoted strongly depends on their seniority and their capabilities in the long run.[11] When Texas Instruments tried to pay and promote its Japanese managers the American way, it did not achieve the motivation or performance levels it had hoped for.[12]

Human-Resource Planning.   Strategically meaningful and personally rewarding headquarters and nondomestic service assignments need to be supported by a human-resource planning system that identifies and moves appropriate employees across business units or national borders. Poor human-resource planning may, for example, be the major reason for the high failure rate to be found among U.S. business expatriates. That is, U.S. managers often have to be recalled to headquarters or dismissed from the company because of their inability to perform effectively in a foreign country.[13] Managerial inventories, including detailed profiles of the best managers from all parts of the company, regardless of nationality, may help to lower such failure rates.

On the other hand, managers and personnel who are transferred must not feel that they risk being forgotten "out there" in their new assignments. Clear career paths, based on a management-development plan, should exist to assure employees that they will not be forgotten or necessarily passed over for promotion.

The global marketing manager can choose from a broad range of human-resource-management tools to motivate employees. Managers should keep in mind, however, that conditions that motivate one person can frustrate another. Because of many cultural differences, this risk is particularly aggravated in a global environment. The marketing manager with global experience and the human-resource manager must cooperate to establish and maintain management processes that adequately motivate the company's international personnel.

Training.   Training is another tool to motivate personnel. It not only improves their skills, but it can also be used to encourage self-development. Japanese companies have more specialized training programs to prepare managers for nondomestic assignments than do U.S. and European firms. These programs include language training, career training, field experience, and graduate programs abroad.[14]

Decision Making

The impact of decision-making styles on the speed and effectiveness of decision-implementation processes was discussed in Chapter 8. Different cultures have different dominant decision-making styles. People in the Middle East, for example, assume that successful leaders impose their wills on the firm.[15] Managers in Thailand,[16] Malaysia, Indonesia, and the Philippines favor an authoritarian style as well, whereas those in Singapore and Hong Kong are less authoritarian.[17] Many successful U.S. companies emphasize participative decision-making processes.[18]

The "right" decision-making style varies by culture and decision situation.

As comparative international studies have shown, processes ranging from highly autocratic to highly participative or democratic can be equally effective, depending on the particular decision situation.[19] It seems that there is no one best style of decision making. Successful managers fit the decision-making process to the situation at hand. Because objectively similar situations will be subjectively perceived in varying ways across cultures, however, the problem of choosing an appropriate decision-making style is further complicated in global marketing. Global managers have to adapt the decision-making process not only to their interpretation of the given situation but also to the perceptions of local personnel. What the U.S. manager of a subsidiary in Indonesia perceives as overly authoritarian behavior may be regarded as weak behavior by the firm's employees. Similarly, what a German manager may regard as an emotionally based decision may be seen as a bureaucratically correct decision by Italian colleagues.

Conflict Resolution

Due to the greater risks and conflicts associated with international business, resolving conflicts is a particularly important function of global business leaders.

A business firm can be viewed as a group of people who join forces to attain their individual goals. Conflicts are therefore inevitable. One of management's leadership functions is to resolve them.

Conflicts in a global business are different from, and often greater than, conflicts in domestic firms. Different groups perceive the strategic importance of business units, resource allocations among them, and market situations differently. Business units and local subsidiaries often feel they are undervalued by top management. Some European Black & Decker managers, for example, could not see that centrally directed global marketing was needed as a defense against Japanese competition, because their subsidiaries dominated the consumer power-tool markets in Europe. In another case, local Parker Pen managers resisted pressure to implement standardized advertising and packaging.[20] Conflicts may also arise between the company and its external environments, such as governments, unions, special-interest groups, or trade organizations.

Some managers aggravate conflicts by denying their existence. Others try to resolve conflicts by replacing employees or managers who resist direction, as was done in the Black & Decker case. Managers who perceive such replacements as losses of important management know-how or experience may seek to resolve or even avoid conflicts with improved information and greater participation by the people concerned.

Just as there is no one best decision-making style, there is no universal best conflict-resolution strategy. The best strategy for any given situation depends on both the objective features of the situation and the global interpretations of different cultural and interest groups. Successful global marketing managers have to be alert to potential conflicts in their internal and external environments. They have to be sensitive to the interests of all the parties in a conflict, and they must try to resolve conflicts in an exchange-oriented manner (where both parties "win"), to safeguard the long-term interests of the company.

Organizational Change

Business globalization leads to growing complexity and faster change both within the company and in relation to relevant environments. Company leaders, therefore, need to constantly evaluate their functional processes and the underlying management systems in view of the firm's changing goals and strategies.

Most changes occur incrementally. That is, new solutions to existing or anticipated problems are tried out by employees or even occur by chance. For example, instead of faxing a letter about all the wrong products sent during the last two months, the merchandising manager in a sales office in Buenos Aires may decide to invite the distribution manager at the headquarters in Seoul to visit. If that is successful, it may be added to the merchandising manager's arsenal of potential behavior. Functional processes change continuously. Not all changes are automatically in line with the firm's strategy, so management has to be attentive to change in order to guide it in the desired direction.

Management systems are often more formalized than functional processes and will not change as easily by incremental steps. If a misfit develops between management systems and the business environment, radical change may become necessary. The firm may have to replace internalized policies and rules of behavior with new ones. Such a resocialization process is very difficult to manage. It requires a great amount of time, energy, skills, and money. Also, management must be able to tolerate uncertainty and ambiguity, and be willing to learn new attitudes and rules of behavior.

Radical change is risky. It requires careful consideration of the original problems, the feasibility of the proposed solutions, and potential outcomes, positive as well as negative,[21] as well as the tools necessary to induce and direct the change process.

The problems of managing organizational change are manyfold under any circumstances. They are even more complex in a cross-cultural business environment. Communication, sources of change, the conceptual ability and participation of personnel, and management's involvement in and commitment to the change process all may differ from one business environment to another. For example, Indian and Egyptian managers are greatly influenced by religion, while Nigerians are not.[22] Therefore sharp changes in the religious environment will probably result in more radical business changes in India or Egypt than in Nigeria.

Certain tools of organizational and personnel development may be difficult to apply because of labor union resistance, the general educational level, social structure, or traditions in a society. For example, U.S. articles on easing internal change[23] frequently advise managers to include the personnel who will be affected by change in company planning, to reduce their resistance to the change. This advice may be appropriate for most organizations in the Western industrialized countries, but it may be of no value in parts of the world where more authoritarian processes are common.

ORGANIZATION

The company's organization structure must fit its needs and global marketing strategy and tactics.

Many companies have developed creative ideas and strategies on how to successfully compete at a global level. Their products and services fit customers' expectations, and their prices are competitive. Their communication and distribution strategies are appropriate. But the companies may still have difficulty in formalizing and implementing an organization that will make their strategies work.

A firm's organization is characterized by its personnel structure and the interactions that occur among the elements of this structure. Successful global competitors have developed an organizational structure that fits their specific needs. Tasks and responsibilities are differentiated among business units. Interdependencies between those units are systematically generated and managed. The most effective global companies simultaneously integrate several elements: functions, geography, and product markets. The basic challenge is how best to coordinate these elements at each management level, and with the organization as a whole. The global marketing manager has a range of organizational structures, each with its own strengths and weaknesses, to choose from.

The International Marketing Manager

Initially, a single person might successfully serve the corporation in its international marketing activities.

In small companies just starting to go global, organizational structure is of minor concern, because one person or a few can handle all of the elements mentioned above. In most cases, however, international marketing responsibilities should not be given to someone whose main job lies in the domestic area. This person will only rarely focus on the more complex and, in the beginning, often less-rewarding job of starting an international business.

Small companies, therefore, are well advised to begin their globalization process by hiring an international marketing manager. The appointment should be made before the company has analyzed potential markets in detail and before marketing strategies, programs, and activities are decided on. The new manager should report directly to top management.

The international marketing manager should have administrative and management ability in addition to selling skills. She or he should be thoroughly familiar with the company's product, procedures, and personnel. Specific markets may restrict the number of applicants who might be successful. For example, if the targeted markets are located in southeast Asia or Arab countries, the manager will probably have to be male, because business partners in these areas are generally not prepared, or even willing, to deal with female business executives.[24]

International Marketing Department

As the importance of international marketing grows, the company will need more international marketing personnel.

As the international business grows, the firm may first add an assistant to the international marketing manager. The assistant will look after the office when the manager is away, gather and update data on specific markets and their relevant environments, and take over much of the administrative work. From that nucleus an international marketing department may develop along with increasing business volume and complexity. Regional managers may be assigned specific geographical territories when the company has expanded its business to a range of different market areas. Regional managers call on distribution-channel members, introduce new products to them, and train their sales representatives and personnel. They monitor competitors and keep in touch with major customers and end users. When the size of the company's international business grows further, sales offices, joint ventures, or subsidiaries may be useful. At this point top management usually decides on one of the following two structural options.

National Subsidiary Structure

When nations have very different marketing needs, establishing national subsidiaries may be appropriate.

If national sales offices or subsidiaries report directly to top management, without intermediate levels such as the international marketing manager or regional managers involved, a national subsidiary structure exists (Exhibit 17.2). This structure is often referred to as a "mother-daughter relationship." Because this structure allows for direct influence by top managers, it is particularly popular with individually or family-owned and -managed small and middle-sized European firms.

However, when a global business increases further in size, this form of organizational structure loses most of its attraction. Concentrating global issues in the hands of one or a few people results in an inefficient use of top management's time. And that concentration also leaves top management unable to properly attend to the vast amount of information necessary to maintain corporate growth.

International Division Structure

A company with one large national market, and many small international ones, may establish a division to manage the international markets as a group.

Due to their huge home market, many U.S. firms starting nondomestic marketing activities are already relatively large. Therefore, their international business operations are usually organized through an international division, similar to the domestic divisions, with all of the operations in one division organized by function, product, geography, or customers (Exhibit 17.3). The division manager coordinates and controls the activities of the units belonging to the division, acting as a representative of upper management. An advantage of this organizational structure is that it encourages a global view of operations, result-

EXHIBIT 17.2   NATIONAL SUBSIDIARY STRUCTURE

A firm that adopts a national subsidiary structure gives each subsidiary manager a great deal of control over the subsidiary's marketing activities.

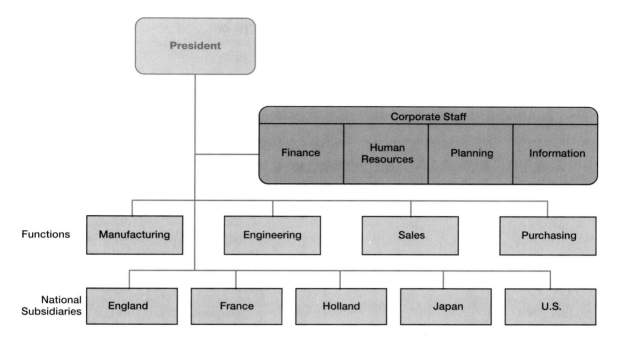

ing in cohesion and concentration of resources. It also enhances the organization's capability to develop a global strategy to respond to global opportunities .

One disadvantage is that the international division is only one among many divisions. Top management may give the domestic divisions higher priority, because they are better established and more visible to top management. Furthermore, technical and product expertise is not easily passed on from the domestic divisions to the international division. The international division will demand higher investments initially but may be more successful than domestic divisions later; for both reasons domestic divisions may perceive their international counterpart as an unwelcome competitor for scarce resources.

Global Structures

The international division structure has proven to be useful as a transitory state for many global firms. Eventually, however, global structures emerge, equalizing domestic and foreign operations so that the distinction between the two is no longer reflected in the corporate structure. The structure of the firm is based on major functions, geographic areas, or product lines. Additional,

EXHIBIT 17.3
INTERNATIONAL
DIVISION STRUCTURE

If the differences among
products are great, firms
often adopt an interna-
tional division structure to
let each product group
be managed
independently.

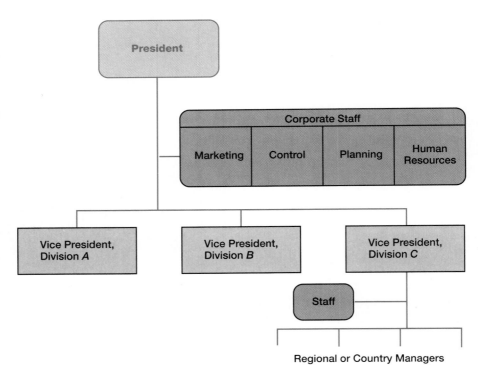

EXHIBIT 17.4
GLOBAL FUNCTIONAL
STRUCTURE

Global firms with similar
products that serve mar-
kets with similar needs
may choose global func-
tional structure.

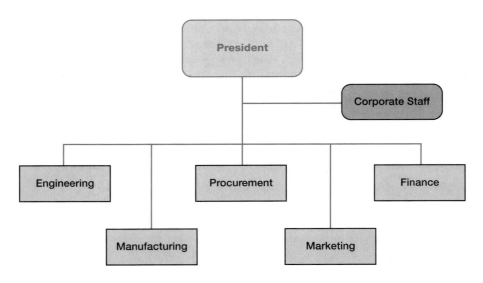

EXHIBIT 17.5 GLOBAL GEOGRAPHIC-AREA STRUCTURE

When a firm with similar global products is faced with significant geographical market differences, it may adopt this structure to gain manufacturing-experience curve effects overall and marketing-experience curve effects within the geographic areas served by local units.

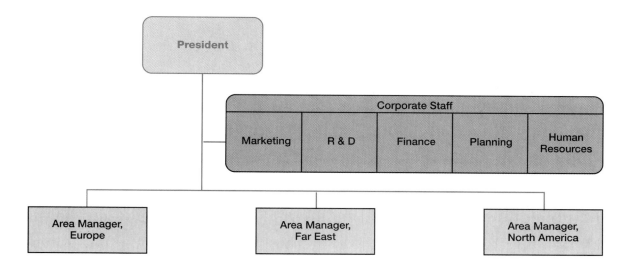

When a company really starts operating on a global scale, it needs a global structure to support its activities.

customer-oriented divisions may be found in companies that deal with a restricted number of important customers or customer groups that need to be treated individually. For example, there may be specific customer groups for selling aircraft to governmental agencies.

Functional Structure. Firms with narrow, highly integrated product lines designed to satisfy globally similar needs (for example, producers of basic chemicals) often choose a functional structure (Exhibit 17.4). Knowledge and experience are concentrated, diminishing operating costs. The biggest disadvantage to a firm structured this way is that it will experience enormous difficulties in reacting flexibly to regional market differences as top management loses touch with local conditions.

Geographic-Area Structure. Where differences among geographic markets make individualized operations necessary, a firm's activities may be grouped according to geographic areas, with regional managers given full responsibility for their area (Exhibit 17.5). Nestlé, for example, given its philosophy that "all business is local,"[25] considers regional management very important.

With a geographic-area structure, products, services, and related operations can be easily adapted to local conditions. The company can readily respond

EXHIBIT 17.6
GLOBAL PRODUCT-
DIVISION STRUCTURE

When the global products
are more dissimilar than
the geographical mar-
kets, a global product-division structure is used to
gain marketing-experi-
ence curve effects for
each product line.

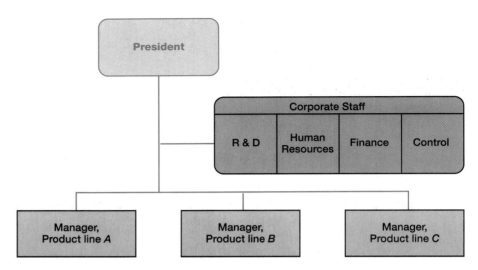

to consumer demands. Economies of scale are achieved within regions, but global product coordination is inhibited and functional efforts are duplicated, increasing costs overall.

Product-Division Structure.   When a company is organized along its major products or product lines (Exhibit 17.6), most often product responsibilities are centralized in corporate headquarters. Marketing strategies for the different products or product lines are developed, coordinated, and partially implemented by the staff located there. This centralization hastens and reduces the complexity of the decision-making process. Problems are resolved in a general manner, and evaluation measures are decided on before regional or local units execute the adaptations required by their markets. Brown Boveri, for example, is organized into divisions for marketing turbochargers for large industrial engines, climate- and energy-control systems, and electrical-energy-distribution control systems.[26]

The product-division structure is most appropriate under conditions where the advantages of a globally standardized marketing mix are higher than the advantages of individualization to accommodate regional or local distinctions. To take advantage of the marketing know-how, creativity, and skills in local units, complete information, planning, and control systems must be in place. The areas of responsibility between the home office and local units must be clearly defined. However, even if all this is done, the local units may struggle to maintain their independence. They may resist decisions made in the home office (the "not invented here" syndrome). Further, too strict an allegiance to a centralized product structure leads to problems such as those encountered by Caterpillar. At one time, its strategic and operational decisions were so central-ized that more flexible competitors, such as Komatsu, had a competitive advan-tage in many markets.[27]

Multidimensional Structures. Each global structure has its own advantages and disadvantages. The global marketer need not choose one or the other, however. The company needs competent functional management to accumulate specialized know-how and skills, as well as to transfer them throughout the company's global operations. It needs strong geographic-area management to detect, analyze, and respond to the needs of different local markets. And it needs product-market management with worldwide product responsibilities to achieve the global efficiency and integration that is necessary to be an effective global competitor. A multidimensional organization, therefore, simultaneously meets the firm's needs for accumulated experience, market responsiveness, and efficiency. The effectiveness of each management group is maintained, and each group is prevented from dominating the others.[28]

One kind of multidimensional structure is a **matrix structure**, where functional, area, and product managers are on the same level in the firm's hierarchy. This forces them to cooperate with each other when making decisions. Global Dimensions 17.1 gives an example of a U.S. company structured in a three dimensional matrix format. The biggest disadvantage of a matrix structure is the increased cost and difficulty of avoiding enduring conflicts.

The development of a multidimensional organization structure does not necessarily imply, however, that functional, area, and product management must have the same level of influence on all basic decisions. Influence can be determined by assigning responsibility for different sets of activities in the various business units.[29] Furthermore, the roles must not be fixed. They should change when the relevant environments in which the firm is operating change.

. . . .

INFORMATION

Global marketing must be supported by a global marketing information system.

Global marketing requires a global marketing-information system. Such an information system will be used to: (a) monitor the global environment; (b) help the firm make strategic decisions, such as decisions about global market expansion or divestment; (c) monitor performance in different product markets and geographical areas; (d) assess resource-allocation decisions and their impact on the company's overall success;[30] (e) exchange and integrate experiences gained by different parts of the company; and (f) communicate information about the firm and its products, activities, and achievements to relevant exchange partners. The information system must be able to gather relevant information from external and internal sources and adequately process, store, update, and selectively disseminate that information.

Information Gathering

Many different sources of relevant information exist both inside and outside the company. Sales representatives, for example, are a valuable source of information regarding existing and potential distributors and customers. They can also

GLOBAL DIMENSIONS 17.1

A Global Matrix Structure

Dow Chemical has adopted a three-dimensional organizational matrix combining six geographic areas, three major functions, and over seventy products.

Geographic Areas. Six autonomous companies headquartered in Hong Kong, Brazil, Canada, Switzerland, and the U.S. (Florida and Michigan), have their own research, manufacturing, marketing, and administrative operations.

Function. Three primary functions—research, manufacturing, and marketing—were selected. One challenge faced by Dow is to make sure its technological innovations and improvements are shared and used by all six companies, regardless of origin. It does so through manufacturing-technology centers and global R&D coordination. At the plant where the product is manufactured, the technology-center manager and staff deal with all aspects of the particular productive technology. Global R&D coordinators, who are also line managers, provide worldwide leadership for product lines, minimize duplication of effort, and measure progress toward R&D goals.

Product. A global Product-Management Unit exists for most product lines. Product vice-presidents develop and manage Dow's global product strategies across geographic areas and functions. Within each geographic area, product departments serve as profit centers and manage all businesses within that area. Business managers within these departments develop product strategies and organize product-management teams, involving key people from each functional area. These teams are the communication link between the matrix organization, corporate strategy, and success in the marketplace.

Source: T. H. Naylor, "The International Strategy Matrix," *Columbia Journal of World Business,* Summer 1985, pp. 11–19.

provide information about competitors' activities, and retaliatory strategies. Sales-administration personnel have information about customer complaints, malfunctions of the physical distribution system, or problems with the terms of delivery. The news media, such as *Business Week,* and trade organizations, such as chambers of commerce, have data on the economic, technical, political, legal, social, and cultural environments in different parts of the world, even within specific industries and product markets.

In order to find and select the best information sources, the relevant elements and processes of the company's global exchange system have to be known. For that purpose an analysis of the business system the company is working in has proven to be useful (see the discussion of the "value-added chain" in Chapter 7). The most important players in this system, as well as relevant environments have to be specified. A matrix can be drawn to show the interrelationships and the direction and strength of each relationship.

In addition, the information requirements of different management levels and business units must be determined. An overly general system of monitoring the firm's environments would not only be too expensive for most global marketers, it would also overburden the company's personnel with information requests. There is widespread feeling among operating managers that the reporting required by headquarters is excessive and that reported information is only partially utilized. Many country managers view the home office as a place where uninformed people frame irrelevant, time-consuming questions.[31] Therefore, the information-gathering process must be highly selective.

Information Processing and Storage

Information is usually consolidated in a **relational data bank,** that is, an information system that retrieves information by starting with a key term that leads to related topics. The relationships among data stored in the data bank model the system, including the external environment, of which the company is a part.

The data bank should contain updated information on the external environments. Internal data stored in the data bank should include the firm's financial status, cash flows, costs, and production capacities. In addition to this operational information, the data bank should contain information about the firm's corporate policy, identity, and strategy, as well as its global programs.

Information Dissemination

Systematic distribution of new information to managers increases sharing of the corporate culture, resulting in more coordinated decisions throughout the corporation. However, too much information is not only costly, it also reduces managers' interest in using information from the data bank. Therefore, new information should not be automatically distributed. It should be available to decision makers when they need it. This objective is not always easy to fulfill. Because the managers in a global company are often located in several different time zones, for example, information can go astray during the dissemination process.

Information should flow to managers not only when they ask for it, but also when unforeseen events affect their area of responsibility. Computer technology permits a management-by-exception approach to information dissemination, which is particularly important for global organizations. Critical events have to be specified in a joint process involving managers and information-system specialists. Procedures for access to and distribution of information, and presentation formats for fast and easy communication, must be developed.

The personnel responsible for the information system in a global firm must be able to effectively communicate across geographic, organizational, group, and individual boundaries. They must be aware of contextual settings on both sides of each boundary. They therefore need cross-cultural experience in addition to information-processing expertise. For example, consider the seemingly simple introduction of a new sales-order form in a global consumer-goods company. A form that serves the computer staff's needs may not be accepted by all the subsidiaries. Even if one country finds it useful, it may not reflect the sales approach used in another country. The personnel responsible for the information system should be regularly assigned to functional units in different countries to learn about their specific information needs.

PLANNING

As companies become involved in more global markets, they need to adapt their planning system to take their market differences into account.

The global firm needs systems for strategic as well as operational planning. **Strategic planning** involves the formulation of key goals and objectives for the entire company and its various business units. It includes the definition of basic strategies that determine the allocation of resources among those units. **Operational planning** encompasses detailed plans, procedures, and budgets for the business units based on the strategic decisions. Operational plans serve as a framework for day-to-day decision making, as well as the monitoring and control systems.

In general, top management has the primary responsibility for determining overall global business direction. It coordinates the strategies of all the business units worldwide. The responsibility for operational planning rests with the line managers of the business units. They are assisted in that task by planning and functional staff members at all levels.

The Planning Process

The planning process should start with a reevaluation of corporate policy. It should then proceed to an evaluation and projection of the environments relevant to the firm. The relative strengths and weaknesses of the firm's business units, compared to major competitors, can be matched with the opportunities and threats identified in the environments.

A useful procedure in this respect is the **scenario technique.**[32] (See Global Dimensions 17.2.) It should be a standard procedure in any global marketing planning system. The scenario technique leads to the identification of key events that can be expected to have the most significant impact on the success of business units[33] and of robust strategic decisions, which are appropriate under all future environmental conditions. Such key events may include important changes in government policy, emerging competitors, or a new technology. A robust strategic move may be to reinforce the firm's relationships with suppliers and intermediaries. The results of the scenario analysis lead to the development or reformulation of global strategies for the entire company and all its business units.

The development of major programs for strategy implementation, and contingency plans to deal with potential environmental changes, is the final step in the strategic planning process. Based on the strategic plans, the firm's business

GLOBAL DIMENSIONS 17.2

The Scenario Technique

The scenario technique is a strategic planning technique. It uses systems analysis to identify the essential internal and external factors that influence the company, and their interrelationships. The complexity of the firm's environments, with all their interdependencies, is reduced to a matrix showing the degree to which the most important factors are active or inactive influences. Extremely positive and negative future developments with respect to each factor can then be formulated and analyzed for their fit. The result is two consistent scenarios, which are interpreted by the use of the most important factors of influence found in the systems analysis. They can be compared to the current situation and analyzed for their impact on the opportunities and threats that face the company. The consequences of specific internal or external events on the scenarios and, therefore, on those opportunities and threats become obvious. A robust basic strategy can be built, that is, a strategy that is right for either of the two extreme scenarios.

The systems approach helps to avoid focusing too much on product markets, which could lead to shortsightedness. The firm must be alert to developments—such as changes in customers' basic values, nations' financial instability, or the development of new technologies—that may have a strong impact on the firm's potential for success. Threats can be detected earlier, and opportunities recognized more easily, by the analysis of different scenarios.

Sources: G. J. B. Probst and H. Ulrich, *Pensée globale et management*, *Résoudre les problèmes complexes* (Paris: Les Editions d'Organisation, 1989); and U. Reibnitz, *Scenario Techniques* (New York: McGraw Hill, 1988).

units develop preliminary operational plans, including detailed budgets. Depending on the state of globalization of the firm, at this point the complexity of the planning process varies. An exporter's planning process may not be much more than planning for domestic business plus an international unit. But in a multinational operation, each business unit has to establish its own operational plan, based on a regional strategic plan.

Mobil Oil has European offices that, for example, develop annual operational plans, based on strategic guidelines from the European headquarters in London. The local units send their plans to the regional and home office, for comments and revision, and the managers of the units present the plans to top management. Home- or regional-office personnel may also travel to local units to discuss the plans. More than one round of discussions is usually required before the plans are accepted.

Local units possess the most detailed knowledge of their markets. Therefore, the integration of this information with the global perspective of the home office is necessary for sound strategic and operational planning. That is, the global planning process has to include both top-down and bottom-up processes.

Planning Problems

Guidance.   Many of the planning problems global marketers encounter revolve around the relationship between the company's home office and local units.[34] Home offices play a range of roles in the planning processes of their nondomestic units. In some cases local units are completely free (unguided) in their planning efforts. In other cases the home office provides information on the global business environment, regional developments expected during the planning period, and the state of the industry. Mobil Oil, for example, provides its local units with information on the development of the world oil market. The home office might also provide information about internal environments, such as new product introductions, price changes, or public relations campaigns. This information then has to be incorporated into the local units' plans. Other companies go a step further and present their business units with a set of strategic goals to be attained and major action programs to be implemented.

Organizational Structure.   Unfortunately, many existing company structures do not provide for direct information exchanges between their local units. This limits experience curve effects, which could be gained through a more global approach to international marketing. Local units could profit from the experience and information available from other units in their planning endeavors. They could, for example, compare the behavior of competitors in different areas of the world (as does IBM in Japan and the United States), or they could gain from unifying their marketing efforts to the different subsidiaries of a global customer. The local subsidiaries of a Swiss watch strap manufacturer supplying straps to the production plants at Seiko, the big Japanese watch company in Germany, the United States, and Japan, could, for example, follow a consistent policy with prices and business terms.

Short-Term Focus.   In many firms involved in global business, too much of the planning activity is focused on the operational instead of the strategic level. These companies primarily rely on financially oriented, short-term budgeting.[35] Very often this perspective leads responsible managers to simply project current sales figures when preparing long-term plans. Such an approach does not provide for changes in competition, the market, and other environments. Nor does it result in information about potential sales that may be lost due to suboptimal marketing efforts. For example, it doesn't indicate that a different distribution system would provide a bigger increase in sales.

Precision and Availability of Data.   Global marketers used to researching U.S. markets should keep in mind that there are not many countries in the world where data on markets and environments are comparable. The plans for local business units outside the United States, therefore, often have to be based on rough estimates due to lack of readily available, comparable data.

In countries with rapid industrial or social development, such as South Korea, Singapore, and Brazil, it may be very difficult to come up with forecasts. The limited data that are available quickly become outdated. In much of the world, political and economic instability make accurate predictions practically impossible. If reliable data cannot be gathered, it may be better not to try to acquire enough information to develop a final strategic or operational plan. It may be more reasonable to maintain the perspective that plans have to be adapted to new information, gathered on an ongoing basis.

Centralized versus Adaptive Planning

The optimal degree of standardization (required to achieve a competitive level of economies of scale) compared to the degree of individualization (required to react flexibly to environmental differences) determines the optimal level of centralization versus adaptiveness of the planning process.[36] Companies confronted with rapid technological change, worldwide sourcing, or homogeneous markets tend to use centralized planning. Global companies, however, have to achieve a balance between centralization and adaptation in their planning processes, to make effective and efficient use of all available managerial resources and to facilitate the implementation of plans. Companies striving for a balance between centralization and adaptation can use the following approach.

Regular Meetings.   Regularly scheduled meetings of local managers (product managers, market researchers, package designers, R&D specialists, production managers, or controllers) with their counterparts from other local units and from the home office improve integration and cooperation.[37] These meetings frequently are used when the firm has decided to use a matrix organization. Regular contact among managers helps ensure that informal and formal communication occurs and that good ideas, which allow a global company to move down the experience curve to great advantage, are shared throughout the company.

Global Coordination Groups.   These groups, composed of delegates from the company's local units and its home office, are given responsibility for fulfilling specific tasks. Depending on the task, a strategic planning group, a communications group, an R&D group, or a personnel group may be created.[38] Bristol-Myers, for example, created a group to assist in integrating a more global view with decision-making processes throughout the organization.[39]

Specialized Planning Forums.   The most effective way to balance centralization and adaptation and to give influence on strategy development to local

MAP 17.1 R&D INVESTMENTS AROUND THE GLOBE

In today's competitive environment, investment in research and development is ever increasing to develop new and more competitive products. This map, based on the 200 largest non-U.S. companies, illustrates the level of R&D spending around the world. As a point of comparison, the 10 largest U.S. companies spent $24 billion on R&D in the same year.

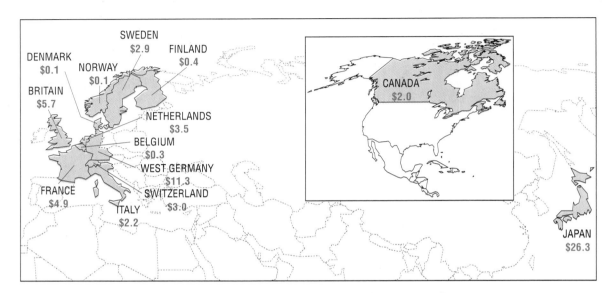

entities is to create entirely new planning forums. Procter & Gamble's "Euro-brand Teams," for example, are business units that were assigned specific roles depending on their strategic importance to the company (market size, home market of major competitor, particularly quality-conscious customers, advanced technologies required) and their specific competencies (in terms of technology, production, or marketing, for example). The company may distinguish between strategic leaders, contributors, and implementors.[40] Proctor & Gamble's Irish subsidiary, for example, is the strategic leader in Europe for the Dash brand, while Germany is Proctor & Gamble's strategic leader in Europe for Pampers. Both had proven to be particularly creative and successful with their respective brands in their home markets.

Despite the fact that one country may dominate the strategic planning for a specific product (line), all other business units marketing the product should be involved in the planning process. Coordination in such teams is self-reinforcing, because cooperation helps all of the units to achieve their own interests.

Top management must consider the motivational as well as the strategic impact of assigning different business units different roles in the marketing planning process. It has to keep in mind that units that must continually implement strategies developed by other parts of the company will suffer from lower motivation to contribute innovative programs to the company's success. Business units in strategically less important markets should, therefore, be assigned lead or contributing roles, even if only for less important products. Philips, for example, awarded its Taiwan subsidiary the lead role in the small-screen computer monitor business, enormously boosting the motivation of management and personnel in this subsidiary to do well in this field.[41]

CONTROL

Control must occur so many options exist as to how to control a global company, to ensure that all parts of the company are working toward common goals.

Companies with widespread activities and interests all over the globe generally have complex organizational structures stemming from specialized tasks and roles. Because of this complexity and differentiation, the organization is particularly subject to disruption. Different environmental demands and competing functional goals and interests lead units to pursue their own strategies. A U.S. company, for example, may be confronted with major internal conflicts when trying to sell its products in countries where side payments (referred to as bribes in the United States) are a normal part of conducting business. The local manager in such a country will probably want to make side payments. Home-office managers may not, being fearful of violating U.S. law or believing side payments are immoral. To ensure that all of its busines units act in accordance with corporate policy and strategy, the global firm has to develop a control system that binds the units into an operational whole and makes their performance sufficiently predictable.

Centralization

For many global marketers control means centralization of decision making and direct intervention in the operations of business units. Local units adapt corporate strategy to the domestic environment after receiving approval from headquarters. This kind of control can be very specific and limited to the short term (for example, the annual budgeting systems, with monthly reporting, used by many U.S. firms). It can be implemented vertically across the organizational structure, with the home office imposing identical roles, functions, and responsibilities on all organizational elements at the same hierarchical level. Centralization can also entail using standardized procedures worldwide, equalizing the influence of business-unit managers on the planning process, and using standardized criteria to evaluate performance.

Centralization becomes increasingly feasible as managers in the home office gain more global experience and as standardization reduces the complexity of the operations for which they are responsible. In addition, improved transportation and communication allow easier evaluation and correction of performance of widely dispersed business units.

The major argument against centralization is that each organizational unit in the global company is itself a complex organization. If every decision or action must be cleared with a higher level, reaction time is slowed and resources are wasted. If control is exerted through strict budgets, the process of coming to mutual agreement on the appropriate numbers generally requires a great deal of time. Similar treatment of the business units leads to overemphasis on small and less important markets, whereas some of the needs of strategically important markets are overlooked. Standardized control also keeps local managers from applying all of their skills and creative energies.[42] Control through centralization should therefore represent a compromise between top management's desire for predictable behavior and performance in each business unit and the need for flexibility and minimizing the cost of control processes.[43]

Coordination

Control can also be achieved through **coordination**. In this case the individual business unit is viewed as part of a network, with responsibilities to other parts of the firm. Coordination integrates the organizational elements of the firm through horizontal associations. Coordination is less direct and less costly than centralization, and it permits a longer time horizon.

Process Standardization.   The simplest form of coordination is **process standardization**, the formalization of tasks to be performed in different parts of the company to ensure similar performance processes and comparable results. Information, planning, and control processes are formally prescribed (usually in a manual), to be followed by all members of the organization.

There is some dispute about the extent to which management processes should be formally structured. Some managers believe in minimizing structured processes, which they believe encourages innovative ideas and entrepreneurial spirit among lower-level managers. Others are inclined to use more structured processes, clearly defining the contribution to be made by each part of the company, which lends itself more easily to tight control of results.[44]

The more decentralized power is in a global firm, the more top management will tend to standardize the processes by which its business units are managed. Philips's project-investment manual, for example, helps ensure top management that investment calculations for different projects are derived in the same manner and therefore can be compared to each other. Rigid guidelines on what figures to use and how to calculate them, however, will not make much sense when precise data are not available. They often only lead to heavy use of intuition hidden by fabricated statistics.

Centralization and process standardization are best suited for **output control;** that is, they ensure *efficiency* of processes. For **behavioral control**, the control of process *effectiveness*, the global marketer will be better off using other coordination mechanisms.

Integration.   Coordination can also be achieved through **integration**. When top management increases the flow of products, resources, and information among local units, these units will recognize the need for coordinating their strategies, programs, and actions. Management can also reorganize the roles and responsibilities of the units to adapt them better to external circumstances, as well as their internal abilities and capacities. An automobile manufacturer, for example, may have a transmission factory in Austria, an engine factory in Ireland, and an assembly plant in Spain. Because these units are dependent upon each other, they will recognize the need for integrating their activities.

Socialization.   A third and equally important way to achieve coordination is by managing **socialization** in the company. Top management should promote company-wide understanding of, identification with, and commitment to its goals, strategies, and programs. If that can be successfully accomplished, informal agreement, information sharing, and cooperation among all the parts of the company will be enhanced (as was illustrated in the International Incident). In addition, less emphasis on a formal structure, such as a sophisticated multidimensional matrix organization, and less-formal control processes will be necessary.[45] A major U.S.-based consumer-goods company, for example, has chosen to train all of its employees, regardless of their national or cultural heritage, "its way" (according to a defined company culture). The company believes this will improve intracompany communication and permit highly standardized management throughout its global operations.

SUMMARY

The successful implementation of a global marketing strategy depends on the existence of an appropriate management infrastructure, that is, management systems that allow coordination of all the firm's activities. The shape of this infrastructure largely depends on the firm's corporate culture and strategies, as well as on the external environments relevant to the company's business.

Company leaders must motivate staff in all parts of the company. Decision-making styles and conflict resolution strategies differ in various parts of the world. The global company, therefore, must decide whether to adapt to local usages or to try to establish a specific companywide style. Either way, the company's leadership system must be able to induce and manage continuous organizational change.

The formal structure of the firm, such as departments, subsidiaries, divisions, or global structures, largely defines how business system elements such as business tasks and responsibilities relate to each other. The stage of development of the firm's globalization process, corporate culture and strategy, and external environments determine what organizational structure is appropriate for the business. Hiring an international marketing manager may be the first step. As they grow, global companies need more complex organizational structures, such as multidimensional structures, to provide for the increasing complexity of their business.

In a similar manner, the firm's information system has to grow with increasing globalization. Information gathering, processing, storage, and dissemination not only increases in volume, but new solutions are needed as well. Internal and external information-exchange partners live in different time zones, are socialized in various cultures, and speak different languages. Nevertheless, the information system has to transmit the intended message, to the right person, at the right time.

The planning process in global companies should be basically the same as that in well-managed domestic companies. Problems may arise from too little or too much guidance from the home office, insufficient internal information exchanges, too much focus on short-term success, and inadequate data for planning in some parts of the world. The firm's decision with respect to centralized versus adaptive marketing planning underlies its control system.

Control can be achieved through centralization and coordination. The more complex the firm's global activities, the less likely it is that centralized control and even process standardization can fulfill top management's goals. Integration and socialization become increasingly important for success in global marketing. All of the firm's management systems—leadership, organization, information, planning, and control—are interrelated. Their fit with the firm's internal and external environments and its global marketing strategy helps determine global marketing success.

DISCUSSION QUESTIONS

1. What influence do external environments have on the optimal corporate management system?

2. What is corporate culture, and how does it affect the potential for global marketing success?

3. How does technology influence a company's management systems?

4. Assume you work for a small corporation based in Utah. Your company is just beginning to be regularly involved in global marketing activities. Which organizational structure would you recommend, and why?

5. What are the advantages and disadvantages associated with a global organizational structure?

6. What is the major purpose of a global marketing information system?

7. What is the difference between strategic and operational planning, and what levels in a corporate structure should be responsible for each?

8. What generates most of the problems global marketers encounter in their planning process?

9. In order to maximize experience curve effects, global corporations may centralize the marketing planning process. What can they do to ensure that such a centralized approach will result in useful plans?

10. What are the alternative ways to implement control in a global management system? Briefly, what are the advantages and disadvantages of each?

11. Providing meaningful and successful leadership for people from different cultures is difficult. In fact, due to those differences, a company will find it necessary to adopt a structure that allows local leadership. Do you agree or disagree with this statement, and why?

C A S E

HIRSCH WATCH STRAPS

George Weber had just started his job as a personal assistant to the owner and CEO of Hirsch, a globally operating manufacturer of watch straps located in Klagenfurt, Austria. After a warm and friendly welcome, Mr. Hirsch talked about the history of the firm, how he perceived the current state of its global operations, and his vision of the company's future.

In 1945, just after World War II, when Austria lacked most basic consumer goods, Mr. Hirsch's father, Hans Hirsch, bought remnants of leather from the shoe industry and cut out watch straps with a knife. His wife finished them with her sewing machine. Only a few years later, Hans Hirsch developed a revolutionary production technique that combined the upper and lower leather strap pieces without a seam. He called it the Hirsch Rebordering System and patented it in the most important consumer markets worldwide.

By the 1960s, Hirsch had become the market leader in Austria. Hans Hirsch and his son, Hermann Hirsch, thought it was time to go international. They exported first to Switzerland, and then to Germany, followed by Denmark and Norway. But systematic expansion began only after Hermann Hirsch bought the company from his father in 1975.

In order to have better control over marketing of the watch straps, of which 90 percent were then being exported, Hermann Hirsch decided to open several subsidiaries: Germany and Switzerland in 1976; the United States in 1977; Canada in 1979; Belgium and Great Britain in 1982; Spain and Japan in 1983; and France, Sweden, and Hong Kong in 1985. More than fifty other markets, such as Portugal, Australia, and South Africa, were served through independent wholesalers. The Eastern European countries were served through a salesforce based in Austria. Average sales growth per year throughout the 1980s was about 15 percent.

In the meantime, Hirsch had developed from a manufacturer of leather watch straps to a globally known marketer of watch "bracelets," made with a full assortment of materials. The company sold only through specialty stores, such as jewelers and watch shops, and specialized departments in department stores. It tried hard to cover all of the price ranges needed by its retailers, to protect its position as a single supplier, but its success was built upon emphasizing quality, service, fashion, and high-priced, high-margin leather items.

Because of the importance of the design of the watch itself for the material of the strap, which is first mounted by the manufacturer and later on replaced by the consumer, Hirsch increasingly sought cooperation with watch manufacturers in the 1980s. Its OEM (original equipment manufacturer) business started slowly. As it turned out, the entire OEM marketing process was different from the refill business with which Hirsch was familiar

In the mid-1980s, two important new developments occurred. First, the company's R&D group had developed and patented an entirely new technique for the production of plastic straps, which it called MARCCO. MARCCO was not only far cheaper than the production of leather straps, but it also resulted in a product far superior in quality to the competition's. The OEM salesforce's first contacts with big potential customers, such as Swatch and Benetton, looked promising. The refill salesforce was eager to get the new product in its assortment as a low-price defense against low-quality, low-price competitors. It thought that such a product would finally open up supermarkets and discount stores. A marketing consultant had warned, however, that Hirsch should not dilute the high-quality, high-prestige image of the existing refill product range (leather) by offering a low-priced item (plastic). He had also suggested that Hirsch reevaluate its distribution policy from a positioning perspective before deciding to serve new customers.

The second major development was Hirsch's acquisition of Rotary, a Swiss-based watch manufacturer and wholesaler of watch-related items. Rotary had a worldwide distribution system, selling its products in all available outlets. Mr. Hirsch perceived the new acquisition as a chance for his company to open up product markets that so far had been closed to Hirsch, because of its core strategy. He ultimately wanted to become the number-one global supplier of watch straps.

Mr. Hirsch handed his new assistant, George Weber, an organization chart. He then said, "I know this will look somewhat strange to you. But this is the current state of our organizational development. We have grown quickly in the past few years and therefore had no time to draw organization charts. Please keep in mind what I have told you about the company and our acquisition of Rotary, and come up with suggestions about how to restructure our organization to prepare for further global growth. I expect your presentation at our board meeting in 2 weeks."

Case Issue

1.   What should the chart look like, and why?

N O T E S

1.   "Grass Beschlage: Mit neuer Unternehmensstruktur multinationalisieren," in Industrie-wissenschaftliches Institut (ed.), *Internationalisierung*, Bd. II (Wien: Reichard-Martini, 1989), pp. 89–92.

2.   H. Mintzberg, *Structuring of Organizations* (Englewood Cliffs, N.J.: Prentice Hall 1979).

3. N. Piercy, "The Corporate Environment for Marketing Management and Marketing Budgeting," *International Marketing Review*, Spring/Summer 1984, pp. 14–32.

4. Y. Wiener, "Forms of Value Systems: A Focus on Organizational Effectiveness and Cultural Change and Maintenance," *Academy of Management Review* 13, no. 4, pp. 534–545; and A. L. Wilkins and W. G. Dyer, Jr., "Toward Culturally Sensitive Theories of Culture Change," *Academy of Management Review* 13, no. 4, pp. 522–533.

5. See, for example, "AT&T's Bob Allen Is Pushing All the Right Buttons," *Business Week*, November 28, 1988, pp. 133–136.

6. G. W. England, O. P. Dhingra, and C. Agarwal, *The Manager and the Man: A Cross-Cultural Study of Personal Values* (Kent, Ohio: Kent State University Press, 1974), p. 32.

7. B. M. Bass and P. C. Burger, *Assessment of Managers: An International Comparison* (New York: Free Press, 1979), p. 131.

8. A. Edstroem and P. Lorange, "Matching Strategy and Human Resources in Multinational Corporations," *Journal of International Business Studies*, Fall 1984, pp. 125–137.

9. E. Schein, *Organizational Psychology*, 3rd ed. (Englewood Cliffs, N.J.: Prentice Hall, 1980).

10. N. Tichy, C. J. Formbrun, and M. A. Devanna, "Strategic Human Resource Management," *Sloan Management Review* 23, no. 2 (1982), pp. 19–28.

11. R. Ballon, "Die Rekrutierung japanischer Manager," in H. Simon, ed., *Marketfolg in Japan* (Wiesbaden: Gabler, 1986), pp. 309–342.

12. A. Kupfer, "How to Be a Global Manager," *Fortune*, March 14, 1988, p. 58.

13. R. L. Tung, "Selection and Training of Personnel for Overseas Assignments," *Columbia Journal of World Business*, Spring 1981, pp. 68–78.

14. R. L. Tung, "Human Resource Planning in Japanese Multinationals: A Model for U.S. Firms?," *Journal of International Business Studies*, Fall 1984, pp. 139–149.

15. C. Pezeshkput, "Challenges to Management in the Arab World," *Business Horizons* 21 (1978), pp. 47–55.

16. F. C. Deyo, "The Cultural Patterning of Organizational Development: A Comparative Case Study of Thailand and Chinese Industrial Enterprise," *Human Organization*, Spring, 1978, pp. 68–72.

17. F. G. Redding and T. W. Casey, "Managerial Beliefs Among Asian Managers," R. L. Taylor et al., eds., *Proceedings of the Academy of Management*, Academy of Management, St. Louis, Mo., 1975, pp. 351–355.

18. "The World's Fastest-Growing Company," *The Economist*, March 19, 1988, p. 68.

19. W. Boenisch, A. G. Jago, and G. Reber, "Zur interkulturellen Validitaet des Vroom/Yetton-Modells," *DBW Die Betriebswirtschaft*, January–February 1987, pp. 85–93; W. Boenisch, J. W. Ragan, G. Reber, and A. G. Jago, "Predicting Austrian Leader Behavior from a Measure of Behavioral Intent: A Cross-Cultural Replication," K. Weiermeir (ed.), *Management Under Differing Labour Market and Employment Systems* (Berlin: Walter de Gruyter, 1988), pp. 313–322.

20. J. A. Quelch and E. J. Hoff, "Customizing Global Marketing," *Harvard Business Review*, May–June 1986, pp. 59–68.

21. H. Mulbacher, W. Vyslozil, and A. Ritter, "Successful Implementation of New Market Strategies—A Corporate Culture Perspective," *Journal of Marketing Management* 3, no. 2, pp. 205–217.

22. S. K. Sokoya, "Impact of Personal and Organizational Characteristics on Personal Values of Managers: Evidence from Selected LDCs," R. L. King, ed., *Proceedings of the 1988 Conference*, Academy of International Business, U.S. Southeast Region, Tulane University, New Orleans, La., November 1988, p. 141.

23. See, for example, S. Spauling and J. Harris, "Staff Suggestions Help Make Computerization Easier," *Marketing News*, November 7, 1986, p. 34.

24. P. Krishnakumar and T. A. Chisholm, "Managerial Profiles: An International Comparison," R. L. King, ed., *Proceedings of the 1988 Conference*, Academy of International Business, U.S. Southeast Region, Tulane University, New Orleans, La., November 1988, pp. 143–146.

25. H. Maucher, "Marketing heute und morgen," *THEXIS*, February 1986, pp. 22–24.

26. S. Pedersen, "Globalisierungstendenzen und ihre Folgen für die Strategiearbeit bei Investitionsgutern," *THEXIS*, February 1986, pp. 5–8.

27. W. H. Davidson and P. Haspeslagh, "Shaping a Global Product Organization, *Harvard Business Review*, July–August 1982, p. 130.

28. C. A. Bartlett and S. Ghoshal, "Managing across Borders: New Organizational Responses," *Sloan Management Review*, Fall 1987, pp. 43–53.

29. Ibid.

30. S. P. Douglas and C. S. Craig, *International Marketing Research* (Englewood Cliffs, N.J.: Prentice Hall, 1983), pp. 289ff.

31. W. J. Keegan, "Multinational Marketing: The Headquarters Role," *Columbia Journal of World Business*, January–February 1971, pp. 85–90.

32. U. Reibnitz, *Scenario Techniques* (New York: McGraw-Hill, 1988).

33. G. S. Day, *Strategic Market Planning* (St. Paul, Minn.: West, 1986).

34. J. M. Hulbert, W. K. Brandt, and R. Richers, "Marketing Planning in the Multinational Subsidiary: Practices and Problems," *Journal of Marketing*, Summer 1980, pp. 7–15.

35. M. H. B. McDonald, "International Marketing Planning," *European Journal of Marketing* 16, no. 2 (1982).

36. B. S. Chakravarthy and H. V. Perlmutter, "Strategic Planning for Global Business," *Columbia Journal of World Business*, Summer 1985, pp. 3–10.

37. D. M. Peebles, J. K. Ryans, and I. R. Vernon, "Coordinating International Advertising: A Programmed Management Approach That Cuts Through the 'Standardized vs. Localized' Debate," *Journal of Marketing*, January 1978, pp. 28–34.

38. R. Kreutzer and H. Raffee, "Organisatorische Verankerung als Erolgsbediungung eines Global-Marketing," *THEXIS*, February 1986, pp. 10–21.

39. C. A. Bartlett, "How Multinational Organizations Evolve," *Journal of Business Strategy*, Summer 1982, pp. 28–29.

40. C. A. Barlett and S. Ghoshal, "Tap Your Subsidiaries for Global Reach," *Harvard Business Review*, November–December 1986, p. 92.

41. Ibid.

42. C. A. Barlett and S. Ghoshal, "Arbeitsteilung bei der Globalisierung," *Harvard-Manager*, February 1987, pp. 49–59.

43. D. Cray, "Control and Coordination in Multinational Corporations," *Journal of International Business Studies*, Fall 1984, pp. 85–98.

44. W. A. Dymsza, "Global Strategic Planning: A Model and Recent Developments," *Journal of International Business Studies*, Fall 1984, pp. 169–183.

45. A. M. Jaeger, "The Transfer of Organizational Culture Overseas: An Approach to Control in the Multinational Corporation," *Journal of International Business Studies*, Fall 1983, pp. 91–114.

GLOBAL FINANCE

INTERNATIONAL INCIDENT

Should You Be Buying Less? (And Saving More?)

Among the Triad nations, the United States has what is generally considered to be the lowest savings rate. Americans are traditionally a nation of spenders, not savers. The current U.S. savings rate is about 3 percent of disposable personal income (down from 7.5 percent in 1981). United States savings are less than 2 percent of GNP, about one-fifth of the savings rate in most OECD nations and only one-eighth of that in Japan.

Savings determine how much a country has to invest. U.S. corporate investment in plant and equipment as a percentage of GNP has fallen consistently since the 1960s. As might be expected, European and Japanese investment rates are much higher. In fact, foreign investment has accounted for much of the investment in the United States.

Because of the low savings rate in the United States, U.S. corporations have to pay higher interest rates for their borrowings than do Japanese and European corporations. That makes them less competitive globally. U.S. companies are falling behind in terms of having the latest, most efficient and productive facilities. They are also falling behind in basic research on new technologies for the 1990s.

The U.S. budget deficit has grown faster than the pool of domestic savings. In order to finance this deficit, the U.S. government is increasingly dependent on investment from other nations. This means that the U.S. government is less able to pressure those nations on trade issues, as it becomes more vulnerable to threats to withdraw foreign funding.

To save more, consumers must spend less. The U.S. tax policy, however, has generally supported consumer spending. The United States is one of relatively few countries that provide a tax break on the interest paid on housing. This encourages people to buy more expensive houses, because they "get some money back" in a tax break. The United States is also one of the very few nations to ever permit interest on credit card payments as a tax deduction. Although that deduction was phased out in the late 1980s, it helped generate a consumption ethic that has resulted in high standards of living, mass markets for consumer—and thus industrial—goods, and low savings rates. Therein lies the problem. Will U.S. consumers, raised to believe consumption is "good," be willing to change their behavior to increase savings? Or will the prediction of some economists be realized, that a drastic economic event will have to occur to "shock" them into changing?

International finance is a business subject in its own right. Indeed, a student interested in international business will find taking an international finance course to be a useful complement to an international marketing course. But international finance and marketing are not unrelated business topics. Marketing, whether domestic or global, cannot occur without sufficient financial resources.

International finance and marketing personnel work together to implement marketing plans and achieve the organization's financial objectives.

For example, a product must be promoted before customers will buy it. This requires a corporate commitment of funds to support the promotion.

This chapter examines finance as part of the global marketing mix. It is critical for the global marketing manager to understand how marketing relates to financial options and alternatives. For example, selling products to customers in less-developed countries presents a considerable challenge in terms of their ability to pay for the products. However, through creative pricing policies, discussed in Chapter 16, it is possible to profitably expand global marketing activities to these countries.

The chapter begins with an examination of the types of financial risks a global marketing manager faces. The global financial framework that affects these risks and determines how they should be managed is then reviewed. The management of these risks and the effects of global marketing management are then discussed. The chapter concludes with a topic of special interest to global marketing managers: debt in developing nations.

FINANCIAL RISKS

Commercial Risks

The risk that a buyer will not pay a seller is higher internationally than domestically.

All marketing decisions have financial implications. Businesses, regardless of their geographic span of operation, all must assume **commercial risks**. That is, will the customers pay the seller what they should, when they should, in order for the seller to achieve expected profits?

While commercial risks are part of any business transaction, the chance of the buyer not paying the seller is higher internationally than nationally. Not only is reliable information on the buyer's credit record less available outside the United States but other factors—such as economics (for example, higher inflation usually means higher risk) or legal issues (for example, when a domestic court discriminates against a foreign company)—also increase global commercial risk. Additionally, governmental seizure, distance (which slows communication), and cultural variables, such as the relative importance of prompt payment, affect risk.

Political Risks

Political risks are higher internationally than domestically, as was discussed in Chapter 5. A domestic firm has a lower probability of nationalization than a foreign one. If the political relationship between two countries declines dramatically, joint ventures between businesses in these countries face the risk that sales will be prevented, or that remission of profits will not be allowed. Political risk, of course, influences the attractiveness of investing in other countries. In fact, political risk also strongly influences the amount of foreign investment in the home country.[1]

The remarkable changes recently in the USSR include political protests such as this one by Latvians in support of the independence movement in neighboring Lithuania.

Exchange-Rate Risks

The need for international trade to occur in two or more currencies raises the organization's commercial risks.

For most international trade, a risk arises from the need to conduct the transaction in more than one currency. The terms of sale state a price in a particular currency. For example, an export from a U.S.-based company to one in the United Kingdom might be billed at $5,750.00, payable in 30 days upon receipt of the invoice. Thus the importer is assuming the **exchange-rate risk**. If the value of the U.S. dollar increases after the price has been set at $5,750.00, the U.K. importer will have to exchange more pounds for dollars, effectively raising the price of the imported product. Of course, if the price of the product is quoted in a foreign currency, the home-country organization bears the exchange risk.

The exchange risk can be assumed by the organization itself, or it can be transferred to a third party in international financial markets, thus covering exchange-rate fluctuations (to be discussed later in this chapter). In any case, the exchange risk must be born by some organization in order for the exchange (sale) to occur.[2]

Inflation Risks

Inflation directly affects the real buying power of the market. While exchange-rate fluctuations are in theory supposed to exactly offset the inflation rate, inflation in fact may be greater or even less than the change in currency rates. For example, devaluation of a currency should increase exports, because export

The price of the product and the profit potential are influenced by national inflation rates.

prices will be lower. But this may not occur if the change is overwhelmed by a high inflation rate.[3]

The **inflation risk** also has a direct effect on international finance. Highly fluctuating inflation rates, for example, not only influence the price that must be set, but also the value of profits that are transferred back to the parent company. There are also certain asset-management decisions that must be made with respect to economies experiencing high inflation. For example, when the Brazilian economy was experiencing 1,000 percent inflation, Brazilian buyers tried to minimize accounts receivable and maximize accounts payable. This is because the value of the money used to settle accounts decreased daily. Thus prolonging payment meant the buying company would pay in "cheaper" (less valuable) money. So while global marketing managers were trying to get Brazilian customers to pay rapidly, the customers were trying to postpone payment.

Interest-Rate Risks

Interest-rate differences impact prices and profits when there is a long time between when the product is sold and when payment is received.

Setting terms of sale also presents the company with an **interest-rate risk**. This risk exists when the inflow and outflow of a currency do not match, and temporary financing is required. This is true either domestically or globally. For example, a U.S.-based seller of cattle to Japan may borrow to finance the costs of the sale and inventory, until an inflow of dollars from the buyer occurs. The loan is subject to interest-rate fluctuations.

A global manager has an opportunity to raise money from a wider set of sources than does a domestic manager. At the same time, funds owed internationally are also subject to changing interest rates. If two or more currencies are involved in the debt of a company and interest rates change, the global corporation will be exposed to higher interest rate risks compared to a domestic one.

Exchange Restrictions

Sometimes a country's currencies are controlled, which increases the global firm's financial risks.

Associated with exchange-rate risks is the risk that the exchange of currencies might be restricted. Governments can either raise or lower exchange rates in order to encourage or discourage the sale or purchase of particular products. This in turn influences the level of financial resources necessary to support the marketing effort, and the profits that will be realized from the transaction.[4] A **blocked currency** means that the government does not allow any transfer of domestic currencies. When selling consumer goods to Romania, for example, usually either a barter or a countertrade pricing scheme will have to be used, because its currency is blocked.

Less severe than blocked currencies are **currency licensing restrictions.** These occur when all foreign-exchange transactions must be done through a central bank, or another agency, at the official (and fixed) rate. This system controls the sale or purchase of products by granting or denying a license to sell or buy foreign currency. Taiwan, for example, requires all exporters and importers to buy currencies through its central bank.

Multiple-exchange rates also restrict currencies. In this case, approved products are assigned exchange rates that facilitate sales by lowering their prices. Nonapproved goods are in effect penalized by exchange rates that make their prices higher.

Import-deposit requirements also influence the real exchange rate by requiring companies selling to a certain country to deposit a specific amount of money with the government or a domestic bank prior to the sale. Once the funds are deposited, a license for foreign-currency transfer or permission to sell is granted. Many developing nations are using this form of restriction, which effectively increases the amount of money lost while those inactive funds are held as the interest-deposit account.

Finally, nations may control the quantity of currency that is exchanged. For example, before 1990 tourists crossing the border from West Berlin to East Berlin, had to exchange a specific amount of West German marks for East German marks. These marks could not be exchanged back when returning to West Berlin. Other countries may place a quota on the amount of foreign or local currency that may be brought into, or taken out of, the country. Several COMECON countries, for example, do not allow their citizens to leave the country with more than the equivalent of a few hundred dollars, or less, in the domestic currency. Quantity control effectively influences the volume of products that can be traded, because it changes the price of the product and the costs of marketing support.

When exchange restrictions are lifted, sizeable adjustments in global financial markets and trade flows may result. As of this writing, the USSR was considering eliminating its exchange-convertibility restrictions. Such a move would affect trade flows, for example, between the United States and the USSR in agricultural products. It might also be an important step in opening up Soviet markets for both consumer and industrial goods to more international sellers.

An organization engaged in international operations has several options available to help manage financial risk, including not engaging in international trade (hence no risk) and direct foreign investment (to avoid being considered a "foreign" company). Before selecting one of these options, the global manager should evaluate the risks and risk-management options in light of the existing global financial framework. Sources of funds and the organizations that regulate financial activity help determine the appropriate financial-management approach.

THE GLOBAL FINANCIAL FRAMEWORK

Not only does each nation represent a somewhat unique market, each also has its own financial system.

Just as global marketing is complicated by the existence of some 150 countries—all with different regulations, cultures, and marketing systems—global finance is complicated by the fact that each country has its own currency, fiscal and monetary policies, and financial-market regulations. But the globalization of markets, with corporations sharing the benefits of the economic integration of

EXHIBIT 18.1

By the end of June 1989, most of the world's busiest stock exchanges had recovered from the world crash in 1987. This exhibit illustrates the performance of some of those markets between June 1988 and May 1989.

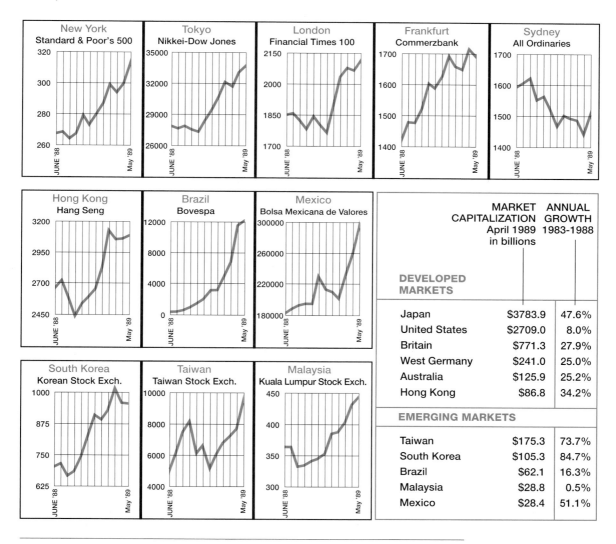

	MARKET CAPITALIZATION April 1989 in billions	ANNUAL GROWTH 1983-1988
DEVELOPED MARKETS		
Japan	$3783.9	47.6%
United States	$2709.0	8.0%
Britain	$771.3	27.9%
West Germany	$241.0	25.0%
Australia	$125.9	25.2%
Hong Kong	$86.8	34.2%
EMERGING MARKETS		
Taiwan	$175.3	73.7%
South Korea	$105.3	84.7%
Brazil	$62.1	16.3%
Malaysia	$28.8	0.5%
Mexico	$28.4	51.1%

Source: *Fortune*, July 31, 1989.

nations, applies to financial markets, too. Even countries that would not seem at first glance to offer a stock market have been developing them, partially in response to increased linkages among nations. China, for example, has opened several stock exchanges since 1986.[5] (For a comparison of the world's major stock markets, see Exhibit 18.1.)

The trading and lending of money, the buying and selling of funds, and capital investing have a history at least as old as the history of international trade in goods and services. The Romans, for example, are generally credited with inventing the bill of exchange that permits the financing of imports and exports by financial houses and commercial banks. Indeed, with today's communication systems, it is easier to trade funds globally than to trade most goods and services.

Given the traumatic losses incurred in the worldwide stock market crash in October 1987, some investors are behaving as if global investment has lost some of its appeal, due to higher perceived risks compared, in particular, to the "bullish" attitudes of mid-1987.[6] The October 1987 stock market crash also illustrates the differences among stock markets around the world. For example, the Tokyo Stock Exchange restricts daily declines in an individual stock to 10–20 percent. After the October 1987 decline, the Hong Kong stock exchange was closed for 4 days to deal with bookkeeping problems and make sure that insurance was available on defaulted contracts in the futures markets. Firms were caught in a liquidity squeeze, unable to raise capital through the sale of stocks for those 4 days. The Australian and New York markets, without such controls, were even more adversely affected.[7] The decision of the Australian and New York markets to remain open to permit firms maximum access to funds contributed to the steep declines in their stocks.

Global finance is the subject of many international agreements among nations. These are attempts to more effectively regulate the transfer of funds and to smooth currency fluctuations. In addition, international currencies (such as Eurodollars) act as a money supply on their own. Also, many domestic and international institutions (including commercial banks, central banks, and government agencies) influence international financial activities. This section examines those agreements, currencies, and institutions in terms of their impact on global-marketing decisions.

International Agreements

International financial organizations and agreements have been developed to facilitate the flow of international trade.

Except in cases of barter or countertrade, international trade requires the transfer of funds. As was discusssed in Chapter 16, the terms of sale and terms of payment help businesses achieve financial stability. Countries have joined together to establish international monetary agreements in an attempt to provide greater stability (and certainty) for the conduct of international trade.

Governments quite naturally wish to maintain as healthy a domestic economy as they can. One way they may attempt to do so is through manipulation of the currency-exchange rate, trying to restore the balance of payments. However, when one country's imports decrease, others' exports must also decrease. Rapid or arbitrary changes in balance-of-payment positions have a ripple effect throughout the global economy, which not only influences trading partners but in the long run returns to influence the initiating nation. One concern about the appreciation of the Japanese yen versus the U.S. dollar, for example, is that if Japanese exports to the United States get too expensive, Japanese firms will lose sales. Japan in turn will suffer an economic slowdown and may not be able to afford U.S. or European exports. To avoid serious economic disruption, therefore, governments have joined in agreements to settle international trade imbalances. They have also established an international monetary system, which facilitates economic growth for member nations.

The floating exchange-rate system now in place stems from the early 1970s when governments, led largely by the United States, began to permit their currencies to fluctuate according to supply and demand in international currency markets. Those markets are basically composed of commercial banks, which buy and sell currencies for their customers' trading needs. Other trades occur as speculators buy and sell currencies in the same way that others "play the stock market."

Before currencies were floated they were fixed in terms of the U.S. dollar. This system was formalized through the Bretton Woods Agreement of 1944. The U.S. dollar, as the currency of the dominant economy at the time, was defined in terms of its value in gold. Currencies were permitted to fluctuate by plus or minus 1 percent around the set rate. For global marketers, this system entailed a low currency-exchange risk in the short term, as exchange rates were essentially predictable.

But under the Bretton Woods Agreement exchange-rate adjustments did occur. Although governments were reluctant to make such changes, when confronted by political or economic crises they were forced to. So when adjustments were put into effect, they tended to be large and unpredictable, providing long-term instability.

As other countries gained economic strength, international currencies became established and the gold standard became difficult to maintain. The value of gold reserves became smaller relative to the increased amount of dollars held in reserves outside the United States. These pressures resulted in floating exchange-rate policies—letting financial markets determine the value of currencies, not governments.

The Bretton Woods Agreement established two international financial organizations, the International Monetary Fund (IMF) and the International Bank for Reconstruction and Development (IBRD, or World Bank). The IMF was established to supervise the new monetary system established by that agreement. It also provides credit to member nations for temporary financing of balance-of-payments shortfalls that are beyond their own financial resources. The World Bank primarily provides credit to governments for development purposes. Both of these institutions have a role in expanding international liquidity, increasing the amount of and access to money that can be used in international trade.[8]

Artificial Currencies

Currencies such as **Special Drawing Rights (SDRs)** and **European Currency Units (ECUs)** are examples of international currencies created through governmental agreements. Eurocurrencies, on the other hand, have been created by

GLOBAL DIMENSIONS 18.1

Eurocurrencies

Eurocurrency markets are composed of banks that accept deposits and make loans in currencies other than those of their own country. U.S. banks are prohibited from accepting deposits or making loans in any currency except U.S. dollars. This regulation does not apply to foreign branches of U.S. banks. Eurocurrencies, including U.S. dollars, Japanese yen, and German marks, exist largely because they are not regulated by the currency's home country. For example, **Eurodollars** (deposits denominated in U.S. dollars in banks located outside the United States) were developed largely because banks wished to avoid many U.S. banking regulations. Banks located outside the United States are not required to keep non-interest–bearing reserves against Eurodollar deposits. Within the United States the reserve requirements are higher. Additionally, interest payments and assets are more fully regulated in the United States. Finally, banks doing Eurodollar business can set up locations in countries with favorable tax treatment.

All of these differences mean Eurocurrency banks can operate on narrower margins between borrowing and lending rates. Borrowing Eurocurrencies therefore is often less expensive (that is, has lower interest rates) than borrowing in the home currency.

Source: M. Goodfriend, "Eurodollars," and A. B. Balbach and D. H. Resler, "Eurodollars and the U.S. Money Supply," both in G. D. Gay and R. W. Kolb, eds., *International Finance: Concepts and Issues* (Richmond, Va.: Robert F. Dame, 1983), pp. 54–64, 86–104.

Both the global financial system and individual nations have developed currencies in order to help control global financial markets.

national financial markets in response to the need for increased liquidity. For example, when the supply of U.S. dollars (as the standard unit of trading) was insufficient to permit the levels of trade that buyers and sellers wanted, non-U.S. banks in Europe began holding U.S. dollars, thus avoiding U.S. regulations and exchange controls. The trend has spread to include Japanese yen, German marks, and other currencies, all held outside the control of their home government. (For a more complete discussion on Eurocurrencies and their impact on global marketing, see Global Dimensions 18.1)

SDRs were created by the IMF. They are basically bookkeeping entries used to settle accounts between nations. An SDR is defined in terms of several major currencies, including the U.S. dollar, German mark, English pound, French franc, and Japanese yen. As such the SDR is not as subject to exchange-rate volatility as a single currency is. The major currency for international trade is still the U.S. dollar. When it fluctuates widely in the financial markets, financial exchange risk increases. Quoting prices in SDRs instead of U.S. dollars makes prices less subject to fluctuations due to changes in exchange rates.

As the European Community moves further toward full economic integration, it is working on integrating member nations' monetary systems, partially through creating ECUs, a common monetary unit. An ECU, like a SDR, is a "market basket" currency. When EC countries contribute some 20 percent of their gold and U.S. dollars, they receive ECU. The ECU is then used in commercial transactions as a more stable monetary unit than a single currency. Today, some salaries of employees within the European Community are even quoted in ECUs instead of a specific national currency. And some European multinationals, like Saint-Gobain, have started to do all of their accounting and to issue their annual statements in ECUs.

All of these international currencies help lower exchange-rate risk, help smooth out different inflation rates in national markets, and provide increased liquidity to countries or companies involved in international trade. They are also an indication of the size and integration of the global financial system, most of which is beyond the control of any one government.[9]

Financial Institutions

The global financial network is made up of banks and other private and public institutions that are active in trading currencies and managing money across national boundaries.

Various banks and governmental agencies play an active role in international financial markets. They combine to form the market for trading currencies, by performing spot- and forward-market services (discussed later in this chapter), which in turn affect global marketers' exchange-rate risks. Some of these institutions also influence inflation and taxation risks.

Commercial Banks. The largest Triad commercial banks actually form the basis of the foreign-exchange market. They buy and sell currencies at two levels: for their customers' (corporations, nonfinancial institutions, and individuals) trading needs and between themselves. Their capability to make transactions quickly, coupled with their expectations as to the future value of currencies, affect the exchange-rate risk faced by global marketers. In addition, the ease or difficulty with which they provide credit to corporations influences credit and inflation risks. For example, the backing of three British banks for the Eurotunnel (a tunnel under the English channel to connect England and France) made the corporate raising of funds through a stock offering easier.[10]

Commercial banks are becoming increasingly global in their orientation and operation. California-based banks, for example, are much involved in Pacific Rim banking operations. Taiwanese depositors, in particular, have for years favored California banks as a safe money haven. And Australia has been issuing licenses to foreign banks at an increasing pace.[11]

Central Banks. Commercial banks' policies are in turn influenced by the nation's central banks. These institutions affect global finance in two ways. First, their domestic monetary policies influence the supply of money, the economic growth rate, inflation, the stability of the banking system, and the availability of credit.[12] These factors, in turn, are taken into account when currencies are traded. For

The privately funded Eurotunnel will directly connect France and England, supporting new levels of trade within the European Community.

example, a central bank may ease monetary controls to allow a potentially high-growth economy to grow faster. This would result in an increase in the supply of that economy's currency in international financial markets. Thus the value of the currency would tend to decrease. The end result would be an increase in the nation's ability to keep its export prices competitive.

Second, central banks influence exchange rates through direct currency transactions. If the Japanese yen, for example, is appreciating rapidly against the U.S. dollar, the Japanese central bank may sell yen to slow the rise. Or the U.S. central bank may buy dollars to support the dollar price. Another example is centralized buying and selling of currencies. Ironically, the central bank of Taiwan has perhaps been too successful in controlling the appreciation of the new Taiwan dollar, to keep Taiwanese export prices competitive. So many Taiwan dollars are now available that commercial banks are actually offering lower interest rates for large deposits than for small ones, in an attempt to discourage new deposits.[13]

Governmental Agencies.   Many governmental agencies play a role in the international financial arena. In the United States, for example, the *Export-Import Bank* (Eximbank) encourages exports by guaranteeing loans, providing assistance to commercial banks that support export sales, loaning funds to foreign buyers, and providing loans or insurance to exporters. Through the *Foreign Credit Insurance Association* (FCIA), Eximbank provides insurance to protect against commercial risks (nonpayment by customers) and political risks. Closely associated with Eximbank is the *Private Export Funding Corporation* (PEFCO). This organization provides loans for overseas purchases of U.S.-produced capital goods, such as aircraft, power plants, and industrial installations.

The *Overseas Private Investment Corporation* (OPIC) provides loans and assistance to friendly developing economies. Usually associated with exports of U.S.-made capital goods, OPIC provides investment-guarantee programs covering currency, expropriation, and political risks. And the U.S. Department of Agriculture, through its *Commodity Credit Corporation* (CCC), supports exports of U.S. agricultural products through programs that support financing, barter, and sale in a foreign currency.

These services help make U.S. exports more competitive internationally by decreasing the total price and improving the terms of sale. Other countries have similar organizations. Those in France and West Germany, for example, provide insurance against commercial, political, and (rarely) currency risks, as well as export-support programs and loans. In the United Kingdom, the *Export Credit Guarantee Department* (ECGD) provides such services. And many state trading companies in centrally controlled economies assist in trade financing. The effect of all such programs (and similar ones provided by the private sector is to lower credit, political, and sometimes currency risks for the company, as well as to support competitive corporate pricing options.

- -
GLOBAL FINANCIAL MANAGEMENT

The financial elements of a sale, which in effect become part of the price, must be competitive.

Finance may serve as either a constraint or a resource in global marketing. In all markets, the pricing package (including terms of sale and payment) must be competitive. This is particularly true in global markets, where buyer options are broader than domestically. Overall, different functional units within the corporation must work together to increase the firm's chance of being globally successful. This is particularly true for the areas of finance and marketing.

Internal Funds

Global firms enjoy experience curve effects and economies of scale with regard to their financial functions, also. An example is their capacity to provide for part of their funding needs internally.

As a company becomes more global and invests in more subsidiaries around the world, the use and allocation of working capital (current assets minus current liabilities) becomes more complex. Global companies can transfer funds internally through loans, equity capital, transfer-pricing mechanisms, or other financial transactions between subsidiaries. Thus the global marketing manager gains considerable financial flexibility through the global corporation's ability to transfer funds internally. This often results in a lower cost of funds for the global company, compared to its domestic competition. In fact, the global trend is toward companies relying more on internal than external finance.[14] (For an illustration of the increasing importance of internal funding, see Exhibit 18.2.) A major device used to transfer internal funds is internal pricing.

Internal Pricing

Goods, services, personnel, and know-how are readily transferred across national boundaries between subsidiaries. As a consequence the company has to determine how it wants to be paid, where, and how much for its deliveries to non-domestic affiliates. This is an **internal pricing** decision, also referred to as

EXHIBIT 18.2   SHIFTING SOURCES OF FUNDS FOR CORPORATIONS

Throughout the Triad markets, internal financing seems to be increasing as a source of corporate funding, most often at the expense of private banks.

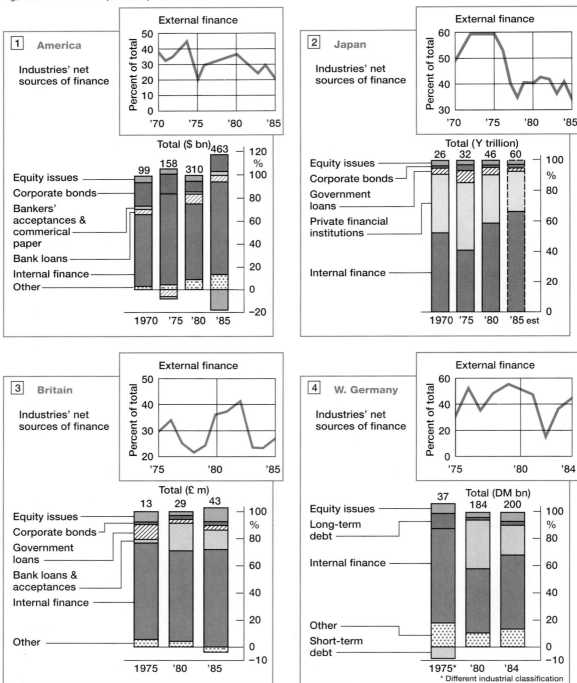

In addition to market prices, a firm can set internal prices, in order to control and audit the transfer of resources and products among its subsidiaries.

intracompany pricing or **transfer pricing.** In effect, a price is set that transfers funds between subsidiaries. The price is not necessarily linked to the market value of the item that was transferred. The decision on what price to charge has to take into account the firm's goals of maximizing and managing profits, the subsidiary's goal of earning recognition of its efforts, and headquarters' need to determine and compare the performance of its nondomestic business units. For example, if profit is transferred out of a subsidiary, the manager of that subsidiary should be evaluated on criteria other than how much profit was generated.

Objectives. The company's tax payments can be lowered by using internal pricing to transfer profits from units in high-tax areas to low-tax areas. In 1988, for example, Australian companies are said to have moved an estimated $2 billion to corporate links in low- or no-tax countries, like Singapore and Hong Kong.[15] In Europe, companies locate a sales subsidiary that officially handles their entire international sales activities in a low-tax country. That subsidiary purchases the products from the factory at cost and sells them at a profit to customers and affiliates around the world.

Internal pricing can also be used to transfer profits from countries with foreign-exchange restrictions or other economic controls to the unit that is supposed to make profits. This transfer is made possible by charging higher prices than reflects their true cost of production for merchandise, royalty payments on licenses, or payment for services delivered to the local subsidiary, as was discussed in Chapter 5.[16] Even if corporate tax rates are similar between parent and subsidiary countries, differences in tariff rates on the transferred goods are important in the determination of transfer prices.[17]

Other uses of internal pricing include counteracting the influences of currency-exchange fluctuations, reducing the impact of inflation on the company's assets, subsidizing new subsidiaries while they build market share, and justifying high prices in one area of the world while making profits in another. For example, some oil companies have justified their high gasoline prices in Europe by claiming they make very low profits, due to high costs, in Europe. They purchase the gas from their own European refineries, which also make low profits. The refineries, however, purchase crude oil from oil-transportation companies that are located in low-tax countries. Of course, the transportation companies, which make substantial profits, are also controlled by the oil companies.

The global firm's internal-pricing policy must permit the achievement of corporate objectives while also allowing the company to live in peace with the local tax authorities. IBM, for example, is proud of being a good taxpayer in the countries where it does business.

Methods. Basically there are two approaches to calculating internal prices. One is to calculate the *market price* of goods, services, or know-how. This approach is easy to justify to governmental authorities. It also allows organizing every affiliate as its own profit center. But it raises the question of what costs to consider in the determination of the price. Market-oriented price determination is well suited to adapt to, and account for, local market conditions. The internal price would be the local market price minus the margin necessary for the subsidiary to cover its costs and expected profit margin. A global marketer introducing a product new to the local market may have difficulties, however, in justifying the chosen internal price to governmental authorities.

For U.S.-based companies, Section 482 of the Internal Revenue Code calls for the determination of *arm's-length prices* for internal pricing. This is the price that would have resulted from negotiations between independent business partners in a similar transaction. Only if this method cannot be applied, because no similar transfers have been made in an open market, can the company use another method to calculate the internal price.[18] This code applies to all allocations of income between U.S. parent companies and their foreign operations, as well as between U.S. operations and their foreign parent companies.

External Funds

The global firm's ability to obtain funds from global financial markets gives it a competitive edge by lowering the costs of funding.

International stock and debt markets present an opportunity for the global corporation to find the lowest interest rate for loans or the highest stock price for equity issues. For example, the Tokyo Stock Exchange has grown to be second only to the New York Stock Exchange. Since the mid-1980s, more foreign than domestic companies have been newly listed in Tokyo.[19] In fact, the international growth of stock markets has changed the corporate financial picture considerably. More and more often, companies in industrial countries are going directly to financial markets, meaning that commercial banks are being replaced by other sources of funds.[20] (See Exhibit 18.2).

However, commercial banks are still a major source of corporate funds. Commercial banks operate quite differently in different countries. In Europe and Japan, they may underwrite security issues, and buy and sell bonds and equities for their own accounts. They may not do this in the United States, where these functions are performed by investment banks. When a commercial bank holds an equity position in one of its customers, it results in a different relationship (usually more supportive) between the bank and customer. This is particularly true in the Japanese banking market compared to the U.S. one. Around the world, other financial institutions play an important funding role. Pension funds and insurance companies, for example, are important capital sources in the United States, The Netherlands, and the United Kingdom. Of course, governmental agencies, such as Eximbank, also provide external funding.

Government-owned or -directed organizations, such as *Hermes* and *KFW* in Germany and *COFAS* in France, provide financial packages designed to increase exports. Export financing is made available either through direct loans to importers or by making credit to importers more readily available.In addition, guarantees that protect against commercial, political, or exchange-rate risks are provided to the exporter. Exhibit 18.3 illustrates these types of guarantees, often provided by a state bank.

EXHIBIT 18.3 BANK GUARANTEES FOR INTERNATIONAL TRADE

Various types of guarantees for exporters and importers are available through banks. *Bill-of-lading guarantees* ensure that the importer or receiver of merchandise will perform as stated in the documents signed by the importer. They cover the shipper against the demand of a third party when the shipper distributes merchandise to the receiver without getting the bill of lading at the same time. *Bid bonds* guarantee the prospective buyer that the chosen bidding firm is willing and able to sign a contract according to the offer made. They are also called *participation guarantees* or *tender guarantees*.

Financial Markets

Technology has allowed the linkage of financial markets around the world.

A global company has a distinct advantage over a strictly domestic one in its ability to tap into global financial markets. Communication systems, deregulation, and the increasingly global scope of investors and speculators has resulted in an interconnected system of debt and equity markets around the world. As firms become increasingly global in their marketing and sales operations, they are also likely to participate more in international stock markets.[21] (A guide to the operations of leading stock exchanges is provided in Exhibit 18.4).

A global corporation interested in obtaining a loan from a commercial bank can, and should, talk to banks based in Tokyo, Geneva, London, and New York, and perhaps other cities. An illustration of the loss of financial-market control by governments related to the globalization of financial markets is foreign investments by Japanese banks and insurance companies, estimated to reach $700 billion by 1990.[22] Because most transactions in international financial markets take place on paper or through electronic transfer, not the actual movement of money, global financial activity is limited only by regulations and the willingness of investors to loan funds.

EXHIBIT 18.4 A GUIDE TO THE OPERATIONS OF LEADING STOCK EXCHANGES

The leading stock exchanges around the world have some major differences in what they trade and how they are regulated.

	Australia	Canada	France	Hong Kong	Japan	Switzerland	U.K.	U.S.	Germany
Bonds	●	●	●	●[1]	●	●	●	●	●
Stocks	●	●	●	●	●	●	●	●	●
Options	●	●	●				●	●	●
Financial futures	●	●	●		●		●	●	
Commissions (approximate range)	Negotiable (0.5-2.5%)	Negotiable (0.4-1.75%)	Negotiable (0.2-0.75%)	Negotiable ($3-1%)	Fixed[2] (0.15-1.25%)	Fixed (0.1-0.8%)	Negotiable (0.1-0.75%)	Negotiable (0.49-10%)	Negotiable ($5-1%)
Margin trading	●	●	●	●	●	●	●	●	●
Settlement period	10 days	5 days	Immediate[3]	1 day	3 days	3 days	6 days[4]	5 days	2 days
Insider trading illegal	●	●	●	[5]	●	●	●	●	[5]

[1] Limited corporate bonds.
[2] 2,500 yen minimum.
[3] Official cash market.
[4] After 10-day account period.
[5] Possible civil penalties.

Source: "Tracking the Leaders," *The Wall Street Journal*, September 18, 1987, p. D–29.

Currency-Exchange Markets

In addition to stock markets, global marketers must understand and use currency-exchange markets.

Markets that buy and sell currencies are made up of commercial banks, central banks, and some individuals and companies. Two different types of currency exchange markets have developed to serve two different financial needs: spot markets for short-term needs and forward markets for long-term needs. Together, these markets average $425 billion volume per day, more than twenty times the New York Stock Exchange's biggest day to date.

The Spot Market.   Corporations and individuals may buy and sell major currencies (blocked currencies do not have a financial market, and financial markets for minor currencies are limited) for their immediate needs. Buying or selling a currency for immediate use or delivery is known as the **spot market**. While there are variations within the spot market, its basic usefulness to the global company lies in the ability to buy or sell foreign currencies at any time. For example, a Mexican company importing products from Germany could buy marks on the spot market, at the spot rate, when its bill becomes due (assuming the price is quoted in marks).

The Forward Market.   But waiting until the bill becomes due means that the Mexican company is incurring a currency-exchange risk. If the mark goes up against the peso between the date of sale and payment, the Mexicans must pay more for the product. If the mark goes down against the peso, the Mexicans pay less. Accurate prediction in any market, in particular one—like the currency-exchange market—subject to political pressures and rapid changes, is very difficult.[23] Therefore, the Mexican company could, on the day the contract is signed, for example, buy marks at a known exchange rate in the forward market. This "locks in" the exchange rate, thus the price, resulting in the Mexican company covering its exchange-rate risk.[24] A forward, or future, market exists because there is uncertainty as to the future value or exchange rate of a particular currency.[25] It is that uncertainty that prompts the buying and selling of currency-exchange risk.[26] For an example of a forward transaction to cover exchange-rate risk, see Global Dimensions 18.2.

Taxation

A nation's tax policies influence the attractiveness of doing business there.

Tax policies affect the entire financial and marketing approach of the organization, including the product's price, profit remission, and funds management and speculation.[27] For example, if a particular country wishes to encourage direct foreign investment as a market-entry option, it can give foreign investors favorable tax treatment. Or if it wishes to discourage foreign direct investment, it can raise taxes on profits generated by foreign firms. Market-entry choices are influenced not only by taxation rates but also the possibility that taxation policies will shift dramatically and quickly, presenting taxation risks to the company. Even the amount of money available for investment in a country, the result of the savings rate, can be significantly influenced by tax policies.[28]

GLOBAL DIMENSIONS 18.2

Spot and Forward Market Transactions

Covering exchange risk means that the company uses the forward market to minimize a potential foreign exchange-rate loss. This process is usually referred to as **hedging**. For example, a U.S.-based exporter may sell $5,000 worth of computer supplies to a buyer in France. Assume the current exchange rate is $1.00 = 5.5 French francs. The terms of payment specify payment in francs in 60 days. At the existing exchange rate, the U.S. firm has a collectable in 60 days of 27,500 French francs. But if during those 60 days the franc appreciates to an exchange rate of $1.00 = 6 French francs, the exporter's bill for 27,500 francs can be exchanged for only $4,583. That is, the exporter will lose $417 due to the exchange-rate fluctuation. Of course, if the franc depreciates or is devalued against the dollar during that time, the exporter will gain additional profit.

Most businesses do not wish to carry exchange-rate risk themselves, as speculation is not their primary business. At the time the agreement was signed, the exporter could have sold 27,500 French francs in the forward market for delivery in 60 days, in effect shifting the exchange-rate risk to the bank. If the 60-day forward rate was $1.00 = 5.4 French francs, the exporter would receive 27,000 francs. The 500 franc difference is $91 less than the $5,000 value. But, the exporter would know about this "loss" in advance, and adjust the price accordingly. Or the exporter may decide that a known $91 loss is more acceptable than the risk of unknown loss or gain if it does not use the forward market.

Franchise Financing

This form of financing is not used extensively in highly developed countries. But in countries that are developing rapidly, such as Turkey, Malaysia, and India, it is quite popular. Most often used in project funding, the investor **amortizes** the investment (gets it back in installment payments that include the principal and interest) through the revenues of the project. Popular as a funding approach for turnkey projects (once the costs of the project, including profit for the investor, are covered by the funds generated by the project), it is turned over to the host government.

Insurance

Global firms can obtain insurance against many of the financial risks they will face, but at a price that may affect their profitability.

Insurance against various types of global financial risks is available from private agencies, governments, and special organizations. Exhibit 18.5 illustrates some of the insurance alternatives available from a U.S. company, a British company, a Soviet company, and a typical state scheme. When private companies provide insurance, they offer the insurance as a product for sale. Insurance against commercial risks in specific countries, for example, is available. The contract value that may be insured, the percentage of the contract that is insurable, and the

EXHIBIT 18.5   COMPARISON OF RISK PROTECTION

Although various agencies offer risk guarantees, their coverage varies considerably.

Item/Underwriter	AIG/CIGNA (United States)	Lloyd's (Great Britain)	Black Sea and Baltic/Garant (USSR)	Typical State Scheme (Command Economy)
Export embargo	Yes	Yes	No	Yes
Import embargo	Yes	Yes	Yes	Yes
Government-buyer nonpayment	Yes	Yes	Yes	Yes
Exchange transfer	Yes	Yes	Yes	Yes
Failure of bank to honor ILC	Yes	No	Yes	Yes
Confiscation/Expropriation/Nationalization	Yes	Yes	No	Yes
Contract nonratification	Yes	Yes	No	No
Private-buyer nonpayment	Yes	No	No	Yes
Barter	Yes	Yes	No	No
Kidnap and ransom	AIG only	Yes	No	No

Source: Mag. Jochen Schwabe, Schwabe & Ley Ges.m.b.H.

fees all vary by the assessment of the risk involved. For example, an insurance policy for Czechoslovakia is available at a rate of 0.5–1 percent. The policy is for 90–95 percent of the value of the contract, with the upper limit of the contract $60 million. But for Iraq, the policy would cost 7.5 percent, be good for 90 percent of the contract, and have an upper limit of $10 million.

State or federal agencies that provide insurance do so to support exports. The Ministry of International Trade and Industry in Japan, for example, provides export insurance covering commercial and political risks in a manner similar to that of the FCIA in the United States.

Debt versus Equity

Global organizations have more choices than domestic ones do concerning whether to use debt or equity financing.

The question of whether to finance global business activities through debt (loans or bonds) or equity (the sale of corporate stock) is influenced by the following: government regulations (for example, local-participation requirements), the value of the company (a high stock price might mean an equity approach is preferable to a debt one), taxation (fast debt-interest write-offs might make debt the preferable option), and management's preferences. Additionally, there is evidence that the culture of the home country influences investors' attitudes, as well as the capital structure of the corporation.[29] For example, debt-equity ratios vary significantly by cultural groupings, as is illustrated in Exhibit 18.6.

EXHIBIT 18.6 DEBT-EQUITY RANKS FOR SELECTED CULTURAL GROUPINGS AND INDUSTRIES

The amount of debt a firm is willing to take on compared to its equity seems to be influenced by its national culture. For example, Latin American countries have much lower debt-equity ratios than do Scandinavian countries.

Cultural Group	Alcoholic Beverages	Auto-mobiles	Chemicals	Electrical	Foods	Iron & Steel	Nonferrous Metals	Paper	Textiles	Country Median Rank	Group Median Rank
Anglo-American											59.5
Australia	8.0	46.0	55.5	51.0	27.5	59.5	14.0	37.5	64.0	46.00	
Canada	68.5		27.5	55.5	30.0	120.0	93.0	117.0		80.75	
South Africa	84.0	46.0	51.0	88.0		59.5	11.5	22.5	120.0	48.50	
United Kingdom	27.5	135.0	46.0	88.0	68.5	51.0	77.0	72.5	55.5	68.50	
United States	51.0	81.0	68.5	64.0	72.5	64.0	81.0	81.0	46.0	68.50	
Latin-American											33.0
Argentina		22.5		25.0	15.0	11.75				11.5	
Brazil		109.0	37.5	59.5	77.0	93.0		17.0		68.25	
Chile			13.0	6.0	125.5	37.5	46.0	33.0		33.25	
Mexico	2.0		33.0	77.0	84.0	59.5	33.0	33.0		33.00	
Mediterranean Europe											130.5
France	72.5	113.0	131.0	131.0	151.0	143.5	113.0	139.0	139.0	131.00	
Italy		41.5	104.0	153.0	160.5	164.0	162.0	149.0	159.0	156.00	
Spain		84.0	101.5	27.5	109.0	156.5	125.5	160.5	24.0	102.75	
Central Europe											90.0
Benelux	20.5	96.5	88.0	51.0	101.5	93.0	41.5	104.0	64.0	88.00	
Switzerland				98.5	64.0	101.5				98.50	
Germany		77.0	72.5	109.0	41.5	88.0	125.5	125.5	104.0	96.00	

	C1	C2	C3	C4	C5	C6	C7	C8	C9	C10	C11
Scandinavia											131.0
Denmark		109.0	33.0	139.0	120.0	55.5	93.0	139.0		109.00	
Finland	19.0	156.5	129.5	135.0	149.0	135.0	131.0	146.5	156.5	135.00	
Norway		143.5	146.5	113.0	153.0	96.5		156.5	143.5	145.00	
Sweden	153.0		113.0	149.0	98.5	113.0	101.5	93.0	88.0	113.00	
Indian Peninsula											125.5
India	1.0	143.5	68.5	125.5		41.5	120.0	139.0	37.5	94.25	
Pakistan		164.0	164.0				129.5	109.0	125.5	129.50	
Southeast Asia											13.5
Malaysia	3.0	88.0	20.5		9.5	17.5	9.5		120.0	17.50	
Singapore		6.0		77.0	6.0	6.0	17.5			6.00	
Industry *median rank*	27.5	88.0	68.5	82.5	80.5	61.8	81.0	109.0	104.0		

Source: W. S. Sekely and J. M. Collins, "Cultural Influences on International Capital Structure," *Journal of International Business Studies*, Spring 1988, pp. 96–97.

Companies can issue long-term marketable securities in the international bond market.[30] For example, a Canadian company may choose to sell a bond issue in Belgium. If it is underwritten and sold by a Belgian underwriting group and denominated in Belgium francs, it is classified as a **foreign bond**. Even more important for raising international funds through the sale of bonds is the **Eurobond** market. These bonds are underwritten by an international syndicate and are sold in countries other than the host country of the issuing company. This market, in particular, has gained in importance due to regulations imposed in the United States, such as banking-reserve and financial-disclosure requirements. In response, U.S. and foreign companies elected to raise money outside the United States. Even though some of these restrictions were lifted, some U.S. and most non-U.S. companies continue to use the Eurobond market extensively to raise funds.[31] Exhibit 18.7 illustrates the volume and home-country affiliation of the ten largest Eurobond traders in 1985 and 1987.

EXHIBIT 18.7
TOP TEN EUROBOND TRADERS (RANKED BY VOLUME)

Major Eurobond traders are not necessarily European, as these charts from the mid-1980s illustrate. In fact, for the first six months of 1987, the three largest traders were all Japanese.

1985		Volume (in billions)	1987		Volume (in billions)
1	Credit Suisse First Boston (Switzerland/U.S.)	$11.5	1	Nomura Securities (Japan)	$12.3
2	Salomon Brothers (U.S.)	4.1	2	Daiwa Securities (Japan)	5.6
3	Merrill Lynch (U.S.)	3.9	3	Yamaichi Securities (Japan)	4.9
4	Deutsche Bank (Germany)	3.4	4	Deutsche Bank (Germany)	4.8
5	Morgan Stanley (U.S.)	2.9	5	Credit Suisse First Boston (Switzerland/U.S.)	4.7
6	Goldman Sachs (U.S.)	2.4	6	Nikke Securities (Japan)	4.1
7	Morgan Guaranty (U.S.)	2.4	7	Morgan Guaranty (U.S.)	3.7
8	Union Bank of Switzerland	2.2	8	Salomon Brothers (U.S.)	3.2
9	Bank of America (U.S.)	1.8	9	Banque Paribas (France)	3.2
10	Orion Royal Bank (Britain)	1.7	10	S. G. Warburg (Britain)	3.0
	Total	$66.2		Total	$39.3

Source: S. D. Moore, "The Battle of London," *Wall Street Journal*, September 18, 1987, p. D-8.

Profit Management

Maximizing profit is the objective of good risk management.

The importance of risk management to the corporation lies in its impact on profit. The risks financial managers are most likely to be concerned about are commercial risk, exchange-rate risk, and inflation risk. During the mid-1980s, for example, companies such as J. C. Penney enjoyed strong sales from their Belgian affiliates. However, due to the rapidly appreciating U.S. dollar compared to the Belgian franc, profit declined.

Obviously, profit is the most commonly used measure of corporate health. As such, global marketing managers must be aware of the impact of their decisions on profitability. For example, if global marketing managers support lenient credit policies in order to increase sales, the corporation is exposed to greater commercial risk. Similarly, if marketing managers too eagerly agree to barter or countertrade, difficulties in completing these exchanges may negatively affect profit.

Taxation and other government regulations may impact investment decisions or the choice of a profit center, as corporations attempt to hold on to as much profit as possible. For example, Costa Rica places no restrictions on the repatriation or remission of profits, in an attempt to attract foreign investment.[32]

Credit becomes part of the price of purchase. Companies generally want to make credit available, but not at the cost of a dramatic increase in commercial risk. Most global corporations are not in the business of financing their customers. But global marketing managers will find an increasing opportunity to increase sales if they are able to help their customers find suitable credit opportunities. This may include referral to or use of governmental agency loans, or even assistance in finding funds through financial markets.

DEBT IN DEVELOPING NATIONS

Debt owned by developing nations poses a problem for global marketers, because it influences the viability of those national markets.

A particular problem for marketing and financial managers is developing-nation debt, especially in the nations commonly referred to as the Third World. (See Chapter 3.) Large numbers of potential customers—consumers, industrial, and governmental—with considerable pent-up demand exist in developing nations. But the financial risks associated with sales to these customers are normally higher than for customers in the Triad markets.

Commercial risks are higher because customers in developing countries traditionally carry a large amount of debt in relation to their assets. *Exchange-rate risks* are higher because financial markets for currencies from developing nations are not as well developed as for developed nations. For example, the forward market for Peruvian sols is quite small compared to the forward market for French francs. Therefore, corporations may not be able to cover their currency-exchange risks through the forward market. *Inflation risks* are also higher in less-developed economies, which have had inflation rates of up to 1000 percent.

MAP 18.1 FOREIGN DEBT

In spite of the U.S. being the world's largest debtor nation, foreign debt is a particular problem for developing countries. Their debt is a large percentage of Gross Domestic Product, as illustrated in this map. This means that their ability to pay off that debt is limited, and having to pay off that debt diverts money from economic activities within the country.

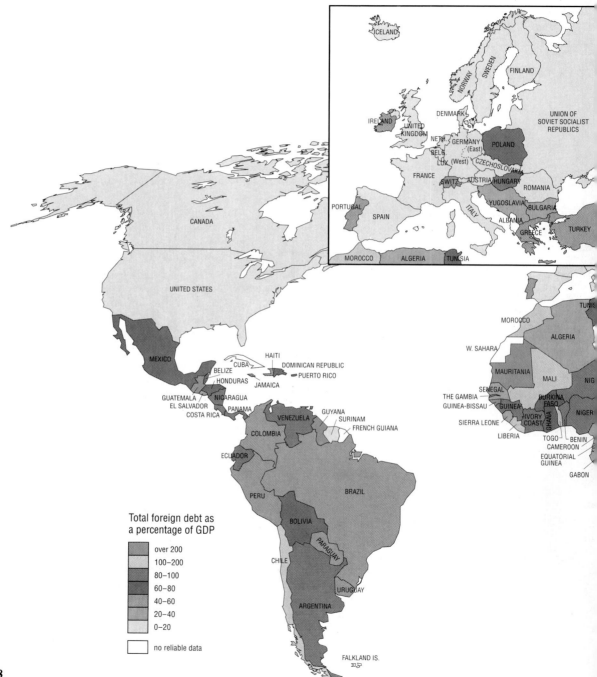

Total foreign debt as a percentage of GDP

- over 200
- 100–200
- 80–100
- 60–80
- 40–60
- 20–40
- 0–20
- no reliable data

UNION OF SOVIET SOCIALIST REPUBLICS

MONGOLIA

CHINA

N.KOREA
S.KOREA
JAPAN

TURKEY

CYPRUS
LEBANON
ISRAEL
JORDAN
SYRIA
IRAQ
IRAN
AFGHANISTAN
KUWAIT
PAKISTAN
NEPAL
BHUTAN

LIBYA
EGYPT
QATAR
UAE
SAUDI
ARABIA
OMAN
INDIA
TAIWAN

CHAD
SUDAN
YEMEN
S. YEMEN
DJIBOUTI
BANGLADESH
BURMA
LAOS
THAILAND
VIETNAM
PHILIPPINES

NTRAL AFRICAN
REPUBLIC
ETHIOPIA
SRI LANKA
KAMPUCHEA
BRUNEI
MALAYSIA

ZAIRE
UGANDA
KENYA
SOMALIA

RWANDA
BURUNDI
TANZANIA
MALAWI
PAPUA
NEW GUINEA

GOLA
ZAMBIA
INDONESIA
E. TIMOR

MIBIA
ZIMBABWE
MADAGASCAR
MOZAMBIQUE

BOTSWANA
SWAZILAND

S. AFRICA
LESOTHO

AUSTRALIA

NEW ZEALAND

609

Taxation rates in those countries are often designed to discriminate against foreign companies, in order to protect domestic companies and raise revenues. In addition, *currency-exchange restrictions* increase the difficulty (and risk) of selling to many less-developed countries. And the success of barter and countertrade agreements, frequently preferred by governments in less-developed countries, depends on the acceptability of the exchanged goods in the world market. Production standards and technology in less-developed countries are often behind Triad standards, making the barter or countertrade transaction more risky.

High debt restricts growth, because in less-developed countries debt payments represent a high percentage of export earnings. Thus funds are not available to support domestic economic growth. Peru, for example, in an attempt to stimulate its economy, did not service its debt in 1985. Foreign banks retaliated by not extending new credit, and Peru ended up with an even worse cash squeeze.[33]

A further complication is the amount of Third World debt held by commercial banks in developed nations. For example, in 1983 Brazil owed U.S. banks some $22 billion. If Brazil had totally defaulted on such a large debt (which was discussed by Brazilian planners, but is considered unlikely by most analysts), U.S. exports would have decreased by $14 billion and U.S. unemployment would have increased by almost 400,000 jobs.[34]

Of the some $400 billion in Latin American debt, about $100 million interest is owed, daily. The area has begun to explore alternative debt-reduction programs. These programs feature such options as swapping loans at a discount for local currency or equity, selling debt back at a discount to private companies, and exchanging debt for new bonds. U.S. banks, in particular, have been exploring ways to help these countries relieve their debt problems, while permitting the banks to recover some of their investment.[35] (Exhibit 18.8 illustrates the economic problems and debt owed by Latin American countries.)

All of these factors increase the financial risks of operating in, or selling to, a developing nation. Companies are likely to try to pass along these financial risks, in the form of higher prices. Of course, higher prices decrease demand. But business is shifting to corporations that have their government's support for exports to developing nations (as in Japan, for example), combined with aggressive marketing and understanding of the host culture.[36]

SUMMARY

Marketing and financial decisions are strongly interdependent. International trade involves higher financial risk than domestic business. Commercial risks, whether the seller will be paid what and when it should be, are higher. Because international trade occurs across two or more political nations, greater political risks exist; and doing business in different currencies adds exchange-rate risks. Since economies grow at different rates and international marketers often find themselves doing business in high-inflation economies, inflation risks must be

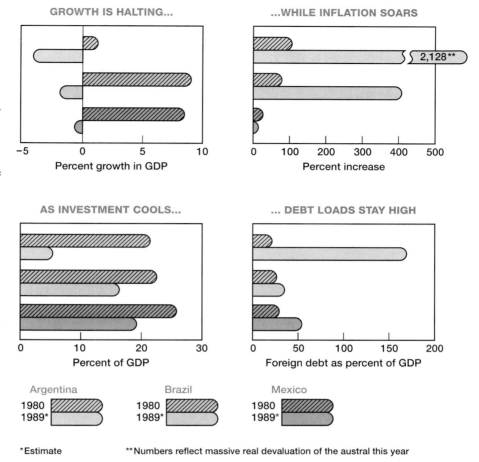

EXHIBIT 18.8
HOW LATIN
AMERICA'S
ECONOMIES ARE
SLIDING BACKWARD

Third world debt, illustrated here for three Latin American countries, has been climbing along with inflation. This decreases investment and economic growth, thereby lowering standards of living.

considered as well. Finally, governments control the right to conduct international trade, often through currency-exchange restrictions, thus presenting another type of financial risk to the marketing manager.

In order to expedite global transactions, a global financial framework has been established. International agreements, artificial currencies, and financial organizations have developed to maintain some order in international financial markets. Stock markets, for example, have developed around the world and are increasingly interconnected. Artificial currencies were developed to provide increased access to funds that support international trade. The financial institutions involved help make financial risks more predictable and manageable for companies engaged in international trade.

Global corporations have more financial options (and higher financial risks) to manage than do domestic companies. Globally operating companies increasingly rely on internal funding to lower their risks. Funds and profit transfer from a unit based in one nation to a unit in another country is often done through internal pricing schemes. The search for low-cost external funds may send corporate financial managers around the world. Currency markets help provide stability and access to short- and long-term currency needs. Taxes affect the financial outcome and desirability of any global marketing decision.

Global companies also must decide whether to use franchise financing or buy insurance against financial risks as part of the financial management activities. These companies also must decide between debt and equity financing, a decision influenced not only by the costs of financing, but by the manager's culture as well. Finally, profit must be managed as it will be influenced heavily by the risks encountered and the management tools selected by the company.

The debt held by developing nations is a topic of special interest to global marketing managers. All financial risks are higher in such nations, as they usually do not have enough resources to pay back debt, buy products, and help the economy grow. Global marketers must be aware that payment for their products may receive a low priority in such markets.

DISCUSSION QUESTIONS

1. What are commercial risks? Does an organization always have to assume them in order to be active globally?

2. Describe an exchange-rate risk and how it might be managed.

3. How does inflation affect international finance?

4. What impact does a blocked currency have upon global marketing?

5. Why does a country manipulate the currency-exchange rate, and what impact does that have on global marketers?

6. What is the difference between a European Currency Unit and a Eurocurrency?

7. What role do commercial banks play in the international markets for currencies?

8. What roles do governmental agencies in the United States play in assisting U.S.-based companies with international financial management?

9. Why do corporations use internal pricing?

10. Why does a forward market for currency exist, and how does it operate?

11. Should a global marketing organization use debt or equity to finance its global business activities? Why?

12. Assume you are the marketing manager for a global corporation. Your major product markets are located in developing economies that carry a large national debt. How are your financial risks affected by that debt?

CASE

HOOPER MACHINE TOOLS: FINANCING INTERNATIONAL SALES

Hooper Machine Tools has an order for a sale in Brazil for $350,000 worth of replacement parts. It has a small sales office in Argentina, and it has been extensively involved in sales in several African nations over the years. In fact, close to 60 percent of its total sales last year came from overseas orders.

Most of its Latin American and African sales have been conducted through sales offices, which it finds necessary to provide sufficient post-sale service to customers. Although its Latin American office is not in Brazil, Susan Kennedy, its overseas marketing manager (who reports directly to Hooper's president, Charles Adams), believes that its office in Argentina could provide the Brazilian customer with proper service.

The customer in Brazil has agreed to pay with an irrevocable letter of credit, through a correspondent bank that has served Hooper's overseas accounts for several years. Susan has already talked with the bank's international-trade specialists, who believe Hooper should have no major problems in receiving payment on time. The customer would like to pay Hooper 60 days after receiving the goods at its plant. According to a freight-forwarding agent, shipment to the plant should take 1 month after leaving Hooper's plant.

Case Issues

1. What financial risks does Hooper face with this sale?
2. What global financial-management activities should Hooper undertake in light of these risks?

NOTES

1. S. B. Tallman, "Home Country Political Risk and Foreign Direct Investment in the United States," *Journal of International Business Studies*, Summer 1988, pp. 219–234.
2. For an additional discussion on the impact of currency-exchange risk on setting prices in nondomestic markets, see J. S. Kaminarides and C. W. Ford, "The Effects of Foreign Exchange Risk on the Pricing and Marketing of a Product in Foreign Markets," paper presented at the Third International IMP Research Seminar on International Marketing, Lyon, 1986.
3. "Why Floating Exchange Rates Aren't Doing Their Job," *Forbes*, October 2, 1978, pp. 121–122.
4. For a more complete discussion of these and related issues, see J. D. Daniels and L. H. Radenbaugh, *International Business*, 4th ed. (Reading, Mass.: Addison-Wesley, 1986), chap. 8.
5. N. Dunnan, "Yuan to Invest," *New York Times Magazine*, November 29, 1987, pp. 28, 34.

6. See W. L. Updegrave, "Assessing Foreign Markets," *Money*, May 1987, pp. 57–84; and R. I. Kirkland, Jr., and L. Kraar, "Global Traders Head for Home," *Fortune*, December 7, 1987, pp. 53–56.

7. R. Meyer, "Around the Rim," *Financial World*, December 15, 1987, pp. 26–27.

8. For a further discussion of these institutions, see R. M. Rodriguez and E. E. Carter, *International Financial Management*, 3rd ed. (Englewood Cliffs, N.J.: Prentice Hall, 1986), Chap. 3.

9. "Stateless Money: A New Force on World Economies," *Business Week*, August 21, 1987, pp. 76–85.

10. J. Joseph, "Leading Banks Agree Backing for Eurotunnel," *Times*, London, June 22, 1987, p. 21.

11. S. Van Collie, "Pacific Rim: New Ocean of Banking Opportunity," *Bankers Monthly*, January 1987, pp. 31–32.

12. For a comparative analysis of the stability of bank systems and the role of central banks and government policies in the banking system, see R. A. Gilbert and G. E. Wood, "Coping with Bank Failures: Some Lessons from the United States and the United Kingdom," *Review* (Federal Reserve Bank of St. Louis), December 1986, pp. 5–14.

13. A. Tanzer, "Liquidity Trap," *Forbes*, April 6, 1987, pp. 37–38.

14. "Survey: Corporate Finance," *Economist*, June 7, 1986, pp. 7–8.

15. "Tax Evasion Millions Go Overseas, Says Risstrom," *Courier-Mail* (Brisbane), May 6, 1988, p. 14.

16. See D. J. Fowler, "Comment on 'Transfer Prices and Profit Maximization in Multinational Enterprise Operations:' Reply," *Journal of International Business Studies*, Spring/Summer 1982, pp. 121–124.

17. T. A. Pugel and J. L. Ugelow, "Transfer Prices and Profit Maximization in Multinational Enterprise Operations," *Journal of International Business Studies*, Spring/Summer 1982, pp. 115–119.

18. See D. P. Donnelly, "Eliminating Uncertainty in Dealing with Section 482," *International Tax Journal*, Summer 1986, pp. 213–227.

19. M. Takeuchi, "Tokyo Stock Exchange Improves Access and Functions," *Business Japan*, June 1987, p. 33; see also "Our Rich Friends: A Special Report—Global Finance and Investing," *Wall Street Journal*, September 18, 1987, sec. 4, and A. Tanzer, "Listing for Success," *Forbes*, December 15, 1986, p. 110.

20. "Survey: Corporate Finance," *Economist*, June 7, 1986, pp. 3–38.

21. See S. M. Saudagaran, "An Empirical Study of Selected Factors Influencing the Decision to List on Foreign Stock Exchanges," *Journal of International Business Studies*, Spring 1988, pp. 101–127.

22. E. A. Finn, Jr., "In Japan We (Must) Trust," *Forbes*, September 21, 1987, pp. 32–34.

23. For example, in late 1978 *Forbes* predicted that the U.S. dollar would continue to decline, causing the U.S. trade deficit to approach $15 billion. Of course, the dollar skyrocketed in the mid-1980s, as did the trade deficit.

24. For a thorough discussion of international exchange markets, see G. D. Gay and R. W. Kolb, *International Finance: Concepts and Issues*, Robert F. Dame, Richmond, VA, 1983, chaps. 20–27

25. For a more complete discussion of the forces that determine forward exchange rates, see M. Ott and P. T. W. M. Veugelers, "Forward Exchange Rates in Efficient Markets: The Effects of News and Changes in Monetary Policy Regimes," *Review* (Federal Reserve Bank of St. Louis), June/July 1986, pp. 5–15.

26.   A review of foreign-exchange risk management, see L. L. Jacque, "Management of Foreign Exchange Risk: A Review Article," *Journal of International Business Studies*, Spring/Summer 1981, pp. 81–101.

27.   For a discussion of the impact of lower corporate taxes on German corporations' fund-management activities, see R. Kuttner, "Still More Reasons to Mistrust Supply Siders," *Business Week*, October 26, 1987, p. 22.

28.   B. Nussbaum, "How to Get Americans to Sock Away a Bit More," *Business Week*, April 13, 1987, p. 86.

29.   G. M. Hampton and G. Bomers, "Comparing Dutch and U.S. Attitudes Toward Foreign Investments," *International Marketing Review*, Autumn 1987, pp. 54–62; and W. S. Sekely and J. M. Collins, "Cultural Influences on International Capital Structure," *Journal of International Business Studies*, Spring 1988, pp. 87–100.

30.   For a more complete discussion of the evaluation of international bonds, see A. Mahajan, J. C. Groth, and B. I. Neysmith, "Risk Evaluation of International Bonds," *Journal of Business Strategy* (Center for Business and Economic Research, Sam Houston State University), Spring 1985, pp. 4–18.

31.   For a discussion of Eurobonds, see R. M. Rodriguez and E. E. Carter, *International Financial Management*, 3rd ed. (Englewood Cliffs, N.J.: Prentice Hall, 1986), pp. 265–273.

32.   "Investment in Costa Rica," *Latin America Times*, Number 70, p. 14.

33.   "Peru's Bad Boy Is Starting to Look Like a Desperate Man," *Business Week*, August 17, 1987, p. 55.

34.   "The World Debt Crises and the U.S. Economy," *U.S. Review* (Data Resources), September 1983.

35.   P. Truell, "Latin American Debt Prompts Action: Banks and Nations Move to Reduce Burden," *Wall Street Journal*, September 22, 1988, p. 12.

36.   See M. L. Rossman, "Japanese Market Strategies in Latin America," *Baylor Business Studies*, October 1982, pp. 7–38.

THE FUTURE: ISSUES, MANAGEMENT, AND CAREERS

INTERNATIONAL INCIDENT

Marketing Management in the Global Village

Kenyan students enrolled in a Dutch MBA program, Hondas manufactured in the United States and exported to Europe, job offers to U.S. students to work in Paris, rain forests in Brazil, Korean television sets sold in New Zealand, and a British rock group's world tour—what do all of these things have in common? They all represent the global village—buyers and sellers linked around the world, increasingly concerned about the political, cultural, and environmental impacts of their economic activities.

Nations are increasingly, and irreversibly, linked economically. Buyers from different nations seem to be willing to purchase similar goods and services, particularly those that are high-quality or low-priced. Groups gather worldwide to talk about the impact (benefits and costs) of economic progress on the environment. National debt has political implications for internal stability as well as relationships between nations.

Such linkages have changed the world. The opening of Eastern Europe has attracted investment that might otherwise have gone to Asian nations. Concerns about erosion in Haiti led the World Bank to invest in planting coffee bushes—in the long run possibly lowering the price of coffee in the United States and elsewhere. And part of the profits from a gold mine in Papua New Guinea go to shareholders in South Africa, potentially slowing the speed of change in apartheid policies there.

The global village has its rewards, including higher-quality goods and services at lower prices. But what political, economic, cultural, and environmental threats and opportunities lie ahead for businesses? And what are the career (and personal) implications for individuals? How should corporate, political, and business leaders prepare for an ever-growing global village?

The forces driving the globilization of business are increasing.

Industrial goods already have a global market, enhanced by the industrialization of developing countries such as Brazil, India, and Indonesia. Globally marketed services have also increased, as service providers follow corporations and consumers on their path of globalization. The globalization of world markets will continue. Other forces behind globalization include improved international communication, increased international travel, and increasing demand (industrial and consumer) for high-quality goods at low prices, regardless of the country of origin, which can only be achieved through global production. These forces, combined with an increase in strategic partnerships focusing on product markets across national boundaries to exploit related opportunities, present an exciting and challenging environment to the marketing manager of the 1990s. This chapter examines the impact some of these forces will have on future global marketing strategy. It also discusses career opportunities in global marketing.

The World's Billionaires

Globalization is reflected in the businesses and investments of the world's wealthiest individuals and families. Most of the world's 192 billionaires made their fortunes in their home countries. But most are now investing in foreign countries to build upon that wealth. David Sainsbury, for example, built his fortune through a supermarket chain in the United Kingdom. Recently, however, he has begun to buy U.S. supermarket chains, in order to continue to grow. Other billionaires made their fortunes largely through international business ventures. The Benetton family, for example, built a $1 billion sales organization over 25 years; the Benetton family itself is now worth $1.3 billion. But saturation in Benetton's global markets has led it to develop new products in new industries.

The distribution and growth patterns of billionaires across nations also reflect trends in global trade. There are more billionaires in the United States than any other country—at least 47 individuals and 20 families, versus 32 individuals and 2 families in second-place Japan, and 16 individuals in third-place Germany. U.S. fortunes, previously made in industry, are now made in media, information, and entertainment businesses, reflecting today's business world. But the ranking of wealth by dollars reveals another pattern, which also reflects today's global trading. The two richest individuals, with wealth of over $10 billion each, are Takichiro Mori and Yoshiaki Tsutsumi, both Japanese. Of the ten next richest, all worth over $5 billion each, three are from Canada, three from Japan, and one each from Korea, Spain, the United States, and Taiwan.

Source: Adapted from "The World's Billionaires," *Forbes*, July 25, 1988, pp. 88–164.

EVOLUTION OF THE WORLD ECONOMIC ORDER

Less-developed nations will increasingly demand a larger role in the new global economy.

Since 1950, world trade has increased twice as much as world GDP; in 1988, world trade grew 9 percent.[1] As nations develop economically, and international trade grows more quickly than most domestic economies, there will be an increased call for a new world economic order, one that shares the economic wealth of nations more evenly. The level of economic achievement and rates of growth among nations are not equal. While most OECD member nations, for example, continue to grow at a positive rate considerably greater than the inflation rate, most developing economies grow at a slow or negative rate. The basic trend is for the economic gap between nations (often referred to as the North-South gap) to continue to widen, although there are noticeable exceptions to this trend, such as the Asian newly industrialized countries. (For an illustration of the concentration of wealth in the OECD nations, see Global Dimensions 19.1,

MAP 19.1 NEW INDUSTRIALIZED COUNTRIES

The economies of the New Industrialized Countries (NICs) have been growing faster than those of the
Triad. If this trend continues, the Triad may need to be expanded to include Asia as an area, instead of
just Japan as a country.

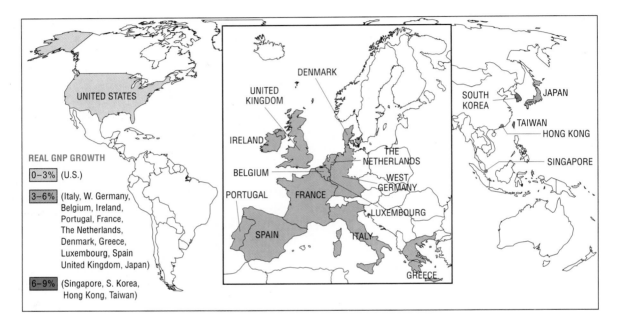

which discusses the world's billionaires.) Wider economic differences will increase
political instability and tensions, resulting in increased difficulty in conducting
business globally.

Developing Economies. Global marketers interested in markets located in
developing countries need to be sensitive to the impact of their marketing decisions on the economic and social well-being of these countries. Many developing
countries already require some level of local participation, such as joint ventures,
as a condition of doing business there. At the same time, Third World nations
are adjusting their economic policies to attract increased foreign investment.
This trend presents greater opportunities for global corporations.[2] For example,
the debt-for-equity swap programs popular in Latin American countries mean
that foreign corporations can obtain discounted capital to invest in those countries.

Even when working with local partners, global marketers in developing
economies may find their activities under increased review and control. For
example, marketing campaigns urging consumers to buy more goods may be
restrained by governments concerned that consumers will spend scarce resources
on noncritical or socially controversial products.[3]

Recent economic growth in South Korea has resulted in traffic jams for the capital city of Seoul, in which traditional methods of transportation such as bicycles and pull carts must compete with cars, trucks, and buses.

Asian-Pacific Basin. Although the economic, political, and cultural differences among countries in the Asian-Pacific Basin are tremendous, there can be little doubt that Japan, Korea, Taiwan, Hong Kong, Singapore, Malaysia, Indonesia, and China are major players in world economic development. The Japanese economic "miracle" of economic expansion and creation of wealth since 1950 is well known. For example, by the late 1980s, Japan had become the world's largest creditor nation, and it was debating how best to assume its leadership role in the "new globalism."[4] (Exhibit 19.1 illustrates Japan's changing investments.)

EXHIBIT 19.1
CHANGES IN JAPAN'S
DIRECT FOREIGN
INVESTMENTS

As Japan's investments grew during the 1980s, its favored investment locations changed.

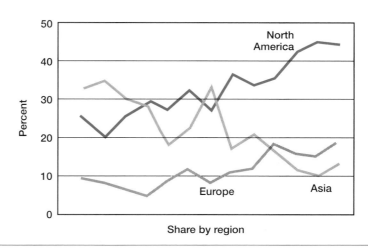

Source: "1988 White Paper on International Trade," *Focus Japan*, August 1988, p. JS-A.

EXHIBIT 19.2   REAL GNP GROWTH

The global expansion is starting to ease. As a group, Asia's Little Dragons—Hong Kong, Singapore, South Korea, and Taiwan—remain the world's hotshots, but their growth will slow dramatically. The Korean rate will be shaved by more than half. Britain appears headed for an economic hangover. Among developed and fast-developing countries, only Indonesia, which has attracted substantial new foreign investment, will boost its rate of expansion.

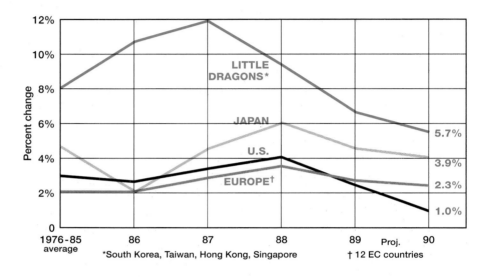

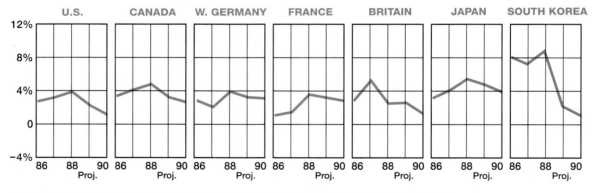

Source: *Fortune*, July 31, 1989, p. 72.

Less well known is the growth of the newly industrialized countries in the area, which have averaged some 200 percent faster economic growth than that in already developed nations.[5] The critical question is whether the NICs' strong growth will continue throughout the 1990s. (See Exhibit 19.2.) If so, they represent increasingly important markets. South Korea, for example, was classified as an underdeveloped nation 25 years ago; today it has one of the largest middle classes in Asia. With its GNP growing at some 10 percent per year, it has strong market potential.[6]

High economic growth is difficult for any economy to maintain. If the NICs do not continue their increased growth, strategic partnerships in these nations will require greater attention and evaluation as to whether they should be continued, altered, or terminated. Financial markets, in particular, are closely monitoring the economic health of these countries. A radical decline in their economic fortune would have major limiting effects on the world capital market, as less capital would be available for global investment.

Raw materials, manufactured goods, food and agricultural products, technology, and tourism are all strong growth industries, fueled by the growing Asian-Pacific Basin.[7] The general expectation is that the less-developed countries in this area will experience a trickle-down effect and add to overall growth in the area during the 1990s.

Centrally Controlled Economies.   Centrally controlled economies underwent many radical economic and political changes in the late 1980s, which will impact global marketing considerably. As free markets become more common, opportunities should increase for global corporations. But so too will competition.[8]

The changes introduced into Eastern European COMECON countries have already changed the economic environment. The Soviet Union, for example, with its "glasnost" and "perestroika" policies began a series of reforms that are increasing market forces within its economy. Central planning, which once

MAP 19.2   EASTERN EUROPE

The opening of Eastern Europe presents many opportunities for global marketers. But each country has its own unique set of strengths, weaknesses, and threats, which must also be taken into account in a market analysis.

included extensive production planning, is expected to be reduced to only an economic planning framework. More ministries, FTOs, and even companies have been authorized to participate in direct international trade. In Poland, companies have been given their own trading rights and foreign currency accounts. In Hungary, FTOs are developing into trading houses. Many state-owned companies now have the right to employ expatriates for special trading purposes. And since the fall of 1988, 100 percent foreign-owned companies have been allowed in Hungary.

Companies in Eastern European countries are getting more independence, authority, and responsibility. In the Soviet Union, companies are now managed following the principle of "self-responsibility." They are even expected to be profit-oriented; production units with chronic business deficits will be closed. (A difficult economic problem may arise from this. Companies will be able to raise their prices to avoid deficits, because most have no or limited competition. This may lead to high inflation and a lower standard of living.) Finally, the Soviet Union is reforming its banking system and developing business banks, similar to the changes already seen in Hungary.

A particularly interesting market, due to its tremendous size and political importance, is China. While still an economic unknown, no marketing manager should ignore its great market potential or, more important, its potential to be a powerful competitor. In 1988 China's GNP increased by 11 percent, while its industrial growth rate was 14.8 percent. Slower rates are expected through the 1990s. China's exports increased to $57 billion in 1988, but imports seem to be declining. Earlier, economic success stemmed mainly from the special economic zones opened for foreign investment along China's coast. The success of the zones is best illustrated by the province of Guandong, which has become China's leading export area, with $5.5 billion in goods shipped in 1987, attracting $5.3 billion in foreign investment. More recently, political turmoil has created economic uncertainty.

Encouraged by such success, Chinese leaders had wished to open up the entire coast from the Gulf of Tonkin to the North Korean border to private industry. Their objective was to bring the country into the world trading system, replacing Taiwan, South Korea, Hong Kong, and Singapore in labor-intensive industries like shoes, toys, and textiles. The biggest problem they faced was to win investors, develop foreign sales, and find managers to lead the companies into world markets.

Such development does not automatically mean that there is a large Chinese market waiting to be filled with consumer goods. In the entire coast region there live approximately 200 million people. If only half of them benefit from the recent economic development and raise their standard of living, the theoretical market is bigger than the neighboring NICs combined. But as experience with NICs has shown so far, China may be an interesting market for direct investments and sophisticated industrial products, but the development of a strong consumer market will take more years to come.[9]

Conducting business with centrally controlled economies is becoming more complicated. Each country has a different economic system, and each is developing differently. The global marketer is confronted with countries like Romania, which has become the poorest country in Europe after years of centrally controlled endeavors to become a leading industrialized nation; Hungary, which is trying to close its economic gap with Western Europe by introducing more and more market mechanisms; the Soviet Union, which has not yet decided what direction its development should take; Poland, where reforms have been announced but have hardly been executed; Cuba and Vietnam, both unable to take off industrially, in part because of their military expenditures; and Yugoslavia, which is wrestling with an enormous inflation rate and is undecided if it should resolve its current economic problems by introducing a free-market economy or falling back to more central planning and control.[10]

The European Community in 1992. The economic, legal, and (to a much lesser extent) political unification of the EC countries is expected in 1992. At that time, at least in theory, any business or product that is legal in any EC member nation will become legal in all. Just as a California-based company can easily expand into Utah, an Italian company will be able to expand freely into Holland. Due to differences in corporate operating efficiencies and management skills, the changes will be tremendous.[11] For example, some forty foreign banks now in Spain will be able to underprice Spanish banks.[12] While there are still many problems to work out (see Exhibit 19.3 as an example of the differences in property rights laws that still exist), customers will experience lower prices, employment will increase, and the European Community GDP is expected to

EXHIBIT 19.3
EUROPEAN PATENT
LAWS AND
DECISIONS

Patent laws—which define how long the patent is valid, how a patent is judged, and whether the patent should be published or used prior to filing—vary across nations. Of course, global marketers must continually update their information on patent laws.

Country	Duration (years)	Patent Criteria	Publication Standard
Belgium	20	Form	No prior publication anywhere or use in country
Luxembourg	20	Form	No publication/patent or use prior to filing
Italy	15	Form and unity of invention with statutory subject matter	Like Luxembourg
France	20	Novelty of subject matter	Like Luxembourg
Denmark	17	Merits of subject matter	Like Luxembourg
Germany	18	Merits of subject matter	Like Luxembourg
Holland	20	Merits of subject matter	Like Luxembourg
Ireland and United Kingdom	16	Merits of subject matter	Like Luxembourg

Source: J. Maronick, "European Patent Laws and Decisions: Implications for Multinational Marketing Strategy," *International Marketing Review*, Summer 1988, p. 32.

grow dramatically. This common market will represent the single largest consumer market in the world and make the "Triad power" even greater.

There should be increasing opportunities for small, medium-sized, and large companies to offer highly standardized marketing mixes, applied across all EC nations. Product design, branding, and packaging, for example, will be more standardized.[13] Barriers such as media access and availability will be eliminated. However, a fully standardized marketing mix may not be optimal. Toothpaste, for example, may still have to be marketed differently, because of national differences in the product concept. In Spain, toothpaste is regarded as a cosmetic, so brand images focus on glamour. But in the United Kingdom, the product is seen as therapeutic and campaigns are quite different.[14]

As economically developing nations exert more political pressure to be fuller members of the world economy, as newly industrialized countries experience slower or faster growth, and as centrally controlled economies permit more free-market activity,[15] shifts in exporting, importing, and manufacturing will occur. In other words, as the rules and relationships of the global economy shift, international trade patterns will also. For example, some of the comparative advantages traditionally enjoyed by OECD countries (such as the availability of capital, and technological skills) will change as trade and investment patterns follow growth markets.[16]

. . . .

EVOLUTION OF ENVIRONMENTS

Economic and Political Trends

Rapid change will be a dominant feature of the new global economy.

To gain the most from international opportunities, managers must be aware of changes in their own country's environments and those of other countries. Although marketing managers cannot be expected to be experts on every nation, a system that evaluates external environments must become a part of the global marketing manager's information system.[17]

Two global trends will heavily influence international marketing: economic integration and political fragmentation. International *economic integration* is clearly evidenced by current investment and trade patterns. At a macroeconomic level, new economic unions are being proposed—between the United States, Canada, and Mexico, New Zealand and Australia, and in effect between Hong Kong and China in 1997. New political problems related to the export and import of labor have followed.[18] (See Exhibit 19.4.) While the United States continues to have an enormous trade deficit with respect to Japan, the Japanese are reinvesting some of that money back into the United States. Estimates vary, but foreigners may own up to 10 percent of U.S. assets, and the figure is rising.

Economic integration means nations are no longer completely in control of their economic destiny. As the vice finance minister of Japan, Toyo Gyohten, has said, "There is no simple national policy any more. Every national policy

EXHIBIT 19.4   POLITICS AND POLICY

The national and cultural backgrounds of immigrants to the United States change over time, which changes the U.S. culture in turn.

	1905		1925		1965		1986	
1	Austria-Hungary	275,693	United Kingdom*	53,822	Canada	38,327	Mexico	66,753
2	Italy	221,479	Germany	46,068	Mexico	37,969	Philippines	61,492
3	Russian empire	184,897	Mexico	32,964	United Kingdom*	27,358	Korea	35,164
4	United Kingdom*	64,709	Scandinavia	16,810	Germany	24,045	China	32,389
5	German empire	40,574	Italy	6,203	Cuba	19,760	Dominican Republic	30,787
6	Sweden	26,591	France	3,906	Colombia	10,885	Haiti	26,216
7	Norway	25,064	Czechoslovakia	2,462	Italy	10,821	India	24,808
8	Japan	10,331	Switzerland	2,000	Dominican Republic	9,504	Jamaica	18,916
9	France	10,168	China	1,937	Poland	8,465	United Kingdom*	16,129
10	Portugal	5,028	USSR	1,775	Argentina	6,124	Canada	16,064
	Total immigration: 1,026,499			294,314		296,697		601,708

*Includes Northern Ireland.
Source: S. McConnell, "The New Battle over Immigration," *Fortune*, May 9, 1988, p. 94.

has an international implication."[19] There is, therefore, a building resentment toward foreign investment in many nations. Just as concern has been expressed in the United States, European countries, Asian-Pacific nations, and less-developed countries around the globe are increasingly concerned about the loss of national control implied by the growth in foreign investment.[20] There is really little cause for alarm, as was discussed in Chapter 1.

Political fragmentation is being experienced in several areas of the world. This may be due to a backlash against international economic integration or the shift in many countries from consensus politics through majorities to confrontational politics through multiple minorities.[21] Perhaps the greatest exception to this trend is the European Community, a strong economic and political cooperative movement.

Of potentially greater impact is the reaction to a generation of more trade blocs. Countries may design new bilateral trade agreements to achieve some of the European Community's projected economic gains. The free trade agreement between the United States and Canada, for example, may expand to include Mexico or, even more radically, Japan. If those trade blocs are created, they may result in higher trade barriers to nonmember nations. In any event, while their potential impact is difficult to project, corporations must be prepared for that eventuality.[22]

Legal Issues

Due to increased strategic alliances and counterfeiting, and the need to adapt to different legal systems, global marketers must pay more attention than ever before to legal issues.

At least three global marketing trends have made legal advice an increasingly important component of the global marketing strategic decision-making process. Those are: (a) an increase in strategic partnerships across markets, which carry a higher legal risk than does direct foreign investment; (b) an estimated loss of $60 billion from product counterfeiting per year; and (c) the need to adapt marketing mixes to the differences in national laws.[23] Product-liability laws in the United States, for example, are so broadly interpreted that they serve in effect as a nontariff barrier to entry.[24] And antidumping suits have been increasing in frequency in the United States and the European Community, as they are used as a strategy to protect home markets against imports.[25] (A strong argument exists, of course, that the long-term impact of protectionism under any guise is to render the corporation less able to survive.)[26]

Another legal area of considerable concern is the protection of intellectual property rights. Protection of patents, trade names, and brand names from unauthorized use is an issue of considerable concern to global managers, as discussed in Chapter 5. The growth of foreign markets is well illustrated by patent applications. For example, in 1984 over 35,000 patents were filed with the European Patent Office, the EC multination patent system. Of those, 30 percent were filed by U.S. firms, and 20 percent were filed by Japanese firms.[27]

Industrial Trends

Just as markets are globalizing, so too are industries, from raw materials through finished products.

Several global industry pressures are gaining force. These are in the areas of competition, production, markets, and supply.

International competitors exist in every industry.[28] Consumers in Korea buy Hondas made in the United States. President Reagan's favorite jelly beans were produced in the United States (on a machine exported from Australia). Financial institutions in the United States, Japan, Hong Kong, and Germany vie for industrial accounts around the world. It is a business truism that every company will be affected by global competition and business in the 1990s.

Production is increasingly shared among nations.[29] For example, the textile industry in the United States has lost several companies as a result of global competitors' (sometimes other U.S. companies) producing in countries with lower labor costs. Close to 95 percent of all the baseball gloves sold in the United States are made in Taiwan and Hong Kong, from hides processed in Brazil, from cows slaughtered in the United States.

While president, Ronald Reagan was famous for his love of jelly beans. His favorite brand is made in the U.S., on machines imported from Australia.

Clearly, *global markets* are driving the other global business trends. Revlon cosmetics are sold throughout the world. Volvos appeal to "yuppies" worldwide. Technology, travel, and communication transcend national market boundaries, increasing the feasibility of marketing to global consumers. Industrial markets—primarily concerned with price, stable supply, and product reliability—cross national boundaries even more today than traditionally.

Global supply systems naturally follow global markets, support global production, and serve global competitors. Raw materials are shipped around the world in response to global supply and demand. Coca-Cola, for example, has invested heavily in Belize to ensure a continual supply of oranges, because of fluctuations in orange crops in the United States. Of the top ten commercial banks in the world, seven are now in Tokyo. And "Black Monday" (or Tuesday, depending upon where the investor lived) in October 1987 sent shock waves through the financial system around the world.

These pressures do not mean that products should be sold exactly the same way everywhere. They do mean that there are not necessarily national market limitations anywhere in the business system, from raw materials through consumption. Global corporations can gain economies of scale and experience curve effects if they present high-quality products at lower prices across more national markets. In effect, the 1990s global environment means that most firms must focus on customer needs across nations. Not to do so threatens the competitiveness, even survival, of the firm. (For a discussion of the attitude changes that need to occur in order to improve the global competitiveness of U.S. firms, see Global Dimensions 19.2.)

GLOBAL DIMENSIONS 19.2

U.S. Global Competitiveness: The Future

The United States is no longer the most dominant economic leader in the world. This change has been due to many causes, including the natural growth of other national economies, the inability of U.S. business to adjust quickly to a more globally competitive environment, difficulties caused by the sometimes overvalued dollar, the highly supportive export policies of other national governments, and the relatively large and open U.S. market compared to other national markets.

Many analysts include in these causes the loss of commitment in the United States to high-quality products. While many underlying causes have led to poor quality, one important, somewhat uniquely American, cultural element merits further discussion. This is the short-term focus on corporate earnings. A quarter-by-quarter perspective, encouraged by institutional investors who control more than 80 percent of the stock held in the United States, leads to decisions that optimize short-term stock prices, often at the expense of long-term market performance.

Corporations based in other nations, in particular Japan, have been able to achieve long-term success through focusing on market share and product quality. Today, many U.S. corporations are not able to compete in the world market. A short-term view, of course, is more a deeply held cultural value than just the result of stock-performance expectations. Chinese negotiators, for example, have often noted that American negotiators are impatient, wanting to get down to business before the Chinese are ready. And the American consumer is well known to be oriented toward immediate consumption, as is evidenced in low savings rates and high consumption rates of high convenience goods and services. At least one business leader is convinced that "until we manage our economic lives in support of long-term strategies . . ." U.S. corporations will continue to be at a competitive disadvantage in the world market.

Source: Adapted in part from E. Spencer, "The U.S. Should Stop Playing Poker with Its Future," *Business Week*, November 17, 1986, p. 20; and R. Kuttner, "Must We Lose the Industrial World Series?," *Business Week*, November 17, 1986, p. 23.

Concurrent Trends: Research, Product Life-Cycles, and Technology

The rapid speed of technological development and diffusion requires firms to increasingly invest in research and development in order to maintain competitiveness. Product life-cycles are shorter, so R&D investments must be recovered over shorter time periods.[30] For example, today's drug companies must be global to maintain the level of research and development required in the pharmaceutical industry. Large global markets are necessary to cost-justify such investments.

The simultaneous introduction, across national markets, of new products is an important preemptive strategy for the 1990s.[31] As with penetration pricing during the introductory phase of the product life-cycle, simultaneously introducing products across national markets raises the barriers to entry for firms that might wish to follow into those markets. It achieves high sales volumes, economies of scale, and cross-market coordination of marketing efforts. All of this allows aggressive pricing (even cross-subsidization). This strategy is an expensive one, however, affordable only to large organizations. Smaller organizations must pursue strategic partnerships and niche marketing (concentrating on their competitive advantages) to remain globally competitive.

EVOLUTION OF THE CORPORATION

The corporation itself must change in response to global markets and global industrial shifts.

In order to react properly to changes in the external environments, the marketing manager's job and the corporation itself must evolve in several ways. Some of these necessary changes are briefly discussed in this section. Together they comprise a major change in corporate culture, as managers must learn to manage multiple identities and loyalties.

Cultural Insight

Understanding customer similarities across nations requires a great deal of cultural insight.

If you want to do business, you need to understand your markets. An obvious statement certainly, but one too easily forgotten by firms that do business in several national markets. An advantage of the global approach to strategic marketing is that the focus is on the customer, not the country. This should lead to marketing mixes tuned to the culture of the *product market*, which may be relatively consistent across nations. Thus, while cultural sensitivity is increasingly important, it should not necessarily be based on a nation-by-nation analysis. Of course, adjustments need to be made to different national laws, customs, and other environments. So sensitivity to national cultures must be maintained or even increased. But of overriding importance will be proper attention to the culture of the customer.

Language Training

Language skills will increasingly be required of managers.

U.S. marketing managers may be pleased that English is the lingua franca of the European Community as it moves toward economic integration in 1992. In fact, it may well be that international managers everywhere need to be fluent in English. It is the dominant language of business transactions and is likely to remain so. But tomorrow's international manager should know at least a second language. In the "new Europe" of 1992, managers should actually speak *three* languages—English, French, and German. Even if the principals in an agreement or the architects of a marketing strategy communicate perfectly with one another in English, those responsible for implementation will not necessarily be fluent in that language. Upper management has a responsibility to stockholders to increase the language skills of managers and other personnel.

Daewoo (in Korea), for example, has its workers come in an hour early at 7:00 A.M. every day for a 6-month course in Mandarin, even though Daewoo does not currently have much corporate activity in China. After the course, Daewoo supports good students for 5 months of intensive study at a nearby university. It then supports the best of those for an entire year at the University of Taiwan.

Another "language" every global marketing manager needs to master is "computer." For those who have not tried to do a spreadsheet analysis or run a statistical package on a computer, this may not seem to be a language. But information is power. The 1990s global marketing manager must be able to access various data bases and transform them into useful information to aid in management decisions. Not to be able to do so is to have insufficient communication skills as surely as if you spoke no Spanish and were stationed in an office in Peru where no one else spoke English.

Megamarketing

Global marketers will need to be more involved in the nations where they do business.

International businesses used to "keep a low profile." However, the increasingly complex and interlinked global business environment means that global marketers must begin to play more of a role in the political and economic environments.[32] Those environments very much determine what opportunities will exist for, and what options will be taken away from, marketers in the 1990s.[33] The following examples illustrate some of the important areas where the global marketer must be willing to serve as an agent of change—"the spokesman for the interest of society in producing, in performing, in achieving."[34]

Education shapes the most important corporate resource—people. A strong education system, in fact, may be the best lever for corporate success.[35] Japan, for example, has a highly acclaimed education system. Although this system has been criticized for its social costs, it produces well-educated graduates who have become part of one of the most productive work forces in the world.

Trade policies are an important element in the political environment where marketers should become more involved.[36] Rather than resisting trade policies affecting business, marketers must help to formulate policies that build comparative advantages for nations and industries.

Marketers need to take a stand on *fiscal policies*, such as R&D incentives, consumption or value-added taxes, and inflationary controls. Without stable long-term economic growth, market and political stability is unlikely. Marketers can contribute to a more positive economic environment by influencing such policies.

GLOBAL MARKETING STRATEGY IN THE 1990S

Strategic Partnerships

In response to the globalization challenge, many firms are entering into cross-national alliances with suppliers, customers, and even competitors.

The increased need for research and development, investment capital for state-of-the-art production facilities, and simultaneous marketing in multiple nations has made strategic partnerships a corporate necessity for the 1990s.[37] **Strategic partnerships** go a bit further than joint ventures, which are essentially market-by-market alliances combining the international skills and resources of the home corporation with the local knowledge and management skills of the host business. Strategic partnerships are proactive, part of an ongoing global business strategy to form cross-market alliances that gain and maintain market leadership. Partners often combine manufacturing skills with national marketing competencies. They may also combine R&D, distribution, or management skills.

Large organizations must form strategic partnerships with other global organizations, especially potential competitors. This permits global access and power while co-opting ruinous competition. Medium-sized and small organizations must try even harder to form strategic partnerships, to take advantage of their special market skills and niche potential in a wider setting. Concentration will occur worldwide, as scale economies drive less competitive firms out of business. Small, medium-sized, and large firms have to either be niched into less price-resistant markets or offer increasingly competitive prices. Either way, a strategic partner makes the process more attainable.

Marginal versus Full-Cost Pricing

To be competitive in global markets, firms must view price setting in different ways.

As successful Japanese marketers have shown, redefining competition in the process,[38] penetration pricing generates mass-market entry, long-term market share, and thus profits. This will be a necessary strategy for success in the 1990s.[39] NIC firms are now adopting this strategy. U.S. and European corporations currently prefer cost-plus pricing, which does not sufficiently recognize competition as a major survival threat.[40] Niche marketing, of course, offers global opportunities for corporations that choose to (or must) use full-cost pricing.

Focus on Triad Markets

Competition within the Triad markets will increase even faster than for global markets overall.

Over 600 million relatively affluent customers cannot be ignored. The Triad markets (at least two out of the three, and preferably all three) need to be considered in the development of any corporate marketing strategy, especially for mass-market goods. Clusters of customers across all of the Triad nations can be identified, which will prove profitable. On the other hand, attacking any of the Triad members individually will give too large a window of opportunity to the competition to preempt your campaigns in the other two.

GLOBAL DIMENSIONS 19.3

Pall Corporation

Medium-sized and small companies can be, and are, successful in the new global market. Pall is a $429 million sales company based in New York. It has evolved from an export-oriented domestic company to a global organization. It has turned itself, in the process, into a leader in its market niche, specialty filters.

Pall's sales strategy is to select industrial distributors that will dedicate a substantial part of their organization to Pall's product line. Pall supports these distributors with regional managers and manufacturing plants in the United States, Japan, and Europe.

Its filters are manufactured to high-quality standards and sold and supported by excellent service organizations. Pall has found that the product market for its filters is global; in other words, the market will profitably support a firm with a global view.

Source: Based on M. G. Hardy, "Going Global: One Company's Road to International Markets," *Journal of Business Strategy*, November–December 1989, pp. 24–27.

World Resourcing

Globalization has business implications beyond the marketing function.[41] Global production sharing, purchasing, and financing are also necessary to achieve competitive prices. For example, a personal computer to be marketed in Europe may be assembled in Mexico, with chips from Korea, a shell from the United States, a board from Taiwan, and software from India. Another example is the corporation's ability to raise capital and place investments 24 hours a day, in debt and equity markets literally around the world.

Finding a Niche

A company need not be large to be globally competitive.

Small and medium-sized organizations, through careful planning, can do very well in the global marketplace. (See Global Dimensions 19.3.) Their strategy should be to find a market niche, form strategic partnerships (often with potential competitors), raise barriers to market entry as high as possible, and be assertive in entering and defending the market niche and similar niches in as many nations as possible. Small and medium-sized companies have seldom competed successfully on price alone against large companies in domestic markets. There is no reason to believe they will be able to do so globally, either. But through careful target marketing global success can be achieved regardless of size. Indeed, smaller companies may need to enter an even greater variety of national markets than large companies do. Smaller businesses can find niches in similar customer segments across nations. In effect, they will follow a market portfolio approach to ensure corporate survival.[42]

Services

Globalization, which has already affected goods, is increasingly changing service industries.

Already contributing some 30 percent of world trade, service industries will be the next great opportunity for global corporations. In particular, telecommunications, business services, entertainment, banking and finance, insurance, tourism, and (perhaps surprisingly) education are experiencing their own global revolutions.[43] Japanese tourists going abroad, for example, have increased over 550 percent since 1950. Advertising agencies link the world to service their globalizing clients better. Even education will globalize, especially business education, as corporations demand the best possible managers for the 1990s.[44]

Trade is shifting away from goods across the Atlantic to services across the Pacific. Global marketing managers in service organizations must be prepared to do global battle in the 1990s, just as their manufacturing counterparts had to during the late 1980s. It appears that GATT will soon begin to play more of a role in the regulation of services.[45] Additionally, manufacturing managers will learn to take advantage of global organizations that offer high-quality services worldwide, at competitive prices.[46]

Centralized Decentralization

Just as marketing strategies must adapt to globalism, so too must the entire organization moving toward new, perhaps "stateless," forms.[47] Global managers are currently evolving away from a geographic focus to a worldwide brand or product focus. The current trend is toward centralized strategy, to gain experience curve effects, combined with decentralized implementation, to achieve market flexibility. (Thus the popular phrase "Think global, act local.")

As a "supermatrix" evolves, with global brand managers along one axis, local managers along another, and functional managers (for example, in production, logistics, or finance) along a third, companies must increasingly turn to marketing to match customer needs with the objectives and resources of the organization. Other new forms of interaction, such as product-development teams, will also be useful.

Quality

Product quality must continually be improved if the firm is to remain competitive.

Within the increasingly complex set of issues faced by global marketing managers, one point must remain clear. High quality, whether the product is a good or a service, must be the mainstay of the organization if it is to survive. Customers have too many choices, and competition is too fierce, to permit poor-quality products to succeed in the marketplace. The cost of gaining a customer is much higher than maintaining one. Even low prices cannot in the long run compensate for poor quality. The appropriate level of quality must be defined from the customer's perspective. Too much quality can be engineered into the product, due to a technological orientation. Too little quality can result from a cost and price orientation.

Quality is dynamic. A corporation that wishes to sustain its competitive advantage must continually increase customer benefits. However, high quality must be coupled with low costs, so that the corporation can make or react to competitive price cuts.

Global Products

Preplanned modification and standardization are increasingly popular product strategies. **Preplanned modification** refers to the careful analysis of market tastes and preferences, and building those differences into the total product before it is launched. This permits the firm to make relatively minor product and marketing-mix modifications while enjoying the maximum economies of scale and experience curve effects possible.

Globally standard products and marketing mixes also maximize economies of scale and experience curve effects. Combined with low prices to gain market acceptance, they can be used for mass-market products. As the purchasing power of developing countries continues to grow, and as the European Community moves even closer together, tomorrow's opportunities for standardized product and marketing mixes will continue to increase. Companies need to continually analyze whether new markets exist for global products. They may have to redesign the marketing function (possibly the entire firm) to take advantage of global opportunities.

CAREERS IN GLOBAL MARKETING

All business managers are affected by globalization—through international jobs, global markets, suppliers, and competitors.

As the number of global markets grows and as global corporations pursue those markets, career opportunities should also grow. But there is a major difference between yesterday's "international" career opportunities and tomorrow's global career opportunities. During the 1960s, for example, U.S. corporations hired American business-school graduates to go overseas and be their representatives there. During the 1970s the pattern evolved to their hiring graduates, training them domestically for several years, and then sending them overseas. The 1980s saw another pattern of hiring: U.S. corporations hired foreign nationals, frequently trained in U.S. business schools, and returned them to their home countries as management teams for the corporations.

But if global markets grow as expected, these patterns will not prove adequate. Rather, career paths will have to include international service to reach the top in almost any corporation. More international business training and language training will also be needed.

Of course, some companies are by nature more likely to have international jobs. These include the large, "Fortune 500," companies. (A list of U.S. companies already active in the international field is included in Exhibit 19.5.) Additionally, local and state chambers of commerce have lists of local companies that are active internationally. Foreign companies are likely to hire Americans to work for them in the United States.[48]

Corporations are, and need to be, increasingly sensitive to hiring the best-qualified employees, regardless of nationality or location of operation. (In 1988, for example, 26 out of the top 500 executives listed in the "Forbes 500" were born or educated outside the United States.[49]) But they should keep in mind that compensation for similar jobs can vary significantly by country, based in part on costs of living, tradition, and the availability of good personnel. (See Exhibit 19.6).

Given the need to employ the best people possible to meet global competition, compensation packages need to be realigned. As was discussed earlier, the current approach to global compensation is to pay foreign nationals differently from nationals doing similar jobs. This happens even when they work side by side in the host nation. If corporations can develop a global orientation, where all markets are equal, unequal compensation systems will be sharply reduced, and employees will view foreign assignments as a necessary, even desirable, step up the corporate ladder. Some evidence exists that such an attitude is beginning to build, particularly in the United States and the Pacific areas. A 1988 study found that managers there were much more likely to consider an international job than they were 10 years ago.[50]

SUMMARY

In the 1990s, marketing students and managers must bring a global orientation to their careers and their companies. The world economic order is changing, and with changes, there are new opportunities. Many of these changes, including the economic, political, and social revolution in Eastern Europe, the high debt carried by developing economies and their struggle to improve standards of living, the increased economic importance of the Asian-Pacific Basin, and the economic integration going forward in Western Europe, must all be monitored carefully. Companies must understand these shifts in order to identify appropriate corporate opportunities and to develop programs that take advantage of those opportunities.

Similarly, international environments are changing even more rapidly. Economic integration has a strong political impact, with stronger reactions leading to political fragmentation. As economies merge, legal issues assume greater importance; and global competition, production, markets, and supply become more critical in all industries. Simultaneously, research and development has become more expensive, product life-cycles have shortened, and new technology has eclipsed the old.

EXHIBIT 19.5 OVERSEAS SALES OF LEADING U.S. COMPANIES

Exports, including intracompany transfers of U.S. companies, are on the rise, in response to global market challenges.

Rank in 1989		Products	Export Sales ($ millions)	Total Sales ($ millions)	Exports as Percent of Sales
1	Boeing	Commercial and military aircraft	11,021.0	20,276.0	54.4
2	General Motors	Motor vehicles and parts	10,185.1	126,974.3	8.0
3	Ford Motor	Motor vehicles and parts	8,602.0	96,932.6	8.9
4	General Electric	Jet engines, turbines, medical systems	7,268.0	55,264.0	13.2
5	Int'l Business Machines	Computers and related equipment	5,476.0	63,438.0	8.6
6	E. I. Du Pont de Nemours	Specialty chemicals	4,844.0	35,209.0	13.8
7	Chrysler	Motor vehicles and parts	4,649.0	36,156.0	12.9
8	United Technologies	Jet engines, helicopters, cooling equipment	3,307.4	19,765.5	16.7
9	Caterpillar	Heavy machinery, engines, turbines	3,291.0	11,126.0	29.6
10	McDonnell Douglas	Commercial and military aircraft	2,896.0	14,995.0	19.3
11	Eastman Kodak	Photographic equipment and supplies	2,874.0	18,398.0	15.6
12	Hewlett-Packard	Computers, electronics	2,634.0	11,899.0	22.1
13	Unisys	Computers and related equipment	2,400.1	10,096.9	23.8
14	Motorola	Communications equipment, semiconductors	2,319.0	9,620.0	24.1
15	Philip Morris	Tobacco, beverages, food products	2,288.0	39,069.0	5.9
16	Digital Equipment	Computers and related equipment	2,103.3	12,866.0	16.3
17	Occidental Petroleum	Agricultural products, coal	1,995.0	20,068.0	9.9
18	Allied-Signal	Aircraft and vehicle parts, chemicals	1,692.0	12,021.0	14.1
19	Weyerhaeuser	Pulp, paper, logs, lumber	1,574.0	10,105.6	15.6
20	Union Carbide	Chemicals, plastics	1,561.0	8,744.0	17.9
21	General Dynamics	Tanks, aircraft, missiles, gun systems	1,522.1	10,053.2	15.1
22	Raytheon	Electronic systems, aircraft	1,340.0	8,796.1	15.2
23	Textron	Aerospace, consumer goods	1,210.0	7,440.1	16.3
24	Archer Daniels Midland	Protein meals, vegetable oils, flour	1,208.5	8,056.5	15.0
25	Dow Chemical	Chemicals, plastics, consumer products	1,157.0	17,730.0	6.5

(Continued)

EXHIBIT 19.5 *(Continued)*

Rank in 1989		Products	Export Sales ($ millions)	Total Sales ($ millions)	Exports as Percent of Sales
26	Westinghouse Electric	Electrical products and electronic systems	1,131.0	12,844.0	8.8
27	International Paper	Pulp, paperboard, wood products	1,100.0	11,378.0	9.7
28	Monsanto	Herbicides, chemicals, pharmaceuticals	1,070.0	8,681.0	12.3
29	Hoechst Celanese	Chemicals, plastics, fibers	1,039.0	6,016.0	17.3
30	Merck	Drugs, specialty chemicals	1,038.6	6,698.4	15.5
31	Minnesota Mining & Mfg.	Industrial, electronic, and health goods	1,019.0	11,990.0	8.5
32	Exxon	Petroleum, chemicals	1,019.0	86,656.0	1.2
33	Intel	Microcomputer components and systems	997.9	3,280.7	30.4
34	Aluminum Co. of America	Aluminum products	935.0	11,161.5	8.4
35	Compaq Computer	Computers and related equipment	896.1	2,876.1	31.2
36	Rockwell International	Electronics, automotive parts	800.0	12,633.1	6.3
37	Xerox	Copiers, printers	770.0	17,635.0	4.4
38	Bayer USA	Health goods, chemicals, photographics	759.5	5,424.7	14.0
39	Lockheed	Aircraft, electronics, missile systems	754.0	9,932.0	7.6
40	Sun Microsystems	Computers, related equipment	751.0	1,769.2	42.4
41	Deere	Farm and industrial equipment	742.0	7,221.0	10.3
42	Honeywell	Control and flight systems	718.0	7,241.6	9.9
43	North American Philips	Components, electronics, lighting	693.6	6,202.6	11.2
44	Abbott Laboratories	Drugs, diagnostic equipment	685.0	5,453.5	12.6
45	Amoco	Chemicals	668.0	24,214.0	2.8
46	Tenneco	Farm, construction, and auto equipment	644.0	14,439.0	4.5
47	Bristol-Myers Squibb	Drugs, medical devices, consumer products	638.0	9,422.0	6.8
48	FMC	Armored military vehicles, chemicals	631.4	3,461.0	18.2
49	Ethyl	Specialty and petroleum chemicals	592.7	2,754.9	21.5
50	Cooper Industries	Electrical equipment and compressors	571.5	5,129.4	11.1
	Totals		110,081.7	979,614.6	

EXHIBIT 19.6 AVERAGE COMPENSATION FOR EUROPEAN MARKETING MANAGERS

Even with similar jobs and responsibilities, international marketing managers receive very different compensation packages.

Country	Average Age	Years in Job	Annual Base Salary* (thousands)	Annual Total Remuneration** (thousands)	Percentage Getting Cars	Most Likely Car Brand
Austria	42	5	$94.6	$105.1	91%	BMW
Belgium	44	6	76.3	86.7	86	Audi
Denmark	44	6	68.6	72.5	57	Mazda
Finland	45	6	71.7	72.8	100	Mercedes
France	46	8	72.9	80.8	68	Renault
Germany	46	6	105.1	116.6	82	Mercedes
Greece	47	9	27.6	29.8	75	Honda
Italy	44	5	74.0	79.1	70	Alfa Romeo
Luxembourg	42	6	85.4	88.7	88	Audi
Netherlands	42	8	79.0	83.6	100	Ford
Norway	45	5	65.6	68.9	100	Ford
Portugal	46	5	24.9	25.9	84	Alfa Romeo
Spain	45	8	64.6	69.7	50	N/A
Sweden	44	6	63.8	69.0	100	Volvo
Switzerland	43	6	120.8	136.9	60	Audi
United Kingdom	44	5	63.5	68.6	88	Ford

*Based on exchange rates for January 1988. **Base salary plus bonus.
Source: Wyatt Co.'s 1988 Top Management Remuneration Study; *Advertising Age*, September 12, 1988, p. 85.

As the world changes, so too must corporations. Business managers must respond to global challenges with cultural and language training programs for their employees. Companies must become more involved in their environments, using the influence of megamarketing to achieve freer market access. Perhaps most important, top management must have a strong commitment toward achieving a global orientation and provide resources to achieve that goal.

As corporations change, they must also change their strategies. Long-term, mutually beneficial strategic partnerships must be considered. Pricing approaches must be reevaluated in light of global competition. The Triad markets need to be considered simultaneously. Small firms must become as globally oriented as large ones (perhaps more so, by finding global market niches). Service as well as goods marketers must adjust to the global marketplace. Finally, high-quality, global products must be delivered consistently to product markets in multiple nations.

These changes and challenges bring tremendous career opportunities for individuals. For students and managers who are willing to respond and pursue international training and experience, the 1990s will bring exciting chances.

DISCUSSION QUESTIONS

1. What forces behind the globalization of markets do you see as being most important in the 1990s? Give an example of each.

2. Will developing economy markets become less important to global marketers, or more important, during the 1990s? Why?

3. Why have Asian-Pacific Basin countries become so successful in international trade? What is your prediction for their future success?

4. What is your opinion of the future value of China as a market for global consumer goods?

5. What is the relationship between economic integration and political fragmentation?

6. Identify three global industrial trends that you anticipate for the 1990s, and indicate how each affects the corporation.

7. How important will cultural and foreign-language training be to U.S. marketing managers in the future?

8. As corporations invest in other national markets, will strategic partnerships and other cooperative strategies increase, or decrease, in importance? Why?

9. Given the increased need for marketing activities in multiple national markets, and increased costs of operation, how can the small or medium-sized firm survive in the global environment of the 1990s?

10. Given the intangible nature of services, and the fact that production and consumption occur nearly at the same time, how is it possible they are expected to become increasingly global?

CASE

MURRAY MANUFACTURING: PLANNING FOR THE FUTURE

The Board of Directors of Murray Manufacturing, a medium-sized manufacturer of household appliances based in Cleveland, was scheduled to meet in a week. Murray manufactures small home appliances, such as electric mixers, can openers, and other kitchen equipment. It is not in the major appliance business, such as dishwashers, and it has avoided consumer electronics, which are too capital-intensive for the corporation. John Johnson, vice-president of international marketing, and Kristie Carlson, director of strategic planning, were discussing their initial thoughts on the report they had been asked to give at the board meeting, outlining major problems and opportunities in international markets for Murray for the next 5 years.

Murray had extensive international experience. It had manufacturing plants in Indonesia, Argentina, and Ireland, and subsidiaries for Western Europe, Africa and Latin America, Southeast Asia, and North America. Johnson and Carlson thought Murray needed to adopt an even more global orientation. But several political and economic developments looked as if they might present problems for Murray in the years ahead.

Case Issue

1.   What issues should Johnson and Carlson be concerned about in preparing their report for the Board of Directors?

NOTES

1.   "Shifting Trade Patterns," *Fortune*, July 31, 1988, p. 88.

2.   G. Pollio and C. H. Riemenschneider, "The Coming Third World Investment Revival," *Harvard Business Review*, March–April 1988, pp. 114–124.

3.   M. C. Gilly and J. L. Graham, "A Macroeconomic Study of the Effects of Promotion on the Consumption of Infant Formula in Developing Countries," *Journal of Macromarketing*, Spring 1988, pp. 21–31; and D. G. Howard, "Developing a Defensive Product Management Philosophy for Third World Markets," *International Marketing Review*, Spring 1988, pp. 31–40.

4.   "New Globalism and the Formation of a Balanced Japanese Society—Japan's Choices," *Focus Japan*, October 1988, p. 1.

5.   See D. I. Riddle and M. H. Sours, "Service-Led Growth in the Pacific Basin," in W. C. Kim and P. K. Y. Young, eds., *The Pacific Challenge in International Business* (Ann Arbor, Mich.: U.M.I. Research Press, 1987), p. 226.

6.   L. Kraar, "Korea: Tomorrow's Powerhouse," *Fortune*, August 15, 1988, pp. 75–81.

7.   See, for example, A. G. Pepper, " 'Goofing Off' Becomes Socially Acceptable," *Business Japan*, July 1988, p. 130.

8.   R. I. Kirkland, Jr., "The Great Rebound: Britain Is Back," *Fortune*, May 9, 1988, pp. 114–119.

9.   M. D'Anastasio, "Soviets Now Hail China as a Source for Reviving Socialism," *Wall Street Journal*, September 18, 1988, p. 1; T. H. Naylor, "Fashion Gives Life to Soviet Reforms," *New York Times*, September 13, 1987, p. 3; and D. J. Yang and M. Shao, "The Reformers Say Let a Thousand Businesses Bloom: Zhao Aims to Turn China's 'Gold Coast' Into an Export Powerhouse," *Business Week*, April 11, 1988, pp. 36–37.

10. J. Naor, "Towards a Socialist Marketing Concept—The Case of Romania," *Journal of Marketing*, January 1986, pp. 28–39; W. M. Mallard, "Hungarians Seek to Boost U.S. Trade," *Atlanta Constitution*, November 13, 1987, p. 3-c; and "Special Section on Marketing in Poland," *Journal of Business Research*, August 1986, pp. 285–327.

11. For a more complete discussion of the business implications of the "new Europe," see "Special Report: Reshaping Europe: 1992 and Beyond," *Business Week*, pp. 48-73.

12. "Will Business Succeed Where Armies Failed?," *Forbes*, July 25, 1988, p. 92.

13. J. Ashby, "European Unification in 1992 Challenges U.S. Export Packaging," *Marketing News*, October 10, 1988, p. 12.

14. L. Wentz, "1992: A False Sense of 'Europhoria'?," *Advertising Age*, October 10, 1988, p. 2.

15. A. C. Samli, "Changing Marketing Systems in Eastern Europe: What Western Marketers Should Know," *International Marketing Review*, Winter 1986, pp. 7–16.

16. R. L. King, "An Examination of Shortages of Consumer Goods in the Polish Market-place," in K. D. Bahn, ed., *Developments in Marketing Science*, Blacksburg, VA, VPI University, 1988, pp. 398–402.

17. J. F. Bolt, "Global Competitors: Some Criteria for Success," *Business Horizons*, January–February 1988, p. 39.

18. S. McConnel, "The New Battle Over Immigration," *Fortune*, May 9, 1988, pp. 89–102; and "Go South Young Man," *Economist*, March 10, 1990, p. 40.

19. S. Simson, "New World—New Markets," *Business Review Weekly*, February 12, 1988, p. 40.

20. See, for example, A. Steward and R. MacDonald, "Japanese Takeaway," *Business Review Weekly*, March 31, 1988, pp. 46–53.

21. See P. Drucker, *Managing in Turbulent Times* (London: Pan Books, 1981), pp. 152–224.

22. S. Barlas, "Trading Blocs May Block World Trade," *Marketing News*, October 10, 1988, pp. 2, 23, 25.

23. See W. C. Kim and R. A. Mauborgne, "Cross-Cultural Strategies," *Journal of Business Strategy*, Spring 1987, pp. 33–35; and K. Cote, "Heinz, Mars Target Europe TV Rules," *Advertising Age*, September 5, 1988, p. 46.

24. C. Rowling, "Liability Blues," *Pacific Way*, June 1, 1988, pp. 54–58.

25. "Business: The Anti-dumping Dodge," *Economist*, September 10, 1988, pp. 77–78.

26. M. Levinson, "Asking for Protection Is Asking for Trouble," *Harvard Business Review*, July–August, 1987, pp. 42–47.

27. For a more complete discussion of patent law, see T. J. Maronick, "European Patent Laws and Decisions: Implications for Multinational Marketing Strategy," *International Marketing Review*, Summer 1988, pp. 31–40.

28. R. I. Kirkland, Jr., "Entering a New Age of Boundless Competition," *Fortune*, March 14, 1988, pp. 40–63.

29. See, for example, "U.S. Exporters That Aren't American," *Business Week*, February 29, 1988, pp. 38–39; and D. Hefler, "Global Sourcing: Offshore Investment Strategy for the 1980s," *Journal of Business Strategy*, Summer 1981, pp. 7–13.

30. P. Ghemawat, "Sustainable Advantage," *Harvard Business Review*, September–October, 1986, pp. 53–58.

31. "Global Business Strategies," *Journal of Business Strategy*, Spring 1987, p. 3.

32. One example of the call for increased business involvement in the political environment of a host country is the demand that U.S. firms take a more active role in fighting apartheid in South Africa. See M. Loeb, "What the U.S. Must Do in South Africa," *Fortune*, July 18, 1988, pp. 88–90.

33. The term "megamarketing" derives from P. Kotler, "Megamarketing," *Harvard Business Review*, March–April 1986, pp. 117–125, which argues that managers need to be more involved in influencing their environments, specifically in the United States.

34. P. Drucker, *Managing in Turbulent Times* (London: Pan Books, 1981), p. 213.

35. A. M. Whitehill, "America's Trade Deficit: The Human Problems," *Business Horizons*, January–February 1988, pp. 18–23; and T. Peters, "Closed Minds Can't Open Markets," *U.S. News & World Report*, March 3, 1986, p. 59.

36. See, for example, S. Nasar, "What Governments Should Be Doing," *Fortune*, March 14, 1988, pp. 63–68.

37. For a description of this trend in the commercial aircraft industry, see R. W. Moxon and J. M. Geringer, "Multinational Ventures in the Commercial Aircraft Industry," *Columbia Journal of World Business*, Summer 1985, pp. 55–62.

38. See, for example, W. P. J. Boichel, "Why the Massive Trade Imbalance? The Japanese Phenomenon," *Unitas, Finnish Economic Quarterly Review*, April 1987, pp. 100–106; and P. Kotler, L. Fahey, and S. Jatusripitak, *The New Competition* (Englewood Cliffs, N. J.: Prentice Hall, 1985).

39. J. C. Abegglen and G. Stalk, Jr., "The Japanese Corporation as Competitor," *California Management Review*, Spring 1986, pp. 9–27.

40. See G. H. Rott, "The Magic Mix of International Marketing Strategies," P. D. Grub, et al., eds., *East Asia Dimensions of International Business* (Englewood Cliffs, N. J.: Prentice Hall, 1982), p. 127.

41. T. Hout, M. E. Porter, and E. Rudden, "How Global Companies Win Out," *Harvard Business Review*, September–October 1982, pp. 98–108.

42. J. Larreche, "The International Product-Market Portfolio," paper presented at the *1978 AMA Educators' Proceedings*, Chicago, 1978.

43. The student interested in a graduate program focusing on international business may wish to read D. A. Ball and W. H. McCulloch, Jr., "International Business Education Programs in American and Non-American Schools: How They Are Ranked by the Academy of International Business," *Journal of International Business Studies*, Summer 1988, pp. 295–299; and M. Morita, "Future of International Business Education in Japan," *Journal of International Studies*, Summer, 1988, pp. 1–6.

44. An interesting discussion of how a manager should prepare for an assignment in Japan is available in J. Frankenstein and H. Hosseini, "Getting Ready for Japan: A Preliminary Survey," *Journal of International Studies*, Summer 1988, pp. 29–41.

45. S. F. Rasky, "Groping for a New Order in Trade," *New York Times*, August 30, 1987, pp. F1, F30.

46. See, for example, "McDonald's Ready to Cook Up Big Mac Attacks in Moscow," *Atlanta Journal*, April 30, 1988, p. C-1.

47. See "The Stateless Corporation," *Business Week*, May 14, 1990, pp. 98–102; and J. F. Bolt, "Global Competitors: Some Criteria for Success," *Business Horizons*, January–February 1988, pp. 34–41.

48. For a more complete discussion of the trade-offs involved in working for a foreign company in the United States, see F. Rice, "Should You Work for a Foreigner?," *Fortune*, August 1, 1988, pp. 123–134.

49. "Corporate America's Most Powerful People," *Forbes*, May 30, 1988, pp. 154–203.

50. "Worldwide Executive Mobility," *Harvard Business Review*, July–August 1988, Table 32.

GLOSSARY

Absolute monarchies: A form of government with a royal head who rules by holding centralized power.

Accessibility: The marketer's ability to reach a market effectively.

Advertising: Any nonpersonal presentation, through any medium, that is paid for by an identifiable sponsor.

Aesthetics: Everything (colors, forms, shapes, and sounds) that is considered attractive or unattractive in a given culture.

Agents: Representatives that fully represent a company in a particular market, but do not take title to the products.

Amortize: Receive investment back in installment payments that include the principal and interest.

Analytical plan: A plan for analyzing data, as part of the research design.

Anticipatory groups: Groups we would like to belong to.

Back-to-back letters of credit: An intermediary uses an irrevocable letter of credit to ask the advising bank to open a similar letter of credit in favor of the ultimate supplier of the merchandise.

Balance of payments: The account that records all the economic transactions that occur between one nation and other nations.

Balance of trade: The merchandise account that keeps track of the nation's exports and imports.

Barter: The exchange of goods or services without transfers of money in a short time frame, generally one year or less, formalized in one contract.

Behavioral control: Control of the effectiveness of a process.

Bilateral agreement: A pact betwen two countries concerning trade in one or a few product groups.

Bilateral barter clearing agreements: Barter agreements between governments in which a clearing account is established by the participating countries.

Bill of lading: A document in which the carrier acknowledges receipt of goods from the shipper; serves as evidence of title.

Blocked currency: The government does not allow any transfer of domestic currencies.

Branch offices: Offices normally staffed by employees of the home organization, who are compensated on a salary or salary-plus-commission basis.

Break-even point: The point at which costs equal revenue and the firm is neither making nor losing money.

Broker: An independent individual or organization that brings together prospective buyers and sellers to facilitate sales.

645

Business definition: The organization identifies the customer needs it will satisfy and the technologies it will use.

Business ethics: Moral standards for business behavior.

Business evaluation: An analysis of demand, costs, and profit potential.

Business partner reliability: The level of trust and the strength of the relationship between two business partners.

Business philosophy: States how a firm's relationships with different exchange partners should be managed.

Buyback arrangements: Compensation contracts used when plant, equipment, or turnkey plants are sold to firms in developing and/or centrally controlled economies, whose governments may sign the contract only if the suppliers are willing to take back the products manufactured by that equipment over an extended period of time as part of the payment.

Buying committees: Groups into which industrial customers, especially large companies, are organized.

Bypassing strategy: A confrontation strategy, used by relatively small companies that are unable to confront major competitors in the global markeplace, so they can either satisfy customer needs in existing markets that are not served in a comparable manner by any competitor, or they can enter geographic markets for existing products that no important competitor has yet served.

Casual exporting: An indirect entry involving marketing functions only, this market-entry technique offers the lowest level of risk and the least market control to an expanding firm.

Centralized decentralization: Evolution by global managers away from a geographic focus to a worldwide brand or product focus.

Centralized organization: Power in an organization is controlled by a few top managers

Centrally planned economy: Decisions made by the government regarding what goods will be offered to consumers, and their prices, as part of an overall economic plan.

Certificate of origin: A document specifying the exact origin of the product; needed for specifying the applicable tariff.

Channel power: The ability to control activity within the channel.

Classic barter: Both parties function as buyers and sellers in a mutual exchange of products with offsetting values.

Clearing-account barter: A barter agreement based on bilateral clearing agreements between governments.

Closed-end barter: One of the business partners already has a buyer at hand for the products to be traded before the contract is signed.

Cluster sample: A researcher selects a sample of units from an area (e.g., a particular city) divided into equal-sized units or neighborhoods; within these clusters, a random sample of members would be taken.

Coalitions: Political groups formed when there are several parties, none of which receives a majority vote.

Code of business ethics: A set of moral standards for business behavior.

Code law: Legal system based on Roman law.

Commercial invoice: A statement or bill of the goods sold, describing the transaction in detail.

Commercial risk: The possible risk that the customers won't pay the seller what they should, when they should, in order for the seller to achieve expected profits.

Common law: Legal system based on English law.

Common market: Member countries, in

addition to removing tariffs between them and harmonizing their tariff policies vis-à-vis nonmembers, also remove all barriers to the free movement of production factors among them.

Communication: The transmission of information from a source to a receiver.

Company-bound distribution systems: Companies that use intermediaries, but also largely control them.

Comparative advantage: A theory that world trade occurs because a nation has a relative or comparative advantage in the production of a product compared to another nation.

Compensation arrangements: Used for industrial projects, an arrangement that involves technology or capital transfer from industrialized to developing and/or centrally controlled economies. When plant equipment or turnkey plants are sold to firms in those countries, their governments may sign the contract only if the suppliers are willing to take back the products manufactured by that equipment over an extended period of time as part of the payment.

Competitive advantages: Corporate competencies that are demanded by the market and that competitors cannot easily match, except at high cost and/or over an extended period.

Competitive market strategy: Certain behaviors or actions in the market that the company must choose to ensure success.

Competitive position: The strengths and weaknesses a business unit has compared to its major competitors.

Competitive structure: The number, size, relative market share, rate of growth, and technical sophistication of firms in a particular industry.

Concentrated demand: As a result of high-volume demand, industrial marketers can focus their marketing campaigns on specific buyers.

Concentration: Centralized decision making, which is normally combined with a high degree of standardization of marketing activities, in which all or most of the sales volume in an industry is accounted for by a small number of firms.

Concentric expansion: A company starts from a strong competitive position in its home market and enters neighboring markets first, gradually expanding its marketing activities from those markets to their respective neighbors.

Confrontation strategies: Marketing strategies that include flanking, frontal attack, encirclement, and bypassing.

Consignment: The marketer or consignor delivers the products to the customer but retains the title to them until the customer has sold them to a third party or has consumed/ used them and paid the marketer.

Constitutional monarchies: A form of government with a royal head who has limited and specific roles.

Consumerism: Protection of consumer well-being through legal, moral, and economic pressures on business.

Control: A process that brings about adherence to a goal or objective through the exertion of power or authority.

Convenience sample: A nonprobability sample that allows the researcher to choose respondents who are readily available.

Coordination: The individual business unit is viewed as part of a network, with reponsibilities to other parts of the firm, and the organizational elements of the firm are integrated through horizontal associations.

Core strategy: Broadly defines the company's competitive posture, outlines how the company will reach its goals and objectives, and specifies the direction in which the company will develop in the future.

Corporate culture: The sum of values shared by the members of a company and the rules of behavior (social norms) they follow; it represents a general frame of reference that the members of the organization use to interpret events and facts in the company's environments.

Corporate mission: A company's statement of what it seeks to do in the long term, the rationale for its existence, and the major objectives it hopes to achieve.

Corporate policy statement: A statement that clarifies the mission and philosophy of a business.

Corporate strategy: Determines in general terms how business is conducted; strategic choices flow from managers' perceptions of environmental conditions, including market characteristics, barriers to market entry and exit, the specific characteristics of customer demand, and competitors' advantages.

Cosmopolitan employees: Citizens of one country who are employed by a corporation based in a second country and are working in a third country.

Cost and freight (C&F): The supplier must cover the costs of packaging, shipment, and documentation until the goods are unloaded in the port indicated in the sales contract.

Cost, insurance, freight (CIF): This term is similar to C&F, but it obligates the marketer to insure the merchandise against damage and loss during shipment.

Counterfeiting: The intentional production or sale of a product under a brand name or trademark without the authorization of the holder of that name or trademark.

Counterpurchase: An indirect form of compensation trading characterized by buying and selling agreements that are basically independent from each other. A form of countertrade, these agreements are either partially or totally paid in cash or in bank credit.

Countertrade: A commercial transaction in which provisions are made, in one or a series of related contracts, for payment by deliveries of goods and/or services in addition to, or in place of, financial settlement.

Country desks: Specialists that can provide the latest governmental import-export statistics for their country and other trade information.

Country-of-origin effect: The transfer of a particular country's image to products made there; customers sometimes assign value to a product on the basis of where it is made.

Creative selling: The process of establishing contacts, locating distributors, and filling orders.

Cross-subsidization of markets: A corporation uses cash generated in one market to subsidize marketing programs in another.

Cultural empathy: The ability to identify with different cultures.

Cultural-social factors: A wide variety of patterns of living, including behavior norms such as those regarding diet or styles of dress.

Culture: A set of symbols, codes, and values.

Customer promotions: Sales promotions directed toward industrial or consumer buyers.

Customhouse broker: Serves as an agent for exporters and importers of goods.

Customs union: A type of cooperative agreement that has the characteristics of a free trade area, but in addition the members establish consistent tariff policies vis-à-vis nonmembers.

Data banks: Sophisticated information systems that store results of portfolio analysis and information on market development, as well as customer and competitor behavior.

Dealers: Intermediaries that have the same function as retailers, plus they have the same type of continuing relationship with suppliers that distributors have, except that they sell the principal's goods directly to final customers.

Defensive motives: Management is reluctant to become involved in international business.

Deferred payments: The marketer is paid by a specific date fixed in the contract.

Delivered duty paid (DDP): The marketer has the entire burden of the costs and risk involved in the international shipment of goods.

Democracies: A government that provides opportunities for the population to take an active role in the formulation of governmental policies.

Deregulation: A movement toward relaxing antitrust rules and laws, along with supporting privitization of businesses.

Desk research: Collecting data from existing, secondary sources, such as statistics published by government agencies or other specialized institutions; also called secondary research.

Dictators: May be either monarchs or civilian or military rulers with centrally controlled power.

Differential formula: Includes all the incremental costs resulting from a nondomestic business opportunity that would not be incurred otherwise and adds them to the production costs; the manager then compares those costs with the additional revenues from the sale to determine if a suitable profit results; also called relevant cost formula.

Diffusion: Acceptance of an innovative product within a culture.

Direct-cost-plus-contribution-margin formula: The production cost of the product is taken as the basis, and additional costs due to the nondomestic marketing process plus a desired profit margin are added.

Direct foreign investment: A market-entry strategy in which a company may make a direct acquisition or merger in the host market, provide venture capital to a firm serving the market, or establish a subsidiary.

Direct investment theories: World trade is examined from the perspective of the corporate need to access business resources (markets, labor, raw materials, and so on).

Direct sales force: A sales force that the firm directly employs and controls.

Direct services: Services that are separate from physical goods and that are traded directly between nations.

Dissociative groups: Groups we would not like to belong to.

Distribution: The flow of products to final customers.

Distribution channels: The means by which goods are distributed.

Distribution system: All the people and organizations involved in transferring the good or service from the producer to the customer, including agents, dealers, wholesalers, and retailers, as well as all the tools and facilities used to carry out this process.

Distributors: Merchants who have a formalized, continuing relationship with the manufacturer, with exclusive sales rights for a specified geographic area.

Document against acceptance draft (D/A): Based on a time draft, the documents are handed over to the customer and funds from the customer are remitted to the marketer's bank, who, in turn, makes them available to the firm.

Document against payment draft (D/P): Based on a sight draft, the documents are handed over to the customer and funds from the customer are remitted to the marketer's bank, who, in turn, makes them available to the firm.

Domestication: Domestic control over foreign investments is increased gradually; the effect may be a partial loss of foreign control, or the loss may be total, similar to expropriation.

Draft for payment: An order written by a seller requesting the buyer to pay a specified amount of money at a specified time.

Dual income distribution: A pattern in developing economies in which 80 percent of the population may share just 33 percent of the wealth; often as little as 10 percent of the population controls 90 percent of the wealth and income.

Dumping: Selling products in foreign markets below cost or below domestic prices.

Economic union: Member nations are fully integrated economically and adopt a common currency.

Embodying: Include services with physical goods to circumvent barriers to trade in services.

Emotional motives: Decisions based on the individual's needs and wants, without much deliberate analysis.

EPRG: Classification of a firm's view as ethnocentric, polycentric, regionalcentric, and geocentric.

Ethnocentric firm: A company views its domestic market as most important, perhaps reacting defensively to international markets, if at all.

Ethnocentrism: The belief that one's own culture is superior to any other.

Eurobond market: Bonds underwritten by an international syndicate and sold in countries other than the host country of the issuing company.

Eurodollars: U.S. dollars, German marks, Japanese yen, and other major currencies that are held by other nations, or by companies based in other nations, and deposited in banks located outside the currencies' home country.

European Community: Members as of 1990 are Belgium, Denmark, France, Germany, Greece, Ireland, Italy, Luxembourg, The Netherlands, Portugal, Spain, and the United Kingdom.

European Currency Units (ECU): A common monetary unit created by the European Community to facilitate transactions.

European Monetary System (EMS): A system created in 1979 to guarantee the internal and external stability of currencies of member countries and to coordinate their economic policies.

Evidence accounts: A type of counterpurchase that usually occurs when an exporter or a trading company in an industrialized country signs a counterpurchase contract with the government of a developing country.

Exchange orientation: The belief that a lasting business relationship can be established and maintained only if all the exchange partners are willing and able to contribute to the relationship so that each benefits.

Exchange rate risk: In most international trade, a risk arises from the need to conduct the transaction in more than one currency.

Exclusive distribution: Severely limits the number of partners in a distribution channel for representing a producer of specialty items.

Expatriate personnel: Employees employed by a corporation in a country other than their home country.

Experience curve effects: Increased efficiency due to economies of sale and increased effectiveness due to accumulated know-how.

Export declaration: A form serving the statistical purposes of export administration agencies.

Export department: Located within the home organization, and organized either by geographic area or product category, this department is responsible for international sales and possibly shipping, advertising, credit evaluation, and other activities related to operating in foreign markets.

Export management companies: Companies that function like external export departments through assuming most or all of another company's risk of market entry.

Export trading company: A company that not only buys products or acts as an export agent, but also imports, invests, manufactures, and engages in counter-trading.

Expropriation: Private property is seized by the government supposedly "in the public interest."

Extensive problem solving: A classification of a buying situation that is unique, such as a one-time purchase of an expensive capital good.

External environments: Economic (including technical), political and legal, and cultural and social environments that affect customer behavior in national markets and marketing decisions.

External stimuli: A source of stimuli, which may cause a firm to begin the process of expansion into nondomestic markets, that includes unsolicited orders from foreign customers, perceived market opportunities, competitive pressures in the home market, or government programs to encourage exports.

Extraterritoriality of national law: The laws of the home country govern the operations of a corporation, including its subsidiaries or branches located in another country.

Ex works (EXW): Signifies the terms of sale most advantageous to the marketer and places all the obligations of shipment, including documentation for export, transit, and import, on the buyer.

Factors: Independent agents, many of which are banks, perform all normal brokerage functions plus financing.

Feedback: A reaction on the part of the communication public (such as a purchase or an attitude shift).

Field research: Data collection and analysis of new or as yet unpublished information that gathers the most specific and targeted information possible for a given research problem; also called primary research.

Fixed exchange rate: A currency may be bought or sold only at specific rates that do not vary.

Flanking: A focused confrontation strategy, chosen by companies that don't have the resources to attack a large competitor head-on, that include geographic and/or segmented flanking.

Floating exchange rate: A currency may be bought and sold for different amounts of another currency.

Focused expansion strategy: A company examines the most promising markets, regardless of location, entering the most attractive ones and avoiding the less attractive ones.

Foreign bonds: Long-term marketable securities in the international bond market, sold in one country, but underwritten by an underwriting group in a different country.

Foreign direct investment: Occurs when a company invests in a subsidiary or partnership in a foreign market; in contrast to investments in stocks, bonds, or funds deposited in a bank, which are generally left alone by the investor, foreign direct investment entails some degree of control by the investor.

Foreign freight forwarder: An agent who provides a broad range of services, including coordination and assistance in all phases of shipment from the company's plants to its markets.

Foreign sales companies (FSCs): Foreign corporations that are not located in the U. S. Customs Zone, which is allowed to pay little or no tax on export sales.

Foreign trade zones (FTZs): Special areas within a country in which companies may ship products for storage, bulk breaking, labeling, assembling, refining, repackaging, and so forth, without paying customs duties or taxes.

Franchise financing: The investor amortizes the investment through the revenues of the project.

Franchisee: An individual or organization that is granted the right to conduct business under the franchiser's trade name.

Franchising: An indirect market-entry technique, usually limited to trademarks, is used by organizations that want to rapidly establish a market presence with limited capital risk.

Free along ship (FAS): Marketer is obligated to deliver the merchandise to the vessel and port specified in the sales contract and is responsible for the costs of packaging, shipment, and documentation until the merchandise has been loaded in the port of departure.

Free on board (FOB): The seller has to deliver the merchandise on board the transport vessel indicated by the buyer at the shipping point and time specified in the sales contract; the seller must provide all the necessary export documents and bear all the costs of packaging, shipment, and documentation, and also bears the risk of damage or loss until the merchandise has been loaded.

Free on board airport (FOA): The seller has to deliver the merchandise at the airport indicated by the buyer at the shipping point and time specified in the sales contract; the seller must provide all the necessary export documents and bear all the costs of packaging, shipment, and documentation, and also bears the risk of damage or loss until the merchandise has been loaded.

Free trade area: All formal impediments to trade for a specified group of products are removed through a multilateral agreement.

Freight, carriage, and insurance paid to (CIP): The marketer is obligated to insure the merchandise against damage and loss during shipment.

Freight, carriage paid to (DCP): The marketer must pay all the costs of packaging, shipment, and documentation until the merchandise is handed over to the first freight forwarder at the location and time specified in the contract.

Frontal attack: Confrontation strategies, appropriate for large companies with substantial resources and a significant competitive advantage, that include pure frontal attack, limited frontal attack, price-based frontal attack, and value-based frontal attack.

Full cost pricing: A formula that takes the full cost price calculated for the product (production plus marketing, etc.) in the domestic market and adding the additional costs resulting from international transportation, taxes, tariffs, distribution, and promotion.

Geocentric firm: A company most committed to global orientation, continually seeking out worldwide opportunities for coordination and concentration.

Geographic bypassing: A confrontation strategy in which a relatively small company concentrates on minor markets and less-developed countries.

Geographic flanking: A confrontation strategy in which a firm chooses geographic areas in which major competitors are weak or nonexistent and offers products that are similar to those that competitors sell in comparable product markets elsewhere.

Global brand: A brand that is used by a global corporation in all the national markets they serve.

Global high-share strategy: A marketing strategy used by a large, dominant firm with sufficient personnel, technology, and capital resources, to make maximum use of economies of scale and accumulated experience

Global marketing: An approach to marketing that concentrates on product markets, emphasizing their similarities, regardless of the geographic area in which they are located.

Global marketing audit: An audit that includes the firm's internal environments (corporate policy, management systems, programs, and actions relevant to global marketing), as well as external environments that influence the company's global marketing success (the economic, political/legal, and cultural/social environments); and the industry in which the firm operates.

Global marketing management system: A system that enables the organization to plan, implement, and evaluate marketing decisions to ensure that objectives, strategic decisions, and resource allocations are compatible.

Global niche strategy: A focused marketing strategy by nondominant firms, whether large or small, that involves focusing on a specialty product that is relatively insensitive to price competition, leading to higher volumes and lower costs per unit.

Global perspective: A strong orientation toward nondomestic markets.

Global portfolio analysis: An overview of how the firm has allocated its resources on the corporate, strategic business unit, and product-line levels.

Global portfolio strategy: A decision about how dispersed the firm's resources will be, with the marketing strategy chosen among four general alternatives: product-market penetration, geographic expansion, product-market development, and diversification.

Global promoters: Marketers that concentrate on the similarities among national markets.

Good: A physical product.

Good-citizen role: A company plays a supportive role in a host country and hires that country's citizens to conduct its operations.

Grey market: The informal sector, or that part of a national economy that operates outside the officially regulated structure of business activities.

Hedging: The forward market is used to minimize a potential foreign exchange-rate loss.

Historical models: Traditional trade and investment patterns.

Import-deposit requirements: Companies selling to a certain country are required to deposit a specific amount of money with the government or a domestic bank prior to the sale.

Import house: An organization based in the host country that provides marketing services through which products are sold to consumers.

Importers: Intermediaries that fulfill the same functions as distributors but generally do not have exclusive territorial rights.

Incoterms: Standard terms of sale developed in international trade over the years that have been precisely phrased by the International Chamber of Commerce.

Independent distribution systems: The company uses intermediaries, either agents or merchants, to establish contact with final customers.

Indirect sales force: A sales force that the firm does not directly employ or control.

Indirect services: Services associated with a physical good.

Industrial demand: Demand for products that are reused in the production of other products; thus it is derived from consumer demand.

Industrial property rights: Corporate assets that have the potential to generate funds, such as brand names, patents, trademarks, and technology.

Industrial sectors: Categories of economic activity, such as mining, manufacturing, agriculture, wholesale and retail trade, construction, transportation, and business and personal services.

Industry analysis: Assessment of a potential market's attractiveness through analyzing a particular industry, including competing firms, intermediaries, suppliers, and the labor force.

Inflation: An increase in prices in an economy that results in a decline in purchasing power for consumers in that economy.

Inflation risk: Fluctuating inflation rates, which may be greater or even less than the change in currency rates, influence the price that must be set and also the value of profits that are transferred back to the parent company.

Informal sector: The part of a national economy that operates outside the officially regulated structure of business activities.

Infrastructure: A nation's communication, transportation, and energy systems.

Integrated distribution system: The company's own employees generate sales, administer orders, and deliver products or services.

Integration: Control of different organizations merges, through the building of a tight network of interrelationships between the elements of a social system, such as a business and its partners.

Intensive distribution: Representation of a mass-production company in as many outlets as possible.

Interest-rate risk: A risk that exists when the inflow and outflow of currency do not match, and temporary financing is required, because the loan is subject to interest-rate fluctuations.

Intergovernmental relations: Relations that exist between home- and host-country governments.

Internal pricing decision: The company must determine how it wants to be paid, where, and how much for its deliveries to nondomestic affiliates; also called intracompany pricing or transfer pricing.

Internal stimuli: A source of stimuli, which may cause a firm to begin the process of expansion into nondomestic markets, that includes strong marketing skills, unique products, or excess capacity in the areas of management, marketing, production, or finance.

International currencies: Money deposited in banks that are not located in the home country.

International firms: Companies that have a domestic market focus, but also service other national markets.

International trade policy: A set of laws and rules that regulates the flow of goods and services across a nation's boundaries.

Intracompany pricing: The company must determine how it wants to be paid, where, and how much for its deliveries to nondomestic affiliates; also called internal pricing decision or transfer pricing.

Investment policy: All the laws and regulations that govern private participation (domestic as well as foreign) in the equity or ownership of businesses and other organizations in a nation.

Joint venture: To join forces with a local partner to enter a particular market.

Judgment samples: A sampling technique in which the researcher chooses "experts" or "typical" representatives on a product or country market.

Jurisdictional clause: A formal statement in marketing contracts that specifies which nation's laws will apply.

Legal environment: The set of laws established by a society to govern its members' behavior.

Length of a distribution channel: A measurement characterized by the number of levels and types of intermediaries in the channel; in general, the more economically developed a country, the shorter the distribution channels in that country.

Less-developed countries (LDCs): The world's poorest countries with stagnant economies and a lack of resources.

Letter of credit (L/C): A written obligation from a bank made at the request of the customer to honor a marketer's drafts or other demands for payment upon compliance with conditions specified in the document.

Level of economic development: A complex criterion formed from combining the corporate policy statement with three general external environments (economic, political-legal and cultural-social).

Licensing: An indirect market-entry technique, which embraces all forms of industrial property, used by organizations that want to rapidly establish a market presence with limited capital risk.

Limited frontal attack: A confrontation strategy in which a firm limits its attack to a specific customer group and tries to win these customers away from the competition.

Limited problem solving: Buying situations characterized by partially structured buying procedures and rules.

Literacy rate: The proportion of the population that can read and write.

Living conditions: Degree of comfort experienced by a society's members.

Local brand: A brand that is specific to a given national market.

Local high-share strategy: A marketing strategy, used by large but nondominant firms, that avoids direct competition with dominant global competitors and usually opts for strategic differentiation, achieved by formulating competitive strategies on a domestic basis.

Long-term perspective: Keeping track of current trends, anticipating future trends, and assessing their implications for the organization.

Major industrial countries: Seven nations with the highest GNP, including Canada, France, Germany, Italy, Japan, the United Kingdom, and the United States.

Management contracts: Contracts that allow the firm to be involved in either the manufacture of a product or in the management of an enterprise in a foreign market; also called production contracts.

Manners: Social codes of conduct.

Manufacturers' representatives: Agents in domestic marketing that fully represent the company in a particular market.

Market attractiveness: An approach to building a product portfolio that is a function of market growth, degree of competition, relative market size, and corporate competencies.

Market-clustering decisions: Decisions concerning whether there is a chance to form clusters of similar product markets, independent of national boundaries, that allow a standardization of the marketing mix or if individualization has to occur.

Market-development decisions: Decisions that concern where to invest, where to hold a competitive position, and where to retreat from.

Market encirclement: A confrontation strategy in which a firm uses product-line stretching and product proliferation simultaneously to attack its major competitor in as many ways as possible.

Market-extension strategies: Extending the product life-cycle through entering new markets, especially those that are culturally similar to its current markets.

Market roll-out campaign: A strategy in which a company uses its experience in a particular market segment to gain a competitive advantage in similar segments.

Market volume: A market's size measured in terms of dollar volume.

Marketing philosophy: Marketing viewed as a basic approach to doing business.

Marketing process: The procedures followed by a firm in making marketing decisions.

Marketing technology: A bundle of management techniques to guide a company in searching for appropriate markets and in gaining and maintaining a competitive position in those markets.

Material culture: Society's standard of living or level of economic development it has achieved.

Matrix structure: A type of multidimensional structure in which functional, area, and product managers are on the same level in the firm's hierarchy.

Membership groups: Groups we belong to, including the family.

Merchandise account: Keeps track of the nation's exports and imports, commonly known as the balance of trade.

Merchants: Representatives that take title to the goods, which they buy, handle, and sell on their own account.

Mission: A company's statement of what it seeks to do in the long term, the rationale for its existence, and the major objectives it hopes to achieve.

Missionary selling: A form of creative selling that involves building and maintaining close and mutually advantageous relationships with intermediaries.

Multilateral agreements: Agreements that regulate trade among more than two countries.

Multinational firms: Companies that view some foreign markets as at least as important as the domestic market.

Multiple-exchange rates: Approved products are assigned exchange rates that facilitate sales by lowering their prices.

National firms: Companies that focus on domestic markets.

Nationalism: The belief that a nation should have complete control over its own affairs.

Nationals: Sales employees who are based in their home country.

Natural resources: Actual and potential forms of wealth that are provided by nature.

Network analysis: Analyzing industry as a system of interpersonal relationships.

Networking: The impact of family relationships and friendship on business decisions.

Newly industrialized countries (NICs): Highly competitive, export-oriented manufacturing countries characterized by high rates of economic growth and low rates of inflation and unemployment.

Niching: Small and medium-sized organizations find a market niche, form strategic partnerships, and raise barriers to market entry as high as possible.

Normative judgments: Evaluations of how things should be.

Norms: A society's underlying set of beliefs about acceptable behavior.

Objectives: Performance measures that permit evaluation of results, to determine whether the company has accomplished its mission.

Offensive motives: Management's aggressive and systematic efforts to locate or respond to global opportunities.

Offsets: Most common in sizable weapon delivery contracts between a supplying firm and a government, these arrangements usually combine domestic-content, coproduction, and technology-transfer requirements with long-term counterpurchase arrangements.

One-party system: A political system in which either the dominant party is the only one that is officially allowed to exist or the dominant party relies on political power or coercion to limit opposition.

Open accounts: Payment method most often used in domestic marketing, it offers full credit terms to the customer.

Operational planning: Encompasses detailed plans, procedures, and budgets for the business units based on the strategic decisions, and also serves as a framework for day-to-day decision making, as well as the monitoring and control systems.

Organization for Economic Cooperation and Development (OECD): A multinational forum based in Paris that allows the major industrialized nations to confer with one another about economic policies and events.

Output control: Controls that ensure efficiency of processes, usually through centralization and process standardization.

Pattern advertising: The theme and components of the advertising campaign are designed for use in several national markets, which gives the campaign a uniform direction and appearance.

Payment in advance: To generate revenue before goods are shipped or services are provided, payment is made by the customer, its bank, or the marketer's bank at the time the order is placed with the marketer.

Personal selling: Direct communication between a seller and a buyer.

Physical distribution: An important strategic tool in global marketing that includes customer service, inventory management, warehousing, storage, shipping and receiving, transportation, and all associated documentation.

Platform expansion strategy: A company starts out in the technologically advanced Triad markets and then expands to other markets.

Political union: An advanced form of economic cooperation in which the agreement among the signing parties results in a new nation.

Polycentric firm: A company sees international markets as a series of domestic (or national) markets, similar to the multinational organizational form.

Portfolio analysis: A firm determines how its strategic business units (SBUs) are distributed in relation to various factors that influence business success (such as political risk, market growth, and competitive position) and to various measures of success (such as profitability, market share, and cash flow).

Portfolio management: Spreading production, distribution, transportation, research and development, financial activities, and facilities across nations.

Positioning analysis: A strategy used to determine whether a desired position has been established in the minds of customers and whether the firm is achieving this goal more successfully than its competitors'.

Positioning strategy: A marketing strategy that chooses a bundle of benefits that is attractive to customers in the target market and distinguishes the product or company from its competitors'.

Predetermined domestication: A company agrees to turn over its operations in a country to the host-country government according to a specified timetable.

Preliminary budget: A tentative budget, based on the research questions, that provides a preliminary understanding of what information is needed and at what level of detail.

Preplanned modification: The careful analysis of market tastes and preferences, and building those differences into the total product before it is launched.

Price adaptation: A global policy in which prices for the company's products are determined in a decentralized manner, according to the local manager's perceptions of the various markets.

Price-based frontal attack: A confrontation strategy in which a firm relies on product features that are similar to those of competitors, offered at a significantly lower price.

Price controls: Governmental controls, which may include price floors, price ceilings, restrictions on price changes, or maximum profit margins.

Price lines: Price patterns that set the company's prices relative to competitors'.

Primary research: Data collection and analysis of new or as yet unpublished information that uses the most specific and targeted information possible for a given research problem; also called field research.

Principle of economies of scale: Whenever the production or sales volume of a product increases, total costs per unit (including production, marketing, and administrative costs) fall.

Probability sample: A sample drawn by a researcher in which each member of the population has a known chance of being drawn into the sample.

Problem orientation: Exchange partner's awareness of the actual or potential problems of the other partners and a willingness to help solve these problems.

Process standardization: The formalization of tasks to be performed in different parts of the company to ensure similar performance processes and comparable results.

Product augmentation: Enhancing products so that customers believe their quality justifies a higher price compared to competing products.

Product bypassing: A confrontation strategy in which a relatively small company develops an entirely new version of its traditional product or service, thereby opening up a new market with little competition.

Product improvement: The company continually augments the capabilities and reliability of its products, extends warranties and services related to the products, and is quick to apply improved technologies.

Product life-cycle model: A model used to explain market-extension strategies.

Product-line stretching: Beginning with a small segment of the market that it has successfully served in the past, a company gradually adds new items to the existing product line in order to reach a broader market.

Product markets: Groups of customers with shared needs.

Product proliferation: The company introduces as many different models or product types as possible at each point in the product line.

Product strength: An approach to building a product portfolio that is based on market share, profitability, and degree of compatibility with the market's needs.

Production-adoption process: A model for analyzing a cultural environment that classifies potential buyers (adopters) into five categories: innovators, early majority, majority, later majority, and laggards.

Production contracts: Contracts that allow the firm to be involved in either the manufacture of a product or in the management of an enterprise in a foreign market; also called management contracts.

Promotional mix: Four promotional tools that include advertising, public relations, personal selling, and sales promotions.

Protectionism: The use of legal controls to protect specific domestic industries or businesses against foreign competition.

Prototype: A working model or sample of a product.

Public relations: A nonpersonal form of communication in which the organization conveys messages to various publics or exchange partners to create a favorable image of the organization.

Public trading agency: An agency purchases, then resells consumer and industrial products to the consumer.

Publicity: "Free" exposure in the print and broadcast media, because the organization does not pay for the media time or space.

Pure frontal attack: A confrontation strategy in which a firm relies on product features that are similar to those of competitors, offered at significantly lower prices.

Rational motives: Decisions based on deliberate reasoning.

Rationalization: The change that occurs within an industry to compensate for some form of imbalance, such as external competitive pressures or the need to achieve greater economies of scale.

Reciprocal demand: Industrial demand in which two companies sell to and buy from each other at the same time.

Reference groups: Groups to which a person looks for guidance regarding behavioral norms.

Regional brand: A brand that is used in more than one national market.

Regional orientation: A firm seeks opportunities for coordinated and possibly concentrated marketing programs, but usually within a geographic or perhaps culturally homogeneous region.

Relational data bank: An information system that retrieves information by starting with a key term that leads to related topics.

Relevant cost formula: Includes all the incremental costs resulting from a non-domestic business opportunity that would not be incurred otherwise and adds them to the production costs; the manager then compares those costs with the additional revenues from the sale to determine if a suitable profit results; also called differential formula.

Representative: An intermediary who establishes and maintains relationships with prospective and existing customers in a specified geographic area on behalf of the principal.

Research brief: A preliminary proposal to be submitted to management for approval states the research problem, the objectives of the research (the benefits that will be realized), and the potential costs of making a decision without the information to be obtained from the research. This document serves as a framework for the research project and provides a basis for deciding whether to proceed with research.

Responsiveness: How favorably potential intermediaries and customers react to a company's offer.

Retail purchasing groups: Groups that service a limited buying group within the host country; also called wholesale purchasing groups.

Reuse: An industrial product will be used in the production or offering of some other product.

Revolving letter of credit: A letter of credit that applies to the sale of multiple shipments over an extended period of time.

Routinized purchase behavior: Buying situations in which products are purchased on an ongoing basis and buying procedures and rules are well developed.

Rules of thumb: Rules based on experience.

Sales promotions: A wide variety of techniques meant to stimulate a short-term response by the exchange partner.

Sales representative: Independent sales agents working on a commission basis.

Sampling frame: A list (such as mailing lists, telephone books, voter registration lists, motor vehicle registration lists, the International Business and Company Yearbook, etc.) from which elements of the target population can be identified.

Sampling technique: The method used to select potential respondents from a sampling frame.

Scenario technique: A technique that leads to the identification of key events that can be expected to have the most significant impact on the success of business units and of robust strategic decisions, which are appropriate under all future environmental conditions.

Secondary research: Collecting data from existing, secondary sources, such as statistics published by government agencies or other specialized institutions; also called desk research.

Segmented flanking: A confrontation strategy in which the firm enters a product market that is not served by major competitors or in which customers are dissatisfied.

Selective distribution: Severely limits the number of partners in a distribution channel for representing a producer of specialty items.

Self-reference criterion: The unconscious application of one's own cultural experience and values to a market in another culture.

Service: Intangible product, which may have some tangible elements.

Sight draft: A form of draft payment in which the marketer must be paid immediately upon presentation.

Skills: A blend of superior knowledge and the ability to apply this knowledge appropriately.

Slotoloy Process: A chemical-electrical process that protects metal surfaces from corrosion by applying a zinc-nickel alloy.

Social classes: Division of people by societies into social categories or status rankings.

Social contract: The generally accepted relationship between society and the individual, which is the foundation of a culture's norms and values.

Social institutions: Organizations, which include the family, reference groups, and social classes, created whenever people join together formally and informally to meet shared needs.

Social norms: Accepted rules, standards, and models of behavior.

Social organization: The framework of a culture, which includes virtually every aspect of how people live from day to day, the assignment of social tasks, and how and why people join together to meet their shared needs.

Social partnership: Describes the alliance among government, labor, and management.

Social roles: An aspect of social organization, which includes roles people play within a society.

Socialization: The process of instilling and reinforcing basic values and behavioral norms in members of an organization in a way that leads to a common set of values and accepted rules of behavior.

Special Drawing Rights (SDRs): Bookkeeping entries used to settle accounts between nations and defined in terms of several major currencies, including the U.S. dollar, German mark, English pound, French franc, and Japanese yen.

Spot market: Buying or selling a currency for immediate use or delivery.

Staff promotion: Sales promotion designed to stimulate a particular response among employees or an external sales force.

Standard formula pricing: The company calculates the price for a product following the same formula in all markets around the world.

Standard pricing policy: The marketer charges the same base price for a product in every product market served.

Standardized marketing programs: Programs that progress toward standardization of product, promotion, price, and distribution.

Statistical clustering: A clustering system that uses statistical procedures to examine variables such as demographics, stage of economic development, or population density to establish clusters of similar geographic markets.

Strategic alliance: To join forces with a local partner (often referred to as a joint venture) to enter a particular market.

Strategic business unit (SBU): A business component that is organized around the customer groups that will be served, the customer needs that will be met, and the products or services that will satisfy those needs.

Strategic clustering: Potential markets grouped according to strategic criteria that are important for the specific product market to be served and that will help the firm achieve its goals.

Strategic decisions: Decisions mainly concerned with the allocation of scarce resources over more than one product or geographical market.

Strategic partnerships: A type of cooperative strategy in which corporate alliances are made between organizations, often between former competitors, that are proactive agreements, part of an ongoing global business strategy to form cross-market alliances that gain and maintain marketing competencies.

Strategic planning: The formulation of key goals and objectives for the entire company and its various business units.

Strategy: The way a firm seeks to compete in its chosen product market to achieve some specified goals.

Subcultures: Groups of people who share a common religion, ethnic origin, or other characteristic that distinguishes the group from the larger culture.

Subsidiary: A market-entry strategy in which a company hires host-country employees and may offer limited capital participation to host-country investors.

Substance of a product: The product market includes the number of customers, their expenditures, and the rate of growth.

Symbols: Abstract characters that represent ideas, feelings, and other aspects of a culture.

System: Consists of elements (structure) and the relationships between those elements (behavior).

Systems orientation: An awareness that the organization's well-being depends on a continuous flow of resources from raw materials through the distributors to the customers.

Tactical decisions: Decisions that relate to the marketing mix for a particular product market or a special target segment.

Technical selling: Selling that emphasizes technical knowledge of the firm's products.

Telemarketing: The use of telephones for marketing.

Terms of sale: Contractual conditions of a sale between business partners.

Time draft: Payment must be made within a specified time period, usually 30, 60, 90, 120, or 180 days.

Total product: A combination of tangible and intangible attributes that may satisfy the customer's needs and wants.

Trade restrictions: Legal restrictions that control or limit trade within a nation.

Transfer pricing: Corporations set internal prices for the transfer of products, technologies, or services to their subsidiaries; also referred to as internal pricing decision or intracompany pricing.

Transnational firms: Companies that have a worldwide market focus.

Triad: The United States/ Canada, Japan, and the European Community.

Triad View: A firm assesses opportunities to standardize its marketing mix for the Triad markets or determine the degree of modification required for particular national markets within the Triad.

Turnkey operation: Through the training of future managers and workers, a company gradually turns over its operations in a country to the host-country government according to a specified timetable.

Two-party system: More than one party plays a significant role in the political process.

Tying contracts: Contracts specifying that a retailer must buy all of a manufacturer's products in order to buy one particular product line (thereby "tying" the distributor to the manufacturer).

Umbrella trade agreement: Two parties arrange that two-way trade between the firm---as well as other businesses designated by it---and firms in the developing country be partially or fully balanced over a specified period of time.

Unit of analysis: The smallest source of information that will be used to answer the research question.

Urbanization: The proportion of a population that lives in cities.

Use-need model: A model that evaluates the market need that is met by a given product as well as how the product is used.

Values: The deeply held ideas (e.g., religious beliefs and morals) that underlie norms and guide social life.

Value-added chain: A marketing approach to analyzing product competitiveness in which a product is viewed as a bundle of related services, and production is viewed as a bundle of processes.

Value-based frontal attack: A confrontation strategy that relies on product differentiation through characteristics other than price.

Venture capital: A market-entry strategy in which a company, bank, or investment firm provides capital to an innovative firm that is developing a new product or approach to a market.

Wholesale purchasing groups: Groups that service a limited buying group within the host country.

Width of a distribution channel: A measurement determined by the number of each type of intermediary in the channel; the larger the number of similar intermediaries in a market, the greater the width of the channel and, consequently, the higher the level of competition.

p. 237: Photo reprinted with permission from Wide World Photos, Inc.

p. 254 (Map 8.1): Reprinted with permission from *Advertising Age* (June 11, 1990). Copyright Crain Comm, Inc. All rights reserved.

p. 261 (Exhibit 8.10): Reprinted with permission from Elsevier Science Publishers, Physical Sciences & Engineering Division.

p. 263 (Exhibit 8.11): Reprinted with permission from *Advertising Age* (November 24, 1986). Copyright Crain Comm, Inc. All rights reserved.

p. 264 (Exhibit 8.12): Reprinted courtesy of NSS/ Marktonderzoek BV.

p. 280: Cartoon courtesy of THE FAR SIDE COPYRIGHT 1987 (p. 86), UNIVERSAL PRESS SYNDICATE. Reprinted with permission. All rights reserved.

p. 286 (Exhibit 9.5): Reprinted by permission of the publisher, copyright © 1985 D.C. Heath and Company, Lexington, MA.

p. 296: Photo reprinted with permission of Wide World Photos, Inc.

p. 309 (Exhibit 10.2): Adapted with permission of K. Labich and *Fortune*, copyright © 1986 Time Inc. All rights reserved.

pp. 318–19 (Exhibit 10.6): Adapted from *Shenzhen Industrial Investment Guide* by Takugin, as illustrated in *China Trader*, vol. X, issue no. 5, 1987, pp. 70–71, 74–75.

p. 323: Photo reprinted with permission from Wide World Photos, Inc.

p. 326: Photo reprinted with permission of Ann Henry, Caterpillar Inc.

p. 329 (Map 10.1): Reprinted by permission of *Wall Street Journal*, copyright © 1990 Dow Jones & Company, Inc. All Rights Reserved Worldwide.

p. 341: Photo reprinted with permission from Wide World Photos, Inc.

p. 342 (Map 11.1): Data from Backer/ Spielvogel/ Bates, Europe.

p. 343 (Exhibit 11.1): Adapted by permission of Prentice-Hall, Inc., Englewood Cliffs, New Jersey.

pp. 350–51 (Map 11.2): Adapted with permission from *The Economist World Atlas and Almanac*, The Economist Books/ Prentice-Hall Press.

p. 352 (Exhibit 11.4): Reprinted with permission from *Journal of Marketing*, published by the American Marketing Association.

p. 353 (Exhibit 11.5): Reprinted with permission from "The International Product-Market Portfolio," 1978, AMA Educators' Proceedings, published by the American Marketing Association.

p. 359: Photo reprinted with permission from Wide World Photos, Inc.

p. 381: Photo reprinted with permission from Wide World Photos, Inc.

pp. 382–83 (Map 12.1): Adapted with permission from *The Economist World Atlas and Almanac*, The Economist Books/ Prentice-Hall Press.

p. 403 (Exhibit 13.1): Reprinted with permission of Routledge Publishing.

p. 405 (Exhibit 13.2): Adapted with permission from *European Journal of Marketing*.

p. 406 (Exhibit 13.4): Reprinted with permission from *Journal of Marketing*, published by the American Marketing Association.

p. 409 (Map 13.1): Data adapted from *Business Week*.

p. 412: Photo reprinted with permission from Wide World Photos, Inc.

p. 418 (Exhibit 13.6): Adapted from *The World Economy*, with permission from Basil Blackwell, Ltd.

p. 420: Photo reprinted with permission from Wide World Photos, Inc.

pp. 424–427: "Swapping Debt for Education: A Proposal to Fitze University," case published with permission of Roger A. Heisler, Emory Business School, Emory University, Atlanta, GA.

p. 438: Photo (left) reprinted with permission from Wide World Photos, Inc.

p. 456 (Exhibit 14.6): Adapted by permission of John Wiley & Sons., Inc., copyright © 1982.

p. 482 (Exhibit 15.6): Adapted with permission from *Advertising Age* (December 4, 1989). Copyright Crain Comm, Inc.

p. 483 (Exhibit 15.7): Adapted with permission from *Advertising Age* (March 29, 1989). Copyright Crain Comm, Inc.

pp. 486–87 (Exhibit 15.8): Adapted with permission from *Advertising Age* (December 4, 1989). Copyright Crain Comm, Inc.

p. 491: Photo reprinted with permission of Wide World Photos, Inc.

p. 505 (Exhibit 15.12): Adapted with permission from *Advertising Age* (August 7, 1989). Copyright Crain Comm, Inc.

p. 506 (Map 15.1): Data from *Advertising Age*.

p. 515: Photo reprinted with permission of Wide World Photos, Inc.

pp. 522–23 (Map 16.1): Adapted with permission of *The Economist World Atlas and Almanac*, The Economist Books/ Prentice-Hall Press.

p. 526 (Exhibit 16.3): Adapted with permission from Publication CCI No. 460, copyright © 1990 (ISBN No. 92.842.00873), published by the International Chamber of Commerce, Paris. Available from ICC

AUTHOR INDEX

SUBJECT INDEX

ECONOMIC AND POPULATION INDICATORS

Country	GDP ($Bil)[1]	GDP/capita (1,000)	Pop. (Mil)	% Chg. in Pop.	GDP Growth[2]	Inflation Rate[2]	Income Group[3]
WESTERN EUROPEAN COUNTRIES							
Austria	$146.0	19.1	7.7	0.1%	2.5%	2.5%	H
Belgium	$173.0	17.5	9.9	0.1%	2.5%	2.5%	H
Denmark	$124.0	23.7	5.1	0.0%	1.5%	4.0%	H
Finland	$123.0	24.7	5.0	0.3%	2.5%	5.0%	H
France	$1074.0	19.2	56.0	0.3%	2.7%	3.0%	H
Greece	$57.7	5.7	10.1	0.4%	4.5%	12.5%	M
Ireland	$36.8	10.2	3.5	0.0%	3.5%	3.5%	H
Italy	$99.1	17.3	57.4	0.1%	3.0%	6.0%	H
Holland	$242.0	16.3	14.8	0.3%	2.5%	1.5%	H
Norway	$107.0	25.3	4.2	0.1%	2.3%	5.0%	H
Portugal	$51.4	4.9	10.4	0.6%	3.2%	10.0%	M
Spain	$408.6	10.4	39.4	0.4%	3.8%	5.5%	H
Sweden	$212.0	25.0	8.5	0.1%	1.8%	6.0%	H
Switzerland	$210.0	31.5	6.7	0.0%	2.0%	2.0%	H
Turkey	$83.7	1.48	56.5	2.3%	3.3%	60.0%	L
W. Germany	$1.4	22.9	60.9	−0.1%	3.3%	2.5%	H
U. K.	$935.0	16.3	57.4	0.3%	1.8%	5.5%	H
NORTH AMERICAN COUNTRIES							
U. S.	$5553.0	22.2	250.0	0.8%	1.7%	4.2%	H
Canada	$683.0	22.3	26.3	1.0%	21.0%	4.2%	H
SELECTED LATIN AMERICAN COUNTRIES							
Argentina	$53.6	1.6	32.9	1.4%	−1.1%	1022.0%	M
Brazil	$341.0	2.3	150.0	2.0%	1.5%	965.0%	L
Mexico	$186.0	2.1	88.7	1.2%	3.1%	25.0%	L
Venezuela	$45.2	2.3	19.7	2.6%	−2.7%	60.0%	M
SELECTED AFRICAN AND MIDDLE EASTERN COUNTRIES							
Nigeria	$26.0	0.236	120.0	3.4%	4.0%	40.0%	L
R. S. A.	$95.0	2.566	37.0	2.6%	1.2%	14.0%	M
Zimbabwe	$6.99	0.739	9.5	3.3%	2.5%	20.0%	L
Egypt	$37.6	0.978	55.4	2.9%	1.6%	35.0%	L
Iran	$261.0	4.6	56.8	3.5%	2.5%	35.0%	M
Iraq	$69.4	3.9	17.8	3.3%	4.5%	40.0%	M
Israel	$29.0	6 4	4.6	1.55%	−1.9%	18.0%	H
Kuwait	$19.0	8.9	2.14	4.9%	−0.9%	2.4%	H
Libya	$21.0	5.5	3.9	4.07%	−4.4%	NA	M
Saudi Arabia[4]	$74.8	5.3	14.1	4.1%	−1.6%	1.9%	H(D)
U. A. R.[4]	$23.5	15.3	1.5	2.7%	−3.3%	3.6%	H(D)